KINGDOM
in the
WEST

The Mormons and the American Frontier

Will Bagley, series editor

VOLUME 16

EADWEARD MUYBRIDGE, "SHOSHONE INDIANS AT CORINNE," CIRCA 1870
Courtesy American Antiquarian Society.

THE WHITES WANT EVERY THING

INDIAN-MORMON RELATIONS, 1847–1877

Edited by
WILL BAGLEY

Foreword by
FLOYD A. O'NEIL

THE ARTHUR H. CLARK COMPANY
An imprint of the University of Oklahoma Press
Norman, Oklahoma
2019

PUBLICATION OF THIS BOOK IS MADE POSSIBLE THROUGH
THE GENEROSITY OF EDITH KINNEY GAYLORD.

Library of Congress Cataloging-in-Publication Data

Names: Bagley, Will, 1950– editor.
Title: The whites want every thing : Indian voices from the Mormon west,
    1847–1877 / edited by Will Bagley ; introduction by Floyd A. O'Neil.
Other titles: Kingdom in the West ; v.16.
Description: Norman, Oklahoma : Arthur H. Clark Company, [2019]. |
    Series: Kingdom in the west ; volume 16 | Includes bibliographical
    references and index.
Identifiers: LCCN 2018057483| ISBN 978-0-87062-442-1 (hardcover : alk.
    paper) | ISBN 978-0-87062-443-8 (leather : alk. paper)
Subjects: LCSH: Indians of North America—Utah—History—19th
    century—Sources. | Mormons—Utah—History—19th century—
    Sources. |Utah—Race relations—History—19th century—Sources.
Classification: LCC E78.U55 W47 2019 | DDC 979.004/97—dc23
LC record available at https://lccn.loc.gov/2018057483

The Whites Want Every Thing: Indian-Mormon Relations, 1847–1877 is Volume 16 in
the Kingdom in the West series.

The paper in this book meets the guidelines for permanence and durability
of the Committee on Production Guidelines for Book Longevity of the
Council on Library Resources, Inc. ∞

1 2 3 4 5 6 7 8 9 10

For Floyd Alexander O'Neil

These Indians and their ancestors have long occupied this country—they very much dislike to leave it—they say they cannot live with the whites, for they cannot live in peace—the whites want every thing, and will give the Indians nothing—that they shoot the Indians if they walk over their grounds.

M. S. Martenas, interpreter, 6 July 1853

The hearts of the Indians are full: they want to think. Wait until tomorrow: Let us go back to our lodges and talk and smoke over what has been said today. The Indians are not ready now to give up the land: they never thought of such a thing.

Tabby-To-Kwanah, Spanish Fork Treaty negotiations, 7 June 1865

CONTENTS

Illustrations

Figures

PLATES

FOREWORD

Soon after discovering what they called a New World, Europeans wondered if its Native peoples were part of the "Lost Tribes" of Israel. Joseph Smith claimed an angel, acting at God's direction, gave him a record of America's ancient peoples, which contained elaborate details of their Hebrew ancestors and their trips to the New World, as well as the names of their leaders and political fights, their wars, and a report of three-day visit to the New World by Jesus Christ between his crucifixion and resurrection. The time had come for the remnant of Israel to be gathered as part of a new religious order that embraced the concept of the Indians as part of the Children of Israel, God's chosen people, which is still doctrine.

I was born and reared on the Uintah Ouray Reservation and lived there until I was fifteen years old. Although I was not of Indian ancestry, I had friends in the tribe and went to school with them. My father, Vaun O'Neil, invited his many Ute friends to visit our home. Being close to the Utes was not popular, so the O'Neil family was often criticized.

American Indians have been at the center of Mormon doctrine from its origin as a church in 1830. *The Book of Mormon* is written for and about them. The ideas used in the religion's founding scripture were not new—the concept that the Indians were part of the Ten Lost Tribes of Israel stretches back as far as the decade of the Columbian discoveries. No set of theories about the American Indians was as well developed or detailed as those articulated in *The Book of Mormon*. It claimed to be a translation of the records kept by the early inhabitants of the New World, and the elaborate dogma contained in the faith's first book of doctrine made Indians central to Mormon theology. They were to be informed of their Israelite origins and would then play a central role in the earthly triumph of the new faith.

In spite of the detailed mandate of *The Book of Mormon*, early Latter-day Saint efforts to embrace the Indians were meager and desultory. Joseph Smith sent a few souls to contact the tribes, but his own work was either highly secretive or virtually non-existent. Perhaps this is understandable given the conflicts and turmoil into which the new and unpopular sect was born. The struggles of the early Mormons are a story told often, and these trials were perhaps the reason they largely ignored Indians. However, the trauma of the early years of Mormonism did not prevent them from making strenuous proselytizing efforts as far away as Great Britain to gather a body of converts who could assist and sustain the new and struggling church. We can assume that those urgent tasks kept the Mormons so occupied that the issue of the American Indians was deferred. That act of deferral would become a pattern in Mormon history.

Missionaries contacted Indians at Buffalo, New York; Sandusky, Ohio; and by 1831 Parley P. Pratt and Oliver Cowdrey and three others crossed the Kansas River to evangelize the tribes in Indian country. The Delaware leader received them with courtesy and fed them. There, proselytizing began. Before long, government agents accused the missionaries of disturbing the peace and ordered them out of the area. It is no surprise that no more work was done on that frontier. The lack of activity is also noted at Nauvoo, Illinois, where other urgent issues demanded attention.

Following the expulsion from Nauvoo, the Indian issue became more immediate. At their new church headquarters on the Missouri River, the Mormons faced the Omahas on the west side of the river and the Potawatomis on the east side. Also in the area was a band of Oto, as well as other tribes, including the Sioux, who visited or raided in the area. After the enlistment of the Mormon Battalion in 1846, the United States granted the Mormons permission to remain on Indian lands until they could remove to the Far West, expecting the outcasts to leave the next spring.

Brigham Young instructed arriving refugees to abstain from interfering with Indian customs and practice. He thought it best not to attempt to convert them to the Mormon faith. It should be remembered that many of these Indians were refugees as much as the Mormons. There was a lack of food and a shortage of timber, and the Mormon camp was so large that the use of timber for homes and fuel led to difficulties, especially with the Potawatomis. Both groups suffered from lack of food, and thus the killing of game and the seizure of Mormon cattle became causes of contention.

The U.S. government gave substantial assistance to the Mormons, but they regarded its officials with great suspicion, an attitude that stayed with the

Mormons for decades. The region's federal officials and many residents believed the Mormons were conspiring with the Indians, a theme that would endure long after the Mormon Hegira. An additional complication was the presence of that busybody of the American frontier, Thomas Leiper Kane. In his ardent pursuit of a Mormon refuge and his own place in history, he succeeded in alienating William Medill, commissioner of Indian Affairs. This was unfortunate, as the Mormon pioneers needed then and would need in the future a constructive relationship with the Indian Office, both in Washington, D.C., and in the West.

As Mormon caravans crossed from Council Bluffs to the Salt Lake Valley, their encounters with the Indians were routine. As was common on the overland trails, Natives took some property and livestock, but rarely and with little impact on the pilgrims. Similarly, the Mormon entry into the Great Basin was remarkably lacking in conflict. A period of quiet was essential to allow the hard-pressed and impoverished pioneers to establish themselves in their new country. They were fortunate to locate their first settlement in an area marginal to both Ute and the Shoshone interests. Their troubled relations with the Mormons began during the settlement's first winter, when curious Utes came to visit and trade. Measles was spread to the Utes, and deadly encounters followed, as they had with such interactions since the arrival of the Spanish. The Mormon expansion into Ute lands was rapid and relentless. In the first five years, the new colonists founded nearly thirty-five communities. The welcoming attitude of the Utes soon turned to fear and anger. Competition began for game in south Salt Lake Valley and for the resources of Tooele Valley, a tale told quite plainly in the documentary history of Utah Territory. These encounters were only a prelude to the contests to come. Utah Valley was soon to be a scene of a more extensive conflict, which the local settlers named the "Walker War," a name taken from the Ute leader Wakara. While a trivial incident ignited the conflict, the fundamental issue was resources. The battle over water and land would entangle the Mormons and their new neighbors well into the twenty-first century.

Sixty years ago, I began collecting documents related to Ute history in graduate school. The most valuable material was found in the Serial Set of the United States, the National Archives, the Denver Federal Records Center, the Museum of the American Indian in New York, and LDS Church Archives. Most of the church's material was not available, so my use of LDS material was sporadic. Today there are vastly more Mormon-created sources available: the key reason this volume is needed.

FLOYD A. O'NEIL

MOSES KING CORPORATION, UTAH TERRITORY, 1891.
This map appeared in Moses King's *Handbook of the United States* (Buffalo, N.Y.)
before Congress opened the Uintah and Umcompahgre reservations to settlement
in the early twentieth century. Small Native colonies survived at Washakie in the
far north, Ibapah in the far west, Santa Clara in the far south, at Koosharem and
Kanosh in central Utah, and elsewhere. Editor's collection.

PREFACE
The Triangle

"The subject of Indian relations on the Mormon frontier deserves more extensive treatment than it has received, since it presents so many avenues of approach and interpretation," historian Juanita Brooks wrote over seven decades ago. She pointed to the region's peculiar social evolution and saw "Mormon philosophy regarding the Indians" as unique, for its ideology largely defined the religion's treatment of its "dark-skinned neighbors." This relationship would "furnish material for a lengthy dissertation," she wrote. More than fifty scholars have now earned advanced degrees exploring the topic. "Mormon-Indian relations are interesting, the Gentile-Indian relations equally so," she wrote, characterizing this Indian-Mormon-American triangle as "intriguing as any provided by fiction."[1]

In an 1828 revelation, before Joseph Smith Jr. organized the Church of Jesus Christ of Latter-day Saints—whose followers were called the Mormons—he put American Indians at the center of his epic, *The Book of Mormon.* Smith claimed he translated it from golden plates so that Indians, whom the book called Lamanites, might know their fathers and "the promises of the Lord."[2] The book was written for and about Indians—"to shew unto the remnant of the House of Israel how great things the Lord hath done for their fathers" and to let them know they were "not cast off forever," for this scripture would restore the Lamanites "to the knowledge of Jesus Christ."[3]

Believing America's Native peoples were Children of Israel is an old concept. "A whole host of arguments had it that Indians were Jews," wrote essayist Jack Hitt. Since at least 1567, Europeans had theorized that American Indians

---

[1] Brooks, "Indian Relations on the Mormon Frontier," 1.
[2] Doctrine and Covenants (D&C) 3:19–20.
[3] *The Book of Mormon*, 1830, title page, and 2 Nephi 30:5.

descended from Hebrews. The Lost Tribes of Israel were the ancestors of American Indians, Amsterdam rabbi Menashe ben Israel concluded in 1644. Massachusetts Bay Colony Puritans proselytized local Natives, believing "the conversion of the House of Israel constituted one of the important events to precede the prophesied return of Christ to the earth." Such speculation essentially defined Indians as "Jews Gone Wild," Hitt quipped.[4] Said to be an abridged translation of ancient American records, *The Book of Mormon* explained Indian origins and made its mandate to inform America's Indians of their Israelite heritage.

This volume presents many long-sequestered primary sources about the first inhabitants of today's Mormon Country. Its primary focus is on Native perspectives after 1847, when Brigham Young led the Latter-day Saints "into very the midst of the Lamanites."[5] It examines the cooperation and conflict that contact created, using the journals, letters, reports, and recollections of the Anglo-Americans closest to the experience. It tries to provide basic cultural, historical, and environmental perspectives to comprehend the Native world. Whenever possible, it relies on the many eloquent Indian voices found in the region's excellent archives.

An insider's grasp of Mormon culture is my birthright, but I have no such insight into Native culture and life, which as someone born into a racist nation and religion are beyond my comprehension. These sources, collected over decades, are mediated translations of white records of what whites said Indians said. Readers must judge if they are insulting and patronizing or eloquent and convincing. As Sherman Alexie wrote, colonialism is "the tired mantra of liberals who've run out of intellectual imagination."[6] This work seeks not to further colonize Native hearts and minds but to let long-silent voices speak.

The wealth of available material imposes its own problems. This collection focuses on Native responses between 1847 and 1877 to an invasion of their homelands. It presents case studies of Mormon contact with the Great Basin's Numic-speaking peoples, whose languages share Uto-Aztecan roots with nations as diverse as Mexico's Aztecs and the Comanche, who ruled America's Southern Great Plains. Europeans imposed imperial leadership

---

[4] Hitt, "Mighty White of You," 41, 50; and Christina Skousen's abstract of her 2005 thesis, "Toiling among the Seed of Israel," v–vi.

[5] Van Wagoner, *Complete Discourses*, 9 August 1857, 3:1315.

[6] Alexie, *The Toughest Indian in the World*, 194.

models on American Indians, who united their families and clans into tribes and nations in response to a brutal alien invasion and economic exploitation. The Shoshonean confederation included the *Nuche* or Utahs, now called Utes; the *Newe, Neme,* or *So-so-goi,* the Shoshones and Bannocks; the *Kusiutta* or Goshutes and the Western Shoshones of the central Great Basin; and the *Nuwuvi,* the Southern Paiutes. These peoples form the core of this study, with only occasional references to Mormonism's substantial efforts among the Hopi and Navajo.

Understanding human prehistory relies on conjuring an interpretation from dusty evidence. Different challenges confront those dealing with the conquest of America's Native peoples, especially in the Great Basin. Nineteenth-century Mormon conflicts, historian David L. Bigler observed, offer two credible but mutually exclusive versions of what happened. In fights between the Mormons and their neighbors, "it was impossible for an impartial observer to figure out where the fault lay," often leaving onlookers to conclude that "one side had engaged in orchestrated falsehood." In the end both sides suffered, but historians must decide what happened in the morass of Utah's "enormous, repetitious, contradictory, and embattled" past, as author Wallace Stegner put it.[7] The challenge is to base such judgments on evidence, not on personal or partisan prejudice.

This study tries to explain concepts essential to understanding LDS interactions with Indians after the religion began its "Great Western Measure" in 1846. Chapters focus on the initial encounters between the two peoples in the Great Basin; armed conflicts in 1849 and 1850 in Utah Valley; initial contacts and clashes with the Northwestern Shoshone; the 1851 campaign against the Goshutes of Utah's West Desert; the competition for resources driving an 1853 war against the Utes; the mission to the Southern Paiutes and Ute resistance to the Elk Mountain Mission, which in 1855 successfully pushed back the first attempt to settle Utah's canyon country; and Brigham Young's failure to forge an Indian alliance during the Utah War of 1857 and 1858. This study ends with the 1865 Spanish Fork Treaty negotiations and only summarizes Utah's Black Hawk War, which began in April 1865 and extended into 1872. It ends with a few documents showing how Mormon millennial dreams continued beyond the death of Brigham Young in 1877.

---

[7]Bigler, *Confessions of a Revisionist Historian,* 11, 141.

Despite the mandate on *The Book of Mormon's* title page that it was "written to the Lamanites," early Latter-day Saints made only desultory attempts to embrace eastern Indians. Joseph Smith Jr. sent a few emissaries to the tribes, but his own efforts were rhetorical. As Juanita Brooks observed, "Troubles of their own in the East and Middle West prevented very extensive proselytizing among the native Americans until after the Mormons had reached the valley of the Great Salt Lake."[8]

Its Indian doctrines helped drive most Mormons into the Rocky Mountains. *The Book of Mormon* set the time for the overthrow of all "gentile governments of the American continent." The "way and means of this utter destruction" would be the "remnant of Jacob," Apostle Parley P. Pratt proclaimed in 1845. In the Last Days, the Lamanites would "go through among the Gentiles and tear them in pieces," until "all their enemies shall be cut off. This destruction includes an utter overthrow, and desolation of all our Cities, Forts, and Strong Holds—an entire annihilation of our race, except such as embrace the Covenant, and are numbered with Israel."[9]

Early believers embraced these predictions, but as Brigham Young's era ended, even the most dedicated Saints had doubts. "The Lamanites will blossom as the rose on the mountains," Apostle Wilford Woodruff said in 1873. When he saw the "nation destroying them from the face of the earth, the fulfillment of that prophecy is perhaps harder for me to believe than any revelation of God that I ever read." It looked as if "there would not be enough left to receive the Gospel; but notwithstanding this dark picture, every word that God has ever said of them will have its fulfillment," by and by.[10] These convictions died along with Mormonism's oldest members as the faith entered the twentieth century.

Native peoples and frontier Mormons inhabited a haunted world of peculiar spirits and endemic violence in a region where less than 4 percent of the land was arable. Latter-day Saints believed the earth itself was a living creation permeated with spirits, while every stream, spring, animal, and plant in the Shoshonean and Athabascan worlds breathed life. Today religious faith remains influential, but Darwin and Einstein have dismantled magical spirituality: science and powerful technologies underlie modern assumptions. The Southern Paiutes and the evangelists sent to them believed

---

[8]Brooks, "Indian Relations on the Mormon Frontier," 3.
[9]Crawley, *The Essential Parley P. Pratt*, 24, quoting Pratt's 1838 "Mormonism Unveiled."
[10]*Journal of Discourses*, 12 January 1873, 15:282.

in spiritual realms more similar to each other's than to their descendants' post-industrial reality.

Given its subject—the struggle of proud peoples noted for "their stern virtues and their fierce instincts"[11] to survive in the Great Basin's harsh environment—this work has been the most difficult of all the sixteen volumes of the KINGDOM IN THE WEST series to compile. These documents describe a ruthless struggle with important consequences, a contested conquest distinguished by its brutality and offering few examples of the better angels of human behavior. The story of the Native and Euro-American war to control the arid heart of the American West is often a pageant of man's inhumanity to man, a hopeless chapter in the history of what Wallace Stegner called "the native home of hope."[12]

These documents tell hard stories intimately connected to the murder and exploitation of African and Native peoples—the darkest chapters in American history. These narratives provide no easy answers to enduring problems, but they contain clues to persistent questions and raise others: Can such mediated documents reveal anything worth knowing about American Indians? Did Latter-day Saint theology affect how Mormons treated Indians? How did the Mormon invasion affect the Great Basin's long tradition of violence? Was Brigham Young a friend of the Indians? Was anything exceptional about Mormon relations with the Numics? And finally, when the lion goes among the lambs, who is the lion, and who are the lambs?

---

[11]Remy, *A Journey to Great-Salt-Lake City*, 2:285–86.
[12]Stegner, *The Sound of Mountain Water*, 38.

ACKNOWLEDGMENTS

"The concept of tribal sovereignty should logically extend to culture and religion," wrote novelist Sherman Alexie. "The real issue is that Indians' relationship to this country is still that of the colonized, so that when non-Indians write about us, it's colonial literature. And unless it's seen that way, there's a problem."[1] As a white, if not delightsome, native son of Utah, a place named after a Great Basin people, I know Alexie's charge is true: I am guilty of cultural pilfering and presuming to speak for a people not my own. Humans can justify anything and everything, be it mass murder or the theft of entire continents, so naturally I excuse my attempt to recover Native voices from Anglo-American sources as an act of pious fraud. Perhaps, if ends justify means, the book's purpose—to provide access to forgotten voices that reveal the intelligence, resilience, and humanity of a brave and brilliant people who survived an inescapable and merciless trap—vindicates my presumption.

The Whites Want Every Thing has been the most difficult journey on a long quest to understand the American West and its peoples. The friendship, insights, and books of five scholars—Ned Blackhawk, Forrest Cuch, Jared Farmer, John Alton Peterson, and Gregory E. Smoak—contributed immensely. Friends and colleagues John Alley, Gregory Thompson, and Logan Hebner deserve special thanks. Ephriam Dickson, the best scout in our National Archives, generously shared his time and expertise. I deeply regret the death at age 90 of Floyd Alexander O'Neal on 18 April 2018, before I could hand him a copy of a book we have worked on for twenty years. Floyd and the late David Louis Bigler made me a better scholar and person.

A host of archivists and librarians helped secure permission to publish the images that illuminate this volume. Space demands that I merely mention the

---

[1]Chapel, "Sherman Alexie," Interview, *Atlantic Unbound* (June 2000), 3, 4.

institutions whose generosity made this work possible: special collections at the University of Utah, Utah State University, Brigham Young University, and the Utah State Historical Society; as well as the curators at Harvard's Peabody Library and Utah's Springville Art Museum, and Pernille Richards of the Maidstone Museum in Great Britain. As always, our National Archives, the Smithsonian Institution, and the Library of Congress provide public access to public history. I deeply appreciate two great archives, Yale's Beinecke Library and Philadelphia's American Antiquarian Society, who have granted open access to their visual resources.

Humble thanks to the Church of Jesus Christ of Latter-day Saints, whose institutional generosity granted access to much of this primary material. I claim no property rights to these documents beyond the rights to my transcriptions and commentary. Friends and colleagues such as Kerry Bate, Christopher C. Smith, Joseph Geisner, Rick Grunder, and Connell O'Donovan generously shared their transcriptions, while Ardis Parshall provided Floyd O'Neil with her formidable transcriptions of Mormon-Indian letters. Whenever possible, I have checked documents against the manuscript sources. I alone am accountable for copying errors.

The historical division of the Church of Jesus Christ of Latter-day Saints' preferred name has changed several times over the decades required to complete the KINGDOM IN THE WEST series, but this volume still abbreviates citations to the Church Library and Archives as "LDS Archives." The access the department has provided to its extraordinary collection of historical records has evolved from a restrictive policy to one of astonishing openness and generosity. Such a wealth of new source material imposes limitations of this volume, which gives short shrift to the influence of Mormonism on many Indian nations, most regrettably the Navajo, Hopi, and Northern Paiute peoples. This abundance of riches explains the focus on the 1850s and the summary of the 1860s and beyond.

Contemporary Great Basin Indians, including former director of Utah's Division of Indian Affairs Forrest S. Cuch, Kaibab Paiute Interpretive Ranger Benn Pikyavit of Pipe Springs National Monument, Goshute tribal officer Mary Bear, and Southern Paiute leaders Gary Tom, Lara Tom, Arthur Richards, Willie Pete, and the late Clifford Jake provided insights into their lives. On 5 February 2004 eloquent Southern Paiute elders, including Cindy Charles, Darlene Pete Harrington, Eldene Snow Cervantes, Eleanor Tom, Genean Tom, Margaret King, Eunice Tillahash Surveyor, Vivian Caron-Jake,

Evelyn Samalar, Clarence John, Phyllis Richards, Arthur Richards, and Will Rogers met in Santa Clara, Utah, and I was honored to attend. Mary Meyer and Tracey Reed of the Timpanogos band provided insights into their conundrum.

Finally, in light of my profound limitations, I will always appreciate everything Laura Bayer has given to my life and work.

Editorial Procedures

This collection of narratives and documents attempts to represent the original records in a readable format. With a few exceptions, transcriptions preserve the grammar, spelling, and diction of the originals but capitalize the first letters of sentences and personal names and end sentences with periods. The abbreviations A.M. and P.M. are set in small caps. Underlined text is italicized, but only significant crossed-out text is rendered as ~~strikethroughs~~. Where the case is ambiguous, I follow standard capitalization. Where a writer employed commas in place of periods, they are converted to periods. Otherwise the sources preserve the original's spelling and punctuation (or its absence). I use [*sic*] sparingly. Brackets enclose added letters, missing words, and conjectural readings. [*Blank*] indicates a blank space, while other bracketed comments, such as [*tear*], note physical defects in the manuscript. Interlined insertions appear in their logical location in the text.

Thomas Bullock, "Clerk of the Camp of Israel" in 1847, continued his clerical functions in the LDS Church Historians Office until 1862 and kept many if not most of the records related to Indians. He used several abbreviations—"av," "bef," "c," "chil," "Fat," "ma," "r," "we"— expanded here to "have," "before," "and," "children," "Father," "may," "are," and "were." I have occasionally inserted apostrophes where needed to clarify contractions, so "well" becomes "we'll."

The material is organized into chapters, sections, and documents. Each document contains an abbreviated heading identifying the source and its location. Headings and footnotes citing newspaper articles contain the complete information needed to locate them. Full citations for other items, including manuscript numbers, are found in the bibliography. Footnotes cite published sources by author, title, and page number. Where available, newspaper citations provide page/column: 2/3. The bibliography contains a complete list of all the books, articles, newspapers, journals, and manuscripts referenced in the footnotes. I have italicized book titles and put article, thesis, and dissertation titles in quotation marks. Manuscript citations appear without quotation marks. Material from the sources reproduced elsewhere in this volume is not footnoted.

Places use the official designations of the U.S. Board on Geographic Names. White renditions of Native names vary wildly, so the text follows spellings used in Forest Cuch's *A History of Utah's American Indians* or the majority of primary sources. Given the likelihood of error, this study does not attempt to identify every Native mentioned. I have done my best to produce accurate transcriptions, but this arduous task encourages no claims to infallibility.

ABBREVIATIONS

BYC	Brigham Young Collection, CR 1234 1, LDS Archives. Citations include box and folder numbers; for example, Brigham Young to Captain Walker, 9 April 1852, BYC 17:1.
Smith Papers	George A. Smith Papers, MS 1322, LDS Archives.
CHO Journal	CR 100 1: Historical Department Office Journal, 1844–2012. LDS Church History Department, LDS Archives.
D&C	Doctrine and Covenants of the Church of Jesus Christ of Latter-day Saints.
LDS Archives	Church History Department and Library, the Church of Jesus Christ of Latter-day Saints, Salt Lake City, Utah.
NARA	National Archives Records Administration.
UTMR	Utah Territorial Militia Records, 1849–1877, 1905–1917, Series 2210, Utah State Archives. Digital copies at https://www.familysearch.org.

INTRODUCTION
A Union with the Indians—
Numics, Mormons, and the Frontier

To appreciate the interactions of American Indians and the Great Basin's first Latter-day Saints requires understanding the Shoshonean world as well as the fundamental role that race plays in Mormon theology. The religion's roots in upstate New York's Burned-over District—"that portion of New York State lying west of the Catskill and Adirondack Mountains"—created an intensely millennial American creed.[1] Its era and birthplace defined *The Book of Mormon*'s romantic view of Native peoples; the faith's adoption of "Anglo-Israelism" defined what follower Jacob Hamblin called its "ideas of the Great Work in the Last Days among the Lamanites." The faith is impossible to comprehend without understanding its racial folklore.

As with all great traditions, Numic stories explain how the *Nuche, Newe,* and *Nuwuvi*—the Ute, Shoshone, and Southern Paiute Peoples—came to be. Ethnographer Carobeth Laird provided detailed insights into Southern Numic traditions, including the Chemehuevi band's Southern Paiute creation stories. The tales of the *Newewe,* the People, or the *Tuumontcokowe,* Black Bearded Ones, offer "intimations of prehistory, although it may be that their most valuable revelations are spiritual, metaphysical, and psychological." Paiutes have multiple origin stories: in one, the Primeval Four—Ocean Woman, Wolf, Mountain Lion, and Coyote (made from dead skin from Ocean Woman's crotch)—floated in a basket or woven boat on the primeval sea, for "there was in the beginning only water"—immortal water. "Ocean

---

[1]Cross, *The Burned-over District,* 4.

Woman rubbed dead skin from her body, formed it into balls, crumbled them, and sprinkled the resulting dust on the surface of the waters. Thus the land was formed." When there was enough to support her, Ocean Woman lay upon it, her head toward the west. She then stretched the land, pushing at it with outspread arms and legs. "Wolf ran up and down from north to south, reporting on how far the land extended, while Coyote ran to the east and back again." When Coyote declared there was enough land to accommodate the beings who would inhabit it, "the earth was finished."[2]

When the world was young and animals were people, creatures in this primeval dream exhibited animal characteristics but thought and lived like humans. When this era ended, the animal people went north or perhaps transformed into the animals that roam the earth today. Besides tales of warfare and magic, Chemehuevi origin myths tell how Mythic Coyote, *Cenawavi*, set the pattern for human life and labor. "His elder brother *Tevatsi*, Wolf, was immensely wise and would have set easier patterns if mankind had chosen to follow him; but the saying goes, 'We followed Coyote.'" Wolf became the prototype magical man, "the all-powerful, all-wise, pompous, and completely humorless shaman. Coyote is typical of sensuous man— erring, lascivious, disobedient to his betters, full of outlandish humor, in every battle the first to be killed and the last to be revived." Coyote became "technological man, for it was he who set the pattern for the making of arrows and for other toilsome human activities involving the use of tools." Note how "the Primeval Four represent four great predators: man, wolf, mountain lion, and coyote." The Chemehuevi believed bears and rattlesnakes also possessed great powers.[3]

For the *Nuche*, the Utes, the man-wolf god Sinauf and his brothers, Coyote and Wolf, "kept the world in balance before humans were created." Here is how Sinauf made people, who took responsibility to care for the world.

CLIFFORD DUNCAN, "THE NORTHERN UTES OF UTAH," 167–68.

Far to the south Sinauf was preparing for a long journey to the north. He had made a bag, and in this bag he placed selected pieces of sticks—all different yet the same size. The bag was a magic bag. Once Sinauf put the sticks into the bag, they changed into people. As he put more and more sticks into the bag, the noise the people made inside grew louder, thus arousing the curiosity of the animals.

---

[2]Laird, "Chemehuevi Religious Beliefs," 19–20, 25n4.
[3]Ibid., 22.

After filling his magic bag, Sinauf closed it and went to prepare for his journey. Among the animals, Coyote was the most curious. In fact, this particular brother of Sinauf was not only curious but contrary as well, opposing almost everything Sinauf created and often getting into trouble. When Coyote heard about Sinauf's magic bag full of stick people, he grew very curious. 'I want to see what those people look like,' he thought. With that, he made a little hole with his flint knife near the top of the bag and peeked in. He laughed at what he saw and heard, for the people were a strange new creation and had many languages and sons.

When Sinauf finished his preparations and prayers he was ready for the journey northward. He picked up the bag, threw it over his shoulder and headed for the Una-u-quich, the distant high mountains. From the tops of those mountains, Sinauf could see long distances across the plains to the east and north, and from there he planned to distribute the people throughout the world.

Sinauf was anxious to complete his long journey, so he did not take time to eat and soon became very weak. Due to his weakness, he did not notice the bag getting lighter. For, through Coyote's hole in the top of the bag, the people had been jumping out, a few at a time. Those who jumped out created their families, bands, and tribes.

Finally reaching the Una-u-quich, Sinauf stopped. As he sat down he noticed the hole in the bag and how light it was. The only people left were those at the bottom of the bag. As he gently lifted them out he spoke to them and said, "My children, I will call you Utikas, and you shall roam these beautiful mountains. Be brave and strong." Then he carefully put them in different places, singing a song as he did so. When he finished, he left them there and returned to his home in the south.

Anthropologists believe Numic religions centered around *puwa*, the spiritual power experienced shamans and song-singers could harness to achieve success in the manly arts of hunting, raiding, and fighting. Women are so prominent in Great Basin society that they seem more powerful than in other Native cultures.[4] Ute traditions, elder Clifford Duncan wrote, connected each person "to the spirit of all living things. This connection makes humans responsible to the earth and all of its creations." No one religion or ritual belonged to the Ute tribe, but the people conducted rites, notably sweat ceremonies for healing and cleansing and the spring Bear Dance to celebrate their "relationship with nature and the universe—connecting all with the supreme intelligence or creator."[5]

---

[4]Miller, "Numic Religion," 337–54.
[5]Duncan, "The Northern Utes," 218–20.

Long before whites reached the Great Basin, their empires made treaties with the Utes and Comanches. Utah traditions assert the Comanches originated in the Uinta Basin before relocating to the southern plains and becoming the largest and most powerful Numic nation. Utes and Southern Paiutes had dealt with Europeans since at least 1638, when Spaniards enslaved some eighty *"Utacas"* to labor in Santa Fe workshops. Spain made its first treaty with the Utes before 1670. French traders began visiting Shoshones and Utes in the 1750s, so Numic peoples had generations of experience mastering transformative technologies such as steel, horses, and firearms. In New Mexico in 1706, Taos feared an expected attack of Utes and Comanches, who would soon build an empire of their own.[6] Our shifting grasp of these changes resembles lore more than history, but Shoshones recall the Comanches "left them and went south in search of game and ponies." They created a Ute-Comanche coalition along New Mexico's northern borderlands and used Spain's colony "as an exploitable resource depot."[7] Silvestre Escalante's description of the peaceful and prosperous Ute villages he found on Utah Lake in 1776 indicates how much the next seven decades changed the region's cultures. When Mexico ceded its control of Alta California to the United States in 1848, the Utes, Goshutes, Paiutes, Shoshones, and Bannocks lived astride the overland wagon roads to Oregon and California and ranged from the Pacific Coast to the Great Plains. These nations controlled the heart of the Rocky Mountains and Great Basin.[8]

Early in the twentieth century, Old Yellow Beads told historian Herbert Auerbach she loathed to leave Fort Bridger where her Shoshone "forefathers for many generations" had lived and were buried:

> She had endless stories of the past to relate. Where Fort Bridger stood there was a village of many lodges and those were happy times. Their men were famous warriors, feared by neighboring tribes and they were great hunters, also they had food in abundance, meat, berries and roots. To the west was a great lake that overflowed its banks every spring [now Utah Lake]. Their old chief "Humpy" who was a hundred years old when Washakie was a boy said that at one time, years before his time their people used to plant corn along the shore of this lake very early before the waters were high and after the waters rose and subsided the corn sprouted and grew tall. When it ripened they packed the ears home and ground the grains into meal of which they

---

[6]Ibid., 173, 180.
[7]Hämäläinen, *Comanche Empire*, 21–27.
[8]Van Hoak, "Waccara's Utes," 310.

made fine cakes. Their young men went hunting and brought back plenty of game. When they came home they were happy and had big dances.[9]

"We know but little of the Indians in Utah, beyond the fact that they are generally peaceable in their disposition and easily controlled," Luke Lea, commissioner of Indian Affairs, wrote in 1850. Like their boss, much of what Lea's agents knew about Numic peoples was wrong. European contact, trade, and horses forged hundreds of small and scattered family bands into the tribes we know today.[10] Shoshone and Ute peoples had dominated their homelands for untold generations but after Europeans arrived, bands battled better-armed and mounted tribes such as the Absarokas and Arapahos to control their homelands. By 1812 the Utes' fame reached north to South Pass, where trappers told explorer Robert Stuart about "the Black Arms, about 3,000 strong," who dominated "the best beaver country on this side the mountains" but were "very friendly to the whites" and whose homeland extended "to the neighbourhood of the spainards."[11]

At Santa Fe in February 1822, Missouri merchant Thomas James met "a deputation of fifty Indians from the Utah tribe on the west side of the mountains. They came riding into the city, and paraded on the public square, all well mounted on the most elegant horses I had ever seen." They came to open trade with the Americans, the youthful, independent, and lordly Lechat told James in fluent Spanish. "Come to our country with your goods. Come and trade with the Utahs," who had many horses, mules, and sheep, and rivers full of beavers that were eating up his people's corn. "Come over among us and you shall have as many beaver skins as you want." The Mexicans had "nothing that you want. We have every thing that they have, and many things that they have not." Lechat convinced James the Utahs were "the true capitalists of the country." They "departed without the least show of respect for the Spaniards, but rather with a strong demonstration on the part of Lechat of contempt for them."[12]

The Utes welcomed American fur traders, notably Etienne Provost, William Ashley, and Jedediah Smith, who quickly responded with "great familiarity and Ease of manner." Smith found "these Indians more honest than any I had ever been with in the country." The Utahs were "cleanly quiet

---

[9]Carter papers, "Remarks," Bancroft Library, 5:5, 2.
[10]For ethnogenesis, see Smoak, *Ghost Dances and Identity*, 6, 85–112.
[11]Alley, "Prelude to Dispossession," 108–09.
[12]James, *Three Years among the Indians and Mexicans*, 145–46.

and active and make a nearer approach to civilized life than any Indians I have seen in the Interior." Mexico's secretary of state complained that Ashley had "caused a peace to be made between the barbarous nations of the Yutas Timpanagos and the Comanches Sozones, and made presents of guns, balls, knives, &c, to both nations" and appointed the "Yuta Timpanago Indian, called *Quimanuapa*" a general.[13]

Mountaineer Daniel Potts described the people he met at "Utaw Lake" in July 1827 as "plentifully supplied with fish which form the principle subsistence of the Utaw tribe of Indians." They were "almost as numerous as the Buffaloe on the prairie, and an exception to all human kind, for their honesty." In contrast, Potts painted the "numerous tribe of miserable Indians" on the Sevier River as "wretched creatures [who] go out barefoot in the coldest days of winter. Their diet consists of roots, grass seeds, and grass, so you may judge they are not gross in their habit. They call themselves Pie-Utaws, and I suppose are derived from the same stock."[14]

On John C. Frémont's visit to the Great Salt Lake in October 1845, explorers Frémont and Kit Carson rode to an island and found "grass and water and several bands of antelope." After killing several pronghorns, Frémont gave Antelope Island its English name. Soon "an old Utah Indian" asserted his rights:

> Seeing what game we had brought in he promptly informed us that the antelope which we had been killing were his—that *all* the antelope on that island belonged to him—that they were all he had to live upon, and that we must pay him for the meat which we had brought away. He was very serious with us and gravely reproached me for the wrong which we had done him. Pleased with his readiness, I had a bale unpacked and gave him a present—some red cloth, a knife, and tobacco, with which he declared himself abundantly satisfied for this trespass on his game preserve. With each article laid down, his nods and gutturals expressed the satisfaction he felt at the success of his imaginary claim. We could see, as far as an Indian's face lets expression be seen, that he was thinking, "I went to the White Chief who killed my antelope, and made him pay for it." There is nothing new under the sun.[15]

When the Mormons arrived in the Great Basin in 1847, its Native peoples had been dealing with Europeans far longer than the United States had been a nation. "The many Ute, Paiute, and Shoshone groups who have inhabited

[13]Alley, "Prelude to Dispossession," 109–10.
[14]Morgan, *The West of William Ashley*, 167.
[15]Frémont, *Memoirs of My Life*, 431.

this region since time immemorial generally appear as distant shadows in historical texts," noted historian Ned Blackhawk. The shift and its associated "terror, horrific violence, and nameless victims" had on Native cosmology "remain lost to historical inquiry, while the social and demographic revolutions unleashed by the spread of Spanish horses, microbes, and economies are only faintly visible." Despite the pain "the waves of violence engulfing their homelands" inflicted, many Great Basin bands remade themselves, responding dynamically to the danger and sweeping changes.[16] Numic peoples adopted and profited from alien technology, adapting swiftly to new realities at the expense of their traditional cultures. The Spanish, Mexican, French, and American traders, trappers, and explorers they met over two centuries all eventually went away. What they could not know was that in every recorded encounter between two civilizations, the culture with the more sophisticated technology always defeated and often destroyed people who stood in its way. The Mormons commanded that technology, and unlike their predecessors, they came to stay.

RED JACKET: TO FORCE YOUR RELIGION UPON US

If Native peoples misread the challenge when the Mormons arrived in 1847, the Latter-day Saints arrived with their own illusions.

During the 1820s, thousands of New York's first peoples lived around four reservations. Upstate was still a rough region, but it was no longer a frontier, the "contested ground" where Native and European cultures wrestled for control of the land. The American Revolution settled that dispute when George Washington ordered Gen. John Sullivan to lay waste to every settlement of the Six Nations allied with the British "in an effectual manner, that the country may be not merely overrun, but destroyed."[17] As American allies in the War of 1812, the Six Nations watched the young republic crush the last effective Indian resistance east of the Mississippi River.

Sogoyewapha, known as He-Keeps-Them-Awake and Red Jacket, appeared in Palmyra, New York, in July 1822. He no longer had the resplendent scarlet coats the British gave him during the Revolution. He wore instead a silver medal stamped with Washington extending his hand to an Indian, a gift from the president in 1792. An "obtrusive white man" once asked the Seneca

---

[16]Blackhawk, *Violence over the Land*, 6.
[17]Cross, *The Burned-over District*, 4; Peabody, *Life of John Sullivan*, 128.

sachem about his feats of arms, and the "spirited, quick-witted, and adroit" Sogoyewapha exclaimed, "I am an orator! I was born an orator!" He is best remembered for his 1805 speech "The Religion of the White Man and the Red," in which he told a missionary named Cram, who wanted to settle among the Six Nations, "You have got our country, but are not satisfied; you want to force your religion upon us."[18] Palmyra's citizens invited him to address their academy one moonless Monday night in July 1822. The local paper summarized Red Jacket's remarks, which merited being reprinted overseas.

"SENECA INDIANS," *THE KALEIDOSCOPE: OR, LITERARY AND SCIENTIFIC MIRROR* (LIVERPOOL, ENGLAND), 12 NOVEMBER 1822, 149/2.

Seneca Indians.—We were last week visited by the famous chief *Red Jacket*, together with four other chiefs belonging to the six nations, to wit—*Blue Sky, William Sky, Peter Smoke,* and *Twenty Canoes,* who arrived here on Monday, about sun-set. To answer the solicitations of our inhabitants, Red Jacket delivered a speech in the evening, at the Academy, which was almost instantly filled with an attentive auditory. His speech, if it had been properly interpreted, no doubt would have been both eloquent and interesting. But as it was, merely enough could be understood to know his object, while his native eloquence and rhetorical powers could only be guessed at from his manner and appearance. He commenced by representing that whole human race as the creatures of God, or the Great Spirit, and that both white men and red men were brethren of the same great family. He then mentioned the emigration of our forefathers from towards the rising of the sun, and their landing among their red brethren in this newly-discovered world. He next hinted at the success of our armies under the great Washington; our prosperity as a nation since the declaration of our independence; mentioned General Washington's advice to the red men, to plough, and plant, and cultivate their lands. This, he said, they wished to do, but the white men took away their lands, and drove them further and further towards the setting sun:—and what was worse than all, had sent missionaries to preach and hold meetings among them; that the whites who instituted and attended these meetings, stole their horses, drove off their cattle, and taxed their land. These things he considered their greatest calamity,—too grievous to be borne. The principal object of this visit by those chiefs was, we understand, to intercede with the Friends, in whose honesty they appear to place the most implicit confidence, to use their influence to free them from the missionaries now in their borders. What are the real grounds of this opposition to the missionaries among these our red brethren, we know not; but the cause of pure religion and Christian philanthropy demand their speedy investigation and public explanation.—*Palmyra Gazette, American paper, of July last.*

---

[18]Stone, *Life and Times of Sa-go-ye-wat-ha, or Red-Jacket,* i, 187, 191.

Sixteen-year-old Joseph Smith Jr. was perhaps in Red Jacket's audience that night. Lori Elaine Taylor described a Native tradition that the Mormon seer was, like Red Jacket, a disciple of Sganyodaiyo, a Seneca prophet who in 1799 reported visions that led him to denounce drunkenness, witchcraft, promiscuity, and wife-beating. His *Gai'wiio*, "the good word of our Creator," predicted a fiery apocalypse if the world failed to follow what became the Code of Handsome Lake. In 1987 a Wabanimkee told anthropologist Nicholas Vrooman the "real story" of Mormonism's birth: Joseph Smith worked with Senecas whose solidity, stability, and strength impressed him so much he decided "what was really needed was an equivalent of Handsome Lake's Gaiwiio, but for the white people," maybe with more Christian emphasis.[19]

Nothing confirms Joseph Smith knew American Indians before publishing *The Book of Mormon*, which showed no awareness of contemporary Native traditions, even though Smith's "Record of the People of Nephi" was "written to the Lamanites, which are a remnant of the House of Israel."[20] But Red Jacket's 1822 remarks reflect issues—problematic communications, the appropriation of Native lands and resources, the desire to turn Indian agriculturalists into European farmers, and the presumed superiority of Christianity to all other religious traditions—that would echo through Latter-day Saint–Indian encounters far beyond Iroquoia.

THE HOUSE OF ISRAEL

The angel Moroni and James Fenimore Cooper's Natty Bumppo first appeared in 1823. Once Native peoples ceased to be a military threat, the American "Era of Good Feelings" spawned romantic Indians. Sentimental savages, noble but savage still, displaced sinister stereotypes. Ironically, the prejudice that pervaded the early republic put Anglo-Americans at a disadvantage in dealing with Native peoples, for it denied the humanity of American Indians, who were every bit as intelligent and resourceful as the Christians who came to contest, convert, and conquer their land. The belief that superior white people were born to rule pervaded American culture and Mormon scripture. Skin color has nothing to do with human intelligence, adaptability, or determination, which prejudice prevented Joseph Smith and

---

[19]Taylor, "Telling Stories about Mormons and Indians," chapter 4; Grunder, *Mormon Parallels*, mp 305, 1120–22.

[20]*The Book of Mormon*, 1830, 128.

Brigham Young from appreciating. Americans went west convinced of their superiority, but it meant they underestimated those whose lands they wanted. The new settlers cloaked their impositions with good intentions, claiming to seek to redeem and "save" Native peoples, when in fact they had come to displace and destroy their cultures.

Today's Mormonism retains none of its original revolutionary fervor, so the language used to refer to American Indians in early sources can be baffling. The first Saints believed they were the chosen "blood of Israel," which they shared with American Indians. *The Book of Mormon* incorporated British Israelism, or the "Anglo-Israelite Theory," which claimed both the English and American Indians were literal descendants of the Children of Israel's diaspora. Thomas Thorowgood published *Jewes in America* in 1650, arguing that Indians "be of the Jewish race." During the 1790s, Newfoundland native Richard Brothers, the self-proclaimed "Revealed Prince and Prophet" sent to gather the Jews to Jerusalem, expanded the theory's popularity in his 1794 bestseller, *A Revealed Knowledge of the Prophecies and Times.* Mormon officials kept the theory alive: "The more of the blood of Israel that an individual has," Mormon authority Bruce R. McConkie said in 1958, "the easier it is for him to believe the message of salvation as taught by the authorized agents of the Lord."[21]

As alleged descendants of the "House of Israel" and the tribes of Ephraim and Manasseh, early Saints accepted Smith's restored gospel naturally. This belief survives in the faith's patriarchal blessings, which "contemplate inspired declaration of the lineage of the recipient." Nine out of ten converts had "the pure blood of Israel, the greater portion being purely of the blood of Ephraim." Joseph Smith "was a pure Ephraimite," Young claimed. Lamanites belonged to Manasseh's "royal seed, of the royal blood." Joseph Smith taught Young "that the Gentile blood was actually cleansed out of their veins, and the blood of Jacob made to circulate in them; and the revolution and change in the system were so great that it caused the beholder to think they were going into fits." These views proved remarkably persistent. "The members of the Church, most of us of the tribe of Ephraim, are of the remnant of Jacob," wrote church president Joseph Fielding Smith during the 1950s. "We are all of Israel!" a later church president, Spencer W. Kimball, taught not long ago. "We are of Abraham and Isaac and Jacob and Joseph through Ephraim

---

[21]Grunder, *Mormon Parallels,* mp 73, 285–88.

and Manasseh," making them part of an implied hierarchy "ranging from most favored to least favored."[22]

The Nephites of *The Book of Mormon* descended from the righteous prophet and king Nephi, while Lamanites originated with his wicked older brothers Laman and Lemuel. They were all the sons of Lehi, "who was a descendant of Manasseh, who was the son of Joseph, which was sold into Egypt by the hands of his brethren." This produced the phrases "stick of Joseph," "tribe of Joseph," "the sons of Joseph," "the seed of Joseph," "the remnants of Joseph," "the remnant of the seed of Joseph," or the stick, tribe, seed, sons, and house of Lehi, Jacob, or Abraham to refer to "Lamanites, which are a remnant of the house of Israel." The terms "Cousin Lemuel" and "Cousin Laman" reflected the belief that American Indians descended from Nephi's unrighteous brothers, who "had hardened their hearts" against the Lord God, who "did cause a skin of blackness to come upon them." Mormons of European ancestry belonged the tribe of Joseph through their descent from Ephraim. This status is important, noted one LDS authority, "for the literal seed of Abraham are the natural heirs to the remarkable promises given anciently to Abraham, Isaac, and Jacob."[23] As scholar John-Charles Duffy observed, *The Book of Mormon* "made America a theater for the redemption of Israel." Early Mormonism required "that Lamanite identity be a *racial* identity, because it was through bloodlines that certain traits and rights to covenantal promises flowed."[24]

Many historians minimize *The Book of Mormon*'s bigotry, but British-Israelism's racism is undeniable. The *Jewish Encyclopedia* connected the Anglo-Israelite theory with the persecutions of the Jews in 1906, while Herbert W. Armstrong's Worldwide Church of God repudiated the doctrine only after he died in 1986. Controversies surrounding a human skull discovered on the Columbia River in 1996 reveal that science is not immune from such chauvinistic nonsense as touting the "Caucasian" cast of Kennewick Man's head.[25]

The distance between Joseph Smith's Lamanites, James Fenimore Cooper's Mohicans, "and the Indian that stands in front of the cigar-shop is not spacious," Mark Twain observed. There was a profound difference:

[22]Ludlow, "Of the House of Israel," 51–55; and Mauss, "In Search of Ephraim," 133–74. See also Young, Remarks, 9 October 1853, *Millennial Star*, 28 January 1854, 52; Young, "The Blood of Israel and the Gentiles," 8 April 1855, *Journal of Discourses*, 2:268–69.

[23]Ludlow, "Of the House of Israel," 51–55; 2 Nephi 5:21.

[24]Duffy, "The Use of 'Lamanite' in Official LDS Discourse," 124, 135.

[25]Hitt, "Mighty White of You," 41.

Leatherstocking's Indians were the last of a doomed race, while Smith's Lamanites were a chosen people—"a remnant of the House of Israel"— destined to usher in the Last Days and the return of Christ. Like other Americans, Mormons appropriated Indian identify, scholar Christopher C. Smith observed, but they "at least generally acknowledged and affirmed natives' right to be alive."[26]

GO UNTO THE LAMANITES: 1830

"Go unto the Lamanites and preach my gospel unto them," the Lord directed Oliver Cowdery before Mormonism was a year old.[27] In October 1830 Cowdery set out for Indian country beyond Missouri's western border, with three companions, including the recently converted Parley P. Pratt. They promised salvation and hope but cast the Lamanites as degraded savages who had fallen from the faith of their fathers. In theory, the Latter-day Saints' sacred stories and promises of redemption for the fallen Lamanites should have had immense appeal to the nation's beleaguered Indian peoples; in practice Mormon scripture spoke King James English and advocated Christian doctrines as alien to Native spiritual reality as ancient Hebrew.

The 1830s were a dark decade for America's Indian peoples. The missionaries set out five months after President Andrew Jackson signed the Indian Removal Act, which authorized the president to trade the lands of any Indians "residing in any of the states or territories" for lands west of the Mississippi. The act directed "the President solemnly to assure" Indian nations making such an exchange that the United States would "forever secure and guaranty" their new lands, unless "the Indians become extinct, or abandon the same."[28]

The Mormon evangelists met the Wyandottes at Sandusky, Ohio, as the tribe prepared to join some 45,000 Native exiles west of the Missouri River. After trudging across Illinois and Missouri during the "Winter of the Deep Snow," Cowdery, Pratt, and Dr. Frederick G. Williams reached

---

[26]Smith, "Playing Lamanite," 165.

[27]*The Doctrine and Covenants of The Church of Jesus Christ of Latter-day Saints* (Salt Lake City: The Church of Jesus Christ of Latter-day Saints, 1921), 38:28.

[28]"The Indian Bill," *Niles Weekly Register*, 29 May 1830, 260. Joseph Smith considered Indian removal "a wise measure, and it reflects the highest honor upon our government." Smith, *History of the Church*, 2:362.

the "Permanent Indian Frontier" known as Indian country. They crossed the frozen Kansas River to a recently established Delaware village, where Cowdery told a council of Lenni Lenape elders of their glorious past when "the whole land was theirs; the Great Spirit gave it to them, and no palefaces dwelt among them," Pratt recalled. If the red men received the message, their Great Father would "raise up prophets and wise and good men amongst them again." The Delaware leader spoke with the courtesy typical of Native responses "to our white friends who have come so far, and been at such pains to tell us good news, and especially this new concerning the book of our forefathers."[29]

The missionaries' visit to Indian country violated a long list of laws, U.S. Indian agent Richard W. Cummins complained. He refused to let them return without permission from Superintendent William Clark. The evangelists planned to ask Clark's consent: if he refused, "they will go to the Rocky Mountains, but that they will be with the Indians. The Men act very strange."[30] Cummins ordered them to depart immediately, either "eastward into Missouri or westward to the Leavenworth guard-house." This clash foreshadowed decades of Mormon conflict with the Office of Indian Affairs.[31]

Oliver Cowdery stayed among Jackson County's "Universalists, atheists, deists, Presbyterians, Methodists, Baptists, and professed Christians, priests and people, with all the devils from the infernal pit." His 1831 report showed Mormon interest had already moved to the Far West:

> I am informed of another tribe of Lamanites lately, who have abundance of flocks of the best kinds of sheep and cattle, and they manufacture blankets of a superior quality. The tribe is very numerous; they live three hundred miles west of Santa Fe, and are called Navajoes [sic]. Why I mention this tribe is, because I feel under obligations to communicate to my brethren every information concerning the Lamanites that I meet with in my labors and travels, believing as I do that much is expected from me in the cause of our Lord; and doubting not but I am daily remembered in your prayers before the throne of the Most High by all of my brethren, as well by those who have not seen my face in the flesh as those who have.[32]

[29]Pratt, *The Autobiography*, 49, 56; Roberts, *Comprehensive History*, 1:253.
[30]Cummins to Clark, 20 January 1831, in Jennings, "First Mormon Mission to the Indians," 298.
[31]John C. McCoy, "Some Thrilling Border History," *Kansas City Journal*, 28 December 1884.
[32]*Times and Seasons*, 15 February 1844, 432–33.

Great Father Writes It in Red Man's Heart

Joseph Smith reached Independence on 14 July 1831 after walking across Missouri from St. Louis. On "the borders of the Lamanites," the prophet "appointed and consecrated" Jackson County as "the land of promise, and the place for the city of Zion." On the site of the Garden of Eden and "the spot for the temple unto the Lord," this sacred ground would serve "for the gathering of the saints," with Independence as "the center place."[33] The scrappy frontier settlement, founded four years earlier, became "the place of general rendezvous, and head-quarters of the Mormonites." The town had a brick courthouse, "two or three merchant stores, and fifteen or twenty dwelling houses, built mostly of logs hewed on both sides," situated "on a handsome rise of ground, about three miles south of the Missouri river, and about twelve miles east of the dividing line between the U.S. and the Indian Reserve." Mormons settled in Missouri "to convert the Indians to the faith of Mormonism," wrote early convert Ezra Booth, hoping to emulate the Jesuits of South America, who had gained "an entire ascendancy over the hearts and consciences of the natives, and thereby became their masters."[34]

Relocating a band of true believers with deep New England roots to America's borderlands entangled the Saints in conflicts over slavery, the forced relocation of Indians, and the suspicions the town's southern "old settlers" had about their Yankee neighbors. The new settlers returned the favor, noting that the Jackson County's inhabitants were "generally an indolent and illiterate people" and "mostly enemies to the cause of Christ."[35]

Joseph Smith spent less than a month in Independence in 1831. He later described standing "upon the confines or western limits of the United States, and looking into the vast wilderness of those that sat in darkness," observing "the degradation, leanness of intellect, ferocity, and jealousy of a people that were nearly a century behind the times" who "roamed about without the benefit of civilization, refinement, or religion."[36] Such contempt did not endear the Saints to Missourians. Undeterred, the prophet's revelations "transformed a bedraggled frontier village surrounded by vast stretches of empty prairie into a sacred place." The process did not improve relations with those who Smith's admiring biographer characterized as "a tough crowd

---

[33]D&C, 54:9, 57:1–3.
[34]Booth to Ira Eddy, "Letter 6," *Ohio Star*, 17 November 1831, 3.
[35]"Extracts of Letters from a Mormonite," *The Unitarian*, 1 May 1834, 252.
[36]Smith, *History of the Church*, 1:189.

of traders and trappers" who tended to scurry into Indian country on the approach of a federal marshal. By late 1833 some twelve hundred Mormons had flocked to Jackson County.[37]

"The Book of Mormon is a record of the forefathers of our western Tribes of Indians, having been found through the ministration of an holy Angel translated into our own Language by the gift and power of God, after having been hid up in the earth for the last fourteen hundred years containing the word of God, which was delivered unto them," wrote Joseph Smith in 1833. The western tribes descended from "Joseph that was sold into Egypt, and that the land of America is a promised land unto them." The tribe of Judah would return to King David's Jerusalem, but the City of Zion would be "built upon the Land of America." The good Shepherd would gather his scattered sheep "and Lead them out from all nations" to the New Jerusalem. The United States would soon "present such a scene of *bloodshed* as has not a parallel in the hystory of our nation." Pestilence, hail, famine, and earthquake would sweep the wicked "from off the face of this Land to open and prepare the way for the return of the lost tribes of Israel from the north country—The people of the Lord, those who have complied with the requisitions of the new covenant" had commenced gathering to Zion, "which is in the State of Missouri."[38]

By year's end, the old Missouri settlers expelled the Mormons from Jackson County. When the news reached Kirtland, Joseph Smith dictated a revelation to go to Missouri, "break down the walls of mine enemies," and "scatter their watchmen." He organized two hundred men as the "Camp of Zion," now recalled as Zion's Camp. The prophet marched his paramilitary across Ohio, Indiana, and Illinois to Clay County, Missouri, seeking to restore the Jackson County Saints to their homes. "The redemption of Zion must needs come by power," the Lord explained, and He would pour out his "wrath without measure."[39] By the time the camp arrived, most of Missouri's Mormons had moved north and Smith's warriors were in no position to conquer anything. Cholera afflicted sixty-eight Saints, including Joseph Smith, and killed more than a dozen of the camp's veterans. Smith returned to Ohio.[40]

---

[37]Bushman, *Joseph Smith: Rough Stone Rolling*, 164.

[38]Letterbook 1, p. 17, The Joseph Smith Papers, accessed 5 January 2019, https://www.josephsmith-papers.org/paper-summary/letterbook-1/29.

[39]*Doctrine and Covenants*, Section 103:2, 15; 101:57.

[40]Smith, *History of the Church*, 2:104–14

A surprising accommodation followed. Missouri's legislature created Caldwell County in 1836 as a virtual reservation for Latter Day Saints. The accord collapsed when Smith returned in March 1838 as his followers expanded beyond Caldwell into neighboring Missouri counties. The ten thousand Mormons said to be in Missouri's northwestern counties shifted the balance of political power. In May Smith established Adam-ondi-Ahman in Daviess County, which had been reserved for non-Mormons. At their new capital, Far West, the Mormons organized three large cooperative "United Firms" as part of a new communal economic order and began bidding for government contracts.[41]

An August 1838 election sparked a violent confrontation that degenerated into border warfare resulting in almost forty total deaths in a series of raids, house-burnings, armed skirmishes, and a massacre at Jacob Hawn's mill. Missouri's "Mormon War" sparked new charges of the Saints forming Native alliances. Two militia officers and a Methodist preacher had it on "the best authority" that Mormon leaders believed and expected "that immense numbers of Indians, of various tribes, are only waiting the signal for a general rise" and accompany the Destroying Angel "through the land, and work the general destruction of all that are not Mormons." John N. Sapp swore he "heard Sidney Rigdon and Lyman Wight say they had twelve men of their Church among the Indians and that their object was to induce the Indians to Join them (the said mormons) in making war upon the Missourians." Another former Mormon, Nathan Marsh, heard Joseph Smith boast "that he had fourteen thousand men, not belonging to the Church, ready, at a moment's warning (which was generally understood to mean Indians)." The Mormons believed "that the time had arrived, when all the wicked should be destroyed from the face of the earth, & that the Indians would be the principal means by which this object would be accomplished."[42]

In September 1838 Smith denied Mormon leaders had "ingratiated themselves with the Indians, for the purpose of getting the Indians to commit depredations upon the people of this state" and had no "communication with the Indians on any subject; and we, and all the Mormon church, as we believe, entertain the same feelings and fears towards the Indians that are entertained by other citizens of this state."[43] Smith was telling the truth.

---

[41]LeSueur, *The 1838 Mormon War in Missouri*, 23, 28, 32–35.

[42]Missouri General Assembly, *Document Containing the Correspondence, Orders, &c., in relation to the disturbances with the Mormons*, 16–17. See also transcriptions and images of items 16A/2/9111 and 16A/2/9112, Mormon War Papers, 1837–1841, Missouri State Archives.

[43]"The Mormon Difficulties," *Niles National Register*, 13 October 1838, 103/3.

Native peoples played a central role in the new religion's millennial visions, but Mormons seldom acted on these beliefs. "Joseph Smith devoted nearly all his energy toward building and expanding the Mormon kingdom," historian Stephen LeSueur observed.[44]

Missouri sheriff and militia captain Cornelius Gilliam, who had fought real Indians in Florida and Illinois and died fighting them in Oregon, "wore a full Indian costume, had his war paint on, and called himself 'the Delaware Chief'" during Missouri's borderlands Mormon War. "They would whoop and yell, and otherwise comport themselves as savages." When confronted with the full force of Missouri's militia, Smith surrendered his six hundred poorly armed men. "This was far better than to have exposed themselves and their followers to the cruel mercies" of the Jackson County "Rangers," the Fishing River "Tigers," and Neil Gilliam's "Delaware amarnjans," a local chronicler observed. Gilliam's amarnjans "committed many excesses," burning Mormon farmsteads and wantonly destroying their livestock and property.[45]

ON THEIR WAY TO THE ROCKY MOUNTAINS: NAUVOO DETOUR

From its origin, Mormonism had its eye on the far West. The church's newspaper reported "Capt. Bonaville's Company, (150) under the command of Capt. [Joseph R.] Walker" passed through Independence in May 1832 "on its way to the Rocky Mountains, to trap and hunt for fur." It noted Nathaniel Wythe's expedition bound "for the mouth of Oregon River, to prepare (as it is said) for settling a territory."[46] At the ecstatic dedication of the Kirtland Temple in 1836, future apostle Erastus Snow recalled being blessed to "perform a good work in teaching and leading the Lamanites west of the Rocky Mountains." This seemed wonderful to his youthful mind, "as the continent west of the Mississippi was known as the home of the savage."[47]

Such marvelous talk led to little interaction between Mormon leaders and Indians until 1839, when the Saints found refuge in Illinois following their bitter expulsion from Missouri. Church leaders bought the village of

---

[44]LeSueur, *The 1838 Mormon War in Missouri*, 14.

[45]Pease, *History of Caldwell and Livingston Counties, Missouri*, 134, 137–39.

[46]*The Evening and the Morning Star*, 6 June 1832, 6/2.

[47]Snow, "Autobiography," *Utah Genealogical and Historical Magazine* (July 1923), 106.

Commerce and renamed it Nauvoo. Smith built his new gathering place on the site of a Sauk and Meskwaki village that James White had traded from Sauk leader Quashquame, giving "a little *sku-ti-apo* [liquor], and two thousand bushels of corn" for the land.[48]

Nauvoo, where he built a temple, served as mayor and militia general, became Joseph Smith's crowning achievement. He expanded his revolutionary theology and had his closest known personal contacts with American Indians. Sometimes Indian leaders joined the prophet on the platform when he spoke before thousands of people.

The Mormon prophet's confidential prophecies force historians to unravel a secret history. In his last two years, "Joseph the Seer" revealed teachings that were only hinted at in his published revelations. He organized the Council of Fifty, the brotherhood of priests and princes who would govern the world in the Last Days during its transition to God's rule, and a Holy Order to enact Masonic-style rites that sealed the Celestial Marriages of elite polygamists. Few of Nauvoo's Saints knew anything about these doctrines and oath-bound orders, but they laid the groundwork for many controversial practices—spiritual wifery, male adoption to create vast hierarchical families of the Royal Blood of Israel, the doctrine of Adam as God, and blood atonement—that make understanding early Mormonism so hard. These "secret things," Joseph's wife Emma Smith said, "cost Joseph and Hyrum their lives."[49]

"In the days of Joseph, a string of guards was set around him on every side," Brigham Young recalled, "lest he should have communion with the remnants of Israel who are wandering on the plains and in the kanyons of this country."[50] Politics limited but did not stop Joseph Smith's meeting with Natives in Nauvoo. On 12 August 1841 General Smith and the Nauvoo Legion band greeted Sauk leaders "Keokuk, Kis-ku-kosh, Appenoose, and about one hundred chiefs and braves." Smith delivered a sermon, advising "them to cease killing each other and warring with other tribes; also to keep peace with the whites." Keokuk claimed "he had a Book of Mormon at his wigwam" that Smith had given him. "I believe," said Keokuk, "you are a great and good man; I look rough, but I also am a son of the Great Spirit.

---

[48]William Whitaker, "Searching for Quashquame's Sauk and Meskwaki Village," *Newsletter of the Iowa Archeological Society* 58:4 (2009), 1–4.

[49]Quinn, *The Mormon Hierarchy: Origins of Power*, 170, 481.

[50]Young, Remarks, 8 August 1857, *Journal of Discourses*, 5:128.

I have heard your advice—we intend to quit fighting, and follow the good talk you have given us." The Mormons feasted their visitors "with good food, dainties, and melons." The Saux "entertained the spectators with a specimen of their dancing."[51]

Thomas Sharp, no friend of the Mormons, mocked the meeting.

"KEOKUK'S VISIT TO NAUVOO," *WARSAW (ILLINOIS) SIGNAL*, 25 AUGUST 1841.

We understand that one day last week, they had quite a pageant at Nauvoo. The Indian Chief Keokuk, with about fifty of his followers—warriors, squaws and papooses—took occasion to pay a special visit to their brother, the Revelator and Prophet, to smoke the pipe of peace with him in his wik-ke-up—and discourse of the wonders of the New Jerusalem.

The distinguished strangers were received with marked attention. The Nauvoo Legion,—ever ready to honor the great ones of the earth, who come to pay homage to the Prophet—escorted them from the landing to the temple, where, in the august presence of the twelve Apostles, and the twelve oxen, these mighty Chiefs held social converse, for the space of half an hour.

They were both dressed in uniform—the Prophet in the splendid and brilliant uniform of the Nauvoo Legion, which he commands—and the Chieftan in the less dazzling habiliments of the wilderness—a dirty blanket and a pair of moccasins.

The Prophet made a speech to the warrior in the presence of the assembled multitude, in which he depicted in glowing colors, and enthusiastic strain the wonders of the Great Temple, the mysteries of the book of Mormon, and the glorious times that they will have together, in these latter days, in the latter day city which they are going to inherit.

All this was perfectly intelligible to the sage chieftain, who, meanwhile, looked unutterable things [*sic*]. He replied in a very effective speech of twenty minutes, which brought tears to the eyes of a number of gallant soldiers of the Legion, and squaws and papooses in attendance. He said he was surprised at the mighty things which had been accomplished by his brother on this side the big river. As to the New Jerusalem to which they were all going to emigrate, so far as he was concerned, it depended very much whether there would be any government annuities—and as for the "milk and honey," which was to flow over the land, he was not particular—he should prefer whiskey!

In short, it was quite an imposing and interesting spectacle—the meeting of those two men—and when next so remarkable an event takes place, in the language of the historian of John Gilpin: "May we be there to see."

---

[51]Smith, *History of the Church*, 4:401–402.

To Start to the Rocky Mountains

The mysterious lands beyond the Missouri River intrigued Americans during the 1830s, especially the Latter-day Saints. Joseph Smith said Sen. Henry Clay advised him in 1839, "You had better go to Oregon." New York editor James Arlington Bennett counseled the prophet to "pull up stakes and take possession of the Oregon territory in his own right, and establish an independent empire. In one hundred years from this time, no nation on earth could conquer such a people." The church's official histories date the prophet's first observation that his people's future lay in the West to August 1842. On a visit to Iowa, Smith reportedly said the Saints "would be driven to the Rocky Mountains, many would apostatize, others would be put to death by our persecutors, or lose their lives in consequence of exposure or disease," but some survive to build settlements and cities, "and see the saints become a mighty people in the midst of the Rocky Mountains."[52]

Anson Call remembered the prophecy. Joseph Smith entered a trance, "his countenance change[d] to white; not the deadly white of a bloodless face, but a living brilliant white. He seemed absorbed in gazing at something at a great distance and said I am gazing upon the valleys of those mountains." The Seer "was wrapt in vision": Call felt "that his voice was the voice of God." He told Call and Shadrach Roundy they would "perform as great a work as has been done by man" in the Rockies. Call did not realize "the vast significance of those prophetic declarations compared with what I do now, with the experiences of the 45 years that have intervened since they were uttered."[53]

Sacred histories ignore Joseph Smith's gift for seizing the moment and his impetuous improvisations, which complicate identifying when the prophet began predicting his people's future in the Far West. Ironically, the first contemporary evidence comes not from the religion's historical records but from Oliver H. Olney, a mystical Mormon heretic who began communicating with the "Antient of Days" in 1842. He converted in Ohio in 1831 and followed the faith to Missouri and Nauvoo, where the High Council withdrew the hand of fellowship in March 1842 "because his deeds are evil." Olney claimed he knew early Mormonism "like a book," but historian Dale

---

[52]*Millennial Star*, 3 October 1857, 630; Smith, *History of the Church*, 6:188.
[53]Tullidge, *Tullidge's Histories, Supplemental Volume, Biographies*, 271–72.

Morgan observed his papers were "of somewhat mixed value." Olney himself admitted he would "not vouch /For the truth of what I have written /As I find I am amongst a Lying set." His papers indicate that by 1842 "Joseph Smith was ready to abandon Nauvoo and take his church west to the Rockies," Morgan noted. In "his characteristically atrocious verse," Olney described these plans "as they were discussed on the street in Nauvoo"; Smith's trial at Springfield in January 1843 "demonstrated the power of habeas corpus to keep him out of the hands of the Missouri courts" and "postponed the Mormon migration to the Rockies. Ironically, this reprieve also resulted in Joseph's being murdered before he could take his church west," Morgan wrote in his comments on Olney.[54]

During 1843 and 1844, "Natives of the Potawate-mys" made multiple visits to Nauvoo as Joseph Smith dispatched "exploring excursion[s] to the west," which was "a code for Indian work."[55] In April 1843, the prophet "had a talk with A deligation of the Indians, who complained of having th[e]ir cattle & horses &c stolen & they were much troubled & wanted to know what they should do," having "borne their greivances patie[n]tly."[56] The delegation consisted of three Potawatomi leaders, notably Apaquachawba, who had heard Joseph Smith "could talk to the Great Spirit and he wanted him to advise them what to do, as the Indians were dissatisfied with the white people bordering on their lands." Already displaced from their upper Great Lakes homelands and Wisconsin, Michigan, and Indiana, the nation had endured forced removal from northern Illinois and western Missouri to Iowa, and now faced being pushed into Kansas. Working through an interpreter named Hitchcock, who suspected the Mormons of "plotting some mischief," the Potawatomi asked if the prophet "would give them any assistance in case of an outbreak on the frontier" for "they had smoked the pipe with ten tribes who had agreed to defend each other to the last extremity." Smith sympathized but "could give them no assistance" for "his hands were tied by the U.S." The Natives gave General Smith "a large silver British Medal" and agreed to return to Nauvoo when the corn reached "the top of their leggins."[57]

---

[54] *Times and Seasons* 3:11, 1 February 1843, 747–48. Olney's papers in the Beinecke Library include Morgan's Foreword and Calendar of the Documents, written for book dealer Edward Eberstadt.

[55] Woodruff, *Journal*, 26 June 1843, 2:246; Walker, "Seeking the 'Remnant,'" 28.

[56] Smith, Journal, Book 2, 18 April 1843.

[57] Coates, "Refugees Meet: The Mormons and Indians in Iowa," 498–502.

Returning in June, they lacked an interpreter, Wilford Woodruff reported, but "manifested a desire to see the Temple & the city. Said they were hungry. I took them home & fed them. Gave them some trinklets &c." The prophet was away avoiding arrest, so the Potawatomies waited "until the Prophet returned" and had "a talk with Hyrum Smith in the basement of the Nauvoo House," though they "did not wish to communicate their feelings until they could see the great Prophet." On 2 July 1843 Joseph Smith "met those chiefs in the court-room."[58]

> The Indian orator arose and asked the Prophet if the men who were present were all his friends. Answer—"Yes."
>
> He then said—"We as a people have long been distressed and oppressed. We have been driven from our lands many times. We have been wasted away by wars, until there are but few of us left. The white man has hated us and shed our blood, until it has appeared as though there would soon be no Indians left. We have talked with the Great Spirit, and the Great Spirit has talked with us. We have asked the Great Spirit to save us and let us live; and the Great Spirit has told us that he had raised up a great Prophet, chief, and friend, who would do us great good and tell us what to do; and the Great Spirit has told us that you are the man (pointing to the Prophet Joseph). We have now come a great way to see you, and hear your words, and to have you to tell us what to do. Our horses have become poor traveling, and we are hungry. We will now wait and hear your word."
>
> The Spirit of God rested upon the Lamanites, especially the orator. Joseph was much affected and shed tears. . . .
>
> When the Prophet's words were interpreted to the chiefs, they all said it was good. The chief asked, "How many moons would it be before the Great Spirit would bless them?" He told them, Not a great many.
>
> At the close of the interview, Joseph had an ox killed for them, and they were furnished with some more horses, and they went home satisfied and contented.[59]

Based on Hitchcock's reports, militia general Henry King alerted Iowa governor John Chambers to rumors he heard in Keokuk:

> What the result of this meeting has been I am unable to say, but it seems evident, from all I can learn, from leading men among the *Mormons* and from various other sources that a grand conspiracy is about being entered into between the *Mormons and Indians* to destroy all the white settlements on the

---

[58]Woodruff, *Journal*, 26 June 1843, 2:246. Although attributed to Woodruff's journal, he wrote this reminiscence in 1855. Dan Vogel, communication with the editor, 11 April 2014.

[59]Smith, "Interview with Pottawattamie Chiefs," *History of the Church*, 5:479–81.

frontier. The time fixed to carry this nefarious plot into execution is about the ripening of Indian corn—This may all be rumour, but I have deemed it too serious a rumour to be trifled with, and have therefore taken the liberty of troubling you with a statement of facts, that in the event of an outbreak we may not be wholly unprepared.[60]

Chambers forwarded the letter to the commissioner of Indian Affairs, dismissing it as "rather indicative of the general suspicion and excitement which prevails against the Mormons than of any treasonable design on the part of their prophet." Smith was "an exceedingly vain and vindictive fellow, and would no doubt feel flattered by the appeal made to him by the Indians if he could bring them into a conflict with the Missouri frontier might do so to revenge his old feud with the people of that state." Chambers asked General King to keep him informed of "further intercourse between these Indians and the 'prophet.'"[61]

As Joseph Smith launched his 1844 presidential campaign, his Lamanite theology became entangled with speculation about moving west. On 20 February 1844 Smith directed the apostles "to send out a delegation, and investigate the locations of California and Oregon and find a good location where we can remove to after the Temple is completed and build a city in a day and have a government of our own in a healthy climate." Three days later, Smith:

> Met with the 12 [Apostles] &c. in assembly Room concerning the Oregon Expidition. I told them I wanted an explosition of all that count[r]y. Send 25 men. Let them preach the Gospel whereever they go. Let that man go that can raise $500, a horse or mule, a double barrel gun, one rifle, and one shot, saddle, bridle, pr of 8 bore Pistols, Bowie knife, &c. Appoint a leader. Let him beat up for volunteers. I want every man that goes to be a king and a Priest, when he gets to the mountains he may want to talk with his God. When with the savage nations have power to govern &c. If we don't get volunteers wait till after the election.[62]

An official church history added colorful details to this report, where the Saints could have "a government of our own, get up into the mountains, where the devil cannot dig us out, and live in a healthful climate, where we can live as old as we have a mind to." The prophet picked a "noble company"

---

[60]King to Chambers, 14 July 1843, Typescript, Iowa Superintendency, 1838–1849, Microfilm Publication M234, Reel 363, 1949, National Archives. Courtesy Christopher C. Smith.

[61]Coates, "Refugees Meet: The Mormons and Indians in Iowa," 501–502.

[62]Faulring, *An American Prophet's Record*, 20 and 23 February 1844, 447–48.

of stalwarts for his Western expedition, notably Daniel Spencer, George D. Watt, Hosea Stout, and Jonathan Dunham.[63]

OPEN THE GOSPEL TO EVERY LAMANITE NATION: THE COUNCIL OF FIFTY

The catalyst for the "temporal establishment" of the Council of Fifty on 10 March 1844 was Apostle Lyman Wight's complaint that Wisconsin's U.S. Indian agent "was using his legal powers to prevent the Latter-day Saints from dealing with the Indians who allowed the Mormons to obtain lumber from Indian lands." Wight wanted to go "with the Indians to the Republic of Texas where they would be free from U.S. laws and could establish a gathering place." The next day, Joseph Smith formally organized the Kingdom of God, drawing largely on men he had enjoined to "perfect secrecy" and ordained as kings and priests in the Holy Order created to sanctify the polygamous marriages. A few non-Mormons drawn from Nauvoo's criminal underworld, such as counterfeiter Edward Bonny and "infernal-device" (bomb) designer Uriah Brown, added diversity to "the grand K. of G."[64]

The new Children of Israel imagined their blood kinship with American Indians would culminate with an apocalyptic nightmare of death and destruction. Until May 1844 clerk William Clayton's record reads like the minutes of a proper debating society, emphasizing the council's support of "universal peace and good will, union and brotherly love to all the great family of man." Joseph Smith's presidential ambitions, imperial dreams, and Indian fantasies usually appear as an appeal for Native peoples to make peace with one another. On 19 March 1844 Smith moved "that brother James Emmett be sent on a mission to the Lamanites to instruct them to unite together and cease their enmity towards each other." He explained "the nature of the nature mission," which the minutes do not provide, but enlisting Native allies was among the Council of Fifty's purposes. At the church's semi-annual conference on 6 April 1844, "Lamanites and interpreter came in and took a seat on the stand," noted Joseph Smith's history. Wilford Woodruff reported "eleven Lamanites chiefs braves &c." occupied an outdoor platform. At one of the council's first meetings on 4 April, "Eleven Lamanites appeared and

---

[63]Smith, *History of the Church,* 5:85, 170.

[64]Ehat, "'It Seems Like Heaven Began on Earth': Joseph Smith and the Constitution of the Kingdom of God," 255–56, 267; Quinn, "The Council of Fifty," 2.

wanted Council. We had a very pleasant and impressive interview."[65] A week later, the Fifty unanimously voted to "receive from this time henceforth and forever, Joseph Smith, as our Prophet, Priest & King," shouting "Hossanna to God and the Lamb Amen and Amen."[66]

Joseph Smith devoted many of his last days to Council of Fifty meetings, developing plans to move his followers to Texas, the Rocky Mountains, Alta California, or Oregon. He sent an ambassador to Texas to convert "Notsuoh"—Sam Houston—and petitioned Congress "to be authorized to raise one hundred thousand armed volunteers to police the inter-mountain and Pacific coast west from Oregon to Texas."[67] After an all-day meeting on 25 April, the Council of Fifty adjourned "sine die" as Joseph Smith turned his attention to dealing with the defection of some of his closest allies, notably his counselor William Law and Wilson Law, a Nauvoo Legion major general.

Even as his enemies secured an indictment against him for adultery and "officers from Carthage" sought to arrest him, Joseph Smith seemed oblivious to the provocative nature of his dealings with American Indians. On 22 May 1844 "about 40 Indians of the Sacs and Foxes came up in front of the Mansion, four or five of them being mounted, among whom was Black Hawk's brother, Kis-kish-kee, &c." Smith "was obliged to send word I could not see them at present," but the next day he talked "with the Sac and Fox Indians in my back kitchen. They said—'When our fathers first came here, this land was inhabited by the Spanish; when the Spaniards were driven off, the French came, and then the English and Americans; and our fathers talked a great deal with the Big Spirit.' They complained that they had been robbed of their lands by the whites, and cruelly treated." Smith agreed that "they had been wronged, but that we had bought this land," and he "advised them not to sell any more land, but to cultivate peace" with all men. The Indians "commenced a war dance" in front Smith's Red Brick store on the

[65]Kenney, *Wilford Woodruff's Journal*, 6 April 1844, 2:376. Potawatomi leaders met on 4 April to enlist Mormon support, for they "did not want to sell them any more land." Smith told them, "we were doing all we could for them and that God would be pleased if they would cease their wars with each other." Samuel Brannan published the lithograph "Joseph the Prophet Addressing the Lamanites" showing him on 4 April 1844 when eleven Potawatomis visited the Council of Fifty. Grow, , *Council of Fifty Minutes*, 58, 74–75, 112–14.

[66]Ibid., 11 April 1844, 95–96.

[67]Faulring, *An American Prophet's Record*, 10, 11, 15 March 1844, 458–462; Smith, *History of the Church*, 6:286, 369–76.

Mississippi. "Our people commenced with music and firing cannon. After the dance, which lasted about two hours, the firing of cannon closed the exercise, and with our music marched back to the office."[68]

These encounters did not go unnoticed. John W. Putnam charged "that the Mormons are endeavoring to seduce the Indian tribes from their allegiance to the United States, and engage them to take up the hatchet against the people of the United States, and that white men are to lead them on to the conflict." Putnam "understood that Lyman Wight has already departed to stir up the savages, and prepare them for the final struggle with the whites." He claimed the Saints wanted "the Indians to attack the people and subvert the government, and establish Mormonism throughout the United States." Indians "had twice held their Powows, or war dances in Nauvoo," Putnam swore.[69]

On 7 June 1844 dissidents published the *Nauvoo Expositor*, whose first issue exposed Smith's "spiritual wife" doctrine, while its prospectus promised "to advocate, *and exercise*," free speech, "censure any *self-constituted* MONARCH," and oppose, "with uncompromising hostility, any *Union of Church and State*." The crisis escalated with the paper's destruction. On 20 June 1844 Gen. Wilson Law of the Nauvoo Legion sent Governor Thomas Ford an affidavit charging Joseph Smith was ready to:

> Set the laws at defiance; for the Government, he said, was corrupt, and ought to be overthrown, and he would do it, for he could get help plenty from the Indians, for he had communication with them all the time, and they were ready. And deponent further saith that he verily believes that said Joseph Smith is, and has been, conspiring with the Indians against this Government, he having agents out among the Indians, passing to and fro ever since last summer; and that a number of Indians have come to Nauvoo, at different times, last winter and spring, and held secret councils with said Smith.[70]

With the governor's promise of protection, the Mormon prophet surrendered to Illinois authorities and was incarcerated with his brother and friends in Carthage Jail. On 27 June 1844 a militia mob with blackened faces attacked. A short gunfight left Joseph and Hyrum Smith "perfectly dead," martyred "by the hands of assassins while under the most solemn pledges from the Governor for their safety."[71]

---

[68] Smith, *History of the Church*, 6:401–402.
[69] Putnam Affidavit, 13 August 1844, in Palmer, "Did Joseph Smith Commit Treason?" 52–58.
[70] Wilson Law Affidavit, 20 June 1844, in ibid.
[71] "Events of June 1844," in Grow, *Council of Fifty Minutes*, 202–204.

Years later, William Byram Pace recalled hearing Smith's last words to the Nauvoo Legion:

I will therefore say to you as Saints and elders of Israel be not troubled nor give yourselves uneasiness so as to make rash moves by which you may be cut short in your preaching the gospel to this generation, for you will be called upon to go forth and call upon the free men from Maine to gather themselves in the strongholds of the Rocky Mountains and the red men from the west and all people from the south and from the north and from the east to go to the west and establish themselves in the stronghold of their gathering places and there you will gather the red men to their center from their scattered and dispersed situation to become the strong arm of Jehovah, who will be a strong bulwark of protection from your foes.[72]

What practical results did Joseph Smith's secretive Lamanite teachings have during his life? Beyond agitating his neighbors, sparking rumors of Mormon-Indian conspiracies, and arousing the polite curiosity of displaced Natives, not much. Six months after Joseph Smith's death, "all the special projects of the pre-martyrdom Council of Fifty had failed." It fulfilled none of Smith's ambitious plans. "No California, Oregon, or Texas scouting parties materialized," wrote research historian Andrew Ehat. "The mission among the Lamanites never got underway." For believers such as Ehat, "the Council of Fifty achieved the 'measures of Joseph' when Brigham Young entered the Salt Lake Valley."[73]

The murder of the two brothers devastated their followers. "The gentiles have rejected the gospel," Chairman Young told the Council of Fifty in March 1845, "they have killed the prophets." Those who did not take "an active part in the murder all rejoice in it and say amen to it" and boasted they were "willing the blood of the prophets should be shed." Where "shall we go to preach. We cannot go any where but to the house of Israel We cant get salvation without it." Bishop George Miller said, "this is all the Land of the Lamanites and the white people are nothing but intruders; the devil gave it to them. If we can form an alliance with the Lamanites we dont care about the whites nor any thing else."[74]

Joseph Smith's death ignited a succession crisis. The Council of Fifty did not meet again until 4 February 1845, after Brigham Young and the

---

[72]Pace, Autobiography, 1904, LDS Archives.
[73]Ehat, "'It Seems Like Heaven,'" 19.
[74]Grow, *Council of Fifty Minutes*, 11 March 1845, 300, 306.

apostles had established their right to lead the Latter-day Saints—at least the ones who did not follow attempted successors James Strang or William Smith. Brigham Young claimed Joseph Smith had committed "the keys of the Kingdom to the Lamanites—he committed them to me—we visited & preached to them. They believed it, we have heard a many times from them."[75]

Forty of the council's members appointed Young "standing chairman as successor to Prest Joseph Smith by unanimous vote" and "rejected and dropped" its non-Mormons and Young's rivals from "the new organization." On 1 March the council met to "fill up the Quorum," adding Jonathan Dunham, Daniel Spencer, Shadrack Roundy, and Lewis Denna, "a Lamanite of the Oneida nation, and the First Lamanite who has been admitted a member of any Quorum of the Church." William Clayton reported:

> The object of the Council was to decide whether we shall send out a company of men with Bro. Dana to fill Josephs measures originally adopted in this Council by going West to seek out a location and a home where the Saints can dwell in peace and health and where they can erect the ensign and standard of liberty of the nations, and live by the laws of God without being oppressed and mobbed under a tyrannical government, without protection from the laws. Many able speeches were made on the subject, and the Council finally agreed to send out a company with Brother Dana to accomplish this important object. The following brethren were selected and appointed by unanimous vote of the Council, for this mission, viz., Samuel Bent to be the first man and president of the Mission, Jonathan Dunham next, Cyrus Daniels, Daniel Spencer, John S. Fullmer, Charles Shumway, Albert Carrington, and John W. Farnham. These brethren are expected to start immediately after Conference and proceed from tribe to tribe, to unite the Lamanites and find a home for the saints.[76]

An Oneida and "one of a very few early Indian converts" who hoped to attract "large numbers of the six nations to a Mormon mission" in Indian Country, Lewis Denna was Mormonism's first known ordained Native elder. He apparently had been Joseph Smith's Potawatami interpreter, but his elevation to the Council of Fifty remains mysterious.[77] Jonathan Dunham, the Nauvoo Legion's commander at the time of Joseph Smith's assassination, was now known as "Black Hawk." Dunham had already "seen much delightful country" on a

---

[75]General Church Minutes, 27 February 1845, LDS Archives.

[76]Clayton, *Journal*, 1 March 1845, 158–59.

[77]Bennett, *Mormons at the Missouri*, 100; Jorgensen, "Building the Kingdom of God: Alpheus Cutler," 196, 199, 200, 205.

six-week "bee-hunting" expedition and "Exploration in the Western Country" to central Iowa in 1843, where he conferred with Sac and Potawatomi leaders.[78]

Generations of historians had no access to the Council of Fifty minutes and had only hints as to what they said about Mormonism's "Great Western Measure." The 2016 publication of the ones from 1844 to 1846 open a window onto Mormon dreams of empire.[79] On 1 March 1845 the council unanimously confirmed "Prest. B. Young as successor of Prest. Joseph Smith and prophet, priest, and king to this kingdom forever after."[80] Young said:

> I tell you in the name of the Lord when we go from here, we will exalt the standard of liberty and make our own laws. When we go from here we dont calculate to go under any goverment but the government of God. There are millions of the Lamanites who when they understand the law of God and the designs of the gospel are perfectly capable of using up these united States. They will walk through them and lay them waste from East to West. We mean to go to our brethren in the West & baptise them, and when we get them to give hear to our council the story is told.[81]

"Joseph committed to me the keys to open the Gospel to every Lamanite nation," Young asserted after being confirmed in late 1847 as Smith's successor, but his claim did not go uncontested.[82] Several of the Kingdom's princes, notably Lyman Wight, James Emmett, George Miller, Alpheus Cutler, and Peter Haws, remained dedicated to the Lamanite missions Joseph Smith had given them before his death. James Emmett, despite George Miller's claim that his pioneering skills were "perhaps never excelled, even by the renowned Daniel Boone," led "a party of misguided saints into the wilderness" in September 1844 and attracted the attention of Indian agents. In July 1846 Young assigned Emmett and Miller to evaluate Grand Island on the Platte as a possible wintering site. Conditions altered Young's plans, and Emmett and Miller led almost four hundred of their followers north to winter at the Ponca villages, some 170 miles northwest of the main Mormon outpost at Winter Quarters. Miller, meanwhile, began agitating for the church to go to Texas: Young had Emmett and Miller disfellowshipped in October 1847.[83]

---

[78]Walker, "Seeking the 'Remnant,'" 28; Smith, *History of the Church*, 5:541–49.

[79]The Church Historian's Press finally released these records as Grow et al., eds., *Administrative Records, Council of Fifty, Minutes* in September 2016 (cited as Grow, *Council of Fifty Minutes*). For a 1998 denial, see Bagley, *Scoundrel's Tale*, 95n55.

[80]Grow, *Council of Fifty Minutes*, 379/192pdf.

[81]Ibid., 1 March 1845, 373, pdf 197.

[82]Anonymous, *Minutes of the Apostles*, 29 December 1847, 1:201.

[83]Smith, *History of the Church*, 7:269–70; Bennett, "Mormon Renegade: James Emmett," 217–33.

Lyman Wight and Alpheus Cutler launched their own versions of Mormonism to carry out the Council of Fifty's plan "to restore the Ancients to the Knowledge of the truth." George Miller cast his lot with Wight, who had already gone to Texas. Wight and some 150 followers boarded flatboats in Wisconsin in late March 1845, floated down to Duck Creek, north of Davenport, Iowa, and made a remarkable overland trek through Missouri, Kansas, and Indian Country, crossing the Red River and entering Texas near today's Georgetown in early November. After building Austin's jail, Wight settled his followers in the Texas Hill Country at Zodiac, "upon the borders of thousands and tens of thousands of Lamanites."[84]

"Father Cutler" updated Brigham Young about Lewis Denna's evangelizing on New Year's Eve 1847 and reported on his own "Mission to the Delawares, & Oneida Indians." Cutler said Fort Leavenworth had a garrison of about 1,500 men—"a man with 600 men co[ul]d kill them all off in about 6 hours"—and discussed the status of the Pawnees, Comanches, Cherokees, and the Kickapoos, who were "three miles from the Fort." Two years later, Apostle Orson Hyde complained, "Everything is precarious with us here. Indian Cutlerism in 500 forms would rage like wild fire through this country if the strong arm of power were not upon it all the time." It required "the utmost care, diligence and watching over this people to keep their eye towards the Salt Lake Valley." Declining to follow Brigham Young west, Cutler settled at Silver Creek, Iowa, and attracted several hundred adherents, notably Lewis Denna. Cutler founded the True Church of Jesus Christ in 1853 and promoted "Indian Cutlerism" until his death in 1864. That year Denna and other Cutler disciples established the town of Clitherall in western Minnesota, where Denna died in 1885 at age eighty-one.[85]

Winter Quarters: Can't Raise Up Our Dead Men

After abandoning Nauvoo in 1846, Brigham Young hoped to lead the Latter-day Saints to Mexico's Alta California, but poverty, bad weather, and politics forced him to delay the religion's great Exodus to the Far West. By June more than five thousand Mormons had reached the Missouri River, where they "built a ferry and were preparing to cross into Omaha country,"

---

[84]Johnson, *Polygamy on the Pedernales*, 54–57; Ehat, "'It Seems Like Heaven,'" 13.

[85]Jorgensen, "Building the Kingdom of God: Alpheus Cutler," 196, 199, 200, 205; Anonymous, *Minutes of the Apostles*, 29 December 1847, 1:201.

still hoping to go as far west as Grand Island. The arrival of Capt. James Allen with orders to enlist five companies of infantry volunteers for the War with Mexico crystallized Young's evolving plans. He now claimed Allen had guaranteed the Mormons "the privilege of staying anywhere we please on Indian lands," though both men knew Allen had no authority to do so. Young met with Big Elk and other Omaha leaders, promising to build a trading house, establish a school, plant crops, and—most importantly— protect them from Lakota raids. The Saints negotiated extralegal "treaties" with both the Omahas and Potawatomis, and by August had crossed the Missouri and started building the "Winter Quarters of the High Council of the Camp of Israel" on Omaha lands at today's Florence, Nebraska. As November ended, Mormon clerk Thomas Bullock found "a city of about 700 houses, and upwards of 4,000 Saints, built in less than three months."[86]

Excellent studies describe Mormon relations with the Omaha Nation during the two years spent on their land. The episode foreshadowed conflicts with federal officers in the Great Basin and violent struggles with Native peoples to control essential water, wildlife, timber, and grass. Along both banks of the Missouri, disputes over resources broke out. Besides the Omahas, the Council Bluffs Agency and its Iowa subagency had responsibility for the Otos, Missouris, Pawnees, Ottawa, Chippewa, and Potawatomis. John Miller, "one of the better men in the Indian service," and Robert B. Mitchell earned the contempt of the Mormons for their defense of Native rights. Both dealt with tribal complaints as the Saints laid waste to tribal lands and killed game. Miller told Brigham Young that the best favor the Mormons could do for the Omahas would be to leave as soon as possible and stop destroying timber and wildlife, "which to the Indians is a great loss." In what was perhaps "the most ferocious Sioux attack of the 1840s," raiders wounded Big Elk within gunshot of Winter Quarters in December—as "the Omahas were being 'protected' by the Mormons." The Lakota "completely destroyed an Omaha village, killing seventy-three women and children"—while the men were away hunting. "You can't raise up our timber," Big Elk complained, and the Mormons "can't raise up our dead men so you are the aggressors."[87]

---

[86]Trennert, "The Mormons and the Office of Indian Affairs," 385–87; "Letter from the Camp," *Millennial Star*, 15 January 1848, 30.

[87]Trennert, "The Mormons and the Office of Indian Affairs," 390–91; Boughter, *Betraying the Omaha Nation*, 53–54; Bennett, *Mormons at the Missouri*, 94–96, 98–99.

PRESIDENT BRIGHAM YOUNG AFTER HE BEGAN WEARING A BEARD IN 1860.
Library of Congress.

"We have more influence with the Indians than all other nations on the earth," Brigham Young boasted in August 1846, "and if we are compelled to, we will use it." Such loose talk bolstered reports, such as one Warren Foote heard from a woman in Iowa in June, that the Mormons had camped among "a great many Indians" and were "building forts and your women are marrying in with the Indians, and that you are combining togather and are coming down here to kill us all off." Young made no attempt to convert

Indians, many of whom were also refugees. He had a hard time suppressing his own followers' violent impulses after the Omahas abandoned a planned buffalo hunt "in expectation of living and sustaining themselves" killing Mormon cattle. "Its a great pity that they were ever permitted to stop here on Indian land, they are cutting timber fast," Presbyterian missionary Samuel Allis observed in February 1847. Omahas destroyed an incredible number of cattle, Hosea Stout complained, but as Robert Mitchell observed, "Jesus Christ could not hinder them from killing the cattle." As the Indian agents expected, the Mormon presence on the Missouri caused "a deterioration in the ability of these tribes to survive in their environment." Historian Robert Trennert concluded that the encounter destroyed "a good portion of the few remaining natural resources," so "if the Mormon encampment was not positively harmful to the Indians, it did them little good."[88]

Despite the mandate of *The Book of Mormon*, the first Latter-day Saints made contradictory attempts to embrace Native peoples. Joseph Smith sent emissaries to many tribes, but his efforts were highly secretive or shrouded in posthumous tradition, such as one of his legendary last prophecies predicting the Saints would "gather with the Redmen to their center from their scattered and dispersed situation, to become the strong arm of Jehovah" and the Indians would be "a strong bulwark of protection from your foes," once the Saints had established themselves in "the *strongholds* of their gathering places."[89]

The "Pioneer Camp of the Saints" sent to establish that stronghold in 1847 had routine encounters with Indians. As was common on the trail, raiders made off with livestock—on Brigham Young's return to Winter Quarters, his train lost most of its horses to thieves—but otherwise Indians had little impact on the pilgrims. The selection of the Salt Lake Valley, vital to the survival of the Goshutes but of marginal interest to the Utahs and Shoshones, made the Mormon entry relatively peaceful, providing a respite for the hard-pressed refugees to establish an empire in Indian country.

---

[88]Bennett, *Mormons at the Missouri*, 96, 99, 102–103; Trennert, "Mormons and the Office of Indian Affairs," 390–91; 396.

[89]Walker, "Seeking the 'Remnant,'" 32.

Chapter 1

INTO THE VERY MIDST
OF THE LAMANITES
First Encounters

Shoshonean peoples stood at the height of their power and prosperity when the Mormons entered the Great Basin. Long before the first Europeans arrived in the region, the vast Numic trading network had spread devastating diseases, including smallpox, measles, and pneumonia. Native winter counts shed some light on virulent pre-contact catastrophes, and fur trader Roscoe Cox in 1811 reported smallpox had "fastened its deadly venom on the Snake Indians." For centuries, the people had survived in a vortex of physical, geopolitical, and cultural changes, but the Numics adapted to them all. Generations of experience indicated they should be able to put new strangers to good use.

In 1840 the Numics controlled a vast domain. The Utahs, now known as Western Utes, had incorporated horses into their annual rounds by 1820, which resulted in the tribe "becoming in the mid-nineteenth century one of the most prosperous and powerful mounted bands west of the Rockies." Native lands had no borders as Anglo-Europeans define them, but Shoshonean *puwa*—power— reached from the Continental Divide to the Sierra Nevada, from the Wind River Range to the Grand Canyon. Ute and Shoshone trading and raiding expeditions ranged north to South Pass, southeast to Santa Fe, and southwest to Los Angeles. Their hunters supplemented their enormous local stocks of fish with bison taken in the parks of the Rocky Mountains and beyond.[1]

The Great Basin's peoples enjoyed a golden age during the twilight of the Rocky Mountain fur trade, while the Latter-day Saints experienced the

[1]Van Hoak, "Waccara's Utes," 310.

hardest of their many hard times before taking refuge in northern Mexico in 1847. With mixed curiosity, fear, and prophetic hope, chroniclers of Brigham Young's Pioneer Camp commented on the Shoshones, Goshutes, and Utes they met in Salt Lake Valley. Indians in their accounts are voiceless, for neither party could comprehend what the other was saying.

The Mormons came west with some extraordinary illusions about the tribes who occupied their temporary Zion. Brigham Young believed the "shoshows" were numerous "and just as quick as we could give them a pair of breeches and a blanket they would be our servants, and cultivate the earth for us the year round."[2] Indian labor, historian Albert Hurtado observed, was one of "the building blocks of nascent capitalism" in the American West. "Indian workers were there in fields, in pastures, in forests, and, yes, even in workshops" on "the shaggy fringes" of frontier society. Indians were "indispensable to the primary purpose of frontier entrepreneurs: to bring Western lands and resources into the marketplace while reaping profits for themselves." The prime source of western wealth was "the Indian business," which required businessmen to be "as calculating and ruthless" as John Sutter.[3] From the beginning, tightly regulated, top-down commerce formed the foundation of Mormon relations with their new neighbors.

Indian traders such as Elijah "Barney" Ward—one of the few mountain men to join the Saints—Dimick Baker Huntington and his sons, George W. Bean, James Allred, Jacob Hamblin, John D. Lee, Lyman S. Wood, and Orrin Porter Rockwell worked as interpreters, while federal authorities often used the translation services of former Mormons such as James Gemmell and Richard W. James. Interpreters were generally young men who seldom acquired even a modest command of the complicated Numic dialects. "I find Dymock, Geo. Bean & other interpreters much deficient in understanding" what Indians said, Brigham Young complained in 1854.[4] Native translators included Lemuel, a Southern Paiute; Enos, a Native "freebooter" associated with various tribes;[5] Peter Berry, known as a Ute "who speaks good English"; Baptiste Kawet, who Capt. Lot Smith said was a good interpreter for Washakie's Eastern Shoshones; and Northwestern Shoshone John Moemberg, Sagwitch's cousin, who learned English serving white farmers near Brigham

---

[2]Grow, *Council of Fifty Minutes*, 11 January 1846, 518.
[3]Hurtado, "Sutter and the Indian Business," in Owens, *John Sutter*, 53, 56.
[4]Brown, *Journal of the Southern Indian Mission*, 30.
[5]M. J. Shelton affidavit, Church Historian's Office Journal, May–June 1859, LDS Archives.

City.[6] They called the whites *how de doos,* "because of the common salute," Oliver Boardman Huntington wrote—and everyone understood "cursing & swearing in broken English."[7]

Besides commerce, another Euro-American legacy characterized frontier Mormonism's relations to Native peoples. "Violence provides the threads that weave Great Basin Indian history together," Ned Blackhawk observed.[8] It would be naïve to expect peace and friendship to follow the Mormon advent rather than the deadly encounters that had dominated the region's experience since the arrival of slave traders and fur hunters, but the newcomers' appropriation of Native lands proved swift and relentless. In five years, the colonists founded nearly thirty-five communities. The contest for resources transformed the tribes' welcome into anger as their neighbors killed their game, netted their fish, turned their earth, consumed their grass, and burned their wood, conflicts told in Mormon records. These initial struggles were but a prelude, for the battle to control the region's water, land, grass, forests, and wildlife continues to this day.

The Latter-day Saints took their prophetic destiny seriously: they had come to the Rocky Mountains to redeem the Lamanites and usher in the Second Coming. After reaching Salt Lake, Brigham Young preached:

> that the Elders would marry Wives of every tribe of Indians, and showed how the Lamanites would become a White & delightsome people & how our descendants may live to the age of a tree & be visited & hold communion with the Angels; & bring in the Millenium. He hoped to live to lead forth the armies of Israel to execute the judgments & justice on the persecuting Gentiles & that no officer of the United States should ever dictate him in this valley, or he would hang them on a gibbet as a warning to others.[9]

"Those guards fought us, whipped us, killed our Prophets, and abused our community, until we are now driven by them into the very midst of the Lamanites," the prophet proclaimed in 1857.[10] After seven years' service as both the territory's governor and *ex officio* Indian superintendent, Brigham Young said:

---

[6]George W. Bradley to Brigham Young, 23 June 1863, LDS Archives; Cuch, *A History of Utah's American Indians,* 45. Peter Berry was known as "Ute Pete."

[7]O. B. Huntington, Diary, 10:63; C. W. West to Young, 16 April 1860, LDS Archives.

[8]Blackhawk, *Violence over the Land,* 6.

[9]Bullock, *Pioneer Camp of the Saints,* 28 July 1847, 243.

[10]Brigham Young, "Remarks," 8 August 1857, *Journal of Discourses,* 5:128.

The people do not realize what they have done by driving us into the midst of the Lamanites. They prevented Joseph from associating with the Indians; but they, through their ignorance, thought that we were going to Vancouver's Island, or on the borders of the Pacific; but lo they have driven us into the midst of the Lamanites. These Lamanites begin to have a knowledge of their forefathers, and they are cultivating the earth. Here were the most degraded classes of Indians to be found; but now there is not a tribe so enlightened, nor one that has so good a knowledge of its real position and standing before the Lord as have some of these Utah Indians. It is now very different with them to what it was when we first came here. It is now becoming a universal practice with them to punish the guilty, and not the innocent: they have been taught that from the time we first came here. Talk with them, and you will learn that they have a good deal of knowledge. They must be saved, for they are the children of Abraham.[11]

The Chambers of the Lord:
The Mormons Meet Their Neighbors

Before reaching Salt Lake Valley, Brigham Young told his scouts "that he felt inclined for the present not to crowd upon the Utes until we have a better chance to get acquainted with them." Mountain man Jim Bridger had recommended the Mormons avoid Utah Valley, and Young took his advice: "The Utes may feel a little tenacious about their choice lands on the Utah Lake, & we had better keep further north towards Salt Lake."[12] Indians proved impossible to avoid in the Salt Lake Valley. "Soon after breakfast" on 27 July 1847, two men "of the Eutaw tribe" approached the wagons and "came to the camp—they were somewhat slightly clad in skins & are quite small in stature, as I am informed this tribe usually are," noted Horace Whitney. "J. Redden exchanged a gun & a shirt with one of them for a pony. They gave us to understand by signs there was a large party of their tribe about forty miles from here."[13]

Shoshone and Ute bands needed technology and gunpowder, while the Mormons wanted horses and furs. "Two of the Utah Indians came to camp early this morning to trade," noted William Clayton. "Two ponies were bought of them for a rifle and musket." That afternoon, "two more

---

[11]Brigham Young, "Remarks," 13 September 1857, *Journal of Discourses,* 5:236.

[12]Willard Richards and George A. Smith to Orson Pratt, 21 July 1847, LDS Archives.

[13]Whitney, 1847 Journal, LDS Archives.

Indians came in to trade. Some of the brethren are making unwise trades, giving twenty charges of powder and balls for a buck skin, while the usual price is three charges. This is wrong." As July ended, Clayton found "from twenty to thirty of the Utah Indians here and some squaws trading with the brethren. They are generally of low stature, pleasing countenance but poorly clad." He described Native discipline:

> While we were there, a dispute arose between two of the young men and they went to fighting very fiercely. One broke his gun stock on the other's head and I expected to see a pretty serious affray, many of the others gathering around. Soon an old man came up, father to one of the young men engaged in the quarrel and he used his heavy whip very freely about both their heads and faces. The antagonist of the son struck the old man and he immediately gathered a long pole and broke it over the young man's head. He succeeded in quelling the broil and gave them a long lecture.

Clayton learned about the contested title of the ground the Mormons now claimed. "These Indians who are now here are of the Shoshones, about fifteen or twenty in number, and several women among them." They began fighting a Ute who "had stolen a horse from one of the Shoshones." An old man separated them, but the thief "saw another horse walking by, which he knew to belong to the Shoshones. He sprang on his own horse and drove the other one before him towards the mountains on the southeast as hard as he could ride." The Shoshones "started in pursuit" and shot "him dead while another one shot his horse." They returned to camp "exhibiting fresh blood on one of the rifles." An ordinary musket would buy "a pretty good horse," which displeased the Shoshones "because we have traded with the Utahs and say they own this land, that that the Utahs have come over the line." They "signified by signs that they wanted to sell us the land for powder and lead."

That evening President Young counseled that "the brethren to keep their guns and their powder and their balls and lead" away from the Indians, who "stole guns yesterday and had them under their blankets and if you don't attend to this you are heating a kettle of boiling water to scald your own feet." He advised: "let them alone and let them eat the crickets, there's a plenty of them." The Shoshones offered to sell the land, but if the Mormons bought it, "the Utahs would want to pay for it too. The land belongs to our Father in Heaven and we calculate to plow and plant it and no man will have power to sell his inheritance for he cannot remove it; it belongs to the Lord."[14]

---

[14]Clayton, *Journal*, 31 July 1847, 328–29.

During the next week, "the Utah and Shoshone Indians visited our camp in Small parties almost daily and traded some horses for guns and skins for clothing &c," wrote Erastus Snow, "and they seemed much pleased at our settling here." So many Indians appeared that the camp adopted a resolution "to trade no more with the Indians except at their own encampments, & hold out no inducements to their visiting our camp."[15]

On 1 August Orson Pratt spoke about "this uncultivated region inhabited by savages." Joseph Smith had predicted the Saints would "congregate among the remnants of Joseph." Now that the gentiles had "rejected the Gospel it was to be taken among the Lamanites" where "the pioneers to this glorious valley" could "build up a city to the Lord," Pratt proclaimed. Once they adjusted to the healthy climate, the Saints would "be able to smite the gentiles. They will grow up strong and will not be in jeopardy from sickness." As for the Great Basin's challenging aridity, "great Jehovah will cause springs of water to gush out of the desert lands and we shall see the lands survive that the gentiles have defiled. Isaiah speaks of the heritage of Jacob being in a high place."[16]

The Mormons disagreed with their Numic neighbors about who owned what. "We have reached the *Promised Land*," said Heber C. Kimball. He advised building "an enclosure made for the purpose of keeping the horses and cattle in nights, for there are plenty of Indians in the vicinity."[17] Before returning to Winter Quarters on 26 August, Brigham Young told the pioneers he left behind to live in a stockade and "raise grain next year. If you only fence in forty acres, make it so an Indian cannot see in, and then they won't be tempted." The Natives knew their rights: "The Indians supposed the land to be all theirs," warned Mormon Battalion veteran Nelson Higgins, "and are in the habit of taking a share of the grain for the use of the land."[18]

"The few passes, and extremely rugged nature of the country," John C. Frémont had observed in 1842, provided "great strength, and secure the Utahs from the intrusion of their enemies."[19] But even their remote mountain citadel could not protect the Utes from a millennial religion and its expansive vision of the earthly Kingdom of God.

---

[15]Snow, Journal, 28 July, 1 August 1847, LDS Archives.
[16]Clayton, *Journal*, 1 August 1847, 331–32.
[17]Whitney, Journal, 25 July 1847, LDS Archives.
[18]Egan, *Pioneering the West*, 126–28
[19]Frémont, *The Expeditions*, 1:493, 705.

A Place and People to Commence With

Levi Jackman of the Pioneer Company kept one of the most revealing records of Great Salt Lake City's first year. Jackman turned fifty on 28 July 1847, the day the newcomers gathered and unanimously "aggread that this was the spot." Brigham Young "gave us an idea how the city was to be built and the order of things. That the Law of God was to be kept strickley and that we should form connections with the differant tribes of the Indians and by that means they would become a white and delightsome people and could be taught the principals of salvation and be prepaired for things to come." Young advised building "a foart to live in for the present that we might not be surprised by the Indians."[20]

The families left behind in Salt Lake Valley totaled perhaps four hundred people. They expected a few Saints from Winter Quarters, but when "the camp began to arrive" in September, Levi Jackman noted, "instd of being 100 famelies there was rising of 660 waggons." Few settlers had brought supplies: Jackman "had not provisions enough to last more than five or six dayes and but little in the camp, and more than one thousand miles from any settemant," he confessed. By October he was "in destitute circumstances" and worked as a carpenter to earn "a little provisions." On 4 October the "High Council met in Great Salt Lake City for the first time at 7 o'clock P.M. There were present President John Smith, and his Counselors, Chas. C. Rich and John Young." Jackman had "the honor of being one" of twelve high councilmen. In November "a few Indians came and camped near us for the winter. They live mostley on grass seeds & roots and woolf meat and we found they used the large thistle root." He regretted "that I could not git enough, for they ware good. They tasted when raw or cooked verey mutch like a persnip and were very healthey." His "Buck wheat & turnips" ran out, and now it was "all the work that I can do and git some provision." Sometimes after he ate, he knew "not where the next bite is comming from."[21]

The population of "our city is 1671; the number of houses 423," the Stake High Council reported next spring. Generally "the people here are disposed to do right and hearken to counsel and uphold the authorities; but as is natural under new and untried circumstance, there are a few exceptions."[22]

[20]Jackman, Diary, 28 July 1847, 35–36.
[21]Jackman, Diary, 35–43.
[22]High Council, Epistle, 6 March 1848, Harwell, *Manuscript History of Brigham Young*, 92.

Levi Jackman's diary of his first winter in Salt Lake focused on survival. He contrasted his faith's Lamanite doctrines with the Native peoples whom Mormons met in the Great Basin.

LEVI JACKMAN, DIARY, WINTER 1847, BYU LIBRARY, 46–48.

A part of oure duty in this would is to bring the Indian from their benighted situation and rais them as a branch of the house of Isreal, to a knowledge of the true and living God, and establish them in the truth of the gospel of Christ.—

In this place we finde a place and people to commence with. They hav not ben paisened with sectarian impositions, nor ware they but a little above the level of the brute creation in regard to intelegance. They live or rather meanely exist in small bands or compenes, dividing off from time to time according to circumstances and always at ware with each other. They have no particular abiding place, but roam from place to palace as circumstances may dictate, and live when stopping for any length of time in lodges made of small poals stuck into the ground fastined at the top and covered with grass or weeds.

They are all the time in fear of there neighbouring bands who each in their tourn will kill his enemy at every opportunity—

Thay have no knowledge of obtaining a living onley by hunting (by which case they are in danger) which is mostley don with bow and arrow, and by digging roots of various kinds, and eating crickets, which are verrey large and plenty in all this Mountain Countrey. As it regards clothing it can a hardley be said they have any. It consists mostley of skins which are the most tattered and filthey that can be immagened—

And finaley thay are the most filthey, degrade[d] and miserable beings prohaps that ever assumid the shape of human beings.

When I reflect and cosider that thay are of the haus of Israel, of the stick of Jacob, and the children of the covenent seed, unto whome belongs the priesthood and the oricals of God. When I see the situation which thay are now in, and rearelise what thay must be brought to by the Church of Jeus Christ, I say to my self O Lord who is able to all this—

But the decree has gon foarth and it must be accomplished, and it will be marvilous not onley to us but to generations yet to come.

Jackman's 1848 description of Native insights into local foods is reveal-ing: "About the 20th of this month (April) the Indians that had spent this winter near us, removed the most of them to an Isleand in the Lake. They fetch from that place many roots that they called sageas [segos] which they exchanged for cloathing, Beef, beans &c. The roots are about the size of a hickery nut and are good eating sum like a potatoe."[23]

---

[23]Jackman, Diary, 50. Jackman described *Calochortus nuttallii*, the sego lily, a bulbous perennial endemic to the American West. It became Utah's state flower in 1911.

At its first meeting on 4 October 1847, the Salt Lake Stake High Council "inferred that to build on Mill Creek would be going too far south, until they knew more about the disposition of the Indians." A week later they "decided that Thos. Williams, Ebenezer Hanks and Chas. Shumway should go and trade with the Indians in behalf of the people for the time being." However singular Mormon beliefs about "Lamanites" might have been, like everyone else who came west, their foremost interest in Indians was commercial. "It was decided that the Council should determine when the traders should start, and whether or not they should trade for the articles handed in or not." Orrin Porter Rockwell, however, "was permitted to trade with the Indians at his pleasure." In May 1848 the council "passed prohibitory regulations against trading guns and ammunition to Indians."

Since the Indian trade inspired conflict, Mormon authorities regulated it closely—or tried to. "Last evening the Indians shot one of our cattle," Stake president John Smith reported on 24 October 1847. "They said they done it because our people had cheated them in trading [so] now we will put a stop to everybody's running & trading without counsel or we will punish them—herdmen who take cattle at a price & loose them & then throw it up, shall be brought before counsel & branded covenant breakers." Parley P. Pratt wanted "to see our trade with Indians established upon righteousnes [and] unmovable principles, but if men go out & cheat them & show them bad examples they will judge this people as a whole by our traders, then either stop all trade with them, or appoint & send our good upright men who are industrious & so much so that they cannot wish to go & until then let there be no trading." Mormon Battalion veteran James Hirons was "the man who trade[d] with the Ind for a horse which caused dissatisfaction, & the ox being shot he gave a blanket & pistol for a pony. Soon after Indian broke pistol & wanted him to take pistol & give him a blanket." The council told Hirons that "these things will not be tolerated & unless we deal honorably with the Inds we will get their indignation."[24]

Salt Lake's first Mormons had a "verrey milde" winter "with but little snow," and the cattle they depended upon lived well without corn or grain by simply grazing. As slender supplies disappeared, though, virtually everyone in the valley was desperately hungry. "The large woolvs killed many of oure oxen and cows," Levi Jackman wrote, "and the Indians who ware camped

---

[24]Salt Lake Stake Minutes, LDS LR 604 109, LDS Archives.

near the Eutaw Lake drove off and killed maney which was a grate loss in our distitute circumstances."[25]

THE EUTAW FISHING COMPANY

In late winter 1848 Salt Lake's High Council informed Brigham Young they had sent "discretionary power and plenty of force" to respond to the cattle raids. Marshal John Van Cott and forty-four men had "just returned from visiting the Indians on the east side of Utah lake and reports that they had driven off and killed seventeen of our cattle and one horse; the only compensation obtained was one gun; the chief whipped several of the band and they all promised to do better."[26]

Mormons began exploring Utah Valley in July 1847 and soon turned their attention to its vast aquatic resources. By 10 August Norton Jacob was at work "on the skiff we are building to fish in Utah Lake," but due to the difficult terrain separating the two valleys, the skiff only reached Utah Valley in December. Parley P. Pratt, John S. Higbee, and others loaded the flat-bottomed boat onto a wagon bed and hauled it south over Traverse Mountain on a fishing expedition to Utah Lake. They surveyed the lake's barren western shore, probably to avoid the populous Timpanogos villages lining the eastern estuaries, so their luck was limited. Later that month, Abner Blackburn, Thomas S. Williams, and Ephraim Hanks embarked on "a trading scheme to barter with the Utas on the head watters of the Severe River away to the south of Utah Lake." A half century later, Blackburn recalled one of the first Mormon-Numic conversations when they came "to Provo and had a palaver with Old Elk, the cheif of the Utahs."[27]

Despite Pratt's failure, the hungry Saints still hoped to catch Utah Valley "fish to help out with our poor beef," one pioneer recalled. Parley P. Pratt "advocated the policy of a company of twelve going to the valley of Utah lake to fish and make a claim and buy fish of the Indians, first making a treaty with them to that effect, and volunteered to go himself." The council authorized Pratt "to raise a company of volunteers who had little or no families, and make a location in the Utah valley, if he could effect a treaty

---

[25]Jackman, Diary, March 1848, 47.
[26]Epistle of the High Council, 6 March 1848, Harwell, *Manuscript History of Brigham Young*, 91–92.
[27]Carter, *Founding Fort Utah*, 40–45; Bagley, *Frontiersman*, 124.

OLD ELK AND HIS WIFE

Howard Stansbury's 1852 *Exploration and Survey of the Valley of the Great Salt Lake*, 150, contained this engraving of Timpanogos Ute leader Old Elk and his wife, both killed in the Fort Utah fight.

with the Indians." He failed to raise the volunteers, make a treaty, or establish a settlement, but on 12 March 1848 Pratt again promoted "the fishing buisiness." If "20 men would go industrious & well armed, & would go for the season, he would see to it, & sd he would prophesy that the Eutaw valley would be filled next season." Pratt confessed "my necessity requires me to go, I have neither milk, meat, nor butter, but I will not go without a sufficient co[mpany]." The High Council chartered the Eutaw Fishing Company on 1 April 1848, granting John Forsgren exclusive fishing rights, ignoring what John Smith called "the poor miserable lot" of Utes who actually owned them. The company was "to go & fish & stay & fish &c 3 months or longer if necessary."[28]

No record of such an expedition survives, but two accounts of short fishing trips to Utah Lake exist. Levi Jackman described his first venture, made with Robert Pierce:

> On wensday April 19 Br Pierce and my self started for the Eutaw Lake to see the countrey and git sum fish—In passing through the farming countrey south all seamed to be hurrey and industrey prepairing for summer crops.—The south end of the valley is not furtile, we found the most of the Eutaw valley as far up as ~~Spanish fork~~ Provo to be rather barron, about the [American] fork the soil looks good. Our carriag turned over twice, the first time I lamed my foot badley. The next time was in a creek, and I got very wet and took a bad colde. We got back the third day.[29]

"In May six of us took a boat and went to Utah Lake fishing," Joseph Harker recalled. "We caught no fish," he wrote, perhaps because they "camped at Pennoakal [Pelican] point" on the lake's desolate west side. Despite this precaution, the fishermen encountered a war party on an odd mission: "a party of Indians came upon us. They had been south and Killed some Indians. They smoaked thir pipes and eat such as we had to give them. They told us that the Indians was following them and they would come upon us and kill us and they would not leave until we had got in the boat to cross to the other side and came home the next day."[30]

---

[28]Harwell, *Manuscript History*, 91, 93; Salt Lake High Council Minutes, LDS Archives; Carter, *Founding Fort Utah*, 56.

[29]Jackman, Diary, BYU Library, 51.

[30]Harker, Reminiscences, LDS Archives, 42.

TOKENS OF FRIENDSHIP: INDIAN TRADERS

"The prospect of subsistance for the comming winter loakes rather gloomey for me," Levi Jackman reflected in September 1848, "as I have neither meet or milk and corn alone. I knew would be rather dry living." Food proved too expensive to purchase, and with a massive influx of almost three thousand Mormons approaching Salt Lake, he "concluded to leave my shop and go and git sum my self."

Jackman's trading venture to Weber River requires introducing a remarkable clan. "In its New England origin and its history of sacrifice, devotion and fanaticism," wrote Wallace Stegner, "the Huntington family is a compendium of early Mormonism."[31] William and Zina Baker Huntington joined the Mormons in April 1835. Their sons William, Dimick, and Oliver became emissaries to the Lamanites: William led the first Mormon expedition to the Navajos; Dimick Huntington's exploits appear throughout Mormon annals, while Oliver Boardman Huntington's eighteen-volume journal incorporated intriguing insights about early Latter-day Saint relations with Native peoples. Despite their existing marriages to other men, Dimick sealed his sisters, Zina Jacobs and Prescindia Buell, to Joseph Smith in 1841. After the Carthage assassinations, Zina married Brigham Young and Prescindia wed Heber C. Kimball "for time." After crossing Iowa in 1846, Dimick Huntington enlisted in the Mormon Battalion as a drummer. His wife Fanny and three children accompanied him to Santa Fe, as Oliver recalled, across "a fathomless desert like the trackless Ocean allmoste, covered with roving tribes of Indians and Buffalo, with but little water and vegtation for teams to subsist upon,—the wife and children sharing with their earthly protector in his fortunes of war in an enemies land over a thousand miles of wild Indian deserts and Oceanlike prairies."

Many Mormon families wintered in today's Colorado near the trapper compound at Fort Pueblo. "The company needed blacksmithing—and no tools were within 1000 miles of them," Oliver wrote. Dimick, "a Smith by trade and a man of no small genius and perseverance," improvised bellows, a coal pit, hammer, tongs, and anvil and "earned 2 or three hundred dollars, principly in doing government work" before reaching Salt Lake in late July 1847, "in good circumstances for an exile who had been through a series of

---

[31]Stegner, *The Gathering of Zion*, 46.

persecutions for 12 years." Dimick did well "smithing for them" and "making arrowpoints and hatchets and trading horses which are cheap there, for the Spaniards have flooded the valley with them and mules." He had "by inspiration applied himself very closely, to learning the Indian languages around there—the Snake & the Eutah, and could talk with either to considerable advantages,—sufficient to do the business of a Church interpreter," Oliver reported. "His Boys too were almoste equal to him, in Eutah, Snake and Spanish."[32] Huntington's linguistic skills led to a successful career: "I have studied and acquainted myself with the language of the Indians generally in this country, and can hold conversation familiarly with almost any of them," he testified in 1861. "I have published a book in the Indian tongue, and revised and re-published the same." Brigham Young trusted him with "some of the most dangerous and delicate problems of Mormon-Indian relations."[33]

Oliver Huntington described the great trade white men carried on for "such articles as guns, amunition, knives, arrowpoints, belts, blankets, tin & sheetiron kittles, cups and cans, paints, beads and various other articles, suiting the Indian taste." Trading posts at Fort Hall and Fort Bridger exchanged them for "very great prices in horses, Deer skins dressed, Antelope, Buffalo, Mountain sheep, Elk, Bear, woolf, panther, Leopard and woolvereens skins—all tanned and dressed in different ways," along with "moste all kinds" of "a great variety of furrs."[34]

IRON TWISTER: WAKARA

Wakara is still the most famous of all the Utes. Best known as Walker, whites gave the "war chief of the Utahs" a dozen names: Wakara and Waccara, Wak-Kuh-rai, Wah-Ker, Wacherr, Wah-cah-rah, Wacher, Walkara, Walkeron, Walchor, Cuaka, and even Joseph Walker, along with many colorful titles: Napoleon of the Desert, Hawk of the Mountain, the Indian land pirate, and "the crafty Indian." "Wakarum means yellow man," explained a Ute elder. Whites struggled with the Ute pronunciation of wahk, so when "they put his name down they spelled it Walker."[35]

[32] O. B. Huntington, Diary, 1848–1849, 10:14, 37–38, 40–43.
[33] Cleland and Brooks, *A Mormon Chronicle*, 2:225.
[34] O. B. Huntington, Diary, 1849, 10:52–53.
[35] Harris, "The Walker War," 178.

According to Sanpete County tradition, the local band pronounced the name "Yawkerraw."[36]

Wakara was already a legend in 1847, but by the twentieth century his myth had so outgrown reality that a historian added almost a foot to the Ute leader's modest stature and gave him an imaginary noble family. "The great Ute chief, Walker, is said to have been six and a half feet tall," wrote stake president William Palmer, "and chief Coal Creek John, of Walker's royal lineage, stood over six feet in his moccasins."[37] In reality, Wakara and other Ute leaders had transformed the Utes into mounted warriors before they met the Mormons. The Western Utes "were distinct among mounted Native American peoples in both their diversification of food resource exploitation and in the geographic scope of their migrations," argued Stephen Van Hoak. The annual rounds they adopted in the late 1830s made them "one of the most prosperous and powerful mounted bands west of the Rockies."[38]

Wakara was first and foremost a businessman who traded in horse and human flesh. It is easy to romanticize the "Napoleon of the desert" as "a great strategist, often out-generaling those he had to meet in war or whom he designed to plunder," as Daniel W. Jones recalled. Despite his economic power and political skill, Wakara seldom acted as tribal leader, and his reputation as a military genius is overblown.[39] Much of what we know about Wakara traces back to "the politeness of Mr. Dimick B. Huntington, Indian Interpreter," who helped Frederick Hawkins Piercy compose this "short memoir of Walker," whose facts allegedly "came from the chief himself."

PIERCY, *ROUTE FROM LIVERPOOL TO GREAT SALT LAKE*, 104–105.

Some of the bands of the Utahs, are the Utahs proper, now under Arapeen and Sau-e-ette; Yampah Utes, under White Eye; Timpanogas Utes, under Peteet-neet and Washear; Pe-ar-a-wats; Pau-van-tees, under Kanoshe; Pah Utes; and Piedes. The late Joseph Walker, one of the leading chiefs of the Utahs, was generally very friendly to the L. D. Saints, and so also is Arapeen, his successor. We here introduce their portraits sketched from a painting [by Solomon Nuñes Carvalho] in possession of the late Elder W. W. Major. Walker, who appears with his cap on, had made himself rich by horse-stealing, and had succeeded by his aggressions upon the minor bands in gaining

---

[36]Belinda Cox Sidwell, "Reminiscences of Early Days in Manti," *Manti Sentinel*, published serially beginning 1 August 1889. Digital copy in Will Bagley's possession.

[37]Palmer, "Indian Names in Utah Geography," 5, 8.

[38]Van Hoak, "Waccara's Utes," 310.

[39]Jones, *Forty Years among the Indians*, 41.

great influence over them. After the L. D. Saints colonized Utah both he and Arapeen requested baptism, and became united with the Church. . . .

It appears that Joseph Walker was born on Spanish Fork (Pequi-nary-no-quint is the Indian name, and signifies Stinking Creek) in Utah County, U.T., in or about the year 1808. When he was about 12 years old the deer, he used to say, were very thick, and the buffalo more numerous than the Mormons' cattle. The first horse he ever saw was brought to Utah by the Spaniards. His father, whose name is unknown, obtained the animal, and, lest it should run away, kept it tied up to the corner of his hut until it starved to death, not knowing anything of the nature of the animal, or that it required anything to eat.

When the first white man came among them, the Timpanogas Utes, to which he then belonged, were quite numerous. In his earlier days, as far back as he could remember, he was with his father in many battles with the Snake Indians, who then occupied the country in the vicinity of G. S. Lake Valley. When he was about 20 years old a portion of the tribe to which he belonged broke off and joined the Snakes, among whom was one of Walker's own uncles and other relatives. This small band of seceders intermarried with the Snakes, and their children are what are now called Diggers—the low race found among the settlements at the present time. They also assisted the Snakes against the Timpanogas band, who were at that time located on the Timpanogas or Provo River, and as Walker and his father's relatives had some scruples about fighting their own relatives who were in the ranks of the Snakes, about 40 in number left the Timpanogas and went on to Spanish Fork to live, that they might not have occasion to join in warfare against the Snakes. This gave offence to the remaining portion of the tribe, who commenced a war with Walker's band, and a company of them stole upon Walker's lodge, and shot his father in the back while smoking. Walker carried his father and buried him in Rocky Canyon, about a mile S. of Spanish Fork. Soon after this, he and his brother Arapeen, whose proper name is Senior-roach, stole into the Timpanogas Utes lodge in the night, and shot 4 persons of the tribe. At his father's death Walker assumed the command of the band. About 2 years after, he went over into Uintah Valley, about 150 m. S. E. of G. S. L. City, to some white traders who were there, where, according to his account, he was taken sick and died. His spirit was absent from his body a day and a night, during which time his body remained warm. While absent from the body his spirit went to heaven where he saw God and a great multitude of angels or beings dressed in white. None of the angels spoke to him, but God talked with him and told him that he must come back to the earth again, for his work was not done, and that some white friends were coming to see him. Before he returned God gave him a new name—Pannacarra-quinker, which signifies Iron Twister. This circumstance occurred about 2 years before the L. D. Saints entered the valleys of Utah, after which time he had occasional skirmishes with the Snakes, but maintained friendly feelings generally towards the whites, and boasted that he had never shed the blood of white men.

In 1872 Huntington released a third edition of his *Vocabulary of the Utah and Sho-Sho-Ne Ne or Snake Dialects, with Indian Legends and Traditions. Including a Brief Account of* THE LIFE AND DEATH OF WAH-KER, THE INDIAN LAND PIRATE. It provides an alternate overview to Piercy's 1854 version.

DIMICK HUNTINGTON, "WAH-KER'S HISTORY," IN VOCABULARY, 27–28.
Wah-ker was born about the year 1815, on the Spanish Fork river, Utah county, Utah Territory, and was one of the shrewdest of men. He was a natural man; read from nature's books. He was very fond of liquor; but when in liquor you could not get him to make a trade.

Wah-ker means "yellow," or "brass." When about twenty-five years of age he had a curious vision. He died and his spirit went to Heaven. He saw the Lord sitting upon a throne dressed in white. The Lord told him he could not stay; he had to return. He desired to stay, but the Lord told him that he must return to earth; that there would come to him a race of white people that would be his friends, and he must treat them kindly. The Lord gave him a new name. It was Pan-a-karry Quin-ker (Iron twister). In 1846, or '47 he went to California with a lot of Piede prisoners. He frightened the Piedes into giving him their children, which he took to Lower California to trade for horses to enrich himself, taking many of his tribe with him. The Spaniards gave him numbers of beef cattle and charged him for them, whereupon he started for home. When out two days he called a halt, held a council, and sent the old men, women and children on towards home. The third day ten men returned to visit the Spaniards. Each man visited different ranches, and took a large number of horses. The Spaniards raised a large force and pursued them, and recovered many, but lost six or seven hundred head of wild horses, for which the Mexicans offered a large reward. The Indians pushed the horses so hard that they lost several on the desert. . . .

Wah-ker had three brothers: Ara-pone, Sampitch, and Tabby. Tabby is at present the head chief of the Utahs proper; and is on the Uintah reservation.

Arapene was a great orator, but a hard-hearted man. At one time in Manti he got mad at his wife and burned her in a fearful manner with a frying-pan handle that was broken off the pan. She crawled to the settlement and the white women nursed her until she recovered. At another time he came down out of the mountains with some deerskins and a Piede prisoner, a small boy, to trade. The price was too high for the child, whereupon he took the child in a rage by his heels and dashed his brains out by thrashing the ground with his head.

In 1849, when fifty of us were exploring the "Dixie" country, in the month of December, we met Arapene on his way from the mountains on the Sevier river, coming down to winter. An old squaw had a long roll of cedar bark, one end of which was on fire so as to light a fire quickly. We all camped together. Arapene had but one daughter, about nine years old, and she was very sick with the measles. She died that night; and the Indians held a council whether to kill one of us or a Piede prisoner, a boy about six years old, to send with the daughter. In the morning two young men came out of Arapene's lodge, loading their rifles and driving the Piede before them. I shall never forget how pitiful he looked, for he knew what his fate was. He asked to take off his moccasins and was refused. It was very cold. They drove him about four rods from the camp, when both fired and the poor little fellow rolled down from off the little knoll on which he stood. He was buried along with the girl.

Brigham Young provided his own assessment of Walker and his band in one of his first official reports as Utah Territory's *ex officio* Indian superintendent:

YOUNG TO LUKE LEA, 13 AUGUST 1851, BYC 55/5.

Now comes the chivalry of the Utahs, Captain Walker and his band, Cheveritts they are called, well known, as they are dreaded in California, for many is the tribute they have levied there. With no particular location they roam at will, making their southern excursions in the winter, fishing in the spring on the Sevier, and trading off their skins and horses, spend their summer generally about the San Petes, sometime makes an excursion against the Snakes, and thus spending their time until fall, hie away again to the south; they visit all the tribes of Utes that I have spoken of, and frequently extends [*sic*] their visits to the Taos, and other Utes in the Territory of New Mexico.

This Captain Walker, has obtained his power and influence by his exploits being successful in stealing, has in his case paved his way to a Captaincy, of which he is as proud and important as any potentate that ever flourished the ensigns of royalty.

This begets a little jealousy on the part of the legitimate aristocracy, thus to see their power stolen from them, but I have not heard of any actual hostilities among them proceeding from this cause.

He is a good judge of property, shrewd and intelligent—but somewhat deceitful in his intercourse with other Indians, thereby bringing down their enmity upon him. This together with their jealousy renders his path rather insecure and requires the utmost tact, and watchfulness, and moreover is the probable cause of his refraining from committing depredations upon the settlements.

Mormon records provide insight into Wakara's origins, extended family, and even his physical appearance. *Wacherr* meant "wears yellow color or brass," wrote Thomas Bullock. In 1852 he was "about 35," stood 5 feet 7½ inches, weighed 164 pounds, had a 37½-inch chest and a 33-inch waist, with "eyes dark, hair black & cut short, complexion reddish olive." Wakara claimed he had "never shed a white mans blood." Probably reflecting Ute matrilineal lineage, which counted cousins as brothers, it often seems every Utah Indian, regardless of age or band, was identified as "Walker's brother," but Bullock identified Peteetneet as "Wakara's Father's brother," while Sowiette was "bro in law Walkers father."[40]

Wakara's power came from California ranchos. With mountain men Jim Beckwith and Pegleg Smith, he reportedly staged "the greatest horsestealing raid in California history" in 1840, making off with as many as 2,500 horses, while exhaustion, hunger, and thirst killed almost as many animals. Reportedly working with sixty American, Canadian, and New Mexicans known as the *Chaguanosos*, "adventurers of all nations," Wakara and an "undetermined number of Indians" allegedly raided as far north as San Luis Obispo. The Spanish Trail from California to Utah, legend claimed, was known as "Walker's Trail." Wakara seemingly made these winter treks part of his annual cycle: "Walker paid a visit to this country some time ago and as soon as they could steal a few horses they put away to their own country, without any molestation from this people, because nobody followed them," California pioneer John Rowland wrote in February 1846.[41]

"The famous Ute Indian chief Cuaka—best known as Walker—was very active about this time and his repeated depredations on the stock of the settlers were very annoying. It was Walker's boast that the rancheros were only allowed to remain in the valley as stock raisers for his especial benefit," wrote the Rev. Juan Caballeria, an early chronicler of San Bernardino. "Nearly every full moon he came down from the mountains with his band of Indians and these incursions generally resulted in loss to the settlers." The raiders would run the stock into canyons, leave the trails and "drive them up over the mountain and down the other side of the range into the desert" and into hideouts such as Horsethief Canyon on the Great Basin side of Cajon Pass. One of "many fierce battles" with Wakara's men wounded three New Mexican settlers of 1841: "Doroteo Trujillo was shot in the back

---

[40]Bullock, Weight, Size &c of Indians, 2 August 1852, Brigham Young Office Files, LDS Archives.
[41]Robinson, "Traders, Travelers and Horse-Thieves," 34–38.

with an arrow; Esquipula Trujillo was shot through the nose, and Teodoro Trujillo was shot in the right foot," Caballeria wrote. But they "succeeded in recapturing the stock."[42] Perchance.

John H. Lyman trekked from Santa Fe to California in 1841 with John Rowland and William Workman. The doctor carried an "assortment of all the articles of Indian trade," including "a good rifle, powder, lead, indigo, vermillion (for painting their faces), coral-beads, knives, looking-glasses, needles, American tobacco, &c, &c." Adventurer Thomas J. Farnham reported Lyman's encounter with Wah-cah-rah. Lyman claimed the "Timpanigos Yutas" were very friendly after meeting Lyman on the Spanish Trail, and were "delighted to have him in their camp":

> Their first and constant greeting is, "Kahche winay—marakah nay," "very good American." They manifest the greatest contempt for the New Mexicans. I travelled through their country with one of their head chiefs, named Wah-cah-rah, who was on his return from an unsuccessful expedition across the St. John's [San Juan] river, in pursuit of his faithless wife, who had left him and fled over the border with her paramour. He was quite sad during the early part of the journey, and was constantly muttering something of which I frequently distinguished the expression, "Kah-che, kai-yah, mah-ru-kah," which, from hearing so often repeated, I recollected, and afterwards, when he became more philosophic, which was the case towards the latter part of the journey, I asked him to interpret for me (he could speak a little Spanish), and he said it meant "very bad girl." He disclaimed all thought of invading the country of his successful rival, for he had, as he said, two other beauteous Helens, who would console him for his loss, and they certainly ought to do so, for he was the very beau-ideal of nature's nobility.[43]

Romantic nonsense clutters virtually every Wakara biography, but his encounters with American topographical engineers reveal the Ute leader's fame. Theodore Talbot was leading a detachment of John C. Frémont's second expedition in 1843 when he met Wakara sporting a tam o'shanter near Fort Bridger. Louis Vasquez and his "gallant party of mountaineers and a band of Indians came dashing into camp at full speed. Having exchanged salutations with the mad-cap party and the rest of Vasquez' Company, and the 15 or 20 lodges of Youta's [*sic*] who were with him having by this time come up, we all went into camp for the evening," Talbot reported. "Vasquez has just returned from hunting in the Youta Mountains."

---

[42]Caballeria, *History of San Bernardino Valley*, 103–104.

[43]Farnham, *Travels in the Californias*, 374–75.

The Youta indians are of rather low stature, dark color and pleasant appearance, they do not compare with Sioux &c. They are well armed, using rifles, and those with percussion locks and double triggers. They are said to be excellent shots, and have a fine country for deer and other small game, on which their subsistence chiefly depends. They are at present great friends to the Whites: about ten years ago they were very inimical towards them. Their principal ruling chief is "Walker" or "Wakaron," surnamed "the little chief." He owes his position to his great wealth. He is a good trader, trafficking with the Whites, and reselling goods to such of his nation as are less skillful in striking a bargain. He is not at all brave, but sustains his position by judicious presents to his principal men. He has also a brother who is a very distinguished warrior, and who acts as generalissimo, leading and directing the motions of the war parties. We had him to dine in our tent. Walker is of small size, good looking and quite young to hold the position which he does. He was dressed partly in the European style, wearing a Scotch bonnet. We gave him a very slight taste of wine, which however had a very visible effect upon him. He was very anxious to trade a fine rifle of me which I had just bought myself, but as he had two hearts, and I had but one, we did not trade.[44]

Wakara met John C. Frémont on 20 May 1844. The legendary Joseph R. Walker, the Ute leader's apparent namesake and a man possessing "an extraordinary firmness and decision of character," guided Frémont's Second Expedition to Utah Valley and on to Bents Fort.

We met a band of Utah Indians, headed by a well-known chief, who had obtained the American or English name of Walker, by which he is quoted and well known. They were all mounted, armed with rifles, and use their rifles well. The chief had a fusee [shotgun], which he had carried slung, in addition to his rifle. They were journeying slowly towards the Spanish trail, to levy their usual tribute upon the great Californian caravan. They were robbers of a higher order than those of the desert. They conducted their depredations with form, and under the color of trade and toll for passing through their country. Instead of attacking and killing, they affect to purchase—taking the horses they like, and giving something nominal in return. The chief was quite civil to me. He was personally acquainted with his namesake, our guide, who made my name known to him. He knew of my expedition of 1842; and, as tokens of friendship, and proof that we had met, proposed an interchange of presents. We had no great store to choose out of; so he gave me a Mexican blanket, and I gave him a very fine one which I had obtained at Vancouver.[45]

---

[44]Talbot, *Journals*, 30 August 1843, 41–42.
[45]Frémont, *The Expeditions*, 1:524, 695–96.

Cartographer Charles Preuss thought the two leaders disagreed about the value of the blankets. "You are a chief, and I am one too. It would be bad if we should evaluate exactly the price of one or the other," Preuss had Walker say. "You present me with yours, and I present you with mine. Fine."[46]

Explorers Kit Carson and George Douglas Brewerton met Wakara's band on the same mission—collecting tolls from the annual Spanish Trail caravan from New Mexico—in May 1848:

BREWERTON, "A RIDE WITH KIT CARSON," HARPER'S,
AUGUST 1853, 323–26.

If I remember rightly, it was not far from the Little Salt Lake that we first met with the Eutaw Indians. At this point we found one of their principal chiefs, "Wacarra," or Walker, as he is commonly called by the Americans. His encampment consisted of four lodges, inhabited by his wives, children, and suite of inferior warriors and chiefs. This party was awaiting the coming of the great Spanish caravan, from whom they intended taking the yearly tribute which the tribe exacts as the price of a safe-conduct through their country. I found a vast difference in all respects between these Indians and the miserable beings whom we had hitherto seen. The Eutaws are perhaps the most powerful and warlike tribe now remaining upon this continent. They appear well provided with fire-arms, which they are said to use with the precision of veteran riflemen. I remember they expressed their surprise that the white men should use so much powder in firing at a mark, while to them every load brought a piece of game or the scalp of an enemy. Wacarra (or Walker, as I shall call him) received our party very graciously; in fact, their attentions, so far at least as my humble self was concerned, became rather overpowering. . . .

Before leaving this encampment, I was invited by Walker to visit his lodge, and accompanied him accordingly. These lodges are made of skins sewed together, with an opening at the top which serves as a chimney for the smoke, the fire being built on the ground in the centre of the lodge. Upon entering the lodge the children crowded round me, admiring the gaudy scarlet cloth with which my leathern hunting-shirt was lined; most of these young people were armed with small bows and arrows which they amused themselves by aiming at me. Walker's wife, or wives, for I think he had several, were busied in their domestic avocations about the lodge, and one of them (a good-looking squaw of some eighteen or twenty years, who seemed to be the favorite), was kind enough to spread a deer-skin for my accommodation. Wishing to repay her courtesy, I called my servant Juan, and directed him to get a brass breast-plate with the letters "U.S." conspicuously

---

[46]Gudde and Gudde, *Exploring with Frémont*, 132–33.

displayed, which I had among my traps, polish it up, and bring it to me. This he did, and I shall never forget the joy of this belle of the wilderness, upon receiving the shining metal. With the aid of a small mirror, which had probably been obtained from some passing trader, she arranged the breast-plate (fully two inches square) upon her raven locks, and then, with the air of a tragedy queen, marched up and down in front of the lodge, looking with great contempt upon her envious companions. It was certainly an amusing scene, and goes to prove that vanity may exist as strongly in the character of a Eutaw squaw, as in the breast of a city belle; with this difference, perhaps, that it is exhibited with much less taste among those whose education should have taught them better things.

WAKARA MEETS THE MORMONS, AUGUST 1848

In 1885 Charles Hancock recalled seeing a large camp of "the Utahs" in Los Angeles while with the Mormon Battalion in May 1847. Their "War Chief was Jim Walker, known as king of the mountains," he wrote, suggesting Wakara's band was far from home when the Mormons arrived.[47] Writer Edward Tullidge claimed Wakara wanted "to go down and clean out the whites from their valleys" as soon as they appeared. The Utes held a council in Spanish Fork Canyon to decide what to do. The "young and impatient braves" looked upon them "as invaders of their country, whom they ought at once to exterminate." Walker, "the great war chief of the Utah nation," gave a "fiery speech" advocating an immediate attack to "clean out the whites from their valleys." Soweite, "the great executive chief" wanted to leave them alone "and pursue a policy of peace towards" the Mormon pioneers. The "fiery young warriors" implied "the old peace chief" was a coward, so Sowiete "in his indignation and royal wrath took his riding whip and flogged the war chief Walker."[48] As historian Jared Farmer noted, this fable never happened.[49]

Curiosity and an irresistible business opportunity brought the Great Basin's most powerful leader to Salt Lake a year later. "A Company of Eutaw Indians arrived in our Camp on the 21st of August," wrote Daniel Spencer in 1848. "War Chiefs name was Walker [with] Som 50 werriors & about 300 Horses for sale. The brethren purches many with Guns & Clothing quite

[47]Bigler and Bagley, *Army of Israel*, 208–209.
[48]"History of Spanish Fork," *Tullidge's Quarterly Magazine* (April 1884), 139–40.
[49]Farmer, *Zion's Mount*, 134.

Cheap."[50] The Stake High Council anticipated the visit: four days earlier it appointed Charles C. Rich, John Young, and Henry G. Sherwood "to superintend the tradeing with Walkers band of Indians."[51]

The Utahs stayed in Great Salt Lake City until the next Sunday, when on "Aug 27th, public meeting, plsnt—on the stand Prst Smith, P P Pratt,—C C Rich, some of the H[igh] C[council] & some of the Bishops &c, Walker & several of his band prsnt on horseback—Captn Walker invited onto the stand,—singing—Pryr by D Spencer, singing."[52]

Parley P. Pratt wrote the best report of the Ute visit.

"To President Orson Pratt," 6 September 1848,
Millennial Star, 15 January 1849, 23.

A few weeks since, Mr. Joseph Walker, the celebrated Utah chief, mentioned in the journal of Colonel Fremont, paid a visit to this place, accompanied by Soweite, the king of the whole Utah nations, and with them some hundreds of men, women, and children; they had several hundred head of horses for sale.

They were good looking, brave, and intelligent beyond any we have seen on this side of the mountains. They were much pleased and excited with every thing they saw, and finally expressed a wish to become one people with us, and to live among us and we among them, and to learn to cultivate the earth and live as we do. They would like for some of us to go and commence farming with them in their valleys, which are situated about three hundred miles south.

We enjoined it on them to be at peace with one another, and with all people, and to cease to war; they have agreed to do so, and have sent a deputation to the Shoshones, their old enemies, whose principal chiefs are now here encamped with them, in the act of establishing a treaty of peace.

We have promised to tell them much in relation to their forefathers, and the will of the Great Spirit, when we are in circumstances to talk with them more fully.

Apostles George A. Smith and Ezra Taft Benson supplemented Pratt's optimistic assessment in December with their own cheerful hearsay:

Walker, the famous Utah chief, has visited the Saints in the valley with his band of riflemen: he said he always wished to live in peace with our people; he wanted his children to grow up with ours as brothers; that his people should not steal from ours, if any of them did, let him know it, and he would punish them and stop it. The brethren told him they did not want his men

---

[50]Spencer, 1848 Diary, MS 1566, 223.
[51]Salt Lake Stake Papers, Minutes, 17 August 1848.
[52]Salt Lake Stake Minutes.

to steal from the Spaniards, for we were at peace with them. Walker replied, "my men hate the Spaniards, they will steal from them and I cannot help it; they love your people, and they will not steal from you, and if any of the bad boys do, I will stop them."[53]

WE BURIED 36 IN ONE GRAVE

In late August 1847 the second wave of Mormon migrants met Ezra T. Benson, "who had been sent back by the Pioneers to meet the companies," recalled George Whitaker. Benson called the Great Basin "a good country and gave us all the encouragement" he could, but when Whitaker arrived, he found "a dry, barren and parched up desert, a few naked Indians and armies of large black crickets that had eaten up everything that had been green."[54]

The Salt Lake Basin had long provided a comfortable home for its Native peoples, but it challenged its first Anglo-American residents. "The site of Salt Lake City was an old Indian camping ground," James S. Brown, "the famous Indian interpreter," told the *Deseret News* in 1900. "One of their burying grounds was in the northwestern part of the Oregon Short Line depot," near the Warm Springs, now about 300 West and 800 North.[55] A string of thermal springs extended along the Wasatch Front faults from Great Salt Lake City to Bear River, creating winter refuges for Utes, Goshutes, Shoshones, and Wanship's "Weber Utes." Runoff from the hot sulfur springs at the junction of today's US 89 and I–15, once known as Beck's Hot Springs, created the now-vanished Hot Springs Lake, a natural home for wintering waterfowl.

Only a handful of Mormon sources from that first winter shed light on how the new settlers interacted with the local tribes. Among the most important was John Nebeker's 1884 interview with historian H. H. Bancroft:

The farming land commenced near the Warm Springs, running thence northwest, thence south to Big Cottonwood. This was all fenced to keep out stock. The crickets covered all this land; they were most destructive in spots. The Indians got fat on them. They would gather them in baskets, then put them in willows and set fire to the willows; by the time the willows were burned the crickets would be cooked. That season a great number of

[53]Smith and Benson to Hyde, 20 December 1848, *Millennial Star* 11:4 (15 February 1849), 53.
[54]Whitaker, Autobiography, 1847.
[55]"Indian Policy of the Pioneers," *Deseret News*, 16 June 1900, 5/4.

Indians came to the Warm Springs suffering from measles. They died off
about as fast as they went into the water. Some they buried and some they
didn't bury. I helped to bury those that were left unburied. We buried 36
in one grave; and 44 dogs in another. Their custom was to kill their dogs
when their masters died. This was the first time measles appeared here. It
was a new disease to them, and they didn't know how to cure it, or where
they got it.[56]

The devastation European diseases inflicted on Numic peoples evoked
one of the few comments a Mormon Indian missionary ever made about
Native religious beliefs. Oliver B. Huntington headed south with Barney
Ward in February 1849 on a trading expedition to the Sevier Valley. They
got no farther than Spanish Fork, where an old Ute warned of bad weather
and worse. Deep snows prevented the southern bands from hunting—"their
horses die with hunger and the people eat them"—and an epidemic had
struck the tribe.

OLIVER B. HUNTINGTON, DIARY, 56–62.

The old man had some very long yarns to spin to our interpreter Mr. Ward,
about the impracticability of proceeding farther on our journey. The story
was about this. "Late in the last fall a party of whites went through there
on their way to California, and soon after they left their village a contageon
broke out among them which killed and drove off nearly all the people."
The old man called the disorder "medecine." [He] "said the whites had left
bad medacine to kill his people off and if any more should go there now,
the few that are left who can not get away will certainly kill them. . . . Thier
disease he said "they had never seen before, and could find no medacine to
cure it." As he represented it was more like the Cholera than any thing else.
He told about some being spoted, which we thought was the Measles, as
they were in the Salt Lake Valley when that company left there. He said the
whites gave that to them by spiting on them.[57]

But here [Spanish Fork] ended our Journey to the Severe [Sevier] Valley.
The Chief of the band and all his young men were gone out on a hunt and
we stayed three days there waiting for them, and three days more trading. I
bought one horse and Ward bought 3.

Considerable many Deer and Antelope skins were bought. The price
of a horse was a gun, 50 charges of poder and lead, and if a cap lock, a

---

[56]John Nebeker, "Early Justice in Utah," *Utah Historical Quarterly* (July 1930), 87.

[57]These New Mexican traders did not visit Salt Lake. On 26 September 1848, diarist Orville Pratt
camped on the Sevier River, "the recognized boundary of the Eutah country" where "the region of the
Pah-Eutah Indians" began.

box of caps, a knife, 15 arrow points (iron) a small piece of tobacco; and if a very good horse, a paper of red paint, and perhaps some other little notions—a great number of articles, seems to be synonimous with a great price, with them.

While here I learned considerable of the Indians ways and language. In fact it was very object, more than to trade. There was a child sick in the village and I had an oportunity of learning one of their modes of doctoring.

The Indian in his native solitary wildness is a very singular being—without a partial knowledge of their language they seem to be mere animals in human form, forming the connecting link between animal and human, but many of those low, degraded, filthy looking animal like humans, have truly great and politic minds.

They only want the means of civilization to develope their true characters, and they would be looked upon by us as a great men—Among themselves they are great.

During our stay at that village it took great care and caution to prevent geting into trouble with them for they were some disposed to be hostile. I will return to a few of their customs and traditions. They believe a great deal in whims and are very superstitious. What we call whims, supersticious customs—even the prayer of faith, a watch—electricity—any power, real or imaginery which they can not administer with their hands nor see the cause or reason of, they call *Medacine*. Ever[y] powerful agency,—good or bad, is *Medacine*. They think there is a great charm in singing, to cure the sick. The administrator of medacine to the child I spoke of, kept me awake nearly all one night singing to it, with all the force of lungs & muscles of body he had. They sometimes rub the part affected creating great friction. Sometimes bury in clay or sand—wash with a paste of certain kinds of clay—they seldom eat when sick—

The most supersticious or religious, use a great deal of *medicine* while well—such as to wash, or paint themselves from head to foot with a certain kind of whitish clay; which they do to prevent sickness—and just before going to hunt, to keep the wild beasts from having power over them, or accidents befalling them. Some are more tenacious about these ceremonies than others. . . .

We at last started for home glad to leave them and their superstitions. Their traditions of God and the origin of their race I have not yet spoke of but which I will briefly touch. God they think is their Father and of course has a wife, both of which they call Peo-ap, signifying Father and Mother—this is their turm for God—They think he made everything and lives in the sun. Every thing but the sun must die. The moon does die often (every old moon)—the earth must die at some distant period.

RELICS: ANOTHER THING THAT SHOULD
HAVE BEEN PRESERVED

"The Indians around us in this valley are Singular beings," wrote Mormon Battalion veteran Robert Bliss early in 1848. He had heard of how "they took some Indian Prisenors from another tribe soon after our People came here & killed them after trying to sell them to us with the exception of one a female & soon as our People saw they killed their Prisenors they bought the Squaw & clothed her & she is now living in town & learning our Language fast." (This was Kahpeputz or Sally, who Charles Decker bought in 1847.) An Indian expedition "had one lame Indian among them who was unable to go with them or get a living. They therefore for fear he would fall into the hands of their Enemies decided he should die. He was accordingly killed; we frequently saw the poor fellow in Town & did not know they had killed him untill a few days ago."[58]

Indians seldom speak in the records celebrating America's pioneers, but the Anglo-European conquest eliminated more than their voices. The settlers "chiseled out and carried away" Native contributions to the Great Basin's artistic heritage of parietal art—rock art—inflicting incalculable and on-going damage.

Mormon stalwart Howard Egan built his first cabin at the foot of today's Capitol Hill next to "a couple of small mounds on the south side of the lot just where the fence was to be placed," his sons recalled. These graves "had to be cut down to the level of the surrounding land, and by doing this there was dug up a large number of human bones," along with petrified berries, black and white flint arrowheads, "and some few pieces of pottery of a dark brown color," relics of the indigenous people who preceded the Numic.[59]

The "red ravine" the Egan brothers described in *Pioneering the West* is today's Red Canyon. "Nothing lasts except the earth," an Indian proverb said, but technology changed that—Salt Lake's Victory Road now bisects the canyon, whose mouth still opens into the valley above the Warm Springs. In 1848 Robert Bliss visited the foot of Ensign Peak and noted "a bed of Red paint on the side of the mt," perhaps iron oxide precipitated from the springs—a valuable resource for local Natives.[60]

---

[58]Cooley, "Robert S. Bliss Journal," 29 February 1848, 393.
[59]Egan, *Pioneering the West*, 154.
[60]Cooley, "Robert S. Bliss Journal," 26 February 1848, 392.

William Monroe Egan (1851–1929) wrote these recollections of Red Canyon's Native art gallery.

EGAN, OBSERVATIONS & EXPERIENCES AMONG THE UTES, BEINECKE LIBRARY.

The native Utes of my childhood days were very peaceful and I have watched the young children at their play many times. They made their camp on the vacant block near the cornorner [sic] of our residence block and so I was in close contact with all their maneuvers. The boys were taught to make their own bows and arrows, which they could easily do from the willows growing near the creeks and in the Canyon [City Creek].

They put the wood in shape by scraping it with flint, which they could get just on the side hill a few blocks away. They learned from their parents how to extract the sinews from the animals they used for meat. The muscle part they cut out and, separating the fibre into as small parts as would answer the purpose, they would wrap the feathers on their arrows and the flint spike after having dressed it into shape. The sinew also answered for a bow string after that had been got into shape.

A bunch of a half-dozen little boys would start out in their play, which was also real practice. One would shoot at some mark ahead of them, and the next, and all would run up to see which had come the nearest. Then they would select another object and all shoot and follow up to the mark, continuing the play and practice.

They would chase butterflys and inscects [sic] the same as the white children and seemed to have just as much fun at it. We enjoyed the wild life in the open as much as they did, and roamed the hills frequently. It was only the next block to ours where the hill commenced and it was less than a mile to Ensign Peak. This was my playground and it is only a block or so from where I am living now to where they got their red paint to decorate their faces.[61] The little boys enjoyed doing that as much as their parents. I have played on this hillside days and days. It amused us to note the native's drawings on big flat stones at this place which we called red holler. A cliff of cement cobble rock with some big flat faced ones, made a good place to show their ability to draw objects, men and beasts.

EGAN, "THE INDIAN PORTRAIT," PIONEERING THE WEST, 154–55.

In the largest red ravine that leads down from Ensign Peak bench, and about half way to the bottom, was a cliff of rocks from side to side, and about twenty-five or thirty feet high. It was more than perpendicular, for the top

---

[61]R. L. Polk's 1897 Salt Lake City Directory, 237, listed Tamson Egan (widow of Howard and mother of William) living at 312 N 2d West on today's 300 West in the Marmalade District.

leaned over to such an extent that water coming down the gulch would fall clear off the face of the cliff, which was composed of a conglomeration of different kinds of stones all cemented together with hardpan.

On the right hand side as you go up, and some ten feet above the steep sloping earth at the bottom, was embedded in the walls a boulder about, three feet in diameter, flush with the face of the wall. On this boulder was painted, with red, blue, and black material, the figure of an Indian sitting on his horse. He was a big, broad-shouldered man, dressed in the Indian fashion, large plumes of feathers on his head, a long spear in one hand, the other held the bridle reins. Just close back of him on the same rock was a small band of Indians all on horses, apparently some distance away, but all could be seen very plainly.

The horses were almost as perfectly drawn as could be by a camera. The Indian was in the correct position for sitting a horseback, and must have been taken from life, but by whom? and what kind of paint used, to stand the weather so long? It could not be washed off and when I last saw it, it was just as bright as ever, only where the boys had tried to chip off a piece that would have some of the paint on, by throwing small boulders at it, thus marring the painting badly.

That is another thing that should have been preserved. It could have been easily chiseled out and carried away.

During the first eighteen months of contact with the Latter-day Saints and the Native peoples of their new Zion, Mormon-Indian relations followed a pattern common across the American West. During the next year, typical tensions increased conflict that pushed the initial friendly relationship to bloodshed.

Chapter 2

WHITE MEN
WERE NEVER SATISFIED
The Mormons Move South, 1849

The rush to California in 1849 upended and transformed the American West. A hundred thousand forty-niners flooded the West Coast, and the Mormon settlements saw about 10 percent of them, along with Capt. Howard Stansbury's topographical expedition and the region's first U.S. Indian agent. The newly organized Mormon militia killed four Ute cattle raiders in March in Utah Valley, initiating the systematic displacement of the most prosperous Western Ute band, the Timpanogos. A month later Mormon settlers began building Fort Utah astride the traditional Ute fishing camp; by late summer Native leaders complained to forty-niners about their new neighbors. Wakara and Brigham Young, the Great Basin's two most powerful men, met in June. Mormon settlers reached Sanpete Valley in November; measles followed in December, along with Parley Pratt's Southern Exploring Expedition on its way to survey the South's warmer valleys.

After returning to Salt Lake in 1848, Young said it was "a matter of great rejoicing to me that this people are in this valley." The hand of the Lord had brought them there to "have the privilege of shewing to God and angels what is in us." He rebuked his followers:

A many elders have prayed to be among the Lamanites and now they want to kill them—they are the children of Abraham, the descendants of Israel—there is the remnants of Israel—there is a reckless band—the mountaineers want us to kill them—some are desperadoes—if this community knew how to treat the natives they never would meet with difficulties—treat them kindly—let every act and deal and move show we are their friends. If they abuse our friends treat them with decision—I don't much believe in killing them—I would not kill them half as quick as a white man—we have been taught all the days of our life not to steal but they have been taught to steal—if the men who had gone up had shot every dog, then every horse—and when elk [Parriots] shot in the camp—you should have shot him dead—old Wanship has done it—my council is—walk into their camp kill their dogs and then kill their horses—until they come to terms—the natives we are obliged to sustain.[1]

Brigham Young was convinced the world was out to get him and his people. "All hell was on our tract," he said in 1849, telling his flock to "build a first rate arsenal." He vacillated between relying on inspirational, compassionate leadership—"I want you to drive away your fears—you wont starve to death in this valley"—and tyranny—"I want this people to know I am boss in this valley." No one who left his Kingdom could "carry off the gold and silver without he pleases to let them, that they can not get away unless he sees fit and those who go away contrary to council he will confiscate their property, for he is boss."[2]

The next year revealed the chasm separating Mormon Indian policy and its prophet's Lamanite rhetoric.

KILL THEM MEAN EWTES: THE UNCIVIL LAW AT BATTLE CREEK

Whatever enlightened hopes the Mormons had for their neighbors in 1849, the year opened with bloodshed. Oliver Huntington, with his nephew Allen, and Thomas S. Williams and his father, Alex "Elie" Williams, made a trading trek to Utah Valley in February 1849, which set the stage for what followed.

O. B. HUNTINGTON, DIARY, 62–66.

[W]e stayed on dry creek [now Lehi] where there was no water at that time of the year and had to melt snow to drink. Late in the evening we heard some one of the natives calling to us "how de doo," a name they some times gave the whites, because of the common salute. We answered them. They were far down the creek towards Ewtah Lake—They cried out again & wanted to know if *Wandship* (a leader in Salt Lake Valley with whom they had been at war lately) was there. We said no.

---

[1]Van Wagoner, *Complete Discourses*, 26 November 1848, 305. The "men who had gone up" were probably Mormon traders; Elk was a Timpanogos leader.

[2]Van Wagoner, *Complete Discourses*, 312–13.

They then kept hallooing in friendly terms until they came to us—four brothers—*Blueshirt* Roman nose and two younger brothers. They have a kind of play which they call "*Nalowich*," by which they gamble. It is attended with a song, and is quite interesting. They wanted we should play with them. Thomas and Allen were used to the game and started with them, while the old man and I looked and kept ourselves as a guard. The whites soon won the Indians bows and arrows. We gave them back their implements . . . and sent them away, on friendly terms.

The next day two of them followed on foot all day to get a smoke at night—when night came, as we were encamped around a good fire on the banks of the Provo river, a number of Indians were around our fire and a village near by. These two who followed us were yet in the village, and the curiosity of those around our fire was attracted by the sight of my "six shooter," or revolving pistol. I told them it was "bad medicine" and they must not touch it, and I motioned with it what I could do with it—They seemed to laugh at the idea—I held it out over their heads and suddenly let off two of the barrels.—They all droped onto their nees, seats, or bent down—I gave a fierce look at them and discharged the remaining four barrels, and by the time I was done they were all laying on the ground shaking with fear.

I then laughed at them and told them I would not hurt them, that I would only kill those that stole cattle out of the other Valley. The next morning they came to us from the village and told us, that those two young men who came with us were scared when them guns were fired the night before, and ran off immediately and had not been seen since—They had probably gone home in the night.

The Chief or Capatan of the village then told us that there was that family of boys [and] great thieves, & for that he had driven them away from his band because they would not hear him and stop stealing the Mormons cattle, and that since he drove them away they had told one of his men that they had eat nothing but "Koot-sem-bongos" or cattle all winter and did not hunt any.

He said he did not know where they lived—but he wanted the big white Capatan to send up some men and kill those mean men—mean Ewtes, he called them—and, said he "if the big Capatan (or captain) does not kill them I will—but it will look better for you to kill your own enemies—if they are not killed now, they will soon get more men to stealing cattle and then you will come up and kill me, my men, women and children." "Tell the big "Tababoo Capatan" (white captain) to come up and kill them mean Ewtes." These particulars he told us through "Parbeleau" the half Ewte and spaniard.

This we reported to the Presidency when we returned home and on the Second day of March a company of 30 men were raised and fited out at the public expense.

Hosea Stout described what happened in late February. "This evening was called on to go with an expedition to the Utah Valley against some Indians who had been stealing a lot of horses from Brighams herd," he wrote. On 1 March Stout and thirty-five men marched south with orders "simply to take such measures as would put a final end to their depredations in future." Young's horses turned up: Indians had not stolen them, but now Col. John Scott's orders were "to proceed with the Indians for killing cattle . . . so that the nature of our expedition was not in the least changed."[3]

A hard slog through deep snow brought the posse to Provo River on 4 March. The Utahs "recieved us friendly but were much excited being evidently afraid of us." That night, as "a bright moon shone beautifully," Little Chief's sons led the Mormons to the renegade camp. The ravine, soon known as Battle Creek, sheltered Blueshirt, Roman Nose, and their two brothers and families. Both sides opened fire as dawn broke. The troops quickly blew the top off Roman Nose's skull. The Utes hunkered down and fought for two hours "with the most determined resolution to die rather than yield," Stout reported. The interpreters called for the survivors "to send out their women & children that they might be spared if they would not yield but all to no effect." Eventually "13 women & children came out, among the rest a lad about sixteen gave up. He had fought manfully during the engagement." After a four-hour fight, the Mormons killed two more men; they shot Blueshirt "before he ran far," Stout wrote. "Thus ended the battle without one of our men even being hurt although they shot hundreds of arrows at us sometimes at only a few yards distance."[4]

O. B. HUNTINGTON, DIARY, 66–74.

The third and fourth of March we spent in hunting for them, but could not find them. On the afternoon of the 4th we came to the Provo, where The "Little Chief" and "stick=in=the=head" were camped—Leaders of two bands—one village on the North and the other on the south side of the river. Little Chief was a noted friend to all white men. He said one of his men had found where the mean Ewtes were—and that we must go under cover of night to get to them, for we would be in sight of them all they [sic] way after we should leave the banks and timber of the Provo, as they were up in the side of the Mountain.

---

[3] Brooks, *The Diary of Hosea Stout*, 1 March 1849, 2:344.
[4] Ibid., 345–47.

He sent three of his men with us. Barney Ward and Dimick were along as interpreters.

The Chief and all the Indians were wonderfully frightened to see our martial array, and order on horseback.

Those mean Ewtes were 10 miles back towards the other valley.

About Eleven O'clock we took up our line of march—the Moon was full which gave us a good view of our road and course. In this country the Moon is seldom obscured by clouds. We were a novel and grand spectacle to ourselves, and a cause of great astonishment and admiration to our native guides, as we moved along softly and slowly in the moonlight.

We took to the side of the Mountain so high up that there was a perceptible difference in the atmosphere—being much colder than down in the vale. We wandered along to within 2 or 3 miles of them, as near as the make of the country and our knowledge of their situation would admit. We did not like to trust too much to our guides.

Here we halted in a cove in the Mountain where were a plenty of large sage brush and Juniper trees. There 4 or 5 men were detached to reconoitre the country and find the Indians which is easily done by night as they never let their fires go down. We that were left to take care of the horses, (as those that went on, went on foot) made a fine fire, warmed ourselves and proceeded to lay down on the ground and took a nap.

The horses we hitched to trees and sage brush with not much to eat that night with their saddles all on, ready to start. After about 3 hours, Judson stodard returned with orders from John Scott our leader to bring on the company in all silence—we were soon on the march, and in a short time came to a small fire in a deep ravene, with the remainder of our company hovering over the few coles they dared to keep, having found the camp of the "mean Ewtes," which was near half a mile distant from us then. Here we waited in silent suspense and anxiety for day light to make its first appearance, upon which the company was divided into five squads or parties, one on horseback, one up the creek, one down the creek, one to the north side and one to the south side of the creek, were the positions of the different little parties [where] the horse men were [stationed], in case they should any get away from our circle.

They had three houses built in the usual stile of those poorer indians. A number of small poles are stuck in the ground forming a circle—the tops of these poles are all brought into the centre and fastened. This is the frame, and it is covered with long grass barks, skins, or any thing most handy, save a little hole at the top and a small hole at the side for a door. The fire is in the centre, and smoke goes out at the hole in the top, some of it; the rest they manage to breathe into their lungs and get into their eyes some way, which gives them a very peculiarly disagreeable look. The situation of these houses were where the crick once run, and near the edge of the creek as it then was. Their situation was a strong hold,—a great place of defence.

About ¼ a mile from the abrupt and allmoste inaccessable mountains, on the banks of a small creek, running swiftly down a very steep small ravine or gutter which was filled with almoste impenetrable small timber, brush and thorns. Their retreat could not be discerned in the day time until within 5 rod of it.

When day broke upon us we were on the south side of the creek—I was in the division that crossed the creek, and we were the most tardy in geting our places, and in seeing this we hurried a little, which made so much noise we started the victims from their secrete retreat. It was the plan, for all to get their stations unobserved and then send in a committee to wait upon them out, and invite them to give themselves up to our law; but they saved themselves the trouble of civil law, and chose the uncivil law.

They only saw us, and started to run up the creek for the Mountains, where they found a wall of whites—they started for the South where they found another blockade—they tried the west and found the same and there we were by this time on the north in a line circling in upon them,=retreat they could not—As yet not a gun had been fired. Our interpreters talked to them and told them our errand, and asked them to give themselves up—They refused—Our guide talked to them and reasoned with them, but all to no purpose—fight they would unless we wend [sic] away—then they said they would come out.

The guide told them they must come out then or die—

Then the Arrows began to fly; but from where we could not see; yet could hear the twang of the bow=string.

Our orders were, every man to take care of himself and as many of the enemy as we could—I.E. to fight them their own way. Occasionally one would put his head up to see the enemy—and the enemy always had their guns up to take advantage of such incidents, but we always shot in such haste, that nearly all our shots, being at such smal objects, missed, and hence we were a long time firing—sculking in the brush—looking—peaking & trying to get a shot.

We knew nothing [about] how many there was—but from their crying, howling, moaning and loud talk supposed there was 15 or 20.

The women and children were called to come out—that we wanted not to hurt them—They would not come. The first one shot was their leader. Then such a howling and crying, I think white men never heard before.

It was enough to move the stones, but our work had to be done, as Little Chief said, to set an example to the others around. All those indians are of that nature, that you must conquer them or they will conquer you. One or the other must prove their mastery. We fought on—and could tell when one was hit, by the loud cries of all—howlings like wolves and crying. Finally they saw their fate, as we had closed in on all sides, death was certain to them; and despair drove one young man out bounding like a deer into our midst almoste, throwing arrows at every jump.

Seemingly the very hills were torn to pieces with the report of our guns discharged at him—but he returned to his den again—having stuck three arrows in the belly of one man; the most dareing of our company—but not sufficiently to injure him. They were not thrown with much force one would suppose—Soon the women wished to come out—Dimick built a fire out back for them, as they were very cold having laid in the creek and ice in the creek—women and little infants, and all who could not fight had laid there as long as they could live, to keep from the firing, but then two had got wounded slightly in the head. Everything was hit in the head, as that was all they would show.

After the women were all out, we were about to go down and take them by storm, and one young woman came to our midst and wanted us to stop—for she had a brother in there that she loved and she did not want him killed. The interpreter told her to go and fetch him out—She went down talking in a low tone, and soon appeared again, pulling and hauling him along—He was either afraid or did not want to come; but she got him out—and as soon as he was with us unhurt, was as insolent as the Devil. He ordered us all to go away; and wanted to know what we were there for. Three or four times he motioned and said "go way." Dimick steped up to him and told him we had come to open their ears—that he came last year and talked to them and told them they must not steal our cattle, but said D "you would not open your ears and hear us. But you have stole our cattle all the time—now we have come to open your ears for you." And pulled his ear—asked him how many guns they had in there. He said only one.

Dimick told him to go and bring it out to him. He then told us all to go away. D—cocked his gun and told him to move and bring that gun or he would shoot him.

His sister told him to go, and he went and brought it. Wit[h] this they had fired at us as often as they could get it off. At first we were at such a distance that we could see their arrows and dodge them.

Now their gun was gone and their arrows nearly exausted and our men nearly all on one side of the creek they began to run, and *"Blew Shirt"* nearly succeded in geting away, but finally fell from a shot which unjointed his neck. He fell with 18 ball holes, mostly through his body, and when he fell was running at the speed of a horse. I believe none got away.

This was on the Morning of the 5th of March 1849.

When the firing had ceased it was perhaps 8 o'clock—the sun was high up and Little Chief had come from his home on horseback, since he first heard our guns. The morning was clear & calm as God ever made, and the vollies of our guns rolled down the mountain and lighted upon Little Chiefs ears, and seemed to him, with all the horrors of his own death nell.

The thought "Oh! his countrymen"—those once of his own band are now being hewn down by the Magic White men—his heart was filled with pity, although but a few hours previous he had signed their death warrant by sending his men to guide us to them, without which we could never have got them. His pity overcame him—he mounted his best horse and dashed up the mountainsides for ten miles with almoste one breath—His horse, a noble animal with large extended nostrils, was as wet as the poor squaws who had laid in the creek. Little Chief was wet with tears and his horse wet with sweat.

The old man howled, cried, moaned hollowed, screamed and smote his breast in the greatest of agony of mind; when he come to us He blamed himself and cursed the whites, and said it would not be good medicine for 2 or 3 to come up there alone as they had done before. But it was not long before a settlement and Fort was made close to his village in the Ewtah Valley, and I went up there and pass that battle ground alone.

The women and children went to the Salt Lake City, or near it, to live with some of their relatives. After they came out of their retreat in the creek, they were no more afraid of us, but seemed as though we were their friends—and indeed such we were. We only wanted to stop their men stealing our cattle and teach all the indians around us, a lasting lesson. There was not an individual in our company injured in the whole fracass and the lesson was well understood by all the surrounding indians.

The fight ended about 9:00 A.M. The Mormons gathered the bodies of the "seven great, fat stout men" they found for burial. Oliver Huntington recognized the Roman Nose family, "tall stout men with that very prominent facial sign of aggressiveness" as "they were well known and closely watched by all mountaineers. They were not to be trusted at any one's back."

Forty years later, O. B. Huntington wrote again of the battle and Little Chief's grief:

We all went away to our horses, at which place we found "Little Chief" weeping and howling over the death of his countrymen, saying that it would probably come his turn next, for the white men were never satisfied—that he had never heard so many guns and such loud noises before, and he could not keep away; had run his horse from where Provo now is in a short time, and he wanted to know what we had done. We told him all; that the women and children were going home with us and that we would give them good clothing, plenty to eat and houses to live in. Well, he thought that was a heap to do for women whose husbands were mean enough to kill.

The surviving women and children followed their conquerors home, where they "were made to clean themselves, and were clothed and fed like whites. All that submission and apparent content lasted but a few days, and they disappeared like young quails."[5]

A week after the fight, the Mormons formed the provisional State of Deseret, whose stupendous borders encompassed "perhaps a sixth of the entire modern area of the United States."[6] On the afternoon of 12 March 1849, the Saints celebrated with a thirteen-gun salute. Wanship's Utes, who identified as Shoshones, wintered at the thermal springs northwest of the Mormon fort. The cannons "dreadfully scared" Wanship, who "thought the white men were going to war."[7]

OUR ADVICE IN FRIENDSHIP: BRIDGER AND VASQUEZ

History often raises the question, Who is lying to whom? The letters Brigham Young exchanged with Jim Bridger and Louis Vasquez are full of professions of friendship and accusations of skullduggery, including counterfeiting, murder, and plotting Indian massacres. Is everyone lying, or are only villainous conspirators twisting the truth? A fair conclusion is that all those teetering on the Mormon-Indian-mountaineer tripod lied whenever it was convenient.

Brigham Young disliked Jim Bridger at first sight. Bridger's July 1848 letter to John Smith, then "President of G.S.L. City," could improve the relationship: "I am truly Sorry that you Should believe any Reports about me having Said that I would Bring any Indians or any number of Indians upon you or any of your Community. Such A thought never entered my Head and I trust to your Knowledge and good Sense to know if A Person is desirouse of living in good Friandship with his Neighbours would undertake such a mad Project."

Bridger complained "about A Number Coins of Base or Bogos Money in my Possession." Jack Redding had "Passed two five Dollar Bogos gold Pieces upon us last fall." He expected President Smith would "see into it" and was "willing to Say no more about the matter." An astute businessman, Bridger was "desiraus of Maintaining an Amical Frendship with the People in the Valley and Should you want a Favour at my hands at any time I shall allways think myself happy in doing it for you," Bridger assured him.[8]

---

[5]O. B. Huntington, "First Battle with Indians in Utah," 227.

[6]Morgan, "The State of Deseret," 93.

[7]Huntington, Diary, 88–89.

[8]For the complete letter, see Gowans and Campbell, *Fort Bridger*, 40. Mormon scholars doubt Bridger incited the Indians against the Latter-day Saints.

Brigham Young contemplated colonizing the most remote Ute strongholds in 1848. He asked the most experienced men in the American West for their advice about sending "a small portion of this community next spring" to the Uintah Valley "to raise grain, taking a few mechanics, a Blacksmith, Tailor, Shoemaker &c. with them."[9] Thomas Williams apparently was not "able to cross the Mountains in Weber River Canyon" until spring, when Young received "advice in friendship and as your good nabers." Bridger said the Utes were "badly disposed towards the whites, for it appears that they have been fighting with sum Americans in the direction of Taos," and the Mormons had "kild four this spring." This alarmed Bridger. He and Vasquez thought "the scope of cultivable land" was "not extensive enoth for a large settlement."[10] Discussing this letter with church leaders in April, Young recalled Joseph Smith "speaking of the Lamanites—we shall see a time when we shall have to kill them to save them from killing us." Smith knew how hard it would be to convert Indians. Young told his advisors "to get a military" organized.[11]

In May 1849 Louis Vasquez asked Young about the murder of a Bannock who had left his fort with Barney Ward and a man named Jacobs with "two Horses and sum beaver skins." He "was found Murderd below the Junction of Hams & Blacks for[k]. He had his head splated by an axe or Tomahack and stabed under the arm." The Bannocks spoke of making war in the Salt Lake Valley. "So Sir, you know best what to do for the safety of your People and all other whites in this country."[12] Vasquez asked "how many horses Ward had brought into the valley," for the Indians "were much incensed and talked of coming to the valley to war upon us." In response, Young attacked Old Gabe:

I believe I know that Old Bridger is death on us, and if he knew that 400,000 Indians were coming against us, and any man were to let us know, he would cut his throat. But Vasquez is a different sort of a man. I believe Bridger is watching every movement of the Mormons, and reporting to Thomas Benton at Washington.[13] That letter is all bubble and froth. It is good for us. Every particle of the wrath of man is handled by the Almighty, and will operate

---

[9]Young to Bridger and Vasquez, 19 December 1848, BYC 16:2.

[10]Bridger and Vasquez to Young, 7 April 1849, BYC 21:15.

[11]Carter, *Founding Fort Utah*, 100.

[12]Vasquez to Young, 8 May 1849, BYC 21:17,

[13]No evidence supports Young's repeated charges that Senator Benton plotted against or even disliked Mormons. Benton showed congressional representative John Bernhisel "a most gentlemanly courtesy and kindness." Benton pleasantly remarked "that he was opposed to poligamy for he thought that four legs between a pair of sheets at one time was enough." Bernhisel to Young, 21 March and 9 August 1850, BYC 60:9, 10, and 15.

to our advantage in the end. We should be prepared for all emergencies with the Indians or whites. As for the old Indians now alive entering into the new and everlasting covenant, they will not do it, but they will die and be damned. How long does it take to train a white man? We have been training eighteen years. And how much longer an Indian? They will not be converted in many years. Men who want to get knowledge, you can't drive away from us. You can't whip them away. Stay at home and mind your own business, and the Indians will do the same. And if they come and are not friendly with us, put them where they won't harm us. If we stay at home, they will send their children to our schools. I am opposed to James Emmet's method of converting Indians—he and his company never washed their hands or faces for months. I recommend the herding of horses. We are scattered all over the valley, men, women and children. The Indians would rather have our horses than us. If those Indians believed that Barney Ward had stolen two of their horses, and they could get them back, and two or three more, they would dance for joy.[14]

"This presant race of Indians will never be converted," Young said. "It mattereth not whether they kill one another off or Some body else do it":

But we will take their children & shool them & teach them to be clenly & to love morality & then raise up seed amoung them & in this way they will be brought back into the presance & knowlege of God & as for appointing men to trade among the Indians who will deal honestly amoung them & represent us in our true character, this cannot be done. If we wish to change the course of a stream we must first cut channels for it to Run in & gradually lead it where we want it to go. But the moment we undertake to dam up the stream, we have a pond of water which will rise as fast as we can dam against it & will ultimately brake over the dam before we can controle the Stream. Just so we must do with this People. Let Tom, Dick & the Devil go & trade with the Indians & by degrees we will controle them.[15]

We Called It "Fort Utah"

Historian Robert Carter has shown the push to build an outpost on Provo River "evolved more from profit motives than from a prophet's motives." The settlement of Utah Valley began with "the common man rather than from the leaders" of the State of Deseret. Colonies spontaneously spread north and south from Salt Lake Valley, much as settlement developed elsewhere

[14]Harwell, *Manuscript History of Brigham Young*, 201–202.
[15]Cleland and Brooks, eds., *A Mormon Chronicle*, 12 May 1849, 1:108, 130n161.

in the United States. Three days after he fought at Battle Creek, Alexander Williams announced he was taking "some cows for Pres. Young" to graze in Utah Valley and "instruct" the widows and orphans "of the Four Indians killed last Monday—to farm, &c."[16]

"The Legislative council," John D. Lee recorded on 10 March 1849, considered "the policy of sending some 30 Families to the utauh valley to setle & put in spring crops, open a fishery, introduce schools, teach the Natives how to cultivate the Soil, raise catle, & in fine to improve their Morals, to make Fishers of them, & then the Saints can buy the Fish of them for a trifle, which will preserve their feelings good as they claim the right to the Fish." Ten days before some thirty men set out for Utah Lake, the council appointed "John Higbee, Bishop & President," with Isaac Higbee and Dimick Huntington as his counselors. This allowed Brigham Young to put the imprimatur of the Council of Fifty and those "fit to Sit in the councils of the Gods" on the project. "Mormon leaders had not yet formulated a set plan that they could follow when establishing new settlements," historian Robert Carter noted, but the fishing colony struck a discordant note. Provo's first settlers "went without the advice of the recognized authorities of the people," which James A. Little thought proved "they were not the proper persons to plant a successful colony among savages."[17]

Angatewats of the Timpanogos confronted Utah Valley's first Mormon invaders. George W. Bean later explained why. Angatewats "placed himself on horseback across the trail in front of the foremost wagon and forbad them from proceeding farther." Dimick Huntington pleaded with him "to try the emigrants a while and see if they could not live in peace together, and after about an hour's delay they were allowed to proceed in peace." Their fort stood on the Provo River's southern or left bank, "near the lower crossing. . . . enclosing an ancient mound near the center." Pickets "about 12 feet long, set in the ground close together [provided] protection in case of attack from hostile Indians."

> They got along pretty well with the natives the fore part of the season, although some of the worst Indians of this western region belonged to this tribe, and they soon found that Provo was the great annual gathering place for all the Ute bands of the valleys for two hundred miles, east and south, on account of the wonderful supply of fish, moving up the stream from the lake to their

---

[16]Carter, *Founding Fort Utah*, 71–73.
[17]Ibid.; and Cleland and Brooks, *A Mormon Chronicle*, 1:100–102.

spawning grounds every spring, indeed so great were the number of suckers and mullet passing continuously up stream that often the river would be full from bank to bank as thick as they could swim for hours and sometimes days together, and fish would be taken in all ways and places. The Indians could feast from morning until night for weeks together, free of all cost, except a little labor catching the *Pahgar* (suckers), or *Mpahger* (speckled trout, good fish). At the time of their arrival at Provo the Timpanodes were governed by a chief called by the whites, Little Chief, but in about a month after this, he led a party of warriors to attack Warship's band, north of Salt Lake City, and was killed in a battle up at Ogden hole, or north Ogden, then Opecarry (*Stick-in-the-Head*). There was also Old Elk, (*Pareyarts*), Old Battiste, Tintic, his brother, Portsorvic, Angatewats and other noted ones here, Old *Sawiet*, old *Petnich*, Walker and his brother, and old *Uinta* and his sons, Tabby, *Graspero*, and *Nicquia*, old *Antero*, and some times Kanosh. These with their bands had been accustomed to meet at Provo, and have a great good time, horse racing, trading, gambling and eating fish, for several weeks every year. There were some additions made to the population at Provo during the summer, and in the fall when Indian troubles broke out, they were situated in the fort.[18]

GEORGE WASHINGTON BEAN, AUTOBIOGRAPHY, 46–47.

On April 1st, my eighteenth birthday, we moved on to within about 2½ miles of Timpanogos River (Provo R.) when we were met by a young Indian Brave on horseback dashing toward us as fast as he could ride, throwing his arms and performing all sorts of wild gesticulations. When he got within about six rods of our head team, he jumped off his horse, threw his buffalo robe across our path and warned us not to pass that designated point. The Indians had got some idea of our intention to make a settlement at the Timpanogos River and this young Brave named Ang-a-Te-Wats volunteered to stop us until an understanding could be arrived at. Dimick Huntington, our Interpreter, told over all our good desires and intentions and that President Young, the Great Mormon Chief had sent us, and that we would like to be "Too-ege-tik-a-boo"—good friends—with the natives and do them much good if allowed to settle with them.

The little Brave dashed off to report to the tribe, and we slowly moved on. Presently a large party met us with the War Chief at their head and we all stopped and talked the matter over again. The party seemed satisfied and we moved on and were allowed to camp on the North side of the River.

Inter- and intra-tribal violence raged throughout North America. As they pushed deeper into critical Native homelands, Mormons like the Higbee brothers did not know how to avoid being caught in between.

---

[18]"Journal of Judge George W. Bean," in Gottfredson, *History of Indian Depredations*, 20–21.

JOHN S. AND ISAAC HIGBEE TO BRIGHAM YOUNG,
12 APRIL 1849, LDS ARCHIVES.

Utah Valley April 12th 1849

To President B. Young
Sir

Since we have been here we have enjoyed health and peace among ourselves and peace with our neighbours the Indians. On the evening of the 7th inst an indian from Goships band came here to make peace with the indians here, and had we not protected him and they would have killed him. Little Chief is situated about ½ mile below us on the Creek and this morning about breackfast time we heard the firing of guns in that direction and soon found they had been attacted by One Ship [Wanship] and Goship's band. The result of the battle was that Little Chiefs son got shot through the arm.[19] They killed two horses and wounded two more and drove off all their horses and one or two of ours.

Now Little Chief says if we are his friends he wants us to proove it by getting back their horses for them. Now we wish you would give some council concerning the matter.

John S. Higbee pres
Isaac Higbee Clerk

O. B. Huntington provided additional details of the raid that tore the Utes apart immediately after the Mormons settled on their Provo River fishing grounds. Little Chief, "a noted friend to all white men," was the dominant leader of the Timpanogos band, while Parriots—Elk or Old Elk—served as their main warrior. Elk was "a daring, intreagueing, bloody villain," Huntington wrote. "They all called him a great warior, but a bad Indian." In 1848 Elk had treacherously murdered Wanship's "extraordinary smart son," Jim, who had been the Salt Lake band's "first warrior—it was said that he was a great Marksman and a great hunter and that & never missed his aim." Huntington began his tale one month after the fight at Battle Creek with the Mormons settled in "Ewtah Vally in the very midst of the Indians, all living in peace togather," when at daybreak, his nephew Allen saw "a cloud of dust specked with horsemen" descending on the Ute village: this was Wanship, whose men "took all the horses of the assailed save one which was not worth taking." Little Chief soon "came over in tears and implored the whites to help him," for he had brought on the attack "by helping them. Said he had shown himself to be the friend of the Mormons and now if they were his friend he wanted they

---

[19]This was Tintic.

should show it by geting his horses back." The Mormons told him they could do nothing without "orders from the Governer." Governor Young "called out an armed force and went to the camp of indians—only to scare them to terms of compliance, but there was sufficient force to accomplish the end."

Wanship defied all the "power on earth to take those horses from him." He confronted the captain "and fired a gun immediately over his head. Saying, he was ready to die—that his men had periled their lives for those horses, and according to all their laws they belonged to them; and every man woman and child in his village should die before the horses should go back—That all of them did not pay him for his son and horse." Brigham Young "came down alone with the interpreter," Dimick Huntington, and "tried pacific means. The old Chief was friendly and cheerful but unyielding." The governor claimed he "was a friend to all 'red men' and he did not want to fight them, nor want them to fight one another, but if they would fight he wanted they should remove to another country." Wanship agreed to leave and "took a northern rout" to Weber River, where "he was overtaken by Little Chief and his band," now "swelled to as great a number as possible." Little Chief recaptured his horses and "a number of the enemies, killing 2 men and wounding several more." That night Wanship marched around the Timpanogos and ambushed Little Chief's band when it was "entangled in a very heavy bank of snow." Here he "fought Little Chief, killed him, three other men and retook more than half of all the horses."[20]

The Historian's Office minutes of 20 May 1849 reported that LDS leaders discussed how "the Utah fight at Ogden's hole—killed Little Chief and one of his men," apparently to avenge "Wanship's Son." Huntington recalled Little Chief died on the road to Fort Bridger and placed the fatal confrontation in Ogden Valley, as the region is now known.

O. B. HUNTINGTON, "FIRST BATTLE WITH INDIANS IN UTAH,"
PARRY'S MONTHLY MAGAZINE (MARCH 1890), 228–29.

Then followed something else: trouble between Salt Lake Valley Indians and Utah Valley Indians. The prisoners [captured at Battle Creek] were relatives of the Salt Lake Valley Indians, whose Chief was a large, bony, stout man, with strong warlike proclivities and getting old. His name was Wandship, and had quite a large family, several sons grown to manhood who were wise, valiant men. About the 8th of April, some of Wandship's men went to Utah Valley, and at dawn of day took all of Little Chiefs horses but one. A

[20]O. B. Huntington, Diary, 95–99.

few shots were fired but no one hurt except Little Chiefs son, Tintic, who followed on the one horse and kept up a running fight alone, until he was shot in the leg just above the knee.

Wandship's men brought the horses into Salt Lake just at daylight the day after the capture. Little Chief followed close upon their track, and appealed to President Brigham Young for his friendship and aid to recover the horses, in consideration of the fact that he, (Little Chief,) had been a friend, and delivered the bad Indians into the power of the whites. Now the whites should prove that they are his friends by returning their horses.

The appeal was not altogether in vain. President Young sent Dimick to Wandship for the horses to be given up peaceably. This demand met with a determined, obstinate refusal. Wandship stated that what they took in war was theirs, and they would die rather than give it up.

President Young returned word that he must do one of two things immediately: either return the horses taken from Little Chief or leave the valley; and if he would rather die than do either he should die in a very short time.

Wandship was camped near the big springs in the 19th Ward, Salt Lake City, but during the night following every Indian disappeared, going north.

Little Chief had lost too much to let matters pass over easy. Indeed, there had always from time immemorial, been a deadly hate between the people of the two valleys, according to the Indian accounts and legends. Years after these events I became intimately acquainted with one of Wandship's sons, while in government employ, and so great was his friendship for me that he offered to have his blood drawn for my relief.

Wandship undertook to pass through Ogden Canyon to Bear River, and on the second or third morning after leaving Salt Lake Valley, he found himself in trouble with Little Chief, who had got in ahead of him and had possession of all the horses of both bands. A fight followed, in which Wandship came out second best, being wounded himself, three or four of his men were killed and all the horses taken.

That deadly hate continued; for on the next morning Little Chief found himself cut off from retreat by Wandship's men. Another fight took place in which Little Chief and several of his men were killed. The rest of his men escaped with a part of the horses.

This was the last difficulty that ever occurred between the two bands. They were too much used up and demoralized ever to rally against each other again. Wandship's band never appeared as a band any more, nor gave us any trouble as a people, but not so with Little Chiefs band, they gave us a vast amount of trouble in a fight at Provo and a few years later a general war on the people under the direction of Tintic, a son of Little Chief.

In the wake of this carnage, Brigham Young laid the foundation of his Indian policy while conveying to Fort Utah his fear of nefarious plots.

Tom Williams claimed that "old Elk and Capt Walker are going amongst the different bands of the Utahs to incite them to join him" and attack the unfinished stockade. "Never be caught away from your Farm—and while you are building your Fort, have your Guns and ammunition fast by your side—and as quick as you can hoist your cannon to the top of your Fort," he advised. Keep "a good quantity of good round cobble stones, to be convenient for any hour of necessity" and "secure your horses and cattle in a coral at nights, keeping up a vigilant guard" day and night. "Look out for the Indians, for they will be on you, in an hour that you do not think they are near." If the Utes wanted "to make peace, do not give them any presents—but if they will be friendly, teach them to raise grain—& order them to quit stealing your cattle."[21]

The next day Dimick Huntington sent a letter to Salt Lake with Jefferson Hunt confirming that a Timpanogos "warparty gone to day in pursuit of Wanship to retake" their horses. "Patsowet an influential Indian a brother of one that we killed came in yesterday and cut up high swells," but Huntington had "made him our friend." The colonists had "twenty muskets in camp & no catterridges" and asked for "twenty rounds a piece for each gun if you think it best."[22]

The festival of bloodshed that followed the founding of Fort Provo was no coincidence, for it was built atop the main Ute fishing camp. The disruptions proved enduring. One consequence of the white invasion, alien infections, became increasingly apparent. "Upwards of 30 Indians have died this month from measles, including Wandsip & Goship the two chiefs," clerk Thomas Bullock noted in March 1850. They were "a miserable looking set."[23]

They All Want Hats: Young and Wakara Meet

To celebrate the annual Timpanogos spring fish run, Wakara's band reached the Provo River on 10 May 1849, as did twenty lodges of "Timpany Utes" and probably every ambulatory Indian within 150 miles. Dimick Huntington visited Salt Lake with good and bad news.

---

[21]Young to John S. Higbee 18 April 1849, BYC 21:16.

[22]D. B. Huntington to Young, 19 April 1849, BYC 21:16.

[23]Church Historian's Office, Journal, 23 March 1850, 1/13, 39. The tenth volume of O. B. Huntington's journal-memoir ended 14 April 1849, when he returned east to persuade his wife to join him in Utah. She declined. Carter, *Founding Fort Utah*, 93–98.

Dimick Huntington sd on Thursday last Walker with 20 lodges came to Utah. 20 lodges of Timpany Utes pulled up Stakes for this (Utah) Valley—Walker shook hands with me—his heart was warm—his bro. came in Sunday previous—we crushed log—he made a Medicine Pill—told me his bro. was coming—Walker came & sat down in my home—we smoked all round—then made a binding—they were satisified. He traded a horse for a flint[lock] gun—in evening they felt happy, sung round the Fort—they slept round the Fire—Walker lay in his arms—at night we talked. He said I am their friend—he said their were lots of Indians coming—as the Mormons were friendly to them. He wants them to stop fighting—Walker is a smart sensible man. I told them of the Book of Mormon. They must be our friends, & we yours—they said Tou (done)—after Walker left, Elk came—four of the Indian boys helped to drive the cattle down to the Fort. Old Elk came with a pistol in belt—bowie knife in case—& Gun on hand.—we smoked.—Mrs. [Catherine] Orr hit Old Elk a blow with her fist & reeled him. Walker wanted his boy to learn our language & wants B.Y. to write him a ltr what to do. Walker s[aid] it was good to kill the Tinpenny Utes & we ought to kill some more—Walker want us to go & settle a c[olony] in his valley—200 miles South of this—I s[aid] if a few Mormons go there wont the Piedes steal our cattle—he s[aid] he will watch them. The Wood, the Water & Soil is good. There is a mountain of salt & a Spring of Blown Salt.

Brigham Young responded that morning to "Mr. Walker, Utah Chief." Huntington had told him of Wakara's desire "to have our friendly feelings and to be at peace with us, and to have a letter from me." Young wanted to be friends with the Indians and "not do you or your people any hurt." He wanted the Utes "to be at peace with us—if you hear any thing from any Mountaineers bad news, you go straight to Dimic Huntington and he will always tell you the truth." He arranged to trade in the fall. "If you want, we will send a company of our men down to your Valley, to make a Settlement and raise Grain," and "sell you Cattle, supply you with seed and perhaps some Clothing," if not that fall, "as soon as we can, but before we do so, we want to know from you that you and your people will not attempt to molest them or do them any injury. We want to make peace, and a good peace that will last for ever and we will do you good." The Mormons had "very little ammunition but Mr. Huntington will sell you a little, that you may hunt and live till Fall, and then we may sell you more when the Companies come in, or sell you grain for horses."[24]

---

[24]Bullock, Minutes and Letter to Walker, 14 May 1849, BYC 16:17, 17–18.

Four days later, Huntington assured Young that "we are all well, peace prevails through the camp & gentry," but "We have a plenty of company every day." Utes were "comeing in from all quarters, & say thare is more a comeing" for the fish festival from as far away as Taos. An "influential Indian" told him the French said "the Americans are not the Marmans friends & byandby they are acomeing to kill off the mormans and go back again." Wakara had moved his camp, but Huntington would visit him as soon as he could find it.[25] Young quickly responded and again urged him:

> to finish your Fort forthwith, keep continually on your guard—and do not admit the Indians inside your Fort—unless it be a few at a time, and then do not let them in, armed. You cannot be too cautious, or too much prepared for defense. You may be deceived by their apparent over kindness and at a moment when you are off your guard, you may suffer loss—but my constant prayer is that you may not suffer—And that you may act in wisdom and prudence all the time.[26]

On 28 April 1849 Mormon leaders reorganized the Nauvoo Legion and "voted D[aniel] H. Wells to be Major General." As May ended they discussed "Capt Walker & Indians—Indian Warfare," how to herd horses, and trading furs and firearms with the Natives. Wakara was expected to visit Salt Lake in early June: he looked at the Mormons as his fathers, mothers, brothers, and sisters, he said, and promised "that none of his people shoud meddle with our Cattle any way." The hierarchy granted Higbee's wish "to be relieved from the Presidency of Utah" with "*all hands up.*" Young promptly filled the station with his brother, Isaac Higbee, and noted there was no hurry bringing Walker to Salt Lake.[27]

Two days before the first California gold seekers reached the Salt Lake Valley in June 1849, the two most powerful Americans in the Great Basin met near the Council House. Their discussion reveals much about Brigham Young and Wakara as both strove to tell the other what they thought their opposite wanted to hear. These sharp traders discussed how many charges of gunpowder to trade for buckskins, noting the rates that traders Richard Grant and Jim Bridger offered. Wakara claimed the Tinpenny Utes had killed his mysterious father in 1845, which might explain his hostility toward the Timpanogos band.

---

[25]Huntington to Young, 18 May 1849, BYC 21::16, 26.
[26]Young to Huntington, 19 May 1849, BYC 16:17, 19.
[27]Bullock, General church minutes, 14 and 27 May 1849, LDS Archives.

Thomas Bullock, General Church Minutes,
June–July 1849, 9–10, LDS Archives.

June 14–1849–4 P.M.

Council met near Council House. B. Young, H. C. Kimball, W. Richards, John Smith, J. Taylor,—N. K. Whitney, J. M. Grant, I Morley, D. B. Huntington—

Walker Utah Chief & 12 of his tribe.

Walker asked for Tobacco which Young gave.

D. B. H. wanted us to go down to his land & make [a] Settle[men]t.—he wanted to no how many Moons before we go & build at his place,—& he will do what we want him to do,—coming down yesterday by American Fork he said the Piedes said that Americans & Mormons wd come in their midst. Walker manifests a very friendly feeling towards us, & his ppl,—they have more idea of God than I was aware of—their tradition is God cut a man in two—the upper part was man, the lower part made woman—

When Walker had filled his pipe—they offered the Lord the first smoke,—pointing the pipe stem towards the Sun.—he then smoked it—& passed it round by the right hand round the ring to H.C.K. who smoked— then passed by the left & to B. Y., W R., J .Smith., D.H. Wells., I Morley., J. M. Grant, N. K. Whitney,—G. D. Grant,—D. Spencer, L. Snow,—J. Taylor,—D. B. Huntington, & on to Indians.—

Walker says he is now friendly with the Snakes, they are at peace & he can go among them—a few of the Snakes & Tinpenny Utes wont hear—he never killed a White man & sd he was always friendly with the Mormons as he hears what the Mormons say & he rem[em]bers it—it is good is like all Mormons & their children—He dont care about the Land but wants the mormons to go & settle it.—

B. Y. we shall want some of his men to come & pilot thro' some of our men to his place this fall.—we will school his Children here—in 6 moons we will go to his place with a co—we have our understanding with Goship & Wanship about this peace—its not good to fight the Indians.—& tell his Indians not to steal—we want to be friendly with him. We are poor now but in a few years we shall be rich—we will trade cattle with him.

Walker thats good.—

B. Y. We'll build a house for him & teach him to build houses them- selves—he can pay us his own pay—

Walker his land is good,—no stones—big hi timber & plenty of it—

B. Y. We'll raise grain for him, till they raise—we'll find them ammunitn. to hunt till they raise grain—will take sheep & teach his women how to make blankets—we want some of them to learn to read the B[ook] of M[ormon] that they may know of their forefathers.—

Walker—All the Utes want the Mormons to go. They all love them—but a few here—here there is lots of Snow,—but there he once saw it white.—But they have no game now—

B. Y. They must raise cattle for game.

D. B. H. They live on thistle tops now.

B. Y. They must raise all they want in cattle,—Sheep, & hogs.—We will teach them that in a few years they can have plenty.—

Walker. Do you want to trade cattle for horses now—

B. Y. I wo[ul]d give him a bull, if his was not alive.

Walker. It is alive & does good bus[iness]—

B. Y. In 6 moons we'll send men to look out the ground—probably 3 or 4 moons we want to go where there is no Snow.

Walker that does us good—

B. Y. enquired about the Gulf—& Country—

Walker. He has been to Cal[ifornia]—If you go S[outh] there is no grass. It is best abt. the Salt Mountain[28]—from my house not a stalk—

B. Y. We want to settle by Little Salt Lake.

W—Beyond the mountain plenty of Streams—From Salt Spring over a mountain, Lots of Timber—then next Sleep, good land plenty of timber & good grass. All his land clear. The Tinpenny Utes killed his Fat[he]r 4 yrs ago.—He wants the Mormons to go down where there is no Snow.—He hates to have us stay on this land and if they come on my land they shall not steal your cattle nor whip them & wants the Mormon Child to be with his—he hates us to be on such poor land—when Passawitt hea[r]d the Mormons killed his brother he had told them to stop—he is not mad but glad—it is not good to fight—makes women & children cry—but let women & children play togr. He told the Piedes a great while ago to stop fighting & stealing—but they have no ears—

They passed the pipe again—

W. One of these days Sowiet is coming—he wants the mormons to go among them—

B. Y. I want him to come.—I dont want to kill anotr. Indian—but they dared us to do it—

W. he want you to hunt Passawetts wife—

B. Y. I wrote to Wanship & Smith—both of them—[29]

W. Wants the bre[thre]n to give 40 changes for a heavy buck skin—

B. Y. Grant has given 10 or 12—Bridger to 25—30 is enough as scarce as it is here now—

W. From 10 to 12—then big heavy ones up to 30 & 40—

---

[28]Wakara's Salt Mountain was in today's Juab County.

[29]Young wrote to Pegleg Smith on 14 May 1849 and asked him "to enquire among the Snake Indians for Te emps Wife and child" so he could "see that they are restored to Mr. Walker and his family." He asked Pegleg "to hunt up Patsawett's Squaw that went away with the Shoshone Indians and send her down."

B. Y. We shd make most by giving 10 for small, 15 & 20 larger—30 for good ones & 40 for big bucks Skins—

B. Y. We will give for the biggest & 10 to 15 for small ones.

W. Good.

B. Y. We ought to buy all.—Do they want hats—

W. They all want hats.—

B. Y. When they are ready to go,—Peace a good peace go with them—if we settle the land we want good peace, that our children can play tog[ethe]r.—

W. Good.—

They then adjourned—B.Y. went & gave them half an ox—

Forty-niner Encounters: The People in Utah Were Quite White

Both President Young and Captain Wakara faced a busy summer dealing with similar tasks, the first being how to profit from the tide of forty-niners about to surge through the Great Basin. Wakara sold horses to the gold seekers, while the Mormons traded livestock, produce, and blacksmithing services for desperately needed clothes, manufactured goods, and tools. Their second mission was to secure enough food to get their peoples through the coming winter. To do this, Wakara journeyed to the Rocky Mountains to hunt bison. Brigham Young found several hundred emigrants "arrived in the Valley too late in the season to continue their journey on the northern route" and warned that "so large an accession of mouths, in addition to those of our own emigration, threatened almost a famine for bread." Young wanted the hungry "Gold Diggers" to move on. They eagerly obliged—no one wanted to reach the golden west to find the gold gone—and many happily signed up to pay Capt. Jefferson Hunt $10 each to guide their wagons down an untested wagon road to Los Angeles.[30]

The Saints received favorable reviews from most (if not all) of the gold seekers. Heber C. Kimball recalled how overland emigrants rejoiced to once again "dwell in the midst of white people. They never thought for a moment we were white men and women; but when they came, they found out, to their astonishment, that the people in Utah were quite white, and right from their own country."[31] Whites gave Wakara mixed reviews: some

[30]Madsen, *Gold Rush Sojourners*, 33, 109–12. An excellent harvest eliminated fears of famine: Young, "From the Valley," November 1849, *Frontier Guardian*, 10 July 1850, 3/1.

[31]Heber C. Kimball, 17 September 1854, *Journal of Discourses*, 2:224.

praised his leadership and enterprise, while others denounced him as a scoundrel and brigand. When he met "Walker the Utah Chief" for the first time at Hobble Creek in 1851, Apostle Wilford Woodruff called him "an ugly cunning chief."[32] Topographical engineer John Gunnison repeated the common mythology about hereditary Numic leadership but published an astute analysis of Wakara's character in 1852:

> Chieftainship descends from father to son. A late chief, acting on the plurality law, left above thirty sons, most of whom have small clans under them. His true successor is a fine brave Indian, with the largest band immediately around him; and he [Sowiette] exercises control over all when he chooses. He is a friend of the Mormons. A half-brother of his, named Walker, has become rich and celebrated for his success in stealing horses from the Mexicans. He has a large drove of cattle, with many followers. He lately located near the San Pete settlement, and professed a strong desire to learn agriculture from his civilised neighbors, and promised conformity on the part of his band. This is the man who, regarded in the mountains as a petty adventurer, has often been so romantically eulogised in the States, and furnishes a theme of praise among the Mormons, being esteemed a trophy to the power of their religion, a kind of first-fruits of their policy. But ere this he may have resumed his robber habits, and frustrated the intention of his Mormon friends of making him the head chief of the tribe.[33]

California-bound forty-niners produced several classic American narratives and captured some of the best surviving Native perspectives on their Mormon neighbors. Ohioan Jerome B. Howard reached Salt Lake Valley at the end of July and observed two used horse dealers in action:

> Cattle are quite plenty among them. Horses and mules were very plenty. An Indian, by the name of Walker, with his band, make a regular business of going to California, stealing droves of horses, and taking them back to the valley for sale. The Mormon interpreter Dimmock [sic] Huntington, holds great influence over him, and acts as his agent in the disposition of the horses. Many of the emigrants got fresh animals of Walker, Huntington receiving a per cent for his services. I witnessed some of these bargains. The Mormons count upon Walker's tribe as allies, should they need their services in any emergency, and no doubt they would prove faithful ones.[34]

Overlander Ansel J. McCall admired the quality of the horseflesh Wakara offered for sale:

[32]Kenney, *Wilford Woodruff's Journal*, 25 April 1851, 4:20.
[33]Gunnison, *The Mormons*, 149.
[34]Howard, "California Correspondence," in Clark, *Gold Rush Diary*, 177–79.

Thursday, July 26.—We have just learned that the famous Indian, moss trooper,[35] Walker, chief of the Utes, returned to the valley from a foray into Mexico, with a large drove of horses and is now encamped about six miles up the valley. It is hinted that the Mormons encourage this great horse thief to make these plundering expeditions in order to obtain a supply of good horses at low figures. Jim Singleton, an expert in horse flesh, and myself were at once deputed to visit his majesty's court and purchase such stock us we might need. After a pleasant ride over the grassy meadows that skirt the Jordan we reached Walker's camp and found the great chief on the out side of his *tepe*, unconcernedly smoking his pipe. He was a big-headed, short, bandy-legged Indian. A bold and magnificent horseman, he furnished a tolerably good representation of the Centaur of old. His natural intelligence and long intercourse with the whites enabled him to understand English well and drive a good bargain. He received us courteously and proceeded to show us his stock. We had hoped to be the first to interview him, but to our surprise some other emigrants had anticipated us and were now attempting to subdue a magnificent iron-gray that seemed indisposed to submit to new and strange masters. There are some very fine animals in his herd, such as could only be handled by skillful horsemen, such as *Vaqueros* and Indians are. Finding nothing to suit our character or our price, we set out on our return.[36]

Brigham Young successfully diverted more than a thousand emigrants to open a new wagon road from Great Salt Lake City to southern California. Their journals, letters, and recollections provide unique insights into Utah Valley's Native peoples. "This valley is settled by about forty Mormon families, who live in a Fort built for protection against the Utah Indians, who, however, are not dangerous," noted future U.S. senator Adonijah S. Welch, while camped about a mile from the fort. "We came here on account of better grass for our cattle, and the chance of getting horses from the Indians, which we hope to accomplish by a trading expedition to the mountains."[37]

Gold seekers noted details of Native culture that escaped Mormon notice. Distinctive pieces of pottery with "the rim & flowers painted on them & impressed figures" caught William B. Lorton's attention: "Naturalists attribute it to an intelligent race that once inhabited this region." They were right. "This afternoon several pieces of broken pottery were found by the cattle guard near a small mound," Adonijah Welch noted on 14 October. "They

---

[35]A moss trooper was a Scottish brigand.
[36]McCall, *The Great California Trail in 1849*, 60–61.
[37]Adonijah S. Welch Letter, 30 August 1849, *Milwaukee Sentinel and Gazette*, 17 January 1850.

were fragments of clay ware far superior to any possessed by the present Indians. The same men found some fine specimens of variegated tiles."[38]

The longer they had to age, the more colorful overland memories became. W. B. Taylor's "reminescences" show how experiences become folklore.

TAYLOR, "PIONEER REMINESCENCES [SIC]," CLOVERDALE REVEILLE, 11 APRIL 1896, 2.

The first three days our route was down the valley, passing the old Mormon fort at Provo, and I remember camping one night near boiling springs, where eggs were soon cooked, that have become one of the wonders of the valley, since then. An incident occured here that I must relate. About a dozen Indians visited us in this camp, among whom was the notorious Elk, famous for his misdeeds all over that country and among his tribe considered a dead shot. He evidently was seeking trouble and bantered the company to select their best man and shoot with him at a mark for a dollar a shot. There was no such thing as getting rid of him, until he had exhibited his skill, so Charley Merchant, one of the best shots I ever knew, was pitted against him. Thirty paces were measured off and a piece of paper, dollar size, was placed upon a tree. Elk had the first shot, the ball striking about an inch from the mark. Merchant fired, remarking before doing so that he would just break in to the inner side of Elk's bullet hole. This he did and won the first dollar. Another dollar was up and Elk was beat again, and this was continued until Elk broke the lower edge of the paper by a shot, when the Indians raised a shout, thinking that his luck had changed. Merchant drew up, fired, and the paper fell to the ground, having made a center shot. Elk wanted no more, but grasped Merchant's hand, saying, "Big white chief, you come to my 'wakeyup' and Elk give you young squaw." The offer, however, was declined, and soon the Indians left us and a quiet night was had.

The next day we continued along the shores of Utah Lake until the trail led through a rocky gorge in the hills that opened out finally into a small valley surrounded by high mountains. Here we went into camp about 2 o'clock to rest until morning as the dreaded desert was just ahead and we expected to enter upon it the next day.

We had no more than unloaded our packs and turned our animals out to grass, when unearthly yells from apparently a thousand Indians came from every mountain top in the vicinity, with an occasional report of a gun, but no Indians could be seen. McIntosh, the Cherokee, said it meant fight, and sought a convenient place among the rocks to defend himself, and advised the company to follow his example. Clements, on the contrary, thought they wanted to talk and suggested a white flag should be raised. A white shirt was found, which Clements tied to a ramrod and shook above his head. A flag in

[38]Welch and Lorton diaries, Dale Morgan Papers, Bancroft Library.

answer was hoisted and soon a stream of Indians descended the mountains and came into camp. Clements had a pow-wow with their spokesman who said their great chief, Walker, who resided at Salt Lake, had sent him to inform the many tribes along the route, that a big emigration of whites would pass through their country and for them not to molest or steal anything from them. That he would start that night on his mission across the desert, and that we and other companies behind us, would not be molested in any way, and that he would meet us again at Salt River, where a large tribe of Piutes lived. After furnishing him with a supply of tobacco and hardtack, he with other Indians disappeared in the direction they came. Of course we all breathed easier after the interview.

At age thirty, Swiss emigrant Vincent A. Hoover kept one of the best narratives of opening of the road from Utah Valley to Los Angeles. He illustrated the tension between the Fort Utah settlers and the Timpanogos—especially with their leader, Elk.

VINCENT HOOVER, DIARY, HUNTINGTON LIBRARY,
DALE MORGAN TYPESCRIPT.

Tuesday, 25 Sept 1849. We bought an ox this morning and while in the process of skinning him (their being Some of the Ladies looking on and also many indians waiting for their share). One of the indians fired his rifle off into the ox, the ball passing between Mr & Mrs [Jefferson] Hunt. The face of Big Elk & another indian had some powder burnt in their faces. He said he intended to frighten the indians. Their are considerable of them here of the Utah tribe but are friendly or seem so. The[y] have a dislike to the mormons. A short time ago Big Elk went out into a field where their was a mare & colt belonging to a mormon and delibertly shot both of them. By signs they express great friendship for the emigrants. This afternoon we left for Hobble creek arriving late in the evening. . . .

Wednesday, 26 Sept 49. Their are a good many emigrants here. Their are two guides one a Mr Hunt a mormon whose price per wagon is 10 dollars for his services. The other is a spaniard by the name of Antonio who charges nothing except to take him and [his] baggage through. Antonio has recently come through from Santa Fe with a pack train. This evening we met and arranged for the trip. Some twenty-five wagons of us have determined to go with the Spaniard while over one hundred will go with Mr. Hunt the mormon & pay ten dollars. We have formed and called our train the Independent Pioneer Company and intend to leave in the morning. Their was an indian sold a horse which he had stolen from an emigrant.

Thursday 27 Sept 1849. This morning the Independent Pioneer Company left camp for California. This is called the Southern route to Los Angeles and has never been traveled by wagons before. As we proceed the Country wears an aspect of desolation. The mountains on either side reaches the clouds. They are the Wasatch range. Camped on a small stream which we gave the name of Spanish creek. As all of the Pioneer train did not leave today we are expecting them [so we are] making short drives. To day has been very warm. Distance 12 miles.

Friday 28 Sept 49. We are camped to day expecting the ballance of the company. Several indians came into camp of the Utah tribe.

Saturday 29 Sept. Left Camp early. The day has been clear & pleasant. We have traveled down a nice valley some ten miles in width. The mountains are not so high as in Salt Lake valley nor is the soil So furtule. Utahs in camp. They informed us that a pack train ahead under the guidance of Mr. Waters killed some of the indians.[39] They did not state why. Distance 16½ miles.

The forty-niners who visited Utah Valley, some 1,068 men, women, and children, guarded livestock with the Mormons. Together they outnumbered the Utes, who consequently "acted less belligerently toward the colonists." After trading firearms and ammunition for the Utes' excellent horses, most gold seekers left Utah Valley in October and the rest were gone by mid-November, leaving behind two peoples to resume their intimate but uneasy relations.[40]

Nepoed: Old Bishop

A murder lies at the heart of the violence that engulfed Fort Utah, a crime entangled in faithful mythology and outright lies. The details and perpe-trators of this gruesome homicide are well known; its greatest mystery is when it happened. Sources place the crime from August 1849 to January 1850; much evidence and many of the best historians date it to the summer, but the recollections of two Provo pioneers show the murder led to more bloodshed.

"We made a treaty with the Utah Indians to keep them from stealing our cattle," Thomas Orr Jr. recalled. "By provisions of this treaty they agreed not to molest our cattle if we agreed not to kill the wild game which they depended on for a living." In June 1854 James Bean said he heard one of the men describe the killing and two of the murderers boast of it. "Jerome Zabriskie, Richard A. Ivie and John Rufus Stoddard were going from the fort in Utah Valley, professedly to hunt cattle"; Bean's use of "professedly" suggests the three Mormon Battalion veterans were hunting something else. The men "met an Indian who was wearing a shirt which Richard A.

---

[39]Mountaineer James Wesley Waters, "a mountain trader" and slave trader from near today's Pueblo, Colorado, led more than one hundred packers to southern California in 1849, murdering Paiutes on the way.

[40]Carter, *Founding Fort Utah*, 123, 147.

Ivie claimed, alleging that it had been stolen from him and demanded it," Bean said. The Ute refused, "saying he had bought it; whereupon they tried to take it from him forcibly, he struggling all the time against them." The Indian drew his bow to defend himself, and "John R. Stoddard shot him through the head killing him instantly; they then dragged his corpse to the Provo River and sunk it near the Box Elder Island."[41]

Orr's story involved Zabriskie, John Stoddard, and "a four-inch fall of snow." Downriver from the fort, the men "scared up a dear unbeknown to the Indians"; as they "were out hunting they met up with an Indian who greeted them and asked what they were hunting. The whites replied nothing." The Indian, however, "knew full well the whites were hunting deer and that they had violated the treaty. A quarrel between the Indian and the two men ensued." "Doc" Stoddard was "prepared for action": when the Indian moved on Zabriskie, "Stoddard fired first and the Indian dropped dead." The Mormons hid the body in a nearby backwater, but first "one of the men stuck a knife into his belly and ripped him open so that his body would sink and efface all evidence of the crime." Instead of sinking, the corpse "floated downstream and caught against a limb of a cottonwood tree."[42]

The Indian whom Stoddard shot "was known among the whites as the 'old Bishop' on account of his appearance and gestures which somewhat resembled" the late presiding bishop Newel K. Whitney. He "had a Greek nose, with a hump and a hook, and had a peculiar way of snapping his eyes when excited" that inspired the only name by which history remembers the slain Ute.[43] James Goff recalled "that the murder of the Indian was talked of at the time by many of the settlers, and that it was asserted that the men who killed the Indian ripped his bowels open and filled them with stones preparatory to sinking his body"—a process called "nepoed," based on "open." Whether a broken treaty or an argument over a stolen shirt inspired this murder, "The Indians assert that, annually, on the anniversary of his death, the old Bishop appears on the bank of the river, and slowly takes the rocks one by one out of his bowels and throws them into the river, then disappears. Some (white) fishermen have watched in hopes of having an interview with the 'Bishop's ghost.'"[44]

[41]Ibid., 114–15; Bagley, *Frontiersman*, 152–54.

[42]Ibid.

[43]Carter, *Founding Fort Utah*, 114–15.

[44]Harwell, *Manuscript History of Brigham Young*, 284–85. Hosea Stout described the fate of Patsowett of Wakara's band, who was "arrested & tried & nepoed to day" after "trying to way lay & kill all the whites he could catch alone." For Juanita Brooks's analysis of the term, see *The Diary of Hosea Stout*, 29 April 1850, 2:368.

By mid-October intercultural relations at Fort Utah had collapsed. Frontier Mormonism's hierarchical nature distinguishes its Indian relations: religious leaders decided matters that most western communities would settle themselves or defer to government authority. Isaac Higbee's questions about the escalating conflict on Provo River reveal how Mormons relied on top-down leadership.

ISAAC HIGBEE TO BRIGHAM YOUNG, 15 OCTOBER 1849, BYC 21:16.

Utah Valley Oct. 15th 1849

President Young

This is to inform you that we wish council from you respecting the course we shall take respecting the Indians. They have been troublesome a few weeks past. They shot at Brother [Jabez] Nowland & [Robert] Thomas about two weeks since while at work in the field. Last week they shot at James Ivie while passing near their camp early on Wensday morning last. We told two of the indians that we were mad at them because they shot at our men and stole our corn. The indians went back to their camp and in a little while the indians was seen to sally out from their camp and stop except three of them two of them were naked and without arms one of them carrying a stick with feathers tied to it. We met them out side of the fort well armed and preparred to fight and it was as much as we could do to keep some of our boys from shooting them. They said they heard we were mad and come to make peace and that they did not want to fight. We made peace with them and told them they must not steal our corn &c but they continue to steal our corn and are saucy and some of them say that we are affraid of them and that they intend to kill the men and take the women themselves &c. Their number at present is not much less than ours.

One of Walkers band came in to day and says Walker will be here in two days to sell horses. Some of the indians are in the fort every day and appear very friendly. D. B. Huntington at present has gone to meet his brother [Oliver] who is on his way to these valleys.

The Indians have also shot a mare and colt belonging to John Wheeler.

Isaac Higbee Pres.

Young's "council concerning the indians" reveals the origins of what became his central "forting up" Indian policy. "Stockade your fort,—& attend to your own affairs and let the indians take care of theirs." Let the "women & children stay in the fort, and the Indians stay out." If the settlers became too familiar with the Utes, "you will find the less influence you will have with them." To have dominion over them, "for their good, which is the duty of the Elders, you must not treat them as your equals, you cannot exalt them by this process. If they are your equals, you cannot raise them up to you." Mormon children had mixed "promiscuously" with the Utes and "some of the brethren have spent too much time in smoking and chatting with them, & instead of teaching them to labor, such a course has encouraged them in Idleness and ignorance, the effects of which you begin to feel." Finally, "You had better finish your fort, bring all your grain into it, and continue to live in it."[45]

THE SOUTHERN EXPLORING EXPEDITION

After he traveled "the splendid road" to the "magnificent valley" on 9 November, forty-niner Joseph Hamelin camped by Utah Lake "with a large band of Utahs and a company of Mormons on their way to Sand-pitch Valley." He found the Utes "inoffensive but troublesome, adepts [at] slight of hand &c." He said nothing about the 224 men, women, and children following Isaac Morley from Salt Lake to Sanpete Valley.[46] When the Sanpete colonists "arrived at the place that is called Manti," on 19 November, Albert Smith recalled many of them were "wonderfully disappointed with the place," but "it was decided that this was the place where we was sent and that here we would settle." "Sage and rabbit brush, the Redman and the Kiote," C. M. Madsen recalled, "were the most prominent features of the landscape." Eventually most of the new settlers "went to other parts of the Territory, on account of the forbidding aspects of things generally and the severity of the first winter." Smith pitched his tent, built a stone wall, added a chimney to his wagon bed, and "went to work getting out logs" for a cabin. "We had hardly got ourselves settled before there came so much snow that our stock liked to starved to death, the snow was over two feet deep." More snow fell than the Indians had ever seen in one winter.[47]

Albert Smith remembered his first impressions of his new neighbors:

Those Indians that was in the vally when we moved here was sanpetes that was thare name. There was another large band called Walkers band of Piutes. The sanpete indians had no guns & not A pony & no clothing nor bedding

[45]Young to Higbee, 18 October 1849, BYC 16:17.
[46]A follower of Alexander Campbell, Isaac Morley (1786–1865) joined the LDS church in November 1830 and became stalwart member of the Council of Fifty, the State of Deseret senate, and in 1849 the stake president of the Sanpete Valley settlements.
[47]Antrei and Roberts, *History of Sanpete County*, 5, 24–25.

save rabits skins soad together & no houses save what they made out of sage & grease wood brush. Thare living was on fish wich sanpete was full of & rabits berries & grass seed. While Walkers band had good bucksing (or deer skin) lodges & clothing made out of the same materials & they were provided with plenty of poneys & guns. Walker and his band owned all of Sanpete and the surrounding country. They spend much of there time in summer in hunting in the mountains & in the winter much of there time on the Sevier River, there being a large valley that they claimed & but little snow that winter. This band, Walkers band, came and pitched thare lodges close to where we had stopped & stayed there all winter and they lived on the cattle that we lost. They became very frendly & attended our meetings. Three years later there was A great number of them Baptised.[48]

Parley P. Pratt's Southern Exploring Expedition, the third major element of Mormonism's southern expansion, arrived twelve days after Morley's company reached Manti. Pratt had a Brigham Young letter for "Cap. Walker," "Chief of the Utahs."

It asked Wakara, or "one of your brothers, and one or two of your Indians" to join the company sent "South to search out another Valley in a Warmer climate" so that when they met "any Indians of another nation, we may be able to talk with them and let them know that we are their friends, and we will do them good, and we want them to be at peace with us." He asked Wakara "to instruct your people to let" the Mormons settle "Sanpitch Valley" in peace, "and do not molest them, or hook any of their Grain—and keep your animals away from their Grain Fields." Keep "your men & people to your part of the Valley, but if your people molest ours, and steal our Grain, and dont behave themselves we shall have to take our Colony away out of that Valley."

We wish you to understand decidedly that if your Utahs, and the different nations in this country do not injure any of our people, in any of our Settlements that you will all be blest, for we are sent here by the Great Spirit to teach you, and do all of you good. Be at peace one with another—dont fight, but love one another and you will soon be taught to become a great, united, and good people, and you will realize all the blessings that have been told you by your forefathers—and you will prove that we are the people, whom you have long waited, and looked for.

Young sent "a Bag of Flour according to your request—and if you cannot go with this Company yourself—I wish you to send two or three of your

---

[48]Smith, Reminiscences, 1876, 55–56.

good Indians with them to talk." A postscript directed Dimick Huntington to interpret the "letter to Capn. Walker" and ordered him "to go with this company to explore out a good location in a Warm Country" and "have every facility to talk with other Tribes."[49]

When Pratt's explorers reached "the Sandpitch settlement" on 4 December, they learned "Captn Walker and his Indians are 70 miles from here up the Sevier river." They "sent for Walker to come and trade" and met the Ute leader north of today's Salina. Captain Walker faced a catastrophe: measles.

ROBERT CAMPBELL, JOURNAL, DECEMBER 1849.

Frid. 7th T 10°. Snowed a little during night, cold day cloudy start at 20 to 9 A.M. As the wagons started Capt Walker & another Indian rides into Camp said Glad to see us. Knew he would see us soon, for he dreamed he would. He told us he had lots to trade, wished us to go back down the Sevier about a mile where there was a good bottom with feed. Parley wishes him to go ahead & camp with us. Said no feed. Parley send messenger after the wagons to tell them come back & go down stream to where Walker would shew us—Camp had gone on nearly a mile, turn back & camp on the Sevier 1½ miles below this mornings encampment. Cold day, 155½ miles. Parley reads letter from Brigham to Captn. Walker. Dimic interprets it tells about the sack of Flour for him, he makes no answer till he sees Arrapin his Brother, all the band is coming & will encamp with us. Tells Parley no pass over these mts S.E. & no good country over there, little Water, don't run far, Rocky. Shewed him the map. He showd points in it & told what country he was acquainted & what he was not, like an experienced geographer, all astonished at him point[ing] out on the map, says some country where we could raise corn on the Rio Virgin, says the pi Gads [Paiutes] dying off fast, whole wika up die in one sleep . . . Indians come in by the dozens, good many nice horses and packs, & Dogs &c. Blowing from the west, snowing, cold, many of them sick with the meazles, hear them making medicine, see them sucking one anothers feet, forehead &c. Stabed a Dog because their village sick. Barney Ward gives Parley some information.

Sat 8th T 21. A horse traded for few Buckskins & very high priced. James Allred, Charles Shumway came in last night, find coal, Salt & iron ore, their iron ore questioned & other curiosities which Shumway was going to

---

[49]Young to Cap. Walker, 22 November 1849, BYC 16:18.

inform Brigham of. Parley, Dan Jones & Dimic goes & prays for Indians at Walkers request, rebukes their meazles, by laying hands on them in the name of Jesus. Walker makes long speech, said he [would] come with us but his ppl [people] are all sick. The best he can do for us send his Bro Ammomah with us—he wished to do right that he might come back on the earth and live with Shinaub [the Ute god] after he died & his Spirit went to Shinaub who gave it, he always listened to the good words of ours, wished all to come American and Mormon & live in peace, he would not fight any more, had done fighting. Start about 10 A.M. Dimic brings Indian guide Ammomah along with 2 horses, reach Coal creek. Difficult turn in crossing, 18 ft Wide, 14 in deep gravelly. Willows on banks. Walkers mother laying here sick, 162 miles. Cold cloudy. Indians shoot a Pi Ute boy, they had bought for a Gun because they were sick & afflicted in camp, sing over one another, & suck their feet and hed. Parley gives instructions to Camp about travelling together. Coy going with him to explore. Capt [Ephraim] Green & some of his ten a head fixing roads to day, good hard claying soil Beautiful prairie road, through sage & greasewood. Ravine, steep 164¼—Pass over small creek 10 ft wide 4 in deep & Camp on banks of the Sevier 165. Willows, sage & greasewood, Sevier nearly froze over. Indian guide sick. Camp prayers & singing.

The party headed south down the Sevier River along the general line of today's Highway 89 as the thermometer plunged far below zero. "Ammomah says we don't make enough medicine for him," Campbell noted on 11 December. Ammon found "an old medicine squaw, at Indian Camp, he is going there, & if gets better in 2 or 3 days he will come on & overtake us."[50]

Campbell reported:

The thermometer has been at 21 below zero on the Sevier bottom, been nearly in snow ¾ of our time, seen but few Indians, different Utes. Had a good time with Capt. Walker, whose band family were much afflicted with sickness (measles). Gave him the flour, but seen his brother Ammomah who in two or three days got so sick, he was compelled to stay with some lake Utes who had a medicine squaw that could make medicine for him to cure him, he to come on, if got better soon. We have passed thro' since we left Sandpitch, a barren, rugged, mountainous country, at present fit only to be a habitation for those who live by idle Indian arts and that of the scantest kind.[51]

---

[50]"Ammomah" is probably Ammon. He did not rejoin Pratt's expedition.
[51]Southern Exploring Papers, 25 December 1849, MS 2334, LDS Archives.

Now on their own hook, the party struggled south for the next ten days through the rugged country to reach the Little Salt Lake Valley. They met few Indians. On Christmas Day at the site of today's Paragonah, Pratt sent messengers to Salt Lake and chose twenty men and "the Mules and horses that were fit" to head south "to explore over the rim of the Basin."

Dreams illuminated the trek. Along Ash Creek on 29 December, Dan Jones dreamed "about the Indians coming to meet us." The next day Pratt dreamed "about talking with the Indians down a little ways who grow corn." When the party camped, three "Pi Utes, called by the American Pieads," reported "there's no Water between here & Colorado to go South. Walker comes this way to go to California." They said the Navajos grew wheat, but they did not "know anything about the White Indians," deflating the explorers' hopes to meet a tribe of white Lamanites, "which was apparently the reason for including Welsh-speaking Dan Jones in the exploration."[52]

The Mormon leaders smoked "the pipe of peace" and invited the three Paiutes "to stay till morning." Campbell portrayed them as "fat, tolerably clad for this warm climate, one of them has a Cassimere coat. Black hair, no beard nor whiskers nor hair under their arm pits, all under the medium size." He then described their powerful laminated "bows made of Mt sheep horns, wound round with sinew of which their bowstring is. Their arrows have 3 large feather in the buts & piece cane break, then ash wood points, round the tip of the arrow, sinew is wound to prevent their arrows from splitting, some have arrow points of Iron."[53] The Paiutes "had heard of us from the Utah Indians," John Brown wrote. "Soon after we camped three Indians came to us they were Pahutah and were a little shy at first but soon got acquainted our interpreter could talk with them in the Utah language We told them who we were and what we wanted. They were almost naked, and they were glad we had come into their country and wanted us to settle here and teach them to farm and make clothing."

"Dimic tells them we were Mormons not Americans," Campbell noted. "Horses feet sore with walking over the rocks, one of the Indians says he sold his wife to Walker. When he gets any, its from a horse."

---

[52]Smart and Smart, *Over the Rim*, 124.

[53]Campbell, Diary, 30 December 1849. On "a long ride with a couple of Shoshonees" who "were as lively and good-humored as could well be," Charles Boyle "told one of them that his bow made of mountain sheep horn backed with sinew was only fit to shoot mosquitoes. To this he answered that he could shoot through a buffalo." Boyle, "The Gold Rush Diary," 23 June 1849.

A few days later, Isaac Haight met a band on the Escalante Desert who told him a story they probably thought the Mormons would like:

> Capt Walker had told them about us, that we were his friends. They said they were our friends and would not kill our cattle or horses. Walker told them the Mormons raised Shaunt Tickup [much food] and they wanted us to come and raise it among them. They said they loved the Mormons. They are very poor and have no horses or skins. They live upon rabbits which are plenty in their valley, now Cedar Valley, and clothe themselves with their skins."[54]

Pratt's explorers crossed the "broken rugged country red sand" and twice forded the Virgin River's "swift, rocky stream" to a large bottom, which Pratt thought "would make a good Settlement." On the site of today's St. George, Campbell noted a knoll with "lots of hard earthenware, streaked." The Indians described the land and road downriver, confirming what Barney Ward had said: "if we go down the Virgin we must go round many Kanyons, Red Knolls, high Red bluffs perpendicular like Mts. no timber, for a long way South East nothing." The Paiutes feared the Mormons, for they did not know whether they came "in peace or war." A hard rain drove many of the "mean, dirty almost naked creatures" into camp. Pratt asked Campbell for a song, and both Mormons and Paiutes gathered "round & sing, all the Indians join us & try to sing with us—say they have no families died in sickness about 17 of them." The "rude, dirty mean & filthy" Indians all spoke at once but said the Mormons heard them say they were "willing we should come & live with them." They "wanted us to feed them," Campbell noted, "which we have done always when we eat ourselves." Charles Hopkins found a "corn stalk 11 feet long, some Pumpkins & squash vines" in a nearby "Pi Ute garden patch"—so much for the need to teach them to farm. "We saw many little Indian plantations where they raise corn. They varied in size from a few rods and up to an acre, having their irrigation ditches &c.," John Brown wrote. Two Indians camped with the Mormons, and "soon after we eat supper one of them said he wanted a blanket to sleep on. One of the brethren gave him his saddle blanket." The Paiute "wrapped it around his shoulders and after a while stepped out to one side and was seen no more taking the blanket with him leaving his bow and arrow in camp," considering it a fair exchange.

As 1850 began, the Southern Exploring Expedition explored Mountain Meadows and began an arduous trek north during a bitter January, having

---

[54]Smart and Smart, *Over the Rim*, 89–90, 117.

fulfilled Brigham Young's mission to find "another Valley in a Warmer climate." The men left at Paragonah had explored Parowan Valley, Cedar Valley, and the Red Hills that divided them, finding the cleft now known as Parowan Gap. Summer and winter solstices naturally aligned with the canyon whose petroglyphs are now listed on the National Register of Historic Places as a cultural treasure. Wakara called it "Gods own house."

The expedition's two elements reunited on 8 January at today's Parowan. They celebrated with "a bounteous feast of roast beef, pumpkin sauce, apple pies, mince pies &c," toasts to the "founding of the city of the Little Salt Lake which will hereafter be built," cannon fire, speeches, and Parley Pratt's "Song of the Southern Pioneers." Composed for the occasion, the song celebrated the extension of "Imperial Zion" to "where Joseph's sons are roaming / In solitude and manners rude," with a promise to "teach them there the Gospel true / Their ancient covenants to renew." Before 1850 ended, the Mormons would move to occupy these warmer valleys.

Pratt's advance return party reached Fort Provo on 28 January, and dispatched rescuers to save the exhausted explorers "from starvation and death." As the consequences of Old Bishop's murder came to roost, Pratt found "the people under considerable excitement on account of the Indians who had become hostile and were killing cattle and shooting at the whites." The stage was set for the first mass slaughter of a Great Basin Indian community.[55]

---

[55]Ibid., 92, 116, 123–25, 143.

Chapter 3

WE CANNOT LIVE
WITH BAD INDIANS
Expansion, Expulsion, and
Extermination, 1850

Common threads run through America's Indian history, notably the red threads of vengeance and violence. The pressure of expanding white settlements and contracting resources had created conflict since the Virginia Company launched the First Anglo-Powhatan War in 1609 and the Puritans battled the Pequots and Metacom in King Philip's War. Leaders avoided violence except when they could bring overwhelming force to bear. Conflict intensified during winter's hungriest times, when the tribes were most vulnerable to disease. When Natives or Anglos faced famine or other contests for resources, fear fueled atrocities.

Bitterly cold weather marked the beginning of 1850 as the Timpanogos villages on Provo River and their new neighbors at Fort Utah faced a crisis. The coming year would witness critical developments in Mormon-Indian relations and singular events, such as what historian D. Robert Carter dubbed the Battle of Provo River, the only pitched battle the Mormons ever fought within the State of Deseret's visionary borders.[1] Thanks to the presence of the Stansbury Expedition, church and federal officials united to kill Indians, a common purpose that church and state seldom shared in Brigham Young's Kingdom.

Mormon ideas about Indian rights were typically American. The nation's legal authority was James Kent, author of *Commentaries on American Law*, written

---

[1]Robert Carter, the bard of Utah County, wrote far and away the best account of the Fort Utah fight in *Founding Fort Utah*, 141–239.

in 1830. The idea that Indians "as original lords of the soil" held right and title to American land was a pretext, Kent wrote. Like Emmerich de Vattel, the Swiss *philosophe* who influenced Washington and Jefferson, Kent argued that moral necessity drove American land law: "To leave the Indians in possession of the country was to leave the country a wilderness," while to mix with Natives or grant them privileges was impossible. Indian character and habits "rendered them incapable of sustaining any other relation with the whites than that of dependence and pupilage." They must be kept "separate, subordinate, and dependent, with a guardian care thrown around them for their protection." The helpless condition of Indians "and the immeasurable superiority of their civilized neighbours" precluded "the application of any more liberal and equal doctrine" to Indian lands and contracts. Immemorial usage and "numerous compacts, treaties, laws, and ordinances" had established the "pretension of converting the discovery of the country into a conquest." The colonized country was "now held by that title. It is the law of the land, and no court of justice can permit the right to be disturbed by speculative reasonings on abstract rights."[2]

For years Congress wrangled over how to integrate the vast provinces the United States had conquered and purchased from Mexico in 1848. The new lands aggravated regional conflicts over slavery and inspired the Compromise of 1850, which would create Utah Territory, contribute to the nation's first civil war in 1857, and fuel the irrepressible conflict that tore the Union apart in 1861.

John Wilson: Wards of the Government

President Zachary Taylor appointed former Missouri militia inspector general John Wilson "Indian agent at the Salt Lake, California." Wilson arrived in late August 1849 with the new president's scheme to integrate Mexican territory into the nation. President Taylor felt the Mormons had "been unjustly dealt with," and "so far as his power constitutionally extends he will do us all the good he can," Wilson told the Saints. Taylor proposed "a temporary amalgamation of Deseret and Western California" that would immediately admit both as one state to the Union. Once it had sufficient population, Deseret would become its own state.[3]

[2]Kent, *Commentaries on American Law*, 3:380–81.

[3]Culmer, "'General' John Wilson," 326–37; Wilson, Pension File S.C. 20,387, RG 15, National Archives.

Mormon leaders endorsed the proposition and instructed Apostle Amasa Lyman in California to support creating "a general constitution for two States," which would be "consolidated in one." Each would become "a free, sovereign, independent State, without any further action of Congress" in 1851. Lyman and Wilson submitted a petition proposing the arrangement to California's provisional government: Gov. Peter Burnett concluded the two communities were too far apart to ever be combined, and that Texas and Maine might as well have been made one State as Deseret and California."[4] Brigham Young felt betrayed on that matter, but federal and Mormon leaders still agreed about Indian rights: they had none. At Fort Bridger in August 1849, John Wilson picked up "information in relation to the Utah and Sho-sho-nie tribes," including their reaction to recent events:

> Mormon settlement in the Salt Lake valley has not only greatly diminished their formerly very great resource of obtaining fish out of the Utah lake and its sources, which to them was an important resource; but their settlement, with the great emigration there, and to California, has already nearly driven away all the game, and will unquestionably soon deprive them almost entirely of the only chances they have for food. This will, in a few years, produce a result not only disastrous to them, but must inevitably engage the sympathies of the nation.[5]

Wilson proposed an ambitious solution. The central Rockies were "better fitted than any other portion of the United States" to settle "a large number of the original inhabitants of the wilderness" beyond "the reach of the millions of Anglo-Saxons, who are pressing towards the setting sun with almost race-horse speed." The *"large and fertile country"* of the Green and the headwaters of the Platte and the Arkansas rivers, were "the only *fitting* and sufficiently secluded spot that seems to be left" to attempt "to extend that national philanthropy to the Indians." Great Basin peoples "ought to be treated entirely as wards of the government," Wilson proposed. He wanted "to unite the Sho-sho-nies and Utahs into *one* nation" at "a great council" at Fort Bridger in 1850. The government should "buy of them such parts of their country as we need" and pay for "this valley now set- tled by the whites, its adjacent country," along with "a highway through their country" and spots for "forts and other public agencies." It could provide the tribes with "useful implements of husbandry and clothing"

---

[4]Bancroft, *History of Utah*, 446–47.
[5]Wilson to Commissioner of Indian Affairs, 22 August 1849, *Annual Report*, 1849, 67–68.

at cost. It should "send proper men amongst them" who would "establish farms—model farms—not models of extravagance" but "plain, simple, and well conducted farms, with inducements held out to the Indians to work upon them." The "Sho-sho-coes," the desert tribes "too poor to have horses," could be "trained, *by the right sort of men*, to engage in the labors of husbandry." Some Utahs, Wilson noted, were already "raising corn and potatoes."

Agent Wilson wanted to transform "the red men of the forest" into yeoman farmers. It was "radically wrong" to suppose "the untutored Indian to be capable of dealing with the Anglo-Saxon race, especially those who have descended from the first settlers of America." Indian management "ought to be confided to the true philanthropist, and not intrusted to the brawling, and often bankrupt politician" who "instead of teaching them the beauties and benefits of civilization, leaves amongst them disgusting evidences that he has, by his example, encouraged them to continue in their basest immoralities." Wilson then addressed the great mystery of American Indian policy: why did the government try to make farmers out of natural ranchers? The herdsman's habits, Wilson argued, might feed Native families but would make them into corrupt cowboys.

> In the Snake claim of boundaries there are many large valleys, where I believe cattle could be reared even with profit; and, therefore, it may be said that it would said that it would be good policy to endeavor to turn them into herdsmen and teach them to raise and herd stock. This, if accomplished, would perhaps better their condition, because thus they might secure for themselves and families meat enough for food, which now they do not get; but I very much question whether their moral condition would in any way be bettered, whilst their physical constitution would unquestionably be enervated in the lazy habits of the herdsman. But, while you may easily and rapidly cause a civilized man to approximate toward the savage life by turning him out a herdsman, alone, to eat the beef he tends for his support, still it will be absolutely impossible to make a civilized man out of a savage by teaching him the idle and lazy employment of herding cattle in a barren wilderness amongst the mountains. There is no employment like that of agriculture, which ties them to a local spot of land, to cultivate the feelings of virtue and social intercourse, which are essential ingredients of civilization even in a savage.[6]

_____

[6]John Wilson, 4 September 1849, U.S. House, *California and New Mexico*, 104–12.

THE WORST INDIANS & HARDEST FIGHTERS:
BATTLE ON PROVO RIVER

Victors write history, especially after eliminating the vanquished. The Timpanogos band suffered such a crushing defeat in 1850 that there survive no known Ute accounts of the Fort Utah fight. To try to capture Native perspectives of this critical battle requires consulting the settler, surveyor, and soldier reports of their "quarrel with the Indians" found in church and military records.

A letter drafted in the elegant hand of Stansbury Expedition artist John Hudson described how Fort Utah's cattle seemed to conspire with the weather and the Timpanogos to imperil its future.

WILLIAMS TO YOUNG AND ISAAC HIGBEE, 7 JANUARY 1850,
BYC, 22:3, 36.

Utah Valley Jany 7th 1850

Prests. Young & Higbee,
Dear Brethren,

On behalf of the Citizens at this place, I apply for counsel under the circumstances detailed as follows. The Indians still continue their depredations, four oxen being stolen on Saturday Eveng, a party on Sunday started for the Indian encampment they discovered the butchered cattle and endeavoured to procure restitution, but this was refused & the Indians raised the war whoop prepared for an encounter; Our Brethren not being sufficiently numerous safely to attack them returned home without accomplishing their object. The Indians have further acknowledged to stealing two mares & threaten still further depredations.

The advice given by you for the preservation of ourselves & cattle has been strictly followed, the fort is secured with the exception of some few gaps in the old pickets which will be done this day. The cattle have been herded in the farm & every precaution taken but despite this the Indians contrive to kill the cattle by lurking in the high grass armed with bows & arrows. On Saturday the Brethren unanimously turned out & commenced building a carall about one mile east of the fort & collecting the cattle, with the intention of guarding them there, where there is good feed. The completion of the work was however prevented by a snow storm which compelled them to leave it unfinished. This was done as the cattle was materially injuring the wheat, & on this account it became necessary that they should be removed out of the farm. Capt Conover the Bearer of this will acquaint you more fully with the facts of the case but we consider the circumstances warrant us in applying to you for advice. Waiting for your reply. We remain dear Brethren

> Your Humble Servts
> Alexander Williams
> J. Y. Willis
> John Hudson Clerk

Dimick Huntington had "sworn by the sun" not to "drive the Indians from their lands, nor take away their rights." The settlers promised to respect Native rights to the local game if the Timpanogos agreed not to hunt the Mormons' cattle, but by January the "treaty" was as dead as Old Bishop.

A letter to the legislature reported whites at Provo had killed an Indian while attempting "to take a shirt from him which the Indian had stolen," Hosea Stout heard on 8 January 1850. Such murderous facts "were kept hid at the time," Brigham Young later claimed, and his "feelings were opposed to going to war with the Indians."[7] Perhaps what Young learned later was that Old Bishop had caught his murderers poaching his band's deer. To avoid trouble, Young suggested the settlers could abandon Utah Valley.

YOUNG TO THE BRETHREN IN THE UTAH VALLEY, 8 JANUARY 1850,
BYC 16:19.

> G.S.L. City Jany 8, 1850

To the Brethren in the Utah Valley

We received your letter of yesterday in hand [from] bros Conover & Weaver, complaining of depredations committed by the Indians and asking counsel on the subject. We have considered the matter and send this epistle in reply.

We will repeat the counsel we have previously given in regard to Carrolling your cattle, and guarding them especially in the night in such a position that the Indians cannot get at them. Secure your cattle and horses so that the Indians cannot get them and that will prevent any quarrel with the Indians. And again, as we have said before, secure your Fort, and on no consideration suffer an Indian to come inside that Fort, for if you do you will be harassed, and have difficulty with them more or less all the time. As to warring with the Indians and killing them there is no necessity for it if you act wisely, and if you do kill them, you do it at your own risk.

We wish you, and would advise you to listen to the counsel of brother Isaac Higbee in all things, and if there is any person or persons who will not

---

[7] Carter, *Founding Fort Utah*, 153.

abide his counsel, but are rebellious, we say, turn all such persons outside the Fort and have nothing to do with them, do not let them have a place among you. Let them come here, where they will find men who can bear with, or else conquer their rebellious conduct, or if they prefer it let them go to the Gold Mines or wherever they choose. We want men who will listen to counsel and do right all the time, and if they will not do it, let them go where they please, but dont suffer such characters to bring you into dificulty and jeopardize the lives of innocent men, women and children. We would also propose to you, that if the brethren have got more cattle than they can take care of, let them send their surplus cattle here, and it will be sold, and the proceeds thereof be put into the Perpetual Emigrating fund, for it is far better to let your surplus cattle benefit the poor who are coming here and cannot for lack of a team, than to have your cattle destroyed by the Indians, thereby irritating your own feelings and laying yourselves liable to trouble and much difficulty.

We would also say that if it is the minds of the brethren to return to this place, and evacuate the Utah Valley, they are at liberty to do so, any, or all of them. If it be their choice we have no objections, let them do as they choose on this subject.

We would take this opportunity to refer your minds to another subject of one part of the subject under consideration. Suppose an Indian steals a Shirt, an ox, a Horse or anything else, there appears to be a feeling in the minds of a few individuals to kill them for it on the spot. Suppose a white man commits precisely the same crime, or worse, do those individuals or any person feel like killing them for it. We leave you to answer this. Now look at the moral, the Indians are wild, uneducated, naked destitute, and they mostly steal from necessity and think it no harm, but there is no white man in this region of country who either steals from neccesity or ignorance, yet they do steal, and if it is right to kill an Indian for stealing, surely on the same principal, it must be an honor to the man who will kill a white thief. Now remember we do not give this as counsel but as a moral for your serious reflection and consideration.

The cultural conflict over Old Bishop's murder intensified as 1850 began. Old Elk contracted measles and asked Jefferson Hunt's wife, whose husband was in California, for medicine. "Alexander Williams saw him and took him by the nape of the neck and kicked him out of the fort," James Bean said in 1854. The simmering crisis exploded. "That same evening the Indians stole three cows out of Mrs. Hunt's yard and continued stealing, which was the commencement of Indian difficulties."[8]

---

[8]Bean Statement, 12 June 1854, in Harwell, *Manuscript History of Brigham Young*, 285.

On 31 January, Isaac Higbee met again with church leaders in Salt Lake:

The Indians are intentionally killing our cattle & stealing our horses. They shot at our boys—we have lost between 50 & 60 head. They cannot sustain themselves there. We drive our cattle down in the morning & bring them up at night—the Indians fired two guns at our boys & they found one ox with 4 arrows—another with a tomahawk in it. They say the Mormons are no count—they want to fight & will live on our cattle—they say they mean to keep our Cattle & go & get the other Indians to kill us.

"We cannot defend our cattle unless there is a company of men," said Higbee. The Utes had twenty-five warriors "close by & 50 or 75 on the other side of the lake" at Spanish Fork. The Mormons had three choices, Parley Pratt claimed: abandon their southern colonies, defend them, "or leave them to destruction."

"My voice is for War," said Willard Richards. "Exterminate them."

"I say go & kill them," Young agreed. The council voted: every hand went up. "We shall have no peace until the men are killed off—never treat an Indian as your equal," he advised.[9] Maj. Gen. D. H. Wells immediately issued orders to Col. John Scott and Capt. George D. Grant:

You are hereby ordered to raise forthwith a company of fifty efficient men and see they are provided with horses, arms, and ammunition and rations sufficient for twenty days, and proceed with said company to Fort Utah in Utah valley with a little delay as possible, There to Co-operate with the inhabitants of said Valley in quelling and staying the operations of all hostile Indians and otherwise act, as the circumstances may require, exterminating such as do not separate themselves from their hostile clans, and sue for peace.

Both officers also received "Private Instructions":

In carrying out the above order you will keep in exercise, every principle of humanity compatable with the laws of war and see that no violence is permitted to women and Children unless the same shall be demanded by attendant circumstances. The Utah Indians have been notified repeatedly of the consequences that would ensue to them if they did not cease to molest the white inhabitants and their herds. You will therefore proceed against them without further apprisal or notice and execute your orders.[10]

Mormon leaders called on the U.S. Army for support. Capt. Howard

---

[9]Bullock, General Church Minutes, 31 January 1850, CR 100 318, 2:17, 8, LDS Archives. See also Carter, *Founding Fort Utah*, 157–58.

[10]Campaign against the Utah Indians, UTMR, 1:2.

Stansbury assured them "the contemplated expedition against these savage marauders was a measure not only of good policy, but one of absolute necessity and self-preservation." He offered such assistance "as it was in my power to afford, consisting of arms, tents, camp-equipage, and ammunition," and assigned Lt. George Washington Howland "to accompany the expedition."[11]

The Fort Utah fight foreshadowed the events, relationships, alliances, and conflicts that would characterize Indian relations in the Mormon West for decades. Many of its "minute men," including Ephraim Hanks and William Hickman, "soon became famous in the Indian service,"[12] while George Grant, William H. Kimball, Robert F. Burton, Lot Smith, and James Ferguson later served as Nauvoo Legion generals.

On Monday, 4 February 1850, the company prepared to march "against the Indians in Utah Valley who have been committing depredations on the Inhabitants in that vicinity for some time past." At 2:30 P.M. Lieutenant Ferguson "with about 20 men started for that place." By Wednesday they had assembled "provisions, forage, wagons Horses &c" and "about 105 men including Officers, Teamsters &c." at Little Cottonwood, where Young and Wells "expressed their Gratification at seeing every one look and feel very well." On Thursday's "tolerably cold" morning, new-fallen snow made the militia's start difficult, and "We found the snow in Utah Vally much deeper than S.L.C. Valley." They reached Fort Utah after dark on 7 February with the Utes "camped in the same position they held before the company started from the city."[13]

No one questioned the courage of the "Lake Utes"—the "very large grizzly skin" Lieutenant Gunnison traded for a blanket testified to that.[14] "This Provo band was considered very brave," recalled Hickman, who attended a council of war "to fix the *modus operandi* of an attack on the Indians the next morning." The "new and high-minded officers" passed around a canteen, "which inspired their minds, and made assurance of an early victory next morning." Hickman did not like his orders and wondered "whether it was the want of brains or too much canteen that had caused such plans."[15]

Two feet of snow covered Utah Valley. The "fortified camp of the Indians" was the Timpanogos village on a brushy bend of the Provo River, a

[11]Madsen, *Exploring the Great Salt Lake*, 235–36, 257.

[12]Tullidge, "History of Provo City," 236–37.

[13]Report of Expedition against Indians in Utah Valley, BYC, 74:20.

[14]Madsen, *Exploring the Great Salt Lake*, 235–36.

[15]Hickman, *Brigham's Destroying Angel*, 58–59.

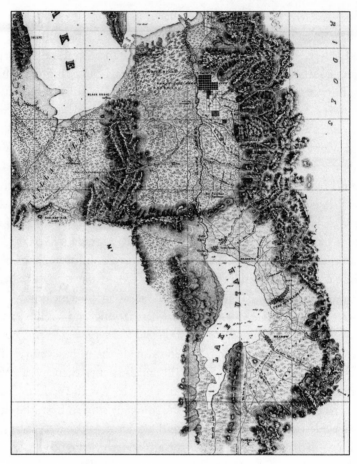

MAP OF THE GREAT SALT LAKE AND ADJACENT COUNTRY
John Gunnison and Charles Pruess preserved the Ute names for the creeks flowing
into Salt Lake and Utah valleys when they drew the "Map of the Great Salt Lake
and Adjacent Country" for the 1852 Stansbury Expedition report.

mile above the fort. By May 1849, the Mormon settlers, operating on what
one historian called "the strictest and most perfect system of colonization," already "had 225 acres of land laid out and apportioned off to forty
families." Much of the action over the next two days centered around two
abandoned cabins. James Bean's log cabin was a stone's throw from the Ute
camp behind "a heavy grove of timber on the river bottom, with a bank six

[16]Tullidge, "History of Provo City," 234, 237.

or eight feet high, and strong breast-works constructed of the big cotton-woods." Mormon Battalion veteran Miles Weaver's stood midway between the village and the fort.[16]

Captain Stansbury considered Elk "a crafty and blood-thirsty savage, who had been already guilty of several murders, and had openly threatened that he would kill every white man that he found alone upon the prairies."[17] Big Elk "was brave, cool and determined, standing over six feet high," Edward Tullidge wrote, and he commanded "about seventy warriors possessing arms equal to those of the expedition sent out against them." Upon seeing "the force that had come against his band" on 8 February, "the superior chief," Ope-Carry (or "old Stickinhead") "forecast their doom to his warriors." He began a "talk" with Dimick Huntington, but "the influence of Big Elk prevailed with the warriors, who opened fire," Tullidge claimed. Two contemporary reports indicate the militia attacked the village without any preliminaries.

FERGUSON, REPORT OF EXPEDITION AGAINST INDIANS IN UTAH VALLEY, BYC, 74:22.

Friday 8th. Council was held this morning. Propositions were made by several of the members but the one chosen was as follows. "That the forces be formed in 8 divisions. 3 of Horse under the command of Lieuts [William H.] Kimball, [James] Ferguson & [James] Little 4 of Foot under Capts. [Andrew] Lytle [Daniel S.] Carn [Peter] Conover and Lieut [Edmund] Elsworth also 1 company of Artillery under Lt. Howland. The horsemen were stationed on the prairie, 2 companies Lts. Kimball and Little on the east side of the River and Lieut Ferguson on the West in order to cut of[f] the Indians retreat should they leave the brush. The foot companies were to enter the brush on the north and South to drive them from their ambush. The artillery was stationed at Bro Miles Weaver's house about ½ mile [from] the camp of the Indians.

The engagement commenced about 12 o clock by the Indians who commenced firing on Lt Littles company as they passed by the river to their post. The Artilery then commenced firing the Canon. The Indians returned the fire with Spirit. Bullets flew lively. One struck John Topham on the arm and bruised it but not materialy. The canon was then moved closer to the Town to protect the men who worked it. Capt Grant feeling anxious to know the situation of the different companies and receiving no intelligence, went across the River to ascertain if possible. Returned in about an hour without any success since the Brush was to[o] thick and the draw so deep it was impenetrable to run on horse back. Firing now commenced in the brush

---

[17]Stansbury, *Exploration and Survey*, 149.

the foot companies having got close to the camp of the Indians they were so near they could see their wickeups and hear them talk to each other but could not see them. About 3 oclock express came from Capt Carn company informs us one man was wounded Samuel Carn, and wanted a blanket to carry him out of the brush. About the same time Alex Stevens was wounded in the thigh while loading the canon and almost immediately after Albert Miles was shot through the fleshy part of ~~Back~~ ~~Thigh~~ in the brush after having shot an Indian out of a tree. It now being near night and almost impossible to see in the brush the different companies retreated from their positions towards the fort. The Bugle was sounded and the horsemen and Artillery also left for their fort. As the Artillery and horsemen was leaving the Indians followd them down the river some ways keeping up a sharp fire which however did no injury it being returned with spirit which kept them from coming too close. It ~~was~~ could not be ascertained how many of the Indians were killed but it is supposed 4 or 5 besides several ~~mortally~~ badly wounded among whom was one Chief old Stick-inhead as he is named

HOWLAND TO WELLS, 8 FEBRUARY 1850, UTMR 1:3, 15, USHS.

I have the honor to state to you an account of our proceedings and also the state of the command as regards provisions &c. We started from the Fort this morning in order to give the Indians battle. The command was divided as follows: three parties were sent out on horseback under command of Lt Little, one under command of Lt. Kimball and the third under command of Lt Ferguson. These parties were sent out as guards to prevent the indians from escaping should they be driven out of there position. 2 parties were sent out on foot as skirmishers to drive from there position, and the ~~Art~~ Cannon were sent out for the same purpose. The indians were strongly fortified and displayed a great amount of skill in selecting their position. They had torn down Mr. Bean's house in order to make breastworks, and fortified themselves in a ditch which was some feet below the natural surface of the ground, their ditch was in the midst of thick under brush and trees and we were not able to get any advantage of them whatever. Capt Grant the commanding officer reconoitered their position in nearly every way, in fact every way possible but we could get no place where we could get them with our fire. The balls flew pretty thick from them but with little effect. We have not been able to ascertain how many of the indians were killed but we think three or four and several wounded, as trails of blood were seen in several places. Among our wounded was Mr Samuel Carn, he was wounded severely but not dangerously.

Mr. Albert Miles the same. Mr. Stevens was wounded slightly, two or three others with spent bullets, which merely bruised their skin. We are going at them again tomorrow, it is not known how many there are, but it is supposed the indians from the Spanish Fork and south of the lake have joined them. The Cannon could not be used with any effect.

As to provisions, we have enough or can get it here. But we want more forage. It is estimated that we shall want 100 bushels of Grain. The snow is so deep that there is no grazing for the animals and there is very little hay here. The express will come back and let us know what time we will have the have the wagons at the Summit, and we will send 2 sleighs to meet them there and help them along.

I forgot to mention that we had one of the red faces as prisoner, and Captured six horses and one colt.

It is generally wished by the Officers here that you were present in order to help us along. We have plenty of men, as many as could be used conveniently.

I have no more to State.
I have the honour
Very Repsecfully to be Your Obedient Servt
Geo W Howland

P.S. It is to be hoped that the Grain will reach us soon, as we are nearly out.

The prisoner was Antonga (or Antonguer), known as Black Hawk and said to be Wakara's half brother, who had camped across the river and refused to fight. He may have moved voluntarily to the fort with his family. Howland's report reflected army tactics, which tried to stop Indians from disappearing at any show of force. The militia followed Stansbury's "explicit advice to attack them while the snow keeps them from their mountain hiding places."[18]

The first day's fight lasted seven miserable hours, but the musket and cannon fire produced few Indian casualties and no Mormon fatalities. After sunset, a bugle sounded retreat, and "the Indians set up such a yell of victory that one would think ten thousand devils had been turned loose." The Utes followed, "shooting at us all the way," local militia commander Peter Conover recalled. Weary, hungry, "dispirited somewhat by the repulses, and nearly perished with the cold," the militiamen sought the safety of the fort. Howland's report reached General Wells in Salt Lake by morning.[19] Wells responded immediately.

WELLS TO GRANT, 9 FEBRUARY 1850, UTMR 1:3, 17, USHS.

Special Orders No. 10   Head Quarters Nauvoo Legion
Major General's Office G. S. L. City Feby 9th/50

To Capt. G. D. Grant

Dear Sir—Your express forwarded by Miles Weaver and Joseph Clarke arrived here this forenoon, giving me intelligence of your battle yesterday

---

[18]Tullidge, "History of Provo City," 239; Madsen, *Exploring the Great Salt Lake*, 257.
[19]Carter, *Founding Fort Utah*, 177–78.

with the Utah Indians, of which I was anxious to heare, and tenders my thanks for the same. I would enjoin upon you, to preserve your men if possible, under all circumstances compatible with duty. You state that your cannons could not be brought to bear upon them, I would therefore suggest the propriety of erecting a Battery upon wheels, under cover to screen your men from their arrows, and bring the same to bear upon them if possible. Take *no hostile Indians as prisoners,* those friendly and sue for peace, take them under guard and place them in the Fort, well guarded, and at no time leave the Fort unprotected. If you have a surplus of horses, more than are necessary, assort out the best, and return the others to this place, as you will want your feed for those necessary to be retained.

Keep a vigilant watch upon the Indians, *and let none escape, but do the work up clean,* as you have commenced and are engaged in it. I have forwarded three teams today, loaded with coin, which will arrives by tomorrow evening at the mountains, and I wish you would send up some teams to meet them and take their loads into the Fort, and let those teams sent by me today return, unless it is necessary to retain them, and send back the teams with weaker ones. I expect to send as much corn tomorrow as you will need perhaps, until the work is done, what I sent you today will supply you until more arrives. I have no more to add, only what I have reiterated before, be *vigilant, be careful and preserve the lives* of your men. I would be happy to be with you, but duty requires my presence here.

Daniel H. Wells
Major-General

At Fort Provo, the subdued officers knew they must capture the Bean cabin. Lieutenant Howland suggested they use a log "battery" to protect the men making the assault. They spent Saturday morning building the A-shaped wooden sled.[20]

REPORT OF EXPEDITION AGAINST INDIANS OF UTAH VALLEY, BYC 74:22.
Saturday [9 February 1850]. The Battle was commenced at One oclock PM The Artillery gained their position at the first Log Home Leut. Kimballs company station and about five hundred yds South of the Indian wigwams on which the Indians commenced firing.

It being puposed [*sic*] in council that morning that there be breastworks made in this shape ^ on sleighs in order to get near the Indians without being exposed to their fire these breastworks were made in the Fort and taken out [and] got ready at one Station near the first Log house. They were Started as they were arranged. As soon as they were discovered by the Indians they set up a tremendous howl as they observed that their shots had no efect on those

---

[20]Ibid., 179–80.

within. As the batteries moved up Capt Grant ordered Lieuts Kimball and Ferguson with their companies to make a charge on the upper Log House which had been previously held by the Indians.

The Charge was gallantly made though a heavy fire was Kept up by the enemy. Every man reached the house not one wounded in the charge. The House is so situated that in order to enter the horsemen were obliged [to ride] in front of the Indians not more than ~~one hundred~~ thirty yd. distant. They succeeded in entering the house in safety and commenced firing with commendable effect—the battries doing the same. Some of the Artillery station on the prairie with the six pounder knowing they would be of more service at the house with Lieut Kimball and Ferguson made a rush on foot and all reached it even though one man was badly wounded being shot through the nose and cheek.[21] A call was made from the house for some Cartidges and an axe, which in the distance was mistaken for doctor and Bandages—and accordingly—Dr. Stephen Kinzie [Kinsey], accompanied by Lt. [Hiram] Clawson—Aid-de-Camp—joined, sustaining a considerable fire from the Enemy though without any injury save to the Doctors hand—a rifle ball.

The capture of the Bean cabin meant Saturday's fight had been an essential success for the Mormon forces. The "very hard fighting," the death of a comrade, and the loss of so many of their horses seem to have left the sometime soldiers rattled. The determined and resilient Native resistance apparently made the Nauvoo Legionaries reluctant to face the Ute rifles again the next day. They chose instead to have U.S. Army lieutenant G. W. Howland draft a report of the day's action that highlighted the distinct lack of civilian support they received from Fort Utah's inhabitants. That night they sent Howland's letter via another express to Daniel Wells in Salt Lake.

HOWLAND TO WELLS, 9 FEBRUARY 1850, UTMR, 1:3, 19.

As the request of a Council was that another express should be sent to the City I have the honour to make a statement to you in the name of Capt Grant & others, an account of the day's proceedings. The indians were not yet routed, that are near the Fort. There are still some left, but it is not known how many. To day we had some very hard fighting, with the loss of one life (Joseph Higbee) he was shot through the neck. Mr. Alexander Williams was shot through the shoulder, but not dangerously. Jabus Knowland was shot though the cheek and nose, not as dangerously. Mr. [Isham] Flynn slightly,

---

[21]This was Jabez Nowland, who "had a verry large nose. His wife told him in the morning if he was shot it would be in his nose. And sure enough he was, while charging a strong position held by the Indians," Abner Blackburn recalled. "The bullet hit on the side of the bridge of his nose, which made a verry painful wound but not dangerous." Bagley, *Frontiersman*, 170.

three horses killed, four wounded, among the wounded was Lt. Kimball's. The fire was kept up on the enemy for some time when the command was given by Capt Grant to Lts Kimball and Ferguson to charge on the upper Log House (Mr. Beans) which was within a few yards of the indian Camp. They made a grand Charge, and took the house in the charge. One man (Mr. Flynn) was slightly wounded, no others suffered. We had two batteries made in the shape of the letter A put on sleds into which 12 men got and approached near the enemy all the time keeping up a hot fire, but could not get into their Camp.

Some of the inhabitants of the Fort feel as if they should leave or abandon the place were the command to be withdrawn without routing the enemy— and some do not seem to care whether they are routed or not as they are going to the Gold mines in the spring. "They never had any trouble with the indians and do not intend to.["] I am directed to state for Capt Grant that he would like to have you come to the ~~scene~~ Fort.

We are going to try them again tomorrow and see if we cannot route them altogether, by force or strategem. Our men from the city are very much discouraged on account of the manner of *some* of the inhabitants of the Fort act, it seems to put a damper on their Courage and patriotism. It would have been far better for them to have gone and encamped close by the indians, than to have gone to the Fort and heard such remarks as "I had sooner the indians should have my Cattle than kill them for you to eat," and "I want them to go to California with." Such remarks as these are not calculated to inspire our men at all.

As I have nothing further more to state as regards the expedition I will now close and forward.

Very Respecfully Your Obedient Servt
Geo W Howland

The demoralized Mormons did not renew the attack on 10 February or even leave the safety of the fort until Antonga reported the Utes, as Stansbury warned, had decamped to "their mountain hiding places." They "had retired in the night after the battle, leaving their dead on the ground, carrying their wounded with them," supplying "themselves abundantly with the horse beef killed in the charge upon the log house."[22]

Brigham Young reacted to the "sad news from Fort Utah," attacking those who had "traded guns and powder" and would "rather the Indians eat their cattle than the saints from this valley—I have sent word to confiscate all their property—and then put them in the front of the battle and kill them." He blamed the trouble on "shooting with the Indians, gambling, and

---

[22]Tullidge, "History of Provo City," 239.

running horses with them—they now turn round and say they have picked no quarrel—they are going to the gold mines." His followers must be ready:

> to fight preach or pray as it is necessary—if those Indians cant be come at—they must either quit the ground or we must—we have to maintain that ground, or vacate this—we were told three years ago—if we don't kill those lake Utes, they will kill us—every man told us the same—they all bore testimony the Lake Utes lives by plunder and robbing—if we yield in this instance, we have to yield this land. Walker advises us to use them up—I am going to keep up a standing army to lick them up—this is the place to begin—Joseph prophesied many of the Lamanites will have to be slain, many of them by us.[23]

In a noonday blizzard, General Wells headed for Fort Utah with Young's orders "not to leave that Valley until every Indian was out." He arrived Monday morning at 3:00 A.M. Wells deserved the title "Brigham's sledgehammer": he immediately declared martial law, put James Little in command, and ordered all "provisions, forage, teams &c will be held for the purpose of the expedition." No person could "leave the settlement for any purpose whatsoever" without a permit. Finally, George Grant's company would "make arrangements for Capturing the remaining Indians" on Provo River.[24]

The commander-in-chief kept in daily contact with Wells. On 12 February Brigham Young ordered Capt. Andrew Lamoreaux and a company of men to Utah Valley as reinforcements. "We would suggest that the poisonous arrows of the Indians are more to be dreaded than Rifle Balls." Young suggested they use "white clay to extract poison from meat," a point worth remembering if "any should be wounded by poisoned arrows."[25]

Let It Be Peace with Them or Extermination

The militia pursued the survivors relentlessly. On 11 February Grant's men followed the "traces of blood on the ground" from survivors and their "foot prints in the snow" to Rock Canyon. Grant left ten men to guard the trapped Indians. Wells joined Capt. Andrew Lytle's 110 men tracking the Utes south to Spanish Fork, where scouts had spotted the survivors. The Utes disappeared, leaving the Mormons to spend a miserable night in the

[23]Van Wagoner, *Complete Discourses*, 2:365–66.
[24]Wells, General Orders No. 1, 11 February 1850, UTMR, 1:3, 20.
[25]Young to Wells, 12 February 1850, UTMR.

snow. On 13 February 1850 George Grant found most of the warriors near Table Mountain. Some claim Grant induced the Utes to surrender and camp near him, but they refused to disarm.

Before heading to Table Point, Wells ordered Robert Thomas's worn-out horses and men to scout Peteetneet Creek. Thomas recalled what they found.

> About 30 rods from in the willows we could see a wiki; we sent an Indian (Black Hawk), an Indian scout to see how many there was. He came back and said, "There is a blind Indian in the wigwam. He said that there were two Indians close by and had a pistol and the blind Indian said "Rustle no go won't stand roost." We concluded to let the two warriers and the old blind Indian be. We went about 2 miles; the snow laid in great drifts. We had a great deal of work before we could beat the snow down in the drifts and it was midnight [before we camped]. I froze my feet. I told them about the blind Indian. That night a company from Salt Lake City under Captain Lumrow [Lamoreaux] went to hunt up the Indians. They took a cannon and wagon. At daylight they charged on the three Indians and killed them and then returned. Wells heard of it and Court marshalled them. Next morning the word came about 12 o'clock to send some wagons to get the squaws. We were ordered to return home.[26]

"We are passing a sleepless night on account of keeping a vigilant watch over Indians changing the guard every hour on account of the cold," Wells reported.[27] Not long after Wells awoke at Table Point and turned his attention to his prisoners, Lieutenant Howland delivered his letter to Brigham Young, who responded immediately:

YOUNG TO WELLS, 14 FEBRUARY 1850, UTMR, 2;1, 1,312.

To Maj. Gen. Daniel H. Wells

Sir, your Dispatch of the 13th just, from Camp Utah, was received this hour—per hand, Adjunt Howland—

We were not disappointed by the intelligence communicated, and are satisfied that you have done all you could under the circumstances; and all that you can do, at present in fighting the enemy unless circumstances shall materially alter, for they can traverse mountains, over deep snows, when your men are not prepared to follow, consequently they will not stop to fight you unless they can choose their position and I do not believe they want to fight any more at present.

When Indians flee as they have done, they consider themselves whipt and if they are "not conquered" they will no doubt remain quiet until after another harvest.

---

[26]Thomas, Autobiography, 25.

[27]Carter, *Founding Fort Utah*, 199–205. Wells's letter is missing from the digitized militia records.

Should things remain as they were, on receipt of this, you will withdraw your troops, and close the Campaign, after having organized all the men belonging to Fort Utah in the most efficient military body possible with instructions to hold themselves ready for any emergency. Should you be so far advanced that it will not be tedious for a portion of the command to return home by way of Tuille Vally, and Great Salt Lake, and you have provisions it might serve a useful purpose, in the appearance, and lead to useful discoveries.

You will not suffer Indians who are known to be hostile and have come in your possession, because they were sick and could not fight to want for *any thing* neither suffer them to go free until they are cured. Your surgeon Mr Blake, is no doubt well provided with medicine and will be ready to prescribe that which will effect that most desirable of all objects, *perfect health.*[28] The inhabitants of Utah can resume their several occupations with safety if they will learn from the past, that great caution directed by *Wisdom* is the surety of that safety—and not again put powder, balls, and rifle in the hands of their enemies, to their own destruction.

Little Indian children taken captives, may be retained by the Captns, and trained to service—Peaceful woman and children, voluntarily surrendered as prisoners, may be set at liberty, unless it shall appear that their relatives have been killed or they claim protection, in which case you will bring them with you, for further counsels.

In all things pertaining to the Campaign, should circumstances change, so as to require it, you will exercise a discretionary power.

This will be dispatched early in the morning, and teams loaded with wheat and corn will follow after without delay.

Friday Morning 9 Oclock

Feb 15th. We have just received another Dispatch from you by the hand of E. Ellsworth, and Lieut. Little, giving us the cheering and gratifying intelligence of your success over your enemies yesterday morning in which the courage and valor of the *boys* as heretofore was manifested—If the Indians sue for peace, grant it to them, according to your discretionary Judgment in the case.—If they continue hostile pursue them until you use them up—*Let it be peace with them or extermination.*[29]

Keep the Provo Kanyon well watched and guarded when those Indians have fled with Stinking Head, and Old Elk—make sure of them all, if you can. These two noted ones if possible.

I would also suggest the propriety of examining the Lake from the Fort to the West side of the same. If found practicable to carry your waggons stores &c there, and make your encampment on the west side of the Lake.

[28]Historian Gary Maxwell, *Robert Newton Baskin*, 102–104, listed sixty Mormon frontier euphemisms for murder; "perfect health" may be another.

[29]The 1850 edition of Webster's *Dictionary of the English Language* defined "exterminate" as "To root out; to drive away; to destroy utterly." As events indicate, Brigham Young's extermination order was conditional.

If so inform us by the Earliest opportunity so we can dispatch our wagons with stores From here to the west side of the Lake, without going by the Fort.

I propose that the friendly Indian (Walkers relative) that is with you, live at the Fort, as heretofore with those that are friendly with him.[30] I also recomend that the Interpreters converse with those Indian prisoners— Women & Children, and ascertain their feelings—whether they are willing to come here, and go to work, and be brought up in usefulness among the white men &c. We are sending you some tobacco for your men—we will send a bill of the same = 109 lbs.

In further consideration I have deemed it prudent for you to send all the Women and children Prisoners here as soon as you possibly can wether they are willing to come or not. We will find them plenty of Work, plenty to eat &c.

Yours &c
Brigham Young

For decades, Young and Wells proved remarkably compatible. In this case, the general had anticipated his orders. James Ferguson reported the executions at Table Mountain to John Gunnison, but "seemed disposed to paint it in as soft colors as possible."[31] There was nothing soft about the Legion's actions.

> Lt. Ferguson says that the party surprised on Table would not give up their arms or smoke the pipe of peace—that some come in voluntarily & one warrior was warned not to come to camp by others but who said that was his land & he would then die there—These were taken about dark & kept under guard till morning, & forcibly disarmed—some tried to run off & were shot—The rest *were also shot.*[32]

The Utes resisted bravely but suffered terribly. "In the deserted camp were three males & three females dead and one old Squaw in one part of the camp & a pappoose in another—a small child was also found on the road thrown away," wrote Gunnison. "The Elk was found dead in the snow." The artillery Howland had dismissed as ineffective "did some terrible execution": the Mormons found "one of the dead women in a wickiup with her legs cut off by a chain-shot."[33]

"On the approach of the troops near the wickiups, there was a general scattering of the squaws and children. Big Elk's squaw fled and attempted to climb a precipice, from which she fell and was instantly killed. She was

---

[30]"Walker's relative" was probably Angatewats or Antonga, Black Hawk.
[31]Gunnison, *The Mormons*, 147; Madsen, *Exploring the Great Salt Lake*, 264.
[32]Madsen, *Exploring the Great Salt Lake*, 265.
[33]Ibid., 264; Tullidge, "History of Provo City," 239–40.

young and said to be the handsomest squaw in the Ute nation; she was also very intelligent," wrote Tullidge, telling the folktale of how "Squaw Peak" got its name. On 17 February 1850 Wells told Young of "one squaw killing herself falling from a precipice." Grant "followed the warriors up the canyon," fought a skirmish, and captured a woman and two children. Some of the Utes escaped over the mountains. The survivors came down Provo Canyon in the spring, "having been as far as the Weber River," Tullidge wrote. "They were thirteen in number and were all that were left of the seventy or eighty warriors who had engaged in the Provo battle."[34]

Historians have long used such traditions to make rough estimates of Ute casualties, but General Wells made a body count for the secretary of war: "In our engagements with them as our reports will show, only one man was killed, and five wounded; while of them 26 warriors are known to have been killed, five wounded, while some have died through exposure, want and fatigue, in being routed from their retreats at this inclement season of the year. Many more are supposed to have been killed and surrounded but in accordance with Indian custom, carried away by them."[35]

"The expedition was completely successful. The Indians fought very bravely, but were finally routed, some forty of them killed, and as many more taken prisoners," Captain Stansbury reported. The women and children "were carried to the city and distributed among the inhabitants." The hope to "wean them from their savage pursuits" and instill "the habits of civilized and Christian life" failed: most of the prisoners escaped at the "very first opportunity."[36]

John Gunnison summarized the campaign for his wife, expressing the common "doomed race" view of American Indians:

a plenty of whooping we have among the Indians here—A party in the Utah valley above were so bold as to steal cattle from us last fall & this winter they troubled the colony of Mormons there to such a degree that forbearance was pushed to the test & they ordered out 150 men and pounced down upon the red brethren in a *savage* manner and whipt them unmercifully, killed about thirty and drove the balance into the mountains where many are perishing with the measles. They brought in squaws & children which are placed in

---

[34]Tullidge, "History of Provo City," 239–40; Madsen, *Exploring the Great Salt Lake*, 265; Farmer, *On Zion's Mount*, 275.

[35]Wells to Crawford, February 1850, Utah State Archives, Series 2210, Box 2, fd. 1. Courtesy Christopher Smith.

[36]Stansbury, *Exploration and Survey*, 149.

families as servants to make white people of them. Our old woman went off the other night with her new petticoats & some knives,—the old ones will decamp when warm weather comes round no doubt; they may make something of the children. One bad thing occurred during the week's war. The militia managed to cut off several squaws & children who were flying from their wigwams, & men were beyond on the sides of a mountain within call. They were induced to come in on the assurance of the whitemen being friendly to them—and the warriors & women were kept under guard that night & in the morning all disarmed & the male Indians were all shot. But the thievish rascals have been so thoroughly trounced and the measles have used up so large a number, that we shall probably have no annoyance from the few scattered & frightened ones left. This band which has been so fully thrashed & nearly exterminated, has been called the worst Indians & hardest fighters in the mountains,—and as the whole country of natives have suffered extremely from the measles, we hope that they will be peaceable for a few seasons. It is astonishing what infatuation has seized on the race of red men. They are not only at war with each other as tribe against tribe, but bands of the same tribe are fighting and destroying one another. It is a doomed race;—and following the law promulgated by God, that a people adhering to murderous, idolatry practices shall be extinguished.[37]

Brigham Young summarized the campaign for two distant apostle-editors.

YOUNG TO ORSON HYDE AND ORSON PRATT, 28 FEBRUARY 1850, BYC 16:19.

Since our last communication the Utah Lake Indians have been very hostile, killed many scores of the brethrens cattle, and threatened, waylaid & shot at the brethren at Utah, until self defence demanded immediate action. The case was stated to Capt. Stansbury of the Corps of United States Engineers stationed at this place; also to such officers of the United States army, stationed at Fort Hall, as happened to be here, and they all agreed that it was necessary that the Indians should be whipped or corrected, that it belonged to the United States troops at Fort Hall to do it, but the snow was so deep those troops could not be come at, therefore it was necessary for the citizens to proceed against the Indians, which they did, accompanied by some of the United States officers—A portion of the Indians entrenched in the brush near Fort Utah, and fought two days, with the loss of several of their warriors, and one of our brethren, and a few wounded, now convalescent, on the night following the two days fight the surviving Indians retreated to the mountains, whither they were pursued—peace was offered them, and other claims of the same tribe in

---

[37]Gunnison to My Dear Martha, 1 March 1850, Madsen, *Exploring the Great Salt Lake*, 269–70.

various Kanyons around the Lake, but they all said they would fight till they died—they would have no peace—when our men proceeded to slay their warriors, and take their squaws and papooses prisoners. Many of the Indians fled, and could not be found—peace was apparently restored after Killing some twenty or thirty indians, and the squaws and children prisoners were distributed among the citizens, clothed fed, and taught to work. There are many tribes called Utahs from many of whom we have heard, and they appear satisfied with our course, and say "The Lake Utes, are bad indians" There is no probability that the remaining Utes will offer any further violence at present, and we hope, never.—

Not all the participants had a positive view of the fight. "An Indian war was forced upon us at the river by a man named Ivie, who shot and killed an Indian for stealing a shirt," Provo pioneer Jane Park Jones recalled. "A battle was fought, in which one of the pioneers lost his life and many Indians were killed. The Indians were suffering with measles at the time." Elk, "the fighting chief," was killed, and his head "brought into camp and hung pendant by its long hair from the willows of the roof of one of the houses," the seven-year-old recalled seven decades later. "I well remember how horrible was the sight."[38]

Bill Hickman claimed he "took off" Elk's head: he "had heard the old mountaineer, Jim Bridger, say he would give a hundred dollars for it."[39] James Blake, Stansbury's surgeon, hired two Mormons to desecrate the unburied Ute corpses at Table Point, "for he wanted to send them to Washington to a medical institution," wrote Abner Blackburn. Other Saints expressed disgust. "I can never forget the horrible and frightening scene when the boys brought into the Fort a number of Indian heads with their nasty bloody necks and their tongues sticking out of their mouths," recalled Anna Clark Hale. "It was horrible."[40]

John Hudson, a Stansbury artist, probably sketched "Utah Indian Prisoners Under the Common Platform at Fort Utah." No other source captures the Ute response to the systematic annihilation of the Timpanogos as vividly. George W. Bean recalled that Pe-teetneet, Tabby, Grospene, "and about twenty others" discovered the corpses left for two months on the frozen lake and confronted militiamen at Table Point. "Grospene rode up and struck Allen Huntington over the shoulders twice, demanding why he killed his

---

[38]"Provo Pioneers of 1847," *Provo Herald*, 24 July 1923, 1.
[39]Hickman, *Destroying Angel*, 68.
[40]Carter, *Founding Fort Utah*, 222–24.

"Utah Indian Prisoners under the Common Platform at Fort Utah."
This engraving from Howard Stansbury's 1852 *Exploration and Survey of the Valley of
the Great Salt Lake*, 148, showed the suffering of Ute prisoners after the 1850 Battle
of Provo River.

friends and relatives."[41] Wakara favored "what we have done," Barney Ward
told a meeting of Mormon leaders, "and he will let the mormons know that
he is their friends." He told the Yampa Utes "not to help the Tinpenny
Utes."[42] Isaac Morley also reported Wakara's reaction:

> The information of the circumstances in Utah Valley caused considerable
> excitement here with the natives. Walker says that a number of his friends
> are killed by the mormons but he says he does not wish to fight them. He
> sais that I am his Father and he will give me this land—how desirable his
> friendship may be is more than I can say or trust at present—I believe there
> is good feelings at present.[43]

General Wells now removed the mailed glove from his iron fist and
assumed the role of peacemaker and power broker:

> The Indians prisoner last taken you will release with instructions to him
> to apprize the Survivors of his nation that they may return and dwell in
> peace, if they cease their depreadations and refrain from Stirring up the

[41]Bean, *Autobiography*, 63.
[42]Minutes about Indians, 28 February 1850, BYC, 74:41.
[43]Morley to General Wells, 20 February 1850, UTMR.

neighbouring indians to enmity with the Settlements. The friendly Indian *Black Hawk* must be their chief and they must obey him. If they will do this we will return them their horses and become again their friends. We do not wish to continue to war with them, but merely teach them to do right.[44]

The Fort Utah fight taught Mormon leaders the effectiveness of selective extermination. They cloaked their policy of "exterminating such as do not ... sue for peace" in murderous euphemisms about *"perfect health,"* doing *"the work up clean,"* and staying "until every Indian was out." It produced immediate benefits, including the approval of U.S. Army officers for its "absolute necessity and self-preservation." What did Native peoples learn from the slaughter of the Timpanogos? Wakara now knew his survival depended on winning Brigham Young's goodwill, but many Natives refused to believe resistance was futile.

BAD MORMONS AS WELL AS BAD INDIANS: TOO MUCH TRUTH FOR A SMILE

Captain, bishop, patriarch, senator, and Council of Fifty member Isaac Morley personified how Mormon prophets concentrated power among the favored princes of the Kingdom of God. A nineteen-year Mormon veteran of proven loyalty when he became president of Sanpete Valley's Latter-day Saints in November 1849, Morley listened closely to what his Ute neighbors said during Manti's first hard winter.

MORLEY TO YOUNG, 20 FEBRUARY 1850, BYC 22:2.

It falls to my lot this morning to communicate to you the state of things in this place. We are in as good circumstance as could be expected with the measles in our midst, and Mormon fare which you well understand.[45] Measles have made a general sweep through this part of the country. Many of the Natives have died. When Walker came within 2 days travel of our company, he sent for me. I met him eight miles out, and gave medicine to 24 the first visit. Arapenes Child which was then dying as I though[t] lived till the next day, and died on the way to this place. In obedience to council I have attended on them ever since. Three have died, but [only] one under my care. Walker say, the sandpitches would all have died, and many of his men to, had we not been here. There has been 2 deaths in the camp. . . .

---

[44]Wells to McBride, 23 February 1850, UTMR, 1:5, 22.
[45]"Mormon fare" referred to the settlement's scant rations.

Mr. Ward arrived her[e] yesterday bringing the express from Genl. Wells giving an account of the battle that was fought in Utah Valey the day before he left. We called a council and invited Walker who came with his attendanse, the case was made known to him through Mr. Ward, he said let them fight it out all is wright, if your big Capt. does not interfere I will not. All right. The Utah are bad they wont take my counsil. They have killed my son Battee. I feel bad. I want they should make me some presents of Guns, Blankets, &c. and I will be satisfied. I want to have the Mormans stay here and plant and sow, and do us good, and we will be friends. If they [the Utahs] will fight and be killed, it is well. We all parted with good feelings of friendship. . . . Walker says this morning he has sent 2 men to Arapenes tent to stay home and not to go fight and that he will take the same message to all of the Natives in the region round about to stay home and not to go fight. Walker says there are bad Mormons as well as bad Indians. Too much truth for a smile. . . .

Walker arrived December 13th in the neighborhood and pitched his tent about one mile from the fort, and has been very friendly, his sick are made well for which he is glad, they want Tieyup, or food, and are hardly willing to take a denial, our breadstuff is wearing away and our cattle for the most part, are too feeble to haul any as soon as will be needed. If we had corn or bread stuff of any kind, we could sell it for skins, and relieve their wants, and keep a good friendly feeling towards us, and between us. He does not wish us to go away but stay here and be friends, and work, and his sanpitch folks will work, and learn to raise their food. Walker says he has got some oxen and we may have them if we want, 2 yoke I think he said. Walker has a lot of Ponies some very good ones I think he would probably exchange for grain, how would a move of that kind do?

. . . Walker says the saints had not better travel in company of less than 8 or 10 well armed at present to keep a good watch a[t] Nights.

Isaac Morley Presidnt
P[hineas]. Richards Clerk

MORLEY TO YOUNG AND COUNCIL, 15 MARCH 1850, BYC 22:2.

Sanpitch Valey March 15th 1850

President B. Young and Council,

In as much as we have taken in hand a great and good work, agreeably to the Councill imported to us while we were with you, we feel to say the hand of the Lord to this time has been over us for good. We arrived here on the 22d day of Novr with 224 souls in Camp 124 males, 100 Females, we commenced to make our selves as comfortable as circumstances would permit, a few put up log homes, some pitched their tents, and others lived in waggons until now. The winter has been severe for this place, we have verry little wind but a plenty of deep snow, from 3 feet & downwards, the prospects of cattle are brightening, we have lost 71 Oxcen, 34 Cows, 14 young stock, and 3 horses. Walker says that if we had not come, the sandpitches would all have died, and a great share of his people also. Now if the Mormons had butchered enough of thier best cattle to have made themselves comfortable, and helped the Natives some, would the Lord have taken the course he has, to show the Mormons the effects of a coveteaus principle and teach them, that the liberal soul is made fat, all the day long. I do not write to instruct my teachers, but that you would bear with me a little in my folly, and indeed bear with me. We are glad to have it to say that Walker and his people, are on the most friendly terms, and the bonds of union seem to strengthen. . . . On the 13th of this month, Walker was led down into the waters of baptism, by Prest. Morley and took upon him the name of Christ. A number more is looking for the door

> To find the right way to walk in,
> Walker says ten, both of women and men
> Desire to find where, they wash away sin.

This will be attended to the first opportunity.

Brother Walker says that he and his folks are short run for food, and he wants that President Young should send him provisions to the price of a good horse. (and I know that he has good ones on hand.) He says that a horse commands a good price, he will keep the horse till you come next and get it, or leave it with Br. Morley or any other one, at your order, he wants a lot of bread-stuff, and he needs it soon as he can get hold of it.

Br. Walker says that he wants that you would send him some whiskey, as he says it makes him feel good. I write you the word from his mouth, &c. He also wants you to send him a good supply of rice, or I may say a good quantity of Rice, without fail. It is a favorite dish with him.[46]

We have tried on some new points, as they form a part of all things, so we expect it, every new turn shows us a new wrinkle. Some times the Natives appear to live in Luxury, at other times eny with the emty beley-ache, come in and plead for some Tyseup, and present their sick Children and say Pappoos sick inch Tysheup, it tries the sencebilities of a benevolent heart. Our provisions are sufficient for ourselves to last until we could get a recruit from the Valey of head quarters, but when the Natives (who have expressed the warmest friendship, and kind feelings towards us, and that friendship and feelings that we above all things wish to cultivate,) come and say we want Tysheup and Shirteup inch sick and faint, it tryes the soul not to be able to afford some relief.[47]

---

[46]Young sent "Mr. Walker in compliance with his request" 306 pounds of corn meal, 10 bushels of wheat, and 25 pounds of rice, with an itemized bill for $119.75. Young to Morley, 4 April 1850, BYC 16:19, 32.

[47]The Utes apparently asked for food and medicine.

If means would be devised that would add to their comfort at this time in releaving their occasional, pressing wants, it would bind more closely their good feelings, and facilitate the object of our mission. Br. Walker and some of his people express a wish to go to farming raise grain get houses to live in and to live as the Mormon do and have their women learn to cook, and work, and learn how to manage Domestic affairs. But how can that be done without feeding them for the time being, and perhaps some little clothing to make them decent for to be in company. We should be glad of Council from you, that we may take the best course to accomplish this desired object. As yet we have not heard a word direct from you since we left the Salt Lake Valey. A word from you would be like cool water when thirsty.

> We remain as ever yours in the bonds of the Covenant,
> Isaac Morley Presidt

Valuing Wakara's friendship, Mormon leaders quickly responded. From the relative comfort of Salt Lake, they suggested if Morley had the means, he should translate *The Book of Mormon* into Ute. They also lectured the hard-pressed settlers about temperance and trade.

PRESIDENCY TO MORLEY AND SAINTS AT SANPETE, 24 MARCH 1850, BYC, 16:19, 22–25.

We rejoice to hear that [the] spirit of the Lord is beginning to operate upon the hearts of the Lamanites, & incline them towards the waters of baptism. And we pray that it may be continued unto them till they are all inclined to do good. The Book of Mormon might be a great blessing to Walker if he would learn to read it & through him to many of his kindred and this he can do in a very short time if he will apply himself diligently by study & also by faith, and you will do well to instruct him particularly on this point. Secure his attention, & give him all the attention you can, & also if you have the means, to translate it into his own language. . . .

"Walker says he wants we should send him some whiskey, it makes him feel good." We canot send it, for we have not got, & we are sorry that we have occason to suspect that this request came from Walkers tongue, by some one or more professing to be good brethren, having placed a cup of strong water, to his lips, even if it was nothing more then the rinsing of the whiskey keg. Big chief says whiskey is no good, & he does not drink it. And good 'Mormons' do not drink it only as a medicine. And the counsel of our great chief to bro Walker is not to drink whisky—& persuade his friends not to drink it and he will have more of the great spirit in his heart.

Walkers counsel for the brethren not to sell the indians guns powder lead &c is good: it has been our counsel ever since the pioneers came to this valley.—And we hope that those brethren who have hitherto neglected to heed our counsel on this matter,—will no longer refuse to hearken, when the indians begin to counsel for their good. Let your trade to the indians be in clothing, & food as you have the opportunity & not in weapons of war,—It is time to look about; when indians begin to teach the elders of Israel; though we believe there are very few of you, who need this caution, the experience of others must have shown you the fact before this.

In a confidential letter dated 13 April, Morley brought up "a delicacy upon my mind" involving Lamanite redemption: "I would like to know if you have ever given Walker any encouragements of a mormon woman for wife. He has intimated this ideah to our interpreters here—they say they do not know but it is all romance." Young had expressed the hope "that the Elders would marry Wives of every tribe" in 1847, but whenever Mormon leaders proposed marrying Native wives, Indian men asked about marrying white women—a point of contention that survived Wakara. The Ute's "requests and performances in the ordanances" appeared sincere, Morley wrote, but "as to motive it may not fully be under stood. I believe he is our friend. He informs us there is a secret plot going on against this people—and he Walker is soliseted to joine in the plan—on this point you will be made better acquainted."[48]

MORLEY TO YOUNG AND COUNCIL, 17 APRIL 1850, BYC 22:2, 23–26.
[W]e at present enjoy a degree of good health as also the Natives, who had much sickness this winter past, but are now injoying better times. Walker & Arapene are determined to put down stealing and Murder, if possible. A Sanpitch killed a Calf for Br. Case, he tracked him up to his lodge, then notified Walker, who readily entered into the merits of the case, drove him from their midst, the same Indian went to Arapene about 30 miles off, and made his boast of killing two creatures, a Calf & yearlin & shot two arrows into an Ox, but did not prove fatal. Aropene took his rifle, and two others took him a few steps and put three balls through him. . . .

John Baker, a young man left the wagons in the Kanion soon after our Brethren left there for S. L. City, he went where he was met by two Natives near summit Creek, when he was shot down by the powder they had obtained of him. Walker on hearing the same sent two men to search out the murderers and bring him word, the result is still to be learned. The friendship of Walker is good and increasing. Walker you know has joined us by Baptism, and Quáets, Toy-a-amp, Show-wer-yocket, were baptized March the 20th. The land has been set off for Fields and Gardens, field, 5 Acres and Garden 10 rods square. . . . We rejoice in the bright prospect before us, we feel confident that no mission to the scattered sons of Joseph was ever attended with brighter prospects of

---

[48]Morley, Confidential to Father Brigham Young, 13 April 1850, BYC 22:2, 16–17.

doing good than the one in which we are engaged. The door is opened and they are coming in, with expressions of good feelings, and kindness as could probably be expected from uncultivated minds. a stone from the quarry needs polishing to become useful, and we believe there are some here that may be made, (with watchful care) to shine as bright gems in the Temple of the Lord, yes, stars that may spread their twinkling light to distant Tribes. (Brother Walker expresses a wish to be Ordained and do what he can for the spread of the gospel to others as he may be able according to his best understanding) Walker said that too morrow, Arapene, and 6 or 8 others will come forward to be baptized about noon, when it was mentioned to him about going to Little Salt Lake he said I shant be here then, when Br. Young comes along, I shall be away. He is calculating to be off on a trading expedition for 2 or 3 month before he returns. we feel to say that there never was a mission opened with brighter prospects to the scattered children of Ephraim than the one in which we are engaged, and should be unwilling to leave unless called away by as good authority as that by which we were sent here. Did we come here to enrich ourselves in the things of this world? No, we came here to enrich the Natives, and comfort the hearts of the Long, Long oppressed. Let us try the experiment and if we fail to accomplish the object, then say, Boys come away. Amen. We are on hand. Walker is a man of noble mind, he has an Eagles eye, nothing escapes his notice, he sometimes speaks of men, talking two ways, and acting two ways, then says, bats wino, meaning no good. He counsils us to be guarded against the disaffected natives, with as much feeling and anxiety, as a father does his children. . . . If Walker leaves we are still weaker [for] the disaffected Natives are as mad with him as they are with the Mormons.

No Earthly Mercy:
Last Religious Rites for Patsowet

If the Fort Utah winter campaign hoped to bring peace, a violent spring proved that it had failed.

MORLEY TO B. YOUNG, COUNCIL & BRETHREN, 21 APRIL 1850,
BYC 22:2, 27–28.

We just heard by two Utah[s], of the situation of affairs in Utah valey. We learn by them that Pat-sorr-e-ett have been over into S. L. Valley and killed 6 Cattle 2 mules and 2 Horses, and threaten to kill all that they find of the Mormons by laying round Nights, or anytime when found alone, and also will come to kill Walker's cattle, and the Mormons in this place. This is their threatning. If Walker or others make peace with the Mormons they say they are women. Walker says that he wishes the Mormons to go and take Pat-sor-re-ett, Un-ker-wer-kent and Tish-u-nah, and put them out of the way, so that he and others may be at rest and peace so he can lay down and sleep good. Walker says that the Utes, Sowe-ett the Capt. are coming here this season, and wishes to have the trade come here, so that they need not travel among the hostile Indians in the Utah Valey. They want Cattle, Blankets, Hats, Knives, guns, and amunition, all kinds of articles for Indian trade. The Brethren at Utah fort, are hereby requested to be on their guard, as they threaten to kill Mormons & Cattle where they can find them nights are the times for such ones to operate.

The report seems to be confirmed that Grant, Vaskus [Vasquez], Bridger and all the Americans, as expressed by Walker, how many this will imbrace we leave it to you to qualify. Walker seems to wish to expose evry plot and contrivance laid against the Mormons as fast as it comes to his knowledge. Grant has written a letter to Vascus [Vasquez] and others to stir up the Natives to go over into the Newinty Valey they say and see your friends, we are rich and will pay you for your land [but] the Mormans want to get it for nothing we don't kill you for st[e]aling fromm us, and killing our Cattl[e], the Mormoans do that is wrong. Walker says it is not us they love but our trade, the Buckskins when they have settled in the Newinty Valey then Grant & Vascus will write to the states to the big Capts and to have him send on men to come and settle the Valey, and when they have stird them up to gather them, then they will gain and drive the Mormans out of the country. Walker having heard of these movements concluded to stay here till President Young comes. There leaders wish to have the Natives keep this calculation a secret but Walker say[s] he shall tell of it, he wishes to be friends with all white people.

We remain as ever yours in the bonds
Of the Gospel,

Phineas Richards, Clerk   Isaac Morley Prest

N. B. [P.S.] This by request of Br. Walker that we send this information.

Wakara's "secret plot" remains murky, even after he named names for Morley, implicating an unlikely alliance: Hudson's Bay chief trader Richard Grant at Fort Hall and Louis Vasquez and "Old Gabe" at Fort Bridger. If not impossible, such a conspiracy was improbable. Wakara's tale might reflect his insight into how to exploit Mormon paranoia.

The killing of Patsowet (also Pat-sorr-e-ett/Patsovett/Patsowits/Pat-sorr-e-ett), the Ute freebooter who allegedly shot Joseph Higbee at Fort Utah and John Baker at Santaquin, became "almost a lost episode in Utah history," Dale Morgan observed. Isaac Higbee informed General Wells on 28 April 1850 that Patsovett and his brother had "been killing cattle since

JAMES FERGUSON, ADJUTANT GENERAL, NAUVOO LEGION, 26 DECEMBER 1856. Ferguson led many of Utah Territory's early Indian operations before his death in 1863. While heading east to Salt Lake in 1848, Indians near today's Elko "brought a child into camp and made motions to show that his mother was dead and brother Ferguson took him and called him Laman," Mormon Battalion veteran John Borrowman recorded. A headstone near Ferguson's grave in the Salt Lake City cemetery reads, "Pregio de Fusil, Indian Protégé of James Ferguson, Died March 7, 1865 Age 16 Years." *Courtesy John Sharp Ferguson and the Beineke Library.*

the war with the Indians and threaten to kill every white man that he can." "We have been searching for him to kill him, but have not found him yet. But we found his brother and have killed him. We wish you would search for him, and, if he can be found in your valley, to kill him before he can do any more mischief." The next day, with coded ambiguity, Hosea Stout described the Ute's fate: "Pat Souette was arrested & tried & nepoed to day. He escaped over the mountains with some others in the Utah war & came back & was trying to way lay & kill all the whites he could catch alone. One man had been killed coming from San Pete here lately."

Thomas Bullock at the Historian's Office provided the most detailed account:

> Walker had tracked Patsowet to this place & sent a demand for him—Sheriff Freguson, [Chauncey] Webb, & Cap. [George] Grant went up to Camp & brought him down to office, where he was tried—D. B. Huntington Interpreter & condemned to die—he was very boisterous, talking long and loud, but after some force was used, he became quiet, was taken outside the City, where Chaplain [John] Kay, & the Sheriff administered his last religious rites before he died. Several persons were present and witnessed his execution—Patsowet killed Joseph Higbee at Utah.

John Gunnison reported a company near Mill Creek was appointed "to shoot & bury him. He strove manfully against being bound in the council house—but no earthly mercy is shown." The "last religious rites" James Ferguson and John Kay administered may have been evisceration (Stout's "nepoed"), but Gunnison's revised report probably reveals what happened: Chief Patsowits was "caught and killed by the bowstring"—that is, garroted. Gunnison praised such "thorough work," which so impressed the tribes "that they will fear to offend, which is the humane policy." Patsowit's legalized murder was called "the first formal execution in Utah history," but its informal brutality describes a lynching.[49]

THE BIG MORMON CHIEF:
WE CANNOT LIVE WITH BAD INDIANS

Only a profoundly presentist historian would characterize Deseret's Indian policy as passive-aggressive, but on the Mormon frontier, ruthless aggression against Native peoples consistently followed benign peacemaking. Major General Wells claimed in the wake of the Fort Utah fight on 21 March 21, 1850, "we are their friends and not their enemies."

> We send the Indian Horses we took from them—by Gosephine—to Chief Black Hawk, at your place to deliver them, to the owners, or their nearest relatives living. We wish you to see that, evry thing is done up right. We want to show the Indians that we are their friends and not their enemies, We do not want their Horses, Women or Children. We have delivered them up, to Gr[os] ephine, that is all his relatives, except those that have died. If you will come down to conference (and bring Black Hawk along with you if you see proper) we will get the remainder of the Horses together, and you can take them back with you to the Fort, for to dispose of to the rightful owners, or nearest kin.[50]

In early May 1850 Big Chief Brigham sent Wells, his big war chief, to explain "the difference between good Indians and bad Indians" to the good Indians.

BIG CHIEF TO PE-TETE-NETE, WALKER, SOW-EE-ETTE, BLACK HAWK, TAB-BEE AND OTHER GOOD INDIAN CHIEFS, 6 MAY 1850, BYC 16:20.

To Pe-tete-nete, Walker, Sow-ee-ette, Black Hawk, Tab-bee and other good Indian chiefs,
  Friends. The Big Mormon Chief sends you his big war chief, Captain Wells, to talk to you, and do you good. I know the difference between good Indians and bad Indians. There was some bad Indians. They killed our cattle,

[49]Gunnison, *The Mormons*, 147; Church Historian's Office Journal, 28, 29 April 1850, LDS Archives. Madsen, *Exploring the Great Salt Lake*, 380–81n80, summarizes Morgan's notes on this event.
[50]Wells to Higbee and Conover, 21 March 1850, UTMR 1:6, 16.

and shot at white men; and I sent and talked to them, but they would not hear: They had no ears, and kept killing and shooting. They were deaf and bad, and I sent my war Captain and killed some of them. We cannot live with bad Indians. We can live with good Indians, and will do them good. The winter has been hard, and the Indians could not hunt, and they have no bread. I send you some powder and lead for good Indians to hunt with, and kill Deer, Antelope and Bear; but you must not let bad Indians have any of it, for they kill white men and cattle. I give you the Powder and lead to give good Indians, and you must look to them, and not let them fire it away at a mark, and waste it; but kill Deer. You have been friends and we want to do you good, and your good Indians. We will learn good Indians to raise corn. You must bye cows, and raise cattle. We will swap cows, and guns, for Horses and skins. We will give you bread for skins when it grows. We have got but little corn now, so we give you powder, that good Indians can live till corn grows. All Mormon chiefs work, and I want you to work and make a good example to your Indians, and learn them to work, and you will have bread when snow is deep. Deer are few, and you must make corn this year, and learn to work like white men. When you want guns mended, go to the Fort at Utah, and pay in skins. If you want guns for good Indians, bye some, with Horses, Skins &c. If bad Indians kill our cattle you must furnish them, and make them pay for the cattle.

You must take care of your own Indians, and govern them. If bad Indians kill white man, you must kill them, or bring them to us and let us kill them. Where are the Indians who killed Baker?—We do not know all the Indians. You know them. You must attend to these things; you know who they are. We shall look to you to take care of your own bad Indians, for you know them. Indians must not fight. Mormons must not fight. They must kill nobody but bad men, red or white. Bad men, not fit to live, they kill. The Great Spirit says we must kill bad men who kill others. We will swap clothing for skins. We will trade with you for all your skins. You need not go away to trade. I give you this powder and lead. Mormons must not trade powder and lead to Indians. I don't want Indians to try to swap skins with Mormons for powder. Mormons must not trade in powder, and Indians need not ask them. I cannot do Indians good if they don't hear me. I want to do you good. You need not leave this land, good Indians can stay in peace. The Great Spirit give land for all his children. Enough for red children. Enough for white children. All can have as much as they need. They need not leave this land. We like good Indians to stay and learn to work, to raise grain and cattle. There is room for all good men. The Great Spirit loves his good red children, and good white children, and wants them to live in peace. All Indians must live in peace with each other. The Great Spirit loves peace. Tell all Indians, every where, to stop fighting, and be good. Sometimes Mormons sold Indians powder and sometimes they would not sell, and Indians complain. Indians must not complain. Sometimes the Great Spirit (God) send rain, and then he dont send rain. Sometimes God sends high water, and sometimes he dries up the Creek. Sometime ago, God send Buffalo, now he has taken them away. All things belong to God. Mormons do as God does, and when Mormons no swap powder, Indians must not cry. God talks to Mormon chief, and he will tell it to Mormons and Indians if they have ears. Indians must do as God tells them, through Mormon chief, and be good and learn to work, raise grain, and learn all Mormons know. Pe-tete-nete has done good, and brought back our cattle. We will do him good, when we can. You must all do us good, and we will do you good.

Walker, Sow-ee-ette, Pe-tete-nete, Black Hawk, Tab-bee, may come here next September, and Mormon chiefs will make a dinner. You may each of you bring some of your best men, principle men, chiefs, and stay one day. You must send us word what day you will be here, ten days before hand, and we will eat, and smoke together.

You, chiefs, must take care of the powder and all your Indians, and learn to do right. Open your ears to my great war chief; his words are good. He does not love to fight. When bad Indians make him fight he is terrible. Indians cant live when God tells him to kill. He will tell you what God says. Hear his words, and remember them.

This is from your best friend.
Big Chief.

Big War Chief Wells "waited three days to see" Petetenete, Walker, Sowaette, and Black Hawk,

but you did not come. Now I must go back. I leave the Powder and lead for you, you will hear the words of the Big chief and come and see us next fall. I would like very much to see you and talk with you but have no more time to stay. I will say to you that the Mormons Big Chief talks with the Great Spirit and he tells us what to do, and we do as he says. We have nothing against you—you have been our friends, as yet, and we think you always will be. We do not give you the powder and lead to make friends for you are our friends without it, we give it to you because you need it to hunt with, and because we love you, and wish to do you good. If you should see some Mormons going through the country you will not be afraid or displeased because we shall travel all about. We want to see the country and are going to look at it. Good Indians are not afraid of us but they will come to us, when they see us and talk. Listen to the words of the Mormon chief in Utah Valley Bishop Higbee he is a man of peace and will be a Father to you. Now go, and do good, live in peace govern yourselves and all of your men right and you will feel good. And next fall we shall be glad to see [you].[51]

---

[51]Wells to Peteetneet, Walkara, Sowiet, and Black Hawk, 13 May 1850, UTMR 1:6.

As Isaac Higbee told President Young, this did not win over the Utes who gathered on Provo River for their annual fish festival.

> This is to inform you that Walker Sowette and other Chiefs and Indians are here, and not satisfied with out seeing you. They say that they have got a great many horses, and skins to trade for bread stuff and cattle, Gun Powder and lead. They want you to say how they shall trade horses, for Cattle &c. I have read your letter to them. They say they want whiskey and every thing else. They want you to bring Breadstuff to sell to them, they cannot get it here, for we have not got it for them. They want Hats, Caps, Clothing Kettles &c.[52]

The mountain would not come to Muhammad, so Muhammad and the brethren met in Walker's tent two days later.

"MEETING WITH UTES IN UTAH," 22 MAY 1850, BYC 74:42.

May 22nd 1850　10 min to 11

A meeting in Walker's tent in Utah Valley; between B. Young, H.C. Kimball, and the brethren, with Walker, Sowiett, Carrican (Yampabh) Arrapene, Tabba, Shinab, Shinents, SanPitch, Ammaron, Black Hawk, Antaro, Parravohoe (Yampa) Ouaback (Yampa) Poroboach (greyheaded) Toquets, Pasago, Poigan (Medicine man) Stick ma head Ankatush (B.Y's boy) Grosaphene, Tocowetum (Sowiett's bro.) Sieu (Yampabh) Incum

The ceremony of shaking hands occupied a long time and scores yea hundreds came into the tent to shake hands with all of the Whites, and then walked out again, the tent was frequently crowded at a time, which required a good stock of patience in our cramped up situation, being squat down all round the inside of Walker's tent.

Walker opened the conversation; he feels bad, he has lost 8 relations, his heart feels sorry; they were killed beyond the Sandy, on the Wind River Chain; he dont know if it is the Bannuck or Shoshones; at the time we were fighting the Tinpanny Utes.

B.Y. Dimic, tell him our business. We would have brought the wagons over the river but could not. We have brought trade, and will doctor him up.

Walker wants B.Y. to find out who killed his friends, and then to send word to Walker what to do; he is a friend and he loves you. I dont want you to throw me away.

B.Y. I wont throw him away.

Walker. If his folks die when hunting something to eat, all right, but he dont like them to be killed in the night. Last Summer the snakes scalped a squaw, but he did not care about that, he did not get mad at that, but does at this, but let it rest.

---

[52]Higbee to President Young, 20 May 1850, Copybook, 1844–1853, BYC 50:1.

B.Y. Tell him of our journey here, we want to smoke the pipe of peace and be friends, and make an everlasting covenant, and we are come to trade with them.

Walker. I dont want to break friendship.

T. Bullock read a letter from big Chief to Walker. D. Huntington interpreted.

Walker said he understood the letter and would tell Sowiett and others all about it afterwards.

B.Y. We have selected some men to trade with them.

Walker. Will do so to[o].

B.Y. You are my brother, let us be brothers, we want you all to be brothers.

Walker: It is done

B.Y. Will you let some of your young men go and build houses and raise grain &c, and if they will send some of their children to school and we will clothe them and we will make settlements for other chiefs if they like and if some of them will go and make farms.

Walker wants to stay in San Pete close to Mormon's house. At [Little] Salt Lake the Piedes will steal our cattle and run away.

B.Y. We want to raise cattle and grain that they need not go away and be killed.

Walker. I understand it.

B.Y. We have bought the 7 horses back, we want to buy them, altho' some had been stolen from us; we started with the 2 children but one ran away back.

Bro. Wadsworth. We have just seen Holliday's mare here, she was stole about 30 days since, She is in the "Lake" Ute's band.

Tabba. There is three stray horses here.

B.Y. Do you wish to sell your land to the Mormons?

Walker. Dont want you to buy, but settle on it. Mormons love us, we love them, we are hungry now, but let it rest.

Walker. Wanted to know why we took bro Taft from San Pete, he wanted Taft to take him back.

BY (to D.H.) Tell him the Great Spirit loves them, and will bring them to the knowledge of the truth. It makes me feel bad to have to fight and hope I shall have no more of it.

We will leave men to trade with Walker and Sowiett, we are not used to it; our business is to make them our friends and show them the difference of trading. Ask them to come and help us harvest, and we will pay them in grain.

Sowiett: I'll do it.

B.Y. Wants a man to come and herd horses and cattle for him and will feed him and clothe him.

After some further conversation B.Y., H.C.K., T.B. went to Isaac Higbee's at ¼ past I.

After dinner all went down to Sowiett's lodge with Walker and Carrican & Grosaphine.

B.Y. I want Sowiette to be a friend and brother. We esteem him a good man we are his friends, if he knew about us, what we know about them they would be our friends. I want to know if we must make a settlement anywhere in his place (yes). We want them to stay here and help us to harvest (yes).

"Come all ye Sons of Zion" was sung, and "All is well"

When all the Utahs were called in a large round ring, BY then said to these my friends I want you all to be brothers tho' we are strangers. Now, we expect to be intimately acquainted (yes). We have come here to settle on your land but our Father the Great Spirit has plenty of land for you and for the mormons. We want you to learn to raise grain and cattle and not have to go and hunt and be exposed to other Indians, but build houses, raise grain and be happy as we are. If any of you have esteemed us to be your enemies, it is because you have been enemies to us, and what has passed this last winter we want forgotten and not have another occurrence, but be as friends and your children go to school and learn and always do right. We have many things to say to you when you understand them, to tell you of your forefathers, who they were, if you stay here a time and trade. We hope you will get all the powder, guns and clothes you want, and not go anywhere to trade, and if you help us to harvest will pay you in bread that you may have bread next Winter. We want you to be happy, here is one of you men, bro. Walker is now my bro. Arrapine is my bro. Sowiett is a good man, and the Great Spirit teaches us what to do, and he told us to come to this country to do you good. We want you never to fight any other tribes but get your neighbors not to take what is not their own, never to be enemies to each other, and when people steal it makes me mad and then they want fight, it is not good to fight. As soon as we can get you to understand that the Great Spirit wants you to be like your father and you will not have any enemies (and spake in Tongues) Do you understand? (yes)

Dr. Sprague spake in tongues (Arrowpine says he spoke Sioux[])]
B.Y. blessed them in the name of the Lord. Amen (About 5 PM.)
Sowiett rose and spoke.

Another Blood Banquet:
Indian Title Should Be Extinguished

In response to the July 1851 horse thefts, Lorin Farr of Ogden seized Ute hostages, shot a Shoshone leader, and appropriated a band's horses to "let them know that we are their superiors."[53] Brigham Young was not pleased:

In regard to policy, whether is it better to suffer the loss of a few horses than to slay an Indian, who has all his life been taught that it is the sure

[53]Farr to Young, 8 July 1851, BYC 16:21.

way to advancement to steal. Whether it is better to suffer the inconvenience of guarding and watching property, and thereby preserving it from the depredations of Indians, or by neglect and inatention to their own interest, throw temptation in the way of the ignorant Indians, and then pursuing them, slay them, and take their property in retaliation not knowing even to any certainty whether they are the guilty ones, or peradventure it may be some others. I hate to be compelled to think of such things. In all of our intercourse with the snake Indians, they have shown themselves friendly, the very moment our trains entered their country they have always felt safe, and it is believed that the nation at large are decidedly friendly; tis true there may be some among them who will not listen but will steal, now what if they should? does it become us to make a wanton attack upon the nation in consequence thereof, and take their property in retaliation, with *their spirit* and failings; instead of exercising and giving heed to the wisdom which superior intelligence should dictate?[54]

After the May meeting in Wakara's crowded tent, Ute raiders retaliated for the alleged February 1850 murders of eight relatives near South Pass. "Sheriff Ferguson reports Walker & Arapene very discontented & gone up the American Fork so as to fight the Snakes. Sowiette said he would take the Big Mormon Chiefs Council & stay at home," wrote Thomas Bullock. As July 1850 began, overland emigrant John W. Jones gave a brutal description of blind vengeance.

On the 27th June a band of Utes fell on a lodge of Snakes 6 miles west of Bear River at day break & killed 11. They also fell on a lodge of Snakes West of Weber River & killed several—they burnt several lodges—one old Indian was scalped, all appeared dead shots, as each one fell & died on the spot—several being squaws—& one old squaw was apparently secreted behind a sage brush.[55]

Following this report, the Utahs began their rounds and for a season disappeared from history, if not from national politics. Four years after the army's conquest of the Mexican southwest, Congress took action to integrate the vast region into the Union. Dr. John M. Bernhisel, Dartmouth graduate and Council of Fifty veteran, capably represented Deseret's interests, keeping provisional governor Young informed with timely reports. The doctor "had a pleasant interview" with Thomas Benton, who entirely concurred about "the necessity of a regular mail," along with a railroad and wagon road. "You also need a strong military force in your vicinity, which will

[54]Young to Farr, 11 July 1851, BYC 16:21.
[55]Church Historian's Office Journal, 27 June and 1 July 1850, LDS Archives, 14:37, 39.

make an imposing appearance in the eyes of the Indians, and keep them in awe without the shedding of blood," the old bull of the Senate advised. "He also said I do not like the name 'Deseret,' it can never go on the statute book; it sounds too much like desert, and that sound is repulsive." But the "quite friendly" politician "observed that it was clear that we ought to have" a territorial government, and "said he should be happy to see me again on any evening." Stephen Douglas, "though an ardent friend of our cause, is not willing to give us all the territory contained within the present bounderies of Deseret," Bernhisel wrote. "If we be admitted into the Union as a State, Commissioners would be sent out to extinguish the Indian titles, and remove the Indians, and where, he asked, would you remove them to? A portion of it he said must be reserved for Indian territory." Douglas, too, did "not admire the name 'Deseret,' and says he shall insist on the territory or State being called Utah."[56] Mormon leaders had much to ponder.

FIRST PRESIDENCY TO JOHN BERNHISEL, 20 NOVEMBER 1850, BYC, 60:1.

Great Salt Lake City
Nov 20th 1850

Dear Sir:

It is our wish that the Indian title should be extinguished, and the Indians removed from our Territory or Utah: and that for the best of reasons, because they are doing no good here to themselves or any body else. The Buffalo had entirely vacated this portion of the country before our arrival; the Elk, Deer, Antelope & Bear, and all eatable game, are very scarce, and there is little left here (abating the white population,) save the naked rocks and soil, naked Indians and wolves; the first two we can use to good advantage, the last two are annoying, and destructive to property and peace, by night and by day, and while we are trying to shoot, trap and poison the wolves on one hand, the indians come in and drive off, butcher our cattle, and steal our corn on the other, which leaves us little time between the wolves and Indians to fence and cultivate our farms: and if government will buy out and transplant the indians, we will endeavor to subdue the wolves, which have destroyed our cattle, horses, sheep and poultry by hundreds and thousands.

But even this will be no easy task for us, situated as we are in the midst of hills thousands of miles in extent, and beasts for wolf prey scarce, except around the settlement: when deep snows come over the earth, they come

---

[56]Bernhisel to Young, 21 March 1850, BYC 60:9. Benton's sentiments are noteworthy since Young, to rouse "a bitter vindictiveness against the Government," long alleged that Benton conspired "to take troops and pounce upon your wives and children" at Winter Quarters. Bigler and Bagley, *Army of Israel*, 44, 429, 443.

down in droves, and devour all before them, till their voracious appetites are satisfied, then skulk to their burrows till hunger forces them out to another blood banquet; thus during the mist of midnight, when the marksman's eye is dim, have we lost stock enough, to sustain all the inhabitants of Deseret for a long time. Is not this alone bad enough for pioneers of the wilderness to contend with? Most certainly but worse by far, are wild men than wild beasts, for they possess not only the cunning and ferocity of the beast, but by trade with Hucksters, licensed or unlicensed, and by robbing and killing the mountain travellers have become possessed of many excellent fire arms, which added to their native bow and arrow, make them a fearful foe, insomuch that emigrants to California are not safe, except in large companies, well armed, added to close watching, and even then are liable to be divested of all their teams in a dark or thoughtless moment, as many travellers have experienced the past season.

Do we wish the Indians any evil? No we would do them good, for they are human beings, though most awfully degraded. We would have taught them to plow & sow, and reap and thresh, but they prefer idleness and theft. Is it desirable that the barren soil of the mountains valleys should be converted into fruitful fields? Let the indians be removed. Is it desirable that the way should be opened up for a rapid increase of population into our new state or Territory, also to California or Oregon? Let the Indians be removed, we can then devote more time to agriculture, and raise more grain to feed the starving millions desirous of coming hither.

For the prosperity of civilization, for the safety of our mail routes; for the good of the Indians, let them be removed; at least, from the interior of the country, now destitute of game, to sustain their shrunk sinews, to some remote part; suppose on the borders of the wind river chain, where fish, and at least a part of the year, buffalo abound; or on snake river, where are fish and game; or on the eastern slope of the Sierra Nevada, between the northern and southern route to California, where no white men lives, and forests and streams are plenty; or on the western slope of the Sierra Nevada, above the dwellings of the whites, if there be space, so as not to interfere, and where Elk and other game are abundant; or any other point of compass, more congenial to their good.

Should the proper authorities think it best to gather on the east of the rocky mountains, in the [blank] of others, hitherto gathered in like manner, and by their teachers farmers and missionarys teach them agriculture, the arts, sciences, and religion, they would improve faster, being thus removed from old hunting grounds, knowing as many of them now do, the value of bread, then they would be instructed in this region, where they have been accustomed to hunt, and long remembered exploits would be constantly brought to mind by daily observation. Not wishing to dictate the Modus Operandi, or place of their removal, we submit these few suggestions to your disposal, with full assurance that the sooner the Indians of this country are removed to some better country, and instructed properly, the better for them, the better for Deseret, the better for California, the better for the Union, the great whole of the nation.

"It was no part of the policy of Brigham Young and the church leaders to be unduly familiar or treat as equals these degraded tribes of the Salt Lake region," a venerable Mormon historian noted. "President Young was too deeply read in human nature generally, and in Indian nature in particular, to think that the Indians could be helped by the whites."[57] Mormon Indian policy involved seizing their land, destroying anyone who resisted, and enslaving the survivors. Historian Howard Christy characterized Brigham Young's "regrettable strategy of selective extermination" as one of "open hand and mailed fist." It might be better characterized as a choice between handouts or the iron hand, which gave Native peoples a choice between support and submission or suppression. "My text, borrowed from you, is, 'cheaper to feed than fight them,'" Apostle Orson Hyde told Young in 1865. "Yet it is not cheap to feed them."[58]

[57]B. H. Roberts, *Comprehensive History*, 3:457–58.
[58]Christy, "Open Hand and Mailed Fist," 235; Hyde to Young, 23 April 1865, BYC 40:4.

Chapter 4

SPADES, STRYCHNINE, AND ARSENIC
The Dry Earth Utes

Quiet, if not peace, marked Mormon-Indian relations after the Fort Utah fight. The Nauvoo Legion had sown the wind on Provo River, the campaign scattering warlike Utahs across the territory soon to be named after the Indian nation. Congress at last integrated its Mexican conquests into the Union with the Compromise of 1850, which created Utah Territory. Brigham Young became governor and superintendent of Indian Affairs of all the land from the crests of the Rocky Mountains to the Sierra Nevada and between the thirty-seventh and forty-second parallels.

Young and his agents attempted to forge a peace between the territory's Shoshone and Ute nations, but the slaughter and servitude the Mormons inflicted on the Timpanogos would reap a whirlwind for twenty years. Hundreds of "gold diggers" gained firsthand experience with the revolutionary religion's millennial politics when they wintered in the state of Deseret in 1850–51, and many left after unhappy legal and financial struggles with its authoritarian theocracy.[1] Utah's contempt for the federal government and its officers poisoned the well of sympathy that had led a president to pick a Latter-day Saint prophet to administer a federal territory. That Governor Young used his power to promote Mormon interests was true but not surprising. He soon deployed his new military powers against some of the Great Basin's most destitute but resourceful desert peoples.

---

[1]Bigler, *A Winter with the Mormons*, 49–50.

DRY EARTH UTES: GOSHUTES, GOSIUTES,
GOSHIPS, AND GO-SHA-UTES

Americans pronounced Kusiutta, "dry-earth Utes," as Goshute, with many
variations. Usually they simply dismissed Native bands living south and west
of the Great Salt Lake with the epithet "Digger." Culturally close to the
Te-Moak tribe of Western Shoshone, the Kusiutta ranged from the Great
Salt Lake Desert to Spring, Steptoe, Sierra, and Goshute valleys in today's
Nevada, and south to Utah's Sevier Lake, while Western Shoshone bands,
notably the Tosawihi, dominated the Humboldt River from its headwaters to
its great bend at today's Winnemucca. Whites crossing their "miserably and
sparsely" peopled homelands viewed "the miserable Digger" with contempt.
"Humanity here appeared in its lowest form, and in its most elementary
state," Frémont charged. They excited "Asiatic, not American ideas." The
"Goshoots" he saw "along the road and hanging about the stations were small,
lean, 'scrawny' creatures," the "wretchedest type of mankind," Mark Twain
wrote, who inhabited "one of the most rocky, wintry, repulsive wastes that
our country or any other can exhibit." Diggers lived "on roots principally,"
Indian Agent Jacob H. Holeman reported. "It is said they eat anything that
has life in it, from a cricket to a buffalo." To those often called Shoshokos,
meaning "one who goes on foot," Digger was "a term as insulting to a Shoshonee as nigger to an African," noted Richard F. Burton.[2]

"The set called diggers chochoukos are misserable objects nearly altogether
naked and starving the greater part of the year," Hudson's Bay trader Richard
Grant reported in 1844.[3] Brigham Young said overlanders "sometimes without
cause or provocation shot them indiscriminately," which raised a spirit of
"blood for blood and a disposition to plunder and rob, and steal" among
the "exceedingly troublesome" Humboldt River bands "during the rush
to the gold mines in the summer of 1849." "Very many guns were thrown
away as well as traded for little or nothing which enable these Indians to
obtain arms, an article of which they were previously destitute, and which
they have learned to use to good effect—in addition to which many of them
have obtained horses, which made them far more formidable than formerly."

West of the Shoshones and extending to the Sierra Nevada, Young reported,

[2]Frémont, *Expeditions of John Charles Frémont*, 1:701; Twain, *Roughing It*, 146–47; Holeman, 29 March 1852, *The Utah Expedition*, Serial 956, 141; Burton, *City of the Saints*, 476.

[3]Grant to Simpson, 15 March 1844, Hudson Bay Company Archives, D.5/10, folio 426.

are the snake diggers, called Cumembahs, who can scarcely be said to have any habitation, clothing, arms, or any thing else which is generally supposed would contribute to a persons comfort or even be necessary for simple existence. In my first acquaintance with them, they appeared inoffensive and in fact utterly incompetent, and unable to be otherwise, [being] of small stature which appeared to be the result of suffering with cold and hunger, and filthiness, they presented the lowest, most degraded and loathsome specimen of human existence that I ever beheld.[4]

The White Indian Expedition

Across the Oquirrh Mountains from Salt Lake Valley, Tooele Valley (also spelled Tuilla or Tuela) apparently took its name from Goshute shaman Tuu Weta (pronounced Toowuda), meaning Black Bear.[5] Beginning in February 1851, hungry Goshutes, wintering overlanders, and Mormon militiamen met in a series of clashes and campaigns during the Nauvoo Legion's "White Indian Expedition." After dark on 11 February, Ira Willis arrived from the new settlement at Tooele to report "Indians shooting horses & cattle from his herd." Daniel Wells ordered an immediate response but weather postponed action. George Grant "started on the 19th in pursuit" of Indians "or other cattle thieves in Tooele Valley. Twenty more started the next day for Utah Valley, to meet those gone to Tooele." Ever suspicious of outsiders, Mormon leaders had "appointed two men from each ward to keep strict watch over all emigrants in their wards," to search for "stolen animals and white thieves."[6]

By 1843 western tribes were "already well known to be led by desperate white men and mongrels, who form bandits in the difficult passes, and at are all times ready to cut off some lagging emigrant," wrote Marcus Whitman. He "feared that organized banditti will be instituted."[7] Porter Rockwell warned Richard Burton to keep his "eyes skinned" for "'White Indians,' the worst of their kind," as Burton rode a stagecoach west from Salt Lake in 1860.[8] Most of "the robberies and murders which have occurred during the past season" along the California trail were "encouraged and assisted

[4]Young to Commissioner Luke Lea, 13 August 1851, BYC 55:1, 6–7.
[5]Madsen, *Exploring the Great Salt Lake*, 267n21. Professor Wick Miller, a Shoshone language expert, provided this information.
[6]Church Historian's Office Journal, 11 18–21 February 1851, LDS Archives.
[7]Drury, *Marcus and Narcissa Whitman*, 2:397.

by white men," Jacob Holeman reported in May 1852. "The white Indians, I apprehend, are much more dangerous than the red." These "renegades, deserters and thieves," mostly fugitives from California justice, were "more savage than the Indians themselves; by their cruelty to the whites, they have stimulated the Indians to acts of barbarity which they were never known to be guilty of before." Mormons too belonged to "a company of white men and Indians" near Carson Valley planning "to plunder and rob the emigrants." His friend Jack Redden advised him "to paint the horns of his cattle," for the bandits did "not wish to molest the brethren," Tom Williams told Holeman.[9]

Latter-day Saints focused much attention in 1851 on "the emigrants for California, who had been wintering in the Territory." Converted mountaineer James Gemmell charged they "were forming into a band of thieves, for the purpose of plundering cattle and horses, to make their outfit for the gold mines." Gemmell claimed "they had got up a petition, signed by all the emigrants in the valley to send to the U.S. troops at Fort Hall, for the purpose of asking assistance to escape from the hands of the Mormons, whom they represented as robbing them of their all to pay taxes, &c."[10]

Despite much ado, the Legion's winter campaign produced few results. "Strong boisterous wind" proved "very severe on those of our brethren who are under the necessity of being out in pursuit of the Emigrant thieves" at Tooele Valley. "They had arrested Kingsley King—attached Harvey Whitlock's property for debt—and got two yoke of Turner's cattle in addition," officers reported. G. L. Turner, awaiting payment on a contract with Brigham Young to develop roads up City Creek, appears to be the primary cause of the trouble. An exploring expedition of "twenty men to discover stolen animals and white thieves in Utah Valley" arrested two suspected rustlers "armed to the teeth with guns swords & pistols," but accomplished little else. "Sent word to Tooele for the brethren to come home," Thomas Bullock reported on 24 February. The campaign ended on 1 March 1851 when a "secret guard" at the Jordan River bridge shot Brigham Young's brother Lorenzo out of the saddle, supposing "him to be one of the thieves they were laying in wait for."[11]

---

[8]Burton, *City of the Saints*, 173, 449–50.

[9]*The Utah Expedition*, Serial 956, 141, 150

[10]History of the Church, 21:9, 28 February 1851, LDS Archives.

[11]Church Historian's Office Journal, 22–27 February, March 1851, LDS Archives. Turner was the subject of a "general manhunt." See Bigler, *A Winter with the Mormons*, 95n11, 114–15, 216–17.

Shot through the Heart:
The Murder of Lorenzo Custer

The White Indian Expedition proved ineffective, so the war on the Goshutes began again in April 1851 with a "company of volunteers going out against those thieving Indians under the charge of O. P. Rockwell."[12] As the West Desert campaigns dragged on, this one resulted in the execution of four or five Goshutes and the death of Ohioan Lorenzo Custer, who had built a dam for Apostle Ezra T. Benson and was waiting for a final payment of $500. A rare Porter Rockwell letter told the strange tale.

"Last night a man named Custer was killed by the Indians in Toolie Valley," wrote Hosiah Stout. "They had been taken prisoners by the whites & attempting to break away they were pursued by the whites & Custer was shot. The Indians were taken but permitted to keep their arms. A party is going out to night to Toolie against the Indians."[13] Rockwell, relying on Sam Brannan's nephew as his amanuensis, provided an eyewitness report.

ORRIN PORTER ROCKWELL TO BRIGHAM YOUNG, 23 APRIL 1851, BYC 22:19, LDS ARCHIVES.

Tuela Settlement April 23 /51

Prest Young
Dear Sir

We have been out about Eighteen miles from the saw mill and found 30 Indian[s] whom we ordered to go to the settlement. Some of them of the men hurried ahead and under guard. Reached the Settlement before the Rest while the remainder were coming up and a short distance from the Settlement. Some reluctance on the part of the Indians to come in was shown. One of the Indians fired upon Mr Custer who fell from his horse Instantly dead. Mr Custers pistol was found one barrell discharged and three caps bursted. The Indians then made their escape with the exception of four who are now with us as prisoners whom I intend to take along with us as guides. We shall start again to day and wish to have William Kimball Raise as many men as he can to come on our trail with Judson Stoddard. Word will be left behind us of our movements so that the company will understand the route.

The body of Mr Custer will be sent into the City this morning.

P O Rockwell
per Alexander Badlam

---

[12]Wells to Wright, 21 April 1851, UTMR, 29.
[13]Brooks, *The Diary of Hosea Stout*, 22 April 1851, 2:397.

Overlander John J. Galvin of Massachusetts was one of a volunteer company "consisting of sixteen men," including ten Mormons, "to go against the Indians, who, it was thought, had stolen and driven off some cattle and horses from a herd in Toolie valley." Galvin swore an affidavit at Fort Hall on 14 June, saying the company captured ten Indians, hoping to use them as guides to show the volunteers "where the Indians were who stole the cattle and horses." Rockwell spoke to the Indians "in Indian dialect" for some twenty minutes and "thereupon the Indians desisted from warlike operations." Some "wanted to take the guns" from the Indians, but Rockwell said, *"no d——n them, we will make them pack their own guns."* He put Custer in charge of five Indians. His Mormon comrades left "Custer alone with the Indians, who were on foot; *that Custer, about this time, was shot through the heart, and fell from his horse dead."* Four or five days after Custer's death, five Indians "were shot in cold blood by said Rockwell, Lot Smith and Ed. Walker—all 'Mormons'—who gave no reason for shooting them; nor was there any evidence whatever against the Indians, of their having committed any offence." Like others who spent that winter in Deseret, Galvin believed "Custer was murdered for his money and property."[14]

LET NO HOSTILE INDIAN ESCAPE: WAR ON THE GOSHUTES

The Nauvoo Legion renewed its war against the West Desert tribes in June 1851. Gen. D. H. Wells ordered George Grant "to raise some forty Mounted Men" equipped for twenty days' service. Twenty more infantry selected from William McBride's company would "accompany you in wagons." If possible, "let no hostile Indian escape." Wells issued similar orders to Peter Conover at Provo: "The Indians known as the Snake Diggers and probably some others who are associated with them have for a long past time been committing depredations upon the property of citizens of Toole County and notwithstanding every effort has been made to reconcile them and peaceable means used to prevent their predatory excursions they still continue until forbearance has ceased to be a virtue."

Major Grant and Captain Conover lead a two-pronged assault "to cut off the retreat of the Indians." Wells sent Conover west "to the Desert," where

---

[14]Galvin, Affidavit, 14 June 1851, in Bigler, *A Winter with the Mormons*, 133–37.

he would follow the west side of the Mountains," rendezvous with Grant's force to "seek to cut off the retreat of the Indians," and "if possible let no hostile Indian escape you." Wells warned them to protect the lives of their men.[15]

The next day, Wells directed Conover to keep a careful guard and "have your men ready to go at the firing of a gun." Having apparently thought it over, he continued: "The Indians are disposed to feel a little aggravated for various reasons, they are poor and very ignorant and if we pursue the same course towards them as people usually do, we may expect to continue our Expeditions one after another until the Expense will be more than the loss otherwise sustained when all ought to be saved by proper care and watchfulness. And the lives of the Indians saved." If the brethren would be ready and watchful, "we shall hear of no more depredations from the Indians."[16]

According to Peter Gottfredson's chronicle, the "successful expedition" against the Goshutes in Skull Valley that spring was not about saving lives. It was an attempt "to surprise and chastise the savages," who could see William McBride's troops approach "and laughed and jeered at them from the rocky heights" of the Cedar Mountains. Grant's cavalry crossed the desert at night, and the "savages were surprised in their wickiups just at daybreak, and the males almost annihilated."[17]

William McBride: Without a Moment's Hesitation

Of the countless ways humans have devised to murder each other, poison is the most insidious. Tradition and folk tales do not prove that Mormon leaders poisoned "bad" Indians. The documentary evidence is less ambiguous.

Daniel H. Wells to Captain McBride, 20 June 1851, UTMR, 126.

G.S.L. City June 20, 1851

Capn Wm McBride

Dear Bro. We have just received yours of yesterday and are truly gratified to learn that you have discovered the retreat of the Indians, and that you have hopes of recovering some of the stolen cattle and horses. We send this by express to inform you that we shall send the number of men required

---

[15]Wells to Grant and Wells to Conover, 13 June 1851, UTMR.
[16]Wells to Conover, 14 June 1851, UTMR.
[17]*History of Indian Depredations*, 36–37.

during today and night. We shall send them off in small companies of 5 or 6 at a time in order to avoid excitement.* We shall also forward baggage wag-gons, with provisions, water Barrels &c during the day, so that by tomorrow sometime you will have a sufficient reinforcement to proceed with safety, to endeavor to route the Indians and recover the stolen property. In the mean time we wish you to keep a sharp lookout on the foe, and be careful not to be surprised by them either night or day. We trust to your good judgement and prudence, for the safety of you company and for a wise and careful attack when the balance of the men reach you. We wish to avoid excitement here, but still desire your movements to be prompt and decided as soon as your number are sufficiently strong. We should like to be informed as often as anything happens of any importance.

Praying for you success and prosperity in all your lawful undertakings. I subscribe myself your friend and Brother,

D. H. Wells
Maj Gen N.L.

*for we are sick of making so many moves and accomplishing so little.
P.S. Brothers Beers & Romney will bear this to you.

In his after-action report, "Minutes of the Campaign Against the Hostile Indians in June 1851," McBride listed Wilford Hudson, James Ure, William Jones, Benjamin Baker, and Phineas R. Wright as among those sent "to discover if possible the dens and lurking places of the hostile Indians."[18]

CAPT. WM McBRIDE TO GEN'L WELL, 24 JUNE 1851, UTMR, 1328.

Head Qrs. Tooele Expedition No. 3
Third Pasture Creek June 24th, 1851

Sir:
The detachment of Guards joined us at Mountain Spring on the night of the 21st having made the trip (seventy-five miles) within the day and night. Being out of sight of the Indians we lay in camp on the 22d (Sunday) and made arrangements for attack. We divided the command (consisting of fifty-five men) into five parties. I took charge of the first. Lt. Hudson of the second. Serjt [James] Ure of the third. Lt. [Nathaniel V.] Jones of the 4th (composed principally of the officers of the Guards) and Capt. Wright of the fifth. We assembled at Sunset, gave the men some necessary instructions and after an impressive and appropriate prayer from Lt. Jones we started for the plains. At Pasture Creek we filled our casks. The company under Lt. Jones (intended for Cavalry service) here left us for the 2d Pasture Creek,

---

[18]Captain McBride's Report, May–June 1851, UTMR, Doc 102.

with instructions to be on the march before day-break: in order to attract
the attention of the Indians from the other companies; as we intended to
be above and around them to help their retreat. We continued our march
in the dark. At the edge of the plains under cover of the mountains we left
our horses and baggage under Capt. Wright. Our pilot was deceived by the
darkness and struck the mountains too far north. We were on the march
and daylight overtook us before the Mistake was discovered. We here separated the companies; giving each their instructions. We intended to remain
in our anticipated position until Lt. Jones should draw the Indians from
their retreat; when we intended to occupy the position they left while the
cavalry exchanged salutations with them. At four O'C A.M. of yesterday Lt.
Jones made a start. When he arrived at the mouth of the supposed cañon
he found it to be an extended valley filled with pinions and cedar. There
he scouted round a little, and pretty soon about seven or eight Indians were
discovered [in] about half a mile. He then formed his men (nine in number
including himself, two having laid back with the carriage) and made a charge
on the Indians, who were just in the vicinity of the principal camp. ~~Three
of the In~~ They broke for a rocky mountain close by; when he was obliged
to halt. Only three of the Indians could be seen. He fired on them and
wounded one who threw away his gun. They fired only one shot in return,
but it came close enough, to cut a hole through Capt. Kimball's neckerchief.
Four of the men having necessarily been thrown into a group. The scarcity
of Jones's men, and incapacity of the horses prevented their pursuing their
charge after the Indians and he soon discovered them on the top of a lofty
peak, their number having now increased to about thirteen or fourteen. He
then detached two parties, one in pursuit of the Cattle trail, and the other
in search of the foot companies. The Cattle trail gave out, and the horses'
trail spread into numerous single tracks. Lt. Hudson was discovered on the
top of a mountain having joined some of Ure's Co. to his: nearly half of his
men were melted down, and now fainting from exhaustion: he gave the same
report of the other Co: they having taken a more circuitous route. They had
marched afoot ten miles over the mountains; before they ~~observed~~ reached
their destination. Lt. Hudson, after some rest went up with a few men to
the peak where the Indians were seen. They had principally retreated: three
however still remained. One of his men, Baker, a most excellent shot, fired
at one, and brought him on to his all fours. Further pursuit that evening
was impossible. Some of the men had not yet come in and little [William]
Jones (the tailor) had not been heard of (nor was found till a scout party
went out for him and found him at Sunset, accidentally).

The Indians at their camp dug a hole in a ravine and found water enough
to suit them—but of no use to us. They had at least fifteen head of cattle
and horses butchered recently, and concealed in the cedars—they also left
many of their traps and camp equippage, consisting of frying pans, water

cans, tin dishes, baskets, powder horns, bullet-molds, fishing nets &c &c. We went round and burned everything we could find, including the meat, which was principally dried. The density of the cedar forests prevented our making any discovery ~~retreat~~[?] ~~of the~~ of the hiding places of the squaws. We then formed and marched back to this place on the opposite side of the valley. Tonight we intend sending a party across to try them again, though we shall all soon have our seats burned—for the brush and cedars are raising hell with our clothes. We want you to send back instructions whether we shall continue. It will take a good many misfortunes to discourage us now. We wish you *without a moment's hesitation* to send us about a pound of *arsenic.* We want to give the Indians' well a flavour. Also a spade to dig for water. A little strickenine would be of fine service, and serve instead of salt, to their too-fresh meat.

Most obediently &c &c
Capt. Wm. McBride

Don't forget the arsenic!
Don't forget the spade and arsenic!
Don't forget the spade, stricknine and arsenic!

Upon receiving this, Wells characterized McBride as "on the hunt" and assured him the general felt "the highest Esteem" for him, but then threw in the towel. Routing the men while seizing the women and children was the best policy, Wells wrote.

D. H. WELLS TO CAPT. MCBRIDE, CA. 25 JUNE 1851, CHURCH HISTORIAN'S OFFICE LETTERPRESS COPYBOOK 1844–1853, 108–109.

Capt. McBride & Company
    Your express of 24th inst. was received 11. Oclock P.M. same day. We feel as though your enterprise was a difficult and dangerous one to accomplish.
    The Indians will be able to subsist upon insects, and Juniper Berries, under every bush; and will probably scatter in every direction, one or two in a place. Want of water only, will bring them together and after the routing and surprise, you can then through the detachment of Lieut. Jones. They will most probably be cautious of assembling together in that vicinity, soon again; it may be possible they have other watering places; of this however you have the best chance to know. You cannot for any length of time remain nearer than 15 miles of them for the want of water. You cannot track them at this season of the year.
    These considderation seems to preclude the possibility of effecting any thing against them at present; and yet it appears necessary for the peace and security of our settlement, that they should be routed. We prefer routing them

and bringing in their squaws, and Children if possible, as the best policy, and one that will have the best and most lasting effect upon the residue. (If there should happen to be any left which must nescessarily be the case) as well as upon other tribes.

This morning you are again on the hunt, to night you will receive this express, after yours, this days hunt we doubt not. Your strongest efforts will have been brought into requisition before this reaches you; if so, and you have no better, or more certain prospect, we think you had better close this expedition; beliving the lessons they have already received, will be a salutary lesson to them. The articles you sent for as mentioned in your letter are not to be obtained, except some articles which we send, together with some other things, which we all believe you need; We are well aware how desireable it is to use up the Band of theiveing Indians, both for the safety of property and to prevent expense.

But how far you will be able to accomplish any thing, we canot judge; We must leave the matter to your own discretion. If you seek to continue your efforts it will be right, and if you think it best to cease for the time being, it will also be right; act according to your best judgment and all will be well.

We offer our unceasing prayers in your behalf for your success, and support, and believe us when we tell you that we should considder it a dear bought victory, no matter how complete it might be, if it were in preserveing the expence of any one of you.

With sentiments of the highest Esteem I remain
Truly yours/D. H. Wells

The order's priority was "to use up the Band of theiveing Indians" to protect property and save money. The requested "articles," perhaps strychnine and arsenic, were "not to be obtained," but being "well aware how desireable it is to use up" thieving Indians, Wells sent McBride something, perhaps cyanide and spades.

The third 1851 Tooele Expedition ended ambiguously. At McBride's camp on 25 June at 1:05 A.M., "prayer was offered to the God of the armies of Israel by adjutant James Ferguson." At daybreak, detachments "continued up different ravines—& discovering a fresh Indian Track the Charge was ordered and the Indians Soon overtaken—firing then Commenced and in one hour eight Indians were Killed and another went off Bleeding profusely—The Squaws & Children being a Secondary Consideration were left for future pursuit." The soldiers "made another war offering"—an execution?—"and hunted again," running down a man who dismounted, ran an arrow into a mare's lungs "up to the feathers" and escaped. "We held A Council," McBride wrote, which "Concluded Considering that we had no horses fitted for the arduous Service of a Charge among the rocks & cedars to return."[19]

Blood on the Rocks: Lieutenant Hamblin

"Apostle to the Lamanites, friend of the Indians, frontiersman, pathfinder, peacemaker, Mormon Leatherstocking, and Dirty Finger Jake. These are a few of the designations that have been used to characterize the Indian missionary, Jacob Hamblin," wrote historian Charles S. Peterson. Critics charged that Hamblin was "reckless with the truth, a tireless self-promoter, or a coward," but the rough frontiersman became a western legend.[20] The apostle in buckskin was seen as a shaman to the Hopi, Navajo, and especially the Southern Paiute, who believed he had the power of life and death. "Paiutes don't see Jacob Hamblin the way Mormons do," Shivwits elder Glenn Rogers said in 2016. Hamblin "was very powerful, but Paiutes feel he used his power against them."[21]

After reaching Utah in 1850, Hamblin's family settled in Tooele, where the people "built their houses in the form of a fort, to protect themselves from the Indians, who frequently stole their horses and cattle. Men were sent against them from Salt Lake City, but all to no purpose. The Indians would watch them during the day, and steal from them at night." Years of this border warfare left "no safety for our horses or cattle." As a Nauvoo Legion lieutenant, Hamblin went "on several expeditions against the thieves, but without accomplishing much good. They would watch our movements in the canyons, and continually annoy us."

Hamblin was deeply superstitious and devoutly religious. He recalled planning to camp overnight with his wife in a nearby canyon while gathering wood and fruit, but "a feeling came over me that the Indians were watching with the intention of killing us during the night." He packed up and went home. His wife asked how he knew the Indians were there. He had not seen or heard them, but "knew it on the same principle that I knew the gospel was true." Investigating the next day, he concluded "an Indian known as 'Old

---

[19] Ibid.

[20] Peterson, "Jacob Hamblin," 21, 23.

[21] Will Bagley, Monumental Mistakes: Mountain Meadows, 2014 to 2016, 10 September 2016, 17, Bagley, Papers, Accn1937, Special Collections, Marriott Library.

Big Foot'" had robbed other wagons that night. Hamblin "thanked the Lord that he had warned me in time to save my wife and child, as well as myself."[22]

Capt. P. R. Wright's report to Judge John Rowberry of the "Indian Expedition Commanded by J Hamblin 3 Lieut" between 12 and 15 March 1852 survives in the territorial militia records. Hamblin's papers at LDS Archives include his "Record of the Life of Jacob Hamblin as recorded by himself," while James A. Little's faith-promoting tale show how time transforms real events into legends.

Hamblin reported his twelve-man 1852 expedition:

> March the 12th we received an express from Grantsvill that the Gosutes Indians were in the Tooile valley fresh tracks being seen by the Indian that lives at Grantsville. We Procceded forth with to Grantsville. The next day about 10 oclock came upon the Indians 6 in number camped on the side of the mountain 18 miles west of Grantsville. The company being discovered by there sentinal in about half a mile before reaching the camp which gave the Indians a chance to scater on the mountain before our men could git to them or Break off there Retreat. However the most active of them succeeded in heading one Indian who was skulking behind some Rocks. The Indian Jack socalled that Lives at Grantsville being along with the company shot at the Indian skulking behind the Rocks and mist him. At this the Indian sprung after Jack with a volley of arrows Jack running towards Liuet Hamblin who was watching the movements and Leveled at his Brest on the aproch of the Indian which did not see Hamblin until he was within 25 ft of him when Hamblins gun missed fire. The Indian then directed his arrows at him and kept coming closter [sic] at which Hamblin gathered a rock and hit the Indian full drive in the Brest which made him turn on his heels and run. This gave Hamblin time to put another cap on this gun and fire at him on the run but his cap Busted the second time and the Indian got away. The caps were some that he had Borrrowed which proved no good however the rest of the company were Blazing away at them the Best they could and some of the Indians was Badly wounded so supposed by the Blood on the rocks as they followed them some 5 miles. In there flight they Left there moccacines, all but one and took there flight Barefooted.[23]
>
> P. R. Wright   Capt

Hamblin's manuscript autobiography begins mid-sentence in 1851 but was written much later.

---

[22]Little, *Jacob Hamblin*, 27–28.

[23]"Itims of the Expedition," UTMR 2:4, 1332. Wright signed the report but Hamblin probably wrote it.

JACOB HAMBLIN, AUTOBIOGRAPHY, 1850–1854,
MS 14654, LDS ARCHIVES.

[After settling in Tooele in 1850,] we ware pesterd with the Indians. They ware continualy coming out from the mountains which was their lurking plases and Steeling Cattle and horses. Thare was Several attempts maid to Stop them but to no affect. Thare was one expedicion under the command of Capt Porter Rockwell. He took Some 20 or 30 Eutaws nere fresh Lake [Rush Lake] 7 or 8 miles from our Settlement. While comeing in an affrey took plase in which one Mr Custer was kiled an Emigrant. The [Ute] Prisioners maid their ascape and fled except 5 they ware taken out and shot. This act alarmed the Setlers of toela they asked for council. It was decided that a Fort S[h]ould be built of the houses, that we Should be on the watch. We tore down our housees built them in order, guarded our Cattle and cultivated our fields. We managed in this way for 18 months, the Indians takeing our cattle whenever opertunity presented.

Capttain wright Sent me with 14 men to asertain Somthing with with [*sic*] regard to them if possible. I acordingly proceded to willow creek the distance of about twelve miles. Lerning thare had ben alight seen on the west mountains I took Bro Sevier [Harrison Severe] with me and road untill about 12 oclock at nigh[t]. When we Saw alight in the moutains we returned as quick as possible. Took the company and Started for the Spot. We began to assend the mountain [as] daylight appeard. I then devided the company. Asended the mountain in two Canions with the intention of Surpriseing the Indians and all we could. When we came up to the camp we found but to familys. The two Indians their women and childrin run up the mountain Schreching as they fleed, expecting to be Shot. We run in a hed of them and they Stopt. Thare was several Shots fird at them none took affect when I herd the Schreems of the chirldin. I could not bare the thought of killing one of them. We brought them home with us. Gave them povisions blankets and treated them k[i]ndley.

In a bout one month from that time a portian of the Same band came again to Steel cattle and was discoverd by one of the Indians we brought in. I took charge of another company and was on our way by 12 oclock at night. The next morning about Sunrise we discoverd their trail. Road about 10 miles. Found whare they had buried a larg pile of roots. The Indian I took with for a pilat Said we would find them at the nex water. We acordingly found them thare drying them selves by a fire. We came upon them Sudently. They left their legins mogisohn and fled among the rocks. We heded Some of them. I met one of them as I raised my gun to fire. The poor fellow begd for mercy. I thought it would be a neglect of duty if I let him pas but my gun mist fire. As quick as thought he threw an arow at me but fortunately it Struck the gard of my gun. We boath Sprung for a rock that ly betwene us.

I evaded two more of his arrow threw threw [*sic*] a Stone at him and So he past by. I burnt two more caps at him but my gun would not go. Several of the company had fair Shots clost by but their guns mist fire. We felt vexed at our first of our ill Success as we killed none of them but we finily concluded it was all wright that the Lord had youse for them. So we returnd home. The manner we had treted the Lamanites that we had taken prisoners had good influance in that tribe. In three months from that time the hole tribe came in and wanted to liv with us and be brothers promiceing to S[t]eel no more.

In July 1853 Walker the King of the Eutah nation commenced depredations on the Saints in Iron County killing three or fore of the Brothering and Steeling catle. The gouvner Brigham Young advised all the Settlements in the Teritory to Fort up and enclose their Cittys with good Subtantial walls. Tharefore I was employd moveing my houces and putting them up again and cultivating the Earth until April Conferance 1854 when I was chosen to go South with P.P. Pratt on a mishion to open up the Gospell to the Lamanittes.

Fifty years later, Thomas Atkin recalled the war on the Goshutes. Grantsville settlers "requested assistance from Tooele to route them. Accordingly about eight of us under the direction of Jacob Hamblin started about midnight" with "no saddles Indian fashion." Before daylight they began their pursuit in the Stansbury Mountains. They

> suddenly came in full view of the band of Indians we were in search of camped by a spring near the mountains. As soon as they saw a troop of horsemen riding rapidly towards them they made a break for the mountains, leaving all of their effects and by the time we were opposite to them and dismounted the Indians were half way up the mountain side. We left our horses at the foot of the mountain and pursued them on foot a considerable distance in the mountains, firing upon them when an opportunity permitted. Our captain, Jacob Hamblin, overtook one of the Indians and tried to fire on him, but his rifle missed fire on account of the dampness of the weather. The Indian then turned on him with his bow and arrows, but Jacob finally put the Indian to flight by using one of the abundant supply of rocks in self defence. Our short expedition checked their depredations for a while.[24]

James A. Little edited Hamblin's recollections in 1881 in his "Faith Promoting Series," recasting his bloody story as a hero's tale in which Hamblin "asked for a company of men to make another effort to hunt up the Indians." They "traveled at night and watched during the day." They discovered a band and at daybreak "surrounded their camp before they were aware of our presence." Their chief "sprang to his feet," and said, "I never hurt you, and

---

[24]Atkin, Life Sketch, circa 1901, Typescript, MSS A 6019/5, USHS, 1–2.

I do not want to. If you shoot, I will; if you do not, I will not." Hamblin could not speak the language, "but I knew what he said. Such an influence came over me that I would not have killed one of them for all the cattle in Tooele Valley." The running women and crying children aroused his sympathies: "I felt inspired to do my best to prevent the company from shooting any of them." He asked "some of the men to go" to Tooele. The Goshutes accepted Hamblin's "assurance that they should not be injured." But his "superior officer ignored the promise of safety I had given the Indians, and decided to have them shot." Hamblin claimed he said that "if there were any shot I should be the first" and placed himself "in front of the Indians. This ended the matter and they were set at liberty."

This exasperated his neighbors, but Hamblin claimed "a different feeling actuated" him. Yet "the presiding Elder directed me to take yet another company of men, go after the Indians, to shoot all we found, and bring no more into the settlement." His men surprised the Goshutes "near a large mountain between Tooele and Skull Valley." Hamblin "secreted myself behind a rock in a narrow pass" where he thought some Indians "would attempt to escape." One soon came within a few paces. "I leveled my rifle on him, and it missed fire. He sent an arrow at me, and it struck my gun as I was in the act of recapping it." A second arrow "passed through my hat; the third barely missed my head; the fourth passed through my coat and vest." He "defended myself as well as I could with stones. The Indian soon left the ground to me."

Hamblin later claimed that "a special providence had been over us, in this and the two previous expeditions, to prevent us from shedding the blood of the Indians." A skeptic might attribute the lack of bloodshed to defective firing caps, since Hamblin learned "that not one was able to discharge his gun when within range of an Indian" and the only injury the fight inflicted was a slight arrow wound. His memoir claimed more:

> The Holy Spirit forcibly impressed me that it was not my calling to shed the blood of the scattered remnant of Israel, but to be a messenger of peace to them. It was also made manifest to me that if I would not thirst for their blood, I should never fall by their hands. The most of the men who went on this last expedition, also received an impression that it was wrong to kill these Indians.

Despite this, on "a fourth expedition against them, we again surprised their camp," but when Hamblin saw barefooted "women and children fleeing for their lives, over the rocks and through the snow leaving a trail of blood," he finally made up his mind "that if I had anything more to do with Indians, it would be in a different way." Except for one: "learning that 'Old Big Foot' was there, and feeling that he deserved killing," Hamblin "found his trail and followed it." A feeling came over him not to go near "a cedar tree with low, thick foliage." Big Foot later told him, "placing his finger on his arrow, if, when you followed me in the cedar hills, you had come three steps nearer the tree where I was, I would have put an arrow into you up to the feather."

After the expedition, Hamblin "dreamed, three nights in succession, of being out west, alone, with the Indians that we had been trying about three years to destroy." He saw himself "walk with them in a friendly manner, and, while doing so, pick up a lump of shining substance, some of which stuck to my fingers, and the more I endeavored to brush it off the brighter it became." The dream so impressed him "that I took my blankets, gun and ammunition, and went alone into their country." He hunted deer and duck with them for several days, "occasionally loaning them my rifle, and assisting to bring in their game. I also did all I could to induce them to be at peace with us."[25]

SUFFERING BORDERING ON STARVATION

Thanks to the diplomatic skills of Thomas Kane and John Bernhisel, President Millard Fillmore appointed Brigham Young governor of Utah Territory on 20 September 1850. When Congress created "a Utah Territory" as summer ended in 1850, it did so "regardless of all our feelings in the matter," Brigham Young complained the day after the president signed "An Act to establish a Territorial Government for Utah." The Saints could only "yield our quiet acquiescence" and urge "the early adjustment of our boundaries and acceptances of our constitution and admission." Having recently "repelled Indian invasion" and explored the country, "all at their own expense," the king of the Kingdom of God wanted a sovereign state named Deseret, not a federal territory named after savages.[26]

Young learned of his appointment on 27 January 1851 after visiting Ogden. Irony attended the occasion, for wintering overlander Jotham Goodell had

[25]Little, *Jacob Hamblin*, 28–32.
[26]Young to Bernhisel and Babbitt, 10 September 1850, BYC 60:1.

just heard Mormon leaders proclaim "their determination never to be the 'territory of Utah.'" They were "the 'state of Deseret,' and they would be nothing else."[27] Young now had much to celebrate, for he was now commander-in-chief of the militia and would "perform the duties and receive the emoluments of superintendent of Indian affairs," for an annual salary of $2,550. In February 1851 Congress authorized the appointment of Kentuckian Jacob H. Holeman as Indian agent and Missourian Henry R. Day and Stephen B. Rose, a New Jersey Mormon, as subagents for Utah Territory. Young began acting as Utah's *ex offico* superintendent of Indian affairs after Day and Rose arrived on 19 July. (Holeman followed on 9 August.) Rose adapted to Superintendent Young's singular style, but controversy embroiled his fellow officials.[28]

Governor Young's appointment produced mixed results. His enhanced power immediately began alienating non-Mormons. Four days after territorial secretary Broughton Harris arrived, the governor told him, "Politicians are a stink in my nose." Terrified, Justices Lemuel Brandebury and Perry Brocchus fled Salt Lake on 28 September with $24,000 in federal gold hidden in Secretary Harris's carriage. Young outmaneuvered the "runaway judges" in the ensuing scandal, historian John Turner noted, "partly because the appointees lacked powerful political allies in Washington and partly because of the church's adroit and coordinated response."[29]

The Prospect of Peace and Friendship: Jacob Holeman

Conflict flourished in Young's Indian office. Due to Mormon hostility "to the government of the United States and its officers," Henry Day returned to Washington and soon resigned. Jacob Holeman was made of sterner stuff. Young initially praised the agent for sparing "no pains to make himself useful." Historians often dismiss Utah federal officers as political hacks: some were, but as Dale Morgan noted, "Holeman showed himself a zealous public servant" who did his best to protect Native interests.[30] He objected to Young distributing Indian goods as presents "for the purpose, no doubt,

---

[27]Bigler, *A Winter with the Mormons,* 49–50.

[28]Morgan, *Shoshonean Peoples,* 58.

[29]Turner, *Brigham Young,* 201–204.

[30]Morgan, "The Administration of Indian Affairs in Utah," 61.

of conciliating the Indians and getting their permission to extend his settlements, thus making use of his office, as superintendent, and the money of the government to promote the interest of his church." He had "no doubt but every effort will be made by the Mormons to prevent the government from peaceably extending her laws over the Territory"—and when Holeman told Indian Commissioner Lea that "no Mormon should, officially, have anything to do with the Indians," Mormon politicians and judges began systematically harassing him. Holeman persisted, noting Young "has been so much in the habit of exercising his will, which is supreme here, that no one will dare to oppose anything he may say or do." Holeman intended "to discharge my duty to the government faithfully, without fear, favor, or affection to any one." Brigham Young never hid his contempt for his responsibilities as a federal officer. "I do not care a groat," he told the Indian commissioner in June 1855, "whether the department or the government ever contribute a penny towards the support of the Indian relations, for the suppression of Indian hostilities, or any other public purpose or object in or for the Territory of Utah."

Primary sources seldom give Goshute and Western Shoshone peoples voices; the reports of federal agents about the western Great Basin are an exception. At a time when American explorers such as Frémont could only speculate about the unexplored "almost unknown" lands between the Humboldt and Mojave rivers, desert peoples were the masters of its vast geography. Jacob Holeman stands out, for he alone failed to denounce the desert dwellers as "filthy looking beings" who subsisted "mostly on roots, crickets, insects, &c.," as Henry Day did. Holeman's 1852 and 1853 Humboldt reports identified their bands and leaders, demonstrating an appreciation of their intelligence and skill as survivalists.[31]

During the summer of 1851, Subagent Day held councils with Ute leaders, who showed "much deference to Walker," acknowledging him "as their war chief, and Sow-er-ette as their head civil chief; but the majority obeyed Sow-er-ette, including Wakara. They all expressed a willingness and desire to cultivate the soil, provided the Mormons would not drive them off from their lands." Day talked with Soweitte and Shoshone leader Cut-nose at Fort Bridger on 1 October 1851, hoping "to make peace between them."

---

[31]U.S. House, *The Utah Expedition*, Serial 956, 125, 131–35, 140–41.

Day to Lea, 2 January 1852, U.S. House, The Utah Expedition,
Serial 956, 130–32.

These nations have been at war for many years, and there seemed to be a
deadly hatred between them. After a council of several hours, during which
time they recounted their alleged causes of quarrel, I told them their Great
Father wished them to be at peace with all the different nations of Indians
and with the whites, and that they must not steal; which, after smoking the
calumet of peace again, they all clasped hands and agreed to. The Indians
complained bitterly of the treatment they had received from the Mormon
settlers from the time they first entered the Territory up to the present, such
as driving them off of their lands, stealing their stock, &c.

I can, perhaps, convey their ideas better by giving you the language of the
old chief, Sow-er-ette, who, raising himself up to his full height, said to me
"American good! Mormon no good! American friend. Mormon kill, steal."

The chiefs said they claimed all the lands upon which were settled the
Mormons, and that they were driving them further every year, making use
of their soil and what little timber there was, and expressed a wish, if their
Great Father was so powerful, that he would not permit the Mormons to
drive them out of the valleys into the mountains, where they must starve.

Jacob Holeman devoted much of 1852 to peacemaking—a challenging
task, since that year saw the largest overland numbers. Holeman noted in
May 1852 that two hundred Bannocks "had made a move for the Humboldt,
for the purpose of joining in the plunder of the emigrants." In July he visited
a village of some 350 Northern Paiutes. He found them "friendly disposed
but somewhat excited, on account of the frequent abuses which they had
received from the whites."

I held a talk with them of several hours—four of their chiefs and many
of their principal men were present—in all of which they manifested the
greatest friendship, and seemed very much pleased with the idea of being
on friendly terms with the whites. They said they "did not wish to be mad
with the whites, or to war with them; but that the whites had got mad with
them, and were always at war with them; that they could not hunt or catch
fish for their squaws and children, for fear of the whites, who were constantly
shooting them; that the whites would profess friendship, call them to their
camp, and shoot them; that the whites would steal their horses, and sometimes
take them by force," with many other charges of an aggravated character. All
this they said "they had borne for a long time; at length, some of their young
men determined to retaliate, and that they had killed as many whites as the
whites had killed Indians, and taken as many horses from the whites as they
had taken from them. They were now satisfied, and if the whites would let

them alone, they would disturb the whites no further." They said they had "never wished to be at war with the whites; that they wished peace, and had kept from the road to be out of the way; that they could see them passing every day, but had not interrupted them in any manner, and that they would not, if the whites would let them alone." The candor with which they talked, and the seeming justice of their course, induced me to put much confidence in their professions of friendship. That they have been treated badly there is no doubt. These whites who loaf about the country, pretending to trade with the emigrants, are principally men of a reckless character, and care but little what they do; they even talked of driving me from the country, because I had manifested a disposition to protect and befriend the Indians. These Indians seem to be very poor; but few of them have guns; they use principally the bow and arrow. Two of the chiefs and six warriors returned with me to my camp. I gave them some provisions and a few presents, and sent the other two chiefs also a present. They were much pleased, and promised me that none of their men should disturb the whites in future. If the whites would pursue a friendly course towards these Indians, and treat them kindly, I do not think there would be any trouble with them.[32]

Holeman made a similar report to Brigham Young that fall about "this mountain tribe" who "professed friendship and great respect for the whites." He met many Indians on the Humboldt in small parties, but "it was difficult to get a talk with them." Those he met "seemed remarkably friendly, and were much pleased with the kindness and friendship shown them by our company." They "had no wish to be at war with the whites," but the whites "were always at war with them" and "they could not hunt or fish on the river but the whites were shooting them." The whites lured them into their camps and "without any cause or offence on their part, would shoot them down." Holeman gave them presents "and advised them to keep off the road—move their lodges into the mountains while the whites were passing." He could not "believe that the depredations and murders which have occurred on this route can be attributed to them."

The "Pi-utah tribe" on Carson River proved friendly and "expressed great anxiety to be on friendly terms with the whites. They said they had never disturbed the whites or their property until the whites commenced killing them, and robbing them of their horses." They long submitted "but, finding that the whites continued to harass them, they determined to retaliate" and "had killed as many whites as the whites had killed Indians, and taken as

---

[32]Holeman to , 30 August 1852, U.S. House, *The Utah Expedition*, Serial 956, 151, 155–56.

many horses from the whites as the whites had taken from them, and no more." They were satisfied, "and if the whites would let them alone, they would let the whites alone, and that their hearts would be glad." Holeman gave them provisions and a few presents "as a gift from their Great Father." The Northern Paiutes "seemed much pleased at the prospect of peace and friendship with the whites," and promised "they would not disturb them or their property again."[33]

The Whites Who Infest the Country:
Jacob Holeman, 1853

Jacob Holeman filed a report the day after he returned from Carson Valley in 1853, giving Brigham Young, "as minutely as time and circumstances will admit, an account of my expedition" using "the substance and language of the Indians on all the most important matters." The agent described bands he called Shoshonees, Pa-nacks, Pintahs, and the "very troublesome" Washaws—today's Western Shoshones, Bannocks, Northern Paiutes, and the Washoes who dominated the central Sierra Nevada and spoke a unique, non-Numic language. He named their leaders and estimated they numbered about three thousand souls. Holeman identified the white criminals among them as principally men from California who occupied "every point where good food is to be found." Their attacks on Native bands caused most of the violence on the Humboldt. Trading posts now lined the trail from California to within 150 miles of Great Salt Lake City. "Their stock in trade consists principally of liquors; scarcely an article is found that the emigrants stand most in need of." They took advantage of conflicts "and steal, and commit more depredations than the Indians, all of which they manage to have charged to the Indians." Some of them persuaded Indians to "steal stock from emigrants, and run them off into the valleys in the mountains." After the emigrants passed, "they would bring out guns, ammunition, blankets, &c., and trade with them for the stock stolen." When Holeman threatened putting "the laws in force against them," they laughed: "they defied me and the laws; they told me there were so many of them that they could and would do as they pleased, law or no law." It was useless "to attempt what I had not the power to enforce," he wrote. In his last official act as Utah

---

[33]Holeman to Young, 25 September 1852, in *Annual Report,*Serial 658, 151–52.

territorial Indian agent, Holeman wrote the best surviving description of mid-nineteenth-century Native culture in the western Great Basin.

HOLEMAN TO YOUNG, 30 SEPTEMBER 1853, LEA, COMMISSIONER
OF INDIAN AFFAIRS, SERIAL 690, 203–207.

By instructions from your excellency, dated June 30, I left this city on the 6th July, for an expedition to visit the Indians on the Humboldt and Carson rivers. In the course of my journey I met with various small parties of Indians, principally of the Shoshonee or Snake tribe, until I arrived at Thousand Spring valley, where I met with the chief of a band of the Shoshonee tribe, by the name of Too-ke-mah, (the rabbit,) whose band numbers about 600. I had previously met a party of his band on Goose creek, who informed me that their village was in the mountains, some distance from the road. I employed one of the party to proceed to the village and invite the chief and his band to meet me in Thousand Spring valley. He, Too-ke-mah, and a portion of his band, met me accordingly. After a talk, having found them friendly disposed to the whites, and he having promised a continuation of his friendship, I gave him some presents, to be distributed among his tribe as he might think proper, leaving to him the selection, as I had not presents to give to all. He seemed much pleased with the kindness and attention shown him, and promised that no difficulties should occur to the whites, so far as he was concerned; that he and his band would not only treat them with kindness, but that they would render them any assistance in their power. Too-ke-mah and his band claim the country adjacent to Thousand Spring valley, and west as far as the Humboldt. When I arrived on the Humboldt I met various straggling parties of the Shoshonee tribe, who belong to a band under the chief, Ne-me-te-kah, (man-eater,) whose band numbers about 500. I laid by two days, and sent two of his band in search of him; they brought him to my camp, accompanied by his son and several of his braves. I found him quite an intelligent Indian, noble in appearance, and a particular friend to the whites. He had never permitted any of his bands to disturb the whites; he told me there were bad Indians on the Humboldt, they would sometimes steal from the whites; but if they did not cease their depredations upon the whites, he would collect his band together and make them. I gave him some presents, which he received very friendly, but told me he did not take them as pay for his friendship; he was, and always had been, a friend to all the whites who travelled the road; that as his great father the big captain (meaning the President) had sent them to him, it made his heart glad, and he never would forget it. He sent two of his braves with me; one Paut-wa-a-raute, (the drowned man,) who has a separate band of about 200, occupying the country around and about the first crossing of the Humboldt, and directed them to find a chief, a friend of his, who resides near

Stony point, called Oh-hah-quah, (yellow-skin,) who has a band of about
450, also of the Shoshonee tribe. They accompanied me to the village, but
Oh-hah-quah was absent on a hunt, and could not be found. I gave them
some presents, and sent some to their chief. All promised friendship to the
whites, and seemed much pleased.

Two of Oh-hah-quah's band accompanied me down the Humboldt upwards
of one hundred miles. They enabled me to see many Indians, as they knew their
haunts, all of whom promised friendship. About seventy-five miles from the sink
of the Humboldt I met with a party of Bannacks, belonging to a band under
their chief, Te-ve-re-wena, (the long man.) Two of them accompanied me to the
sink for the purpose of finding the chief; he, with many of his braves, was out
in the mountains on a hunt. They promised to meet me at their village, near
the Big Meadows, on my return. After crossing the desert to Carson valley, I
found but few Indians until I arrived at the Mormon station, near the head of
the vally. There I met with a number of the Pintahs and Washaws; they were
stragglers from their bands, hunting and fishing on the river. The Washaws
reported that they had two chiefs, who were at that time in the mountains,
they knew not where. The tribe is and has been very troublesome.

The many depredations which have been committed on the whites in
crossing the Sierra Nevada no doubt have been by this tribe. The Pintahs
are in two separate bands, commanded by two chiefs, one estimated at three
hundred and the other at three hundred and fifty. They reside on the Carson
river, and in the mountains east and southeast of the river. They have been
generally friendly to the whites, and are very poor. . . .

I left Carson valley on the 7th instant. On my return I met with many
of the Pintahs tribe on Carson river, but saw neither of the chiefs; they were
both absent from their bands on hunting excursions. All were very friendly;
no disturbances on the river during the present season by the Indians. I
gave them some presents and sent some to their chiefs. At the sink of the
Humboldt I met with a few of the Bannack tribe, who belonged to a band
under the chief, Te-ve-re-wena, (the long man). They accompanied me to the
village at the head of the Big Meadows. This chief, with many of his braves,
was also on a hunt—his band numbers about six hundred. I held a talk with
them; all appeared very friendly; seemed much pleased at the friendship of
their great father in sending them presents. They assured me that the whites
should not be disturbed by any of their band.

The Humboldt river runs through a narrow channel for some seventy-five
miles above the sink; the bottoms are very narrow, affording but little grass,
and of course no game. The Indians do not reside near the river, and I met
none until I arrived within fifty miles of Stony point.[34] I here met with a
small band of Shoshonees belonging to Oh-hah-quah's band. I gave them

---

[34]For the best analysis of this spot, some seven miles northeast of today's Battle Mountain, see
Barrett, "Stony Point: Nevada's Bloody Landmark," 2–21.

some presents, and engaged a brave to accompany me to their village near Stony point I found them much scattered on hunting parties; I gave them presents of various kinds, which seemed to please them very much. They promised friendship to the whites in future, and from their conduct generally I think they will adhere to their promises. Oh-hah-quah sent two of his braves with me for the purpose of finding; some parties of his band who were off hunting, but they were not to be found. He informed me that there had been some trouble with the whites and Ne-me-te-kah's band, and that Ne-me-tekah had sent for him and requested that he and his band would join him for the purpose of killing all the whites that passed the road, as the whites had killed his son and five of his braves, without any cause whatever. But Oh-hah-quah refused to join him, and told him he was afraid I would be mad with him; that he had promised me to be friendly to the whites—that he was afraid to tell me a lie; that he would be friendly with the whites until he could see me, which he knew would be in a few sleeps, (meaning days,) and advised Ne-me-tekah to wait until my return.

Near Stony point I met an emigrant train, who informed me that a party of Californians, who had been on the Humboldt on a trading expedition, had killed six Indians, taken their horses, and left for California. They travelled on the north side of the river, and passed me unknown. I hastened up the river, and on arriving at Gravelly ford I met two emigrant trains, both of which had been attacked by the Indians, and had four men badly wounded, and lost many of their stock, with one wagon and a quantity of provisions, with much other valuable property. I sent the two Indians given me by Oh-hah-quah to see Ne-me-te-kah, and to request him to cease further attacks on the whites, and to request him to meet me as soon as possible. They travelled all night, and brought him to me next morning. After much persuasion he was induced to come. He said he was afraid to see me; that his conduct had been so different from what he had promised me, he feared I would be mad with him. He still expressed a great desire to be friendly with the whites, but said the whites would not be friendly with him; that the whites had killed his son and his men, and taken their horses and guns, without any cause; that it had made his heart sick—had made his men mad, and he could not restrain them; they were determined to be revenged on the whites. Having learned the cause of these troubles from an emigrant who witnessed the attack and robbery of the Indians by the California traders, I explained to him the difference between those traders and the emigrants—that the emigrants had no acquaintance with them; that the emigrants were much opposed to such outrages on the Indians; that their great father did not allow his white children to harm the Indians, &c., &c. When he became acquainted with the true situation of the emigrants, and the difference between them and these traders, he seemed to regret the course he had taken, but said his heart was sick at the murder of his son, and believing the whites all to blame, he had sought revenge upon the first that passed; but now, that he understood who had killed them, he was better satisfied, and that all further troubles should cease.

I distributed to his band all the presents I had; sent some to the relatives of those who had been killed; all of which were received, apparently, with much good feeling and entire satisfaction. They promised that no further difficulties should occur on their part. I then proceeded on my journey—met Paut-wa-avante with several of his band, and gave them the presents I had reserved for them. He was much pleased; and I left the Humboldt with the strongest assurances on the part of the Indians of their friendly feelings towards the emigrants. And I feel confident that if the emigrants who have to pass the road this season (and they are few) will treat the Indians with any degree of kindness, there will be no further difficulties. When I arrived in Thousand Spring valley I found but few of Too-ke-moh's band. He and the most of his band had left for the neighborhood of Fort Hall, where there is more game, and where they intend to winter. With these Indians I have had considerable intercourse. By giving them a few presents, and always feeding them when they came to my camp, I have gained over them an influence and friendship which seem to inspire them with confidence in me, and great respect and friendship for the government. I feel assured of their amicable and friendly disposition at present. . . .

In a previous communication I gave you my views in relation to this section of the Territory. From my recent trip I am more strongly impressed with its importance. I feel satisfied that until government throws protection over this route, and places the means within the reach of the officers to enforce their authority and the laws, there can be no safety to travel. The whites who infest the country are far more troublesome than the Indians.

Bloody Chief, Sergeant Haws, and White Indians

Before first visiting the Humboldt in 1852, Jacob Holeman outlined the information he had picked up about the desert Shoshones.

The tribe of Shoshonies, or Snakes, is very large, and being divided into many bands, they occupy a large portion of the Territory, but are all on friendly terms with each other. They have nothing like a settled residence, but roam the country from the headwaters of the Platte, near the South Pass, to St. Mary's river, including a portion of the Territory of Oregon. There are two bands of Utahs of considerable size; one residing south of the city, and are very friendly towards the whites; the other, who are called the "Diggers," reside north, and range over a portion of country lying between this and California; they are said to be a tribe formed by the poorer classes of the Utahs, the Snakes, the Pa-nacks, the Crows, and the Flatheads. They have heretofore been considered as the most worthless and trifling Indians in the Territory, subsisting on roots principally, from which they take the name of Diggers. It is said they eat anything that has life in it, from a cricket to a buffalo. It is principally in their country that the robberies and murders which have occurred during the past season have been committed. Many are of the opinion that they have been encouraged and assisted by white men; and judging of their past character and their bold and daring conduct now, it would seem that there is strong grounds for the opinion. There are many bands of the various tribes above named, of a more elevated character, who pursue the chase for a living, and travel the country in search of game, from the Platte river to California, and from this city to Oregon. I visited a village of the Snakes about 80 miles north of this city, in January last. It was reported here that they had information of two white women, who were said to be held as prisoners by a band of the "White Knives;" all the information I could gather seemed to justify the belief that they had been killed by the Indians. The name of White Knife has been given to these Indians who have been committing the robberies on the California and Oregon routes, in consequence, they say, of white men being connected with them and their being so completely armed with almost every description of weapon. The Indians I visited professed great friendship for the whites, and seemed disposed to enter into any arrangement with the government which would have a tendency to secure, permanently, this friendship.[35]

The name White Knives, Garland Hurt wrote, derived "from a beautiful flint found in the mountains of that region," at the Tosawihi chert quarry north of today's Battle Mountain. Anthropologists know little about the Tosawihi, and historians may know less. They ranged through the traditional Western Shoshone–Northern Paiute borderland, but since 1938, when anthropologist Julian Steward argued they "had no organization and were not a band," scholars have debated Great Basin social structures and who and what constituted the Tosawihi. Whatever the White Knives might have been, today the Battle Mountain band of the Te-Moak Western Shoshone has "taken the lead in protecting the Tosawihi Quarries."[36]

Late in 1854, Edward Steptoe of the U.S. Army hired Oliver B. Huntington to scout a shorter trail to California—the destination of the U.S. soldiers who had wintered in Utah.[37] The scouts reached Carson Valley on

---

[35]Morgan, *Shoshonean Peoples*, 169.

[36]Hurt to Young, September 1856, Commissioner of Indian Affairs, *Annual Report;*Clemmer, "Tosawihi Quarry," 1; see also Stephanie Woodard, "Tosawihi Lost Bones, Damage and Harassment at Ancient Sacred Site," *Indian Country Today*, 13 January 2016.

[37]"New Route from Carson Valley," *Deseret News*, 7 December 1854, 2/3–4; and MacKinnon, "Sex, Subalterns, and Steptoe," 77–86.

15 October, four weeks after leaving Salt Lake, finding "the Indians as peaceful and about as wild as the antelope, with the exception of a band of the White Knife Tribe." They returned in November on a trail "well supplied with grass," and after "a most extraordinarily successful trip of 24 days we arrived in this city on the 27th." Thirty-three years after seeking the "best route known by white men" across the Great Basin, Huntington wrote an account of the trek "to show the inspiration of the Lord." He described Western Shoshone culture during a period of tumultuous transition in what he described as "an almost unknown wilderness, a country inhabited only by Indians and wild game." The explorers included traders John Reese and Stephen Kinsey; two gamblers with a "very fleet race-horse"; and a Native guide named Natsab, "son of the Indian chief who was ruler in Salt Lake Valley when we first settled the country," perhaps Wanship. Natsab disappeared at Mormon Station, fearing Huntington would "make him stay too, and that was too long to live among the whites; he would have got sick and perhaps died." On 28 September in Ruby Valley:

> an Indian, naked except for a covering about his loins, with gun in hand, stood before us suddenly and stopped our movements. After a very short and unedifying oration he fired his gun in the air, and instantly there arose an Indian from behind every bunch of grass and greasewood all around us until there was quite an army in view, and we saw it was necessary to talk in persuasive tones and our orders were enforced with many presents, in giving which the interpreter was very expert. The Indians guided us to some very fine springs of water and small ponds not far distant, where we distributed quantities of tobacco, pipes, paints, calico, etc.

By morning, the Indians had disappeared, "which to men acquainted with Indian natures, indicated hostile intentions."

O. B. HUNTINGTON, "A TRIP TO CARSON VALLEY," 80–81.

We had chosen an open piece of ground where we could not be surprised in daylight. We were preparing an early supper so as to have it over before any surprise might be undertaken. Just as we were sitting down to eat, seven Indians on horseback rode slowly towards our camp, came past our horses which were grazing near and dismounted near our fires. We saluted them kindly with "how-de-do," and they replied. They were all dressed in coats, pants, overcoats, caps, etc, and rode well shod horses, excepting one short, thick-set Indian, about twenty-three years old, who wore buckskin pants, a hickory shirt, a Panama hat and with his hair cut short and straight around his neck; he was very wide between the eyes, rode a very large mare without a saddle. He came to my mess where I, my nephew and Natsab were just sitting down to eat, and shook hands.

We sat with guns and pistols in our laps. I told all our company to be very careful, as this one could talk English. The interpreter [Clark A. Huntington] tried to talk with him, but to no effect until he spoke in the Snake language, when he answered some. They were observing our actions, habits, etc., and making their calculations how and when to take our scalps. I felt that under the Panama hat was a dreadful chief for blood and plunder, and that he could talk English; and I was right in my judgment or feelings.

As soon as the interpreter and I were done eating, we walked around the horses after cautioning the men. While driving the animals a little nearer camp he asked if I had noticed a secret sign, a strange motion, the Indian made as he shook hands with us, and he showed it to me, stating that he believed these Indians were of the tribe and party who had done so many murders on the Humboldt, among the California gold seekers, and that he believed they were banded with whites by secret oaths, signs and pass-words. Immediately after he told this I felt a strange but bright sensation come over my mind and I could see with my heart, or my spirit could see without my eyes. I told him we would leave the horses and go quickly to camp, where he should go up to that Indian (the chief), give him the same sign he had given us, and that we would then be safe among them.

He did this and the effect was astonishing. The Indian shook hands and hugged him heartily.

I gave further instructions to the interpreter what to say about a certain man whom we knew lived on the Humboldt River, where so much murdering had been done, and with whom I went to school in Nauvoo. Every word had its effect as I anticipated, and the chief understood that this man who lived on the Humboldt, and whom very many believed to be the cause of all the murdering done there for money and plunder, was our friend from boyhood; but the opposite might be said to be nearly true, as we held no sympathy in common, although we had been boys together. The chief called that man his "daddy," meaning father. . . .

When we told "Bloody Chief," for such was the name of the chief who visited our camp, that we were special friends to the bad young man we thought not of the terrible consequences that might result from that deceitful stratagem to save our lives then. We told the Indians frankly that we were coming back in a little more than one moon, but did not tell them there would be but three of us.

On the morning of September 30th, the same seven Indians came into our camp without a gun, pistol, bow or arrow. All were merry and jolly, and traded everything they could, and ran foot-races. They wanted to run horses, but ours had too long a journey before them to admit of racing. The main object and effort of the Indians was to get that race-horse, but they did not succeed. They escorted us about eight miles on our way and told us all they could of the country ahead in the direction we wanted to go. They showed us a great deal of gold and silver coin, jewelry and pocket-knives, which they doubtless obtained by killing people on the Humboldt.

We left the valley at the south end, passing over a low divide and through a narrow, rocky canyon, full of scattering cedar trees, making as nice a place for ambush as an Indian could ask for the massacre of whites.

Parallels—age, dress, and intelligence—between Huntington's Bloody Chief and French traveler Jules Remy's Sokopitz are clear. But who was Daddy? Who taught Huntington's stocky Tosawihi leader the "secret oaths, signs and pass-words" the Mormon temple endowment shared with Masonry? Huntington implied it was former Mormon Battalion sergeant Alpheus Peter Haws, then "about twenty-four years old, a very tall, muscular man, not less than six feet, two inches in height, with black eyes, set wide apart under a heavy forehead and over high cheek bones," whose "whole countenance indicated a cruel and heartless disposition." Haws lived in "his lone log house on the Humboldt, about sixty miles from Ruby Valley."[38] But "Daddy" perhaps referred to A.P.'s father, Council of Fifty veteran Peter Haws. He shared Alpheus Cutler's devotion to "Lamanism" and "the old gentleman's natural parabolical, allegorical, symbolical, mysterious, secretative way of telling things." As a priest and prince of the Kingdom of God, Peter Haws stayed true to Joseph Smith's vision of a Mormon-Indian alliance.[39]

Jules Remy reported Peter Haws was "among the first to emigrate to the Salt Lake, where he earned his livelihood for several years by making whisky." As early as 1853, Haws was ranching in Huntington Valley between today's Deeth and Lamoille, Nevada. He sold "garden sauce" to passing migrants and, like Ruby Valley Indian agent William Rogers, probably traded "peltries of the mink, wolf, woodchuck or ground-hog, fox, badger, antelope, black-tailed deer, and others." Haws "managed to secure the confidence of the Indians to a great degree" and felt "no danger from them," wrote Apostle Orson Hyde. "His stock roams unherded and unguarded without molestation, unless by some strange and transient Indians. He keeps no locks upon his doors; but the strings hang out day and night." Hyde claimed Haws had restrained Indian "depredations upon the whites as they pass," but they were "getting 'tobuck,' angry," because Major Holeman's

---

[38]Huntington, "A Trip to Carson Valley," 83.
[39]Hyde and Bird, Reports, 5 April, 15 March 1849, BYC 39:18; Quinn, *Mormon Hierarchy: Origins*, 196–97.

promises were unfulfilled. Haws stood charged "with being colleagued with the Indians in robbing emigrants," which Hyde considered "unjust and cruel."[40]

In 1854 Brigham Young denounced overland outlaws who proved "much more dangerous than the red":

> From information brought in by the last California mail, the emigration, on leaving Bear River, must prepare to run a still harder gauntlet, for it is reported that a numerous and well organized band of *white* highwaymen, painted and disguised as Indians, infest several points on the road, and drove off stock by wholesale, and recent murders are rumored from that quarter. It is presumed that the Arkansas murderer, and a large number of associated outlaws, and fugitives, compose this robber band; men who have heretofore been in the habit of killing Indians, and probably some whites, for the sake of their stock, and a little booty.[41]

Scholars know little about most "white Indians" but a lot about the "renegade" Mormons plying the trade, including their names—Return Jackson Redden, Carlos Murray, and Alpheus and Albert Haws. Redden was "associated with a company of white men and Indians" near Carson Valley whose object was "to rob and plunder the emigrants," Jacob Holeman reported in 1852. Redden warned Thomas Williams "to paint the horns of his cattle so that he may be known, as they do not wish to molest the brethren," but Redden was "now held by them in utter contempt, and looked upon as a great scoundrel."[42] Remy had an "unaccountable aversion" for Carlos Murray, Heber C. Kimball's nephew. Besides killing at least one Indian, Murray "had murdered two pale-faces to secure their money, and the Mormons suspected that more than one other victim attributed to the Shoshones should be laid to his charge." Salt Lakers assumed Remy and his companion Jules Benchley had "fallen victims to the much dreaded Carlos." Remy regarded Peter Haws as one "of the worthiest of men that we have met in the course of our wandering life" and believed he was unaware of the nefarious character of his son-in-law, Carlos Murray.[43]

---

[40]Remy, *A Journey to Great-Salt-Lake City*, 1:139; Burton, *City of the Saints*, 473; "Letter from Elder O. Hyde; Haws Ranch," 31 May 1855, *Deseret News*, 27 June 1855, 128.

[41]Brigham Young, "Emigration," *Deseret News*, 13 July 1854, 2/6.

[42]Return Jackson Redden was a bodyguard for Joseph Smith and a scout for Brigham Young's 1847 pioneer camp who later served as a justice of the peace in Tooele and Summit counties. He died at Hoytsville, Utah, in 1891. See Bagley, *The Pioneer Camp of the Saints*, 343.

[43]Remy, *A Journey to Great-Salt-Lake City*, 1:122, 137–38, 148, 150.

Alpheus and Albert Haws had been "notorious for their horse stealing and counterfeiting operations" since Nauvoo. Whenever threatened, they sought "the protecting wing of the Mormon Church, under which they repose for awhile, when they again sally forth in search of plunder."[44] During the explosion of violence on the California Trail in 1857, California papers charged: "Alph Hawes, who left this State last spring, took with him twelve dozen muskets which he furnished to the Indians, and it is these guns with which they are shooting the emigrants with [sic]. The Hawes had a partner, whom some of the emigrants caught and shot, putting thirty bullets through him, and would have served Hawes the same way, had he not escaped them."[45]

Alpheus Haws denied such "disreputable allegations."[46] Agent Garland Hurt authorized him "to call upon the Indians to punish those emigrants who should commit any offence against the natives," Peter Haws told Remy.[47] Whether Haws properly understood whatever authority Hurt gave him, he regarded himself as an agent of the U.S. government—at least that was what he told his European visitors. Even California newspapers praised his achievements:

> About forty miles below the head of the Humboldt, and divided from Ruby Valley but by a slight range of hills, is a finely cultivated ranch, owned by Mr. Peter Hawes. This enterprising settler has grown grains, vegetables and other products of the soil very successfully and profitably. These he disposes of to the emigrants, traders and Indians, although he carries on no little trade with the latter in the way of exchanging firearms, ammunition, &c. for peltry. He raised, also, some two hundred head of stock last season, which he has driven into Great Salt Lake City.[48]

Disgusted with Brigham Young, Peter Haws left Utah to practice Joseph Smith's "holy doctrines his own way, without having to bow to the authority of the President of the Church. Nevertheless, Haws was not an apostate. He remained true to the doctrines of the founder, but refused a blind obedience to his successor," Remy observed. Haws "had fixed his farm at the foot of the highest mountains, close to a clear little brook." His "long wooden cabin with two large chimneys" was 250 miles "from the nearest house," making Haws the sentinel "of Mormonism in the desert." Remy's extended stay at

[44]"The Bandits of the Plains," *San Francisco Weekly Chronicle*, 22 August 1857.
[45]"Arrival of Emigrants.—Myers' Train," *Stockton Daily Argus*, 17 October 1857, 2/2.
[46]"From the Plains—Mr. Hawes' Statement," *Alta California*, 19 October 1857, 2/1.
[47]Remy, *A Journey to Great-Salt-Lake City*, 1:124.
[48]"Salt Lake and Carson Valley Wagon Route," *Sacramento Daily Union*, 11 October 1855, 3/1.

this "stout, good-natured-looking" zealot's ranch in 1855 provided a wealth of information about the Shoshone neighbors whom Haws considered "honest and trustworthy, but lazy and dirty." Most remarkable were the portraits Remy provided of "Sokopitz, the chief of the valley":

> The chief soon arrived with his band of hunters. He was a man of about twenty-five years of age, rather small, thin, well-made for one of his race, and possessing some intelligence. His countenance indicated cunning and ferocity, notwithstanding which, Mr. and Mrs. Haws were well satisfied of his gentleness. He had no distinctive characteristics, except that he was perhaps more reserved than the generality of Indians. His hair, worn long, as is their custom, hung in plaits at the side of his head. His entire clothing consisted in a coloured shirt, black pantaloons, and a felt hat, and a revolver was suspended from his belt. He was the husband of the two best-made women of the tribe. He knew a few words of English, and invariably answered Mrs. Haws, "Yes, Sir!" The other Indians did not appear to show any deference whatever to him. He was constantly accompanied by a younger brother, who was remarkably stout. Some Canadian trappers, with whom this brother had passed several years beaver-hunting, had given him the name of "Bourgeois," and he was known by no other. More careful of his person than his brother, he was dressed in a blue blanket and deer-skin trousers; his hair was ornamented with trinkets and a copper disk, a sign of his rank. His white horse was also handsomer than those of the others. He frequently wore a cap of rabbit-skin, to which were suspended several tails of that animal; and he was excessively fond of painting his face.[49]

In fall 1855 a Mormon posse arrested Carlos Murray for the murder of an Indian, hauling him to Salt Lake for a trail that failed to convict him and charging the government $20,000 in expenses.[50] When Garland Hurt met A. P. Haws in Thousand Spring Valley on the last day of May 1856, Haws reported "the suspected massacre of Carlos Murray" and his wife. The well-dressed "and quite intelligent" Setoke "appeared ignorant of the affair, but said he thought it was right, for he understood Murray was a very bad man, and had killed an Indian the year before." Peter Haws suspected a mixed band of some 150 Utahs, Snakes, Bannocks, and Diggers, had collected "for

---

[49]Remy, *A Journey to Great-Salt-Lake City*, 1:121–23, 133–34, 145–48.

[50]After a Mormon jury acquitted Murray of murdering the Indian, raiders killed Murray and his wife. "Some Facts about Mormonism," *Oregon Argus*, 11 July 1857; and People vs. Carlos Murry [*sic*], 1855, U.S. First District Case Files, Utah State Archives 25011, 2:39. For more on the Haws clan, Murray, and other Mormon renegades, see Morgan, *The Humboldt*, 213–21; and Hickman, *Brigham's Destroying Angel*, 110–11.

SOKOPITZ, LEADER OF THE WESTERN
SHOSHONE TOSAWIHI BAND
Few Western Shoshones found
themselves immortalized in an
engraving published in both France
and England, as did Sokopitz, leader
of the Western Shoshone Tosawihi
band known as the "White Knives."
Two images of him survive: the
engraving in Jules Remy's *A Journey to
Great-Salt-Lake City* and the original 1855
daguerreotype, showing Sokopitz with
his brother, known as "Bourgeois." It
is now found in the Julius Brenchley
Collection. *Courtesy Maidstone Museum
& Bentliff Art Gallery, Image 017.*

the purpose of plunder" and killed them, for he recognized a gold pencil and earring "as the property of Mrs. Murray."[51]

Scholars may know more about the impressive Sokopitz—also known as Setoke, Chyukupichya, Sho-cop-it-see, Sho-kup, Sho-kub, Tsu-kup, and Cho-kup—than any other frontier Western Shoshone. In 1859 topographer James Simpson met "Cho-kup, chief of the Ruby Valley band of Sho-sho-nees" riding the mail-stage to Camp Floyd to visit Garland Hurt. Simpson said he was "the best-looking Indian I have seen in the Territory." Cho-kup was an intelligent "friend of the white man, and a good, respectable, and well-behaved Indian" and "chief of the Sho-sho-nees south of the Humboldt River." In May 1859 Simpson "had a sketch of him taken. . . . I should suppose he was about thirty-five years. He is dressed in buckskin pants, a check under, and a woolen over shirt; has a handkerchief tied around his neck, wears shoes, and has a yellowish felt hat. His air is that of a man who, while knowing his own powers, is capable of scanning those of others."[52]

On the October afternoon of a "Tuscan day" in 1860, Richard Burton noted that the name Chokop meant 'earth.' "His lands are long to the north and south, though of little breadth. He commands about 500 warriors." Sokopitz was collecting hunters for the autumn rabbit drive. "In 1849 his sister was wantonly shot by emigrants to California," Burton wrote. "He attacked the train, and slew in revenge five men." His father and grandfather were both alive, but reserved "their voices for the powwow," while his "rather pretty" younger wife had "a newly-born papoose." The Tosawihi appeared happy, "and for the first time I heard an Indian really laugh outright." Burton found them unclean, but "the existence of old age, however, speaks well for the race."[53]

As Burton observed Sokopitz in 1860, the Overland Telegraph Company's technology was about to transform Native life in the Great Basin.

JAMES GAMBLE, "WIRING A CONTINENT," THE CALIFORNIAN 3:18 (JUNE 1881), 557.

[Construction supervisor James Street] made it a point to see some of the Indian chiefs, to gain, if possible, their good will, as well as explain to them

---

[51]"News From Agent Hurt and Party," *Deseret News*, 18 June 1856, 5/1; Hurt to Young, September 1856, in Commissioner of Indian Affairs, *Annual Report*, 227–28

[52]Simpson, *Report of Explorations*, 46, 67–68. Two days later, Simpson met "an old man of at least sixty years" who told him "a number of his people died last winter from starvation and cold."

[53]Burton, *City of the Saints*, 471–72.

the object of the work. At Roberts Creek, he met Sho-kup, the head chief of the Shoshones, who received him in a very friendly manner. The chief told Mr. Street that he and his tribe were desirous of knowing and understanding the ways of the white man, and to be upon friendly terms with him. He expressed himself as anxious to do always that which was to the good of his own people, and provide for their wants. He added, with much feeling:

"Before the white men came to my country, my people were happy and had plenty of game and roots. Now they are no longer happy, and the game has almost disappeared."

Sho-kup exercised great influence, not only over his own tribe, but also over the Goshutes and Pah-Utes. The Indians there, as everywhere, are very superstitious and put great faith in the teachings of their medicine men. At the time of the visit of Mr. Street, one of Sho-kup's wives (he had two) was dangerously ill, and one of her doctors had said the cause of it was the overland mail. The chief asked if this was true. The interpreter replied in the negative, and on behalf of Mr. Street invited Sho-kup to get on the stage and go to San Francisco where he was assured he would be kindly received, and be as well in all respects as if he had made the journey on horseback. The chief accepted the offer and started with them the next stage, but on reaching Carson City he resolved to return, as it was taking him too far from home. The telegraph was explained to him by the interpreter, and he afterward called it "We-ente-mo-ke-te-bope": meaning "wire rope express." On being pressed to continue his trip to San Francisco, he said no; he wanted to go back and learn how his wife was. He was told that when the telegraph was completed he could talk to her as well from there as if by her side; but this was more than his comprehension could seize. Talk to her when nearly three hundred miles away! No; that was not possible. He shook his head, saying he would rather talk to her in the old way. His idea of the telegraph was that it was an animal, and he wished to know on what it fed. They told him it ate lightning; but, as he had never seen any one make a supper of lightning, he was not disposed to believe that. During his stay in Carson City, Sho-kup was kindly treated, and, as he refused to go farther, he was told he could talk with the Big Captain (President H. W. Carpentier) of the telegraph company at San Francisco. Thereupon he dictated the following dispatch:

"Sho-kup, Big Chief of the Shoshones, says to Big Captain at San Francisco, that his Indians will not trouble the telegraph line. Sho-kup is a friend of the white man. His people obey him. He will order them to be friendly with the white men and not injure the telegraph. He would like to see Big Captain, but must return to his tribe, and cannot go to San Francisco."

On receipt of this message, General Carpentier, President of the Company, sent Sho-kup several friendly messages, and ordered presents of food and clothing to be made him. The importance of having a good understanding and keeping on friendly terms with the Indians was well understood, and everything was done, both then and during the period of the construction of the line, to prevent the occurrence of anything that would lead to trouble with them.

Fate was not kind to these men. Not long after the completion of the talking wire, Indian Agent Warren Wasson reported Chief Shokub died on 28 June 1862.[54] Albert Haws murdered several lawmen in Nevada and Utah and died in May 1870 under the guns of Porter Rockwell's posse.[55] Alpheus Haws ultimately settled in Berkeley, California, and died at Sonoma on 3 November 1906.[56]

Federal commissioners reported 460 Goshutes lived in Utah and Nevada in 1873. "The Goshute people are survivors," wrote historian Dennis Defa. They outlasted "the unjust epithets, lies, and outright barbarity of the white invaders." By the late twentieth century, more than 524 Goshutes were enrolled members of the Confederated Tribes of the Goshute Reservation and the Skull Valley Band of Goshute, while another thousand belonged to the Te-Moak tribe of Western Shoshones.[57]

---

[54]Stewart, "Temoke Band of Shoshone," 253.

[55]Schindler, *Orrin Porter Rockwell*, 216n66, 355.

[56]Larson, *A Database of the Mormon Battalion*, 119.

[57]Pritzker, *A Native American Encyclopedia*, 241–242; Cuch, *Utah's American Indians*, 110, 121–22.

Chapter 5

HOSTILITIES AND TREACHERY
The War on Wakara

T
he 1853 war between Utes and Mormons resembled the border war that abolitionists and slaveocrats soon fought in Kansas Territory. Moreover, the Nauvoo Legion's campaign against the Utes had similarities to the war against the Plains Indians that exploded in 1854 when an arrogant young officer fired a howitzer into a peaceful Lakota camp near Fort Laramie. Both race wars pitted Native peoples determined to defend their land against white invaders intent on the conquest and colonization of contested ground. The beatings, skirmishes, and ambushes Utah settlers habitually inflicted on Native peoples had not relented since 1849; what was different about 1853 was the apparent resolve of Deseret's strongmen to make war on their foes, regardless of race. Utah's leaders had long since decided to draw borders around Native peoples, segregate them, compel the dependent Lamanites to become "white and delightsome," and exterminate all who resisted. The Saints had "invariably given them provisions and clothing, furnished them with guns and ammunition to kill game, and in various ways administered to their relief," claimed Brigham Young. "In many places, grain has been raised for them, and houses built for their chiefs and principal men. This policy has a tendency to correct their vile habits and propensities, and sometimes induces them to labor for their own support."[1] Simultaneously, Young ordered "forting up" to centralize scattered villages within adobe strongholds that separated Mormons from their increasingly desperate neighbors.

The Brigham Young–Wakara power struggle erupted in July 1853 in a conflict long called "the Walker War." That year's documentary record shows

---

[1]Roberts, A Comprehensive History, 4:50.

Utah's military, political, and religious rulers had resolved much earlier to suppress Ute power by any means necessary. Edward Beale's independent railroad survey through southern Utah produced several outside perspectives. The Nauvoo Legion purchased "government" military supplies and wagons from Fort Hall and sent the "Fort Bridger & Greenriver Expedition" to capture and perhaps kill Jim Bridger. Finally, on 23 August 1853, Salt Lake's bishops "reported all their wards unanimous for walling in the whole of the city, with a good ditch upon the outside of the wall [to] be built of mud taken from the ditch, and mixed with straw or hay and gravel," which was "deemed to be the cheapest and in the end most durable method that we can at present adopt."[2]

WAKARA: I WOULD BE A FOOL TO WANT TO FIGHT

It often seemed the left hand of Mormon Indian policy had little conception of what its right military fist was doing. On a warm evening in June 1851, Presidents "Young Kimball Richards ordained Walker, Sowiette, Arrapene, Unhoquitch," Elders in the "Ch-JC-LDS Lamanites," wrote Thomas Bullock. "Mormon authorities likely hoped these ordinations would be a positive step," noted historian Robert Carter.[3] Later that month, following the bloody Tooele campaign, General Wells turned his attention to Wakara, issuing an odd challenge through Fort Utah's Peter Conover.

DANIEL H. WELLS TO CAPN P. W. CONOVER, 30 JUNE 1851, UTMR.

G.S.L. City, June 30, 1851

Capn P. W. Conover,

Sir: We understand that Indian Walker is quite saucy to the people of your County, feeding his Horses on their wheat fields &c. Also saying he does not want you to sow [*sic*] wheat there &c.

Now we want you to ask Walker, if he wants us to leave his lands, and go away; and if so, how far his land extends. We also want to know, if he is mad, and wants us to fight him, and if Sow-ee-ette, Arapine, Grosapine, Tabbee, Pe-tete-nete, and Antero feel the same way. If they do not we want them to leave Walker, unless he will do better, for if we hear of him committing depredations upon our settlements of San Pete, Iron County, or elsewhere,

---

[2]"Indian Difficulties," *Millennial Star*, 12 November 1853, 738–39, citing *Deseret News Extra*, 25 August 1853.
[3]Carter, *From Fort to Village*, 69.

to such an extent as to compel us to act in self-defence. We shall not like it, and he may share the same fate as Pat-sow-ette, or those other Indians who have persisted in such a course after having been repeatedly told better, and borne with for a long time.

We do not wish to provoke a quarrel with Walker, but we wish him to behave himself and make his men do so too; and if he wants us to leave his lands, tell him we will *talk* to him.

Bro. D. B. Huntington is the bearer of this letter, and I want *him, Elijah Ward, and George Bean to accompany you to Walker, and then report to me.*

Respectfully yours
Daniel H. Wells

Wakara pled his innocence. Conover said the Indian trade was the problem.

I went to see Walker and took the interpreters and red the letter to him. He appeared perfectly astonished and quieted down and said he did not want us to leave his land but wanted us to stay and rais wheat and bee good friends. Why he said I would be a fool to want to fight. Now I have come because there was some mean utes that would not hear him but would through [throw] the fence down and would not keep out of the wheat and he did not want a fuss. He started yesterday and we had to follow him to the Spanish fork. . . . Walker talked very different to what he did the other day but Jest as long as everybody is alowed to come from your place and trade the Indians cattle and guns and ammunition their will be a fuss with them. Their is som of our folks . . . say they have as good a wright to trade as they [Salt Lakers] have so there is more or less trading with them every day.[4]

Wakara meanwhile sought to master the white man's magical technology, notably their ability to "make paper talk." Thomas Bullock identified his experiment as "Walker's writing 1851." Apparently based on the letters translated, read, and given to him, he imitated their form on a folded sheet now in the Brigham Young papers. "The title or salutation is underlined; two words per line," historian Ardis Parshall observed. "One sheet is folded into an envelope, and the markings on the outside are 'rotated' to run the way an address would."[5] The writing is bold and confident; a single blot at the end of the first line on the address fold shows a struggle to master quill-and-ink technology. What Wakara said is a mystery, so these images must speak for themselves.

---

[4]P. W. Conover to Wells, 2 July 1851, UTMR 1:12.
[5]"Walker's writing," 1851, BYC 74:44.

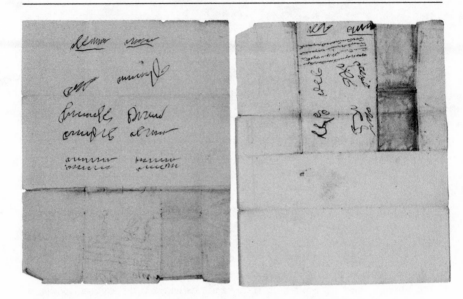

WAKARA'S WRITING

Wakara imitated the form of letters sent to him in a document now in Brigham
Young's papers. Wakara struggled to master these seemingly magical powers.
Sequoyah developed a Cherokee syllabary, making reading and writing in Cherokee
possible. Given Wakara's intelligence and curiosity (if not his character), could he
have created a Ute alphabet and written language? *Editor's collection.*

To Save Them from Starvation, Abuse, and Even Death: Slavery

New Mexico governor James Calhoun issued a license in August 1851 to
Abiquiú farmer Don Pedro León Luján, authorizing him to traffic with the
Utah Nation until 14 November. After crossing the Rockies, Luján sought
out Brigham Young to determine if his license "was good to trade with the
whites and Indians also," and if not, "to get one from the Governor." When
Luján found him in Sanpete Valley on 3 November, Young "pointedly for-
bade" the Mexicans to trade with the Utes, who resented their compliance
and began stealing the traders' horses. Arapene rode into the Mexican camp,
threw down two children, seized five of Miguel Archuletta's horses, and
said that "if he had a mood to trade he would trade and if he had not he
would trade anyhow." Officials arrested Luján and his men, who appeared
before federal judge Zerubbabel Snow in December. Isaac Morley testified

Latter-day Saints purchased Native children "to save them from misery, starvation, cruelty and death," which was echoed by Brigham Young, who claimed citizens bought Indians "to obtain their liberty And to save them from starvation, abuse and even death." Young testified:

> Indian Walker has been in the habit for years of trafficking in Indians. He has never been here with his band, without having a quantity of Indian children, as slaves. He offers them for sale, and when he has an offer that satisfies him in the price he sells them; and when he cannot get what he thinks they are worth, he says he will take them to the Navaho Indians or Spaniards, and sell them, or kill them, which I understand he frequently does.

He had seen Wakara's slaves "so emaciated they were not able to stand upon their feet. He is in the habit of tying them out from their camps at night, naked and destitute of food, unless it is so cold he apprehends they will freeze to death. In that case he will give them something to sleep on, lest he should lose them. That is the general character of the Utah Indians."[6]

The Mormon legislature passed laws regulating slavery and "An Act for the Relief of Indian Slaves and Prisoners" in 1852. New Mexico had laws to control indentured servitude, but its legal euphemisms "made Utah the only part of the Mexican Cession open to black slavery." As governor, Young believed the Bible justified slavery and polygamy, and so enforced the fugitive slave act.[7] Journalist Albert Browne found Utah had "not more than fifty or sixty negroes" in 1858, but there were "several hundred Indians, held in servitude."[8] Since ancient times, this ruthless business has dehumanized both slavers and slaves. Indian slavery was no different, though Utah's legislature called it "a worse than African bondage." The suppression of human trafficking in Utah was a noble cause that challenged Wakara's economic power and became yet another cause of conflict.

PEACE MIGHT BE MADE

For about a decade before 1851, Wakara had led his band of freebooters, sometimes associated with the Elk Mountain Utes and called the Cheveriches, Cheverets, Shiberetches, Shibereche, or as agent Henry Day reported, the Cho-Ver-ets, "Known as Walker's Band." Wakara's bold, "if somewhat

[6]Jones, *The Trial of Don Pedro León Luján*, 62–70, 73, 125–26.
[7]Turner, *Brigham Young*, 226–27.
[8]Browne, "The Utah Expedition," *Atlantic Monthly* (May 1859), 581.

variable, following of Western Utes" fluctuated, as some "joined him only for a few hunts or raids and then returned home to more traditional activities." Resources kept his following small, never numbering "more than forty to fifty families, with about seven horses per family."[9] When Wakara's band returned from wintering among the Hopi and Pima peoples in 1852, Brigham Young advised him to be "at peace with all men" and then got down to business.

YOUNG TO CAPT WALKER, 9 APRIL 1852, BYC 17:1.

Great Salt Lake City, April 9th 1852

To Capt Walker, Chief of the Utahs,
Friend.

We hear you are at Pauvan Valley, and as Dimick Huntington is going that way we write you, to say we are well and happy. This is the fourth day we have held a great council in the new house we have been building, to worship our heavenly Father; and the Good Spirit has been with us very much, and our hearts rejoice.[10] We feel good, towards you, & all the Indians, and we want you to [tell] them all, we love them: we are their friends. And they must live in peace, as we do, and learn to work, and hearken to the Good Spirit, and God will bless them, and they will have bread, and clothes, and be happy as we are. We hear some bad white men tell indians, mormons are their Enemies. This is false. We are friends to all good men, and to the indians. We are your brothers & you are our brothers and will always do them good when we can, if they will hear us, and [do] right.

We hear you have visited the white indians, who have houses, cows, sheep, and make cloth, and other tribes on the Gila, & Colerado, and that you talk good to them, and tell them about mormons. That is good, and we want you to talk good, what the Good spirit say, to all Indians, all the time. We want to hear more about the white Indians, when you come you can tell us.[11]

You have a right to trade with any body, but the united States, our Great Father, the President, says white men must not trade with Indian[s], without our license. So when you come here to trade you can find a good place for your horses, between here and Provo, a little North west of Utah Lake, south of the west mountain, where you can trade your horses to the emigrants and get clothing, blankets, guns, powder &c & we will appoint

---

[9]Morgan, *Shoshonean Peoples*, 165; Van Hoak, "Waccara's Utes," 322–24.

[10]This adobe building, later known as the "Old Tabernacle," was on Temple Square where the 1882 Assembly Hall now stands.

[11]The "white Indians" reflect Young's belief that the Hopi people descended from Welsh wanderers. "I was carried away south until I found the Welsh Indians, and conversed freely with them," Welsh missionary Dan Jones wrote in 1851. He was so elated to find the Colorado navigable "that it awoke me to lament that it was only a dream!" "Local Correspondence," *Deseret News*, 10 January 1852, 2/1.

some one to trade for the Emigrants, perhaps friend Dimick, so our Great Father will be pleased; and we mean to give Friend Walker a suit of clothes when he comes to see us.

Now Brother, Be at peace with all men, & talk peace, & all the good things you can think of all the time, and pray the Good Spirit to bless us, and every body, & we will pray for you, and all the indians. Peace be with you.

Remember we are your friends all the time. Dont beleive [sic] what bad men say about about [sic] us. O our heavenly Fathy [sic], may thy servant Walker have the Testimony of thy Spirit, when he shall read this, that he shall know of us & of thy work, and the good spirit that prevails at this conference in the name of Jesus, Amen.

The American invasion of their homelands did not simplify the relations between the Shoshones and Utes, two peoples often portrayed as mortal enemies. Fight they did, but they also intermarried, creating independent bands hard to fit into white categories. As warrior societies in which battle and theft were rights of passage, Numic competition for resources sometimes resulted in violence, but just as often, Native leaders sought the blessings of peace.

Keeping peace was Superintendent Brigham Young's prime responsibility. One of his first official acts in 1851 was to direct his agents to assemble Native leaders for the Fort Laramie treaty ceremony. Holeman, Rose, Jim Bridger, and Louis Vasquez headed east with eighty-three of the Shoshones' "principal chiefs and braves," including Washakie.[12] Day stayed in Utah to persuade prominent Utes to go. They declined, believing it was "a trap set by the Mormans to Kill them," reported Commissioner Luke Lea. "They seem to have but little Confidence in anything the Morman [sic] people say to them, and decidedly stand in Much fear of them and from all the Information I could gather not Without good Cause." Nonetheless, Day felt "a treaty held of all the different Tribes in the Territory Would be of incalculable benefit."[13] The treaty proved elusive. Six Shoshones rode into Salt Lake in August 1852 to ask about trade and if "possibly, peace might be made with the Wachor and the Utahs." Brigham Young gave them presents and told Isaac Morley at Sanpete he wanted "Walker, Arapine, Grosepine, Tabbee, Petetenete, Sowerette, Antero, and as many of others as convenient of their chief men" to meet the Shoshones as soon as possible, promising "they will be perfectly safe."[14]

[12]Chambers Letter, 1 September, *Missouri Republican*, 26 September 1851.

[13]Morgan, *Shoshonean Peoples*, 58, 60, 166.

[14]Young to Morley, 9 August 1852, BYC 17:3.

SHOSHONE CAMP NEAR THE UNION PACIFIC RAILROAD
Andrew Joseph Russell photographed this Shoshone camp near the Union Pacific
Railroad in 1868 or 1869. Washakie is the man raising his arm, while Bannock leader
Pocatello may be wearing the flat-brim hat next to him. *Courtesy Beinecke Library.*

Coy as ever, Wakara wished "to consult with the rest of the Utes." Four
days later, Wakara told Morley he "not wish to come to Salt lake at this time,
but is friendly to you & to the Snakes he says he wishes the snakes to come
here and trade and he Walker wil be there friend." Meanwhile, Indians had
been "gathering here from all Quarters of the Utes tribes. I think there are
as many as fifty lodges now in sight of my place. There has ben som little
threats." Morley met with Wakara and "wished to know his feelings. He
told me he was friendly to wards me [but] some of the mormons ware fools
& some of the Utes like wise, he says." Morley understood Young's call for
patience, but the Utes were "very trouble some in our houses," and "some
of the brethren apeer to have a bout as much as they can stand."[15]

In August 1852 Young wanted Morley to tell Wakara he "should make as
much haste as possible," for the Shoshones were coming to Salt Lake. Wakara

---

[15]Morley to Young, 12, 16, August 1852, BYC 17:3.

seemed ready to go to when Morley "discovered they were in councell" for "there had just arived a Ute mesenger from the east over the mountain. Some where in the vicinety of the Snake Indeans this mesenger informed Walker that a band of Snakes or Sues hd fell up on a band of Utes and had killed ten men and ten Squas." The Utes were "much excited [and] we soon found that we could have no conversation," so Morley went home. "Ammon came to my hous and wanted me to write to you reletive to this Circumstance [for] they say they want you to inform the President of the United States of there situation."[16]

After "many fruitless efforts," on 3 September, Wachor, Sourette, Antaro, Anker-howhitch, and thirty-four Utah lodges met twenty-six Shoshone lodges, including "Wah-sho-kig, To-ter-mitch, Watche-namp, Ter-ret-e-ma, [and] Pershe-go." About fifty "braves" from each side attended the parley, along with Jacob Holeman, D. B. Huntington, and Elijah Ward. "The main object seemed to be accomplished in getting them together upon a friendly footing."[17]

THOMAS ELLERBECK, UTE/SHOSHONE MINUTES, 4 SEPTEMBER 1852,
LDS ARCHIVES.

State House (Lower Room) Saturday Sep 4th 1852 10 AM.

B. Young, Supt Indian Affairs, H. C. Kimball, W. Richards, Genl Wells, E. Hunter, Maj. Holman, Indian Agent, D. B. Huntington Elijah Warde Interpreters. F.D. Richards.

[Utes] Walker, Sowerette, Antaro, Anker hawkitch. Utah Chiefs. Arrapene is sick. 36 lodges.

[Shoshones] Wahshokiq, Totermuch/MarPok Waichenamp, Terretema, Pershego Snake Chiefs. Arwatce/Tamny 26 lodges.

B.Y. asked Major Holeman if he wanted to ask questions.

Major. I wish you to take the lead.

B.Y. asked Walker and Was-sho-kiq if they had made good peace. If it will last that will please me.

Walker got up and asked the Utes.

B.Y. I want them to lift up their right hands if they have made peace (all up)

Was-sho-kiq got up and asked the same question (all up)

B.Y. Tell them they must never contend again.

I want you to ask Walker and all the Utes if we have been friends to them and used them well.

[16]Young to Morley, 21 August 1852, BYC 22:17; Morley to Young, 23 August 1852, BYC 17:3.
[17]Morgan, *Shoshonean Peoples*, 185.

D.B.H. asked the Utes; answer "yes" "do you love Brigham"? and "ooa" we all love you.

Walker got up and made prayer, lifting his pipe to "Toowats" and asked him to bless the pipe, then smoked and passed it around.

B.Y. Have the Utes had any objection to us settling on their lands or are they glad. If they are glad, tell them to raise their hands (All satisfied).

B.Y. Ask Sowiette if we shall settle his lands ansr "ashante" he wants. It is good. He wants to be right side of him (B.Y.).

B.Y. Aske them if they want to trade with us ans—"yes they want to trade with every body white.["]

The Shoshone land goes over to the 'Sweetwater'—goes clear to the mouth of Pe nar par, Sugar Water. (Sweetwater)

Tell them I love them all. I want them to be friends to each other, and we know the Shoshones are the friends of the whites and have always been so.

Tell them to tell all the Indians to be kind to the Whites. And if they steal anything from each other or from the Whites tell the Chiefs to return it.

Ask Walker if I shall ask how many horses he shall return for the Shoshones (indians) he has killed.

Tell the Shoshones Walker had no horses now.

Walker got up and preached to the Utes. Said he will give them [the Shoshones] 9 horses next winter on Green River and be at peace, and that he was not going to be the man to cut the peace in two; I am sorry I did not do as Brigham told me, I will hear now what he says to me: it is good. I was a fool.

To-ter-mitch then talked to the Shoshones. He said his ears were open wide: it is good. Brigham is our father. It is good.

B.Y. Major shall we not give these five chiefs a suit of clothes?

Say to Wah-she-kiq we shall now give them some presents—some clothes.

We will give two beef creatures to each tribe. Tell them we have done now and feel good.

D.B.H. then gave ammunition to each tribe and gave them all some knives.

B.Y. Tell them all this is a happy day. I feel good.

Young officially reported on the intertribal conference:

I led off by asking Wachor and Wash-o-kig if they wished to make peace and be friends with each other. They replied they did. Will you make good peace that will last? Answered yes. I then said to Wachor, tell all of your tribe this, and ask them if they will do the same, and, if so, let every one arise and hold up his right hand. It was done unanimously. And the same explanation being made to the Shoshones by their chief, they also responded unanimously in the same manner. I then told them that they must never fight each other again, but must live in peace, so that they could travel in each other's country, and trade with each other. I then asked the Utes if we had been friends to them, and if they loved us? As soon as the question was explained to their understanding, they answered in the affirmative by acclamation, with evident signs of joy and good feeling. The pipe of peace, being first offered to the Great Spirit, was often replenished and sent around by the Shoshone chiefs, until every one had smoked in token of lasting friendship. The Utahs were then asked if they had any objections to our settling on their lands, and, if they had not, to raise their right hands; which they did unanimously. Sow-er-ette, being the chief of the Uinta Utes, (two of his sons being present,) was also asked the same question. He replied that it was good for them to have us settle upon their lands, and that he wanted a house close beside us. I then asked the Shoshones how they would like to have us settle upon their lands at Green river. They replied that the land at Green river did not belong to them; that they lived and inhabited in the vicinity of the Wind River chain of mountains and the Sweet river, (or Sugar Water, as they called it;) but that if we would make a settlement on Green river they would be glad to come and trade with us. I expressed unto them my good feelings for their kindness in always being friendly to the whites, and for the safety in which all the emigrants had ever been able to pass through their country, and hoped they would always continue the same. If any of the whites should steal anything from them, it should be returned if I could find it; and if any of their tribe should steal anything from the whites, they must do the same. The Shoshones were expecting that Wachor and the Utes would give them some horses, according to their usual custom, for a certain number of Shoshones which they had killed in their last conflict, which occurred something over a year ago. Ten seemed to be about the number which had been killed, and the same number of horses were required, but finally agreed upon nine head. Walker now led off in quite a lengthy speech, in which he said that he had done wrong and was sorry for it. His friends had been killed on the Shoshones' land, and he had supposed that they had done it; but now he was satisfied that it was not them; that Brigham told him not to go, but he would not hear him; he had been sorry ever since, and so forth; had no horses now, but was going to trade with the Moquis next winter, and would bring the horses to Green river when he should return. I will hear now what Brigham says to me good, placing his hand on his breast; have been a fool, but will do better in future. To-ter-mitch, Shoshone chief, then said a few words. His ears were open wide to hear; it was good, and he felt well; his heart was good. I then directed that the chiefs should have some clothes and ammunition given to them, and some beef-cattle and flour, having been procured for the purpose, was distributed among them, when they left in apparently high spirits, and good and friendly feelings towards each other, as well as to the whites.[18]

---

[18]Young to Lea, 29 September 1852, Lea, Commissioner of Indian Affairs, *Annual Report*, Serial 658, 147–48.

"The Shoshonees or snake Indians came into the City to day to make peace with the Utahs & Walkers Company. They smoked the pipe of peace & shook hands in friendship & fellowship," wrote Wilford Woodruff. "They have been at war for many years but through the wise course of President Young they are brought to peace." Peace seldom endured long on the frontier's contested grounds. Two years later, "The Snake Indians fought the Utahs & killed & brought in the Indian scalps on poles through our streets & had a war dans."[19]

TO ROB PLUNDER AND KILL: THE MORMONS MOBILIZE

Ute bands often wintered in southern Utah. In December 1852 "a part of Peteetneet's band of Utahs, about 40 in number, encamped at Parowan." They had "near 100 horses, which they regardless of our request" let eat the wheat "in the big field," John D. Lee reported. The Mormons impounded their horses, but quickly returned the animals to "Green Jacket, one of their war chiefs," who promised "to keep them out of the field in future." Another Ute band went west and "fell on a party of the Piedes while encamped 7 miles south west of the Iron Springs and killed and wounded about 20 men and took as many more women and children prisoners." On 20 January 1853 Wakara and sixty Utes camped at Fort Harmony, Lee wrote, with about "10 Indians of the wild tribes in the south" who found "the face of a white man" to be a terror. Lee celebrated the start of a beautiful friendship.

LEE TO RICHARDS, 5 FEBRUARY 1853, *DESERET NEWS*, 19 MARCH 1853, 2/4.

I gave them a dinner to show them the difference between civility and barbarity. Before partaking of the festival, I preached to them the gospel of peace, and told them that the refreshment's [sic] then prepared in part had been raised by the natives. When I was done, Walker continued the subject, and said "take back the news to your friends, and tell them to cease committing depredations upon the whites, and be at peace among yourselves and come and work, raise grain, herd cattle and sheep every day, and live like white people;" said he had left the natives on the Santa Clara, 7 milch cows and requested me, when I got my blacksmith up, to make them some hoes to cultivate the soil with. He further declared his hands was clear of the blood of the Piedes, that had been shed by his nation; neither had he ever shed the blood of a white man. He then turned to me and said this looks like true friendship.

---

[19]Woodruff, *Journal*, 21 August 1852 and 23 September 1854, 4:144, 4:289.

On the 24rd, Walker came and said that one of their dogs had caught one of my sheep, and one of his unruly boys had shot an arrow into one of my hogs, and asked what I wanted for the damage. Keep your boys and dogs from doing so again, and the damage is settled, was my reply. After pausing for a moment, he said, "you ask a hard thing of me, for some of them won't hear; please tell me what you do with your men and dogs that have no ears?" We cut off the dogs tails where their ears should be, and then they will do no more mischief, and punish the men. "Very true; but if I was to do so, I soon would be without dogs, for those that have ears do not keep them open all the time.["]

The same night a council was held. The next morning the Hawk of the mountain and lady breakfasted with me. During his conversation remarked that wise captains should never keep their men and dogs that have no ears, within barking distance of each other. He had therefore concluded to remove his encampment to the next water, 10 miles off, the same day his policy was consummated. 25th, Nephi returned with two of my horses which had strayed to their encampment. Up to this date friendly feelings prevail among the natives and the Utes towards out people.

Warm feelings seldom endured in Utah's extreme southern settlements. On 6 April "a company of California emigrants partly made up of apostate mormons" came to Parowan with "a horse branded with a recorded brand of This Territory, and not reversed," wrote Mormon Battalion veteran John Steele. It was "retained as stolen property according to law," and the party "went away much dissatisfied" and "made threats that they would be revenged before leaving the territory." After staying nearby "about two days near a band of Utah Indians," they "purchased a Pieute boy for the purpose of traffic with the Mexicans." They sold the "Indians rifles and a large amount of powder lead and caps, cloths &c. at the same time exciting the indians to come against us." The Mormons dispatched an armed posse after them, but at Summit Creek "they were very unexpectedly intercepted by the Utahs, some thirty in number," with Wakara at their head, all well armed and mounted. The Utes leveled their rifles and told the posse to stop, "that the Americans were good, but that the mormons were not good and that Brigham was not good &c." The greatly outnumbered Saints "thought proper to return to the fort" and held a council "to deliberate upon the affair." After due deliberation and in consideration of the number of Indians being egged on by the apostates, they "thought best to waive the matter for the present and obtain your council upon our course of proceedure" and sent Young an "epistle in charge of brothers Samuel Lewis and Barnabus Carter." Few frontier settlements would dispatch riders on a five-hundred-mile round trip to ask for such advice, but in Utah this was standard.[20]

Young replied immediately after receiving Steele's letter "conveying the intelligence of the threatened hostility of the Indians." He trusted he would "have no trouble with Wacher's band, but what can be amicably arranged." It was "better to conciliate and make peace with the Indians, than be at the trouble and expense to pursue so far after such a worthless set" of apostates.[21] Young sent a sterner message to Wakara.

BRIGHAM YOUNG TO CAPTAIN WACHER, 14 APRIL 1853, BYC 17:7.

G.S.L. City April 14th 1853.

Captain Wacher
Chief of Utahs:

We have heard from you, by way of the Brethren in Iron County, that you have become angry with them, and leveled your Rifles at them, and threatened to shoot them, when they were trying to go after some bad men, who had been stealing. That you stopped them, and would not let them go, and so the bad men who had been stealing got away; and that you say, that they were good men, and that I, and my people were not good.

Now Wacher, I am writing a Letter to you, that you may know my feelings towards you, and that I may know your feelings towards me, and toward my people.

You have always pretended to be my friend. Now, if you wish to throw me, and my people away, just say so, and let me know that this is your wish; but if you do not wish to throw me away, nor have me throw you away, and blot your name off from my Books, you must be friends with me and my people, and not believe all the lies, which other people that steal from us, and seek to do us all the injury they can, tell you.

I have been friendly with you, and still wish to be, and wish, and intend to do you all the good I can. I was anxious to have you to make friends with the Shoshones, that you might live in peace with them, and am always glad to hear from you, when you feel well with me, and our great Father wants us to be friends.

I am expecting to start South in about a week, and shall expect to meet you somewhere on the route; when we will have a friendly talk as usual.

I send Dimick, our old friend to you, that you may see him, and hear him talk; you know him, and know that he tells you the truth. I want you to hear him, for the Great Spirit loves Dimick, and will love you, if you hearken unto him.

[20]Steele to Young, 10 April 1853, BYC 23:7.
[21]Young to John C. L. Smith and John Steele, 14 April 1853, BYC 17:7.

When I see you, and your braves, I shall also expect to see Arrowpin, Grospin, Taaba, Peetetneet, Blackhawk, Anton, and all of your Brothers, and I will be your Brother, and you will be my Brother, and I pray unto my father in heaven, to peaceably dispose you towards all of my people, and make you feel glad and happy until I see you, Amen

Brigham Young

Despite Wakara's attempt to accommodate his white neighbors, tension escalated. Brigham Young quickly headed south. At Provo on 23 April 1853, a buckskin-clad stranger, Dr. Wallace Alonzo Clark Bowman, confronted him and "wanted a private conversation." Bowman had his pockets "filled with deadly weapons," Young said, and had come "to buy Indian children, and sell them again for slaves." He told the prophet that he had "400 Mexicans at the head waters of the Sanpete making threats, and the Indians are making threats. The Mexican has bought 40 rifles and says he has money enough to by Governor Young and all his women." The encounter made suppressing the slave trade personal. As for Bowman's plans, Young said, "I had my own thoughts." He issued a proclamation denouncing the "horde of Mexicans, or outlandish men, who are infesting the settlements, stirring up the Indians to make aggressions upon the inhabitants, and who are also furnishing the Indians with guns, ammunition, etc., contrary to the laws of this Territory and the laws of the United States." Young "gave orders to the Lieutenant General, and he has done what he has."[22]

However Wells dealt with Bowman, Mormon historians have circled the wagons around the charge that Indians murdered Bowman, a lie the Utes resented. Long before the incident that allegedly ignited the "Walker War," Utah's military leaders had moved to subdue Wakara and the Utahs. Acting on Young's "horde of Mexicans" proclamation, D. H. Wells sent Capt. William Wall and forty-four men on an "Expedition to the extreme Southern Settlement of the Territory of Utah." Captain Wall found "Spanish Traders" at Payson on 24 April. He "went with a Guard and took them prisoners, according to my Orders, after I had them safe delivered into the hands of Civil law." Bowman was arrested, for when a Salt Lake court released him, Young told Payson's bishop to return his property "and also release the Spaniards, or Mexicans who are in your charge, and give them their property."[23]

---

[22]Van Wagoner, *Complete Discourses*, 8 May 1853, 2:665–67; Whitney, *History of Utah*, 1:512.

[23]Wall, Report, 24 April, UTMR 177; Young to Cross, 20 May 1853, BYC 17:7.

Back in Salt Lake, General Wells forwarded Young's proclamation and instructed Tooele's militia to prepare for war. Exposed regions must be vigilant, and "a good thing if the People of Grantville would build a good Fort," for it was "in the immediate vicinity of ignorant savages liable to be incited to rob plunder and kill for the most trivial reasons and even for no other reason than to glut their own savage propensity for blood and plunder." God had so far protected them, but "it would be heart rendering indeed to hear the tidings which we acknowledge we have especially feared many times we should hear of some lone settlement having been masscreed by the Indians."[24]

While camped at Nephi on 25 April, Superintendent Brigham Young ordered William Wall to find Dimick Huntington and learn "the where-abouts of Walker & the conditions of the Indians." Young planned to visit Sanpete with a small escort, but if all was peaceful, Wall could return home after "delivering a copy of the governors proclamation" to each southern settlement. However,

[i]f Walker is not disposed to live peacefully with his band of Indians while in this Territory, but has made his threats to the danger of the Inhabitants & you have an opportunity without too much endangering your command you will take him prisoner with those of his band who are determined to follow him; but if he & his band are too strong you will immediately send a messenger informing me thereof, that a sufficient company be raised to meet him.[25]

At Nephi George Bean told Wall "that Battice an old Utah Indian" was camped nearby. The shaman "came down very much excited, stating the he had been told that Governor Brigham Young had sent out the company to kill him, together with the Chiefs *Peteetnea* and Walker." Battice "was assured that was not the case but advised to behave better, as he had been troublesome to the Citizens."[26] The "Executive" ordered Wall "to take 30 men and go south through Millard, Iron, and Washington Counties, to inspect their military strength and preparations—to visit the several Indian tribes and learn their dispositions toward the whites—with instructions how to proceed in case of a war with the Utah Indians:—also to arrest any and all persons whom I should find trading with the Indians without

[24]Wells to Wright, 25 April 1853, UTMR 235.
[25]Young to Wall, "Orders to capture chief Walker if possible," UTMR 236.
[26]Wall, Report, 24 April, UTMR 177.

license." Wall wrote on his return, "Walker was willing to live in peace, if he can have his own way in stealing other Indian children to sell them to Mexicans for guns and ammunition, or if we will buy these children of him and give him guns and ammunition, to enable him to continue his robberies."[27]

Young visited Sanpete County "prepared for whites, reds, or blacks, by night and by day." The Saints had quieted the tribes, he said, "because when we first entered Utah, we were prepared to meet all the Indians in these mountains, and kill every soul of them if we had been obliged so to do." This policy "secured to us peace." New settlers "received strict charges from me, to build, in the first place, a Fort, and live in it until they were sufficiently strong to live in a town; to keep their guns and ammunition well prepared for any emergency; and never cease to keep up a night watch." Utah had suffered nothing from Indians "compared with what we have suffered from white men who are disposed to steal; and I would rather take my chance to-day for good treatment among Indians, than I would among white men of this character." He had only a single recollection of Indians killing anyone, a man "who had started for California, on foot and alone, against counsel." Young said "the men who follow Walker, who is the king of the Indians in these mountains, do it out of fear, and not because they have real regard for their leader." If he became hostile and committed depredations upon persons or property, Wakara would "be wiped out of existence, and every man that will follow him." If the Saints had "the faith they ought to have, the Lord Almighty would never suffer any of the sons of Jacob to injure them in the least; *no never*," Young said. His advice was to "*be on the watch all the time.* Do not lie down, and go to sleep, and say all is well, lest, in an hour when you think not, sudden destruction overtake you." As for Walker, Young expected he would "be peaceable, and the rest of the Indians also. I have no doubt of it. Why? *Because they dare not be any other way.*" The "wretched remnants of Abraham's seed" would "be kind and peaceable, because they are afraid to die, and that is enough for me." His advice was "*keep your powder, and lead,* and your guns in good order."[28]

Wakara visited Sanpete to try to defuse "the Supposed difficulties," as Isaac Morley promptly reported.

[27]Wall to Editor, 31 May 1853, *Deseret News*, 28 May 1853, 3/3–4. Its erratic schedule meant the *Deseret News* occasionally contained items that post-dated its official publication date.

[28]Young, "Indian Difficulties—Walker," *Journal of Discourses*, 8 May 1853, 1:104–108.

MORLEY TO YOUNG, 30 APRIL 1853, BYC 23:4.

Walker and four of his men have Come into this place to see me in relations to the Supposed difficulties which are existing. He says he wants Peace and is a friend to the Mormons. The Council you have sent him, he has returned with, and the tobacco you sent him, he has Smoked in the Pipe of Peace with the Utahs, and he manifested a very good Spirit. He has expressed a very friendly feeling towards you, and myself and the Mormons generally, and in relation to the Spaniards he says there are but eight or ten in the Country. He also Says he will not trade with them if you say so; he says that he has traded a great deal with them, and is a friend to them, but he understands now, that the Spaniards makes Slaves of them, and we, when they become Men and Women, Sets them free, and Walker says he will tell the Spaniards not to Come here any more and trade for Children. Walker says he has a good number of Skins of various Kinds to trade and wants to go to Salt Lake City to See you, and to trade, &c, and wishes you to send him and expression of your feelings in relation to the matter. This appears to satisfy Walker better than any thing that we Can do to him here; for you to write to me, for information upon the subject, [about] that Company of Utahs from the East which you was Appraised of when you was here, write to him [illegible]. Walker also says in relation to the difficulty which has existed at Cedar City, that he interfered, to prevent any difficulty at the time. Walker wishes to visit you as soon as you Can Conviently.

Walker also Says if you will let the Spaniards go, he will not trade with them.

Young was "pleased to learn of the pacific disposition of Walker. You can tell him that it is just what pleases me, to have him come and trade." He expected "a small amount of ammunition can be found, shirts, clothing and Blankets, &c. and perhaps some money."

I am glad if Walker understands that the Mormons are his friends, and friends to his people. I know that we are, and that we seek to do them good all the day long, and if Walker and the Utahs will do right the time will come when they will become a "white and delightsome people," but if they continue to sell their children into slavery, and rob other Indians of their children to get them to sell, and they persist in this course they will continue to decrease until they become extinct, until there is no man of them, you can tell Walker this, and also tell him to come and see me and trade, and be my Brother; if I talk to him plain it is to do him good. I could not believe that he would turn out our enemy after all his professions of friendship towards us. I want to talk to Walker about trading hereafter, I think some of sending for Indian goods, and having a stock kept continually on hand to trade with them. If he comes we can talk this matter over with him, and make arrangements with him for the future.[29]

The next day Brigham Young addressed his followers at Salt Lake.

Yesterday morning, we received a communication from father Morley, in which we were informed that Walker and Arapeen came down to pay him a visit. The morning that we left San Pete, we sent back by the hands of Arapeen's two messengers, some little presents in the shape of shirts and tobacco. Walker said to Father Morley, "Tell brother Brigham, we have smoked the tobacco he sent us in the pipe of peace; I want to be at peace, and be a brother to him." That is all right. But it is truly characteristic of the cunning Indian, when he finds he cannot get advantage over his enemy, to curl down at once, and say "I love you." It is enough for me to know that Walker dare not attempt to hurt any of our settlements. I care not whether they love me or not. I am resolved, however, not to trust his love any more than I would a stranger's. I do not repose confidence in persons, only as they prove themselves confidential; and I shall live a long while before I can believe that an Indian is my friend, when it would be to his advantage to be my enemy.[30]

On 2 July 1853, a warm Saturday, Wakara accepted the invitation to visit Salt Lake and trade. The "Govr saw Walker Ammon Peteetneet [and] other Indians this morning" while their "'band' camped above his house." As the Nauvoo Legion drilled nearby, Wakara "came into Prests office," manifesting a "peaceable disposition showing hypocrisy," wrote Thomas Bullock.[31] The Utes were not the hypocrites: the when, where, and how of Dr. Bowman's murder may be a mystery, but the killer was not a Ute. After Wakara visited Salt Lake, Jacob Holeman engaged a New Mexican interpreter who had traded with the Utahs since the 1830s to find out what Wakara, Sowiette, and others had to say.

M. S. MARTENAS, STATEMENT, 6 JULY 1853, HOLEMAN PAPERS, MS 2178, LDS ARCHIVES.

At the request of Maj. Holeman Ind. Agt for U. Ter. I held a conversation with Indian Chief Walker, respecting his feelings and wishes relative to the Whites setling [sic] on his lands, and on the lands of the Indians generally.

He said, that he had always been opposed to the whites setling on the Indian lands, particularly that portion which he claims and on which his band

[29]Young to Morley, 7 May 1853, BYC 17:7, 48.
[30]Young, 8 May 1853, Journal of Discourses, 1:106.
[31]Historical Department Office Journal, 2 July 1853, LDS Archives, 98.

resides and on which they have resided since his childhood, and his parents before him—that the Mormons when they first commenced the settlement of Salt Lake Valley, was friendly, and promised them many comforts, and lasting friendship—that they continued friendly for a short time, until they became strong in numbers, then their conduct and treatment towards the Indians changed—they were not only treated unkindly, but many were much abused and this course has been pursued up to the present—sometimes they have been treated with much severity—they have been driven by this population from place to place—settlements have been made on all their hunting grounds in the valleys, and the graves of their fathers have been torn up by the whites. He said he wished, to keep the valley of San Pete, and desired to leave the valley of Salt Lake, as he could not live in peace with the whites—but that the Whites had taken possession of that valley also—and the Indians were forced to leave their homes, or submit to the constant abuses of the whites. He said the Gosoke Utes who formerly lived in the Salt Lake valley had been killed and driven away, and that now they wished to drive him and his band away also—he said he had always wished to be friendly with the whites—but they seemed never to be satisfied—the Indians had moved time after time, and yet they could have no peace—that his heart was sick—that his heart felt very bad. He desired me very earnestly to communicate the situation of the Indians in this neighborhood to the Great Father, and ask his protection and friendship—that whatever the great father wished he would do. He said he has always been opposed to the whites settling on his lands, but the whites were strong and he was weak, and he could not help it—that if his great father did not do something to relieve them, he could not tell what they would do.

I have had sincere talks with Sou-we-reats, (the man that picks fish from the water) Tos-kah-boos (Black belly) who have always expressed themselves in the strongest terms against the whites setling on their lands. Sow-we-reats in Uwinty Valley and Too ke boos, on the river of the same name—it is a fine valley, well watered, and has plenty of game. These Indians and their ancestors have long occupied this country—they very much dislike to leave it—they say they cannot live with the whites, for they cannot live in peace—the whites want every thing, and will give the Indians nothing—that they shoot the Indians if they walk over their grounds.

I have been acquainted with his country, and these Indians for upwards of thirty years. I have known Walker, Souwahreats, and Tookeboos since they were children—I have always been on friendly terms with them—they talk freely with me—and express their feelings and wishes without reserve. One prominent cause of the present excitement is the interference of the Mormons with their long established Spanish trade, and the killing of an American by the name of Bowman, from Santa Fee, and charging the murder to the Indians. I greatly fear that much difficulty will grow out of the

present excited condition of the Indians,—should the Mormons continue
their unkind treatment. I have just had a long conversation with the Chief
Walker and make the above statement of his feelings with his expressions
fresh in my mind.

    Great Salt Lake City July 6 1853   M. S. Martenas, Interpreter[32]

BLOOD MUST ATONE: ANOTHER INDIAN WAR

After Ute leaders left Salt Lake in July, they camped along Spring Creek,
a mile north of today's Springville. Historian Howard Christy concluded
"efforts to stifle the slave trade precipitated the Walker War," but as scholar
Ryan Wimmer noted, "it was more complicated than that." Mormon "land
encroachments, laws regulating trade of many kinds," and "the murder of
one of Wakara's band" drove the conflict traditionally mislabeled as the
"Walker War."[33]

    The Nauvoo Legion had prepared to fight an Indian war long before
15 July 1853, when James A. Ivie laid low three Utes with a musket barrel,
including the "squaw" he said he was defending.[34] Ivie sought to profit from
his story with an 1897 Indian depredation claim:

> In '53 there was two Indians and a squaw came into my house wanting to
> trade some fish for flour; I was digging a well at that time, my wife came
> to me and called me to come out and make the trade; I came out then and
> went into the house, and traded flour for those five fish; shortly two other
> Indians came in with their guns and bows and arrows in their hands; went
> into the house and commenced fighting amongst themselves; one of those
> Indians caught the squaw and knocked her down, knocked the blood out of
> her, and the blood flew over the house, the Indian; then my wife called on
> me to protect the squaw, I taken [*sic*] the Indian and let him out the door;
> then he drew his bow and arrow on me, presented it and I caught the arrow
> and broke it in two; then I struck him with my fist and knocked him down;
> he arose with his gun and attempted to shoot me; I caught the muzzle of
> the gun and broke it in two; having the barrel in my hand, and then I struck
> him over the head with the gun barrel and knocked him, and he lay on the

[32]Martinez was a common New Mexican name. Otis "Doc" Martin noted Manuel Martinez's
1827 report of a party sent "to retrieve some caches in the direction of the lands of the Utes." Hafen,
The Mountain Men, 7:185. Bancroft mentioned a Miguel Martinez at San Bernardino in 1846. I have been
unable to make a more precise identification. The name has appeared as "M. S. Marlenas," but the "t"
is crossed in the manuscript.

[33]Christy, "The Walker War," 396; Wimmer, "The Walker War Reconsidered," 4–5.

[34]Accounts of this incident are error-ridden; Carter, *From Fort to Village*, 163, first identified the location
of the Ute camp and the correct date.

steps in front of the door; the second Indian drew his gun on me, and it was a flint lock gun and missed fire, and I struck him over the head with the same gun barrel, knocking him down, and falling over the other Indians I had just hit; then the squaw that I was taking her part, she arose to her feet and struck me with a billet of wood across the lip, cutting it through to my teeth; I also struck her with the gun barrel, and she fell across the other two Indians that had fell on the outside of the door; Mr. [Joseph] Kelly, a man by that name, rode up and said he "Ivie, you've got into a fight, and I'll stay with ya and see it over with." Then I sent my wife and children to her father's a quarter of a mile away; Mr. Kelly remained with me there for a half hour, waiting for the Indians to recover from their wounds, and then those two Indians who had taken no active part in the fight called on me for a bucket to get some water to pour over those wounded Indians; I gave them a bucket and they carried water and threw over those Indians to bring them to; I stayed there about half a hour waiting for them to come to, and they didn't come to, and Mr. Kelly and I then went to Springville and left them laying there; those other two Indians went off to Spanish Fork, where Walker was camping with about 300 lodges of Indians; two hours and a half later there was 40 Indians mounted and come over and carried off those wounded Indians, and went back to Spanish Fork. That night those Indians killed a man by the name of [Alexander] Keel, at Payson, shot him when he was on guard.[35]

That fall Salt Lake merchant William H. Hooper explained the "Origin of the Indian War" to a Sacramento newspaper. A Mormon wanted to buy some fish from an Indian woman, "without however, paying to her the price demanded." Her husband "became exasperated, and wreaked vengeance upon his guiltless wife by cruelly beating her." The purchaser "obtained the services of another 'saint,' and immediately searched for and found the Indian, whom they bound and beat to death. For this act the Indians have declared war upon the Mormons." The *Daily Union* expected "to hear of a battle at Salt Lake before many days, as Indians seldom forgive an injury of the kind which has been done them. Their whole history denotes a belief in the doctrine of blood for blood. The history of this war will, however, be like all others in which white men engage with Indians—the white wins and the red loses." Hooper's honest reputation suggested his tale was not "in every respect 'a fish story.'"[36] But Peter Conover recalled the Utes had a "row" with Jim Ivie "over trading guns. Ivie knocked an Indian down and that was the first start of the Walker War."[37]

---

[35]Indian Depredation Case File 707, RG 123, NARA, in Wimmer, "The Walker War," 97–98.
[36]"From Great Salt Lake," *Sacramento Daily Union*, 5 November 1853, 2/2
[37]Conover, Sketch of the Life, typescript, 7.

GUNS, BOWS, AND ARROWS: CHARLES HANCOCK

Now the "Walker Indian War commenced," wrote Luke Gallup, naming Joseph Kelly and James Ivie as "the first cause of the disturbance. They whipped an Indian for abusing his squaw." His neighbors "were much to blame as they let slip a good opportunity to settle the matter for a trifling sum of a little over $50, damages claimed: only a selfish & wilful course" prevented a peaceful resolution. "Some of the Whites & Indians it seems have long fostered a spirit of war & now it seems the time had arrived to foster the same," Gallup noted.[38]

Before the Ute died, events moved quickly. On 16 July 1853 Nauvoo Legion captain Charles Hancock saw three "lion looking braves" enter his wife's cabin near Payson. He "followed them in for fearing some mischief might be done as I did not like their looks." Such "impudence needed correction," but he "had no weapons and was alone with his wife and two children." Hancock thought "a collision had better be avoided." From the comfort of the twentieth-first century, it is impossible to grasp the revulsion and dread such encounters created, for Ute warriors terrified Anglo-Americans. Hancock persuaded the Utes to go to their camp, telling them he "would soon be there to see their chiefs." No one would go with him, but Hancock kept his word, finding "the well known and much dreaded blood thirsty savages known as Walkara's Band" gathered around a low mound. By 1882 this probable gravesite was a "well cultivated garden and orchard."[39] The Utes wanted traditional justice.

> I soon became satisfied that their intention was to use me as their victim. Soon came Arapeen into their circle and talked to Walkara and his men a few moments and then took me to his tent which was nearby, and told me to go in and lay down which I did, and he threw buffalo skins over me and he stayed in the door and none others entered. I know the others gathered around by their talk although I did not see them. After laying in my sweat for about two hours Arapeen told me to go home and as I arose, Arapeen pushed me ahead of him, keeping himself, with his hands on my shoulders, between me and many others that sat at the tent, with their guns, bows and arrows.[40]

Both Mormons and Indians tried to avoid another conflict. Hancock's vivid memoir illuminated the drama of two cultures unable to comprehend each other.

---

[38]Gallup, Diary, July 1853, LDS Archives, 175.

[39]Hancock, Autobiography, 12 April 1882, LDS Archives.

[40]Hancock, Reminiscences, LDS Archives, 15–16.

CHARLES B. HANCOCK, REMINISCENCES AND DIARY, 15–20.

Their manners and Conduct seemed plainly to show that they were ill disposed and not friendly. I had learned Considerably of their character when in California 1847 and having some experience in indian Battils there I dreaded the now evoked for Task. They encamped on a selected place suitable for their Battil ground near the watter and deep ravenes for shelter and defense on the upper part of the town site. Three of their Braves Came down to my Cabin and went in. I was out but soon followed them in. My wife [and] 2 little Children were in the house. Their appearance was frightening they had butcher knives and bows and arrows. I told them to go back to their camp and I'de Come there and see them. . . . On reaching their camp I was soon surrounded by many well armed warriers. They were naked and only a brich clout and were Striped with Black as war parties. Walker and aropiene came to the center and I got between them and began to talk to them. Arapiene pled for no execution and Walker raised his hand to the Executioner as to hold on these ceremonies and talk continued for over an hour. Then Aropine took me to his tent clost by and I went in and lay down. He throwd a Buffilo Skin over me and Sett down in the door of the tent. Many gathered around as their talk Planly [plainly] sounded to me & probably was there an hour. Then arapiene told me to go home. I came out of the tent and there was many indians with their arms. Arapiene walked beside me untill I was safe from their Shotts and then went back saying that he would soon be down to see me. I went home and soon he came and said the Indians were going to kill me and he had kept them from it and he could not keep them any longer than one day and in that time if I would go to Salt lake and see the Govenor and have a compromise made and [be] back by one Sleep there would not be any body killed. By that time it then being at dusk. I instructed my officers to Collect the People to gather and keep the best of guards [and] take Care of their stock Closely. The People being scatterd out for large farms and ranches made it Bad to battel with Indians and they did not realize the Perilous war just Opened upon them.

I at once started with my team which had been standing half of the day without feed. On arriving at Springville I called on James Ivy having heard that he had had difficulty with Some Indians while they were there the even[ing] before. Ivy said that an Indian and Squaw Came into his house and the squaw wanted to trade some fish for Bread and Iveys wife did not want to trade for fish was Plenty and Bread Scarce.

James McClelan dashed off a letter, which Hancock rushed to Salt Lake.

McCLELAN TO B. YOUNG, 16 JULY 1853, BYC 23:4.

B. Young, dear sir.

I have learned from Arepeen and from other reliable sources, that in a difficulty near Springville on yesterday between James Ivy, and some of Walkers band, Ivy knocked down three, and one of them it is thought uncertain whether he will recover. In the scrape there was two guns broken belonging to the Indians.

Arepeen says if the Indian gets well, and the guns are made good, it will all be right, but if he dies Ivys Blood must atone for it—nothing else will satisfy the Indians—he wishes you informed of the event and let you settle it. He does not want anyone interested but the guilty. Walker has just sent a runner for Arapeen, and is opposed to sending to you, and from the report of the runner the Indian will not live long. Arapeen has gone to talk to the Indians and try to reconcile them

Payson July 16th 4 P.M. 1853. James McClelan

Hancock reached Salt Lake "in good time and got instructions from the governor to settle the matter and he would back me." He returned immediately after Brigham Young dashed off a message to the "Chiefs of Utah Tribe."

Ivy not willing to have the Indian kill the Squaw in his house pushed him gently out of doors, and told him in a friendly manner to behave himself. The Indian turned back and abused her more severely then Ivy lead him out of the house the second time and took him about six paces from the house, and told him forcibly to keep quiet; the Indian returned again and kicked the squaw the 3rd time, then Ivy's wife and children became alarmed and commenced crying, when Ivy seeing his family much distressed and no further use of seemingly peaceable to the Indian he kicked the Indian down. Indian made an attack intending to kill Ivy.[41]

Hancock failed to find a fresh team in Salt Lake and did "not git back in time." Young advised "Wocker and Arrowpin" that the whole affair "would counsel you to be peaceful quiet and not hasty, angry and for war." It was too late. Arapene could not restrain his men: a shot "from the gun of a tetcherous Indian" killed Alexander Keele "while on Post as guard." So began "the Grand Walker War of 1853 which lasted for 4 years," at immense cost in lives, dollars, and "much Experience and anxiety," Hancock recalled. Orders to mobilize and consolidate "were willingly Obeyed through fear of Indian Raids."[42]

---

[41]Brigham Young's Letterbook No. 1 is water damaged and often illegible, but see Edyth Romney's deciphered typescript, MS 2736, 108–10.

[42]Ibid.; Hancock, Reminiscences and Diary, LDS Archives, 19–20.

War Was Forced upon the Settlers: Lewis Barney

Lewis Barney came west with the Pioneer Camp in 1847 and returned to Winter Quarters that October.[43] Five years later, he again "rolled into Salt Lake City, which had by this time become quite a settlement." The lot and acreage allotted to Barney in 1847 "had been given to another party," so Heber Kimball advised him to join his brother Walter at Provo. The Barneys went to "Peteneet Canyon and put up a saw mill through the winter" and "suffered very much with cold, and for the common comforts of life. About the first of July 1853 we got the mill started to making lumber." Barney recalled the morning of 18 July 1853.

Lewis Barney, Autobiography, Typescript, Family History Library.

Through some unwise conduct of some of the Mormons the Indians became affected and broke out, and killed one man by the name of Alexander Keel, while on guard at Payson in the evening. Then they came up Peteteneet Canyon and camped a mile and a half below our saw mill. As we had just got the mill running I was up very early in the morning and had just started the mill to sawing. My son Walter was out with me on the mill to work. As soon as it was light enough to see, two Indians came galloping up the Canyon, and rode up to the mill and motioned for us to come down. Accordingly we went down to see what they wanted.

They said, "You kill one Utah, and we kill you," pointing to myself and son Walter.

They wheeled their horses round and started down the canyon full speed, but seeing a mule tied they stopped to get it, but the mule was tied with a trace chain and fastener so they could not get it loose, so they galloped on down the canyon. While the Indians were trying to get the mule I ran into the cabin and roused up the men, and told them to get up for the Indians were upon us. By this time the guns were firing and the bullets were whistling around us tearing up the ground and cutting the brush at a rapid rate in every direction.

I ran across the creek and woke up the Stuerts family. I then went up to the dam and shut off the water and while I was coming down the trail to the cabin two bullets whistled by me so near that I could feel the wind of them. We knew nothing of the Indians until they were upon us. Neither did we know of their being mad, consequently we were without fire arms or anything to defend ourselves with. While Brother Walter was trying to get his mule loose the bullets whistled around him so fast he was forced to abandon the mule and run around the house. He stooped down to get his saddle and a bullet struck the house just missing his head.

I then spoke to him and told him that we had better try and get down to the settlements and give them the alarm. We looked around and found men, women and children had all hid themselves in the brush. So brother Walter and I started up the mountain to try and get to the settlements. When we got up a little way on the side of the mountain we looked back and saw the hills and canyons full of Indians. They had gathered up all our stock, cattle, horses and milk cows and were driving them off into the mountains.

It was out of our power to stop them. We continued on our way up the mountain. Finally Walter's shoes hurt his feet so he could not travel, and he stopped and took them off. I continued up on up the mountain, but knew nothing of Walters coming. I made my way over the mountain into the head of Loafer Canyon, and down the canyon to Pond Town, a small settlement between Payson and Spanish Fork. Here I found the settlers in a state of great excitement, expecting every minute to see the Indians coming to take their lives. They also supposed that the whole camp in the canyon were massacred. I then proceeded on to Spanish Fork, here also the settlement was wonderfully excited, and Colonel [Stephen] Markham was raising a company to go to Peteneet Canyon to see what had become of the families at the saw mill, supposing them to be all massacred by the Indians. As soon as they heard of my arrival he came to me to inquire after the folks at the mill. I related what occurred in the Canyon and informed him that the folks were all right. But their stock were all driven off by the Indians. This allayed the excitement considerably. In a short time after, brother Walter came in all right with the exception of his feet being very sore.

Through the foolishness of two or three men, by the name of J Ivy the Indians were exasperated and broke out, and the Walker War was forced upon the settlers. Many a precious life was lost, much property destroyed, and we were forced to abandon the mill our only source [of income] for our families. I was then under the necessity of working by days work for my provisions and clothing to support my family. I also took up a lot and a piece of farming land in Spanish Fork and moved onto it.

I built a house and helped build a fort wall around Palmyra. The next spring I put in five acres of wheat and six acres of corn, a patch of potatoes and other garden stuff, from which I gathered one hundred sixty two and one half bushels of wheat, one hundred fifty bushels of corn, and enough potatoes to supply the wants of my family. The Indians through the influence and kind treatment of President Brigham Young and the Mormons became a little reconciled, but were not altogether safe. But through necessity we were obliged to venture into the canyon for lumber at the risk of our lives.

---

[43]Ronald Barney, *One Side by Himself*, 294n18, is an excellent Lewis Barney biography.

Perfect Folly and Wickedness: Who Began the War?

Who started Utah's Indian war of 1853? The *Deseret News* blamed Wakara, who took no active role in the conflict.

> It is well known to the inhabitants of this territory that the Indian Chief, Walker, has been surly in his feelings and expressions at divers times and places within our borders for more than one year past, and that he has repeatedly endeavored to raise excitement and open war out of small pretexts that in former times he would have smiled at. It is equally well known that, in the midst of all Walker's folly, Gov. Young has pursued an invariable and manifestly mild course towards him and his tribe and has counseled our citizens so to do, and that counsel has been followed in all the settlements without any deviation worthy of notice, but it at last appears that all this does not prevent a still greater exhibition of perfect folly and wickedness on the part of Walker.—His cunning and treachery, his thieving and murderous propensities have outweighed the constantly open and extended hand of utmost kindness, and on a mere pretext which he could have satisfactorily arranged in a moment had he possessed a spark of good feeling, he has declared open war.[44]

Why did Mormon leaders order campaigns against Native peoples? One reason was the federal government paid them to do it. General Wells told Capt. Henry Standage that he supported "issuing rations to citizens of all classes males females and children as tho all were in the service" of the Nauvoo Legion. It was "a safe conclusion that in these vallies of the Mountain we as a people have to sustain ourselves build our own roads bridges and defence and defend ourselves from all aggresion whether Indians or otherwise," so it was "perfectly reasonable to conclude that all of our settlements have to be based upon a permanent system of defense and that we should institute such an order of things." Extraordinary times required extra exertions, so it was "right for the government to pay all of these expenses and we intend they shall if we can make them." Standage should keep close financial records even though it was "extremely doubtful if the government does pay them"—it would be "like their paying us for eating our own beef and bread"—because Wells needed the accounts "to present them for payment in the proper form." He contended the statehouse being built in Fillmore belonged "to the church just as much as the tithing property does only being set apart and denoted for the particular purpose" of the government: in Utah it was "one and the same."[45]

---

[44]"Indian Difficulties," *Deseret News*, 30 July 1853, 2/5–6.
[45]Wells to Standage, 31 August 1853, UTMR 1365.

Utah policy always had a theological edge, for a millennial lens colored all of Wells's and Young's religious and military orders. They believed they acted as agents of God's will, which helps explain their aggressive campaigns against real and imagined enemies. The 1853 war over land and livestock degenerated into atrocities on both sides, with bloodshed leading to more bloodshed. As wars go, the "Walker War" was not much, but for Mormons such as Alexander Keele, John Dixon, John Quail, William Luke, and the twenty-five to thirty Utes that "friendly Indians" said died in the conflict, it was war enough.[46]

Pursue and Capture Walker the Chief of the Utahs

The Nauvoo Legion mobilized on 19 July 1853. Drafts of its "Special Orders" exist, but no final copy is known to survive. Orders to Lt. Col. William Kimball and Col. Peter Conover, now with four lines crossed out, are in the Brigham Young Collection, ordering Young's personal "Life Guards" to join forces "engaged against the Utah Indians" at "Peteet Neet Cañon or thereabouts." Colonel Conover would "take charge of the Expedition and pursue the campaign until Walker the chief of the Indians is executed. To him, when found, you will show no quarter."[47]

General Wells's special orders, in James Ferguson's hand, expands on Young's draft.

> IV. Col. Conover will take all possible measures to pursue and Capture Walker the chief of the Utahs and prosecuting the campaign until he is executed. He will also give directions to the several officers Commanding the Separate divisions of his district, to keep a strict guard, around their Settlements, and prevent any surprise. He will also communicate immediately with the settlements South, informing them of the Commencement of hostilities and directing them to keep a strict guard. He will also be careful as far as the execution of these instructions, will admit, to preserve the lives and health of his command, and in no case act upon the offensive, but where a sure and effective blow may be struck.[48]

In a letter to Horace Eldredge, his business agent at St. Louis and a Nauvoo Legion general, Brigham Young described how quickly violence spread:

---

[46]Wimmer, "The Walker War," 105–107, 128, 132–33.
[47]Special Orders, 19 July 1853, BYC 17:9, 57.
[48]Wells and Ferguson, Special Orders No 1, 19 July 1853, UTMR 258.

Indian Walker, unable to restrain himself began open hostilities on the 18th at Payson, in Utah County. Alexander Keele has been killed, Wm Jolly, Clark Roberts, & John Berry are slightly wounded, & some horses & cattle have been driven off. On the 23d Six Indians were killed, more of the brethren being harmed in the skirmish. This includes losses on both sides up to date. The brethren in the settlements south & west are instructed to consolidate & fortify, be constantly on the alert, use every exertion to secure their persons & property. How long, or how extensively Walker will carry on depredations I do not know, but no longer than the Lord deems it necessary for our good.[49]

As July ended, Brigham Young tried to persuade Wakara to meet him face to face and make peace. One letter in D. H. Wells's hand gave the governor's communications a poisonous edge.

I send you some tobacco for you to smoke in the Mountains when you get lonesome. You are a fool for fighting your best friends, for we are the best friends and the only friends that you have in the world. Every body else would kill you if they could get a chance. If you get hungry send ~~down~~ some friendly Indian down to the Settlements or come yourself and we will give you some beef cattle and flour. If you are afraid of the Tobacco which I send you, you can let some of your prisoners try it first and then you will know that it is good. When you git good natured again I would like to see you. Don't you think you should be ashamed? You know that I have always been your best friend.[50]

Young delivered a rambling discourse claiming that he had "not made war on the Indians, nor am I calculating to do it." Walker was "now at war with the only friends he has upon this earth"—and Young planned to "let him alone, severely." The Lord would use "our brethren, the Lamanites," to "purify and sanctify the Saints, and prepare the wicked for their doom." Men teased him, saying, "Just give me twenty-five, fifty, or a hundred men, and I will go and fetch you Walker's head." It was not Walker's head Young wanted but for "him and the Devil to chastise this people for their good." The Indians were "continually on the decrease; bands that numbered 150 warriors when we first came here, number not more than 35 now." The southern tribes "towards New Mexico, have not a single squaw amongst them, for they have traded them off for horses, &c. This practice will soon make the race extinct." Walker was continually "killing and stealing children from the wandering bands that he has any power over, which also has

---

[49]Young to "Dear Brother Horace," 29 July 1853, BYC 17:9.
[50]B.Y. to Capt Wacher, G.S.L.C., 25 July 1853, UTMR 289.

its tendency to extinguish the race." Walker was now "hemmed in, he dare not go into California again. Dare he go east to the Snakes? No. Dare he go north? No, for they would rejoice to kill him." He was "penned up in a small compass, surrounded by his enemies" and "the Elders of Israel long to eat up, as it were, him and his little band." Soon not an Indian would be left "to steal a horse. Are they not fools, under these circumstances, to make war with their best friends?" Their wickedness was so great, even the Lord Almighty could not get reach their hearts.

> Joseph Smith said we should have to fight them. He said, "When this people mingle among the Lamanites, if they do not bow down in obedience to the Gospel, they will hunt them until there is but a small remnant of them left upon this continent." They have either got to bow down to the Gospel or be slain. Shall we slay them simply because they will not obey the Gospel? No. But they will come to us and try to kill us, and we shall be under the necessity of killing them to save our own lives.[51]

Mormon authorities regarded the confrontation as their best chance to destroy Ute power. On 19 August 1853 Governor Young issued a proclamation declaring "the Utah Indians" were "in a state of open and declared *war* with the white settlers, committing injuries upon them at every opportunity, killing them, driving off their stock, and burning their mills and dwellings." Affidavits filed with the U.S. District Court charged that "certain white inhabitants of this Territory, in defiance of all law, justice, and humanity, have trafficked and still do with the said hostile Indians, selling them Powder, Lead, and Guns, and threaten to continue to do so." Every person was "strictly forbidden to give, trade, or in any way voluntarily put in possession of any Utah Indian, any powder, lead, gun, sword, knife, or any weapon, or munition of war whatever; or to give, or in any manner render to any Utah Indian, any aid, shelter, food, or comfort, either directly or indirectly" without permission from the authorities, "and every license to trade with the Indians in this Territory, is hereby *revoked*."[52]

The "Walker War" was one-sided: the Nauvoo Legion conducted aggressive campaigns while Ute leaders such as Sowiette sued for peace and Wakara traded on the Colorado. Wyonah, brother of the man James Ivie killed, and a handful of Utes raided Mormon livestock. Indians at Fort Nephi told George A. Smith on 21 August:

---

[51]Young, "Indian Hostilities and Treachery," *Journal of Discourses*, 31 July 1853, 1:168, 170–71.

[52]"Proclamation by the Governor," *Millennial Star*, 12 November 1853, 737.

QuanDuEtts shot Keel, that Wyonah and To Ah Bish were with him—Watcher and most of his men are gone to meet the Spaniards on the Coloradeo to trade—Wy-O-Nah is the one carrying on the war. One of his brothers died at Provo while the Indians were camped there in the spring, and it was another one of his brothers, and a particular favorite that was hurt at Springville in that affray, he died and Wy O Nah is very mad.[53]

The Mormons "published a reward of fifteen thousand dollars for Walkah's head, but it was a serious question among them who should 'bell the cat,'" Gwinn Harris Heap wrote when he visited Parowan.[54] Heap's cousin, California Indian superintendent Edward Beale found this "flourishing Mormon settlement" in a state of alarm. "Walker, the Utah chief, had made war upon the Mormons, had killed several men, and driven off upwards of three hundred head of cattle. He had sent them word that the war was to continue four years, and that he was determined to capture all their horses and cattle," wrote an unknown reporter. The settlers had abandoned Paragonah, "a beautiful little town, leaving their houses and grain-fields" and moved to Parowan, "to give it greater strength." He concluded: "Walker is a remarkable Indian. He is not a chief by hereditary right, but has risen to his present position as supreme chief of the Utahs, solely by his own energies. He makes annual incursions into this country; and it is estimated that within the last four years he has driven off not less than two thousand horses."[55]

"Soon after sunrise" on 2 August, a few Paiutes ran down a hillside to greet Beale and his men "and, accosting us in a friendly manner, asked whether we were Mormons or *Swaps* (Americans)." Heap's book added to Wakara's legend.

GWINN HARRIS HEAP, CENTRAL ROUTE TO THE PACIFIC, 91–92.
The excitement occasioned by the threats of Walkah, the Utah chief, continued to increase during the day we spent at Parawan. Families flocked in from Paragoona, and other small settlements and farms, bringing with them their movables, and their flocks and herds. Parties of mounted men, well armed, patrolled the country; expresses came in from different quarters, bringing accounts of attacks by the Indians, on small parties and unprotected farms and houses. During our stay, Walkah sent in a polite message to Colonel G. A. Smith, who had military command of the district, and governed it by martial law, telling him that "the Mormons were d—d fools for abandoning

---

[53]Smith to Wells, Report, August 1853, UTMR 357.
[54]Heap, *Central Route to the Pacific*, 93. No publication of this reward is known.
[55]J.A.L., "Arrival of Lieut. Beale and his Party," *Sacramento Daily Union*, 8 September 1853, 2/4.

their houses and towns, for he did not intend to molest them there, as it was his intention to confine his depredations to their cattle, and that he advised them to return and mind their crops, for, if they neglected them, they would starve, and be obliged to leave the country, which was not what he desired, for then there would be no cattle for him to take." He ended by declaring war for *four* years. This message did not tend to allay the fears of the Mormons, who, in this district, were mostly foreigners, and stood in great awe of Indians.

The Utah chieftain who occasioned all this panic and excitement, is a man of great subtlety, and indomitable energy. He is not a Utah by birth, but has acquired such an extraordinary ascendency over that tribe by his daring exploits, that all the restless spirits and ambitious young warriors in it have joined his standard. Having an unlimited supply of fine horses, and being inured to every fatigue and privation, he keeps the territories of New Mexico and Utah, the provinces of Chihuahua and Sonora, and the southern portion of California, in constant alarm. His movements are so rapid, and his plans so skilfully [*sic*] and so secretly laid, that he has never once failed in any enterprise, and has scarcely disappeared from one district before he is heard of in another. He frequently divides his men into two or more bands, which, making their appearance at different points at the same time, each headed, it is given out, by the dreaded Walkah in person, has given him with the ignorant Mexicans, the attribute of ubiquity. The principal object of his forays is to drive off horses and cattle, but more particularly the first; and among the Utahs we noticed horses with brands familiar to us in New Mexico and California.[56]

Whooping & Yelling & Singing Their War Song: The Shoshones

As the Nauvoo Legion battled Utes, Maj. David Moore "endeavoured to Carry out the general Orders to the letter" and reported "the movements of the Indians in these Northern Settlements"—the Shoshones—to General Wells, along with the lackadaisical militarism of local militia units. The Mormons had not yet invaded their neighbors' most critical and productive land, such as Cache Valley, so they had maintained relatively good relations with the Bannock and Shoshone bands, even as settlements expanded north in the Salt Lake Basin. But on 21 August 1853 Moore received a panicked message from what is now Willard, Utah:

---

[56]Heap, *Central Route to the Pacific*, 91–92.

Received a Note by express from Willow Creek Settlement, stating that some Indians had been seen on the mountains east of the Settlement that day & that the Shoshones Stated that the pah Utes were near by & would in all probability would [*sic*] attack the Brethren at Willow Creek that night. I accordingly sent four men to their assistance that evening and went with two more next morning early & arrived there about 10 A.M. [and] found that the Camp had been much affrighted the evening before by the Shoshones & Bannocks, some 150 in number Comming into their Camp the evening before, on a Rush & at full speed, whooping & Yelling & Singing their war song, saying at the time that a Utah had stolen a horse & buffalo Robe from the Bannocks.

Such a terrifying "rush" was a typical mountaineer and Indian greeting. After looking around for a few minutes Moore found Willard's "Brethren were in a poor state of defense. At that place every one was for himself & taking little or no heed to the danger that surrounded them." He spoke "& told them that if they would go & pull down their school house & put it up inside their fort & then build a good Breast work around it some 40 & 50 feet square they would then be enabled to get the women & Children inside & there defend them in Case of an attack." They did and "had Quite an amount of work done before dark." Taking three men with him, Moore left for Box Elder, now Brigham City.

On arriving I found the Brethren there in a good fix to be Raked down by any War Party which might come along. I gave them the same advice, but not having time to stay there over night I accordingly returned to Willow Creek, but before I left Box Elder News Came in that the Company of Bonnacks that was at Willow Creek the night before had come about 4 miles beyond Box Elder Fort & had turned themselves & horses into one of the Brethrens wheat field[s] & had taken the liberty of helping themselves to wheat Corn & potatoes. I told the Brethren to go & endeavour to get them out of the field in the most peaceful manner possible, [but] the Indians are very bold & Saucy in those parts.

On 28 August, Moore reported:

[T]he whole Shoshone Band that are now camped at Willow Creek assembled to a man and went with their weapons of war, to the Brethrens Camp and Challenged them to Come out and fight, said they were not afraid of the americans there. Young [John Francis] Grant from fort Hall was there or nearby at the time. Capt. Wells sent and got him to Come & talk to the Indians after which they left. The excitement was occasioned by a Squaw that lives at Br. Crandells [John A. Crandall?] telling them that the ammericans were a going to Kill them. . . . The Shoshones are very bitter against us & say that this is their ground & what grass wood & all the Brethren had is theirs & they intend to have it. I cannot see how we can avoid a fight with them much Longer under the present position of affairs.[57]

EXPEDITIONS TO FORT HALL AND FORT BRIDGER

Making war in Utah Territory proved costly: "The expense incurred in this 12 months' difficulties amounted to 200,000 dollars," one source claimed in 1855, and Congress had "merely refunded a small portion."[58] With arms and ammunition scarce, in August 1853 Mormon leaders dispatched expeditions to Forts Hall and Bridger to address some of their materiel shortages. They also planned to end Jim Bridger's dominance of the Indian trade and settle old grudges with the mountaineers who threatened Utah's legislative monopoly of the lucrative Green River ferries.

The Snake River had overflowed in mid-July and flooded Fort Hall's dilapidated adobes and the high "water washed away the trail." Neil McArthur now commanded the Hudson Bay Company's decrepit outpost, but Richard Grant remained the region's dominant trader. When Celinda Hines took tea with him on the Snake River on 13 August 1853, Grant said he "had been to Ft. Hall to dispose of some government property, also to Salt Lake," apparently to negotiate the sale. (Grant apparently sold the Mormons the military stores left behind when the U.S. Army abandoned Cantonment Loring in 1850.) Anticipating "a protracted war," wrote Andrew Love at Nephi, "The Church Bought out Capt Grant of Fort Hall of all his ammunitions ordinance & other fixtures."[59] The purchase included "wagons and other property." Wells ordered Col. Thomas S. Smith of Farmington to send fifty oxen and men "without delay" to pick up the goods.[60] The next day, the general, agitated that his orders been ignored and at least one man openly defied them, issued a stern directive to retaliate, fort up, and take care not to start a war with the "saucy" Shoshones.

> I have issued an order to you to make up the deficency of oxen which were called for to go to Fort Hall. We have not got a report from all of the wards yet but have learned from Bro Bryant Stringham that there requisition

[57]Moore to Wells, 29 August 1853, UTMR 1362.
[58]Piercy, *Route from Liverpool to Great Salt Lake*, 108n33.
[59]Journal of Andrew Love, July 1854, LDS Archives, 24–25.
[60]Wells to Smith, 31 August 1853, UTMR 374.

has not been complied with by a large amt. I have therefor sent an order expecting that you will fill it with out fail or delay. I have issued similar orders to other Districts but it is not necessry to wait for them. The President instructs me to say that if the Men resist or refuse to obey orders like Jas. Davis put them in irons with ball and chain or picket guard and in no instance permit him or anyone else from those weak settlements to lean on any pretense whatever but seek to strengthen by sending more to them. Let the Brethern [sic] at East Weber Fort on both sides of that River and let the Willow Creek and the Box Elder Settlements be concentrated unless they can render themselves secure immediately, by Forting up. Be sure that you save the grain and all kinds of provisions and proceed with your defences as fast as possible. Major Edward A Bedal Indian agent for this territory with D. B. Huntington are on a visit to your place. You will render them what aid they may need by assisting to get access to the Indians. We think that although the Indians May be a little saucy that still they will not commit any very great depredations unless the people continue remiss in taking care of and defending themselves. You must be careful not to give any occasion but bear and forbear and give them no pretense or cause of provocations. The Brethern should be careful at the same time not to proceed to extreme measures for light and trivial causes as is sometimes the case and thereby plunging the settlements into war unadvisidly and perhaps with friendly tribes—I have no more.[61]

Driving Jim Bridger from the Mormon Kingdom proved complicated. Brigham Young had been accusing Bridger of conspiring against the Saints since 1849, so it was hardly surprising that when he made war on the Utes in 1853, Young charged that Bridger had armed the tribe and was the primary cause of conflict.

Brigham Young, J. H. Holeman wrote in 1852, had "been in an ill humor" since receiving the U.S. Indian commissioner's annual report containing Holeman's description of "the excitement of the Indians on account of the whites settling their lands." The Uintas had told James Bridger "in the strongest terms" they did not want "the Mormons making settlements on their lands; that they understood they intended to do so, and were anxious to know what they should do, or if they had the right to prevent it," telling Holeman "in such a manner that I could not hesitate to believe it." The agent subsequently met a deputation of "Uwinty Utes, sent by their chief Soweates" who "expressed their decided disapprobation to any settlement being made on their lands by the whites, and more particularly by the Mormons." The

[61]Wells to David Moore, 1 September 1853, UTMR 375.

Utes asked him to send them traders: Holeman sent men from Fort Bridger, "who they treated with great kindness and respect," and traders from Salt Lake. "Such was the feeling of hostility expressed towards the Mormons, that if they had been known to be so they would have been driven from the village." The Shoshones were opposed "to the Mormons settling on their lands in the strongest terms."

> The Indians in this Territory have, in the general, been badly treated; upon some occasions so much so as to produce resistance. Then, upon the most trivial occasion, would follow, as the Mormons call it, an " Indian war," and being better armed and equipped than the Indians a most brutal butchery would follow. For all these services in all these "Indian wars," I understand that there is a petition presented, or will be presented, to Congress for the government to pay the bill. Before they do so, however, I hope they will inquire into particulars, as these people seem more inclined to fleece the government of her money than to render her any important service or friendship. I have thought it to be my duty to inform the department of all matters calculated to produce excitement or dissatisfaction among the Indians. With this view I have made you the several communications relative to matters and things here. I shall continue to do so as circumstances may occur; and while I confine my statements to facts, I feel confident I shall be sustained by the department.[62]

Holeman believed "he had no other responsibility than to the Indians, and he was prepared to defend their interests against anyone," wrote Dale Morgan. But he resigned in March 1853 "as my duty to the government compels me to act in such a manner as to give offence, frequently, to the Mormons, who seem to recognize no law but their own self-will."[63]

Utah officials drafted laws to dispossess the mountaineers of the lucrative overland trade. The territorial legislature created Green River County in 1852 to assert its power over the region. Governor Young launched his "open and declared *war*" on the Utahs in 1853, declaring every "license to trade with the Indians in this Territory, is hereby *revoked*."[64] Church attorneys persuaded federal judge Leonidas Shaver to issue writs charging Green River traders with selling liquor, arms, and ammunition to the Indians.

The "Fort Bridger & Greenriver Expedition" began the next day when Young ordered James Ferguson to "raise from your command fifty Men

---

[62]Holeman to Luke Lea, 29 April 1852, U.S. House, *The Utah Expedition*, 144–45.
[63]Morgan, *Shoshonean Peoples*, 63, 66.
[64]"Proclamation by the Governor," *Millennial Star*, 12 November 1853, 737. .

fully equipped for service with rations for twenty days." He would take "two or three good spy Glasses and keep a vigilant Lookout that you may not be taken in ambush or surprised by the Indians." He should "exchange friendly Tokens with the Shoshone Indians" and "with Sowiet and his band who are supposed to be friendly," and "be cautious in your movements not to create any unnecessary alarm." He was to arrest "all persons engaged in furnishing Indians with Guns or Ammunition," and take charge of "all such guns or Ammunition and spill upon the ground any and all Spiritous Liquors that you shall find in or about the premises." He should rout "from their lurking places any and all hostile bands of Indians" and "perform all such necessary and prudent things as shall be best calculated to quell the Indian hostilities now unfortunately existing." He must preserve his camp's "order and decorum cleanliness and sobriety," make a full report of "your doings herein," and keep headquarters advised of all important occurrences. Young signed the order as "Governor and Superintendent of Indian Affairs & Commander in Chief of the Militia."[65]

Donning his hats as sheriff, Nauvoo Legion major, and commander of the "Battalion Minute Men," James Ferguson set out on 21 August to hunt down Bridger with a posse eventually numbering seventy-nine men. He carried Young's message to incoming Mormon overland companies: "Major Jas. Ferguson is out on an expedition designed principally to quell Indian Hostilities (& executing process & writs accusing some white people who have been guilty of the laws of the U.S.) maintain the Laws of the U.T. and promote friendly ralations with the Shoshone Indians and all others who are friendly disposed."[66]

General Wells granted "liberty to take the twelve pound Howitzer with you" but feared Ferguson's fifty might not be enough men to capture Bridger. When William Kimball returned to Salt Lake on 26 August from his southern campaign, Wells ordered him to saddle up again. A day later, Kimball informed Major Ferguson he was bringing reinforcements, in case Bridger planned to give what Kimball called the "bayhos b'hoys" a hot reception.

> I arived with my Detachment at Salt Lake City yesterday at 4 Oclock P.M., & Received orders to Raise 30 Men out of the military of Salt Lake City & those of my Detachment that were south that could go with me to start Immediately to accompany & aid you in carrying out your Orders. I am En

[65]Young to Ferguson, 20 August 1853, MS 17205, LDS Archives.
[66]Young to Captains of Companies, 21 August 1853, UTMR 350.

route with 42 men. We shall make our way as fast as we posibly can with our animals, Some of which were with me south. Just as I left the city today Thos Grover Reached there Stating that Briger was Expecting a Detachment from Salt Lake Valley, & was makeing preprerations to Defeat them In their plans, had gathered forces untill he was 200 strong.[67]

Despite such fears, Ferguson had already occupied the fort and "found BRIDGER gone." He seized "all the arms, ammunition, and everything else."[68]

FERGUSON TO YOUNG AND WELLS, 28 AUGUST 1853, UTMR 1361.

Head Qr. Ft. Bridger & Green R. Expedition
Fort Bridger, Aug 28th 1853

His Excellency
  Brigham Young Governor & Comd in Chief U T
  & Lieut Genl Danl H. Wells Comd Nauvoo Legion
Gentn
  I send in charge of Lieut Ephr. Hanks, Lt. Walker, Wm. A. Hickman, & Rufus Stoddard the prisoner Elisha Ryan charged with resistance to the Territorial Marshal in the service of the process from the U.S. Dist. Court. He came to our camp at the head of a Posse of Shoshones with the Chief White Weazle, yesterday morning armed cap-a-pie [head-to-foot] in rather a bragadocio Manner and was arrested by Capt. [Robert] Burton, the U.S. Depty Marshall. The Shoshones became Scared and after I had engaged to meet them at their lodge, they made tracks.[69]
  We arrived here on the evg of the 26th and found everything as usual at the fort, but Bridger gone. [James] Baker tells me he went to Laramie, but I do not believe him. It is more probable to me that imm'y on our approach he concealed himself in the impenetrable brush thickets that cover the valley and is now in the vicinity. I formed camp in front of the fort and placed in the charge of Genl Robinson all the contraband stores I found here, which included 4 Barrells and a part of liqior, 4½ kegs and 1 sack of powder, a large quantity of lead & balls, and a case of guns. The ammunition was claimed by a Flat-head trader Ben Keizer, as having been bot by him but I declined giving it up and he has left. The fort I keep under a sort of moderate martial rule allowing no one to enter or leave after Tatoo at 8 PM. The horses are also coralled nights under a vigilant guard and herded in sight during the

[67]Kimball to Ferguson, 27 August 1853, UTMR 308. Kimball's force included notables such as O. K. Whitney, Seth Blair, Samuel Gould, William Staines, Thales Haskell, Lot Huntington, and Brigham Young Jr. Grover's rumor fed fears that Bridger would rally his Native and mountaineer allies to resist Mormon authorities.

[68]"Later from the Plains," New York Times, 13 October 1853, 8.

[69]Elisha B. Ryan, whose close relations with the Eastern Shohone nation made him a constant thorn in Mormon sides, survived this encounter with the Saints.

day. Agreeably to your instructions I sent Capt. [Andrew] Cunningham with
[Alexander] McCrae [McRae], Snow, & Geo Boyd ahead on the 24th A.M,
instructing them to continue on to Green R and call at Ft. Bridger returning
for this purpose. We marched slowly but finding that further delay might not
be good we came on in, and in the nick of time to prevent the distribution
of the ammunition.

Captn. Cunningham and McCrae returned to day leaving Boyd and Snow
a day longer on Green R. to watch movements. All is as usual there, the every
day routine of filth and drunkenness without respect to classes. If nothing
further is brot in by the boys from that place we shall start a party of fifteen
out in the morning, there to arrest the law-breakers & attach their property.
It is considered that number is sufficient as our presence has created a good
deal of alarm among the mountaineers. The arrest of Ryan will have a good
effect. He is a dangerous man and should not run at large. His connexion
and acquaintance with the Indians won't do us no good.

We have pretty busy times having on our hands some 40 head of cattle
attached and taken yesterday by Lt. Hanks which however I shall turn over
to Bro Miller till we overtake him. This together with a patroling party
kept out every day, and a heavy guard at night keeps the boys from rusting.
We live well, principally on fat beef. When White Weazle ran off, Bazil
the Shoshone chief that lives around here was about picking up his duds
complaining he was hungry. I directed the QTMR [quartermaster] to buy a
beef of Mr. Vasquez, Bridgers agent, for them and they were satisfied. We
had a good talk with him and I gave him some small presents. Wahshaki
is on the Sweet Water and I cannot send to him. He wants to see you. If I
can send to him in any way I'll send for him to come and see you. He likes
you, but says Holeman is a double tongue.

This morning Joshua Terry came down and told us of some Twenty
Yampa Utahs that had come down. I went up and asked them down to
our camp. They came. Three chiefs were with them: two sons of White
Eye and a Son of Sau-e-ette. We smoked and talked. Their camp is fifty
miles or more from here. Sau-e-ett is there; and I hired one of their Indians
to run and bring him and White Eye down. He will be here the day after
tomorrow noon. The YampaUtahs wanted to go and see you. I asked them
to go with us and I think they and Sau-e-ett and White Eye will go in. I
thought this course prudent if for nothing else but to draw them from the
influence of this place. Their feeding will cost something but it will be an
advantage in the long run.

The officers meeting in Council, we all thought it prudent to consult you
upon our course with the fort, as well as turn Ryan over to speedy justice.
There are here some 4 or 500 head of Bridger's stock together with some
few dry goods. You have marked out our course in regard to the contraband

stores. What shall we do with the rest? and what with the fort? what with Bridger's family? With the help of God there is not difficulty in anything.

Respy & obdly [Respectfully and obediently]
James Ferguson
Major Commanding

My ink is all gone.
Excuse penciling—

Meanwhile, William Kimball made his "way as fast as posible; but on account of some of the animals being thin & Weak," he had "to Movee Slower than we could have wished" and had two animals give out. He had learned "maj Furgerson & the Boys have posesion of the fort & that Bridger has fled" but marched on, for "I know nothing Better than to movve on there & keep a vigilant watch & Govern our Selves according to circumstances." Kimball's postscript indicated how much the Mormons wanted to capture Bridger: he proposed securing "the Guns ammunition & Spirits & Retreating to the mountains and camping in Some Secluded Place & keeping out Small Reconortering parties" in hopes of seizing him.[70]

Brigham Young had good reason to order his officers to be examples of sobriety. James Ferguson and William Kimball were both notorious alcoholics, which might explain the two-day delay after 26 August, when overlander Thomas Flint noted the Mormons had "driven old man Bridger out and taken possession" of his fort. William Hickman claimed Ferguson was drunk, for the expedition destroyed Bridger's whiskey and rum "by doses: the sheriff, most of his officers, the doctor and chaplain of the company, all aided in carrying out the orders, and worked so hard day and night that they were exhausted—not being able to stand up. But the privates, poor fellows! were rationed, and did not do so much."[71]

August 1853 ended with a blizzard of communications between Salt Lake and Fort Bridger. Quartermaster Lewis Robison occupied the "Old Ford" on Green River and asked Ferguson to have Attorney General Seth Blair provide documents "so that we can have a fair chance to settle all things up on the river. So far as Possible." He wanted F. M. Russell, a mountaineer, "Arrested and Safely kept as one of the Rioters. I doonot know his name But think there is no doubt but the charge can be sustained against him." It also "would be well to out a Warrant For Tayler Davis Ryan Jack Sweny

[70]Kimball to Wells, 29 August 1853, UTMR 363.
[71]Flint, "Diary," 97; Hickman, *Brigham's Destroying Angel*, 92.

Big Bill For Resisting Teritorial Martial."[72] Governor Young signed an order endorsing Kimball's plan to capture Bridger. It would "probably be best to leave Bridger Property undisturbed except the Articles Mentioned as Contraband, to wit powder lead coffee Liquor, Guns &c." This might make it "probable that Mr Bridger will return and We may have a good chance to get him by throwing him off his guard."[73]

Wells was dismayed that Bridger and Ryan had escaped, foiling Ferguson's plan to turn Ryan "over to speedy justice." The general's letter to Robison suggests the motive for the costly Green River campaign:

> I am a little astonished at Ryon Escape. I think you are mistaken about Bridger going to Laramie and perhaps he may have Cached Ammunition Guns &c. Colwell [Samuel M. Caldwell] and him I understand purchased all of Addous & Kinkeads [gunpowder] or at least a large proportion of it. This should be looked to so far as relates to leaving any quantity there for the purpose of supplying the Indians for hunting purposes. If we only had some Judicious persons to remain there it might prove beneficial. But that can be assayed hereafter. One of the agents will probably be located there or in that vicinity and the Indians can procure their supplies by coming to the city and perhaps that this would also prove beneficial as it would bring them in more direct commerce with us, and perhaps exert a more salutary influence over them. The President says that if you would like to go there and trade with the Indians that he would give you Licence.[74]

As messages flew between Bridger and Salt Lake, express riders often crossed on the way. Kimball and Ferguson told Wells that while Ryan had escaped, his "former property" had not.

> We send you by Bishop Daniel Miller 2 mares & a colt, one horse, and 47 head of cattle, and 5 calves, the former property of E. Ryan the escaped prisoner. The firm are under obligations after paying the Court expenses to let the property go for the collection of the Judgment. You will please to see that the property is secured in that way. Nothing new since [our] former communication. The reinforcement arrived yesterday morning. Captn Burton started with 13 men including Genl Robinson on the 29th. We look for him to night, and lay on our oars till you[r] express comes in. We have directed Mr. Kinkead to account to His Excellency for the cattle he takes from this

---

[72]Robison to Ferguson, 30 August 1853, UTMR 367. Tayler, Davis, Ryan, Jack Sweny, and Big Bill (perhaps ferryman William Ashton) were mountaineers.

[73]Young to Ferguson and Kimball, 31 August 1853, UTMR 370.

[74]Wells to Robison, 31 August 1853, UTMR 369. Wells refered to a James Kinkead, not Charles Kinkead of the firm Livingston & Kinkead.

place, and to take the ammuntion in with him. We are now 79 strong in aggregate. Bro's [Christopher] Layton & [Thomas A.] Dowell accompany the stock. All well.[75]

In a postscript, Colonel Kimball and Major Ferguson asked General Wells to "please consider on the propriety of retaining this post." Wells had already consulted with federal judge Leonidas Shaver about the legal implications of seizing James Bridger's fort, property, and livestock. Shaver thought "it might be seized under the Indian laws providing it could be proved that he sold Spiritous Liquors" to the Indians, and "if a case could be sustained against him it would unquestionably be *forfeiture all*." Young and Wells regretted the "most unfortunate the Escape of Ryan, but things that *are are* and who can help them, so we say all is right again and go on." If the men lived "close to the line of their duties" and prayed with great faith, they "would not be at a loss how to act in almost any Emergency that might occur." Bridger's "Liquor should be spilled" and "the Guns and Ammunition taken," while other property should "placed in the hand of the Officer of the Court." They assumed the expedition had "gone to Green River and done whatever you Could and are ready to return." They should "leave about thirty Men to keep things Safe in regard to the Emigration" and hope "those villians [*sic*] might return and could yet be caught." They "should be glad if Sowiett and some of the Snakes would come in with you, Especially Washikik." The "good many animals" they had "taken from the range" should be "returned in as good order as possible." Bridger probably was "not far away and probably Looks out upon you from those impenetrable thickets," so they should "be careful you do not get ambushed." The letter ended ironically: their letter should have been shorter, but "The less we have to say the longer it takes to say it." A postscript was the key: "We consider, that if you leave men enough there, to take care of the emigration, that you have finished your Mission and done good work."[76] So the "Ft. Bridger & Green River Expedition" marched home on 7 September "with Cooked rations for 3 days," leaving James W. Cummings and twenty-one men to "use all possible Measures to Consolidate & Secure the Emigration" bound for Zion and "Carry into Execution all the Instructions to the Expedition from the Executive & Head Quarters."[77]

---

[75]Kimball and Ferguson to Wells, 31 August 1853, UTMR 373.

[76]Young and Wells to Ferguson and Kimball, 31 August 1853, UTMR 1366.

[77]Kimball and Ferguson, Orders No 2, 6 September 1853, UTMR 378.

"The most of those that call themselves white men that live in this part of the country are a notorious set of robers & cut throats and are the enemies of all good people, and will do wright no longer than they are compelled to by force of arms," Cummings told Brigham Young. He believed "there are near a hundred whites in this part of the country within fifty miles of here." Whenever Mormon trains passed through the country, he warned, the mountaineers would need watching, "unless we send them home the Short cut"—meaning the mountaineers, not the Mormon trains.[78] By next spring, Green River County officials, including "Sheriff, Prosecuting Attorney & Assessor & Collector" William A. Hickman, had visited "several of the Mountaineers, Assessing their property and collecting their taxes." Louis Vasquez, Jim Bridger's agent, paid "near fifty Dollars taxes without a murmur."[79]

Bill Hickman's notorious memoir provides insight into what was at stake: control of the Green River ferries and overland trail trade. Hickman netted over nine thousand dollars trading at South Pass that summer. The mountain men "had always owned and run the ferry across Green River; but the Utah Legislature granted a charter to Hawley, Thompson & McDonald, for all the ferries there." The mountaineers "claimed their rights to be the oldest, and a difficulty took place, in which the mountain men took forcible possession of all the ferries but one, making some thirty thousand dollars out of them," he recalled. Young sent Hickman back to Fort Bridger, so he "might be of special service." Bridger heard the posse was coming "and left—no one knew where to. We searched around several days for him." The "*posse* went to Green River, shot two or three mountaineers, took several hundred head of stock, returned to Fort Bridger, and what whisky they could not drink they poured out, reserving, however, enough to keep them drunk until they got home." Ferguson ordered Hickman and Ephraim Hanks to escort Ryan to Salt Lake. They "started in the afternoon. Hanks was full of rum," and the "necessary supplies" consisted of a few canteens of liquor. "We intended to travel forty miles before we slept, but when night came on it was very dark. The canteens made things lively until we came to some brush, when the prisoner, Elisha Ryan, slipped off his horse, and in an instant was in the brush out of sight." The posse's confiscated property "went to pay a few officers" and expedition expenses, but the men, "poor fellows, I never knew

---

[78]Cummings to Young, 19 September 1853, BYC 23:1. William P. MacKinnon provided this reference.
[79]Appleby to Brigham Young, 29 May 1854, BYC 23:09.

of one of them getting a dollar." The money was "all was gobbled up and turned over to the Church, and Hawley & Co. never got a cent."[80]

When the Salt Lake mail reached St. Louis in October, Utah congressional delegate John Bernheisel claimed Bridger had boasted "he intended to give the Utah Indians guns and ammunition for the purpose of exterminating the Mormons at Salt Lake. Writs were issued to take BRIDGER and bring him to Salt Lake, and a company of men were sent for that purpose."[81] Bridger surely knew that all the arms and powder in the West would not let the Utes dislodge the Saints from their strongholds. (Ironically, they charged Bridger with plotting to carry out a version of the future they envisioned when Mormons and Lamanites, united as the Blood of Israel, ushered in the millennium.) By January 1854, Bernhisel reported, Bridger was in Washington, "telling marvelous stories about his being driven from his home in the mountains," charging the Mormons "had sent a number of men to pursue him on the plains to murder him." He wanted Congress to redraw Utah's boundaries to exclude Fort Bridger.[82]

Mormon historians cite confusing and contradictory documents to prove Bridger and Vasquez sold their fort to the Mormons in 1855. "Mormon leaders greatly feared that the image of James Bridger meant as much to the Indians as that of Brigham Young meant to the Mormons," biographer Cecil Alter wrote, which could be dangerous, so "the Mormons continued their devious efforts to establish themselves as equal or superior to Bridger." The documents about the sale of the fort were "not even up to frontier standards," and by no means were they "in accord with the usual Mormon standards of integrity and quality." Bridger and the Mormons were swindled, Alter concluded, but "ample evidence" showed "that Bridger had no knowledge of the sale of Fort Bridger." Alter had examined every vestige "of authentic firsthand information about James Bridger, whether good, bad, or indifferent," which made it "very difficult to charge him with duplicity or dishonesty in his dealings with the Indians or the Mormons."[83]

The evidence indicates some sort of sale did take place. Bugler William Drown, who in 1857 marched west with Bridger, "the best and most experienced guide in the country," was present on 3 November 1857 when Col. A. S. Johnston gave him a regular army appointment "as principal guide through

---

[80]Hickman, *Brigham's Destroying Angel*, 90–93.

[81]"Later from the Plains," *New York Times*, 13 October 1853, 8.

[82]Bernhisel to Young, 13 February 1854, BYC 60/15.

[83]Alter, *Jim Bridger*, 254, 280–81.

Utah" with the rank of major. Bridger had "realized a considerable fortune trading with the Utahs and other Indians" before the Mormons "gave him his choice—to receive from them $8,000 for his place here, leaving all his cattle and everything as it was, or to be forced to leave without any remuneration. He chose to leave, although the stock he had here at the time was well worth the amount proffered, saying nothing of the buildings, goods, etc., that he was obliged to leave."[84]

"You are probably aware that I am one of the earliest and oldest explorers and trappers of the Great West now alive," Bridger complained in 1873 to senator (and Mormon eater) Ben Butler. Before joining the Utah Expedition, "I was robbed, and threatened with death, by the Mormons, by the direction of Brigham Young, of all my merchandise, stock—in fact of everything I possessed, amounting to more than $100,000 worth—the buildings in the fort partially destroyed by fire, and I barely escaped with my life."[85] The Mormons did pay $8,000 to Louis Vasquez, but had the Nauvoo Legion caught Bridger, they probably would have killed him.

Soldier and explorer Randolph Marcy, who met Bridger in 1857, concluded Bridger's prosperity

> excited the cupidity of the Mormons, and they intimated to him that his presence in such close proximity to their settlements was not agreeable, and advised him to pull up stakes and leave forthwith; and upon his questioning the legality or justice of this arbitrary summons, they came to his place with a force of avenging angels and forced him to make his escape to the woods in order to save his life. Here he remained secreted for several days, and through the assistance of his Indian wife, was enabled to elude the search of the Danites and make his way to Fort Laramie, leaving all his cattle and other property in possession of the Mormons.[86]

THE INDIANS ARE NOW AT OPEN WAR: SARAH DE ARMON PEA RICH

"Utah is a good country for men and horses," locals told overland traveler Luther Goold in 1863, "but a hell of a country for women and oxen."[87] Moving and meaningful Mormon women's voices have often eluded historians.

---

[84]Drown, "A Trumpeter's Notes," 3 November 1857, 214.

[85]U.S. Senate, Report 329 (53:2, Serial 3,192), 1894, 13.

[86]Marcy, *Thirty Years of Army Life*, 401.

[87]Goold, Overland from California to Omaha, 20 April 1863. Janet Skidmore generously shared her ancestor's journal.

As the first wife of an absent apostle, Sarah de Armon Pea Rich belonged to Deseret's aristocracy, but her life was hard. Brigham Young's plan to "commence a ditch & wall around the entire city, the wall to be 12 feet high, with suitable gates, & bastions" did not reassure her.[88] Few sources capture how much the war on Wakara and the propaganda that drove it terrified Utah's most vulnerable citizens, even in its capital.

SARAH RICH TO CHARLES C. RICH, 25 AUGUST 1853,
TYPESCRIPT, HUNTINGTON LIBRARY.

Dear Companion having a few retired moments this evening whilst all is hushed and still except our city guard, I improve the same in writing to you. I feel lonely therefore I prefer a lonely time to write to you. . . .

The Indians are now at open war with us as a people and are killing our brethren whenever and wherever the opportunity presents itself and are skulking around in the canyons and watching us all the time. Among the good brethren they have killed is Brother John Dixon and John Quail who was killed last week in Parleys Canyon whilst hauling lumber from the mill and young Hagland [John Hoagland] was wounded in the arm. Him and Samuel Knight succeeded in making their escape into the city whilst the Indians were taking the horses and mules. But John Hagland had the courage to cut his horses loose and him and Knight rode into the city. The dead bodies were brought in the next day and buried. All settlements are now ordered into forts. The fort near your farm is laid out where your old log house stood. The president is now going into measures to wall in the city which plan is going to use up property for certain and, how I wish you was here to arrange your part to suit yourself for the talk is now that all unoccupied lots will have to be sold to accomplish this wall. I have attended one ward meeting on the subject but it was only to get the feelings of the people to know whether they was for having the city walled in or to have the wards forted in. All were in favor of having a wall around the city. If you was here now I would not begrudge a considerable sum for I know not what to do. I wish I was on our other lots. I wonder if I wouldn't feel more safe than I do here at the foot of the mountain where the Indians are liable to come down in the night and do damage. How do you suppose I feel with seven children and not a man person in the house and we are counciled to keep our doors and windows well fastened in the nights and our guns well loaded by our bedside expecting an attack before morning. Those that do not experience the like cannot tell my feelings that is for sure. The president sais the trouble is only now only just commencing but we must prepare ourselves for the worst. If you can possibly come hoem [sic] safe this fall and situate

[88]Young to W. H. Hooper, 30 August 1853, BYC 17:10.

us in a safer condition than we now are I would be thankful but do not run any risks for we had better dye than you. . . .

Old Bridger is at the head of all the war and says he will now make a clean work of the Mormons. There is a company of men gone out to take him. What the results will be I know not. I fear they will be serious. Some emigrants has come in and made oath to what they have heard Bridger say. He is furnishing the Indians with guns and amunition [*sic*]. He told these men that he was just waiting for California Emigration to pass by and then the slaughter was to commence on the Mormons. The men that went out had orders to take Bridger dead or alive and tear down the fort if they resisted. The president sais this church never was in such danger as it is at the present time but if all will obey his council he will take them through safely. . . . All these settlements south of this all will not do for some are rebelling [so] their houses are torn down and gone into forts. The Indians have broken Uncle James Allred up by driving off his stalk. I sleep with Charles little gun loaded by the bed but know not whether I should have the courage to use it or not if the war hoop should be raised at my door but I now think I should be good for one Indian for running would be useless with so many children for I never should run and leave them behind if they must die I will die with them. Perhaps you will think I am scared. If I am scared our leaders are also for they keep a strong guard around their houses and advise all to do likewise.

Brother George A. [Smith] has just returned from Iron County. He sais a good company can come from your place in *saifty* if they keep a good guard. You can do as you like about coming but you are needed here more than you ever was. No one can arrainge your affairs to suit as you can yourself but I have nothing to say in the matter for your father is your agent and of course he will see to it but he is discouraged and knows not what to do for this is something he did not expect when you left but I keep having forshadows of the trouble with the Indians.

President Young has offered all his property east of his office for sale and offers to turn it all into walling the city for he says we are going to have worse than Indians to incounter [*sic*] and the time has come to fortify ourselves. He says there is men among us that keeps our enemies informed of all that is going on. . . . I can get along with all this if the Indians will let us alone. I do not want them to get our children and you may be well ashured that I keep them in close quarters such times but it is almost like holding them by the hair.

Sarah Rich signed her letter "your affectionate companion forever."

Chapter 6

BLOODY HANDS
AND HOSPITABLE GRAVES
Atrocities, Massacres, Tragedies

Wakara was "making war with the Mormons" in August 1853 when William R. Brown visited Salt Lake on his way to California. The Utes had "already committed some depredations. The Mormons keep a guard out in the Valley and mountains day and night." When Brown departed, the Saints at Ogden were "all forting up throughout the whole valley and making ready to receive the Indians with bloody hands and hospitable graves."[1] Mormon authorities initially regarded their Numic neighbors as a strategic problem and their 1853 Indian war as a tactical solution with long-term benefits. Leaders use mass violence under the illusion they can control it, but once unleashed, war becomes as unmanageable and as vicious as the atrocities that follow in its wake. Wakara showed little interest in fighting losing battles with his powerful neighbors, but Native resistance to aggression caused uncounted complications for the territory's political and religious powers, driving internal dissent in surprising ways. As their war with the Indians and mountaineers ground on through 1853, unexpected massacres of Anglos and Indians challenged the status quo. When an opportunistic Pahvant hunting party ambushed Capt. John Gunnison's railroad surveyors on Sevier River in October, the Nauvoo Legion had to pick up the pieces as Governor Young managed the complicated national response.

"They used to say, in Utah, I was a pretty good sort of a fellow until I got to be a Colonel," said George A. Smith, "and then I became more savage."[2]

---

[1]Brown, *An Authentic Wagon Train Journal*, 20 May, 3 August 1853, 59, 61.

[2]Smith, "Disobedience . . . Indian War the Result," 7 October 1853, *Journal of Discourses*, 1:194; Wells to Lee, 21 May 1854, UTMR 442.

GEORGE A. SMITH
Because of his wig, dentures, and
glasses, Indians called Joseph Smith's
cousin George A. Smith "Man Who
Comes Apart." He was celebrated as
"the father" of southern Utah and
served as an apostle, church historian,
and brigadier general of the Nauvoo
Legion's cavalry during the war on
Black Hawk. *Editor's collection.*

Appointed southern Utah militia commander in July 1853, Smith directed
the hierarchy's unpopular policies until "called to higher and more important
duties" in May 1854. General Wells ordered "all the people to assemble into
large and permanent forts and no man is at liberty to refuse to obey this
order without being dealt with as an enemy." Smith dismantled isolated
villages, including Paragonah, demolishing a tannery, machine shop, and
eighteen log and adobe homes with "not a murmuring word." In contrast,
at Cedar City "defiance and insult" greeted Smith's order to confiscate the
settlers' cattle and drive them to Salt Lake, allegedly to protect them from
Ute raiders. A few settlers "threatened to shoot anyone who tried to move"
their animals, Maj. Mathew Caruthers resigned his command, and twenty
men left for California with their families.[3]

The "peace policy" of forting up, consolidating settlements, and confis-
cating community cattle aroused resistance even from Mormon officials.
Acting on George A. Smith's complaint, on 25 August Wells temporarily
removed Peter Conover from his Provo District command for "non-com-
pliance of certain orders," probably for not posting guards and building
forts quickly enough. Smith called for a vote to sustain [William] Wall in

---

[3]Christy, "The Walker War," 407–408.

his appointment" to replace Conover. Joseph Kelting refused to support Wells, causing Smith's persistent headache to increase "to that extent that it produced blindness": a man had to lead him home. Conover persuaded two men to contribute six hundred cattle to the church roundup, "but a great many of the people are not willing to sustain the herd but want to turn out their work oxen promiscuously."[4]

From the extreme southern settlements, John D. Lee complained that breaking up the town of Harmony to assume command at Cedar City in its "exposed and reckless condition" increased his arduous labors. In "one or two instances a few rebellious & refractory Spirits" opposed his orders, "attempting to raise a mutiny amoung the People." He strapped on his sword and swore to carry out his orders "if it need be by the shedding of the Blood, of those cursed wicked apostate fault finding wretches." He would "rather walk into them th[a]n to Slay Walker & his Band." Other southern Legion officers promised to back him up with "Pouder & Ball," which made peace. Lee had started two "Adobees Mills which if properly attended" would produce two thousand bricks per day, "the most speedy & best method of enclosing our city" in a wall. "The Natives arround us are harmless & peacible," tending abandoned crops at empty settlements, "& nothing has been disturbed or molested in the le[a]st by them. They say that Walker & his Band are on green River, about 250 Miles South East of this place." Wakara had sent his brother "to trade with the Spaniards for Pouder & to enlist their aid as well as the Navijoe Indians" to attack the southern settlements when the snow fell. (Lee claimed "2 Squaws that made their escape from Walkers Encampment" confirmed this.) The Paiutes wanted to butcher the cattle Walker had left at Fort Harmony, but Lee "told them that the Big captain did not want us to retaliate upon past wrongs & injuries; but to act uppon the defensive." The local band explained why they resented the Utes:

> I apprehend but little danger from the native Piedes; they are not disposed to be Friendly with Walker at all; they Say that his promises are to[o] ea[s]ily broken to be of much force: & his Friendship cost the sacr[i]fice of their wives & children; to be carried off & used by them, or traded off to the Spainards as Slaves.[5]

---

[4]Geo. A. Smith to Young, Provo, 27 August 1853, UTMR 359.
[5]Lee to Young, 24 September 1853, BYC 23:4.

I Got Their Hoodoo Bag

Santaquin, whose name was given to Summit Creek and a southern Utah Valley town, led a band of Utes that had its way with the Saints, killing men and seizing cattle. From Palmyra near Spanish Fork, Maj. Stephen Markham led "an Expedition of Sept 25 and 26 to Salt Creek," looking for the raiders at Goshen Valley, one of the last Ute refuges in Utah County.

Markham to Wells, 5 October 1853, UTMR 397.

As a band of Indians had been very troublesome in the vicinity of Sumit and Willow creek stealing grain vegetables and any other articles that was of Benifeit to them and of late had commited depredations of a more cerious nature by shooting at John Brimhall this side of Payson in search of his cattle also robing a man going to California by the name of Yager of Clothes money and a revolver. Also who was firing upon one [Henry Wesley?] Wheaton Betwixt this and Springville, and it was ascertained that they had colected together at or near the mouth of Salt Creek in the Open Valley S.W. 10 miles from Sumit Creek; I ordered out a portion of my comand and marched to Sumit Creek on the 25th [September] at which place we were obliged to Encamp in consequence of a heavy rain. Capt. C. Hancock and Co. proceeded on and discovered the Indians camp and returned. At night at 2 o.c. on the morning of the 26th took up our march and a little after sunrise surprised and nearly Sourounded the Indians whose suposed number was 15 to 30 who was in great confusion and after a parly of some time a charge was ordered which Efectivally routed them upon which they took up refuge in a heavy Cane Toole and wilow swamp and under the Banks of Salt Creek which was only a few rods from their Wikiups and very steep. A brisk fire was kept up on both sides for some time in which Capt. C. B. Hancock of Payson Cov[e?] was slightly wounded in the back of his head. It is believed that 4 or 5 Indians were killed although hard to ascertain for a certainty as they were [hidden] in the creek.

There was found and recovered 8 bushels of wheat also corn tools Iron and various articles which had been stolen from various places at their camp. As their Situation afforded them sure protection the command was ordered to return which was acomplished on the 26th. Soon I wish to know your will concerning these Indians as they have done much injury [and] if they shall be allowed to remain where they are if they continue Heostile [sic] & Theiving.

Decades later, John W. Berry recalled details of the skirmish.

We came to an Indian camp just at day break and took the savages by surprise. As they begged for peace, we told them if they would give up their arms and go to the settlements, we would not hurt them. We dallied with them for some time, as they did not like to give up their arms, that being the last thing an Indian will part with. But at last Colonel Markham gave them five minutes to decide. Not complying with his order the colonel gave the order for our company to attack. The Indians returned the fire very lively for some time, but our men pressed them so hard that they soon silenced the firing of the Indians. Those of them that were not killed retreated into a cane swamp and got away. Casualties on our side were small, considering the smartness of fire of the Indians. One man (Bishop Charles Hancock) was slightly wounded in the head, and one horse shot in the hip. The Indians being in the cane and in the swamp dragged their dead in there; Consequently we could not tell how many were killed.

A Ute later "told us we only wounded two or three; but they reported at Nephi that we killed nineteen or twenty of them." In response, the band "made a haul of sixty or seventy head of cattle" and "got away with them to Uintah Valley." They eventually "returned what they had not killed and eaten."[6]

George McKenzie recited a bizarre doggerel "true statement" to a reunion of Walker War veterans at Springville in February 1895. His epic celebrated Markham's 1853 raid, later called the "Goshen Valley Battle." Like many young Mormons, at age seventeen McKenzie was wilder than the Indians he grew up with. Armed with guns, army pistols, and sabers on their "dashing rides," buckskin-clad teenagers carried "war expresses," stood picket guard, and did what McKenzie called "sometimes pretty hard" duty. Under Major Markham, a "grand old Utah man" who was in it if "fighting was on hand," they set out "to do a band of hostiles" that had "murdered without fear" and "sacked the fort at Santaquin." At sundown Markham sent ten scouts to find "the hostile camp" and led half of them to "Goshen land." McKenzie rode with Markham "through the hills on Salt Creek" (now Currant Creek) "to deal out frontier justice" to their "wily foes." Five advance scouts marched in silence to a village at Utah Lake's southern end in "a large cane-break" with high banks. This sandy, swampy, isolated site was one of the last refuges of the Utahs of Utah Valley. McKenzie forgot about the "parly of some time" and described a dawn surprise attack.

---

[6]Berry, "Further Particulars of the Walker War," in Gottfredson, *Indian Depredations in Utah*, 51–52.

GEORGE McKENZIE, BALLAD OF THE WALKER WAR, 3–4.

We rode right down amid the boys
Who gave us a welcome yell,
We formed in cowboy fashion;
Old Steve says, "Give them hell."
We fought the battle bravely
And when the fight was won
We took their camp and sacked it
And then began the fun.

Some took their bows and arrows,
Some dressed in Indian tags,
Some took their robes and buckskins,
But I got their hoodoo bag.
And I painted my old comrades
In yellow, red, and gray
And some of the times we had that night
We remember to this day.

There was Acy Boyce who had a nose
Which might have been the pride of Rome;
I painted it a crimson red
With some yellow on the end.
And on old Proc some stripes of gray
Which showed quite plain you see
And then we danced the Highland Fling
In all our boyish glee.

McKenzie's "fun" consisted of sacking the village, donning plundered war paint, and doing a Scottish war dance: young frontier Mormons often proved more savage than saintly. Nineteen-year-old "Acy Boyce" came to Utah about 1850; fifty years later he was an inmate at San Quentin Prison.[7] McKenzie's "hoodoo bag" was a sacred medicine bundle containing precious, valuable and important materials of great significance and herbs, tools, ochre, roots, bones, and potions, related to the owner's spiritual journey or immediate task.[8] Bundles belonged to individual men and women but protected the entire community. The paint suggests the stolen pouch belonged to a Ute warrior.

---

[7]"Redwood City's Aged Burglar: Asa Boyce, Sixty-Four Years of Age and a Physical Wreck, Sentenced to the Penitentiary," *San Francisco Call*, 2 February 1897, 4/5.

KILL THEM AFTER ROLL CALL: FORGOTTEN ATROCITIES

As war spread through Deseret in August, four Utes smoked the pipe of peace with Manti's leaders. Promised protection, the band brought a teenage boy, five women, and four children to the village. Surrendering their arms, they camped near the fort's gate and began working for the settlers. Nervous Saints soon suspected they were spies and thieves. A council decided their fate: death for the men and slavery for their families. The cycle of Biblical eye-and-tooth vengeance threatened to leave central Utah's entire population blind and toothless. Azariah Smith wrote: "Yesterday morning there was six Indians came in camp with their squaws pretending to be friendly, but some of the brethren tracked them back to their camp and found some things that had been stolen and hid by them. And in the evening the Indians were taken down the street and shot."[9]

Andrew Lafayette Siler's graphic report of the Manti slaughter and his critique of Isaac Morley's authoritarian rule show Brigham Young was not boasting when he said, "I am watching you. Do you know that I have my threads strung all through the Territory, that I may know what individuals do?"[10] Siler's account of this atrocity—a "pigg shaved with a rusty nale"— reveals how poverty, autocracy, and fear inflamed internal conflict in one of the hardest of Utah's hardscrabble settlements.

SILER TO YOUNG, 13 NOVEMBER 1853, BYC 23:6.

Manti U Territory Nov 13 1853

President Brigham Young
    Dear Sir; At the request of a number of my friends amongst whose names Levi W Hancock, Dani[e]l B Funk, & Sylvester Hulets are to be found I write to you to give you an outline of affairs as they exist. You know probably that in the latter part of August last four Indians came into this place. They it seems came for peace, gave up their arms, and remained quietly here during the night. The pipe of peace was smoked with them and they were promised that if they would return with their families that they should upon their giving up their arms remain in place and work for us and be protected. They after being gone several days returned with their families. There was four men one boy about 16 years old, five squaws, and four children. They gave up their Guns, posted their Camp inside of our sentinels and near the stone fort gate.

---

[8]Harrison, "Botanical Parts of the Patterson Bundle," 53–61.
[9]Azariah Smith, Journal, MS 1834, LDS Archives, 83.
[10]Young, 8 October 1855, *Journal of Discourses*, 3:122.

After they came in some of the Brethren took the Back Track, went to their camp and found a Cache containing buckskins, a Buffalow robe, and some of the Lead that had been stolen. They returned with the plunder when Bro Higgins the Major in command of this Military Dist went to President Isaac Morly and asked him what should be done with the Indians.[11] Prest Morly replied that his mind was to kill them after roll Call. The four men & the boy were led out. One of the men jumped at Bro Hamilton whether for that purpose or to take his gun from him I do not know. Hambleton threw him off.[12] He then made for President Morly when he shot him through. This was a signal for firing and the five was then shot down, the bullets flying into the Corell where women were milking & in all directions. After they were killed the word was given out that all that wished to see the pigg shaved with a rusty nale to turn out. I then went to where they were buried [and] I see them by moon light. Some of them were shot several times when either of the shots would have proved fatal. They were all burried in one hole for grave it could not be called. The Second Morning afterwards their property, their wives, and their children was brought into the ring. The property & children were sold to the highest bidder. Prest Morly bid 3 Bushels of wheat for a Girl 8 or 9 years old [but] she was runn up to 16 Bushels & Knocked off to William V Black Jr.

Some time after President Morlys return from Conference [6–9 October 1853] he said at in the morning that it had been revealed to him that it was a gr[e]vious sin in the sight of heaven to sell the indian children and took a vote to rescind the sale. (Just as if that would help the cause.) This was done. He then couniled those who had bought the children to give them away. This his son Isaac done & I heard Mother Black say that she was called to examine the child and that its back was horably brused from beatings that it had recived lately. The child that Wm V Black bought having passed into Mother Blacks hands she positively & pointedly refused to give up as she had cleaned the child up & dressed her warm and Comfortably. Upon her refusing to give the child up President Morly spoke of the spirit that Father Blacks family were possessed of saying that the family were ruled by a woman. Wm V Black said that there were other persons who had spirits. At this President Morly grew angry and told him that he would put him under guard if he did not hush as he had not come there to be tantalized. This took place at Roll Call.

President Morley about the same time said that the Bigg feild on the North side of the Creek must be thrown out to pasture next year without ever

[11]Nelson Higgins (1806–1890) served as a Mormon Battalion captain, pioneered Manti and Sevier counties, and later led disastrous Black Hawk War campaigns. Manti's other Mexican War veterans included Elisha Averett, Levi Hancock, Sylvester Hulet, and Albert and Azariah Smith.

[12]In February 1851, Madison Hambleton shot his first wife's non-Mormon lover, Dr. John Vaughn, after church in Manti. As Hambleton's attorney, Brigham Young won his acquittal.

Consulting the feelings of the Proprietors of it therby throwing your Land & Bro Kimbles out to the Comons. A few days since the Brethren returned from GSL City bringing the report that you had said that we as a branch of the church might lie under the Censure of not obeying your counsel just as long as they would. Also the report of what Bro Kimble said in relation to President Morly not being fit to preside [over] the Temperal affairs of this branch. Upon these reports Coming in peoples minds were stired up and they began to investigate the matter. In the mean time I drew two Petitions which I enclose with a view of having them signed & sent to you. Bros Cox & Whiting came to me [and] requested me to let them lay over for a few days saying that they thought that president Morly would resign rather than push the petitions. I let them lay over. This morning Bishop [John] Lowry said there was feelings and he wished a Conference calld today to set matter[s] right. At 10 oclock A.M. the People assembled for conference when Bishop Lowry arose and stated the object of the meeting saying that the Tithing in this place was going to waste for the want of a store house and that he had been trameled by President Morly to such an extent that he had not been able to build a store house to preserve the Tithing in. Bro Hancock then spoke of the rights that every quorum should enjoy and said that the Bishop, High Council, City Council &c had been overruled and put down.

Bro Averett told what he had heard you say about the Presidency in this place. I then spoke in relation to the sayings that had come from you, spoke of the Bigg field being thrown out and of the old System of herding & said that under existing circumstances that I did not feel willing to uphold President Morly unless you would say. So President Morly said that he would leave the Bigg field matter with the People. Father [Titus] Billings said that the reason every man was called upon to herd his day cattle or no cattle was because every man had land in the field. This is an original idea never having been advanced before. Bro Jordan and others spoke upon the Principle of obeying council. Bro Higgins said that as he understood matters that President Morly ought not to preside over this Branch any longer that President Youngs mind was that the People chose a new President and if they did not that they would still be Censured with not obeying your Council.

After Bro Higgins had concluded his remarks President Morly arose resigned the Presidency and Called upon the People to choose a new President. This was not instantaneously done and a number of brethren expressed their minds, some in favor others against President Morly Presiding. There was a sympathetic speech made by Bro Warren Snow for President Morly and a speech made by Bro Jno Lawson (the man who sold ACW Bowman the flour) in which he brought Provo City forward as a figure to prove that if we did not take President Morly back as our president that we would be like they were in Provo (ie) all by the wool and all on the road to hell. There were many motions made and the conference became a confused Mass. There was then a motion made to sustain all of the officers in San Pete including President Morly. Of Course this was hurried through Many voting for it who did not understand it and who are sincerely sorry for what they did. I and others did not vote as I always intend to stick to my assertions untill I find they are wrong. President Morly has said in Public that he did not want the Brethren to go to you with his little weaknesses therefore I have avoided the little things as much as posable. Bro Levi W Hancock said in meeting today that he wished the scribes to write to you as he had as leave they would as not and as they could write to no better place this side of heaven.

Tomorrow evening a number of the Brethren meet to make arrangement for Bro Jezrel Shoemaker to act as President of Temporal affairs and as Bishop in Temporal affairs as President Morly thinks that Bishop Lowry is no better versed in Carrying on the Temporal affairs of his office than he. President Morly is what the issue will be. I know not [but] Time will tell. Bro Hancock has had a talk with Bishop Lowry in which he told him that Did he Bro H fill his station that he would not be trameled in that way but that he would act in the station that he had been called to fill untill he was removed from that station by the Proper authority.

Nov 16. Nothing further has Transpired worth noting. As I have been charged lately with writing to you and telling you of everything that transpired in Manti I will merit the name in part and writing to you when anything of note comes up. My Mottoe is

Naught Externnale Naught Set down in Malice.

I Remain yours to command
And[rew] L Siler

Albert Smith witnessed the murder at Manti and its grim consequences.

ALBERT SMITH, REMINISCENCES, 1876, MS 1835, 60–61, LDS ARCHIVES.

Thare was A small band of Sanpeps Indians that wsaid [sic] that they wanted to be good frends they came & went wer [where] they pleased for A long time. The first first [sic] of september I think it was it was ascertained that they ware stealing & surmised that they ware Spies or that they ware acting falsly. Let that be as it may: thare was A council hild & at the same time thare was eight Indians in camp with thare wifes & the desision of that council was to kill the indians & imprison the Squazes. The Indians ware perswaded to go with some soldiers outside the limits of the town & started for that perpos. When in front of my house they mistrusted sumthing I suppose for they started to run.

The fireing then commenced. At that they all broke to run but ware all kiled. I have no comments to make but will only say that it was A sad afare as the sequel will show. Shortly after thare was A company of 20 wagons with horse tems started for salt lake. The night preavious thare was 3 ox teams started loded with weat & cantry [contrary] to council wen they got to the head of the vally they camped & went to bead. Wen we came up the nex day we found them all massecred. Some ware kiled wile others ware found baried in the w[h]eat in the wagons. Thare was four kiled. We put them in one of our wagons & took them to nephy & thare they ware buared. [Wh]en we got to Salt crick or Nephy we found that thare was A band of Indians that ware friendly & had bin in town that day (Saturday) & they looked for them the next day, Sunday. Just at dusk the Br that rode with me came into the wagon ware I was, & told me that the Br[ethren] thare at Nephi & the Br[ethren] with us from Manti had counciled together & had come to the conclusion to kill on the morow all the Indians that came to town. I replied that it was the worst move that they could make & counciled him to stay in the wagon with me. I need not say that thare council was car[ri]ed into exucation.

"It is my painful duty to report to you the barborous Murder of three of our brethren," Maj. George Bradley wrote from Fort Nephi on 2 October 1853. Four men left Manti bound for Salt Lake City with two wagonloads of wheat on 30 September. The next day, Isaac Morley found the "horribly cut and mangled" bodies of William Nelson, William Luke, and William Reed at Uinta Springs, now Fountain Green. Thomas Clark's corpse "had been covered up in the wagon with wheat that the Indians had emptied out of the sacks."[13]

The men had camped on 1 October, "just East of Salt Creek kanyon, where some Indians killed them all, and horribly mutilated their bodies, which were brought into Nephy, and buried," the reported. Three bodies, Bradley wrote, "were brought to this place and buried to day."

This morning I sent for Seven Indians and one Squaw whom were camped near our Fort, to come and have a talk. I told the Indians to lay down their arms but they refused and Showed fight. I ordered their arms taken whereupon two shot arrows and wounded one white in the Arm and one arrow through the coat of another, upon which I ordered them to be fired upon. Seven Indians were killed and the Squaw was taken prisoner, about one hour after one other Indian and a boy came up. The Indian was shot and the Boy taken prisoner.

Bradley presumed the "Indians killed were 4 of the Willow Creek Band, 2 Sandpitches, 2 Pabawat." That evening nervous guards "discovered an Indian and fired upon him and Suppose they Killed him." They probably

---

[13]Gottfredson, *Indian Depredations in Utah*, 74.

did, for the reported "a skirmish at Nephi" in which "eight Indians were killed, and one squaw and two boys taken prisoners."[14]

U.S. Marshal Joseph Heywood described his September meeting with three familiar visitors, "Sandpitches," to Governor Young. They told him Wakara wanted peace, but they left Nephi:

> in consequence of being afraid that our people wanted to get them into the Fort & then Kill them. They seemed very hungry & had a quantity of squirrels with them about the size of the Eastern Chip squirrel. They manifested a desire to work & I told them they could come & work for their board & when we were able we would give them clothing also, with which they seemed well pleased—They said Walker & most of the Indians had gone to Uinta—that Walker was disposed to make peace, but that Arrowpine said he had "Killed a squaw & two horses in consequence of the war, and that he never would make peace but wanted to fight."[15]

Sarepta Marie Heywood, born on 8 August, "had the honor of being born in the midst of Indian difficulties, when there were express[es] running all over the country and martial law prevading in all the settlements," wrote Martha Spence Heywood. Her husband wanted her employ them and "do all I could to encourage" local Natives. Duty called Marshal Heywood away in late September. "I felt very bad the morning he left me," she wrote; "it seemed I could not bear to be left alone and also what could happen to him on the way." Soon "the San Pete brethern arrived here on their way to the city to attend conference and brought with them the bodies of three murdered brethren, by the Indians, out of four who started from San Pete the day before the company did," continued Martha. "They had not obeyed counsel in camping where they did that night. They were very much mutilated and the other one was found and brought in the next day." Martha then described the summary executions of the hungry, harmless band:

> This barbarous circumstance actuated our brethern, counselled by Father Morley of San Pete (who no doubt was much excited in the time of it) and President [Anson] Call of Filmore to do quite as barbarous an act the following morning, being the Sabbath. Nine Indians coming into our camp looking for protection and bread with us, because we promised it to them and without knowing they did the first evil act in that affair or any other, were shot down without one minute's notice. I felt satisfied in my own mind

---

[14]Bradley to Wells, 2 October 1853, UTMR 396; "Indian Difficulties," *Deseret News*, 15 October 1853, 2/2.
[15]Heywood to Young, 22 September 1853, UTMR 392.

that if Mr. Heywood had been here they would not have been dealt with so unhumanly. It cast considerable gloom over mind.[16]

Juanita Brooks called Martha Spence's narrative "one of the great pioneer Mormon journals," so her report of the atrocity is well known. Historian Stanley B. Kimball transcribed the less renowned memoirs of Adelia Almira Wilcox Hatton Wood Kimball. After her birth in New York in 1828, her family followed the Latter-day Saints west. Her father, Eber Wilcox, was one of the fourteen casualties of Zion's Camp in 1834.[17] Adelia's personal history is confusing, but in 1844 she married William Hawthorne Hatton, who "was not a member of the church and had no sympathy with it," Kimball noted. Hatton rushed to California in 1849, returned, and bought a quarter section of Illinois land before neighbors persuaded him to return west.

On their trek in 1853, the family stopped at Fillmore to visit Adelia's mother, now married to John Webb. Hatton had "said all the time he would never go by Salt Lake," Amelia recalled, but "now it seemed that circumstances would compel him to for it was told us that the Indians wore very bad and it was not safe to go the northern road." Webb told Hatton that "he had better go the southern route." It was bad advice. Adelia dreamed William "had to pass through a dark gulf," which she interpreted to mean "the Indians were so bad that some of us, if not all, would get killed." While standing guard at 3 A.M. on 13 September at Fillmore, "Mr. Wm. Hatton Sentinel No. 4 at the Cattle Carrol was Shot dead on his post. Whither done by supposed friendly Pauvans or hostile Utahs we know not," Henry Standage reported.[18] Here Hatton's widow picked up the story.

ADELIA WILCOX, MEMOIRS, 1849–1868, 12–13.

I was woke up by a noise in the house and I heard someone say, "Hatton is shot by an Indian." I jumped up, dressed myself and was going out. Just then they brought him in to the kitchen. He was dead. They would not let me see him until they had washed, dressed and laid him out. Now this was a terrible shock to me for I never dreamed of any danger while we were here, but all my worry had been for what would happen to us after we left the

---

[16]Brooks, Not by Bread Alone, 1 January 1854, 2, 97.

[17]Smith, History of the Church, 2:116.

[18]Standage to Smith, 13 September 1853, UTMR 384. Pioneer Mormon-turned-critic Josiah Gibbs listed "the Hatton incident" among "those abundantly verified cases of blood-atonement, from the Parrish tragedy in Springville to that of Hatton in Fillmore." The date and other details of his unlikely charge, based on "fearsome whisperings to the effect that a certain resident of Fillmore was the murderer," are wrong. Gibbs, Lights and Shadows, 202.

settlements. We often have forebodings of coming evil, but never know in what shape they will come. After he was dressed I was allowed to see him and where he had been shot. He had been shot twice in the left breast and in his upper lip. It looked like he had been hit with an arrow. The room was full, but today I could not tell one person that was there except my own folks. I don't remember whether they buried him the same day, or not until the next, but this I know he was the second one ever buried in Fillmore graveyard.

Now I was left to look after myself and children, but one thing I was thankful for was that I was not left among strangers for it seemed to me if I had been I could not have stood it. William was eight, Henry six and Mary Eliza was four. One week after my husband was killed a company came along going through to California and Mr. Hart, the man that we left at Fort Laramie with his sick wife, he was along. He tried to persuade me to go to California with them, but I could not be convinced that it would be to my interest to do so, but felt that I would be better off with the Latter-Day Saints and my own relatives. He found he could not persuade me and they soon went on in about four weeks after this. Pa and Mother were going to Salt Lake to see my sister Sarah who was living there and as I wanted to get some dishes and other things to keep house with, we had brought nothing with us, expecting to get such things when we got through to California.

We left Fillmore early in the morning and as there were no settlements between Fillmore and Nephi, 60 miles, it made it quite a hard day's drive. We had crossed Chicken Creek and went about two miles the other side—it now being dark—when we were met by an express from Nephi who had heard we were on the road and did not consider we were safe as the Indians had killed three of our brethren that were coming through the Canyon from Sanpete going to Salt Lake City. We were told that one of the number, an Englishman [William Luke], had come a year or two before and had made a home for himself and family and was then on his way to meet them when he met this terrible fate. And oh, what an awful blow it must have been to them expecting to meet him after a long separation! But such were the scenes that many had to pass through in those days, not all in the same way. Many others have been killed in these valleys and their families left without their aid or support to battle with life as best they could. Some of our folks went to see them but I did not for I did not feel that I could stand the sight.

The next morning before we left seven Indians and a Squaw came into the Fort. The brethren were so exasperated and Father Morley being there ordered them shot down without even considering whether they were the guilty ones or not. It was an awful sickening sight to me. They wore shot down like so many dogs, picked up with pitchforks [put] on a sleigh and hauled away. The squaw they took prisoner. She never made any to do that I heard, but when she passed by where I was, she walked as slip and independent as though nothing had happened. They took her to Salt Lake

City and we heard that President Young soon had her released and was very indignant over the way the Indians had been killed. It was afterwards learned that they were Lake Indians from Parvian Valley and had no hand in the murdering of our brethren, but this was the cause of other hostilities between the Indians and whites.

In August 2006 workers excavating a foundation uncovered seven skeletons, evidence of what the press called the "Nephi massacre."[19] The "seven individuals, all male and all between the ages of 12 and 35," whom state archeologists recovered showed the purported skirmish recorded in traditional histories was actually "a cold-blooded execution." The bodies, tossed into a shallow mass grave showed "clear evidence of gunshot trauma to the head, pelvic region or leg"; five revealed blunt-force wounds, while four indicated trauma to the left forearm or wrist. Archeologist Ronald J. Rood, the site's principal investigator, interpreted the fractures as defensive wounds, suggesting the Natives "were severely beaten prior to being shot."[20]

Historian Robert Carter discovered a letter to Brigham Young that Tovashant dictated, listing his relatives executed in Nephi; the eight names indicate Major Bradley's guards had also killed the Indian they fired upon the night of the murders. Linguists consulting on the case provided possible names and translations for the murdered Natives: Upsavo'a-pu (Hunchback), Tuso'-qa-chi (Early Dawn), Nuu-as-gha-pu (Brave One), 'aka-taa' or 'aka-tuachi' (Red Shirt or Red Child), Tin Ta Dyes (Little Rock), Tachapu-chi' (Little Summer), Paach'a-chi or Paa-ta'wa-chi (Bat or Water Man), and Naso-karu-ru (Sitting Depressed).[21]

As Howard Christy observed, "the grisly cycle of mutual retaliation continued to grind." At Nephi, Andrew Love "soldiered & stood guard as usual." Perhaps referring to the settlement's reckless massacre of Indians that fall, he wrote, "Many things transpired but not to be written in this book."[22]

Violent events followed in quick succession. Perhaps the Utes did not let the wanton bloodshed at Manti and Nephi go unanswered. Major Higgins wrote:

I have to report that on Tuesday the 4th inst [October 1853] John E Warner and Wm Mills went to a small Kanion about 3 or 400 yds above the grist mill to get a load of wood and while in the act of loading there wood a party

---

[19]Myrna Trauntvein, "Native American Remains Reveal Evidence of Being Executed," *Nephi Times-News*, 7 June 2007, 1.

[20]Rood, The Archaeology of a Mass Grave, 10, 21–22, 26.

[21]Ibid., 31.

[22]Christy, "The Walker War," 407–408; Andrew Love, Diary, 25–26, LDS Archives.

of Indians crep[t] up and shot them boath dead on the spot. Br Warner it appears went to the mill to do some grinding [and] after filling the hopper with the grain and starting the mill to running went to help Br Mills get his wood.

That afternoon a visitor found the hopper empty but the mill running. Several men who "went immediately to ascertain the difficulty" found pony tracks "but could not find the Brethren" and left quickly. Higgins gathered more men and "went on above the Mill a short distance [and] found the oxen: one dead the other with severel arrows sticking in him. A few rods further were found the Brethren—stript of nearly all their clothes."[23]

As Hosea Stout later noted, the cycle of vengeance had only begun:

Allen Weeks living in Cedar Valley Utah County sent his two sons William F. & Warren D Weeks on the 8th [August 1854] to the kanyon for a load of poles with an ox team. The Indians a small band of ten or twelve who had seperated from the tribe & would not make peace with the whites untill some of their friends & relations were revenged or a recompense given which had been killed & Salt Creek Juab County last year, had concluded after waiting 12 moon for a recompense and recieving none, to reveng their death on some of the whites & accordingly the[y] lay in wait in the mouth of a kanyon to which the inhabitants of Cedar Valley were accustomed to go for wood and poles and br Allen Weeks two sons happened to be the two unfortunate ones who first came alon & were slain & their bodies mutilated & scalped by the indians.[24]

By October's end, the Mormon campaign against the Utes was losing steam and with winter ground to a halt. Nelson Higgins's October report from Fort Manti explained he had ordered Lt. James T. S. Allred to enlist all the men at his post; Allred reported he had "sixty one men able to bare armes and only two horses one sadle twenty nine guns one hundred thirty rounds of ball and only four and a half pounds of powder to the whole sixty one men." They were "mostly Danes and are very poor so if armes and ammunition could be furnished I think they could defend the place." Higgins asked the adjutant to "have thirty two guns and some powder & Lead forwarded to this place for them."[25]

War weariness spread among the Utes. They stole cattle and horses at Provo and burned buildings at Summit Creek, but a few visited Fort Payson

[23]Higgins to Wells, 5 October 1853, UTMR 399.

[24]Brooks, *The Diary of Hosea Stout*, 31 August 1854, 2:526.

[25]Higgins to Ferguson, Report No 11, Fort Manti, 25 October 1853, UTMR 408.

"and declared their intentions to be friendly," wrote G. A. Smith. "Ponawat said he had walked along the Mountains during the war. Looked down at the houses had been tu ege hungry and thought of the bread and Milk and cried."[26]

BLOOD ENOUGH: THE GUNNISON MASSACRE

Topographical engineer John Gunnison's service with the Stansbury Expedition won him a promotion and command in 1853 of the Pacific Railroad Survey along the thirty-eighth parallel, which brought him back to Utah a year after he published leaving them alone would see the faith "fade away and be forgotten." Meanwhile, the Mormons were more effective "than an army against the Indians on the West."[27]

Geologist Jacob Schiel described the expedition's encounter with Utes, probably near Montrose, Colorado:

> we found ourselves surrounded within minutes by a crowd of Tabawatshi Utes, who seemed to grow literally out of the floor in that country which we believed uninhabited. There were a few hundred men, women and children, the men riding beautiful Navajo horses, which were undoubtedly stolen from the Navajo Indians, famous breeders of horses and sheep. A number of squaws were also riding, sitting in the saddle like the men. Mostly they were well-dressed, had not the starved and filthy look of the prairie tribes, and in general seemed to possess a certain wealth. Their warriors were well-built and strong, of medium height, with broad and high chest, but their legs were bent, feet pointing inward as is usual with Indians. The very broad root of their nose gave their faces an ugly expression. At first their talk was haughty, almost threatening, and they let us know openly that if we would not make presents they would take them.

To impress the explorers, "a few warriors wheeled their horses back and forth in a wild race, which indeed gave the riders a demonical appearance." They pointed at the mountains, "continually chattering and calling, 'Utah, Utah.'" They told interpreter Antoine Leroux "that 2000 warriors of the Utahs were in the neighboring mountains, that they had shortly before had a big battle with the Comanches and chased them over the mountains, that the Utah have not yet been defeated by any other tribe, and that they are on the warpath with the Mormons of which they have killed a great number, and other pleasant things."[28]

[26]Smith to Richards, 14 November 1853, BYC 42:5.

[27]Gunnison, *The Mormons*, v, 165.

[28]Schiel, *Journey through the Rocky Mountains*, 80–81. Perhaps this was Arapene's band.

On 1 October, Gunnison camped at today's Moab, Utah. "Indians thronged our camp for several hours. They are the merriest of their race I have ever seen, except the Yumas—constantly laughing and talking, and appearing grateful for the trifling presents they receive," wrote Lt. E. G. Beckwith. "A wrinkled, hard-faced old savage, with whom I shared my luncheon of bread and bacon, quite laughed aloud with joy at his good fortune." The Utes confirmed the "war between the Mormons and Wah-ka-ra's band of Utahs," and reported Wakara was in New Mexico disposing of Mormon cattle. The expedition hired Tewip Narrienta (Powerful Earth), "one of the best guides" Beckwith ever met. He told the surveyors his people were at war with the Mormons, "boasting of their feats of prowess." He "repeatedly warned us against these people."[29]

Angry Pahvants awaited the expedition as it traced the Spanish Trail into Utah. Samuel Hoyt described their fatal encounter with a California-bound "Emigrant train of forty or fifty men" near Fillmore on 23 September 1853, which was typical of Anglo-Indian relations on the overland trails. Capt. Thomas Hildreth had asked Hoyt "if the Indians in our Valley were peaceable." Hildreth pointed to Indians sitting nearby "and said there are three or four of those who fired on my men." His men returned fire and perhaps wounded a man.

> He wished me to tell the Indians to keep away from his train and not come near his encampment for his men threatened to shoot at the Indians if they came near them. I went to them and told them in their own language what Captn Hildreth said. The Indians laughed turned round and chatted among themselves and appeared to disregard what I said to them. Captn. and his company soon started on their way. In the evening information was brought into our City, by Parashant an Indian of some note, that some of his tribe had been to the American Camp as they called the Emigrant train. Parashant said the Americans had fired on some of the Pauvans and had one and wounded two and had one tied in their Camp. Pant a young Brave, a son of the Indian just killed by the Americans came in with Parashant. They said Kanosh the pauvan chief and Queant leader of the Lake band were absent on a hunt and quite a number of the Pauvans with them. Parashant said he had sent for them to Corn Creek. Parashant and Pant appeared to be full of fight. They said they would attack the Americans the next night. I told him not to do so and tried to reason him out of the idea of retaliation. They tried hard to get Guns and ammunition of me as I had formerly had

---

[29]Beckwith, *Explorations and Surveys*, House Exec. Doc. 129 (33:1), Serial 737, 62.

some trade with them. When they found they could get none, they wanted me to go to the Americans and get two Guns that belonged to the Pauvans.

Hoyt agreed to try to get the guns back and next morning started with three men, overtaking the Americans at Corn Creek. Hildreth said Indians had visited

> his Camp the preceding evening while he was out taking care of his stock, he said that his men told the Indians they must give up their Guns and other weapons and stay in their camp until morning, two or three gave theirs up willingly. But one of the Indians by the name of Tow-ipe who had a high standing in his tribe and who was the Father of a number of Braves he was armed with Bows and Arrows refused to give them up. One of their company by the name of Hart undertook forcibly to take them from him, while in the act the Indian stabbed Hart in the Lower part of the Abdomen, with an arrow. Hart seized is revolver and shot the Indian who ran a few rods and expired. Several of the men seized their Guns and fired on the Indians who made their escape with the exception of the one who was tried [*sic*] to whom they made presents and let him go in the morning. Capt H. said he was absent during the whole affair if he had been in camp no doubt but he could have prevented it he was very sorry the affray, had happened and if property would settle it he would give five or six hundred dollars in stock Blankets &c. Hildreth said his company were strong enough to go through but he knew the Indian character so well that small companies will have to suffer for it. Capt gave the two Guns to me saying he had no need of them but requested me to keep them two days until he could get a little out of the way. He said he did not want the Indians to use them against him. He then said tell Kanoshe to come to his camp and he would try and satisfy him.

Hildreth asked Hoyt how many Pahvants were in Kanosh's band. On being told, he boasted "his men we are strong enough to whip twice that number" and went to a wagon "and dealt out powder to those that needed." The Natives claimed they were firing at game and only went to camp on Meadow Creek to trade with the Americans, who now wounded two more Pahvants. Queant "said the Pauvans had had a council and he and Kanosh would not fight," but Kanosh warned "that some of the Pau-van boys," especially Towisse's three sons, were determined to avenge their father. Hoyt heard they "followed the Company nearly out of the Territory to get revenge," but the agitation soon subsided and the band resumed hunting. In 1855 Hoyt recalled:

The excitement among the Indians appeared to die away in a short time and they were soon off on their hunt again. Every thing appeared to be quiet among the Indians in this Valley until the Massacre of Capt Gunnison and party. Capt Gunnison was at my house a short time before his death. I broke a Draft of five hundred dollars for him. He said he wanted to pay some young men that were going to California.

John Gunnison split his expedition and made a poorly located camp among the willows on the Sevier River on 25 October 1853 A Pahvant hunting party and two of Towisse's sons found it.

The Indians say one of the sons of the Indian killed was out hunting [when] he heard the report of two Guns. He followed in the direction of the sound and found it proceeded from two men that were shooting fowls, cautiously followed them to their camp. Having ascertained the number, He returned to his own camp made exciting speeches, and had a War dance during the night. Determined on having revenge they started very early in the morning and poured a deadly fire on them while they were eating their breakfast.

Hoyt's report preserves the best version of what the Indians said about the attack, which killed Gunnison and seven others:

I have never been at the place where Captain Gunnison and party were Killed [near Sevier Lake]. It is said to be about forty five miles from our City. The Indians that massacred Gunnison and party were principally the band called the Lake Band.

I have been told there were twenty four or twenty six as near as can be ascertained. Nowquick a Brave was a leader of the Company that fell upon Gunnison and party. Nowquick was the son of Towisse the Indian Killed by Hart. Since I have been writing this Nowquick came in Mrs. Hoyt now recognising him asked him if he was a Utah. He said he was not. He said his name was Nowquick he was the one that Killed the Americans cut off both arms and took out the heart accompanying each word with corresponding gesture. This was a voluntary introduction of his own explaining to Mrs Hoyt who he was. Saying that he did it because the Americans had Killed his Father on Meadow Creek. I know but few names of the Indians concerned in the Gunnison Massacre. I have been informed that Scarrip, Pant, Monsoo, Seyo, Pismy, and Queants two sons. Some other names I learned when I was at the Trial at Salt Creek. I think were Whitetree, Anklejoint and Sandyhair. The Indians say they have shed blood enough and are satisfied. The part that each one performed in that bloody transaction can only be ascertained by the Indians themselves.[30]

---

[30]Hoyt to Hosea Stout, 14 August 1855, Governor's Letterbook, BYC 50:1, 355–60.

The murder of Gunnison and seven men on 26 October 1853, initially charged to "Walker's band of Utahs," has been controversial since January 1854, when the observed, "there is more ground for suspecting the Mormons of the murder than there is for supposing it to be the work of Indians." Evidence undercuts the enduring suspicion that Mormons engineered the attack: even the commiserated "with the friends of those who have been so suddenly and unexpectedly cut off, but more especially with the wife and children of Captain Gunnison, who was endeared to us by a formed and fondly cherished acquaintanceship in 1849–'50."[31]

Bvt. Capt. Robert M. Morris, commander of the expedition's military escort, began a journal at Fort Leavenworth on 1 July 1853, stopped it on 21 August, and started again on 24 October at the Sevier River, perhaps to explain the disaster. Gunnison had set out with botanist Frederick Kreutzfeldt, artist Richard Kern, Gunnison's black servant John Bellows, and Mormon guide William Potter with "an Escort of six men to accompany him on the Survey of Sevier Lake," Morris wrote. Yale University's Beinecke Library acquired his diary in 1996, which contains this detailed account of the assault and its aftermath.

ROBERT M. MORRIS, JOURNAL, 24–29 OCTOBER 1853, 2–6.

Oct 26/Weds/[Camp] No 109. At Capt G'[s] request I ordered an escort of four men to accompany Mr. Potter the guide[32] to ascertain whether we could find a camp to the left of the mountains, as he wished to pass on that side of the mountains and come up the side of Utah Lake. Potter & party were just leaving camp when they met Corpl Barton running on foot in breathless haste who reported at 11½ AM that Capt G had been surprised by the Pah Vants (Eutaws) and he feared all were massacred excepting himself. A few moments after Pvt Smith came in on Caulfields horse which was wounded, and confirmed Bartons Statement saying that Caulfield was shot with a Rifle ball through the stomach and [had] fallen from his horse when he jumped on him and escaped—I immediately sounded to horse and at 12 n. with the remainder of the troop hastened to the scene. Rode at a full trot until six PM when I came up to where the bodies of Ms Kern Caulfield & Liptrott lay. The former was shot with a Rifle ball through the heart. Liptrott was killed by numerous arrow wounds.[33] It now [being] dark Mr Potter (the guide) and myself concluded that it would not be prudent to penetrate into the willows until daylight.

[31]*Deseret News*, 12 November 1853, 2/6; 30 March 1854, 1/5.
[32]Gunnison had hired Gardiner G. Potter and his brother William as interpreters at Manti.
[33]The first names of the Mounted Riflemen privates Caulfield, Liptoote, and Mehrteens do not survive.

We therefore selected as clear a spot away from them as we could find and stood to horse until day light.

Five horses gave out on the march which I was compelled to abandon and send the troopers back to join the train, which was moving under Lt Beckwiths command to the town of Fillmore. Between camp & camp 108 I met Whitesides leading his horse with his rifle in hand. He had also escaped. About 6 miles beyond the camp met Mears endeavoring to escape. Sent all back to the train. My force then consisted of half [?] Lt Baker Mr Potter and fifteen soldiers.

At daylight proceeded to Capt G'[s] Camp [where] within an area of ¼ Struck across the basin to camp No 109 where I found the train just getting on at 9 PM. Found that the four men sent back had not got in, nor Corpl Flake [?] whose horse gave out on our return. The statement of the men who escaped is in substance as follows. That Capt G camped on the ill fated spot contrary to the wishes of Mr Potter his guide, who proposed a camp away from the willows [and] that Capt G. said no Indians were about and if they were, that they were not hostile. He camped about 3 PM. that a guard was kept all night until daylight—each taking his turn.

At daybreak they rose and were eating breakfast just before sunrise, when the Indians attacked. A terrific yell accompanied by a discharge of guns and showers of arrows, from the bushes about 20 yds to the left of the camp. That Corpl Barton called out to jump to their arms and that Capt G & Mr Kern exited from their tent the former bare handed extending both hands upwards. Both unarmed that seeing the band was about having surrounded [the camp] they all rushed for their horses. Some succeeded in reaching them and escaped, while those who fired fell. The lowest number of Indians is said to be Sixty. When I reached the camp it was entirely stripped of every thing. All the bodies were stripped. A few shots were returned by the party before retreating.

Had it not been from the fact that the people of Fillmore said that the Indians were all friendly about the Lake, Capt G would have taken a larger escort. I had informed Lt Baker that he would go in command of the Escort and had intended to have sent a Non Com Officer and fifteen men, but Capt G thought Six were enough [interlined: so says Lt. Beckwith].

The next day, Morris visited Fillmore to buy forage and alert the authorities. Nauvoo Legion general Franklin D. Richards, an apostle and "a man of some status among them," visited the army camp on 28 October. He sent an express to Great Salt Lake City so Morris could report "the particulars of the massacre" in the November mail. The Morris journal ended at Salt Lake a week later.

Lieutenant Beckwith's report dismissed statements "charging the Mormons or Mormon authorities with instigating the Indians" to murder Captain Gunnison as "not only entirely false, but there is no accidental circumstance connected with it affording the slightest foundation for such a charge. " Kanosh, "chief of the band of murderers," told Beckwith "that he deeply regretted the tragedy," which "was done without authority, by the young men—boys, as he called them—of the band, who had no chief with them, or it would not have happened."[34] Moreover, trying to prove Brigham Young's Danites killed Captain Gunnison is a fool's errand. Legislator Anson Call's report echoed details in Morris's account. At Fillmore, Hildreth's party "manifested a very hostile apearence towards the Indians" and allegedly "swore they would kill the first Indians that came in to their camp." Call warned them the "Porvine" Indians "took no part with Walker or his men and was friendly with all men," but the emigrants killed a Pahvant at Meadow Creek anyway. "Parishont one of the Chiefts and one of the Sons of the Indian kild met with us and were very mad." The Mormons tried to pacify him, but he said the murdered man's three sons "would fite that Company." Parashont "arose and said they had kild his father and then left." When Gunnison visited Fillmore on 23 October, Call "related to him the circumstance of the Indian bein kild and the feelings of the three Indians brothers and that I then supposed that they ware persuing the Company." Gunnison denounced the emigrants' conduct, said he had never "had any dificuly with the Indians." He "entended to survey the Sevier ~~river~~ Lake and then go to Salt Lake City for winter quarters." [35]

Heading south from Nephi with a mounted guard, Apostles Erastus Snow and Franklin D. Richards "espied two mounted Indians" and induced them to talk, giving them bread and tobacco. They said they came "to tell our people to be kind to the Indians and not to kill them and to say also to the Indians to cease to kill our people and be friends." The Utes had "come from Walker who is in the Navajo country" and "desired the same." After dark on 26 October at today's Holden, the party was "haild by four distressed men of the late Capt. Gunnisons party who had escapd the slaughter, were barefoot and nearly naked and had been about twenty hours without food or water."

---

[34]Beckwith, *Explorations and Surveys*, 74, 75.
[35]Call, Statement, November 1853, BYC 47:37.

We Brought them into camp and today Elder Richards visited Capt. Morris' camp on Pioneer creek in company with Elders Call & King, and after learning the particulars of the late distressing affair advised Capt. Morris to send an express to Great Salt Lake city to acquaint you with the facts and to avail himself of the first eastern mail to convey dispaches to the Goverment at Washington. Haveing no animals in his camp able to carry the express, He employed Prest. Call to ~~send~~ carry the express; and by this conveyenance we send you this hasty scrall, and we would add that the Pauvan chiefs are here and are very sorry about the murder of the Americans. They deny all previous knowledge of or participation in the affair. They say it was the unruly Boys of the Lake band. Knoss [Kanosh] has Sent in one of the Goverment horses and is to start tomorrow to endeavour to recover the papers instruments &c. They say the indians were not aware of any Mormon being in the party untill in striping Bro. Wm Potter they found his garments upon him and left them on him. We have every where endeavourd to impress the saints in all the settlements with the spirit of our late general conference and have felt ourselves abundantly blessed in all our preaching.[36]

Morris returned to Fillmore on 28 October "and said Capt Gunnison and 7 of his party had binn killed by the Indians." He asked Call to recover the expedition's books and property. One of Morris's men "drawed his Pistol to shoot Kanoshe," but Call "sprang be twixt him and the Pistole and ordered him to leave the fort amediately." Kanosh soon retrieved "the books and instruments and a part of the animels and Guns and said it was the Porvine Indians principly that had comit the deed and it was in concequence of the Emigrants killing there man the three sons of the man kild was the means of the slowter [slaughter]." Dimick Huntington brought "orders from the Gviner" to gather the property and bury the dead. Call found the body of Kreutzfeldt at the campfire, near Bellows, Kern, Potter, and the escort, the bodies "torn to peces by the Wolves. We picked up their bones and placed them to each of their bodes as well as we could. They ware scaterd near a mil[e]d from their Camp." Nothing remained of Gunnison "but one thy bone and some Hare." They dug three graves near the Sevier but took Gunnison's femur to Fillmore and buried it.[37]

Josiah Gibbs, editor of the Millard *Progress*, first published a Pahvant account of the Gunnison murders in 1894. It was reprinted in 1928.

---

[36]Snow and Richards to Gov. B. Young, 29 October 1853, BYC 41:18.
[37]Call, Statement, November 1853, BYC 47:37.

GIBBS, "INDIAN MAREER'S VERSION OF THE TRAGEDY,"
UTAH HISTORICAL QUARTERLY 1:3 (JULY 1928), 67–75.

[Mareer] began this narrative, which follows:

During the early afternoon of October 25th, the whiteman's date, Sam and Toady, armed with bows and arrows, were hunting ducks and rabbits on the south side of the river, a couple of miles or so below Deseret.[38] They were startled by the report of firearms from the north side of the river. Peering through the willows, the redmen saw a small number of horsemen, a few of whom wore United States military uniforms, which proved that they were "Mericats." Trailing in the rear of the horsemen, was an improvised cart, on which was packed bedding, provisions and camp utensils. The soldiers were firing at the flocks of ducks then moving southward. Within the shelter of the willows, the Indians watched the movements of the whitemen until Captain Gunnison and comrades entered their last campground. After carefully observing the details of the camp, Sam and Toady hurried down the river and told Moshoquop of their discovery.

The opportunity for avenging his father's death had unexpectedly arrived, and Moshoquop lost no time in planning the details of the attack.

It was about midnight when the braves left their camp for the encampment of the whitemen. Without hesitation Mareer traced the sinuous trail of the redmen out to the river, thence up the north bank to the inlet in the southwest corner of the depression, where Moshoquop halted and gave his final instructions.

The war-chief, accompanied by Pants, Mareer, Carboorits, Nunkiboolits and several others in crossing the inlet, covered with a thin sheet of ice, got their feet wet, which Mareer distinctly remembered as the only disagreeable incident, while sitting motionless during the remainder of that chill October night, they awaited the fatal signal. Stealthily working their way through the willows on the north bank of the river to the Gunnison camp, Moshoquop, Mareer and others secreted themselves in clumps of willows not more than a hundred feet west of where the explorers were soundly sleeping. Carboorits took his assigned position on the river bank a few yards west of the trail made by the whitemen from their campfire in going to and fro for water. The other warriors skirted the north side of the depression, and turning south completed the deadly cordon. Carboorits had been selected to fire the signal gun at the instant the first rays of the sun should strike the camp.

It was a few minutes before sunrise when the cook lighted the campfire, over which he placed the iron tripod and kettles. Professors Kern and Creutzfeldt were standing by the fire, while the corporal and his men were caring for the horses, a hundred yards or so northwest of the campfire, where, the previous evening, they had been picketed among clumps of willows.

---

[38]Founded in 1860 on the Sevier River delta, Deseret has a restored 1865 adobe fort.

Captain Gunnison had walked out to the river, not more than fifty feet distant, and in a stooping position was bathing his hands and face. Startled by the click of Carboorits' gun as he raised the hammer, the captain sprang to his feet, and the bullet passed harmlessly by. Kern, Creutzfeldt and the cook fell dead beside the campfire, pierced with bullets from the guns of Moshoquop, Pants, Mareer and others.

Captain Gunnison, having emptied his revolver at Carboorits, who, illustrated in pantomime by Mareer, ducked and dodged with such agility as to escape injury, turned towards the terrifying babel of warwhoops, shouts of victory, cries for help from those wounded during the first discharge of arrows, and yells from the confused survivors, some of whom were moving the horses to fresh pasturage, or were racing toward their mounts. The corporal and a private leaped on their horses, and by keeping within the clumps of willows reached the higher ground to north, and escaped. Another private ran to the river, plunged in, reached the opposite bank, secreted himself, and during the afternoon reached the camp at Gunnison bend.

Reaching the scene of slaughter, Gunnison realized that all was lost, and that his only course, if possible, was that of escape from the heart-breaking scene. Pursued by a shower of deadly arrows, the captain, doubtless, with the hope of securing his saddle horse, ran towards the northwest and disappeared within the willows.

CLOSING DIABOLICAL SCENE—MAREER'S STORY ENDS

Some two or three hours after the firing of the signal gun, Mareer and a few companions began a search of the willows, a hundred yards or so to northwest, for additional plunder. The redmen were surprised at discovering a whiteman who had been wounded by arrows lying full length on the sward, now marked with crimson stains. Several arrows lying about proved that the wounded man had wrenched them from his body.

At the appearance of the Indians the whiteman slowly and painfully raised himself to a sitting position. Mareer, alone, recognized Gunnison, but remained silent. Not even Moshoquop, until eleven days after the massacre, knew of the Captain's presence with the expedition. Extending his hands, palms up, in mute appeal for mercy, Captain Gunnison awaited the verdict. The red men hesitated. There was something in that silent appeal that touched a stranger in the hearts of the also silent redmen. Suddenly, "Jimmy Knight," the renegade Indian, appeared, and without speaking, raised his gun and fired. The captain's body swayed, then sank to the ground.

Brigham Young summarized his Indian troubles for a missionary in Scotland as November ended:

During the past season the Indian Walker & his band have caused us some trouble, by killing nine of the brethren & wounding several more, & by driving off several hundred head of stock; but at present the Indians are all quiet. In the different affrays nineteen Indians have been killed. From the latest reports we learn that Walker & his band have had a fight among themselves & split up, & a part of them have gone onto the Yampah River to hunt, & will return as soon as they learn we do not wish to kill them, & Walker and the other part have gone to winter among the Navajoes.

"The massacre of Capt Gunnison & a portion of his party," Young wrote, "had no connection with the Walker affair, but was the result of the [39] As scholar Benjamin Madley noted, "it took sustained political will—at both the state and federal levels—to create the laws, policies, and well-funded killing machine" needed to destroy Native peoples.[40]

Young and Apostle Albert Carrington sent the major's widow, Martha Gunnison, "a small lock of hair belonging to your deeply lamented husband," laying "the hair in the letter loose to prevent it from chafing."[41]

To Avenge the Death of Capt. Gunnison

The U.S. Army returned to Utah in 1854 when Capt. Edward Steptoe arrived with Pacific-bound reinforcements. He was to investigate the Gunnison murders and find a shorter road from Utah to California. Governor Young asked Steptoe to rush troops to Salt Lake to witness Mormon justice. "We came in two days sooner than was intended, to be present at the execution of two Indians, for the murder of two little boys," wrote Lt. LaRhett Livingston. "The Governor requested it, and thought this precaution necessary for fear of a rescue. Nothing of the kind was attempted, and there was no reason for supposing such a thing."[42]

The Goshutes had waited almost a year to avenge their relatives massacred at Manti before killing William and Warren Weeks, the teenage sons of the bishop of Cedar Fort, on 8 August 1854 at Pole Canyon, west of Utah Lake. George Bean officiated at the hanging of Longhair and Antelope. "It was hard on me," he recalled, but he "led them to the gallows. They said they were 'Braves' and would not die like a squaw, so walked straight to their doom." Relatives "immediately commenced their depredations in retaliation." The Goshutes hoped to capture "men to take into the kanion to Hang," Bishop

---

[39] Young to Edward Martin, 30 November 1853, BYC 5:1.
[40] Madley, *An American Genocide*, 13.
[41] Young and Carrington to Mrs. J. W. Gunnison, 30 November 1853, BYC 17:10.
[42] LaRhett Livingston, 16 September 1854, Beinecke Library; Bean, *Autobiography*, 109.

Weeks complained to Brigham Young, saying the lurking Indians "were determined to have two men out of this fort to Hang & if they could not get men they would take Boys or Children."[43]

In late October 1854 Steptoe headed south "to make a demonstration in the Indian Country & if possible—get hold of the murderers of Capt. Gunnison. It is an act which should be signally avenged and I hope he may have a complete success," wrote Lieutenant Livingston. Young officers were "paid for fighting, no matter against what odds, and since there is no glory in fighting Indians, it is of no count if they are killed!" The "principal object" in Steptoe's Expedition was "to avenge the death of Capt. Gunnison." It was a "pretty time to do such a thing, and a suitable command to do it with. However, it is to be done in a peculiar way."[44]

The "peculiar way" involved not offending the sensitive Saints. The effort to punish "a few Indians for killing Gunnison" degenerated into a farce that prosecuted a woman, two blind Pahvants, and three men whom Kanosh had "thrown away." Brigham Young recalled he delivered a few Indians who might have been involved, but Steptoe "dared not take them. I told him at the time of the conversation, that there might be some thirty of those Indians; but, if the United States should send 50,000 of their troops here they could not get one of them, if they had a mind to keep out of the way." Steptoe knew enough about Indian fighting to believe it.[45] The search next spring for a "new route was a failure, as the ground was found too soft for a heavy train so early in the season." The troops "were all very glad to get away from the City as it was getting very hot for us. It is a great relief to be free from petty annoyances that we can not treat properly. There was no love lost on either side," wrote Livingston. As the expedition prepared to depart, he was astonished "at the number of disaffected persons here, who would leave if they could. Many are with us under protection of the command & many others just following along, anything to get away."[46] Steptoe and his gallant young officers failed to accomplish any of their objectives in Utah, but the experience stiffened Mormon resolve to keep the army out of Zion.[47]

---

[43]D. Robert Carter, "Carnage in Pole Canyon Avenged," *Daily Herald* (Provo), 19 April 2008, B2.
[44]Livingston to Livingston, 16 September and 27 October 1854, Beinecke Library.
[45]Young, 9 August 1857, *Journal of Discourses*, 5:128.
[46]Livingston to Livingston, 15 May 1855, Beinecke Library.
[47]MacKinnon, "Sex, Subalterns, and Steptoe," 227–246.

Parrah-Shont the Pah-vante War Chief:
The Good and the Brave

In November 1855, Utah Territory's Second District Court tried Levi Abrams, "indicted for the murder of Too-ebe an Indian"—the Pahvant warrior whose murder at Meadow Creek triggered the Gunnison murders. Remarkably, Hosea Stout offered several Indians "as witnesses on the part of the prosecution," including Too-ebe's son Parashant, who described "his belief in future rewards and punishments."

Thursday 15 Nov 1855. Court met at ten A.M. Case of Abrams called up. Several Indians were offered as witnesses on the part of the prosecution. The first was Parrah-Shont the Pah-vante war chief was introduced. When on being questioned as to his belief in future rewards and punishments, He said that if he told the truth and done right in his life, he would go to a good warm Cañon in California, after death, where there were plenty of fat elk and good game. Where there [are] groves and grasses in eternal green. Where ran never failing streams of limpid and cool water; beneath the genial rays of a cloudless sun, in one eternal summer. Where he would live in peace and dwell in the society of the good and the brave and subsist on the choisest game and fattest elk. But if he told a lie, he would go to a barren, dreary and frozen Cañon filled with eternal snows, where he would drag out a miserable exhistence, poor naked and bare foot without good bows and arrows, doomed to persue his lean game and poor Elk over the rugged and frozen steeps of this desolate and dreary Cañon forever in the society of the wicked, the cowardly and the mean. This was deemed quite orthodox by the court and his testimony allowed.

Abrams was a Mormon convert, so the jury "rendered a virdict of not guilty as charged."[48]

---

[48]Brooks, *The Diary of Hosea Stout*, 5, 15–17 November 1855, 2:564–66.

"Joseph the Prophet Addressing the Lamanites."
S. Brannan & Co., 1844
*Harry T. Peters "America on Stone" Lithography Collection,
Smithsonian Museum, DL.60.3141.*

RED JACKET.

SENECA WAR CHIEF.

THE SENECA ORATOR SAGOYEWATHA (RED JACKET)
Sagoyewatha spoke at Palmyra in 1822 near Joseph Smith's home.
This Henry Corbould lithograph shows him wearing the medal
George Washington gave him in 1792. *From McKenney and Hall*, History
of the Indian Tribes of North America, *1837, and the Smithsonian Museum.*

WILLIAM WARNER MAJOR, "SKETCH OF WALKER, WAR CHIEF
OF THE UTAHS. ROCKY MOUNTAINS. TAKEN FROM LIFE BY
W. W. MAJOR SITTING IN COUNCIL, SEPT. 4, 1852."
Courtesy of the Peabody Museum of Archaeology and Ethnology,
Harvard University, PM #41-72-10/427 (digital file #99050027).

WILLIAM WARNER MAJOR, "KONO'SA,
CHIEF OF THE PARSIANTS NEAR FILMORE," 1852
Courtesy of the Peabody Museum of Archaeology and Ethnology,
Harvard University, PM #41-72-10/426 (digital file #99050028).

WILLIAM WARNER MAJOR, "TOOTOOMITCH WAR CHIEF SNAKES"
Courtesy of the Peabody Museum of Archaeology and Ethnology,
Harvard University, PM #41-72-10/424 (digital file #99050058).

Wash'echkick. Chief of the Shoshomas Tribe

WILLIAM WARNER MAJOR, "WASH'ECHICK,
CHIEF OF THE SHOSHOMAS TRIBE (1852)"
Watercolor, 7.63 × 5.25 in. (19.37 × 13.34 cm). This may
be the earliest image of Washakie, legendary leader
of the Northeastern Shoshones.
Courtesy Springville Museum of Art.

Parishont: *Rocky Mountains* ...
Leap of Elk, Chief of Corn Creek. Near Fillmore.

WILLIAM WARNER MAJOR, "PARISHORT OR LEAP OF ELK,
CHIEF OF CORN CREEK, NEAR FILLMORE, PAUVAN (1852)"
Watercolor, 8.38 × 6.13 in. (21.27 × 15.56 cm). Also known as Parashont,
he was at the Gunnison Massacre. The bishop at Fillmore reported he
was a son of Towisse, whom the Hildreth party killed at Corn Creek.
Courtesy Springville Museum of Art.

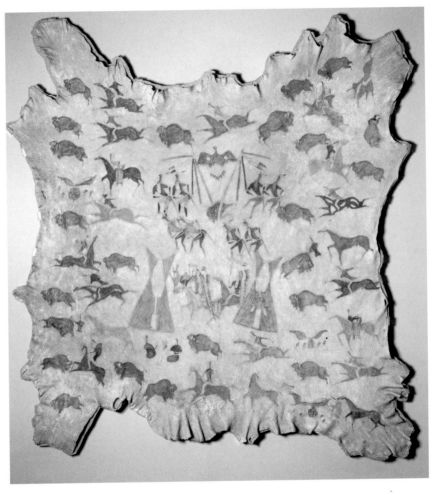

CADZI CODY (COSIOGO) (SHOSHONE, NATIVE AMERICAN, 1866–1912),
PAINTED ELK HIDE ROBE, CA. 1900
Elk hide, pigment. 81 × 78 inches (205.7 × 198.1 cm).
Cosiogo created Shoshone visual history on Wyoming's
Wind River reservation. His image shows buffalo hunters, horses
loaded with meat, ritual dancers, ceremonial lodges,
and women greeting two warriors as they enter camp.
Courtesy Brooklyn Museum, Dick S. Ramsay Fund, 64.13.

Chapter 7

KILLING CAPTAIN WALKER,
THE UTAH CHIEF

"I am the best friend you have on earth, and I wish to do you good all the time," Governor Young told Utah's "peace chiefs" as 1853 ended. "As you are far away, and for some reason keep away, I have to let you know my feelings by this letter." Natives and whites had been killed foolishly, "and it was nonsense to have any such fuss, but let that all pass." If everyone who had been killing, stealing, or destroying property wished "to quit such doings, & be friendly," it would "be all right with me & my people," Young wrote. His peace proposal displayed his grasp of Native justice:

> no Indian who has killed any of my people, nor any of my people who have killed an Indian shall be hurt by either party for such conduct. If in the future any one of my men kills an Indian, he shall be delivered up to the chief of his tribe, to be dealt with as the tribe may please; and if any Indian kills any one of my men he shall be delivered up to the principal man of the settlement where the white man lived to be dealt with as we please, but let all that is now done pass, & be forgotten, & let no Indians nor white men be killed for it. And if in future any of my men, or any Indian commits any depredartion [sic] of any kind upon the other party, such one shall make restitution, or be delivered to the party. If the Indians will all be quiet & friendly I will try to induce my people to furnish them bread, clothing, & other articles for their comfort, & some powder & lead to *hunt* with, but I shall want the Indians to work for what they get from the whites, as we have to do, or pay in skins, & quit begging, for we all have to work for what we have, & I wish to learn the Indians how to work.[1]

Utah's Indian nations seemed "desirous of making peace," Young told territorial representative John Bernhisel. He asked him to persuade Congress

---

[1] Young to Sowiet et al., 3 December 1853, BYC 17:1.

to approve Indian farms at Carson Valley, on the Colorado, and in Iron and Green River counties under agents who were not "hopeless among the Indians and rather desperate among the Mormons." He needed authority "to treat with the Indians for their Lands" with an appropriation for "Treaty stipulations."[2]

As the season of Cold Maker returned to rule the mountains in 1854, misery united all those entangled in the territory's Indian conflicts. Like most border wars, as Albert Smith of Manti explained, hunger and exhaustion ended the conflict in Utah.

> In the winter I had all of my cows & oxen took out of my yard but I got them all back again wile Br Whitting had [h]is took out & drove of[f] & he got none. About January 10th 1854 peace was restored. The fact of the case [was] they got Starved out & two of their braves came in & wanted to be frens & was very ticubu [hungry]. We told them that we wanted peace & for them to go and fetch in the rest of the tribe, which was not fer of [far off] but was up in the hills among the seaders & we would give them some thing to eat. They went & fetched them in not onely thare woryears [warriors] but thare women & children. We cared [carried] in to one place bread meat & any thing we had that was eatible & gave them quite a feast & smoked the pipe of peace together. That ended the Indian ware at that time.[3]

Utah's latest Mormon-Ute war only ended in stages and in theory. The road to "peace" began in winter 1854 and lasted until spring. The official legend tells how Brigham Young met Wakara in May 1854 near Nephi and ended hostilities. In reality, nothing changed: violent cultural conflict began immediately after the kabuki play staged on Chicken Creek and flared on the Mormon frontier's ragged edge for decades.

Pleading the Cause of His People

The crooked path to peace in 1854 generated some of the best Numic accounts of their struggle to preserve the lands at the center of their lives. On 12 March 1854 "five Utah Indians from Walkers camp and one Mexican from Santa Fe by the name of Besueta Shavez" came to Fort Manti and asked "Father Morley or some of the whites" to come to their "camp on the Sevier and

[2]Young to Bernhisel, 28 December 1853, BYC 60:4
[3]Smith, Reminiscences and Journals, 62, LDS Archives.

have a talk."[4] Nelson Higgins ordered four men "to procede to Walkers camp." Mormon Battalion veteran James T. S. Allred, who spoke Ute, described the visit.

ALLRED TO HIGGINS, 16 MARCH 1854, UTMR 1386.

Fort Manti March 16th 1854

Maj. N. Higgins,

Sir agreeable to your order under date of the 13th Inst I with the detachment under my charge proceeded on my journey to Walkers camp. When we had traveled about twelve miles I met Teweep Walkers brother[5] who informed me that Walker had removed his camp twenty miles south of Salt creek in the Sevier vally which makes the distance from this place to his camp about fifty miles; we arrived at willow creek in the Sevier vally about 6 Oclock PM where we encamped, about two next morning about two Oclock. I with one Utah who I had with me as a guide left the waggon & three men (directing them to follow me at day light) for Walkers camp which I reached about 9 Oclock AM 15th. I immediately requested Walker with some of his men to accompany me back to meete the wagon & three men as the team was tired and h[e] avy loaded with provisions for him which request he readily complied with.

On my return with Walker and fifteen of his men I met the wagon & men seven miles south of Salt creek. Here we halted and smoked a pipe of peace. I then red a letter to him from Isaac or Father Morley—with which he was well pleased. He said Father Morley was a good man and had always treated him well, he further said that he was Father Morleys friend. He then put the letter into his boosom and said that he would Keep it for he loved it and father Morley.

He said that our coming and bringing him the letter was in fulfillment of a dream which he had some time ago. He then arose to his feet and prayed some five or ten minutes. He then sat down and said he wanted to talk over our difficulties and tell me what his feelings had been and what they are now; he commenced at the time we came to this valley saying the Mormons about that time and the tenpenny [Timpanogos] Utes had some troubles and that the Mormons Killed some of his friends but it did not make him mad, but some of his men became very mad and wanted to fight; but he persuaded them to be at peace and he had always since tried to Keep them quiet and friendly to the Mormons, and still wishes to be friendly; but that it hurts him when the Mormons accuse him of being untrue and a liar which he says they do as he has heard.

---

[4]The Basurto-Chavez family has been in New Mexico since 1580. Carvalho, *Incidents of Travel*, 195, indicates the trader's name was José; he briefly joined Fremont's fifth expedition.

[5]At Corn Creek on 16 May 1855, Wilford Woodruff said Teweepponakary was the "present name" of "Parashon" (Parashant).

He says this last difficulty, was caused by the mormons (alluding to the assalt at Springvill[e] or Hobble creek) the Indian that received the blow over the head in that affray was his cosin who has since died. He said that made him a little mad and being blinded by the influence of the Dead and not seeing the result of the course he was taking caused him to act as he has.

He was sad at the time that Ivie struck the Indian (*Showereshockits*) with the gun that the Indian was whiping a Squaw which was no difference to the Mormons if he had of Kill her but had it of been a Mormon woman that he was whipping then the Mormons would of been justifiable in interfearing. From this offence they Killed the man at Payson and stole some property, he says that when he left Payson and got over the mountain he began to think and came to the conclusion that his men have done enough for that offence and told them so and tried to get them to hold on, but that they were determined upon more depredations and urged him to come down uppon the Allred & Hambletan settlements and Kill them all off and drive of[f] their stock but that he persuaded them not to Kill the people but be content with driving off their Stock which they were determined on doing. Yet he was opposed to that but could not prevent them and as a proof he says that he made an alarm smoke so that the Mormons might get up their cattle.

He talked a long time amount[in]g to nearly this same thing all the while justifying himself & pleading the cause of his people Saying that we have taken his land and fishing places and now he wishes the Mormons to purchase his land and make peace.

He wishes Gov. Young to send D.B. Huntingdon immediately to meete him at Fillmore and make a treaty with him and purchase his land. He also wishes him to send guns ammunitions & blankets to trade to him (Walker) for horses.

He promises to be at peace until he hears from Gov. Young.

Yours J. T. S. Allred

Young would learn Wakara's "feelings and wishes more fully," Higgins added, "when Mr. Huntingdon gets to talk to him." Governor Young acted immediately. "Indian Walker has come in from his winter quarters, professing friendship, & a desire for lasting peace," he wrote.[6] He immediately "dispatched Agent E. A. Bedell, & Bro Huntington" to deliver a rambling letter to Wakara, seeking to patch up relations while ordering the Saints to "fort up." His message seemed heartfelt, but he spoke with "two tongues and two hearts."

---

[6]Young to Bernhisel, 31 March 1854, BYC 60:5.

Young to Capt Wackor Chief of the Utahs, 24 March 1854,
BYC 17:12.

G.S.L. City March 24 1854

Capt Wackor Chief of the Utahs

I Brigham Young your brother send you this letter, by your old Friend Dimock [*sic*].

I am glad to hear that you feel friendly towards us for I have always said that you were not mad but that you could not restrain your men. I have never been mad with you nor said that you was a liar. But had always held and esteemed you as my Brother. I sent for my Men to come home as soon as I found that they were following you and told them to take care of their Stock and themselves, but not go after you nor your men.

I dreamed that you felt bad for what your men had done and would help it if you could but that you could not. And that you wanted to be friendly but was afraid to come here. And then I thought that God whispered in your Ear, and you though[t] that you would come and see me—and then you did come and we was friends and we put our arms about each other just as we used to, and we felt first rate with Each other and you said that we were brothers, and that we should be good friends—fast friends, and be at peace—good peace—and that our men should fight no more.

Now Brother Walker I do want to see you and I should like to hear you. Come to this city to our Big Meeting ~~which takes place twice a year~~ on the 6 of April—We have this Meeting which takes place twice a year and talk a great deal to the people and you can hear and speak if you wish to and Dimock can be by your side to tell you what is said and what you say.

I have a few things to tell you about the Killing of Capt Gunnison and his party who were slain ~~at~~ near Fillmore on the Sevier by the Pervantes. The Americans think you did that act and are very mad about it, and threaten to send troops against you. But ~~I shall tell them~~ I have told them that it was not you nor your men and that you did not know any thing about it, and I shall use all my Endeavors to make them understand the truth about it so that they may not send their troops either against you nor the Parvantes, altho' the Parvants did not do right in killing them. It always results badly to go to war and kill each other and it is not good—Now you do know that we are your friends, the very best friends that you have got, and that so long as you and your Men do right you will always be safe and well treated by us. We have no desire to harm you not in the least, but on the Contrary, wish to do you good.

I can tell you what is best for you and your men. You should settle down somewhere and get to raising grain and cattle and live in peace with us and every body else—have you never heard how the Indians have always been used up when the[y] warred with the whites and that the Indians have almost always been destroyed when they came in contact with the whites. If you have never heard of this before I now tell you it is the truth. Now we wish to preserve you and your nation. There is not much grain now, you know that yourself, and that you would be much more comfortable if you would follow my Council and raise grain and Cattle. We can live in peace if you will let us. About buying your land I cannot talk about that at present. We shall have to wait for that until Our Great Father the President shall authorize us to do so. But we will send you some presents and do as well as we can by you in trading with you if you will come here to our Great Meeting as I wish you to Listen to Bro Dimock and agent Mr Bedell who has been sent by the President to look after his red children in this country and Come and see me and we can even tell these Matters better than we can write them.[7]

May God Bless and preserve you and Enlighten your mind to see the good and reject the bad is the prayer of your friend and Brother BY

On 25 March Agent Edward A. Bedell headed south with D. B. Hunting-ton. Two days later, he talked "with Panawick a Ute Chief with a Small party of Indians" in Utah Valley who "had used his influence to get the Indians belonging to old Squash-Head's band, who had stolen from the neighbor-hood of Springville, some Eighty head of Cattle a short time previous to return them to their owners, and we ascertained that he had succeeded in procuring the return of 24 Head." Bedell "made them some small presents of Shirts, Tobacco &c. They seemed well pleased & promised to go again into the Mountains, and if the Indians had not killed the remainder of the cattle, to bring them in. I told them to tell old Squash-Head & Peteetneet to come in, & bring the Cattle back if they had not killed them, & be honest, and cease stealing. I also found quite a number of Indians at work on lands that had been ploughed for them by the citizens of Payson."

Bedell met "Ammon, Walker's Brother, with 10 or 12 lodges of Indians" at Nephi. "They seemed very much pleased to see us. Ammon talked very much in favor of establishing a permanent peace, & said he was glad we were going to have a talk with Walker, for he was sure Walker wanted to be friendly." The "citizens also spoke well of the band, they surveyed off & set apart for them 80 acres of land near the Fort, and was assisting such of the Indians as would work to plough and Sow wheat. I gave Ammon two Blankets, and his men some Shirts, & Tobacco." The Utes "seemed much

---

[7]Edward A. Bedell had been a Mormon ally in Illinois, so "the people of Utah felt they had a friend" when he replaced Jacob Holeman in August 1853, but he died on 3 May 1854. Brooks, *The Diary of Hosea Stout*, 2:515n15.

pleased and said, that the Parvan Indians that murdered Captain G had done very wickedly, and they were sorry, for they believed he was a good man."

At Fillmore Bedell "found the celebrated chief Walker encamped near the Fort with about 75 braves with him." He visited him "at his Lodge on the morning of the 31st March, in Company with the officers of the Fort and my Interpreter. He appeared quite reserved, but glad to see us. Said he had a great deal to say, and hoped we would make a stay of several days. I told him I could not spend more than a day: he said Kenosha & other chiefs were there, and he wanted the Indians all as also the officers of the Fort to hear what he had to say, for my Interpreter Mr Huntington could understand him." Bedell "commenced a talk with Walker," Mormon leaders, "& about Eighty Indians." It lasted all day.

I furnished dinner for the Chiefs at the Hotel, & furnished provisions for the other Indians also. Walker said from the first he had been opposed to this difficulty, & that he had done everything in his power to prevent it, but that he could not control some of his men, and when he found they were determined to steal & murder, he went off to New Mexico to get away, for he felt bad. I told him that the Report had gone to the States, that he & his men had murdered Captain Gunnison & part of his Surveying party, and that the people and also the Great father were justly indignant that such a terrible cold blooded murder should be committed upon men in the service of the United States, and sent by the Great father to locate a Road that would enable them to get a much larger amount of presents, by reducing the cost of transportation. He said, he had heard about it, & seen one party South, making a similar survey & had rendered them assistance & was much pleased. He said he was truly sorry the Pauvants had acted so hastily and indiscreetly, in committing the assault & murder on that party, but tried to apologise for them. Said a train of Emigrants a few days before, had killed an Indian without any provocation, and that the friends & relations of the Indians came upon the party while their hearts were bad. I told him Captain G & his men knew nothing of that, & were entirely innocent, & tried to show and explain to them how wrong it was to punish & murder innocent men, for the acts of bad, and wicked men.

The Pauvant Chiefs Kenosh & Parashunt were present, and quite a number of their men. They seemed very uneasy, and much alarmed. Walker wished me to ask you to inform the Great Father, & the people of the States, that it was not him, or his party that done the deed, & also to ask the Great Father, not to send soldiers to punish the Pah-vants, for he was afraid some innocent Indians would be dragged into difficulty. I talked with him in reference to selling his land to the general government. He said he would prefer not to sell if he could live peaceably with the white People, which he was anxious to do.[8]

Superintendent Young sent George Bean—who was known as Purretz to the tribes—Porter Rockwell, and John Murdock south in April with presents for the "Old Chief" and proposals to make "a good lasting peace." They should keep "Chief Walker in hand and peaceable" and "try to heal up the feelings" war had stirred up. Wakara agreed to meet at "upper Chicken Creek in fifteen days and, if plenty of beef cattle, flour, and Indian goods were brought, then all might be well, otherwise not." Bean recalled they softened Wakara's "warlike spirit" and left him camped near Nephi.[9]

Superintendent Young wrote to his "best friend," Pe-teet-neet, recommending the Utes adopt the Protestant work ethic.

Purretz brought me word from you the other day that you was poor, & hungry, & wished to come in unto your lands again & live near the whites, & learn to build houses, & raise grain, & live in peace. Now all this is good talk, & pleases me, for I & my people have been friendly to you, & to all good Utahs all the while, & have not wished or tried to hurt you at any time, but have wished to do you good, & you ought to know that I am the best friend you have, & it will please me much to have you & your band come into your old grounds again, & be friendly & learn to labor for what you need to eat & wear, for I & my people have to work to build houses & raise grain, & cattle & horses, & we do not like to feed & clothe those who will not work when they are able, but we are willing to learn you & your people how to work, so that you can easily raise a plenty to eat, & live much more comfortably than you now do, & then your young men will not be tempted to steal our animals, & grain, nor call upon my people to give them what they are not willing to work for, which my people do not like to do, for they work hard for what they have; & when any of your people wish to be fed or clothed for nothing, & if they are not, get mad about it. I think they are very foolish, & ought to know better. Your ears are & always have been open & I hope the ears of your people will be also be open, & I wish them to understand that I am the best friend they have, & I hope you and your band will come in as you desire, that your men will behave well, & learn to labor as you say you wish to, which will be the best thing for all; & I will instruct my people to use you all well; & if another fuss should arise, do not run off into the mountains again, but come to me. I send you a shirt & some tobacco by my good friend Purretz, that you & your men may have a

[8]Morgan, *Shoshonean Peoples*, 197–99.
[9]Bean, *Autobiography*, 93–94.

good smoke, & understand with open ears, & good hearts, that my heart is good towards you & has been all the time.[10]

At the "Big Meeting" in April 1854, Young said "a word in behalf of Walker," who had nothing to do with "the difficulties we have had." He had "felt at times that he would like to destroy this people," but "a superior power" held him in check. If the whites "had been as kind to the Indians as they have been to the whites from the beginning, there never would have been a single difficulty to this day." The "foundation for difficulties" was "mingling with the Indians" and trading, gambling, racing horses, playing "field-cuff," and cheating them. Young had "fed fifty Indians almost day by day for months together" but lacked soldiers enough to "kill one hundred of them." If he sent twelve thousand men into the mountains, "Indians would escape" and "steal all their horses into the bargain, and laugh them to scorn." Dead-falls and traps were the only way to destroy them. The Utes "came pretty nigh starving to death last winter." If they were driven into the mountains next winter, "they must perish; therefore they now want to make good peace. Treat them kindly, and treat them as Indians, and not as your equals." Tie up your animals, Young said, "so that the Devil cannot get them."[11]

"All the tribes north and south are ready, and want to have us among them," Young had announced in October 1853.[12] Even as war divided the territory, he called more than twenty men to launch a mission to the Southern Paiutes. On 10 April 1854 six apostles set apart the missionaries; four days later, the group started south. At Corn Creek, clerk Thomas D. Brown reported:

> About 20 Indians of Walker's Band came and surrounded our wagons and finally crossed the road and stood ahead of them. After many strange gestures and much loud speaking by the eldest of them, a blanket was thrown down. We all understood this to be a demand of toll for passing over their lands; we all contributed some bread and flour and tobacco. They sat down and seemed to enjoy the bread. We passed on and soon some more came down to the creek, they too had to be satisfied.

The missionaries next met mountain trader James Waters with "a small train of goods & droves of horses," several San Bernardino Mormons, and Wakara, who was heading north with "one of his Squaws & a son." He had

---

[10]Brigham Young to Peteetneet and Band, 3 April 1854, BYC 27:12.

[11]"Proper Treatment of the Indians," 6 April 1848, *Journal of Discourses*, 6:327–29.

[12]Van Wagoner, *Complete Discourses*, 4 October 1853, 2:719.

presented Waters with "a fine indian boy, apparently about 8 years of age." In return, Waters "had given Walker one of the best horses in his drove with goods amounting to about $200," thus evading the ban on trading with Indians "by the law of the Territory of Utah." Porter Rockwell and George W. Bean:

> met Walker & the train on the Beaver, & were using Watter's influence as well as their own to induce Walker to accompany them to Gt. Salt Lake City to have an interview with Govr. Young. Walker declined, urging as an excuse that he wished to remain at home till his wheat was sown. Here interpreter Bean and Walker had two long "talks." I learned afterwards that Walker had said he never yet had been mad, but when he got mad no white man should pass through his lands alive, and that he meant to sell all the lands, as the Indians were all his & the land also, he wanted now 2 tons of flour, many cattle, & horses as part of the pay.

Wakara complained of violence, which he blamed on the Mormons, who blamed it on the Indians. Brown's assessment of Wakara proved astute:

> Walker appears very cunning, big in his feelings & very greedy. We heard of a quarrel that took place the previous day between Walker and Arrowich, a Piede Indian, on the banks of the creek north of the Beaver, in a talk between them. Walker struck this Indian on the face, and he withdrew to his "Wickeup." Walker judging of his intentions, viz to get his gun & shoot him, besought Bean & his company to interfere & hinder the Consummation, they did so & with the aid of the two squaws prevented, where so much ignorance & vice are cowardice dwells—had the Mormons wished him dead, here was a probability of it, but for them. Would Walker see it thus? I think not.[13]

George W. Bean reported peace—even nominal peace—had a steep price.

BEAN TO YOUNG, 1 MAY 1854, BYC 23:10.

Provo City May 1st 1854

Brother Walker desires that Gov Young would come to see him as he is busy farming on Corn Creek.

He says that he has been a little mad since he went to the Navahoes for there he learned that Gov Young had wrote to New Mexico stating that Walker had killed Bowman last summer, but he knew the Mormons done it. Also several other murders that had been committed by the Mormons he wanted inquired into.

When he gets very angry there will be no more travel on the Roads.

There must be no restrictions whatever upon any traders in his country.

---

[13]Brown, *Journal of the Southern Indian Mission*, 25–26 April 1854, 10–12. See editor Juanita Brooks's notes on the murders.

The Governor must bring him two Oxen & some flour some good guns & ammunition & a little Whiskey, if he wants him to be good friends with the Whites. He has sent Ammon to the Pieds to get some Children which if we do not buy he will sell to the Mexicans.

He wants to know how much Money Cattle & Horses the Mormons will give yearly for 20 years for portions of his lands.

He expects many presents from the Governor this spring. Apparently much more than common. He is no doubt afraid to come into the settlements until he has a b[e]tter understanding both with the Mormons & also other Utah Chiefs.

He is at present averse to farming & building houses unless the Whites will do all themselves. He has one or two horses belonging to the whites but will not give them up until paid for.

We seen Grospene at Salt Creek and he says the Mormons are afraid upon no grounds whatever. Uintah and Battice were also there both apparently very friendly.

Peteteneach, Sampich and Wahwoona were at Spanish Fork apparently friendly. Petetenich says he wants the Big Captain to bring him a fur cap, also one of his Squaws ran away and is now at Wanships sons Camp. He wishes it returned to him. Bro O. P. Rockwell accompanies this and will explain more fully,

G W Bean Interpreter

Brigham Young began his annual trip south on 5 May. The next day, "Indian Walker come to Nephi" after a storm covered the ground with hailstones "from the size of buckshot to the size of Meadow larks eggs." The town "gave him a dinner & his braves that were with him together with some presents," wrote Andrew Love. "All good peace now but watch your friends."[14]

At Provo Young prepared to parlay with the Utes. "I am on the road going to see Walker," he informed Grospene, who had promised "that you would go with me." He had sent Porter Rockwell, George Bean, and others with "some cattle for Walker which I am giving to him. I want you to go with these Men and drive these cattle to Walker." He promised he would stand between "all the bullets that My Men will shoot, but for him to meet me like a brother." He asked Wakara to camp near by Nephi or Chicken Creek and he would visit him there. "I dont want him to be mulish and not talk when I come to him but be free and act like a brother."[15] Young wrote Wakara:

[14]Love, Diary, 6 May 1854, 34.
[15]Young to Grosepine, 7 May 1854, BYC 27:12.

I am now at Provo on my way to meet you. I have sent you some cattle as presents and have got some more presents with me for you when I come. I would be glad that you would camp near Nephi so that when I come there, I can go to your camp and see you and have a good Talk and I can get some flour for you then. Dont come riding up to my camp with all your Men to frighten our horses for there is no need for that. And I want to come to your camp with a few men to show you that I am friendly to you and wish you no harm. I also wish you to be free and talk to me and act like a brother and make your Men act like brethren too, for I wish to do you good, and not harm, you nor any of your Men. If you wish to trade we expect to trade with you. Bro Porter Rockwell Amos Neff Geo W Bean and others have gone on ahead to tell you what I want and to give you those cattle which you can do as you please with. They will also tell you about the time I shall be along. I have got a good many with me but we are going on a visit to Iron county to see our friends, and you can go with us if you choose. I will not write any more now for when I see you which I shall in a few days I can talk it better than I can write it. May God bless you Amen.[16]

Superintendent Young ordered Bishop Elias Blackburn to collect "some fat cattle to take to Walker." Provo responded with "delay or defalcation," so Young sent men to seize "eight or a dozen head of good beef cattle" that he "must and will have" without delay. "If the People complain," the "righteously angry" Young wrote, "ask them what they are going to do about it."[17]

On the evening of 10 May at Nephi's schoolhouse, the prophet told the faithful that "ye are the people that God has spoken about, that is to save Israel." The Saints and Indians were both "of the house of Israel, they are our brethren in sorrow because of the sins of their Fathers, & we are called to redeem them." The latest war, "when we take into consideration the breaking up of settlements, moving into Forts, loss of farms, & the raising of troops," had cost more than $500,000. "Now I want peace, *don't you?*" he asked. "I should rather give 10,000 dollars a year to feed the Indians & keep peace with them, than to fight them." He had "told the people to fort up, but has there been one fort built according to my council, *No not one.*" Only one "old Mormon" had proven reliable.

I will tell it right out here, there was an army of Elders called to go to the Lamanites, & there was but one man, that manifested any wisdom about it, & that was Porter Rockwell, he is an old Mormon, he said I think it best go to the Lamanites & live with them, & preach to them, & teach them,

---

[16]Young to Walker, 7 May 1854, BYC 27:12.
[17]Young to Blackburn, 8 May 1854, BYC 27:12.

& make them know that we are there friends, & stick by them, until they know the truth; . . . I expect you will soon come to my house, & see a good squaw in my house, they are the seed of Israel. It will be a very little while before they will be a white & delightsome people, this will be hard upon the women, but they must stand it; I will tell you my feelings concerning Walker. He has not wished to fight, I hope the time will come that I may have the privilege of picking out all the bad Indians, & Mormons, & put them in a pen & let them kill each other. I don't want to do it now, for it will take too many of us.[18]

SOLOMON NUÑES CARVALHO: OLD WAKARA WAS A KING

When Wakara headed north from Fillmore, William Wall advised Brigham Young about "the feelings and movements of the Indians." Their leaders seemed friendly, but "others of Less distinction" were "quite saucy when they happen to find no one except women & children about the house." Wall attributed "this petty Theiving & threatning of cutting throats &c to their low degraded Starving condition. There seems to be a kind of ferociousness of disposition or temper caused by hunger Privation or from some other cause that rules over them and they act regardless of the consequences which their acts may produce." Wakara seemed reluctant to meet "except upon his own Ground."[19]

The Mormon cavalcade of some forty wagons and "quite a large number of the boys" reached the Ute camp at Chicken Creek, near today's Levan, before noon on 11 May with a wagonload of flour, "sixteen head of cattle, blankets and clothing, trinkets, arms and ammunition." Rockwell and Bean arrived early, "just long enough for Porter to slip a bottle of whiskey into the Old Chiefs hands." Half of it disappeared down Wakara's throat "instanter, as it were," Bean recalled, so "when President Young arrived, Walker was half drunk and sulky." The parley lasted two days. The Mormons had intended to drop off the provisions and march on to the Sevier immediately, but "the President decided to stay rather than cause a rupture between parties, as about eighty Lodges of Indians were encamped."[20]

A mounted "guard of honor" occupied the heart of the Ute camp. Some fifteen "old chiefs" surrounded Wakara's lodge—Ammon, Washear, Battiese,

---

[18]Bullock, General Church Minutes, 10 May 1854, CR100, 2:52, LDS Archives.

[19]Wall and King to Young, 1 May 1854, UTMR 437.

[20]Love, Diary, 10 May 1854, 34; Bean, *Autobiography*, 94–95.

Grospene, Peteetneet, Kanosh, San Pitch, "other celebrated Indians," and a "care-worn and haggard" Wakara. He "appeared dogish & was not disposed to talk when we first formed our Carrell within 40 rods of his camp," Wilford Woodruff complained. He gathered his warriors "& made quite a display but we did not go out to meet them at the time." Wakara "lay down in the dirt & did not feel disposed to talk but President Young manifested great patience with him even after the patience of most men was exhausted." Young "lifted him out of the dirt & finally got him to talk some. . . . Walker said he had no spirit. He had no heart. Did not feel as though He Could talk And when I herd that President Young was coming I felt that I had no heart. I do not want to talk. I want to hear President Young talk & he sit still & here others talk."[21]

Thomas Bullock's minutes began: "When I came to see B Y I had the heart but now I have not." He had neither spirit nor eyes nor heart, said Wakara. The men should smoke and "make him a spirit and put it into him." Battiese filled a pipe, rose, "offered it to the Almighty prayed and then sat down and smoked & passed it round by the right hand then came back by the left hand." Walker said, "I have neither heart nor spirit and am afraid." Brigham Young suggested the Utes kill one of the "beef creatures" and have a feast. Wakara agreed and asked to hear "the songs of the Lord. It makes me feel good." The Mormons obliged and sang William Phelps's "Come all ye Sons of Zion." Then Wakara napped.[22]

"Ammon, a brother of the celebrated Wakara," had met John C. Frémont's disastrous fifth expedition near today's Paragonah in February 1854. The starving explorers had buried everything but their clothes in the mountains. G. W. Bean recalled Wakara sent Ammon "with the Mexican Chavez with ten pack animals to raise the Cache" in Rabbit Valley, near today's Loa. The Utes retrieved tents, blankets, kettles, guns, ammunition, tools, an odometer, and even a "daguerreotype apparatus." The Utes then shot Chavez, Bean claimed, so "the whole booty fell into Walker's hands."[23] Parowan pioneer James McGuffy told an alternate history to the *New York Herald* in 1877, charging John Steele "was ordered to assassinate poor Sherman, one of Fremont's men, in 1854." McGuffy, a "most canny, experienced and

---

[21]Woodruff, *Journal*, 11 May 1854, 4:272–73.

[22]Anonymous, *Minutes of the Apostles*, 258–59.

[23]Bean, *Autobiography*, 95. Nelson Higgins reported "Besueta Shavez" visited Manti on 12 March, supporting Bean's story. "Jose, the Mexican, whom Col. Fremont found in the mountains" was "almost naked" when rescued in Mosca Pass. He "proved perfectly worthless." Carvalho, *Incidents of Travel*, 79, 95.

trustworthy" apostate, later claimed he saw Barney Carter take "Sherman" away and heard Samuel Gould boast he had shot Chavez "when he was on horseback and left him at the mouth of a canyon for the wolves to eat."[24]

One survivor who staggered into Parowan was an observant Sephardic Jew, daguerreotypist Solomon Nuñes Carvalho. Born in South Carolina in 1815 to an Iberian family, he described his adventures in one of the American West's best chronicles. After recovering from his Fremont ordeal in Salt Lake City, Carvalho acquired a "superior riding mule" and joined Brigham Young's southern tour in May 1854. Fifty mounted men, six apostles, and about a hundred wagons accompanied the prophet. From a hillside, Carvalho watched "this immense cavalcade, lengthened out over a mile, winding leisurely along the side of a mountain, or trotting blithely in the hollow of some of the beautiful valleys through which we passed." He wrote the most perceptive account of "the Grand Council" at Chicken Creek.[25]

CARVALHO, *INCIDENTS OF TRAVEL*, 189–92.

Wakara sent word back to say, "If Gov. Young wanted to see him, he must come to him at his camp, as he did not intend to leave it to see any body."

When this message was delivered to Gov. Young, he gave orders for the whole cavalcade to proceed to Wakara's camp—"If the mountain will not come to Mahomet, Mahomet must go to the mountain."

The Governor was under the impression that Walker had changed his mind, and intended to continue the war, and for that reason declined to meet him. But old Wakara was a king, and a great chief. He stood upon the dignity of his position, and feeling himself the representative of an aggrieved and much injured people, acted as though a cessation of hostilities by the Indians was to be solicited on the part of the whites, and he felt great indifference about the result.

Gov. Young, at the expense of the people of Utah, brought with him sixteen head of cattle, blankets and clothing, trinkets, arms and ammunition. I expressed much astonishment, that arms and ammunition should be furnished the Indians. His excellency told me that from their contiguity to the immigrant road, they possessed themselves of arms in exchange and trade, from American travellers. And as it was the object of the Mormons to protect, as much as possible, their people from the aggressions of the Indians, and also from the continual descent upon their towns—begging for food, and stealing when it was not given, he thought it more advisable to

---

[24]Kerry Bate shared his transcriptions of "Mormon Rascality!" *Salt Lake Tribune*, 18 May 1877, 3/1; and "Brigham Young's Infamy," *New York Herald*, July 6, 1877, 2.

[25]Carvalho, *Incidents of Travel*, 134, 181, 188.

furnish them with the means of shooting their own game. The Utah Indians possess rifles of the first quality. All the chiefs are provided with them, and many of the Indians are most expert in their use.

When we approached Wakara['s] Camp, we found a number of chiefs, mounted as a guard of honor around his own lodge, which was in the centre of the camp, among whom were Wakara and about fifteen old chiefs, including Ammon, Squash-Head, Grosepine, Petetnit, Kanoshe, (the chief of the Parvains), a San Pete chief, and other celebrated Indians. The Governor and council were invited into Wakara's lodge, and at the request of his excellency, I accompanied them. Wakara sat on his buffalo-robe, wrapped in his blanket, with the old chiefs around him; he did not rise, but held out his hand to Gov. Young, and made room for him by his side.

After the ceremony of shaking hands all round was concluded, our interpreter, Mr. Huntington, made known the object of the Governor's visit, and hoped that the calumet of peace would be smoked, and no more cause be given on either side, for a continuation of ill-feeling, etc.

For five minutes intense silence prevailed, when an old grey headed Utah chief got up, and in the effort, his blanket slipped from his body, displaying innumerable marks of wounds and scars. Stretching aloft his almost fleshless arm, he spoke as follows:

"I am for war, I never will lay down my rifle, and tomahawk, Americats have no truth—Americats kill Indian plenty—Americats see Indian woman, he shoot her like deer—Americats no meet Indian to fight, he have no mercy—one year gone, Mormon say, they no kill more Indian—Mormon no tell truth, plenty Utahs gone to Great Spirit, Mormon kill them—no friend to Americats more."

The chief of the San Pete Indians arose, and the tears rolled down his furrowed cheeks as he gave utterance to his grievances:

"My son," he said, "was a brave chief, he was so good to his old father and mother—one day Wa-yo-sha was hunting rabbits as food for his old parents—the rifle of the white man killed him. When the night came, and he was still absent, his old mother went to look for her son; she walked a long way through the thick bushes; at the dawn of day, the mother and the son were both away, and the infirm and aged warrior was lonely: he followed the trail of his wife in the bush, and there he found the mother of his child, lying over the body of Wa-yo-sha, both dead from the same bullet. The old woman met her son, and while they were returning home, a bullet from the rifle of Americats shot them both down." He added, "old San Pete no can fight more, his hand trembles, his eyes are dim, the murderer of his wife, and brave Wa-yo-sha, is still living. San Pete no make peace with Americats."

The old warrior sank down exhausted on his blanket.

Wakara remained perfectly silent.

Gov. Young asked him to talk, he shook his head. "No," after the rest had spoken, some of whom were for peace, Wakara said, "I got no heart to speak—no can talk to-day—to-night Wakara talk with great spirit, to-morrow Wakara talk with Governor."

Gov. Young then handed him a pipe. Wakara took it and gave one or two whiffs, and told the Governor to smoke, which he did, and passed it around to all the party; this ended the first interview.

An ox was slaughtered by the orders of Gov. Young, and the whole camp were regaled with fresh beef that evening. I made a sketch of Wakara during the time that he sat in council. I also made a likeness of Kanoshe, the chief of the Parvain Indians.

Mormon minutes indicate Wakara slept off Rockwell's whiskey until four o'clock, as Brigham Young "ordered the flour carried down to Walker's Tent. Wakara awoke in a better mood and said, "I want to live good now." Mormons could "build where they please" and travel alone. "I now want a mormon wife to keep my house and when I go awa[y] I will leave her behind with the Cattle." He would join "you on your journey." Before the night ended, Wakara asked the Mormons to sing for him. Young "& others sung All is Well."[26]

CARVALHO, INCIDENTS OF TRAVEL, 192–94.

The next morning the council again assembled, and the Governor commenced by telling the chiefs, that he wanted to be friends with all the Indians; he loved them like a father, and would always give them plenty of clothes, and good food, provided they did not fight, and slay any more white men. He brought as presents to them, sixteen head of oxen, besides a large lot of clothing and considerable ammunition. The oxen were all driven into Wakara's camp, and the sight of them made the chiefs feel more friendly.

Wakara, who is a man of imposing appearance, was, on this occasion, attired with only a deer-skin hunting shirt, although it was very cold; his blue blanket lay at his side; he looked care-worn and haggard, and spoke as follows:

"Wakara has heard all the talk of the good Mormon chief. Wakara no like to go to war with him. Sometimes Wakara take his young men, and go far away, to sell horses. When he is absent, then Americats come and kill his wife and children. Why not come and fight when Wakara is at home? Wakara is accused of killing Capt. Gunnison. Wakara did not; Wakara was three hundred miles away when the Merecat chief was slain. Merecats soldier hunt Wakara, to kill him, but no find him. Wakara hear it; Wakara come home. Why not Merecats take Wakara? he is not armed. Wakara heart very sore. Merecats kill Parvain Indian chief, and Parvain woman. Parvain young men watch for Merecats and kill them, because Great Spirit say—'Merecats kill Indian'; 'Indian kill Merecats.' Wakara no want to fight more. Wakara talk with Great Spirit; Great Spirit say—'Make peace.' Wakara love Mormon chief; he is good man. When Mormon first come to live on Wakara's land, Wakara give him welcome. He give Wakara plenty bread, and clothes to cover his wife and children. Wakara no want to fight Mormon; Mormon chief very good man; he bring plenty oxen to Wakara. Wakara talk last night to Payede, to Kahutah, San Pete, Parvain—Indian say, 'No fight Mormon or Merecats more.' If Indian kill white man again, Wakara make Indian howl."

Wakara "was still in the same unpleasant mood" when the Mormons returned next morning; he refused to talk "& left his tent & went into the willows and others talked," Wilford Woodruff wrote. The Utes had a sick child (perhaps Wakara's daughter) and "wished the Elders to lay hands upon it," which they did. Dr. Samuel Sprague left medicine for the band's sick children. One Ute, perhaps Washear, "said Walker was a great Chief & President Young was a great Chief & what he said was true." He wanted to go with the caravan but not until his child was well. "Petetnet spoke & said that that would be good & not steal nor kill any body. That one Could now go alone & not be killed. Their would be no blood in their path." Walker "wished President Young to write a Letter so he could show it to the people & let them know that we were at peace so their would be no difficulty with the people. President Young wrote one." When the governor left his tent, Wakara said "we now understand each other that they were now to have all peace so all could now go on the road in peace and not be afraid. Could now put in wheat & corn & one alone without [fearing] for somebody to kill them. He now wanted to have the road clear without any blood in it. He wished for peace all the time." The Mormons "swaped blankets for Horses & bought 2 children that were prisoners," Woodruff reported.[27]

Wakara promised the Ute leaders "and about thirty Indian young men, all mounted on splendid horses," would "accompany the Governor's party" to Fort Harmony and "all the way and back, as a body-guard." Young distributed "a great many presents" to the tribe. At Harmony, he appointed four men, notably Porter Rockwell, "to take up a permanent residence with Wakara's band of Utahs" and "follow them in their wanderings," which Carvalho thought would probably "prevent many depredations and murders."[28]

[27]Woodruff, *Journal*, 12 May 1854, 4:273–74.
[28]Carvalho, *Incidents of Travel*, 193, 214–15.

Heading south, Mormon leaders instructed Parowan's officers on "building a wall round the present Fort." Brigham Young said the town had "always done well here in regard to the Lamanites." He assured them that "Walker feels first rate now he has preached to the Indians on this journey. He told the Piedes not to be afraid of the Mormons dont steal from them for if you do I will make you howl. Let the Mormons alone & not kill any or take any thing from them."[29]

"I have visited the Indians from Great Salt Lake to this place," Young wrote to Paiute leaders from Harmony. "Captain Walker Grosepine and other of the Utahs have been traveling with us and have talked to the Piedes and all other Indians on the road. Good peace is now established." The Mormons had "good peace with them all" and wished "that peace may prevail through all the settlements and on the road to California." Young promised to send tobacco to smoke in "the pipe of peace and wish that I could see you shake hands & smoke with you. You can come here and see my brethren who will tell you all that I can not write and who will do you good."[30]

Young returned to Salt Lake on 30 May. All the Indians, "even to the distant Paiedes, rejoiced exceedingly at the visit and were highly pleased with the words and counsel of the Big Captain of the whites," the press reported. "All the talks were favorable to a *good peace*, and the Indians were much pleased and gratified with the presents of beef cattle, blankets, shirts, tobacco, &c., which enabled them to contrast strongly their present friendly and favorable position and prospects with the doubt and wretchedness of the past winter."[31]

WAKARA: WE CANT SHAKE HANDS ACROSS A WALL

For all the talk about "good peace," the Chicken Creek council resolved nothing. Wakara became "very inquisitive" when Nephi's wall began going up in June 1854. The Utes at Nephi were "plenty around us & quite Saucy," noted Andrew Love. "What the result will be I know not & care but little." The result was not good: Wakara met with local leaders to "forbid the building of the wall & says we cant shake hands across a wall." Tensions then escalated. "If we have to fight hurraw for the fight," Love wrote. "If it

---

[29]Bullock, 17 May 1854, in Anonymous, *Minutes of the Apostles*, 260.

[30]Young to Toquer Tutsecupets and To-chints, 20 May 1854, BYC 27:12.

[31]"Return of Brigham Young," *Deseret News*, 8 June 1854, 2/3.

can be all good peace *Amen.*" Terrified "rumors & reports" swept through
Nephi, reporting Wakara had "twice set a time to massacre the people." In
an incident soon repeated, two Utes blocked Love's doorway on 6 June. He
told them to leave, but he spoke no Ute and the Utes no English.

> They seemed sullen & would not get out of the door way so I took hold of
> them to push them out of the way, one had a gun the other his bow & arrows,
> as I took hold of the one with the gun the other strung his arrow for battle.
> I then took hold of him gently to push him along towards the door but he
> resisted and I being the stouter of the two propelled him. When he got within
> a step of the door, he took hold of me to pull me out with him, so finding
> him so stubborn, I took hold of his bough & arrows with my right hand &
> took him by the windpipe with my left & very near met my fingers round it
> for a while thinking the fellow had enough of that slackened up a little. He
> then tried for my neck but finding it not go, I took his bow out of his hand
> & struck him over the head with it several times & broke it & his two arrows
> that he had in his hand & put him out he calling for the one to shoot, but
> John Cazier was their reddy to attend to him, so they left & returned with
> Walker and all his warriors that he could raise armed with bow & arrows
> & some guns, came to Brother Bradley to settle the matter, Walker with his
> armed force set as judge, jury, counsel & all, & decided that I should pay a
> gun to settle the matter. Brother Bradley so decided, (nothing but my life
> or a gun would settle the matter) it being one of Walkers braves, to have
> his weapons of death wrestled out of his hands & broke over his head in a
> disgraceful way was too bad for such a high blood to stand. So this being
> complied with peace declared & court adjourned.[32]

George W. Bean recalled Wakara's anger:

> Walker had come to Nephi and found the people all busily engaged in
> building an earthen wall around their settlement, which exasperated him very
> much, and he forbade any further work thereon, saying it was an evidence
> they intended to keep the Indians away, and was therefore an unfriendly act,
> for after the wall was done, when he came to visit them and get something to
> eat, they would let him stand outside and possibly toss a biscuit out to him
> over the wall like he was a dog or a slave. He reminded them that he had given
> Brigham and the Mormons the privilege of settling on these lands and jointly
> occupying them with the Indians, using land, water, grass, timber together
> as brothers, but if "Whites" separated and fenced off their settlements, they
> would have to stay inside and Indians outside—no more getting wood and
> grass for the "Whites" if they continued the wall business.[33]

---

[32]Love, Diary, 3, 6, 15 June 1854, 42–44.
[33]Bean, *Autobiography*, 96.

Nephi bishop Jacob Bigler put President Young's forting up plan to a vote and never "saw this settlement so united in performing any piece of work and we ware commencing all around the wall and the work is prospering fine," he told his brother-in-law, George A. Smith. Nephi could have "the wall pretty well completed" by August.

> But the Indians look upon us with a Suspicious Eye. Walker brought out some of his Braves a few days since where . . . a company was at work to put a stop to the work, as we supposed, and he wanted to know what we were adoing. They ware told that this wall was to Keep out the Americans and they returned to their weekeups. On yesterday Walker told Brother Bradley that he wanted the building of the wall stopped as it made the Utahs all mad and they were building [walls] in all the settlement and for further particulars I refer you to Brother Bradley's letter to Prest. Young. The natives appear quite independant.[34]

Work stopped on the wall. Maj. George Bradley's letter showed how seldom Utah officials took action without approval from Salt Lake. He described Wakara's anger and negotiating skill—and who the Mormons considered their real enemy.

GEORGE W. BRADLEY TO D. H. WELLS, FORT NEPHI, 10 JUNE 1854, BYC 23:10.

We commenced our City Wall about a week ago and are making very good progress. This morning Walker came to me and wished to know what we were building a wall for. I told him that we expected the Americans would come and try to drive us away from the mountains, and we were building fortifications against them. He, Walker, sais that he thought Bro Brigham ought to have told him when he was here, all about it. He says when we get the wall up he can not come in and shake hands with his friends. He says we cannot throw bread over to him over the wall and when his wives & children get hungry they can not get in. He also says if we want to harvest our wheat we must Stop building the Wall. He says the Utahs say we shall not cut our Grain if we build the Wall. He told me to write to Brigham and tell him what he says, and if Brigham says build the Wall he says of course we will do it and then he will go to the Mountains, and he can not tell what they will do. He says if the Americans come against us, he is here, and he knows how to travel in the night and he will help us to fight them but if we go on and build the Wall he says he will be friends with the Americans and by shutting them out, we throw them all away and he does not like it and gave me to understand that if we wanted to fight he was on hand.

---

[34]Bigler to Smith, 11 June 1854, Smith Papers, 5:1.

I shall stop the work on the fortifications untill I hear from you, in order to keep peace and save lives.

I am sorry to say that we had a little unpleasantness with the Utahs a few days ago. Two of Walker's men went into the dwelling of Bro Love and stood in the doorway so that the family could not pass in or out. Bro Love requested them to go out, but they would not do it. He then took one of them and put him out and struck him, which raised quite an excitement. Walker with all his men came to me to have it settled. I sent for Love. Walker told him he must pay the Indian or they would Kill him the first time they caught him out. He said I might say what he should give him. I told him to say and then I would say. He said he must have a Gun. I agreed to it and Bro Love gave him one. Walker and his men seemed satisfied and went off peaceable. Walker has been here about two weeks. He called upon us for a Beef animal and we supplied him. The Indians manifest a disposition to be quarrelsome and impose upon the people. Waiting your further instructions.

Yours Respectfully
Geo W Bradley
Major Comg/Juab Military/Dist

Confrontations between aggravated Indians and impoverished Mormons were the logical result of Brigham Young's "cheaper to feed them than to fight them" policy. As Indian superintendent, it was Young's duty to provide for Utah's Native peoples, but he conducted his Indian business, Carvalho observed, at the people's expense. Emotionally, women paid the price. At Provo, Utes entered their homes "when the men are off to work and if the women shut the door to ceep them out they will break it open and make a great many threats and scare the women and jest take any thing they can get their hands on," Colonel Conover reported. On 15 June two men forced their way into Epsy Jane Pace's home while her husband, William Byram Pace, "was off to work and one drew his gun on his wife and told her if she said any thing he would shoot her and stood with his gun pointed at her while another took all the ammunition he could find." From the safety of the twenty-first century, it is hard to imagine the terror these encounters inspired. Some thirty warriors, Conover continued, "the ones that done the most mischief last summer," planned "to drive off our cattle and horses and live off of them next winter." Despite friendly treatment, "they think we are afraid to cross them because they say Brother Brigham wont fight nor any of the rest of the mormons."[35]

---

[35]P. W. Cownover to Daniel H. Wells, Provo, 18 June 1854, UTMR 445.

"I am well aware that great patience faith and perserverance is required to get along peaceably with the Native tribes," Brigham Young told Major Bradley. "The truth is their sense of matters & things differ so much from ours that we often find it difficult to bear with their indignities and ignorance." He hoped to make them "depend on us more & more until their interest shall become so completely identified with ours that they cannot injure us or our interest without injuring themselves." He hoped to use "our understanding, led by our superior intelligence, wisdom, and more extended views" to "control them so far as is in our power." Humoring their notions could "often bring to pass our own policy, designs and intentions, they still believing that they have their own way and doing as they please."[36]

President Young "was much disturbed by this new move of the wiley old Chief, and he immediately wrote a strong letter to Walker. George Bean delivered it with Porter Rockwell, Amos Neff, and Washear to the "80 Lodges (tents) of Indians camped one mile above Nephi.[37]

BRIGHAM YOUNG TO CAPTAIN WALKER, 13 JUNE 1854, BYC 17:13, 46–49.

G.S.L. City June 13 1854

Captain Walker

I have been home but a few days from visiting you and now I am informed that you are threatening the people if they do not stop building forts and walling in their cities. You are a fool and do not understand your own true interest or you would not do so. Do you not know that if your enemies come against you that you and the Utahs can go in side the walls where you and they can get something to eat and be safe from the Snakes or any other Enemies which may come against you[?] Do you not see that almost every year more or less of the Utahs are killed by their Enemies[?] You say that your fort is in the mountains. You cant travel an[y]where but what others can travel there too just as well as you. You can you can not travel nights any better than other folks can. I tell you Bro Walker as friend as one friend talks to another that if you do not do as I told you and abide my Counsel to you, your Enemies will distroy you and your nation. The game in the mountains is scarce you told me so. There is not a hundredth part as much as there was a few years ago, when you was young. You said so. Now do you not know that it is better to raise grain and cattle to live on, than to depend on game, and you say that our people cannot harvest their grain if they go on building their wall. You stand in your own light. You can travel off and go to the Navahos and Moquis and trade and get your living but

---

[36]Young to Major Bradley, 13 June 1854, BYC 17:13.

[37]Bean, *Autobiography*, 96–98.

your Men cannot all do so, neither can you support all your men. You can not furnish them guns nor ammunition nor fix them up when they get out of repair. Tis strange that you cannot see that we are the very best friends that you have got and that we want to do you good, give you provisions Ammunition and Every thing which you want, trade with you and always be friends. It is as much & more to your advantage than ours to be friends to us & [illegible]. If you could only see it I hope & trust that you will see it, and continue to be friends and make the Utahs be friendly too. Your *good peace* does not last long if you can break it so soon as this—after trading with you and my men so long I should think that you would know that we were your good friends. Bro Geo W. Bean O P Rockwell and Amos Nef are going to see you and trade with as they agreed at San-pete. Now you must be friendly and trade with them and not go off and act so foolish for that is the worst thing that you can do for your own interest. The more you try to injure us the more you injure yourself and your Men. The more you destroy the less you and your men will have to Eat and wear. We have been poor very poor, and could not help you much, but now we are just beginning to be able to help you, some, we was never able to make you such presents before as we have this year. Now if we can be let alone we shall be able to do more and more for you and your Nation. Every year these Men which we send you will tell you all about me and my people. Grosepeen & Washer [Washear] will go out with them, they can tell you how well they have been treated. Hence [?] why cannot you come here and live with me[?] We would never have any difficulty. You know that. Suppose you come and live here with me, and keep cattle & raise grain. I think myself that if Bro [Andrew] Love had given those two men a little bread and sat down and laughed at them when they would not let him nor his folks go in nor out of the house it would have been better than to get angry about it, but it was a small affair for either you or me to interfere with. Now dont you think so [?] I would a great deal rather give you a gun for good feellings [sic] than for bad ones. If you want me to make you presents you must be good friends and keep good peace. Then I can give you big presents but if you do not I shall not be half as well able to. You must be good and do as I tell you and let me govern my men as I please and may God bless you with his spirit. I ask it in the name of Jesus Christ Amen

B.Y.

Wakara was "*very* impatient" and snatched the letter from my hand in the greatest rage and trampled it under his feet, and then struck into a boastful tirade," Bean wrote. Wakara would not hide behind walls and wanted Brigham Young to know he was here before the Mormons. He "had fought the Sioux, the Snakes, the Arapahoes, and Cheyennes, and the Crow Indian tribes—that his scars were all in front, and not on his back, and if he said so War would commence this very day." Wakara ordered his camp to move. Instantly "there was a great scattering of the crowd around us, and a howl of grief from the squaws, and a pulling down of lodges." Within thirty minutes, "the ground was clear and the whole cavalcade moved toward Salt Creek Canyon." About fifty warriors "including all the old Sub-Chiefs" surrounded the traders. "Battiese, Tintick, Bear Scratch and others" each took great pleasure "in boasting to me and Porter of their brave and bloody deeds during the War the year before." Their "willingness to do lots more of it was plainly manifest, and the snapping of caps, swaying of bow-strings was not very pleasant music to us."

Bean picked up Young's letter "from under Walker's feet" and said he "would return to Salt Lake and tell Brigham how his words of counsel had been treated." Wakara flew into a rage and said: "No, you won't go and get all the Mormons after us again." He asked what the traders planned to do with their guns and trade goods. Bean "told him we would take them back." Wakara said, "No you won't. We have waited till I'm sore for those goods and must have them." Amos Neff was holding the reins of the wagon's team, "ready to move at any moment." Bean claimed Washear saved him. "Walker you talk like a fool," he said. "I was with George when Brigham gave him the letter and Brigham was not mad, but he talked straight and he wants you to do right and not act foolish." Bean was "talking for Brigham, and he wants you to listen and do right and all will be well." Washear "grew very earnest and Walker talked loud, too, and the Braves all began to talk." This let Bean and friends "slip away, get on our wagon and quietly drive down to Nephi settlement, one mile distant, unmolested." Before the traders and their armed escort left for Payson, "we looked across the plain just above the town and saw old Chief Walker coming toward the town on foot, leading his little son, and Washear leading his horse." Bean forthwith concluded the morning's trouble had ended peacefully. "I'm not angry now," Wakara said. "'Shenentz,' my relative, has convinced me I was wrong in my suspicions of Brigham and his Mormons and I'm sorry for all the trouble."

Wakara wanted the Mormons "to overlook everything and go right along with them over to Sanpete Valley, near Fort Ephraim, to do our trading just as if nothing had happened." They agreed, but took Wakara and his son into their wagon, "so that if any treachery was attempted, we could have some show to keep even." Five days of trading with the Indians at Fort Ephraim followed, including "stormy bouts with Walker's impudent greed." He forced them "to take eight little Indians (Slaves), rather than have them butchered by the cruel Utes." They prayed often, "and not always on our knees."[38]

Major Bradley's contemporary report tells a harsher story.

> Our express returned from your City on yesterday morning as also Bros Bean Rockwell & Neff. This morning Bro Bean gave the Governor's letter to Walker, who treated the contents with perfect contempt from beginning to end. He sais that Bro Brigham knew nothing about the Utahs and that the Fortifications South of Provo must stop or they would fight. He said the whole nation was mad about the people building Forts, and that this Land was their's and they would not wish to have it piled up into a Wall. He said they had lived in these Mountains until now and had not starved to death and they could live without the Mormons and they could go and trade with the Spainiards [sic], Americans and others, and were not dependant upon us for their trade. Bro Bean told him that he and the Mormons thought a good deal of Bro Brigham's word, and as he had thrown it all away they thought that they had better not go out with them to trade untill they heard from Bro Brigham again and tried to reason [the] matter with him, to postpone the trading. Walker said they might please themselves but if they did not go with him to his camp in Sanpete near Allreds present Settlement [Spring City] they would commence fighting right off as the Utahs were not ready. Consequently Bean Rockwell & Neff were obliged to start with him this morning. His conversation with his men was of an exciting nature, telling them that Brigham was wrong & he spoke right, and that the Snake Chief told the Parvants that Brigham told him he would feed the Utahs for a while untill they got their Forts built and then they would get them into them, and Kill them all. Old Uinter says that Walker talks bad and is mad, but that he, would not fight the Mormons and he intended to stay with them. There Seems to be an uneasiness among the Indians that is not common, they have a great deal of travel to & fro, and seem to have a good deal of business on hand.[39]

The San Pete trading session failed to calm Wakara's anger. "Said if you don't trade with us, consider us enemies, and ready to fight," Bean reported. All the Indians were angry, and Tintick, Uinta, and others were mad at Wakara and argued with him at Nephi. Tintick complained, "it was calling them squaws, not to let them trade for themselves, and said he was no squaw last summer, when he made the mormons run from Summit and Willow

---

[38]Ibid., 98–100.
[39]Bradley to Wells, 17 June 1854, UTMR, 444.

Creeks." Wakara "demanded a squaw at Allred's settlement while he staid there, and wanted them to levy a tax and pay to him in gold or silver." He complained, "Brigham did not know how to use a Chief like him, for when he came down, Brigham would not allow him a squaw to sleep with like the Moquitches and Navahoes." Finally, Bean shared a rumor: "Grosepene, Sanpitch, Washear and a great many of the Indians have a venereal disease which they got of the Navahoes."[40]

By June 1854 word of Wakara's threats had spread north. The town of Payson found itself caught between Brother Brigham's wall and Wakara's hard place:

> Walker has sent us word that we have Got to stop forting or he will Leave the Territory and he has called all the Indians that are here and elsewhere to come to him unless we Do stop, And advises us if we do Not stop to Not go alone into the Kanyons or travel unless we are in companies, and wishes us to understand that he is Not Going to fight but that if he goes away that there is others that will and he can Not hinder them. His runner Toab came here yesterday and We thought it advisable to tell him that we would stop, and we wish You to counsil us what to Do about it. For the indians here were Making preperations to Leave until we told them we would stop Which pleased them very much for a majority of them are anxious To stay with us but they thought they had to obey Walker. The brethren have made a good begining on the Wall and are anxious to continue If you think it is Wisdom.[41]

Brigham Young now wanted Wakara "to talk good all the time and tell all the Indians to be good too" and sent George Bean back "with the things you wished me to send you." He was always "willing to do anything I can for you but you talk so crooked I cannot always understand what you do want." He did not want the Mormons to abuse the Utes, "nor I do not want the Indians to be ugly saucy and act ugly and bad to my people and if they do not my people will treat them well. Have not I always treated you well and talked one way to you," he asked. "Will you do just as I do and then all your people will feel better and wont be so impudent and act so ugly and then my people will not abuse them." Young wanted "to be a brother to you and all the Utes all the time if you will only let me." Wakara could rely on his friendship "if you will only be friends and make the Utes friendly too and they will be friendly if you talk strait and good to them."[42]

---

[40]Report of G. W. Bean, 24 June 1854. This is historian Jared Farmer's transcription, which cites "Losses in Sanpete County (Manti)," BYC 58:14.

[41]James McClelan et al. to Brigham Young, 25 June 1854, BYC 23:15.

[42]Young to Capt Walker, 29 June 1854, BYC 17:13.

Brigham Told the Snakes to Come

As Brigham Young had observed, Wakara was now truly "hemmed in" and "penned up in a small compass, surrounded by his enemies."[43] Following their June conflicts, Wakara and his band disappeared and communicated only through messengers. When intertribal violence broke out that fall at Provo, they reappeared in rumors.

"This morning by break of Day the peace of Provo was disturbed by an attack of some 80 Snake Indians upon the Camp of Utahs immediately adjoining this City," Sheriff Alexander Williams informed the governor on 22 September 1854. The raiders killed and wounded several Utes, generating more violence.

> The Snakes immediately left & in one hour All of the Utes of the south were here & demanded the wife of John & beset the House. Old Squash burst 3 caps at her before assistance arrived & with much difficulty he was put off. The whole band then left in pursuit of the Snakes & they had a Battle at Battle Creek & then returned & swore vengeance to all the Citizens of the Country & swear that no man shall travel the Road. I make a requisition upon you for an armed force to kill every damned Rascal.[44]

Barney Ward's Shoshone wife Sally and her brother John bore the brunt of the Utes' outrage. She had "hid one of the Utah Children under the floor & preserved its life from her own band the Snakes," wrote George W. Bean. Accidentally wounded in the fight, she "could not be removed in safety." Washear "was slightly wounded but afterwards went and shot Barneys Calf, robbed the house of what was left in it, & snapped his gun twice at the Snake Squaws head." Bean elaborated on these "difficulties."

Geo W Bean to B. Young, 24 September 1854, BYC 23:10, 18–21.

Provo Sept 24*th* 1854

Governor B. Young

I write to inform you more full[y] concerning the difficulties between the Utahs Snakes and Ourselves that have recently occurred at this place.

You were informed by A. Williams's letter of the fight that happened here on the morning of the *22nd* inst. Shortly after the Snakes left the scene of action the Utahs came pouring in from the south to the number of about 40 warriors.

---

[43] Young, *Journal of Discourses*, 31 July 1853, 1:171.

[44] Williams to Gov. Brigham Young, 22 September 1854, BYC 23:17. Williams suggested Young use "Uncle Sams men" who had recently arrived with Colonel Steptoe.

They immediately as[c]ertained from Squash that a Snake Squaw that was crippled in the engagement was lodged in our City. The ringleaders of this band were Tintick Petetenese Highforehead Blackhawk and Quiesh the latter being Walkers brotherinlaw. They forthwith demanded that the Squaw should be delivered to them which was refused on our part we alleging that we had protected their families from the Snakes that morning. They would listen to no reason & threatened they would take vengeance on us as they returned home Petenea said that he heard that Brigham told the Snakes to come on them. If he could find out that was the case the Utahs would know what to do, and talked in a very threatening manner. They were very angry to think we would stand by and see the Utahs killed by the Snakes and us living their lands: two or three of them struck at me and said I should not live.

They followed on to Battle Creek where they overtake the Snakes & fought with them 2 or 3 hours [and] killed none, but lost 2 or 3 horses & came back in a greater rage than ever: declared they would have the Squaw at any risk. We brought the argument that we wished to use all alike that we had protected their families & we should not let them have her now. They then told us that we should go no more into the Kanyons for wood, no more wheat be sown that all travel should stop [and] that we must all move to the Snake Country. The Chiefs said this. Squash threatned [sic] the life of Prest Higbee or Brigham or myself. They shot several head of Cattle as they went on to Hobble Creek.

Today several of them came back at different times and said they must have the Squaw or they would not be our friends. Said they had sent word to Walker & he would be here in a few days. Yontan came in from Lehi and demanded the Squaw saying that Brigham had promised him to deliver his enemies on account of his bringing those Goshutes that had killed Bro. Weeks Boys.[45]

He finally agreed to go see Brigham about it but said he knew you would give her up to him. He will probably accompany this letter. The whole drift of the Indians talk is that is they do not obtain revenge of the Snakes they will have it of the Mormons. . . .

> In haste your most obt srvt
> Geo W Bean Interpreter

Governor Young did not "deem it necessary to call any force into service on this account," and advised Sheriff Williams to "endeavour to make the Utahs understand that this is a difficulty with which we have nothing to do."

The Utahs stole 22 horses of the Snakes while they were peacably encamped near Ogden, and I suppose that they (the Snakes) have gone for them, let them have it out between themselves as much as possible, and let our people

---

[45]See Robert Carter's "Carnage in Pole Canyon Avenged," *Provo Daily Herald*, 19 April 2008, B2.

look out for themselves and their property and not interfere. Do not let the
Utahs interupt Bro Elijah Ward's family and relations, as he is absent and
they have had nothing to do with it. The brethren must be on their guard
and prepared to defend themselves against the Indian whenever they may be
met, but I do not anticipate any regular attack by them upon the whites, but
they should be careful about going out into Kanyons and bye places alone
or unarmed. The loss of a few cattle does not justify a retaliation sufficient
for White men to kill the offenders, this is Indian politics in their savage
state, & the white men's should be of a higher grade.[46]

Did the settlers encourage the Shoshone attack? Probably not. This neu-
trality reflected the Saints' desire to "use all alike." Mormons, David Bigler
noted, "persisted in seeing all natives as one people," the Lamanite "remnant
of Jacob," which ignored "the evidence before their eyes that all Indians were
not the same." Despite vast experience, the Saints never learned an essential
lesson of frontier survival: "the friend of my friend is my friend; the friend
of my enemy is my enemy."[47] Sheriff Williams's request for "an armed force
to kill every damned Rascal" showed at least one Mormon official backed
the Shoshones. The Utes, he told the governor, had sent for Wakara, "but I
do not know whether he will come or not but if you deem it proper you can
give my respects to the Snake Chiefs and tell them that I can be a very good
Snake and render them assistance should it become necessary."[48] Before the
Provo attack, General Wells had ordered Bishop William Draper to "give
Ratah a shoshone Indian chief a Beef." He "must not fail to give them a
beef creature," for they depended on it.[49]

When he reappeared in October, Wakara echoed Brigham Young's peace
policy, stating his desire to be friends "with all Peaple."

JAMES McCLELLAN TO BRIGHAM YOUNG, 10 OCTOBER 1854, BYC 23:15.

Fort Payson Oct 10th 1854

Brother Young

By request of Hongowick an Indian that Claims to be sent on an express
from Walker that I should Wright to you and to state that they want to make
a Treety with the Snakes and they want your assistance in the affair. They
also want to be friendly with the mormons and with the Mearicans and with
all Peaple. Walker has Sent word to all the Indians to quit there stealling and
to be have them selves and to do right. They want tenn head of Cattle and

[46]Young to Williams, 23 September 1854, Letterbook 1, BYC 2:1, 689–90.
[47]Bigler, *Fort Limhi*, 302.
[48]Williams to Young, 22 and 24 September 1854, BYC 23:17.
[49]Wells to Draper, 20 September 1854, Letterbook 1, BYC 2:1, 687.

about 5 dollars in whiskey. He also wants to know the minds of the Peaple in this place and all others in regard to them in this Peaple they have been the best of fealance [feelings] for the Indians but they have done so much that they begin to feal as though they Could not bear with them much longer. They have Pulde down the fences and let the Cattle in to the grain and what the stock did not destroy they have Cut up and packed off them selves and when they are told of it they threaten to shoot or do some other mischieaf but the peaple wants to be friendly with them if friendship can be had on any faverble termes. I will Close as brother Maxwell will state the Peticulars.

Yours in the Bonds of the Covenant
James MClellan

On 7 November 1854 John Steele informed George A. Smith of Wakara's return to Parowan:

A few evenings ago I had a talk with the old Piede Captain, and gave him the suit of clothes you sent him. I told the old Captain that he must talk to his men and tell them they must not steal, nor kill our cattle, nor molest anything that belonged to us. He said he would talk good to his men, and had told them not to steal from us, and with a few exceptions they would hear, but some had no POCKETS in their heads. I told him when any misunderstanding took place between his men and ours, they tell him about it and he must come to our Captains and tell them about it. He said he would do so. I also told him not to trade squaws nor children to the Spaniards to be taken into Mexico, or pretty soon they would have no wives, and of course no children, and there would soon be no Piedes. He said he understood it. I also brought your little Indian girl, and showed him how nice and clean were the Indian children who lived with the Mormons, and he seemed pleased and told us that she was his brother's daughter and her mother was living over on Ash Creek and her father is dead; that he was a great Captain. Sister Smith gave him some tobacco and he said he would have good smoke with his men and talk good to them as I had talked to him. He told us that Walker was coming here, as snow fell, to stay all winter at his house, and that he wanted to be very friendly, and had told his men not to kill the Mormons, but that some of them would not hear.[50]

Wakara appeared the next day "with a very large train of horses about 23 men, 25 squaws, 120 head of horses, 20 head of oxen, some sheep, cows, and goats. From the looks of their equipage they are going to be our neighbors this winter," wrote Steele. "They look friendly, and maybe feel so, for oughts [sic] I know."[51]

---

[50]"Parowan, Iron County," *Deseret News*, 30 November 1854, 3/4.
[51]Steele to Smith, Smith Papers (redacted), 5:4.

On 22 December 1854 Thomas D. Brown reported from the Southern Indian Mission. His letter showed how much it was a trading venture, how Natives regarded land ownership and alliances, and how deeply Indian bondage was entrenched.

BROWN, *JOURNAL OF THE SOUTHERN INDIAN MISSION*, 103–105.

President Brigham Young. Dear Sir,

This should be our second report of monthly sales of Indian clothing: but we have sold none & there is no report.

Perhaps it would be well to examine some of the causes in this "dull trade." The few that have been steady and regularly employed in the settlements have been clothed, those that still prefer an outside & offish course (with or without a cause?) are fully engaged hunting our Small game—rabbits for their food. And the many almost naked we find on the Santa Clara & surrounding country have nothing to give in return for this clothing, at present, but they are very willing to work, and perhaps the days are not far distant when they will be taught & capable of producing more than they need to consume.

Brors [Rufus] Allen & [Hyrum] Burges have just returned from the Santa Clara where they and Brors [Jacob] Hamblin, [Augustus] Hardy & [Thales] Haskell have been residing & laboring with the Indians during the past month. There they have built one log cabin for the missionaries, and one for the chief & his friends. Others of them, have requested to have this increase of comfort—houses, as soon as we can.

The Brethren cut the logs and the Indians carried them, they manifested their willingness to aid us, we in return cut their logs and showed them how to put them up.

While Prest. Allen and the brethren were preparing these logs, Sanpete or Sanpitch, one of Walker's brothers arrived, and the following interesting dialogue occured. With an air of authority he demanded why we built there? The Pahutes did not want us. Bror Allen replied, "because we had been among the Pahutes for some months, and were sent by the Big Captain to live among them and teach them to build, plant & grow plenty of good food, and they were willing we should do so." "How many oxen, horses &c. are you going to give them for the land?" "We have not given them any neither do we mean to, but shall teach them how to obtain & raise them." "This land does not belong to the Pahutes, it belongs to Walker." "This land belongs to the Pahutes they have lived on it for ages, & the Big Captain wishes us to teach them how to use it."—"But the Mormons have shot some of the Indians."—"Many of the Indians have been mean and stolen many cattle & have shot the Mormons also"—"When the Snakes fought and killed the Utahs at Provo, the Mormons stood neutral and did not help us." "Perhaps this was because Squash head & others had acted meanly and were very saucy." During this conversation many more Indians had arrived and manifested much interest in it, Seeming pleased when the missionaries spoke, but hung down their heads when the Ute spoke. At length Bror Allen addressing the chief Pahute there Tatsagovats, said "Do you & the Pahutes wish us to live among you, build houses and teach you to make food, or shall we quit & leave you"? He hesitated for a time, and then replied "Go on and make houses, live among us & teach us to make food & get clothing—we have been a long time naked and often hunger & you are our friends." All the Pahutes approved—"toy"—it's all right, go ahead. Sanpete then put his finger to his forehead, & said, "I am not wise, I do not know much—it's all right" and from that hour he encouraged us and them. He came to trade for some children peaceably, here he gave a horse for a girl about eleven years old, the parents were reluctant to trade, but their chief prevailed & procured this trade for him; he then sent an indian off West, with 2 guns, ammunition and beads—In six days this Indian returned with 2 children—a boy and girl 6 and 7 years of age. For the one he paid a gun, for the other "Shontz of beeds" that is "very many" or a few quarts, and to this Indian he gave a gun for his Commission. Walker, we learn, has now about 10 of these little ones at Parowan, we try to persuade him to sell them to the Mormons—he says they give to little for them. For a young Indian the Spanish and Mexicans will pay $300 to $500, we are told, & there they labor as Negroes do in the states.

I remain, Dear Sir,
Yours faithfully,
Thos. D. Brown Recorder.

David Lewis visited Fort Harmony and carried Brown's letter to Salt Lake, where he delivered a message and a gift from Wakara.

DAVID LEWIS TO BRIGHAM YOUNG, 9 JANUARY 1855, BYC 24:7, 25–27.
. . . During the fall and winter I often visited the camp of Chief Walker, who has until late bin encamped in the canion of Summet creek seven miles southwest of Parowan. After I got acquainted with walker and explained to him my business in that country, he seemed to become mutch attached to me, he strongly solicitied me to accompany him in the spring on a trading expedition to the Navaghoes [sic]. I told him that I would go if the Big Captain would tell me to go, he said Brigham was a good captain and always talked good, and always wanted pease. I told him I was going to see the Big capts pretty soon, he said he wanted to talk with me before I went. He accordingly came to me and said, for fear you forget to take your book and wright it down, he then preseeded, Tell Brother Brigham to talk to the Snakes and tell them that he was not mad at them nor neither did he blame them for what they had done, that Squash and a few of the utaws was not wise and

he did not approve of the course they had taken, and he wanted to be good friends and never go to war with them again.

Tell him that I am all the time preaching pease among the Indians, And the Mormons and Americans may now all pass as they please one or two at a time, as they please. No cattle or horses shall be killed or stold. All might lay down and sleep good, and none need to stand gard or be afraid.

Tell him the captains of Parowan have thrown me away without a cause, that they seem to be affraid of me, and I am affraid they have wrote to you something bad about me, and said he I want you to talk to him your self, and if they have written any thing bad, you tell him that you have bin with me, you talk good to him. Tell him in three moons to send me ten good rifle guns some powder and lead and caps some Shirts and a stud colt two years oald [sic] good large American colt, send them to a small stream south of Filmore and I will pay for them in horses, also some cattle for beef to last me to the Navejoes.

Tell him that I want you to go with me in the spring and that my Brother Sanpete wants Jacob Hamblin to gow with him as he had got acquainted with him whilst he was among the santeclara indians.

Take this poppoos, and tell Brother Brigham that I give it to him, and I want him to give me a good gun a coat a vest and white blanket and se[n]d them by you. Ammon then spoke and said tell Brother Brigham to send my wife a dress. I now have the poppoos in my possession, subject to your orders. It is a small boy I suppose him to be between three and four years old. . . .

David Lewis,
First Counselor to Rufus C. Allen
of the southern mission.

Meanwhile, Brigham Young "sent word to Walker I shant give him or any of his band any more presents but he must work for what he gets & he has been better since."[52]

Wolf Medicine: The Death of Capt. Walker, the Utah Chief

When George A. Smith saw "General Walker, the Utah Chief" at Chicken Creek in 1854, he appeared "to be sulky—said he had lost his heart, and could not talk—his heart was dead in him." But Brigham Young "succeeded in waking up the old tiger to pretty good advantage."[53] Solomon Carvalo noted Wakara's imposing appearance but "care-worn and haggard" look,

[52]Thomas Bullock, 7 January 1855, General Church Minutes, LDS Archives.
[53]Smith to Richards, 21 June 1854, *Millennial Star*, 30 September 1854, 615.

even though he was probably not yet fifty. A month later, when Rockwell and Bean "held a talk with walker & read a letter from Brigham to him," it "inflamed his passions verry much & hurt his dignity." Wakara's dance on the governor's 17 June 1854 letter obviously intended "to trample under foot the authority of Brigham," wrote Andrew Love. "So Brother Walkers End is fast approaching."[54]

After his baptism in 1850, Wakara "intimated" Brigham Young had encouraged him to marry a Mormon woman. George A. Smith claimed Wakara had "teased" him for a white bride, providing fodder for another joke: "if any lady wishes to be Mrs. Walker, if she will report herself to me, I will agree to negotiate the match"—and "close the war forthwith."[55] Wakara's courtships of Mormon women resulted in "two documented refusals—possibly others as well." Mary Artemesia Lowry's story was "told over and over again to her posterity" and became Sanpete County folk history. Lowry was allegedly the "beautiful, innocent young maiden" who inflamed the passions of the old reprobate, famous "for his murders, his pillage, his assassinations."[56] The *Deseret News* retold the tale in 1995: Wakara thought his baptism entitled him "to two things—priesthood 'medicine' and a white wife." He "went to the Lowry home when he thought Mary would be alone and placed a blanket, some moccasins, a beaded headband and other items on the table, followed by a crude proposal." Terrified, Mary Lowry "blurted that she was promised to another man," George Peacock, who was married to her twin sister. Wakara, "according to several accounts, plunged his knife hilt-deep into a table and said he would take the matter to Brigham Young," who had indeed promised that if Mary was not already married, he could have her. Lowry and Peacock were now wed—"a logical solution to the problem."[57]

Peter Gottfredson's *History of Indian Depredations* was "essentially a work of folklore based on foggy memories of aged members of the Utah Indian War Veterans Association," as Jared Farmer observed.[58] But folklore, with all its limitations, often reflects popular memory, and Eunice Billings Warner Snow told a compelling story. When Indian war veterans asked John Warner's

[54]Love, Diary, 15, 17 June 1854, 45.

[55]Smith, "Address," 7 October 1853, *Journal of Discourses*, 1:197.

[56]Antrei and Roberts, *History of Sanpete County*, 72; and Helen Dyreng, "A Most Unusual Proposal," in Spencer, ed., *Saga of the Sanpete*, digital copy accessed 12 December 2016 at http://sanpete.com/pages/lowery.

[57]Twila Van Leer, "Chief Watched Way of Life Vanish," *Deseret News*, 21 February 1995.

[58]Farmer, "Crossroads of the West," 160.

widow to address their annual reunion, she thought she "could not speak in public on such a trying subject," but also felt she owed it to her family. "The Indians were very troublesome from the first of our settling. As we were on their land, they were mad," she recalled. "They would drive off our cattle and kill them to eat, and they said it was as much their right to take our cattle without our consent as it was for us to live on their land and not get their consent." Then they "began killing our brethren," including William Mills and her husband.[59]

Eunice was cooking two rabbits Warner had shot when she "heard the report of the guns that killed the two men, but paid no attention," thinking it was more rabbit hunting. Then a search party found their bodies.

EUNICE SNOW, IN GOTTFREDSON, *INDIAN DEPREDATIONS*, 76–78.

The Indians had been in ambush waiting for an opportunity to do their work. Both men were stripped naked, except that my husband had his garments left on him. I was not allowed to see him as he was so badly disfigured in the face. The Indians, after they had tried to make peace with our people told that Mr. Warner had fought desperately and had killed one Indian.

Soon after the killing an Indian came over to our house carrying my husband's gun, and one day two Indians came to our door, one of whom had my husbands kneck tie on his black kneck; the other had his pocket rule, which he always carried with him, and also his pen knife. The knife was a usefull one, and it contained a number of articals, such a button hook, an ear spoon, etc. Two or three articles they had broken up. They were showing these things to my mother and father as we happened to be eating dinner at the time. I grabbed a butcher knife which was lying on the table and started for them. My father seeing me rise from the table, caught me by the arms and carried me out of the room. It was more than I could stand to see the black imps with my husband's things. This happened a short time before the birth of my son, who was born six months after my husband was killed.

Another serious trouble came of which I will make mention; Soon after my son was born, Chief Walker came to our house one day. He said he intended, when I got around again, to have me for his wife. He told my father and mother his intentions. They did not let me known anything about it until he came several times to see me; when they told me it almost frightened me to death. I was obliged to keep in hidding from him for about six weeks, in fact until the good news came one morning that Walker was dead. He died very suddenly.

---

[59]"Troubles and Trials with the Indians," in Spencer, ed., *Saga of the Sanpete*, 27.

David Lewis left Salt Lake on 22 January 1855, authorized to go with Jacob Hamblin and "Walker & Sanpete to the Navajos" in the spring.[60] Lewis told Brigham Young of Wakara's death on the day it happened.

"DEATH OF INDIAN WALKER," *DESERET NEWS*, 8 FEBRUARY 1855, 3/5.
President Brigham Young:—
Dear Brother—

I improve this the earliest opportunity to inform you of the death of Captain Walker, the Utah Chief after a sickness of 10 days; he died on the 29th inst., at Meadow Creek about 6 miles from Fillmore. His complaint seemed to be a cold settled on his lungs.

I arrived at Fillmore on the 28th inst. I started the next morning for Walker's lodge, and met the Utah's coming with Walker, and supporting him on his horse. He held out his hand, and shook hands, and seemed very glad to see me. He asked me if Brigham talked good and if I was going with him to the Navahoes. I told him that Br. Brigham talked very good and perhaps I would go with him. I showed him the letter you sent to him, and I gave him all the articles you sent to him. He seemed greatly pleased with them and wanted me to come the next morning to Meadow Creek, and read the letter for him.[61]

On the next morning, before day, the Pauvans came running into the Fort, and said that Walker was dead, and the Utah's were mad, that they had killed two Squaws, and two Piede children. Ka-no-she, the Pauvan Chief, sent us word to drive up all our horses, and cattle, and keep out of the canyons; that the Utahs intended to kill two Pauvans, and two Mormons and a great many cattle.

About eighteen of our people went out in the morning, and found that the Utahs had killed two Squaws, Piede prisoners, (slaves) and two Piede children, and about twelve to fifteen of Walker's best horses. The Pauvans had said twenty horses.

They had buried Walker with the letter and articles you sent him.

Yours as ever, in the Gospel of Christ,
David Lewis

P.S. Walker's last words to his people were, not to kill the Mormon cattle, nor steal from them. I was with him until he was struck with death. He was in his senses, and greatly desired to live. He possessed a good spirit and shook hands twice with me. As I was starting for the Fort, he pressed my hand and said, 'Come and see me again tomorrow, for I wish to have a long talk with you, but I am too sick to talk now.'

---

[60]Ellerbeck to Allen, 22 January 1855, Letterbook 1, BYC 2:1, 830.
[61]This letter does not seem to have survived.

"Some of the strongest preaching ever deliverd to the saints" took place on 4 February. After the service, Brigham Young held a prayer meeting in the Beehive House. "Report came that the Indian Walker was dead," wrote Wilford Woodruff. "That He died in his tent with the consumption."[62] A letter Young wrote the previous day indicates this was already old news.

YOUNG TO ARROW PIN AND THE UTAHS, 3 FEBRUARY 1855, 2:1
LETTERBOOK 1, 888–92, BYC.

I hear that you say that Captain Walker is dead—I am sorry if this is so because Walker was always my friend, and I gave him a great many presents, and made my men trade with him a great deal. He was my Brother and I feel bad to lose him—But I do not want to kill any body else because he died as Some say that you do. That is [a] wrong notion, that you seem to have when any body dies that some one else must die, to make peace with the great Spirit as though he was angry with you every time anyone dies.

This is a wrong idea and one that you must get rid of and then teach your People better. Because a man or Chief dies, it does not make it any better to Kill any body else. That would only make it worse, and the great Spirit would be more angry with us for doing that than any thing else. You might as well because one of your horses or Cattle should happen to die go and kill another and another and so on until you had Killed all of them off. You can see what folly this would be, well the other is just as foolish, as that would.

All people have to die sometime and although we may feel bad on account of losing our friends, yet when we die, we shall go to them and all will be right if we do right ourselves, all the time, until we die.—Now if Walker is dead, as you say, and the Great Spirit took him, because he was angry with him, it was because he had done something himself, or Some of the Utes or Pauvantes, had done something wrong—perhaps it was, they killed Gunnison and his party, and one of our Brethren from San Pete, William Potter. It is a great deal more likely that the Lord took him, for this for you know that no person was ever taken, and killed on account of that atrocious deed.

Now when one man Kills another the man that killed him should be tried and killed also because one man has no right to take the life of another—But when a man dies, and no man kills him. Who is to blame for that and who could help it—Why no one. Cant you see the difference[?] So if we do not take and kill a man that has killed another The Great Spirit may perhaps take some one away for it and he you know, would take whom he pleased. Perhaps that is the reason, why he has taken Walker because the Pauvantes Killed Capt Gunnison and Party and Brother William Potter. I do not say that this is the reason but it is far more probable that he is angry about that

---

[62]Woodruff, *Journal*, 4 February 1855, 4:303.

than that he is about Walkers death—because noboddy killed Walker he just took sick and died, just as people frequently do. And the great Spirit is not angry about that, but he would be angry if you or any of your Nation should kill any body else for it. If the Lord wants any body to die for that he will take them himself and does not want you or me to kill them for Him.—I do not so much object to giving gifts when anyone dies although that is a foolish custom too but is not so bad as the other, so I send you a few presents, not because Walker is dead but because, I am Your friend, and want to do you good and if it will be any comfort to you I shall be glad.

It is nothing but natural that you should feel sad because this is a great affliction to lose your Chief and I send Dimic to see you, and try to comfort you up—I want you should feel right about it, and not be angry with the Mormons for they had nothing to do about it—If you want to please the Great Spirit, you will hearken to the words which I said and to the words that Dimic will say to you and if you do this you will feel better, but if you do not, do so, I dont know how you will feel neither do I know what the Great Spirit will do about it—You know that he can do just what he has a mind to and neither you nor I can help ourselves. We should always be careful and not displease him—When you. When you [sic] die, as we all must sometime, you will be glad if you do as I tell you now and follow my Counsel hereafter.

I Remain Your Brother and pray the Lord to Bless and Comfort Your heart
Brigham Young

P.S. I propose that the Utahs all get together and select another Chief one whom they will listen to as they did to Walker, and make him their Captain, and if it suits them I should like for them to select Arrowpin in his place.

Wakara appeared to Arapene in a vision with survival instructions that John Lowry interpreted and his son-in-law, George Peacock, transcribed.

Vision of Arapine on the night of the 4th of Feb 1855, BYC 74:49. Walker apeared unto me and told me to be at peace and not to fight the mormons but to cultivate good peace [and] to talk good to the utes and the Lord said to me that the Land the timber and water and horses cattle &c was the Lords and did not belong to the indians nor the mormons, and that Walker had took Sick and died A natural death; and the Lord had took him to him self &c and if the indians Stole the mormons cattle and horses to put A Ball & chain on them and for me to Whip them but it was not good to Kill them or spill Blood on the Land. And the indians was to here to me and do as I told them and to go to Bros. [Welcome] Chapman, [Nelson] Higgins and Bishop Lowry and relate what the Lord told me and have it wrote down that the mormons might all here it and then if the mormons throwed away the Lords words the Lord would not go to there meetings; the Lord told me that the Danes did not understand the mormon nor indian talk and ways and if they went to meeting it was good and for me to go to meeting. Also, and for the mormons to not trade guns and Ammunition to the indians at present nor untill I should tell them for some of them was bad and would not here to me; it was good to raise wheat and to travel the road in small companys in peace &c &c. The Lord said that by & bye when all People was good and at peace he would come and Live on the earth and not go Back. I saw three personages and there garments where [sic] as white as snow and as Briliant as the sun and by and bye all good People would Apear as they did and the Lord said that he often talked to Brigham and now he had come to talk with me.

And I was to tell the Momons at Allreds settlement to give unto me A young cow or heffer. But I was to not Kill her but to keep her [for] it is the Lord that wants the cow and not me. And as the Lord said for me to not talk to[o] much I will relate no more at this time. But this is the Lords talk and not mine

interpreted by John Lowry, Jr.
by Geo. Peacock, scribe

The vision inspired Brigham Young. "I want to send elders all over the world among the Lamanites to preach the gospel," he said. "I have prayed for the Lord to reveal himself to the Lamanites. Arrapeen has seen three personages arrayed in white, I consider honestly it was the three Nephites who came to him, they told him that Walker died a natural death."[63]

Wakara's death solved nothing.

Tommy the Indian that lives with me, came in to my house and said that there was an Indian told him that Squash had some six or seven days ago killed a cow at Provo, and last Saturday he came up hear and killed 2 more. One of them up in the Cedars South East of hear and the Other between here and provo, Also that over at Palmyra last week, Antongur or Black Hawk shot a Creeter [creature] and then the People took 2 of the Utas and wiped [whipped] them considerable. The next day they went out and Shot two more (I have not heard whether those three cattle died or not) and that Squash had said that he calculated to kill cattle whenever he pleased for Brigham had Lied to him and that the Mormons were afraid to do any thing with him for they had said a great many times that they would do something with him but they had Lied &c. the Indian that told him (Tommy) was his mothers brother who lives at Provo, which was the truth and no mistake. (I have just learned his name it is Tshar-ig-iche) I know of a surety that the

---

[63]Van Wagoner, *Complete Discourses*, 18 February 1855, 2:913–14.

animal that was kill up in the cedars was brother Enos Curtis. Tommy says the Mormons are fools or they would take Squash and put him in Irons, I have not heard Positive about the Fence since you left but Tommy say that they still Burn the Poles. High-forehead came over in 2 or 3 days after you was here and said that he had cried ever since he saw you. I told Tommy to tell him all that you had told him and I told him also. Afterwards he felt better especially after he had got the shirt and the tobacco, I hear that the Indians had began to geather at Salt Creek and expected to have their big council in a few days. And that there had been some cattle shot at that place.[64]

Faithful Saints attributed the Ute leader's demise to causes ranging from pneumonia to consumption to apoplexy. Wakara, D. B. Huntington initially reported, "while gambling with some Pah-van-tes, broke a blood-vessel, which caused his death. Ar-a-peen thinks the Pah-van-tes made bad medicine for him." He "had his senses until the last" and asked "his brothers to kill a Pi-ede woman (who was in a delicate condition,) to strangle, with lassoes, two Piede girls, and bury alive a Piede boy ten years old; to kill sixty horses and six sheep."[65] Huntington (and most Mormon historians) soon joined Lewis's conclusion that pneumonia killed Wakara. He told James Linforth he died "on the 29th of January, in the present year, 1855, on Meadow Creek, about 6 mi from Fillmore, of a cold which had settled on his lungs."[66] By 1872 Huntington had revised his account to say the "king of the mountains" died soon after "he inaugurated what is called the Wahker war." He was taken sick near Fillmore "and was ill but a short time when he was stricken with death, being blind for three days. He would have the men raise him up, when he would talk to them, telling them not to fight the whites as he had done."[67]

Other explanations soon emerged. After several predatory Ute incursions, wrote British traveler William Chandless, "Brigham had Walker their chief, a very determined foe of the Mormons, secretly put to death and buried by Jordan."[68] Mary Ettie Coray claimed Young promised the woman who accepted "the dusky warrior as a husband" would win "a crown of Immortal Glory in the celestial kingdom." The chief "suddenly died from some cause unknown"; the Prophet seldom failed "to accomplish his aims," Coray said, such as "the death of the chief, whether by natural or foul means."[69]

---

[64]J. D. Wood to D. B. Huntington, 20 February 1855, BYC 24:12, 75–76.

[65]Huntington, "A Trip to Manti," 6 February 1855, Deseret News, 22 February 1855, 3/5.

[66]Piercy and Linforth, Route from Liverpool to Great Salt Lake, 105.

[67]Huntington, Vocabulary of the Utah and Sho-Sho-Ne, 27–28.

[68]Chandless, A Visit to Salt Lake, 184.

[69]Coray, in Green, Fifteen Years among the Mormons, 315.

Years later, Charles Wandell charged Young was "determined to form the closest possible alliance with the Indian tribes" through marriage. "Walker, poor innocent soul, supposing that he was on a perfect equality with his Mormon brothers, demanded a white squaw to help fill up his wick-e-up; but he died very suddenly by devouring, as is supposed, an innocent bowl of bread and milk!"[70]

California newspapers closely followed Utah's colorful news, and the "Deseret mail" made William Allen Wallace's *Los Angeles Star* one of the state's best-informed sources about Mormon matters. Courier Griff Williams told Wallace about the charges "reported to the *News*," which the *Deseret News* did not print.[71]

"NEWS FROM GREAT SALT LAKE," *LOS ANGELES STAR*, 31 MARCH 1855, 2/2.

It is reported to the *News*, that Walker, the Indian Chief of the Utahs, had been poisoned. He died January 29th. He requested his brother to kill, at his burial, one Pi-ede woman, to strangle two Pi-ede girls, bury alive one Pi-ede boy and to kill sixty horses and six sheep, as a sacrifice that he might pass in peace to the happy hunting grounds of the Indian. . . .

The Utah Indians are now camped about 60 miles from Salt Lake where they have elected their new Chief, (whose name is Aropene,) to fill the vacancy of Walker, deceased. They appear very friendly, and will continue so. . . .

Mr. Williams, the mail carrier between this city and Great Salt Lake . . . says, three Indian women were strangled with lassos, and one Indian boy buried alive on the death of Walker, all of them being captives. This constituted a part of the burial ceremonies as an offering to the "Great Spirit," for a passport to the happy hunting grounds of the red man. Some of the chiefs best horses and sheep were also sacrificed as a feast offering.

Whether he had a hand in Wakara's death or was blameless since "the Great Spirit took him," Brigham Young had mixed emotions about losing his most talented foe and Native military leader. James Farmer explained why the Saints at Fort Ephraim tolerated "our red brethren" living "in their wickeups close by our small fort" and often entering their homes. "We feed and clothe them, for they will yet be the battle-ax of the Lord, and will fight for the kingdom of God."[72] Similar hopes may have driven Young's alternating accommodation of and anger with Wakara. "By and by they will be the Lord's battle ax in good earnest," Young said of his Lamanite neighbors soon after Wakara's death.[73]

---

[70]Argus, "Open Letter to Brigham Young," *Daily Utah Reporter*, 12 September 1870, 2/1–2.

[71]Juanita Brooks identified Griff Williams in Brown, *Journal of the Southern Indian Mission*, 82n55.

[72]Farmer to Beloved Mother, 10 January 1855, *Millennial Star*, 28 July 1855, 477.

[73]Van Wagoner, *Complete Discourses*, 8 April 1855, 2:929.

In 1871 Brigham Young concluded civilization had killed the dreadful Wakara and most of his people. "There is a curse on these aborigines of our country who roam the plains, and are so wild that you cannot tame them," he said. Jesus himself had the delivered "the oracles of truth" to the Lamanites, and "they received and delighted in the Gospel" for generations, but

they turned away and became so wicked that God cursed them with this dark and benighted and loathsome condition; and they want to sit on the ground in the dirt, and to live by hunting, and they cannot be civilized. And right upon this, I will say to our government if they could hear me, "You need never fight the Indians, but if you want to get rid of them try to civilize them." How many were here when we came? At the Warm Springs, at this little grove where they would pitch their tents, we found perhaps three hundred Indians; but I do not suppose that there are three of that band left alive now. There was another band a little south, another north, another further east; but I do not suppose there is one in ten, perhaps not one in a hundred, now alive of those who were here when we came. Did we kill them? No, we fed them. They would say, "We want just as fine flour as you have." To Walker, the chief, whom all California and New Mexico dreaded, I said, "It will just as sure kill as the world, if you live as we live." Said he, "I want as good as Brigham, I want to eat as he does." Said I, "Eat then, but it will kill you." I told the same to Arapeen, Walker's brother; but they must eat and drink as the whites did, and I do not suppose that one in a hundred of those bands are alive. We brought their children into our families, and nursed and did everything for them it was possible to do for human beings, but die they would. Do not fight them, but treat them kindly. There will then be no stain on the Government, and it will get rid of them much quicker than by fighting them. They have got to be civilized, and there will be a remnant of them saved. I have said enough on the subject.[74]

"Mormons know how to poison, as well as murder, armed 'Gentiles,'" the *Alta California* claimed in July 1857, carrying on a tradition of toxic charges that followed the Latter-day Saints from Missouri to Illinois and ultimately to the Great Basin.[75] Two months later, the *San Francisco Herald* presented "facts" it acknowledged were "too incredible for belief," charging that "the Kingdom of Sin at Salt Lake" had sent missionaries to search for "an insidious but fatal poison." They found many in China, "Some are so slow that long periods elapse before they take effect, while at the same time their fatality may be precipitated by the admixture of other poisons." Young had one, it

[74]Young, Discourse, 9 April 1871, *Journal of Discourses*, 14:86–87.
[75]"More Mormon Mischief," *Daily Alta California*, 7 July 1857, 1/3.

claimed, that would "remain inert in the human system for years before its fatal consequences."[76]

"Wahker's Death has been a good thing, for I tell them they must harken to Brighams words or they will go like Walker Did for he would not hear Brigham when he talked," wrote Dimick Huntington. Indian leaders shared a good spirit "except Tintick," who was badly scared. They believed Young's threat: "if they did not stop thir stealing in a short time thar would be none of them left." The spirit of the Lord rested "upon the Chiefs & they begin to have visions & Dreams & want to hear preaching & are willing to Do any thing that Brigham shall say. By all appearance they will be ready to go when they are called upon to GO." When he slept, Antero said, "Brigham is before his Eyes all the time."[77]

THE LAST RESTING PLACE OF AN ELEPHANT: WAKARA'S RESTLESS BONES

Wakara died on the eve of what historian Ann Fabian called America's "imperial body collecting" project. She concluded, probably incorrectly, that the bones of "Wah-ker, a celebrated chief," became "one of the few skull's in the army's collection with an individual identity."[78] In 1872 Wheeler Expedition surgeon H. C. Yarrow visited a stone cemetery in central Utah "situated at the bottom of a rock slide, upon the side of an almost inaccessible mountain," that "would have been almost impossible to find it without a guide." Native graves had once been lined with pelts "and covered over with saplings of the mountain aspen," while weapons and articles "useful and ornamental" adorned the corpse. The boulders "formed a huge cairn, which appeared large enough to have marked the last resting place of an elephant." The bones of horses, "no doubt sacrificed during the funeral ceremonies"

---

[76]"New Feature in Mormon Tactics," *San Francisco Herald,* 14 September 1857, 2/4. Brigham Young sent three missionaries to China, nine to India, and three more to Siam, now Thailand. If Mormon leaders believed Asia would produce thousands of converts, their efforts failed—people "told them that they had not time to 'talka' religion." Roberts, *Comprehensive History,* 4:71–74. But perhaps they did not fail entirely. Hosea Stout wrote from Hong Kong, "Do not feel that we are discouraged or cast down for we only want the proper *element* to act upon & we feel assured that we can produce the proper compound." Stout to Young, 16 May 1853, BYC 23:7. Might Stout have found his "proper compound" before sailing away after only fifty-six days in Hong Kong? Brooks, *The Diary of Hosea Stout,* 28 April–22 June 1853, 2:476–84.

[77]Huntington to Church Historian, 1 September 1856, Jared Farmer transcription. I have been unable to locate this item in BYC 58:15.

[78]Fabian, *The Skull Collectors,* 171, 199.

lay scattered about. The grave, "said to contain the body of a chief," also held fragments of a child's skeleton, "and tradition states that a captive boy was buried alive at this place."[79]

Charles Kelly visited the site in 1946 with Kaibab guide Joe Pickavit. "White ghouls had removed everything—bones, clothing, rifles and all the other goods buried with the chief," Kelly wrote. "We did not even find a loose bead." Pickavit thought the grave was looted about 1909 but denied knowing who did it.[80]

Two years after the Wheeler desecration, Millard Stake president Thomas Callister described the consequences to Brigham Young, who wrote, "have those bones brought back" on the letter.

THOMAS CALLISTER TO BRIGHAM YOUNG, 18 AUGUST 1874, BYC 35:4.

Fillmore City, Aug 18// 1874

Pres. B. Young,
Dear Bro:

. . . . Kanosh and his Indians are very much exasperated, they have just learned that some of the men composing the Wheeler Expedition took from their burial place at the mouth of Walker's Kanyon the skull and other bones of two indians one supposed to be the remains of the Ute Chief Walker, but upon examining the burial place by Kanosh and his chiefs and some of our people, they find that Walkers bones are not disturbed but the skull and bones of Shot a half brother of Kanosh's and also the skull and bones of Kanosh's son were taken.

The party that took them supposed they had Walker's bones and I hear has exhibited them in the City of Washington as such. Kanosh has been to see me to-day terribly enraged at the wanton sacrilege of his dead, and although we have known him as a man of peace for over a quarter of a century he and his warriors are fired with revenge, and it took what little influence I had to have them keep cool till this matter is thoroughly investigated, we shall hunt up all the evidence that can be found in this case. I am satisfied had we not held a controlling influence over Kanosh and his men, that the warwhoop and the scalping-knife would have been heard and used in our defenceless towns, as the result of this dastardly act.

Respectfully Your Brother,
Thos. Callister

P.S. I have just learned who went with the men of this expedition to the burying place and paid him a sum of money to show them Walker's grave which he supposed he had done.

---

[79] Yarrow, *Mortuary Customs among the North American Indians*, 48–49.
[80] Kelly, "We Found the Grave," 19.

SALLY AND KANOSH

At Pedro Luján's 1852 trial, Brigham Young told of an "Indian in this territory by the name of Baptiste," a Ute slaver who had "followed this business
ever since I have resided in this Territory, of trading for Indian children."

> In the fall of 1847, after we came here, he, Batiste, brought in our Fort a
> young Indian boy and Squaw, that he had stolen in Beaver Valley, from a
> tribe called the Pi-Band; the boy about 16 years old and the girl about 18, as
> near as we could judge. He offered them for sale. The people refused to buy
> them. Batiste then told the whites if they would not buy them he should
> kill them. The whites, not believing his statement, still refused to purchase
> them. Batiste then took out his two prisoners to his camp, and killed the
> boy. He then returned to the Fort with the girl and offered her for sale.
> A young man by the name of Charles Decker (a son-in-law of mine) gave
> Batiste a gun for the girl. She has lived in my family ever since, has fared as
> my children and is as free.[81]

Legends swarmed around this child, including multiple origin stories.
Eliza Snow claimed her "Indian name was Pidash," but it was Kahpeputz.[82]
"She was the saddest-looking piece of humanity I have ever seen," John
R. Young recalled seventy-three years later in his colorful but unreliable
memoir. Wanship's band had lost two men in a fight, but had taken two
girls prisoner. They had killed one and were torturing the other. "They had
shingled her head with butcher knives and fire brands. All the fleshy parts
of her body, legs, and arms had been hacked with knives, then fire brands
had been stuck into the wounds. She was gaunt with hunger, and smeared
from head to foot with blood and ashes."[83] Her brother "gave" the child to
Clarissa Decker, Brigham Young's fourth wife, and she became known Sall
or Sally. Her tribal association is lost: Eliza Snow recalled Sally was "of the
Pibandy Tribe" whose cruel step-father sold her into captivity, while Susa
Young Gates identified her as a Bannock prisoner.

Zina Diantha Huntington Jacobs Smith Young's name reveals her marriages,
but when the spirit moved her to bless several of her sister wives in June 1849,
she noticed "Sall (the Lamanite that Charles Decker brought) was setting by":

> I lade my hands uppon her hed and my language changed in a moment and
> when I had finished she said she understood every word. I had talked in her
> mother tongue. The speret bore testimony but there was positive proof that

---

[81]Jones, *The Trial of Don Pedro León Luján*, 69, 125–26.
[82]Lyman, "Chief Kanosh," 192, 199.
[83]Beecher, *Personal Writings*, 31; Turner, *Brigham Young*, 215; Young, *Memoirs of John R. Young*, 62.

could not be denied. I told her that her mother and sisters ware coming, and She must be a good girl. It was to her understanding it was a great cross but the Lord crowned it with joy for which I fee[l] to praise his name.[84]

Eliza Snow said she shared "mutual care and cultivation" of Sally with Clarissa and recalled spending a wet night in Salt Lake's old fort "reflecting the ludicrous scene" under a "fully saturated" flat dirt roof when "the storm was much worse inside than out." Sally being "asleep on the floor, altogether made the situation rather romantic." At first the captive "cronched bones like a dog," but "very soon became disgusted with her native habits,—became neat and tasteful in dress, and delicate in appetite. . . . She proved to be a good, virtuous woman, and died beloved by all who knew her."[85]

Despite Brigham Young's testimony in 1852, "Sally ultimately did not live as Young's other children," John Turner observed. She was listed in the 1860 census with the female household help.[86] That September Young told a visitor:

it would be cheaper to feed them [the Indians] on fine flour and beef by one fourth than to fight them. Mr. Ruth enquired if it was difficult to rear Indian children. The President said it was. I have an Indian woman who assists in the house Keeping, and is an excellent hand at that work. I obtained her when a child. At first she slept outside, and preferred the meal [meat?] she gathered from the gutters instead of good fried beef, but she is ready to vomit now at the recollection of her former habits.[87]

As early as 1856, Kanosh wanted "to have a talk with Sally" before he returned to his home near Fillmore. D. B. Huntington married the couple at Clara Young's residence on 8 June 1877; the surviving portrait of Kahpeputz may date from this event.[88] She did not join a happy family: the Pahvants allegedly killed Kanosh's first wife after she became insane; his wife Betsykin killed his wife Mary Voreas and then agreed to starve herself to death. John R. Young retailed the tale that Sally was the murdered wife, but he seems to have been misled.[89]

"Sally Kanosh died at 10 o'clock A.M., yesterday December 9th, at the house recently put up at the Indian Farm, and was buried today in the temple clothes presented to her by the late president Brigham Young," George

[84]Bradley and Woodward, *Four Zinas*, 181.

[85]Beecher, *The Personal Writings of Eliza Roxcy Snow*, 30–31.

[86]Turner, *Brigham Young*, 216.

[87]Brigham Young Office Journal, 28 September 1860, 153, BYC.

[88]Huntington to Young, 21 August 1856, Incoming Correspondence, BYC 24:22; Marriage Certificates, Salt Lake County, 1876–1879, CR 100 1:4, LDS Archives.

[89]Carter, *Heart Throbs of the West*, 1:100–102.

Crane reported in 1878. "Quite a number of brethren turned out with teams to conduct the funeral," where leading local churchmen conducted the solemn and peaceful service. "The faithful old chief, Kanosh, was deeply moved at the respect shown to his dead wife." She had been "aware of the near approach of death" for several days. "Beneath that tawney skin was a faith, intelligence, and virtue that would do honor to millions with a paler face," Crane concluded.[90]

Kanosh died about sundown on 4 December 1884. Four years earlier, he had mourned the death of a Mormon friend:

> I behold before me my much beloved friend, Bishop Callister. Have known for some time past that he was sick, have been anxious to see him oftener than I have. I had hoped he would get well again and to die. Now I see him dead before me. You all behold him, the young, the old, the young men and the young women. Like President Young, Kimball, George A. and others he has gone and left us, the beloved of my nation and myself in Council. Now as the generation what will become of us? The great men who have always been our best friends have gone to the spirit world and left us here behind. From them we received words of counsel and comfort. They have supplied our wants, food, clothing, and have never turned us away destitute. We ask, to whom shall we look for comfort protection? Like these of our white friends those of my nation are passing away. Among the many good and leading men of my people I am the only one now left. How long I will remain I cannot tell, and my heart aches within me and my spirit mourns and weeps. While I live I shall try to do all the good I can. I shall live to cherish in memory all the counsel and advice of those who have gone to the spirit world. Although our bodies are laid in the lonesome grave, I believe that our spirits yet live, that they go to the Great Father where all is peace and no sorrow, that our mourning days will be past and in time we will return and receive our babies which we have left, that we will raise up and live, that we will meet all our friends and kindred never to be parted again by death it will be time of rejoicing for all the nations and people who have done right here on earth. Amen.[91]

---

[90]"Funeral of a Lamanite," *Deseret News*, 18 December 1878, 768/1.

[91]Carter, *Heart Throbs of the West*, 1:102. Caroline Callister's scrapbook apparently has a typescript of these remarks. See MS 12282, LDS Archives.

Chapter 8

THE DEVIL WILL RAGE
Millennial Dreams, Ute Resistance,
1854–1856

A fter Wakara's death, nature and politics challenged the lives of Great Basin peoples: drought devastated traditional Native food sources and complicated the Latter-day Saint struggle to adapt their alien farming culture to the arid West. For two years both Mormons and Indians battled locusts, repeated crop failures, and famine. The general privation put a sharp edge on relations with tribes determined to defend their remaining land and resources from destruction. Typically, as the crisis intensified, Brigham Young responded aggressively, saying, "The key was turned, the Gospel should be sent to the lost sheep of the House of Israel," so he called "a good many Elders" as missionaries "to the House of Joseph."[1]

This contradicted Young's stated Indian policy: "This present race of Indians will never be converted. It mattereth not whether they kill one another off or Some body else do it & as for our sending Missionaries among them to convert them, it is of no use." Thomas D. Brown recorded Young telling Southern Indian missionaries, "the day has come to turn the key of the Gospel against the Gentiles, and open it to the remnants of Israel."[2] The signs and portents that the Mormon prophet, seer, and revelator relied on convinced Young that his sanctified Saints and a united Israel would compel the Lord to begin the Second Coming.

Determined to "sanctify Israel" and build an army to handle the violent onset of the millennium, the Indians were essential to this process: the Lord had sent "our brethren, the Lamanites, to chasten this people," Young said

---

[1] Joseph Lee Robinson, Journal, 6 April 1855, Utah State Historical Society.
[2] Brown, *Journal of the Southern Indian Mission*, 21 April 1855, 123.

as the war on Wakara began. "They will purify and sanctify the Saints, and prepare the wicked for their doom."[3] Young poured energy and scarce resources into building the Nauvoo Legion, which effectively served as his private army. He sent many of its senior officers to Great Britain as recruiting officers "to select chosen battalions."[4] He simultaneously launched aggressive missions to persuade Zion's divided tribes to join the Kingdom of God, become one nation in a day, and forge the Lord's battle-ax.

Another round of federal officials arrived in 1855. Only thirty-six days after leaving Independence, Indian Agent Garland Hurt appeared in Salt Lake on 5 February. A southerner, Doctor Hurt believed the inferiority of the colored races was "a fixed and demonstrable fact," which made "the idea of their future elevation to an equality with the Caucasian race utterly preposterous."[5] George W. Armstrong, a Mormon, began work as northern Utah's "Indian Sub Agent" in April. David H. Burr, Utah's first surveyor general, reached Salt Lake on 27 July 1855.[6]

"Elders in the Mountains are appointed missions to the Lamanites with Muskets, yawgers & good rifles as their mouth pieces," wrote Andrew Love as the war on Wakara began.[7] Although war prioritized eliminating Indians over evangelizing them, it merely delayed Young's commitment to fulfilling Joseph Smith's vision, which made it essential to unite *"all Israel"* to *"carry on the work of the last days."*[8] Young's militaristic millennial effort to forge alliances with the Lamanites conflicted with his federal duties as Indian superintendent, but the prophet, seer, and revelator's faith never wavered—and he used his power to prepare his people for the imminent apocalypse. He strove to boost his Kingdom's population and military power, secure the loyalty of the Lamanites, and bind the Latter-day Saint people to his theocracy.

Mormon leaders in Europe used scorching metaphors to describe the swift approach of the Last Days. Smith's 1843 polygamy revelation was "one of the firebrands which the Lord is throwing out in these last days to set the world on fire, in order to burn up the moral filth and impurities." As drought ravaged Utah in 1855, real fires raged: "almost all of our kanyons, north and south, have been burned, some by the Indians, and some by the carelessness

---

[3] *Journal of Discourses*, 1:162.
[4] Kimball to Smith, 23 September 1854, George A. Smith Papers.
[5] Hurt, "Indians of Utah," in Simpson, *Report*, 457–64.
[6] Neff, *History of Utah*, 679.
[7] Love, Diary, 16 July 1853, 25.
[8] Brigham Young to Andrew Cunningham, 4 August 1857, BYC 18:6.

of the whites," complained Heber C. Kimball.[9] The Utes explained the "very destructive fire in our pinerry [pinery]" that burned for several days to Nephi's Andrew Love. "The Indians states that the Mormons cut their timber & use it & pay them nothing for it, & they prefer burning it up rather than let us use it, so the devil will rage in the hearts of the children of men as long as he can."[10]

On Mormonism's twenty-fifth anniversary, 6 April 1855, Young reinforced Fort Supply and sent missionaries to every point of the compass: west to Carson Valley in today's Nevada; north to establish Fort Limhi on the Salmon River, now in Idaho; south to Las Vegas on the California road; and east to the Elk Mountains, now the La Sal Range that towers above Moab. He even dispatched a dozen missionaries to the central Great Basin to seek a refuge in the "White Mountains." They found Crystal Peak in the Wah Wah Range on today's Utah-Nevada border, but concluded the desolate region could support few settlers.[11]

For the first time, the tribes effectively halted the invasion: The Utes attacked the Elk Mountain Mission in September, and none of the 1855 missions lasted three years. Native peoples familiar with Young's millennial vision and expansive ambitions did not rush to the Kingdom of God's standard. They understood what was happening to them: "That's why the white people took everything away from the Indian; because they were snakes," said the Northern Paiutes, and they "told the Indians to go way out in the mountains and live."[12] As hard times intensified the struggle for resources in 1855 and 1856, Utes and Shoshones fought back and briefly turned the Mormon tide.

To Recruit the Army of Our God: Militant Missions

During the mid-1850s Mormons worked to transform American Indians from military targets into allies. On 4 October 1853 the First Presidency met with eight apostles in Brigham Young's office. Orson Hyde "opened on the subject of sending missionaries among the Indians, & marry wives in different tribes." Young ordered "20 or 30 men to go to Green River" with Hyde. Next spring

---

[9]*Millennial Star,* 17 November 1855, 730–31.

[10]Love, Diary, 26 July 1855, 80.

[11]Stott, *Search for Sanctuary,* 14–16.

[12]"White Men are Snakes," in Ramsey, *Coyote Was Going There,* 258.

Young wanted to send missionaries to the Potawatomi, Cherokee, Chocktaw, Sioux, Crow, and Blackfeet nations—and "instruct them in private," he said, aware of the suspicions this would raise. "All the tribes North and South are ready, & want to have us among them." Young expanded on the policy he first announced in 1847: Antaro of the Yampa Utes "wants us to marry with them. Suppose 20 or 30 men marry it will bring all the influence of the tribes. The squaws will work & then the Indians will work. It is our duty to do it to send missionaries to the House of Israel." He "never said go boys but come boys marry chiefs daughters," so which apostles would set the example? he asked. Parley Pratt volunteered, "I am on hand." Hyde promised he would go to "Green River or any other place." "The time has come," the prophet concluded. "I will go," Young promised—if the apostles could find a man to preside in his place. "I say turn to the House of Israel now."[13] As general conference ended five days later, Mormon leaders called more than ninety men to go with Hyde and John Nebeker to Green River.

"The duties of the Missionaries here is to save the remnants of Israel. God planted us here in the valleys of Ephraim, we have been brought to these valleys for a good purpose, to save Israel," Young explained in 1854. "The white men of the east have driven the red men west, and those farther west, are driving them east, and here will be a center. His hand is in all their movements; our duty is to be diligent in saving Israel; if we are not faithful, we will be removed and others placed in our stead."[14] In April 1855 the Saints "never had a Better Conference," Wilford Woodruff reported. "About 160 men were appointed missions mostly to the Lamanites." A year later, he helped bless "115 Missionaries who were appointed to go on Missions to the Lamanites & Gentiles."[15]

Indian missions were only one aspect of Brigham Young's campaign to revolutionize the world. Another was building Mormon military power. "Professor" Uriah Brown, a Nauvoo Council of Fifty veteran, came to Utah in 1851 to sell his "invention of liquid fire to destroy an army & navy"—a weapon useless in Indian warfare. Simultaneously, Daniel Wells asked Samuel Colt about his "most powerful, sophisticated, scope-equipped weapons" and arms "suited to mountain warfare."[16]

[13]General Church Minutes, 4 October 1853, BYC 72:2.
[14]General Church Minutes, 19 May 1854, BYC 72:2.
[15]Woodruff, *Journal*, 8 April 1855, 4:314; 6 April 1856, 4:408.
[16]MacKinnon, *At Sword's Point*, 1:45–46.

"Cannot the 30,000 British Saints do a great deal more than they are now doing to prepare the minds of those of whom is the kingdom of heaven, to become valiant soldiers of that kingdom?" Samuel Richards asked in January 1854. "Depend upon it, on this earth, there is a struggle yet to come, or rather to be concluded, between the kingdom of God and the kingdom of Satan, in which the rising generation will act a most conspicuous part."[17] Apostle and Nauvoo Legion general Franklin D. Richards took command of the faith's European Mission that spring, along with veterans of mountain warfare who were now assigned recruiting duty. Artist William Warner Major soon had "the pleasure to Baptise every week many promising Soldiers. The devil [is] Raging and firing of his Big Guns which I love to hear as it shows he is alarmed, and uneasy, & I hope while he is unbound he ever will be alarmed and do his Best while we are Close by," he wrote. "I don't care How hot the fight is or how close for I know that our weapons are all mighty, all powerful, and the Stronger the enemy the more honor to overcome."[18] After Major died in September 1854, Lt. Col. William H. Kimball described his new mission to his former commanding officer.

WILLIAM KIMBALL, "MISSION ON THE BRITISH ISLES,"
DESERET NEWS, 7 DECEMBER 1854, 2/1–2.

Canterbury, Sep. 23, 1854

Colonel Geo. A. Smith:—

Agreeably to "Order No. 1." I hasten to report a few circumstances which may interest you.

While reading your letter of 19th April to Brother F. D. Richards, it brought fresh to my mind many circumstances which transpired about a year ago, in our arduous but agreeable campaign in the southern part of the territory—suppressing Indian hostilities—engineering—surveying, and locating "forts," and barricades for the protection of the Saints in the more thinly populated portion of the Territory. What a contrast! A year ago I was under military orders in company with yourself; now under ecclesiastical. At that time my brain was racked because of my inability to command such an interesting body of men, and execute orders satisfactory to myself, and those of my superiors, for the protection of those under command. Now I know my inability to perform my numerous duties—commanding upwards of 4,000 sterling volunteers, still enlisting for the great conflict. I feel like the 'Indian hunter' when he expresses himself by saying, 'O give me back my mountain home.' When I was upon my saddle, by the side of those tried

[17]"Home Intelligence," Millennial Star, January 21, 1854, 40.
[18]Major to Young, 7 June 1854, BYC 23:15.

ones, whether suppressing the incursions of the savage, white or red; scaling mountains; bringing offenders to justice, or on parade, or whatever the duties might have been, I find that I was at home.

However, with Generals, Colonels, Captains, Lieutenants, Sergeants, not forgetting Majors, and all recruiting officers sent out to enlist volunteers, we hope to select chosen battalions of sterling soldiers, and march them safely to Zions' standard, there to defend virtue, truth, & genuine liberty.

Our drill is somewhat different now, yet under the same King and Commander; but I find the tactics every different and much more difficult; still, they can be learnt, which is a consolation.

I have to thank the Lord that our worthy chaplain "in arms" is now our dictator and dictated by that same Spirit that he prayed for when we were in action that his knowledge wisdom and inspiration be on us and now on him, F. D. Richards, and furthermore I have "commissions" and "non-commissions" whose motto is "Is the will of God, and his banner display. . . ."

GARLAND HURT:
TO PRESERVE PEACE ON THE FRONTIERS

"Medical men are generally good talkers and good observers," observed Jules Remy after meeting Garland Hurt. These qualities imparted "zest to the animated sketches he gave us of the habits of the savage tribes with which he was, by his position, brought into daily contact." Hurt described "the diplomatic stratagems to which he was obliged to have recourse in dealing with these children of nature, of their deep sense of justice, of their pride, of their dignified bearing of solemn occasions, of the punctilious feeling of their chiefs, of their orations, grave, sensible, and sometimes rising to a very noble pitch, and of their stern virtues and their fierce instincts."[19] One of Hurt's first letters—to Commissioner George W. Manypenny—warned about the character of Indian missionaries but cautioned against exciting prejudice against the Latter-day Saints, who thrived on persecution.

HURT TO MANYPENNY, 2 MAY 1855, U.S. HOUSE,
THE UTAH EXPEDITION, SERIAL 956, 176–77.

Great Salt Lake City, U. T.,
May 2, 1855

Sir: Permit me to call your attention to some facts which I do not feel myself altogether at liberty to remain silent upon.

At the last semi-annual conference of the Latter Day Saints a large number

---

[19]Remy, *A Journey to Great-Salt-Lake City*, 2:285–86.

of missionaries were nominated to go and preach to the Indians, or Lamanites, as they are here called. Now, since my arrival in this Territory, I have become satisfied that these saints have, either accidentally or purposely, created a distinction, in the minds of the Indian tribes of this Territory, between the Mormons and the people of the United States, that cannot act otherwise than prejudicial to the latter. And what, sir, may we expect of these missionaries? There is perhaps not a tribe on the continent that will not be visited by one or more of them. I suspect their first object will be to teach these wretched savages that they are the rightful owners of the American soil, and that it has been wrongfully taken from them by the whites, and that the Great Spirit had sent the Mormons among them to help them recover their rights.

The character of many of those who have been nominated is calculated to confirm this view of the case. They embrace a class of rude and lawless young men, such as might be regarded as a curse to any civilized community. But I do not wish to excite prejudice or encourage feelings of hostility against these people. On the contrary, I think such a course would be unwise and impolitic. They always have and ever will thrive by persecution. They know well the effect it has had upon them, and, consequently, crave to be persecuted. It is due to many of them, however, to say that they are honest in the belief that they are the only Christians on earth, and that God is about to redeem the world from sin and establish His millennium. It is possible, too, that many of them are loyal in their feelings to the United States, but, perhaps, this cannot be said of many of their leaders. But time will convince many of them of their errors; many of their prophecies must come true in a few years, or doubt will take the place of sanguine hope, and will do more to relax their energies and weaken their strength than anything else could do at this time.

My object is writing is to suggest that the attention of all superintendents, agents, and sub-agents, and all other loyal citizens residing or sojourning in the Indian country, be called to this subject, that the conduct of these Mormon missionaries be subjected to the strictest scrutiny, and that the thirteenth and fourteenth sections of the *"Act to regulate trade and intercourse with the Indian tribes, and to preserve peace on the frontiers,"* be properly enforced.

Very respectfully, &c.,

Garland Hurt
Indian Agent for Utah.

Hon. Geo. W. Manypenny,
Commissioner of Indian Affairs, Washington, D.C.

P.S.—In proof of the facts before stated, I would say that I have had great difficulty in procuring an interpreter, though there are many persons in the Territory who speak the Indian language, but they were all nominated as missionaries, and I was forced to the humiliating necessity of imploring the clemency of his excellency Brigham Young to permit one of them to remain with me. I never saw any people in my life who were so completely under the influence of one man.

Hurt might seem to be exaggerating the extent of Mormonism's efforts to evangelize Indian nations, but in 1913 Mormon historian Andrew Jenson celebrated the "many Elders of the Church [who] responded to calls from the Church authorities." He listed "special missions among the Indians" to Delaware, Pottawattamie, Omaha, Pawnee, Ponca, Southern Paiute, Blackfoot, Bannock, Hopi, Navajo, Papago, and Maricopa peoples.[20]

STRONGHOLDS OF THE GADIANTON BAND: NAVAJO MISSION, 1854

"Trade is the best letter of introduction a white man can take among Indians," wrote William D. Huntington.[21] Despite Young's instructions to dedicate themselves to their Lamanite flock, it is often hard to tell if the main motivation of Mormonism's Indian evangelists was religion or commerce. For Natives, trade was always at the center of their relations with Europeans, and trade was often the primary concern of Latter-day missionaries. In October 1854 Brigham Young issued Huntington a permit "to trade with the Utah, and other friendly tribes of Indians, southeast of G.S. Lake City."[22] After conference, Young directed his company "to open an intercourse with a tribe of Indians hitherto but little known to us or any other white men . . . a settled tribe of Indians occupying the same land from year to year, having fixed abodes." He probably referred to the Navajo or Moqui—the Hopi—but he might have hoped the traders would find Welsh white Indians who were "more peaceable and quiet and nearer approach to civilization than those in our midst who are indolent and seemingly use no bodily exertion for a subsistence." Young held the missionaries to high standards: "Teach them also morality both by precept and example; permit no fraud to be used in the transaction of business among them nor the use of any improper language. Do not let the love of money or property swerve you from doing right."[23]

Huntington left Springville in October "with eleven whitemen and one Indian," who was named Sun Cloud but better known as High Forehead, to explore southern Utah and "trade with the Navijos for sheep, goats, and horses." The Dine, "quite a manufacturing people," worked "iron, gold, and

---

[20]Jenson, "The Elk Mountain Mission," 188.

[21]Huntington, "Interesting Account," *Deseret News,* 28 December 1854, 3:2.

[22]Young, 5 October 1854, Gubernatorial Letterbook, BYC 162.

[23]Young to Huntingdon [*sic*] Company, 9 October 1854, BYC Letterbook 1:706–708.

silver into a multitude of forms and articles for the warrior, husbandman, and tradesman." Huntington claimed his party defied "Indian Walker and his allies"—twenty Spaniards—and crossed the "wild, mountainous, and dreary desert." Their five wagons followed Gunnison's trace to Green River and the Spanish Trail to the Colorado River and a "beautiful valley" with good soil, grazing, timber, and water some "50 miles from the Elk Mountain," the dozen 12,000-feet-plus peaks now known as the La Sal Mountains.[24] They "were many times compelled to take their wagons apart and lift them piece by piece up the perpendicular sides of the cliffs, leading their animals by circuitous and dangerous paths to the heights above, until the wagons could be taken no farther."[25]

The explorers continued south from Spanish Valley, crossed "St. John's River" (today's San Juan), and visited a Navajo village near Chinle Wash. The Navajos were "at war with the whites, and three days before we arrived, had killed, boiled, and eaten a white man"—an unlikely tale. The Mormons "did some trading with them, while they were doing some tall stealing from us," Huntington reported. The Navajo "were highly excited, but the chiefs were more cool, appeared quite friendly, and wished us to come again and trade." (Mormon Dennison Harris's family traditions claimed "a company of Elk Mountain Utes" under Sheberetch headman Quitsubsocketts "came up with guns leveled at the head of the Navajo chief" and saved the Mormon venture.) The Navajo "great captain," perhaps Hastiin Ch, for "he did not want to fight us." He traded "corn, meal, flour, bread, beans, dried pumpkin, dried squash, pine nuts, with sheep and goat meat of the fatest [sic] quality to fit us out for our journey home."[26]

The traders turned northwest on what was essentially "a road from nowhere to nowhere." They visited the ancestral Puebloan ruins at Hovenweep and Canyons of the Ancients national monuments, perhaps searching for an imaginary tribe of Welshmen. Their Native guides told the traders they "had heard that a *very long time ago* there was water running there. We asked them who built those houses. [They] smiled and shook their heads and said they never heard, but surely somebody built them a *very long time* back." The Saints were certain that "the ancient possessors of those strongholds

[24]Blanchard, *Going to My Grave*, 193; Huntington, "Interesting Account," *Deseret News*, 28 December 1854, 3:2.

[25]Johnson, *A Brief History of Springville*, 25.

[26]Huntington, "Interesting Account," *Deseret News*, 28 December 1854, 3:2–3.

were robbers of the Gadianton Band,"[27] infamous *Book of Mormon* "murderers and plunderers" consisting of Nephites and "the more wicked part of the Lamanites."[28]

MARTYRS IN THE CAUSE OF OUR GOD:
THE ELK MOUNTAIN MISSION

With many others, in April 1855 O. B. Huntington "was appointed by a vote of the General Conference to go on a mission to Israel—or the indians." Missions "were appointed to different Tribes" across the United States. Authorities set apart some forty men "to go to the Elk Mountain Mission on or near Grand River[29] in the South of Utah Territory among the Utah Indians to make a Fort and open the way for a settlement." They also sent thirty men to establish an outpost on the southern road to California at "Vagos Spring," today's Las Vegas.[30]

Forty years later, Oliver Huntington recalled President Young's instructions "to avoid difficulties with the Indians and to lead them to live better lives by cultivating the earth." Young ordered, "Take no trade with you for Indians. Go among them to elevate them, and not to degrade or rob them. Trading with Indians is liable to make trouble."[31] Indians wanted to acquire spiritual power, but goods and gifts were essential to establish relations with the tribes, so the missionaries set out well stocked with firearms, ammunition, and trinkets. Huntington described the "trade business" to his brother Dimick: about a quarter of the "mostly inexperienced boys" sent to "this old country just being newly settled" ignored "Brigham's council" and made it "a trading mission," which "set the balance in a stew to trade." Oliver asked Dimick to get his son Allen "a License or a Permit to trade with the Indians," as "the easiest & best way to get along without trouble." Even without a permit, Allen would manage "in a roundabout way." Oliver added, "We care not so much about trade as we hate to be put in a kennel."[32]

---

[27]Much of this detail comes from chapter 12 of Mark Blanchard's excellent *Going to My Grave: The Life and Mysterious Disappearance of the Mormon Scout Levi Gregory Metcalf*, 227–54.

[28]*Book of Mormon*, Helaman, 6:18.

[29]The Colorado River above its confluence with Green River was officially known as the Grand River until 1921 when Congress changed the name to Colorado.

[30]O. B. Huntington, Diary and Reminiscences, 6 April 1855, BYU Library, 11:70.

[31]Huntington, "Elk Mountain Mission," *Juvenile Instructor*, 1 April 1895, 255.

[32]Oliver Huntington to Brother Dimick, 16 July 1855, BYC 24:5.

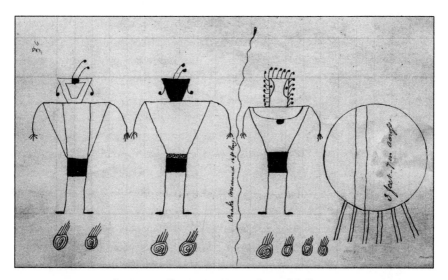

SKETCHED PICTOGLYPHS BY JOHN MCEWAN
On his journey to Elk Mountain in 1855, Indian missionary John McEwan sketched
these pictoglyphs. They can still be seen in Salina Canyon across the highway
from a rest stop on Interstate 70. *Courtesy L. Tom Perry Special Collections, Harold B.
Lee Library, Brigham Young University, Provo, Utah.*

The missionaries left vivid descriptions of the "crooked and sandy"
Gunnison and Spanish trails they followed. Their guide, apparently High
Forehead, showed them pictographs in Salina Canyon, "but that no one
knew how or when it came there." Late on 10 June the entrepreneurial
evangelists reached the Colorado. While moving their cattle across the river,
they met their new neighbors, and on 22 June "Some Ute Indians came to
camp, having swam the river, and in a hurry called for help to take their
families over, as the Snake Indians were pursuing them." Clark Huntington
ferried them in the mission's boat-wagon. The next day, Sunday, "Meeting
was called and the Indians invited. They came, and the Spirit of God was
poured out upon all alike. They were anxious to become as we were, live
with us and do as we did. The spirit of our work seemed to be in them
already."[33] Ethan Pettit noted, "Indian Chief Shorivornoup and five of his
band" attended the service.[34]

[33]Jenson, quoting O. B. Huntington Journal, "The Elk Mountain Mission," 196.
[34]Pettit, Diary, 24 June 1855, MS 419:2, LDS Archives.

On 30 June "the chief of all the Indians in that region came into our camp and three or four of his principal men with him," Oliver Huntington recalled. Known to the whites as St. John, his "Indian name was Quitchup-Sockets. He was a small man, perhaps five feet six inches high, not given to much talk, and was pleased to see us, and more pleased that we had come to stay and teach them how to live by work. He was willing to divide with us the little good land that he had, but he wanted some nice presents as a token of friendship from us, which would show also that we appreciated his surrender of a portion of his land." President Alfred N. Billings tried to pawn off ragged shirts, cheap butcher knives, and mirrors on Quitsubsocketts, but this was not his first trading session. He declined to be swindled and "sat down on a log in sulky silence." Billings asked what was wrong. "The chief got angry, and said that we had come to rob them of their land and run off their game; that the first thing we did was to lie to him; that they wanted new shirts and the interpreter told him he had none. He knew we had new shirts, for he saw a box full of good new ones." Billings asked interpreter Allen Huntington, "a natural diplomat as well as warrior," to "appease the anger of the Big-Little Chief." He sat beside Quitsubsocketts "and remained a long time silent. Finally he got the eye of the chief, and they gazed a moment at each other and 'talked with their eyes.'" The Ute asked a simple question to break the ice. When they finished talking, "Allen called for a lot of presents." The missionaries spread new white blankets on the ground, and piled on gifts for each Ute: "a good new shirt, lots of tobacco, red paint, a butcher knife for each, and I can't tell all," O.B. recalled. They gave Quitsubsocketts "a powder horn with a looking-glass in the bottom"—he looked into the horn and laughed. "Besides that was given him a pound or two of powder, lead and caps to go with it." This "mended matters with the Indians for a time," but exposed the "stock of trade that we were forbidden to bring."[35]

William B. Pace's contemporary journal painted a vivid portrait of the Sheberetch shaman.

> Finished the corrall in the afternoon. The Elk Mountain Chief (i.e Quit-sub-socketts alias St. John) with three or four of his Men Came down to see what was the Matter in the North end of the valley as he said he had seen great smokes (from the boys burning sage) but did not Know we were there until he came in sight of the waggons. After some Little conversation between himself & the Interpreters as to our Business their [sic] on his domains &c.

---

[35]Huntington, "Elk Mountain Mission," *Juvenile Instructor* (1 May 1895), 279–80.

He expressed himself as well satisfied & said we were welcom to a share of his country, but that we were the first white men or red that he had ever [been] given any Privileges to stop on his Premises any longer than they had time to get away—but said I had a dream the other night & I saw the Mormons coming here to live on My land & I got my men to gather & was agoing to drive them off, but the Great Spirit tole Me to Let the Mormons alone that we must be good friends & not fight anymore—& from that he said he [k] new it was good for us to be there. That he wanted us to learn his boys how to Plow raise grain & work like we did &c.[36]

One Mormon thought Quitsubsocketts had "1000 men under his Command."

JOHN McEWAN, ELK MOUNTAIN DIARY, 1855, MSS 1051, 53–54, BYU LIBRARY.

In the afternoon an indian chief by the name of Cuts-sub-soc-its and 4 of his band arrived in Camp, they had a few skins to trade. The corn at the head of this valley belongs to him, he is the same that rescued brother Metcalf from being killed by the Navihoes. We told them our business &c they appeared friendly and satisfied.

July 1st Sunday
    The chief this morning acknowledged that he had dreamed several times of our Coming and being on the road, and it was impressed upon him to live and be at peace with us; thus we see the fulfillment of the sayings and prophecies of the Servants of God Verified unto us, which they told us previous to our departure on our Mission. After breakfast some 4 of the boys left in Company with the indians to the upper end of the valley, and assisted them to irrigate their corn &c. . . . at dark the boys returned and reported that the corn was breast high and topped out. Vines looked well &c. about two weeks ago the corn was only from 8 to 10 inches high on an Average.

What the missionaries heard often had less to do with what the Utes said than with what the Saints wanted to hear. They spent the summer planting, cultivating, and irrigating crops; built a stone fort and log corral; and handled the "many Indians who came to trade." Virtually every Ute band visited the new settlement on their annual rounds, where Mormon elders baptized men, women, and boys, sometimes conferring their Aaronic and Melchizedek priesthoods on the men. Billings baptized at least fourteen Utes in the Colorado on 22 July, and the Mormons ordained "Capt" Conarowats, Shettoaquon, Suppachinpooni, and Showeshint as elders, giving them the "mormon names" Nephi, Lehi, Samuel, and James.[37] They baptized about

[36]Pace, Journal, 30 June 1855, MS 10424, LDS Archives, 21–22.
[37]Pettit, Diary, 22 July 1855, LDS Archives.

fifteen Uncompaghres from the central Rockies that summer and held meetings where "a good spirit was manifested, and at which some of the Indians spoke."[38]

On returning from his annual expedition to the Navajos, Arapene delivered a letter from the busy Spanish Trail crossroads to Brigham Young. Not surprisingly, the Elk Mountain Mission's leaders painted a sunny portrait of "the condition of affairs in this region" and the blessings that "attended us both in our journeyings & our labours here to an almost astonishing degree. We are all snugly stowed in stone houses inside our stone fort. The finishing job of our fortification is the gates which are now in operation."

> Our Corn & vines look excellent—vines in full blossom—Corn beginning to tassle. Wheat looks well but much of it has been eaten of[f] twice or 3 times by our own & Indian horses. The health of the company is good without exception. Our Valley swarms with Natives from every direction, for the news of our arrival & business has run like fire & as fast as they get the word they run to see—& make friends. All are friendly, & fifteen have been baptised of the Taby-wats, living on the otherside of the Mountains.

The missionaries considered most of their neighbors "to be more honest, honorable & manlike than any we have yet been acquainted with." Arapene had done "much good & very essential service to the work. He has preached and taught among his nation all the time—his labours have been unceasing by day & night." He had made peace with the "somewhat neat and comely" Navajos, enabled the Mormons to make "friendly arrangements" so the way was "open that we can go amo[n]g them, and for which they are anxious—In fact nearly every Band wants some Mormons to be sent to live with them for *they* have a better valley than *this*." The missionaries had "killed an ox upon their arrival for the entire benefit of our Red Brethren." Now "Peace prevails universally."[39]

Messages inevitably crossed during the two weeks it took letters to travel the 240 miles between Salt Lake and Moab. Having received reports from "the boys of the Elk Mountain Mission" about "the warm reception of the Elders of Israel by the remnants of Joseph," Young believed the Lord was "pouring out his spirit upon them abundantly through visions & dreams thereby preparing their rude but honest hearts for receiving you and company" to "receive the Gospel of the Son of God, which is able to save them."

[38]Jenson, Huntington Diary, "The Elk Mountain Mission," 188.
[39]A. N. Billings, J. S. Rawlins, and O. B. Huntington to Brigham Young, 10 August 1855, BYC 29:19.

The Lamanites had extended "all the cordiality and sympathy that could be expected from the red men." Young hoped "the Elders will ever walk, and act before, and among them, in a manner so that the native confidence reposed may increase instead of diminishing, and that the scattered and peeled, and forlorn, sons of Jacob may begin to realize that the God in which their fathers trusted and obeyed is their friend if they Keep his commandments, and that the saints in very deed are their only true friends and brethren." When "trading with them, which you all have the privilege of doing as we do here, be strictly careful not to cheat or defraud them, but act towards them as you would wish them to act towards you under similar circumstances."

> I have a word of council to give in relation to this mission, and it is, to branch out, and scatter yourselves among them, go where they go and live with them, and among them, and prove to them by every act of your lives that you love them and that you live among them to benefit their condition by showing them how to live without fighting, and stealing from each other, and the white man.[40]

Young's contradictory policy, first banning and then encouraging trade and "going among the Indians," left Elk Mountain's missionaries confused. Billings warned Young that despite the "abundance of rain for the last 2 weeks," the mission's crops would "not realize more than a plenty for seed of corn, wheat, Buckwheat, Oats," and "rather slim" potatoes. "Indians continue very friendly and our acquaintance & friendship extends wider & wider every day," while the "health of the company is perfect." Joseph Rawlins would "make known more fully than I can write the necessities & wishes with regard to more Brethren being sent out here" and "making an appropriation for the benefit of the Indians who come to visite us."[41]

Meanwhile, Heber C. Kimball celebrated the mission's success:

> We have very favourable report of the Indians from Cache Valley and the regions round about. We have also news from the Alfred Billings company, that went to the Elk Mountain. They report very favourable; they had baptized fifteen, and the Indians were flocking to them in almost every direction. They had built a stone fort, and had also erected stone houses, and had all things comfortable for winter. . . . I can say that the whole world of Lamanites are peaceable with the "Mormons," very peaceable.[42]

---

[40]Young to Billings, 6 August 1855, BYC Letterbook 2:289–92.

[41]Billings to Young, 21 August 1855, BYC 25:19.

[42]"Deseret," Kimball to F. D. Richards, 31 August 1855, *Millennial Star*, 17 November 1855, 730–31.

Despite official optimism, the cultural gap between the Elk Mountain Utes and missionaries was vast. The Elk Mountain Lamanites did not remain peaceable after the missionaries built their stone fort and log corral, planted crops, and traded with all comers in the homeland of the Sheberetch Utes. Few desires better illustrate the divide separating Numic and European ways than human sexuality. In her 1937 folk history of Moab, Faun Tanner recounted this "interesting story" the missionaries told the Utes:

> they had come to live among them in peace, to be one with them, to work with them and marry. The Indians evidently took this literally and the next morning brought a number of young Indian girls to the fort, all dressed and painted in their best. They told the white men to take their choice. This resulted in some difficulty when the men could not accept the invitation and it was only through the influence and tact of the interpreter that trouble was averted.[43]

In September 1856 Dimick Huntington reported that "the Indians occasionally had what they called a whore dance, which was lewd and wrong." Brigham Young told him to "drive away the boys that congregated, round the Indians, and whip the Indians that they might desist from these dances and practices."[44] Blacksmith Sheldon Cutler described a similar fertility celebration in mid-July 1855 following a Sunday meeting when "quite a number of indians was present," including Arapene, on his way to trade with the Navajo. "They all feel firstrate and consider us their freinds. Aropine spoke much in our favor." Quitsubsocketts "came in while he was talking and also spoke good. We had a good meeting. The young men and girls held a dance here this evening such as I had never heard of before for the purpus of illicit intercours with each other."[45] These apparent references to the Bear Dance indicate that what the Utes considered natural, Mormons condemned as illicit. Cutler's ambiguous reference to "young men" did not indicate whether any missionaries joined the dance. Few of the Mormons were over thirty, so some of them probably had "illicit" liaisons with the only women available for hundreds of miles.

The mission's Indian business eventually overwhelmed whatever pious purposes the Mormons claimed. The missionaries may not have planned to trade, "yet we could get a horse or three or four fine buckskins for a little

---

[43]Firmage, *A History of Grand County,* 89.
[44]Brigham Young Office Journals, Excerpt, 8 September 1856, New Mormon Studies CD-ROM.
[45]Cutler, Elk Mountain Journal, 15 July 1855, 22–23.

ammunition, guns, clothing, or flour," so naturally they did "a great amount of trading with natives" for buckskins and horses, "so that nearly every man of us had a horse," Oliver Huntington recalled. The outpost soon "had a boom in trade, and it was all on our side, and we could see no end to it." They swapped so many "shirts, blankets, powder, lead, caps, and even guns," they "had parted with a great deal more than any reasonable men would have spared" and now "needed to go home to get a new supply of trade."[46] Over the summer, half the men left for home, ostensibly to deliver mail and visit families, but few returned.

What Ethan Pettit called "the riches of the Navajos" tempted those who stayed behind. As August ended, A. N. Billings & Company headed south with Shinobby ("Hiram"), "A good Indian for A guide," packing sixty-five buckskins, needles, thread, fishhooks and lines, files, awls, knives, hand-kerchiefs, gun tubes, powder, and some four thousand firing caps.[47] After spending a day among the Navajo, the missionaries returned with plunder but no converts.

During Billings's absence, William Sterrett recalled, "we baptised 18 more of the Natives" on 7 September.[48] On the 15th, an afternoon express arrived from Quitsubsocketts, "stating that he was very sick and requested some of us to come up and lay hands upon him." Six men "arrived at his camp a little after Sun down, we found him very sick," noted John McEwan, who asked a few questions, offered a healing prayer, and anointed the ailing Ute with oil. Then all six men "laid hands upon him in the name of the Lord." A Ute woman then "Commenced doctoring him, and two others joined in Singing, thence one Young Indian got up and danced with a Gun in his arms, flint lock a little powder in the pan. After a while he fired it off, this was to kill the devil or drive him away. They had a great many curious Manouvers and actions." The Mormons "repaired to the banks of Pack Saddle Creek where brother John Crawford offered up prayer. Thence returned to wick-i-up, found the chief sitting up and eating a little boiled Water Melon and Juice, he inquired if any of us wanted to eat some, it was the best he had, but none of us felt hungry." Three days later, "Two of the natives, viz Capruin and his wife came and requested hands laid upon them for their health."[49]

[46]Huntington, *Juvenile Instructor* (15 May 1895), 308.
[47]Pettit, Diary, August–September 1855, LDS Archives.
[48]Sterrett, Autobiography, MSS SC 879, BYU Library.
[49]McEwan, Elk Mountain Journal, 15, 18 September 1855, 90–92, 94.

Meanwhile, more men returned to the settlements. Many simply abandoned the mission, while others planned to return with a fresh stock of trade goods. William Sterrett summarized the tensions that exploded on the autumn equinox.

> We had our first new potatoes on the 20th. The Indians took a good portion of our vegitables, and some of them were getting rather saucy and mean. They had taken some of our horses and cattle also, besides taking our vegitation. Out of the 41 brethren of the mission there were only left at our fort 16 men. The rest had gone to the Settlements to see their families. On Saturday the 22nd two of the brethren went on to the Mountain to hunt sheep. William Buchanon [Behunin] and Edward Edwards, this was the last time we ever saw them. We concluded they were killed by the Indians as were heard seven shots fired on the mountain. The 23rd we changed our [cattle] heard around. This we done for fear that the Indians would steal them. However, about 8 or 10 of them came up to the fort and wanted to know why we changed our heard around. We tried to satisfy them by saying to get them on bunch grass, but they were mad and bent on mischief.[50]

John McEwan and Sheldon Cutler described what happened on 23 September:

> We changed our herd ground this morning being fearful that some of the Indians meant to do some mischief, by stealing or driving off some of our stock. About 10 O'clock A.M. 8 or 20 of them came across the River up to the Fort, they acted very rude and saucy, enquired why we had drove our stock on a new range &c. Some one or more of the boys went to loading their guns, but was discovered, they then drew in their horns and was more civil. Bro Wm H. Freeman overheard some of them talking, concocting a plan to get some of the cattle out of Corall to-night, this goes to verify our suspicions. One of the indians wanted Said Freeman to go and baptize him, he said he would go, but first he [Freeman] wanted two or three more [Mormons] to go along, then the Indian would not go. This also goes to prove that Murder was in their hearts. They soon left the Fort and retired a short distance in Front consulting together. Soon 3 of them started in the direction of the field and stock, in a few minutes James W. Hunt started with a lariat to go catch his horse.[51] Charles, a Son of Quit-sub-soc-its, or St. John followed going with him on horse back. He frequently told [Hunt] to go on a head of him, asking him several times what he was afraid of—as brother Hunt would occasionally turn his head around as though all was not right. They proceeded on in his manner till they were nearly a mile from the Fort, when

---

[50]Sterrett, Autobiography, BYU Library.
[51]Hunt was known by his middle name, Wiseman.

Charles drew said Hunts attention towards the Stock—Charles embracing the opportunity instantly shot him. He then shouted to an indian not far off to run and take 2 Horses.[52]

SHELDON BELA CUTLER, JOURNAL, 23–24 SEPTEMBER 1855–1856, 34–38, LDS ARCHIVES.

Sun 23rd We drove all the stock to a new range this morning east of the fort. Wight and myself saddle our horses and went out to herd. We rode some distance up the vally and came back and found the stock some what scattered. Drove them all together on the field unsaddled our horses and turned them loose to feed. While there watching the stock several Indians came to field aparantly in search of somthing to eat. Shortly we say bro Hunt and an Indian by the name of Charly (the son of St. John) coming towards the field. In a moment more we heard the shot of a gun in that direction and heard bro Hunt call for help and said he was shot. We imediately ran to him and found him badly wounded in the back. This was the *first* intimation we had of them being hostile.

I ran my horse to fort to tell what had happened. Came [back] with bro. Billings and others soon followed and we proceded to carry bro Hunt to fort. The indians all immediately left for the other side of the river but before we had got more than half way to the fort being about a mile when they returned and made a charge upon us and fired several guns. Some of the boys came and met us and returned a few shots and kept them at bay until we reached the fort. Only one of their shots took effect and that passed through bro Billings finger. C [Clinton] Williams came out and drove the cattle and horses all in the carrell in time to save them except for horses that they drove away at onset. The balls flew thick around us as we entered the fort. The Indians then went on to a hill north of the fort and cept up a fire for several hours. Many of the balls fell into the correll but done no harm. In the mean time one of them crept up and fired our stacks of hay and corn and was shot down as he ran away. Two more was shot in the cane in attemp[t] to creep towards the burning stack. Two of the boys Wm. Behanon [and] E. Edward wer on the mountains for a hunt. The Indians saw them a coming and seven of them went to meet them and shot them. They continued firing until near night when C. A. Huntington called them down and talked the matter over with them and they agreed to come the next morning and settle with us.

Mon 24th Bro. Hunt died about 8 Oclock this morning. The Indians came at day light. We let them in to the fort without their arms but they were not altogether disposed for peace. They said that Charly had gone for more help and they did not know how soon they would come and that we

---

[52]McEwan, Elk Mountain Journal, 23 September 1855, 96–97.

had better leave. Bro. Huntington talked with them all the morning but they could not be satisfied. Bro. Billings and 5 or 6 others repaired to a room by ourselves to ask the will of the Lord in prayr. It was finally agreed that we should leave forthwith. We accordingly saddled up gatherd what few articles we could take with us and left the Indians in possession of the fort and all our provisions except what little we took to last us to Manti. We left the fort about 11 o'clock. Crossed the river found an Indian on this side the river [the] bro of St. John that appeared friendly and insisted that we should take our cattle with us. He finely agreed to bring them to the springs that night. Stopt at the springs and bated our stock [until] the Indians came up with 16 head. They give us 8 cows the rest was shot full of arrows and could not travel. We sadled up and traveled 12 miles and campt for the night.

For the first time—but not the last—the Utes successfully resisted Mormon expansion into their homelands—and it only required a handful of angry young men to terrify the Saints. The panicked survivors fled back to Manti, most arriving by the end of September. Others were not so fortunate. After crossing Green River, Billings sent Allen Huntington, Richard W. James, and William Sterrett "to strike the Spanish Fork trail to intercept any of our brethren" bound to Spanish Valley. They took three days' provisions and "after a remarkable and unwilling exploration of twenty-four days," woodcutters found them lost in Provo Canyon, "foot sore, almost naked and weary," having eaten wild rosebuds, a duck, their dog, saddle-trees, moccasins, and most of a horse. Native hospitality in the Uintah Basin had saved them. Black Pine's band of this "very revengefull tribe" served them "first a little bread," then "a little more," and in the afternoon a kettle full of venison "and told us to eat all we wanted." The next year, Garland Hurt hired James as the Spanish Fork Indian Farm interpreter, where Black Pine told James his band had debated until midnight whether to kill the Mormons. "Every Indian but the Chief was in favor of taking our scalps," Sterritt recalled, since the Mormons had killed some of their Elk Mountain kin. But Black Pine "prevailed and we were alowed to live."[53]

Diarist John McEwan "was lost four days with nothing to eat" after attempting to save his three horses. He "could not flee as fast as" his companions, who abandoned him. "This was in the tops of the mountains: with only a dull trail to follow." McEwan wandered back to Castle Valley and failed to recognize the trail he had taken, but "a man lost, is liable to not

[53]Sterrett, Autobiography, BYU Library; Huntington, "Elk Mountain Mission," *Juvenile Instructor*, 15 June 1895, 364.

recognize his own house." He "suffered intensely with hunger and thirst, and cold at night, being without fire or bedding." A Manti search party, "with some friendly Indians to lead," found McEwan near where he had been abandoned, "as near dead as alive." Oliver Huntington heard "he never fully recovered from the effects of his four days' mental and physical sufferings."[54]

Arapene: Go and Kill the Elk Utes

The flight from Elk Mountain inspired responses from both senior Ute and Mormon leaders. Arapene reaffirmed his devotion to Brigham Young and expressed contempt for the heartless Sheberetch, who would not listen to him.

John Eager to Brigham Young, 1 October 1855, BYC 24:1, 31–35.

Manti San Peter Oct *1st 1855*

Br Brigham Young

Late Yesterday afternoon there was considerable excitement in this place on the arrival of the brethren from the Elk Mountain Mission. They report that the Elk Utes have killed Brs Wise Hunt, Edward Edwards and William Behunnin, that the brethren have killed several Utes and succeeded in escaping with 27 head of horses & cows. The rest of their efficts [*sic*] were left in the hands of the Utes whom they left quarreling over the division thereof. Br. A. N. Billings had one of his fore fingers shot off while in the act of conveying Br Hunt to the Fort. Br H was shot about one mile from the fort. Behunnin & Edwards were out hunting at the time and were shot by the utes about 1½ Last Evening there was a company selected to go and hunt the wagons that were on their road for that place and notify them of what had occurred. In the mean time three utes that were here sent an express to Arropine, and Arropine sent to the wagon company also on hearing what was up, and Br Huntington and Arropine came in the next morning.

The brethren were called together with the Utes and San Petches and held council. Arropine offered up a prayer in his own language in usual form after which he stated that he had told Brigham that the Elk Utes were bad and had no hearts and would get mad and fight the Mormons & Navajoes, and that they would not listen to him—perhaps in two or three years they might be friendly if they had no powder and had to use dirt to load their guns with. Said the Mormons would not let him have powder for fear he would Kill them, but they had let the Elk Utes have it and now they had killed three of the mormons. Said the Sanpitches have thrown away his talk and would not listen to him and asked if there was any Utes that had talked good all the time like him, said there were big Chiefs among the Elk

[54]Huntington, "Elk Mountain Mission," *Juvenile Instructor*, 15 June 1895, 363.

utes when he was gone, but when he was there he done all the talk. They
had said they would cut his throat &c all very good. The Mormons have
got lots of women and Children and they ought to stay home and take care
of them and not go among the Elk Utes. There was no one that could call
all the utes together but him and he did not know that he could now or
not, but by the by he would gather them all here. Said he wanted Brigham
to send the snakes down and Kill the Utes out there and take their Horses.
Wanted the brethren & Brigham & Americans to Keep their powder all tied
up from the Utes except him and his band. The indians told him to run
away or the Mormons would Kill them but he told them he was not affraid
to go where he pleased. He was going out to hunt and Kill deer and was
not going to hunt the Mormons and Kill them. When snow fell he would
come in. If the elk utes Killed him all right. Perhaps sometime he would
gather all utes here & sanpitches and Some of the mormons and go and Kill
the Elk Utes off, for they would always keep fighting the Navjoes—if the
Mormons had not killed any of the Utes peace might soon be made good
again but as they had he did not know how it would be. Perhaps the Elk
Utes would come out here and Kill the mormons and take their cattle. He
said that *Soweats* was friendly to the Mormons and was out in Uintah Valley
hunting, & the Mormons must not be affraid when he comes in at any time.
Perhaps Brigham may be mad at what I have said. I want Brigham (said he)
to acknowledge that what I told him was true and that I [k]now most. Said
we need not be afraid here only the squaws stealing potatoes, &c. when they
were hungry. Said if the Utes and Sanpitches Kept stealing all the time by
the by the Mormons would get mad for they do not like to have the Indians
steal all the time. Said he wanted us to write to Brigham about all that had
transpired, & wanted him to answer.

                                          Yours Respt John Eagar Clerk.

Brigham Young to Arrowpine, 3 October 1855, BYC 17:18, 2.

                                          G.S.L. City, Oct 3d, 1855.

To Arra-pin,
Chief of the Utahs.

  I have just heard that 3 of the Mormons who had built a fort on Grand
River, near the Elk Mountain, have been killed. I have not yet learned all
about the particulars of this sad affair, nor do I yet know what Indians were
concerned in it. I am aware that you and your people are friendly towards
me and my people, and we always feel friendly towards you & your people
and wish to do you all the good we can. No doubt it was some Indians who
did not to have killed those 3 whites Perhaps it was some Indians, who did
not know our men, that came in and killed them before they had a chance
to tell them that they were there to do them good. Be this as it may, you

know very well that I do not like to have people fight & kill one another, neither the Mormons nor the Indians, but that I love to have the white & red men live at peace with themselves and with each other, and do good to each other and to all men.

I know that you love peace and have done much towards making peace with different tribes, and I now wish that you would use your influence and try to have the difficulty on Grand River amicably settled, so that the Mormons can go there in peace and do the Indians good, as they were trying to do when this late unfortunate circumstance occurred. And I wish you to let the Indians concerned in killing our men near the fort on Grand River know that we are their best friends and are trying to do them all the good we can.

I learn that you have not powder and lead; I will send you powder & lead by some of our people who will start for Manti in a few days, and I always desire to assist you to such things as you may need, so far as I may be able. But you know that I have to be very diligent to provide for my large family, and my people have to work hard for food, clothing, houses, and such things as they have, and I hope that you and your men will strive to raise horses & cattle and learn to farm as fast as possible, that we may all live comfortably and have a plenty to supply our wants

I trust that your efforts to make peace for our people with the hostile Indians, who have lately attacked the Mormons on Grand River and killed 3 of them, will prove successful, and for which you have the prayers of your Best Friend,

B.Y.

In a letter to the Cherokee mission in today's Oklahoma, Young downplayed the setback. "We continue to enjoy peace with our red neighbors, with only one serious and an occasional slight exception" when "the Yampa Utes killed four of the brethren at the Fort on Grand river, which has caused a vacation of the Elk Mountain mission until the ensuing Spring."[55] Despite this hope, no Mormons successfully settled in Spanish Valley during Brigham Young's lifetime. Young "much regretted the loss of the mission and the misfortunes of the brethren," blaming "the treachery of the Indians there," claiming they were "the literal descendants of the old Gadianton robbers" who would eventually ask the Mormons to come back. But as Oliver Huntington noted, no band "ever wasted faster or disappeared" like dew before the sun than did the Sheberetch.[56]

---

[55]Young to Henry W. Miller, 28 November 1855, BYC 17:18.
[56]Huntington, "Elk Mountain Mission," *Juvenile Instructor*, 15 June 1895, 364.

For the Purpose of Fishing:
The Ute Struggle to Survive

Seasonal rainstorms never reached arid Utah in 1854, and Cold Maker failed to make much snow before winter ended in 1855. By springtime, "the long continued dry weather [was] operating against crops, the streams not affording enough water for irrigation." The mild winter fostered an enormous hatch of Rocky Mountain locusts, famed in Mormon legend as grasshoppers, which had depleted the 1854 crop. Grasshoppers devoured "whole fields of grain" between Salt Lake and San Pete, and "whether they have really concluded to stop eating, die off, or clear out" was not yet known. By May 1855 drought threatened "to destroy all vegetation as fast as it appears," including the spring greens and "garden sauce" poor farm families relied on to fend off scurvy.[57]

At Manti as 1855 began, Arapene appealed to Brigham Young to send Mormons and "more Utes on to a creek twelve miles south of this place and open a farm for them and learn them how to work," Nelson Higgins recorded. "He said he wished to be at peace with the Mormons and with the Americans," but if the Americans "killed the Pavants it was all wright with him as they had stole three of his cattle some tim[e] ago." Many friendly Utes visited Manti, but they had "killed a cow at the Allred settlement lately." Utes "brought in word that you had told the Mormons not to give the Indians anything to eat and that the Ute felt very bad and cried about it," Arapene dictated. Maybe the Ute lied, but he hoped the Mormons would "continue to give them some bread."[58]

Drought and famine sharpened the ragged edge of Utah's already hard life: peoples of all colors shared desperate privation. Brigham Young began his spring visit to the southern settlements on 6 May 1855, leaving D. H. Wells in charge. On 21 May Wells described hard times in Salt Lake:

> The Indians are camped over Jordan west of the field about two miles down. I visited their camp at Ammons earnest request on Saturday and saw Arrowpine. There is about fifty lodges with him some five of which are Shoshones. Ammon interpreted the main drift of their conversation was about being at peace with the mormons and the Shoshones and not stealing cattle or fighting and killing any body and wound up by saying that they were very hungry [and] wanted Tobacco, flour, cattle &c and indeed they looked very miserable. I did not say much to them as Ammon could not very well

[57]*Deseret News*, 25 April 1855, 6:2; and 23 May 1855, 2:1.
[58]Higgins to Young, 21 January 1855, BYC 24:3.

explain, but gave them some tobacco and promised Arrowpine two sacks of flour. They are getting considerable provision in town where the squaws and children are begging every day. I don't think I ever saw them looking so miserable. Arrowpine has not been in town the reason Ammon says is that he has to talk to the Shoshones all the time. He also says that the Shoshones west and north are friendly but that Washikik and the Shoshones are "*heap mad*" and want to fight.[59]

The Mormon conquest's consequences came into sharp relief in May 1855 when "Arapene Tabby Tintic Squash and all their bands" assembled for their annual festival on Provo River. Having found their traditional campsites fenced and cultivated, the Utes "manifested a very bad feeling towards the settlers." Agent George W. Armstrong feared war would break out:

> The chiefs frequently complained that they had now no place of Safety where their animals could feed as in former years in consequence of so much of the land having been improved and fenced in by the settlers, and requested that a pasture should be made for them bordering on the Provo river near their fishing grounds. Where they Could fish and at the Same time protect themselves and animals from the Shoshones or Snake Indians with whom they are almost constantly at war and in continual dread and urging still further that there would be no necessity for encroaching upon the improved land of the settlers. I agreed to their proposals and communicated their wishes to Your Excellency who instructed me to Carry the Same into execution.[60]

The Utes ignored the fences and set up their usual camps, turning their animals out into the crops planted on their ground. Armstrong described the deteriorating situation in early June.

> Sanpitch informed me that he could not control the Indians, that he was here merely to catch fish, that he did not let *his* horses go on to the crops but had his squaw and children herd them across the river. That the land belonged to Tintick and that he had nothing to do with the Indians that is camped in the field. Tintick was present during the talk and took the reins of government pertaining to the Indians into his own hands. After he had talked much about owning the land he informed [me] that a colt about a week old had been Killed by the citizens on Sunday evening. I told him that I did not know that any of their horses had been Killed by the whites, that I had no evidence to that effect. I then asked him whether he would or would not take his horses and cattle out of the field. He replied that he would not without the citizens would pay them for the horses that had been Killed. I

[59]Wells to President B. Young, 21 May 1855, BYC 43:8.
[60]Armstrong to Young, 30 June 1855, Commissioner of Indian Affairs, *Annual Report*, 1855, 202.

then told him that I should demand payment for the horses and cattle that had been Killed by the Indians. He replied that if the Indians had Killed any that it had been done by some mean Indians who are worth nothing and that he would not foot their bills. I then told him that if he would not turn the horses and cattle from the field that I would be compeled to send a company of men and turn them out. He replied that if the Mormons wanted to fight that he was ready. I told him that the citizens did not want to fight them but were their friends. He said he would not turn *his* horses out if the Mormons killed every one of them and further that we had talked long enough that he wanted to know if we would pay for the horses which had been killed, or fight. Since I left their camp ten or twelve Indians crossed the river and were seen driving two cows belonging to citizens, and also of firing two other shots at a cow and calf. When the Indians noticed the whites who saw them they galloped off leaving the cows behind them. I have used my best endeavours to find out the truth of this story of their horse said to have been killed by Snyder but from the best evidence I can get I believe the mare died of folding [foaling]. They have also been seen to Kill one their own ponies and they lay the blame on the citizens.

Black Hawk added to the chorus when he charged "the citizens with killing and threatens unless paid for it he will take four head of cattle." [61] Col. Peter Conover told General Wells:

The Indians are now in posession of the Fort field, and are making threats of what they will do to us if we do not comply with their demands, that is to pay them for a horse that they say the mormons have killed. Also they want pay for the land, or fensing up the grass. They say the Indians that have killed our cattle and horses are poor and have nothing, and they will not pay for the damage they have done. Since this day break they have killed some ten or 15 head of cattle and I beleave the Indians are determined to have a fuss in spite of any thing we can do. Now our president says we must not shed the blood of an indian no matter what they do. Now I want some instruction how to proceed and if you say let them go and do nothing with them they will kill our horses and cattle and destroy our crops as they pleas and then come and say we are cowards and wont fight. Now I want something don forthwith. Yours in hast. Send me an answer as soon as possible no more at present. [62]

The Utes charged that Chester Snyder had killed a mare and colt "belonging to a chief of the Utah tribe of Indians, named Tintick." Armstrong talked with Tintic, Tabby, and Sanpitch's forty lodges camped "in a well

[61]Armstrong to Young, 4 June 1855, BYC 55:20, 9–11.
[62]Conover to Wells, 4 June 1855, BYC 23:21.

enclosed field containing some four hundred acres of grain and grass."
Tintic "was very 'mad,' and complained much at the loss of his animals"
and demanded compensation for his horses. Armstrong "soon learned that
the same bad feeling reigned throughout the entire camp." Tabby, Sanpitch,
and Grosepine seemed "disposed for peace," but "the principal leaders of
the disaffected were Tintick, Squash, and Antan-quer (Blackhawk)." The
Indians "killed five head of cattle and one horse" and "turned their horses
into fields destroying a large amount of grain which had hitherto escaped
the ravages of grasshoppers." Armstrong warned "that unless their men
would cease their depredations I would not pay for the animals which they
had lost and would most assuredly punish the offenders." The Utes agreed
that if the agent paid for their animals, "they would immediately move their
camp out of the enclosed fields and would not encroach upon the property
of the settlers for the future." Armstrong paid them, the Utes "left the field
forthwith, and peace was restored." Now "many of the Indians Came To
My office daily, begging for flour," and the chiefs complained "they could
not catch their usual supply of fish in consequence of some of the citizens
using seins and nets." When Armstrong's efforts to pacify the Utes failed,
Colonel Conover explained why the situation was collapsing.[63]

> PETER CONOVER TO BRIGHAM YOUNG, 6 JUNE 1855, BYC 23:21.
> Since the agent Brother Armstrong started on his last express this morning
> the Indians have offered to sell all the land grass and fish they clame in provo
> and [not] come into any of our enclosures any more with their horses. They
> say the mormons have fenced all the grass and they have no place to turn
> their horses and have never gave them any thing for it but if we will give
> them 1 yoke of cattle some flower [sic] and money they will leave and not toble
> [trouble] our fields any more. It is my opinion if we do not buy them out we
> will have to fight them before we can get clear of them. Sampich says he will
> not have any thing to do with it for the land on provo wrightly belongs to
> Tintic and his brothers. He has it by inheritance from his father the little
> Cheaf. I would be very glad to have some thing done soon for they have took
> possession of the fort field and say they will not leave it without pay for the
> horses that have died since they came here. They say the mormons have killed
> them and their dogs but I beleave they have done it themselves to have some
> excuse or pretence to rais another another [sic] war. They thretton [sic] to fight
> if we donot comply with their requirements. They say they will drive our
> cattle and horses off in to the mountains and we dare not come after them.

[63]Armstrong to Young, 30 June 1855, Commissioner of Indian Affairs, *Annual Report*, 1855, 202.

I have born about as much as I can from them without you say so. Their was two of them come in to my hous on thursday last when I was out at work and my wife sick in bed and wanted to get in bed with her and frightened her ver[y] much. She hollorred to me and I ran to the hous. As soon as I could I put them out. One had a pistol and cocked it and threttened to shoot me. The other drew his bow. I had a considerable scufle with them but no body got hurt. My boys had come that morning and taken my guns all away or I expect I would have killed them boath but they boath went away and I have not seen them since neither do I want to for I am reddy for them now and intend to be. The same ones have been to several other houses and sceared the women allmost out of their senses. I went to the agent and told him about it but he has not done any thing with them yet. I want your advice about it if you pleas as soon as convenient.

Armstrong returned to Provo with George A. Smith, who promised the Utes "a pasture should be fenced off for their exclusive use next fishing time." Dimick Huntington and Armstrong "went to visit the Indians and fish with them all day. They caught a thousand suckers at one haul." (One "seine was over 300 feet long.") The Utes got "half the fish, loading four horses with as much as they could carry."[64] Back in the excessively hot Salt Lake City, where the grasshoppers had stripped the "vegetation the second time," Smith described his 8 June 1855 visit with the Utes. They insisted the Mormons must "throw open the Old Fort field, and also 400 acres of grassland adjoining, for their horses to feed, and had prohibited the people from fishing in the Provo river." Huntington promised to fence a pasture in the lower field before "the Indians want to come again to fish." This "succeeded in pacifying the Indians," and they moved out of the field. "Tintick, Squash and An-ton-guer" led the disaffected Utes but Tabby, Sanpitch, and Grosepine "were first disposed for peace." Tintic explained his anger:

> Tintick was "tooldge niah" (very mad) at first but after a long conversation he became more quiet. Mr. Huntington inquired what he was mad about; he replied he was mad because he had been told that Brigham had ordered Tabba to come and arrest him: he was told that if he did not stop committing depredations upon the Whites he would be arrested, and if he was mad at that he might stay so. The interpreter requested one of the Indians to fill the pipe of peace, and pass it round, when Tintick burst out into a loud laugh, and

---

[64]Church Historian's Office Journal, 7–9 June 1855, 32–33, LDS Archives.

said:—'I see I cannot scare you,' and he then came into the lodge, appeared friendly and willingly agreed to the resolution of the others.[65]

Drought and famine continued into July, when Mormon leaders gathered to counteract the "strange spirit" of the Provo Saints who seemed "Cold & indifferent" to supporting the Utes. At a three-day revival "for Latter-day Saints White and Red," long sermons celebrated the suffering and degraded Lamanites and their millennial role. The authorities recruited Indians to fill Sunday's audience and translated as Brigham Young "Preached upon the subject of the Lamanites" and "told the Latter day Saints plain their duty towards them," delivering what Wilford Woodruff called "strong doctrin."[66] The Lord had "appointed our location in the midst of Israel, which is a astounding miracle," Young said, expressing sympathy for the Utes. "Suppose us to have been the original settlers instead of them, and our enemies or our friends would come and attempt to fence our land, burn our wood, catch our fish. Would we not feel like fighting?" The Saints should teach the Indians "to sow and reap and to spin and sew and to read" and "make them a field and not disturb it." Would they turn the Indians "away empty? Instead of their being our inferiors, they are our superiors in many things, as they are the lawful heirs."[67]

Springville mayor Lyman Wood then translated the "Remarks Tow-om-bu-gah or High Forehead, the Indian Chief." No document better captures the Utes' feelings than Sun Cloud's eloquent remarks.

TOWOMBUGAH, 15 JULY 1855, CHURCH HISTORIAN'S OFFICE REPORTS
OF SPEECHES, 3:13.

Why shall the country be broken, why shall we devide the land? He says it has been a tradition handed down to them from their fathers and their fathers father, for many generations, that they must not sell their country. He says he wants the mormons to live here, and have good feelings. His people say that they are poor, and we have plenty, and that this is the country of their fathers, the land where their fathers and mothers have died. Before the mormons came here they [had] plenty of timber right here on the streams. He says it is true the ground is hard and we cannot eat it, and we cannot take it away, but we love the land where our fathers and mothers have died, and we cannot bear the thought of selling it. We want to live here and be brethren together. We know that we have unruly boys among us and we

[65]Smith, "Home Correspondence," 12 June 1855, *Deseret News*, 27 June 1855, 2/1.

[66]Woodruff, *Journal*, 15 July 1855, 4:331–32; Church Historian's Office Reports, 3:12.

[67]Brigham Young, 15 July 1855, Provo Stake Minutes, Van Wagoner, *Complete Discourses*, 2:996.

would like to be better. (Prest. Brigham Young, I believe that they give as good advice as they are prepared to receive, and it is just as good as the whites can give.) The chief says that when the mormons first came to this country Br. Dimick Huntingdon came up and asked him in relation to the country and asked if we could settle with them, and he told him yes, we could settle with them but they did not wish to sell the land. He says there are many of our Mormon boys as well as many of theirs who are very unruly, and he says that they have killed perhaps one creature belonging to the mormons, but he says he talks to his people by night and by day, and tells them to be good. He says that his heart is good, he is not mad, and has not been mad with the mormons. He says I have seen two ways in my time, but now I wish to see one way. He also says some of our people, men and boys, do not do right, and some of them pretend to understand their language, when they understand but a few words, and they pretend that they understand more than they do, and owing to this many of them are apt to convey a wrong idea respecting the indians, and they may influence the people against his people. He likewise says when these men and boys talk it is all mixed together, they talk every way and it is not good, and the great spirit does not like it but when he talks he talks all one way, and he wants all his people to talk one way. He advises the mormons when they talk to let it be all one talk. He says he has always heard what Br. Brigham has told him: his ears have not been stopped, but he says there is a great many mormons that have stopped up their ears, and many of my people have stopped up their ears, and they have got ears like stone. He says I have one ear, one mouth, one heart, but some of the mormons and some of my people have got two ears, two mouths, two hearts. He says I like to hear what Br. Brigham says, and I have always heard it. He wants all those who have got no ears to get some, for they should not have any mouths till they have ears.

To maintain peace in Utah County, Mormon authorities granted favors to win over Ute leaders. "The Indians were mostly absent on a hunt," George A. Smith reported in 1854, but a house was "in progress of erection at Palmyra for old Peteetneet and several cabins to accommodate High Forehead and the Indian inhabitants of Springville."[68] High Forehead did not have long to enjoy his cabin: the Hobble Creek leader died at Springville in 1856, reportedly from eating too many watermelons. He was buried "with much savage ceremony in the 'Indian graveyard'" high in the Wasatch. Others said his gravesite outside the Mormon cemetery was reserved "for Indians who were friends of the settlers."[69]

[68]"Trip to Utah County," *Deseret News*, 30 November 1854, 3/4.
[69]Blanchard, *Going to My Grave*, 363–64.

By October 1855 the Mormons still had not selected an Indian pasture at Springville or Provo. "Brother Agent" Armstrong blamed his failure to reserve ground for the Utes on "the disinclination of the chief, High-fore-head, or Tanta-buggar, to make any at present, and on the part of Tintick, at Provo, in consequence of sickness."[70]

How Many Shot Him? Death Stalks the Utes

Troublesome Lamanites, notably Washear and "Baptiste, the Ute medi-cine-man," suffered hard fates. "Washear, or Squash, was one of my truest friends," George W. Bean recalled. Washear had saved Bean's life when he deflected the knife of a shaman who "was hunting some good person" to accompany his wife and child to the "Happy Hunting Ground."[71] When "Squashhead" became a thorn in the side of settlers from Provo to Parowan, Bean's friendship could not save him. In February 1856 Washear, Show-ershockits, and Tintic entered Thomas Marston's Cedar Fort cabin before his wife was out of bed. A typical confrontation ensued: Marston pointed his gun "at Tintick and told him he was determined to protect his wife and children." This insulted the unarmed Utes, who demanded the Indian agent surrender Marston "so that they could punish him for ejecting them from his house." George Armstrong wrote:

> This demand I of course refused. They then demanded Ten Kegs of powder or Ten head of cattle. This demand I likewise refused telling them at the same time that I did not come to buy their friendship neither would I do so at this or any other time. I found that I could not bring them to terms by any persuasive means and finally told them that if they did not settle the matter before I left that I should take a course to settle it that would not be agreeable to them in fact I would arrest them and bring them to justice. When they learned that I was not to be intimidated nor would not buy their friendship they yielded and promised that for the future they would not enter the houses of the citizens.

The situation escalated when James Ivie secured a federal bench warrant "for the arrest of Squash on a charge of murder and for Tintick, Showash-oketts, Cotton-legs and others on a charge of stealing cattle and horses." When Deputy Marshal Thomas S. Johnson's Springville posse tried to

---

[70]Armstrong to Young, 30 September 1855, Commissioner of Indian Affairs, *Annual Report*, 1855, 206.
[71]Bean, *Autobiography*, 99–100.

enforce the warrant, "four Indians were killed three mortally wounded [and] three slightly," but Tintic, Showereshockits, and Cotton Legs escaped.[72] Johnson sent George Parrish and six men from Cedar Valley's South Fort to "lay in wait for Squash, Tintick, Cotton-Legs and two other Indians for which he had Writs with orders to arrest them if possible, if I should happen on them." The posse found more Utes than they anticipated, so Parrish sent Elk Mountain veteran John Clark "to see what was up." Becoming uneasy, he recruited four more men from the fort, who "took our pistols under our coats which was 72 shots and no large guns" to the Ute camp.

> The interpreter John Clark was setting in the Lodge talking with the Indians. We dismounted & some three or four of us went into the Lodge. We talked with them near half an hour which was after sunset. I used every means of persuasion & stratigum I was capibal of but to no effect. I then told Tintick if he would go with me to see you, that I would get him some blankets & a Carriage to ride in & plenty to eat as I took him down [to Great Salt Lake City], but he utterly refused. This all pass'd without any excitement or even a weapon in sight. I then told him that the American Captain had sent some papers for him & Squash & some others & that was what I had come for. He then laughed a hearty laugh and said *Cotch*. I then asked him twice more if he would go & he answered as before. He was standing close by me, at that I catched him by the hair with my left hand. He made a pass for his Gun, which lay directly behind him, but missed it. I then drawed my Revolver & Cocked it. He caught it by the mussel with his left hand, while he fastened his right hand in my waistband. I still held my hold in his hair. At this instance Old Battesse raised his Gun Cocked within a foot or two of my head. At this instant John Hoops who stood close by me drew his Revolvers and Shot Batteese down. At almost the same instant my revolver discharged between Tintick & myself, and Tintick, Batteese & myself fell through the Lodge into the sage brush, and about the time we were falling another gun discharged through my pantaloons below the knee. About this time matters were getting tollerable warm outside of their lodge. This is as near as I can tell what happened inside of the Lodge. The Boys outside fought with the true courage of Saints—when a Brothers life was in danger not a man flinched until the alarm was given that a man was Wounded. I then ordered the boys not to shoot, until the man was in the Fort and after administering to him put him on my horse & took him to the Fort. I was told by the Bishop that it was his opinion that they had made their arrangements to attack this Fort last evening had we not come by their sending their Squaws away. With deep regret we are called to mourn for the loss of our faithful brother George Carson (who was the one that was wounded last evening. He died about 2:00 oclock A.M. This is thrown a *Chill* over this place. Their was three killed

dead on the ground (& one Squaw that was killed accidentally) of those that were killed were Batteese Tinticks Brother & the other was Known here by the name of broken nose. Their was at their camp 8 Indians & one boy & two Squaws and there was seven of us. Feb 23d This morning we went to the Camp & found where Tinctick had left. We tracked him by the blood some distance from the camp and this continued as fresh as ever (i.e.) with blood. I think he was shot under the left breast. We got Tinticks horse & Gun & two other Guns & Tinticks Brothers Horse.[73]

So began what Mormons still call the Tintic War.[74]

When "my Brother Battease, through some cause or other" died, Arapene told Brigham Young his "feelings respecting it." For the "Chief of the Utah Nation," justice was a business transaction:

I of course feel bad. He was my Brother, but still I am not mad and do not intend to be. I want good peace with both Mormons and Utahs, though some of the Utahs feel mad, *Tintic* is mad, he is but one, for the majority wish to have good peace. I want the American Captain to send me some beef cattle to feed my Indians with and all will be right, the Mormons can go into the Kanyons and travel the roads, either one or two together and be unmolested by any of my Indians and all will be good peace. I wish to know how many, and if any, of the Mormons have been Killed. If so I do not wish any acknowledgement for my Brother Battease, if not I wish the Indian Agent, Dr Garland Hurt to present me with Blankets, Ammunition Shirts, Guns &c &c and all will be right. I also wish to know the reason of his death who killed him? Mormons or Americans? Why [have] the[y] killed him? how many shot him? and all particulars respecting his death, also how many Utahs shot the Mormons and everything in regard to the fight; providing that all is good peace with the Mormons, ever after this I will give up and throw away all Indians that steal or Killed cattle, or those that are guilty in any criminal offence, but don't want anything done or said of anything that has happened heretofore.[75]

THE NOTED WASHEAR, OR SQUASH

"Squash had left Tintick's camp and gone over to Spanish Fork" before Johnson's ambush, but "friendly Indians" enticed him to Springville, "where he was arrested and well secured," Agent Armstrong reported.

---

[72]Armstrong to Young, 31 March 1856, RG 75, Microcopy 234, Reel 898, nara.

[73]Parrish to Young, 22 February 1856, BYC 25:4, 24–25.

[74]See Walker, "The Tintic War of 1856," 35–67.

[75]Arrowpine to Young, 29 February 1856, BYC 24:14, 25–26. For a description of Baptiste's healing powers, see Kane, *Twelve Mormon Homes*, 36–41.

The Indians that escaped then commenced their system of plunder and murder and succeeded in driving off a large number of cattle and horses and killing seven of the herdsmen. General Conover of the Utah Military District who was ordered out by proclamation of your Excellency succeeded in recovering sixty five head of cattle and eleven American horses that had been driven off by Tintick and no doubt would have recovered many more had not his men and animals been compelled to return from fatigue and want of provisions the weather at this time being very severe and the snow in many places from two to three feet deep yet notwithstanding he succeeded in pursuing the Indians on the Desert where they mounted the best American horses which they had stolen stampeded the cattle and fled in every direction. I received a letter from T. S. Johnson U.S. Dep. Marshall dated feby 28/56 informing me that Squash (or Washear) had that morning committed suicide by cutting his throat with a case knife during the temporary absence of his guard. I obtained a copy of the proceedings of Coroners inquest which I forward with this report. During this time the friendly bands became considerably excited and I deemed it my duty to use all my influence and if possible prevent them from joining the hostile Indians consequently I visited their Camps frequently and assured them of the friendship of the Whites to all well disposed Indians and also protection to such as remain peaceable. I made them a number of Presents which inspired confidence in them and I am pleased to say that it had the desired effect and as far as my knowledge extends but very few if any have joined the hostile band.[76]

The "noted Washear, or Squash," the *Deseret News* claimed, while momentarily not "under the eye of his keepers, so effectually cut his throat, with a case knife furnished him to eat with, that he soon died." Washear swore "he would not go to G. S. L. City to be hung up like a dog," a "mode of death very repugnant to his feelings."[77]

This fable became history. The Springville posse used Aaron Johnson's front room "as a kind of a military prison," keeping Washear "ironed with a ball and chain upon his ankles and wrists." He hated the nickname Squash-Head for good reason, but whites thought it "very appropriate as he had a very large head, round as a squash, and adorned by a huge mouth in which gleamed a set of teeth a chimpanzee might have been proud of." As his guards ate breakfast before taking their prisoner to Salt Lake, "Old Squash-Head settled his case in severing his jugular vein with a sharp bread knife which had been given him with his breakfast. He fell forward upon the hearth, his

[76]Armstrong to Young, 31 March 1856, RG 75, Microcopy 234, Reel 898, nara.
[77]"Disturbance With Indians," *Deseret News*, 5 March 1856, 9/3.

chains clanking so loudly as to attract the attention of his solitary guard, who was standing nearby. It was darkly hinted at the time that some white person had done the bloody deed, but every indication pointed to the fact that the Indian, who feared hanging as a just punishment for his crimes, had been the means of his own taking off."[78]

What actually happened? Alexander Williams cut Washear's "throat with a case-knife" while delivering his breakfast, J. C. Lemmon reported in 1906.[79]

The War on Tintic: His Men Is Most All Dead

Historians often divide history into manageable chunks using arbitrary eras of war and peace. Conflicts named after Ute leaders traditionally interrupt the heroic epic of Utah's progress, but murderous crusades against the state's Native peoples actually began in 1849 and continue with current campaigns to eviscerate Bears Ears National Monument.

As he told Arapene, Brigham Young had bad Indians in his sights long before the Timpanogos leader met his fate.

> You know very well that I love peace, good peace, between the whites and all the Indians, and that I am a good friend to all good Indians, even their best friend, and always expect to be. But there are some foolish Indians, as well as many unwise and foolish whites, and they often cause difficulties like those which have lately happened, and with which you are acquainted. Tintick and some of those with him have been acting very badly, killing the whites and driving off their cattle and horses, and threatening to do more mischief. Now I do not like such conduct, and you know that it is not good, and I wish to secure Tintick and the bad Indians with him, and to recover the animals they have stolen. Some friendly and good Indians have proffered to bring in the stolen animals and the mischievous Indians, if you will give your consent, and counsel to so to do, and I write these lines to you asking you, as my Brother and lover of peace, to counsel the good Indians to bring in the stolen animals, and also to endeavor to bring in Tintick and the bad Indians, if they can do so without fighting, for I do not wish to have any fighting done.[80]

Arapene proposed the Americans, probably meaning Utah's federal marshal, Peter Dotson, handle Tintic.

---

[78]Johnson, *A Brief History of Springville*, 28.
[79]Gottfredson, *History of Indian Depredations*, 42–43.
[80]Young to Arapene, My Brother, 15 March 1856, BYC 17:22.

ARROPIN AND AMMON TO BROTHER BRIGHAM, MARCH 1856,
BYC 24:14, 43.

Brother Brigham

Arropin Cannot go to Tinticks camp. Mormons no go to Tinticks camp. Arrowpins men cannot go to Tinticks. Let the Americans go after them. The Americans have chained the Parowans and the Piedes and now they want to chain the Utes. He says he dont want to go and he has been talking to the Sanpitches and tells them not to steal but some are like women and wont hear. He talks to the Utes and some of them are like some Mormons [as] they have no ears and wont hear. He says Tintick wont hear neither Arrowpin nor Brigham. He will not come back again. When the snow goes away he will go away off and not come back again. Sanpitch and them other Indians have gone to Fillmore to see if they can find Tintick but he dont know whether they can find him. One Ute brought in Six horses ~~and~~ to the Bishops house from the Severe. Dont know how many men Tintick has with him [but] is afraid that he will kill some of his brothers as he Tintick is mad at Brigham, and Arrowpin and all the Mormons. If You leave Tintick alone awhile he will come in and make peace as he has not much powder and lead. Tintick has not got many men with him. His men is most all dead. He may come in and Kill Arrowpin dont know what he may do. The man who brought the horses does not belong to Arrowpins band. He once did but was with Tintick in the fight but now he has thrown him away. Arrowpin say Squash is dead and he is glad and no one is mad about it [for] it is right it is good. Wants the mormons to stay and raise wheat and the Utes to stay and raise wheat. Wants the Americans to go and fight Tintick as they want to chain the Parrowans, Piedes, and Utes. Wants the Americans as they are great Captains to go and fight—Says he always talks good and Brigham talks good and he never chained the Utes but the Americans does and when they have been here awhile they will learn better than to chain them.

Let the Americans pay Brigham and the Mormons for what cattle Tintick has stolen. If the Mormons want to fight Tintick go to where he is and not come here as he dont want to fight in Manti. Wants Mormons to stay and raise wheat so that they will have something to eat and the Utes wants to stay and learn to raise wheat and make shirts and clothes. Wants Brigham and all the Mormons to stay and screw their women and raise children. The Americans have no trigger and cant make children. Dont want Brigham to send any Mormons to Elk Mountain as the Yampa Utes are mad and will kill them all and not to trade them any powder. Arrowpin are now friends with all the good Utes, Snakes and Mormons and dont want to fight—but want to keep good peace. Tintick is alone and them that is with him is mad and he cant get no others to join him to fight the Mormons. He wants the mormons to stay here and build houses and raise grain and not go off to fight nor he dont want the Utahs to fight for nobody is mad but Tintick. He wants the mormons to baptize all the good Utes there is here and make mormons of them and have them go in the kanyon like white folks and work. He wants the mormons and Utes to live and stay together and work together and not to fight. He wants all the good mormons to do just as Brigham tels them and he will talk to his Utahs to do the same. He says his brother has gone out now to see where Tintick is and maybe he has killed his brother because he is mad at Grospine because he wont help them and he dont know but what he will kill them if he gets a chance or he [illegible words] brother will see Tintick and he may be friendly and talk good. When he comes back he will know. He says he will send back word when his brother comes back where tintick is. He may give the cattle up to his brother. He does not know.

Witness Mr. Armstrong

Arapeene [his mark]
Ammon [his mark]
Peter one [his mark]

A mountain range, mining district, and high school bear his name, but his many wounds killed Little Chief's son: few mourned when "Tintic the notorious Ute chief" died on 15 March 1859. "The Indians had a big powwow on the occasion, and killed eight horses to accompany him to the world of spirits." The Saints "acquainted with his history will not much deplore his death," wrote Manti's *Deseret News* correspondent, probably George Peacock.[81]

---

[81]G.P., "Letter from Manti," *Deseret News*, 6 April 1859, 7/4.

Chapter 9

This Is My Country, and My People's Country
Shoshone Defiance

There are no prouder Indians in the American West than the Shoshones, Bannocks, and Utes. Shoshone "horses are said to be amongst the finest of the Prairie, and although they were just from a trip of six hundred miles, they were still of good mettle and in fine order," wrote an eyewitness to their arrival at Fort Laramie in 1851.[1] "They'll never be caught napping," Jim Bridger told Dragoon corporal Percival Lowe. "Awful brave fellows, these Snakes; got the nerve; honest, too; can take their word for anything; trust 'um anywhere; they live all about me, and I know all of them." The Shoshones' attitude, "the cool, deliberate action" of Washakie, "the staunch firmness of his warriors and the quiet demeanor of women and children, who were perfectly self-possessed" impressed Lowe, for this "grand display of soldierly manhood" showed "the faith that band of warriors had in each other; the entire confidence of their families in them; the self-reliance all through."[2]

Shoshone bands were often named after favored foods, be they animal or vegetable—the Kutsundeka, Padehiyadeka, Tukudeka, Kamuduka, and Yahandeka relied on bison, elk, sheep, rabbits, and marmots, while the fish-eating Pengwideka and Agaideka consumed trout and salmon. Sometimes derisively called "dust eaters," the Hukandeka, Tubaduka, and Warradeka peoples ate seeds, pine nuts, and sunflowers.[3] Outsiders arbitrarily divided these wide-ranging peoples into groups based on culture and geography.

---

[1] "Letter from Fort Laramie," *Missouri Republican*, 26 September 1851.
[2] Lowe, *Five Years a Dragoon*, 82–83.
[3] Madsen, *Pocatello*, 16.

Differences between Shoshone and Bannock peoples were few, for they spoke a common Uto-Aztecan language with "slightly different pronunciation for some words" between these nations and their relatives, the Comanche.

The Northwestern Shoshones lived around the Great Salt Lake and so were closest to the Mormons, while the Northeastern Shoshone ranged on both sides of South Pass and west to Bear River. Other bands roamed today's north-central Nevada, throughout Idaho, and west to Oregon's John Day River. In 1860 Pacific Wagon Road surveyor Frederick Lander counted 485 lodges of bands he called Salmon River Snakes, Western Snakes, Bannacks or Pannacks, and Warraricas (Sun-Flower Seed Eaters), who numbered almost 3,400 souls.[4] Shoshone peoples had resisted the invasion of their homelands since at least 1812 but avoided violence and masterfully managed relations with whites. Long experience and skilled leadership helped them handle yet another challenge, the Latter-day Saints.

WARLIKE AND STUBBORN, BEING UNWILLING TO GIVE UP THEIR ARMS

It was the Northwestern Shoshone's misfortune to have the Mormons expand into their country as soon as they arrived in 1847. "The Indian's condition is best when furthest removed from contact with white men," journalist James W. Simonton observed.[5] Jacob Forney, who replaced Brigham Young as Utah's Indian superintendent, found "no tribe in the Territory has been so much discommoded by the introduction of a white population as the Sho-sho-nes."[6] Both peoples got along relatively well until 15 September 1850, when Urban Stewart found an Indian in his garden who "was picking corn & he told him to leave." The Shoshone walked off too slowly to please Stewart, who "went into his house and himself and another man came out with their guns. The Indian had not got out of his corn yet. He told him to go. He did not as fast as he wanted to have him and he busted a cap at him but his gun did not go. The young man fired and missed him. Br Stewart snapt again. His gun went off and killed the Indian."[7]

---

[4]Lander, "Report of F. W. Lander," Serial 1033, 121–38.
[5]Simonton, "Highly Important From Utah," *New-York Times*, 8 July 1858, 1/4.
[6]Morgan, *Shoshonean Peoples*, 241.
[7]Farr to Young, 16 September 1850, BYC 21:19, 53–54.

Stewart had gratuitously murdered Terrikee, leader of the Weber Band. He "hastened, in alarm for the consequences, to his nearby neighbor, David Moore," and woke him. "Aroused to stern indignation, Major Moore severely rebuked Stewart, not only for killing the chief, but for provoking the certain return of the band to take vengeance," chronicled writer Edward Tullidge. Moore refused to hide Stewart, who found shelter with Lorin Farr at Ogden. Farr expected "nothing but the man that shot him" would satisfy the Shoshones. Terrikee's son alerted his band on Box Elder Creek, who "in fierce rage, mounted their ponies and rode furiously back to attempt the destruction of the Ogden settlement, in revenge." Little Soldier's band was "provoked to great rage over the killing of the old chief, and they threatened to burn the settlement and kill the settlers unless Stewart was given up to appease the vengeance of the Indian bands." To balance the scales of justice, the Shoshones killed a "Gentile" mechanic working on Farr's mill. On a peacemaking mission, Moore, "unarmed and alone," survived a rifle shot passing "close over the Major's head," but managed to placate Little Soldier, while Stewart skedaddled for California.

A Nauvoo Temple carpenter and dedicated servant of the kingdom, it fell to Maj. David Moore of Ogden to manage his Native neighbors. Tullidge claimed the band returned with Terikee's nephew, Kattatto (or Catalos) as their new leader. They camped west of Ogden, and "began to make trouble" killing cattle and stealing, and "became so saucy that it was necessary to take some action." Major Moore's cavalry surrounded their camp at dawn and surprised some fifty warriors, who made "a show of resistance" but realized "resistance would be in vain, [and so] passively yielded and not a gun was fired." Aware of the militia's slaughter of the Timpanogas the previous February and knowing the Nauvoo Legion had mustered 150 men to manhandle the Weber River bands if necessary, Kattatto agreed "to make terms for peace . . . with all formality, and a treaty in writing was made." Both parties agreed to pay restitution for stock theft. "The band," Tullidge wrote, "kept their covenant."[8]

---

[8]Tullidge, *Tullidge's Histories*, 16–17, 25. Mormons also practiced eye-for-an-eye justice. George Washington Hill recalled the Shoshones kept stealing livestock, "so we took the warpath again"; they followed them fifty miles, caught one man, "and killed him and recovered a portion of the horses they had stolen." Hill, Incidents in the Life, 41.

THIS IS MY COUNTRY, AND MY PEOPLE'S COUNTRY:
WASHAKIE

Shoshone peoples had long experience dealing with American traders and travelers. Their leaders included "war chiefs" such as Mopeah, Tashepah ("French Louis"), Pushican, Tiwandoah ("Old Snag"), Tentoi, Amaroko, Pocatara (Pocatello), and Pasheco, a noted shaman. Few men have left as enduring a mark on the American West as Washakie, the most renowned of all Shoshones. Obourne Russell met him on Christmas Day 1840 on Weber River: though born about thirty years earlier, Who-sha-kik was already among "the bravest men in the nation," a pillar of his tribe at whose name "the Blackfeet quaked with fear."[9] Indian agent John Wilson identified "Washikick, (Gourd Rattle)" in 1849 as one of four "principal chiefs of the Sho-sho-nies."[10] His father was said to be Salish (or Flathead), but Washikeek's "various feats as a warrior" and "his extreme severity" made him the tribe's most powerful man. (Washakie's tomahawk had left a scar on Pushican's forehead.)

The Northeastern Shoshones had been dealing with fur traders for decades. Their Wind River homeland straddled the overland trails, where they became skilled traders, stockmen, and diplomats. Physical appearance carried great weight with Anglo-Europeans, and Washakie never failed to impress:

> He is tall, straight as an arrow, with features of Grecian mould rather than Indian, and a form full of graceful dignity and conscious power. His hair is slightly gray, and his eyes are keen as the eagle's. Untutored though he is, his every word or step clearly marks the soul of a nobleman of nature's own commissioning. Taught in no school, totally unskilled in the conventionalities of polite society, this proud chieftain, nevertheless, is a nobly jealous of the respect due him, and as truly polite to others, as is any cultivated gentleman of the East. His is a politeness of the soul, born in him, and as natural as are the rays which beam from the morning sun. All feel its attraction, and no white-skinned gentleman fails to respond with sympathetic warmth to his out-spoken demands for the deferential civility, which is the true nobleman's due. Such is Wash-a-kee,—for this is no overdrawn picture.[11]

As "the white man's friend" and a "constant companion of the white trappers," Washakie won the admiration of virtually every American he

---

[9]Russell, *Journal of a Trapper*, 115.
[10]Morgan, *Shoshonean Peoples*, 132.
[11]Simonton, *The New-York Times*, 8 July 1858, 1/4.

met. He was "remarkably tall and well formed, even majestic in appearance," wrote Frederick Lander.[12] James S. Brown thought Washakie's oratorical skills "surpassed any man I ever met."[13]

American authorities at the 1851 Fort Laramie treaty appointed Tibebu-towats (or Tibendewa or SoKaper) official Shoshone leader instead of Washakie. This "quiet, unobtrusive man, who never had been a chief, nor was in the line of chiefs" was called White Man's Son, Dimick Huntington said, "by being made a chief by the U.S. Agents at Laramie." The Shoshones "never recognized him as chief," but Tibebutowats often represented his people with the Mormons.

Utah Territory's original border included Green River, where emigrant trade and ferry tolls generated enormous revenue. William, Dimick, and Oliver Huntington tried to found a settlement and bridge the river in 1852. The "disturbed state" of the Indians he met at Fort Bridger "in consequence of the occupation of a part of their country by the *Mormon Whites*," led one A. Willson to ask Jacob Holeman on 9 October 1852 "to allay, by all the means in your authority, the present excitement." He had heard a Shoshone council "assert, that they intended to immediately drive the whites from their lands, and much persuasion was used to pacify them for the present time." If the agent did not act "speadily, I do believe and fear scenes of destruction and bloodshed will soon ensue." As Willson predicted, the "Indians and mountaineers" soon drove the Huntingtons away. [14]

SAVE THE LAMANITES, NOT DESTROY THEM: FOUNDING FORT SUPPLY

Apostle Orson Hyde "was appointed to make a permanent settlement on or near Green river" in October 1853. At conference, Hyde "read the names of 39 persons selected to accompany him on that mission."[15] Brigham Young privately complained the Elders of Israel "seemed to forget the poor, ignorant Lamanites who surround us, and are in our midst, at our own doors." He called them to "get the Spirit of the Lord and of your mission, begin to save the Lamanites, and not destroy them, for they are of the House of Israel."[16]

[12]"Report of F. W. Lander," Serial 1033, 122.

[13]Brown, Life of a Pioneer, 319.

[14]Morgan, *Shoshonean Peoples*, 189, 213.

[15]Gowans, "Some New Notes on Two Old Forts," 219.

[16]Van Wagoner, *Complete Discourses*, 9 October 1853, 726–27.

Being in "high favor with the powers at Salt Lake," British convert Henry Mogridge was among those "solicited to take a mission to the Green River Indians." He declined, having just returned from hard service in Parowan. Although not part of the mission, he attended its organizational meeting and "heard the charge given to the missionaries to those Indians by Willard Richards, now dead. First they were to establish missions, then they would form treaties and alliances with the Indians; the elders, both married and single, must marry squaws, particularly the daughters of chiefs. Such ties as these could not be broken, and the Indians would be under their control forever." Mogridge concluded his report of the 1853 meeting with remarkable charges.

> "LATER FROM THE SOUTH," *ALTA CALIFORNIA*, 27 OCTOBER 1857, 1/2.
>
> At that time, war against the United States was anticipated, and they professed according to the Book of Mormon, to use the Indians "as the Lord's battle-ax." A time would come when they would be of great service to the Saints, from their knowledge of the mountains. They were to teach the doctrines of Mormon, and baptize them into the church—they were also to monopolize all trade with them, and influence them to keep out the Gentiles.
>
> These missionaries did not at that time, go so far as Green River, but remained in the vicinity of Fort Bridger, to watch the movements of the mountaineers, who were gathering there, indignant that Bridger had been driven off. In the following spring several other missionaries were sent to different parts of the territory. P. P. Pratt was sent to the Santa Clara for similar purposes.
>
> I had been an eye-witness to the baptism of scores of Indians at Parowan, and other southern settlements. The doctrines taught, are invariably, that the Americans are enemies to the Mormons and Indians, and they must kill them whenever they can find them.
>
> The Mormons have a school wherein the young men of the church are taught the different Indian dialects. These dialects are reduced to a system, and are printed in books. Many of the Mormon elders and missionaries have Indian wives, and are raising families of half-breeds.
>
> I have frequently heard Brigham Young declare that he could clean out the United States with the Shoshonees (Snake) and Utahs, and that he intended to do it.

While returning to Washington late in 1853, former Indian agent Jacob Holeman secured a statement of Shoshone sentiments from traders Herbert Papin and Elisha B. Ryan at today's Casper, Wyoming:

... we have had repeated Conversations with Shoshone or Snake Indians relative to the Settlement of their land by the Mormons and thay have always expressed themselves as violently opposed to their Setling on the territory which the Indians Claim and assert when in the City of G.S. Lake to enter into a treaty with the Utahs and the question was asked by the Governor if they were willing that such Settlements should be made, that they told him they wer[e] not, that the land at Green river belonged to a family that were not there, when asked again if they themselves (such as were present) were willing one of their chiefs replied in the negative. They further say that, some time after the above mentioned treaty they were approached again on the subject of buying the lands on Green River by a messenger or agent of the Mormons, and that their Chief Washikique told said agent of the Mormons, that he had no right to sell the land that belonged to all the Snakes, and that the Mormons had no right to buy it, that when their great white Chief wanted the land, he Washikique would send for all the Snake Indian[s] and if they wanted to sell their lands to their white Chief he was willing, for he would pay them for it, but that he did not want the Mormons there. From frequent Conversations with different members of the tribe and particularly with their principal chiefs Washikique, Amapoch & Liabone we are fully satisfied they are violently opposed to the settlement of their lands at green river; and have never consented that such settlements should be made by the mormons.[17]

Papin and Ryan both had reasons to resent Mormons. The seizure of Fort Bridger created "very ill feelings" among the mountaineers, who threatened to take "as much property out of the Mormons as they had lost." Brigham Young feared "they might bother the emigration the next fall," Bill Hickman recalled, and sent him "to quiet them down in some way or other; and if I could not make peace with them any other way, pitch in and kill those that would not come to terms," especially Ryan, who "would do us much harm, and must go up."[18]

After being told "that some of us might have to take Indian wives," thirty-nine men left Salt Lake on 2 November 1853 under John Nebeker, reaching Fort Bridger two weeks later after battling bad roads, worse weather, and grey wolf packs. The country was "held in the fists of a well organized band of from seventy-five to a hundred desperadoes," still angry about Fort Bridger

---

[17]Ryan and Pappan, Affidavit, 26 November 1853, BYC 58:14. The "White Chief" was President Franklin Pierce.

[18]Hickman, *Brigham's Destroying Angel*, 95–96, 102–106. A. O. Smoot warned in 1860 that Hickman's frequent visits to Young's office led people "to suppose he is sanctioned in all he does by the President." Turner, *Brigham Young*, 260–62.

and "having two or three of their numbers killed at Green River Ferry."
The missionaries trudged twelve miles south through the snow to Willow
Creek, a tributary of Smiths Fork, and picked a spot to build a blockhouse
and cabins. At 7,201 feet elevation, the site was five hundred feet higher than
Fort Bridger. After a three-day visit in December, Orson Hyde left behind a
letter for Washakie but did not stay for winter. As 1853 ended, James Brown
recalled, "the weather was so cold that we had to abandon outdoor work."
Wolves began killing livestock, so the Mormons put out strychnine and
trapped their "ravenous enemies." New Years 1854 brought cold and storms,
threats from the Utes, and seven Shoshones "who got starved out and came
to us for help." The men began studying the Shoshone language, but only
six "made even fair progress in learning the Indian tongue," Brown wrote.
Nebeker sent eight men, four empty supply wagons, and this letter to Salt
Lake, but snow blocked their return.[19]

> We are all well and feel well but on account of the cold wether and the
> condition of our stock I have not started any teams yet. But will in a few
> days. I think about six. I have bin bussey in inquiring the whareabouts of
> Washakeat and from the best information he is on the Medicance bow near
> Laramie. On account of the distance we have not sent any men to him. The
> Utes have Killed some Snakes and lately so it [looked] fair for a war between
> them. One hundred or more of the Utes came on to Henrys [Fork] a few
> days back and was verry mad. Four of our men was over at [the] time. Barney
> talked with Sowettes son. He said the Mormons Snakes and Utes ware all
> alike. Some would Obay their big Captain and some wold not but Said his
> Father wanted to be friends. I have not heard from them for some days but
> I think they have gone back to Browns hole. S. Caldwell has returned from
> his trading vo[ya]ge and I sent Brother Bollack down to see him.[20] He gave
> some information on paper which I enclose to you. The Utes likewise told
> Caldwell they Sent Ammon and others in for a Sham for they intended to
> fight in the Spring and we hear should not raise any grain hear as long as
> there is a Ute alive. The Mountain Men on Henrys fork through fear tel
> Utes thay are thare friends and our Enamiys. Thay Expected Some fighting
> and thay gathered on the head of the crick, but giving some presents and a
> few lies about us the Utes left. The Brethren in general are Faithful in thare
> prares and other duties. No more at [present].[21]

---

[19]Brown, *Life of a Pioneer*, 305, 308–309.

[20]Ibid., 310, 323. Mormon courts settled Caldwell's estate; see Brooks, *The Diary of Hosea Stout*, 2:518n20, 528–29.

[21]John Nebeker to Orson Hyde, 6 January 1854, BYC 39:21.

Samuel M. Caldwell "was said to be at the head of the gang of desperadoes who plied their vocation from Bridger to Green River, and back on the emigrant route to Laramie; he was a large, trim built man, about six feet six inches tall, and very daring," wrote James S. Brown. Caldwell died after Louis Tromley plunged a bowie knife into his vitals in January 1854. Elisha Ryan took over his gang.[22] Orson Hyde enclosed "information on paper," apparently Caldwell's last report.

> On the 8 of Dec I Started with an Equipment of Indian goods to the Utah Indians for the Purpose of Trading. I found them very hostile especially Walkers Band. There was about thirty Lodges ten of which came to my camp. The Ballance was camped about five miles distant. The[y] sent me word they did not want to see the whites [and] they would kill them if they came in to Camp. Sowiats came in Traded & Appeared Friendly toward the whites. The Lodges of Walkers Band informed me that the Balance of the Band [was] 5 miles distant [and] had in their Possesion one hundred & forty head of cattle & about Eighty head of horses which they had Stolen from the Mormon Settlements. The[y] also stated Walker had gone to the Navijoes. Some of the young men that went with him has Returned. The[y] Stated that the Navijoes would be up early in the Spring for the Purpose of Stealing horses & cattel from the Mormon Settlements. I was Compeled to Profess great Friendship towards them to Save the life of one of my men by the name of [J. D.] Shockley who they took to be a mormon.[23] They went so far as to Boast of the Depredations they had Commited on the Settlements. One Stated he was the Person that Shot two bullets in the man at the mill. Another that he shot the man going to the mill with wheat. Another [said] he had Stole so many horses So ma[n]y Cattle & So forth.[24]

Alexander Robbins described the brutal winter to Orson Hyde on 5 March 1854:

> The severe weather set in about the first of January, and the thermometer stood on the 6th, 17° below zero at sunrise; on the 20th, 25° below, at sunrise on the 21st, 30° below. A few cattle died, and some who went out to see to the stock got their feet slightly frozen. At this date the thermometer ranges from 8° to 12° above zero, with frequent snow squalls. We had a Shoshone family with us some two months—an old lady with two sons and one daughter; all of whom have been uniformly friendly, and we have mainly supported them, as they could not hunt to advantage during the cold weather.[25]

---

[22]Brown, *Life of a Pioneer*, 310.

[23]The Utes might have been right. James David Shockley, age 23, and eight family members came to Utah in 1847 with A. O. Smoot's train.

[24]Hyde to Young, 11 January 1854, BYC 39:21, enclosure. The men at the mill Caldwell mentioned were William Mills and John Warner.

[25]Jenson, "History of Fort Bridger and Fort Supply," 34–35.

Cold, hunger, and isolation stirred general disaffection. On Christmas Day the outpost's leaders cut off two men, William Spafford and Asa O. Boyce, who told them that "he was part white and a free man and calculate to do as he damn please, and would go to the Fort when he pleased." After weeks of subzero temperatures, other dissenters refused to do camp duties.[26] On 12 March, fifteen very hungry Shoshones camped near the blockhouse: more "almost starved" Indians appeared six days later. The missionaries shared their only food, bread. An antelope hunt failed and the community was reduced to "living on bread and water." March ended with blustery weather and heavy snow. Lacking women "to drive dull care away," James S. Brown said the men held a "bachelor's dance." Harsh conditions continued through 17 April, but the next day the men "started the plows" despite the "very disagreeable weather." By month's end, even President Nebeker abandoned hope; others soon left for home. The rest of the company continued to plow and plant. Apostle Orson Hyde arrived on 7 May with provisions and some twenty-five reinforcements, although several of them came to set up the county court. "Elder Hyde preached to us on the evening of the 9th, and we had good cheer; everyone seemed to be encouraged," Brown claimed in his relentlessly positive memoir.[27]

Orson Hyde's sermon, Henry Sanderson recalled, "informed us that the way the Indians were to become a white & delightsome people was by our marrying their women." Asked what he thought about Hyde's advice, Sanderson replied that it might be all right, but Apostle Hyde should set the example and "then Say come on Boys instead of Saying go on." When Hyde "took a Squaw to wife perhaps I would, but the example from that Source was never Set." Several missionaries followed Hyde's counsel "& provided homes for Squaws."[28]

Hosea Stout called Fort Supply "the most forbidding and godforsaken place I have ever seen for an attempt to be made for a settlement." He had "no hesitancy in predicting that it will yet prove a total failure but the brethren here have done a great deal of labor." Even Apostle Hyde seemed to have "an invincible repugnance" to the place and left three days after he arrived.[29]

---

[26]Nebeker, Green River Company Journal, 14–15, 23–24.
[27]Brown, *Life of a Pioneer*, 310–11.
[28]Sanderson, Henry Weeks Diary, Typescript, BYU Library.
[29]Brooks, *The Diary of Hosea Stout*, 7, 11 May 1854, 2:515n16, 517.

Buffalo Meat: The Shoshone Bread, 1854

Congress appropriated $45,000 in April 1854 to cover Utah Territory's expenses for "negotiating treaties with and making presents of goods and provisions to the several Indian tribes," diplomatic delegate John Bernhisel informed Governor Young. If ratified, the treaties would require a larger appropriation "to pay the Lamanites for their lands. We shall now I trust have peace with our red brethren. Tell them that if they will be good children, and cease to kill, rob and steal, their great father the President will pay them for their lands." In July both houses of Congress appointed Dimick Huntington the agency's official translator, and appropriated $20,940.65 for "expenses incurred in suppressing Indian hostilities" in 1850 and 1851, $45,000.00 for treaty expenses, and $30,000.00 to cover operations.[30]

As superintendent of Indian affairs, Young used this river of cash to support two projects: converting the Lamanites into yeoman farmers and forging them into the Lord's battle axe. The "Saints" he sent to Green River included some of Zion's most notorious operatives—Orson Hyde, Bill Hickman, Porter Rockwell, James S. Brown, and Hosea Stout. On the way to Fort Supply in May 1854, Hyde, Stout, Hickman, and constable George Boyd had murdered J. T. Hartley "after Brigham Young publicly denounced and excommunicated him."[31]

Cash and commerce played a central role in all frontier Mormon enterprises, be they religious or political, and their ferries had been making money since 1847. During the 1850s overland enterprises generated enormous profits: William Sloan estimated North Platte bridge tolls topped $40,000 in 1853.[32] The brothers Peter and John Richard were "coining money" at their North Platte trading post and bridge, J. Robert Brown reported, making "over $200,000 apiece, but that demon, gambling, keeps them down."[33] Bill Hickman claimed the mountaineers made "some thirty thousand dollars" from their ferries in 1853.[34] They intended to keep them, but Utah's territorial legislature organized Green River County in 1853 and granted D. H. Wells its ferry rights. He picked Nauvoo Legion captain William J. Hawley to run the Middle or Mormon Ferry, now a small village with grocery stores, gambling

---

[30]Bernhisel to Young, 11 April 1854, BYC 60:15; and 14 July 1854, BYC 60:16.

[31]Marquardt, *The Coming Storm*, 16–18.

[32]Sloan, "Autobiography," 246.

[33]J. R. Brown, *Journal of a Trip across the Plains*, 5 July 1856, 51.

[34]Hickman, *Brigham's Destroying Angel*, 91.

tables, and even a brewery where emigrants and mountaineers could wind up the day "according to custom by fiddling, drinking & gambling"—or having a knock-down brawl. "The fact is our place is improving fast," Stout noted, "so when Emmegration & law gets in full blow every body can be accommodated." Soon the Mormons were repairing the "miserable old log house which we occupy for a Court house," where defense attorney and tax collector Hickman, prosecutor Stout, and Judge William I. Appleby enforced all the justice overland emigrants could afford.[35]

Before Apostle Hyde departed on 10 May, he set apart four men "to go to Wooshekut and preach among men of the Shoshone Nation." Three days later, James Brown, Barney Ward, Isaac Bullock, and James Davis headed east. Bullock described wandering across the Red Desert for a week to Washakie's camp:

> We followed down and struck the trail of Woosekut band. We followed it and come up to them bout 10 oclock 30 lodgges and we was soon interdused to the main chief Waeshekeet and he came out to greet us and had nothing on but a blanket round his waist and a better looking Indian I never saw. Inteligent. He received us as friendly as we could wish. He asked us in to his lodge. We read the letter to him that we broat and told him our intentions. He appeared glad and said he wuld send for all the chieves have them come and have a talk with us. We gave him the shirts and tobacco and he said the chieves was poor and when they come he would let them have it to divid out amoung all of the men. And he asked us if would have some Buffalo meat as that was the Shoshone bread and we told him we would and got some flour and coffe and his women went to work and made up a supper. They fride the cakes in Buffalo tallow and it was first rate. He was camped on Mudy creek Indian (Poogguat]. We slep in his lodge that night.[36]

James Brown recalled a more colorful encounter. "Who are you, from where do you come, and what is your errand to my country?" Washakie asked. By signs and gestures, he said, 'Tell me the truth; do not tell me any lies, nor talk any crooked talk.'" Brown explained "the big Mormon captain" had sent the missionaries "to learn better the Indian dialects, manners and customs," to warn them that the game would soon disappear, and "to show them how to till the earth, and raise stock, and build houses, like the white man did," so "their wives and children would not starve to death." An "old

---

[35]Brooks, *The Diary of Hosea Stout*, 6 June 1854, 2:519.

[36]Bullock, Diary, 7–29 May 1854, MS 1478, LDS Archives. Muddy Creek north flows to the Sweetwater River. The camp was probably south of the Sweetwater near today's Three Forks junction at Muddy Gap.

and wise counselor" objected to Brown's proposition "that some of us might want to take some of the young Indian women for wives."

> No, for we have not got daughters enough for our own men, and we cannot afford to give our daughters to the white man, but we are willing to give him an Indian girl for a white girl. I cannot see why a white man wants an Indian girl. They are dirty, ugly, stubborn and cross, and it is a strange idea for white men to want such wives. But I can see why an Indian wants a white woman.

The council ended when Washakie said, "the white men might look around, and if any one of us found a girl that would go with him, it would be all right, but the Indians must have the same privilege among the white men." The Mormons next visited a camp of "fifteen hundred and two thousand Indians, principally Shoshones," with some Cheyennes and Arapahos, Brown recalled.[37]

When the four missionaries returned on 1 June, Stout wrote, they reported "the indians somewhat ill disposed but some were friendly."

Whites Sitting on Their Lands: June 1854

In mid-June seven Shoshones escorted Elisha Ryan to Fort Supply, where several lodges were already camped. Ryan "said he was sent by the Head Chief to learn what our intentions were. Whether we intended to take their land & if so whether peaceably or not." They wanted to know the feelings of "the General Goverment & also Governor Young and the mormons, towards them," Hosea Stout reported. The Shoshone "did not want their timber cut or have houses built on their land nor have settlements established." They wanted "to live in peace with all men but at the same time they would not allow any infringement on their lands." The tribe had granted special rights to mountaineers who married Shoshone women, without which "no one had a right to keep a ferry here." Ryan denied the legislature's power "to grant a legal charter without the consent" of the Shoshones who owned the land. "The plot thickens and a considerable excitement." Sheriff Hickman's posse found Ryan passed out at Kinneys Ferry and arrested him. After a "sober second thought," Ryan agreed to behave "and the excitement ended without smoke," Stout noted. "And thus ended the Sabbath day on Green River."[38]

---

[37]Brown's memoir, *Life of a Pioneer*, 316–22, is full of intriguing if suspect detail.
[38]Brooks, *The Diary of Hosea Stout*, 1, 15–18 June 1854, 2:518, 520–21.

James Brown reported "all the mooves that are made by the Shoshoney Indians" to Orson Hyde on 20 June "and Those that have been trying to influence them a gainst the People of Utah." All the Shoshones "design going in to Fort Supply and they don't know but what they will go in to the valley for they are desirous to know what the mormons is going to do on their Lands." They often spoke about trade "and of Bridgers being run off who all ways had furnished them with such things as they kneeded." "Mr Wrine"—Ryan—and the ferrymen on Green River had formed an alliance, and before Sheriff Hickman could deliver proper papers, Ryan seized the Kinney Ferry. Francis M. Russell secured a writ to stop Ryan, but Sheriff Hickman and Constable Boyd found Ryan at the ferry with a dozen well-armed, drunken "backers." Brother Hickman somehow negotiated a compromise, but trader Charles Kincaid met Ryan headed east from the ferries, saying he "was going out to establish him Self some wher to traid."[39] Judge Appleby's report of the Green River rebellion showed how land was always at the heart of the long defense of Shoshone rights.

WILLIAM I. APPLEBY TO BRIGHAM YOUNG, 24 JUNE 1854,
BYC 23:9, 55–58.

Green River County June 24 /54

Br. B. Young

As I have a few minutes to spare before the Mail leaves this morning (which has Just arrived here) I embrace the opportunity of writing a few lines to you informing you in brief how we are getting along out here. In the first place I would inform you that we have had some pretty "*scaly* times" in regard to Elisha Ryan, a Mountaineer and several others that claims the Ferries here on Green River, from under a right & gift of the Shoshone Indians. Ryan is the one, the boys arrested out here last fall and made his escape from the guard that was conveying him a Prisoner to Salt Lake City. He has been with the Shoshone Indians all winter, has married two or three of their squaws. He came here to Green River Ferry about two weeks since with six or eight Indians (some ten lodges having preceded him) and demanded the Ferries in the name of the Shoshone chief who had given him the same. The Chief having deputed a young Indian (his son & Ryans Brother in law) to tell us here his the [sic] Chiefs wishes and concerning the gift of the Ferries to Ryan. We held a council with them. I explained to Ryan the right of the Territory to grant charters, the Organization of this Territory by the United States, its boundaries defined, the Government being organized by

---

[39]Brown to Hyde, 20 June 1854, BYC 39:21.

the United States &c. and that the U.S. did not admit of the Indians owning one foot of the land no[r] anything else, but claimed all upper and Lower California by conquest and purchase of Mexico &c &c. It seemed to take him by surprise. I further informed him that the U. States treated with the Indians, and gave them annuity &c for their lands but that was policy, and not a right acknowledged by the U. States. He then made a Proposition to the Ferry company that he would leave the decision of the right & legality of the Legislature to grant charters here on Indian lands, and would enter into Bonds in the sum of fifty thousand Dollars, which was agreed to by the Parties. I drew up the writings and a letter of Inquiry to the chief of the Bureau of the Indian Department at Washington, with duplicates. This took place on saturday last, and on sunday Ryan went up to Kinneys Ferry, and demanded the Boat running there. [Ryan] claimed it as his own and told the Emigrants he would receive the pay. Several of the Mountaineers were with him that had come up from the Sweet Water. Russell, one of the Owners of the Ferry, said he would have shot him if it had not been for Mr Jones. He wished law to have its effect, so a writ or Complaint of Russell was issued to arrest Ryan & his Posse, and W. Hickman with six of the boys sent up to arrest him, and make him deliver up the Boat. When he saw Hickman & the boys, he said he was drunk, was willing to settle it, and wished peace with the Party on the Ferry—so the Parties settled it amicably between themselves, and on tuesday last they entered into Bonds, and at present things in regard to the Ferry are quiet. How long they will remain so I cannot tell, if it had not been for the law and offices out here, the Ferries would at this time been in the possession of Ryan & his Company. SoKaper the head chief of the Shoshones Indians arrived here last evening. We had a smoke with him, but no time to talk with him. We have a Council with him and his chiefs to day. There is some seven or eight hundred Indians on their way here from the Sweet Water &c. SoKaper wanted to know as soon as he arrived if the Whites had left the Ferries. He is displeased with the whites sitting on their lands here, cutting timber, building Houses &c. and says they must quit it, but I think his mind will alter when we have a talk with him.

We have some few law suits here, chiefly in regard to Replevy [sic] claims, appertaining to the Caldwell Estate. I do not think according to the appraisement that it will pay more than fifty or sixty cents on the dollar, the whole appraisement only amounted to about two thousand Dollars. Next monday the sale takes place at Kinneys Ferry, where the Property is. Br Hickman makes a first rate good officer. His name is enough, among these devils of the Mountains, although there are some Mountaineers that are men of principle, and quietness as far as I have seen. He pursues a course of Wisdom. Br Boyd [G. W. Boyce] makes a good constable also. Tell Br Hyde that *horse trade* is not made yet but will be attended to just as soon as the grass gets a little higher, and when the *"little Bay"* gets tame enough to let him run without a Larriet—so says Br. H[ickman]—.

My health continues poor and has been ever since I cam here but the weather is fine at present, and I hope my health will be better. My kind love and regards to you Brs Heber & Grant and all enquiring Brethren & Friends.

As ever your true and faithful Br & Friend

W I Appleby

NB I think it would be wisdom to send out the Indian Agent here immediately with a few Indian goods to see SoKaper & his tribe.

James Brown and Judge Appleby acknowledged Sheriff Hickman's previously unappreciated talent as a peacemaker. Appleby reported again "in regard to Ryan and the Indians" six days later. "We have had several interesting councils & smokes, with the Shoshone Chiefs *SoKaper* and *'Washakeeke.'*"

They say they want peace, & dont want to fight the whites, but dont want the whites to settle on their lands, building houses or cut down their timber, without their leave,—this the white men among them have imbued in their minds, no doubt. The Indians have all left here now and have gone up towards "Subletts Ferry" in Oregon, where Ryan and other Mountaineers are. I have heard it reported that they intended to take the Ferry up there, and no doubt if it had not been for the law, and vigilant officers here these Ferries on Green River, in Utah Territory, would at the present time been in Possession of the Mountaineers & Indians. The Mountaineers with Ryan at their head made a Pass to take Kinneys Ferry, but a warrant issued against them, and a sufficient Posse for their arrest, they quailed and fled.

Appleby heard "that 'Fort Supply' will be evacuated, before fall, and that there will be no District Court held there in August next." He would not complain: "This Country and climate does not agree with me, and it is enough for to make any one sick to hear the talk of Emigrants & Mountaineers, it is a perfect hell."[40]

Many Abuses We Have Patiently Suffered: Washakie

Mormon records paint a colorful portrait of Washakie, who arrived at the Mormon Ferry on 30 June 1854 and "was not here long before he became intoxicated when he acted very bad," Hosea Stout wrote. He sobered up

---

[40]Appleby to Brigham Young, 30 June 1854, BYC 23:9.

and "professed to be all very good," but "left mad creating considerable excitement." The next day, William "Hawley moved two waggon loads over the river & cached his liquor for fear the indians might come & get drunk and thereby create a difficulty."[41]

James S. Brown recalled Washakie inspected the ferry's "boat and its fixtures, or tackle; then he went to the brewery, the bakery, store, court room, whisky saloon, blacksmith shops, card tables, saw much money changing hands, and observed that money would purchase about anything the white man had." Washakie saw Hawley "handling considerable money," including "two or three fifty-dollar gold slugs." He wanted one, but "the captain laughed at him, and offered him a silver dollar." Outraged, Washakie walked away, "got hold of some intoxicants," and contemplated the injustice "going on in the land of his forefathers."

> This is my country, and my people's country. My fathers lived here, and drank water from this river, while our ponies grazed on these bottoms. Our mothers gathered the dry wood from this land. The buffalo and elk came here to drink water and eat grass; but now they have been killed or driven back out of our land. The grass is all eaten off by the white man's horses and cattle, and the dry wood has been burned; and sometimes, when our young men have been hunting, and got tired and hungry, they have come to the white man's camp, and have been ordered to get out, and they are slapped, or kicked, and called "d—d Injuns." Then our young men get heap mad, and say that when they have the advantage of the white man, as they have often, they will take revenge upon him. Sometimes they have been so abused that they have threatened to kill all the white men they meet in our land. But I have always been a friend to the white man, and have told my people never to moisten our land with his blood; and to this day the white man can not show in all our country where the Shoshone has killed one of his people, though we can point to many abuses we have patiently suffered from him. Now I can see that he only loves himself; he loves his own flesh, and he does not think of us; he loves heap money; he has a big bag full of it; he got it on my land, and would not give me a little piece. I am mad, and you heap my good friend, and I will tell you what I am going to do. Every white man, woman or child, that I find on this side of that water," pointing to the river, "at sunrise tomorrow I will wipe them out" (rubbing his hands together). He went on: "You heap my friend; you stay here all right; you tell them to leave my land. If they are on the other side of my water, all right,

---

[41]Stout reported the District Court indicted "Capt W. J. Hawley" for selling liquor to the Indians on 19 December 1854. Brooks, *The Diary of Hosea Stout*, 2:522, 534.

me no kill them, they go home to their own country, no come back to my land. Tomorrow morning when the sun come up, you see me. My warriors come, heap damn mad, and wipe them all out, no one leave.[42]

The following obsequious and imperious letter makes it possible to compare Brown's embroidered memoir with his contemporary report.

JAMES S. BROWN TO ORSON HYDE, 1 JULY 1854, BYC 39:21, 39–40.
Green River County Mormon Crossing July 1st[?]/54

Brother Hyde Respected Sir.

Washakeek, came in here yesterday whilst I was up at Henrys Fork, and the Brethren here Say that he drew his sword and Smote the Rafters of the Grocery, and Pushed some of the men out of the haus and Cast his B[uffalo] Robe on to the Ground and Stamped it in anger. He also thrust his Sord thru the Roof of the haus, and then he raised an excitement. And they sent for me to come down and talk to him (Washakeek). I came down in hast[e] and he, Washakeek Came out of the haus and Shook hands with me all so his comrad, one other Indian.

They knew me and said that they was pleased to meet with me, for they had come to hav a talk. We then went with him in to the Court room and had a smoke with them. He then told me what he had heard and also what his eyes now be held. That was many roads threw his land, and Fords established & crost all the rivers, Butifull Groves cut down and houses Built and said he, all of this is Washakeeks and I am the man that It Belongs to, Washakeek is my name and I fear not for the roof that is now over our heads also the Seats that we Sit on is mine; And now I want you to Write a letter to Brigham Young, the mormon Chief that I and all the Shoshoneys Will come in when Corn, Wheat, and Potatoes Get [ripe] and the mormons hav plenty to eat for the whites has killed of[f] all our Game and we cant come in their to have a talk without Some thing to eat. So we shall wate and come in when the Serves Berrys Get ripe and by that time the mormans will have plenty. I told him I would but hope that this may answer the purpess.

They unsaddled their muls and was agoing to stay all Knight But he either had or Got Some thing to *drink* that made him drunk. However, he was partly Drunk when he came, as he walked around and knocked about. He said his feelings was hurt to see what the whites had done on his lands; and whilst he talked a bout it his eyes sparkled with an heathens rage and said that he was Going home and pict up his saddle and started And Said he I want this land and all that is on it the houses the Boat and every thing hear is mine and now I want them. He then mounted his mule and Started on the loss

---

[42]Brown, *Life of a Pioneer*, 338–40.

[?] and said that he would yet see the mormans and Brigham Young, to talk with them. I encisted on having him Stop but he would not but he told his comerad to Stop. So I gave him 2 of my Bead blankets and some one & I gave him some Tobacco and said that Washakeek would receive half when he Got Sober. So from every appearance the Fordmen and traders will have trouble hear in a few dayes and every Body that Stops here has now moved all their affects a crost the River and shall try to taken [*sic*] of what they hav.

Hickman read this and added a postscript: Brown was correct but Hickman did "not aprehend as much danger as most of the Folk have." They needed a government agent to explain "what to promis the Indians or what the agent will give them." They told the Shoshones Hyde "and our great chief B. Young are good friends to them and we wish to live here and be friends, but that is not what they want to know"—what the Mormons would give them. Someone should explain Utah Territory to them "and what they may expect." These issues, Hickman wrote, "are the things that cause all their bad feeling."

As June ended, Brigham Young wrote to Washakie and Tatowats, the official Shoshone leader known as White Man's Son. "I love you very much and have always loved you. I know that you are the very best Indians in all the mountains" and had "always been friendly." The Mormons wished "to cultivate some of your land and raise grain and vegetables if they will grow there" and hoped to "buy as much of it as we want to use." He would "furnish plenty of trade so soon as we can obtain it to trade with all the Shoshones." He had driven James Bridger away for breaking the law, and if he had not "fled or resisted the officers but stood his track, perhaps he might have got clear and not even been fined." He promised to "send you some trade, all we can at present, but will send more when we can obtain it." If anyone said the Mormons were "going to kill off the Indians or would do it if they should come against us, you just tell them that they lie for we are your friends and brethren and not your enemies." If they all lived "friendly with each other" and did "each other all the good that we can the Great Spirit will be pleased with us and make us happy." Meanwhile, O. P. Rockwell and G. W. Bean would "take out some trade and talk with you and I hope transact business to your satisfaction."[43]

Sheriff Hickman explained how he resolved the crisis.

---

[43]Young to Wash-e-kik and Tatowats, 28 June 1854, James, "Brigham Young–Chief Washakie Farm Negotiations," 246–48. Tatowats was a Shoshone also leader known as Tibebutowats, or White Man's Son.

WILLIAM A. HICKMAN TO BRIGHAM YOUNG, 13 JULY 1854, BYC 23:13.

Green River Ferry July 13th 1854

Dear Bro. Brigham Young

By request of Bro. Appleby and others of the brethren here I address you a line of information concerning affairs in this country. We have used every exertion to [al]lay all excitement and bad feelings that has existed amongst the indians and Mountaineers which we have succesfully done—It has been no small job to do this it has we have had to use much stratagem. We have not failed in anything which we have undertaken to do with the Inidians [*sic*]—In the first place we learned Ryan was East with a large portion of Indians. I was satisfied that it was best to see him—I therefore wrote him a letter with some flattery and at the same time learned the feelings of the Mountaineers which I found with but verry few exceptions to be good towards Ryan. Jack Robertson who is the man of most influence thought Ryan to be a good fellow but high strung and would do what was rite if he thought he would not be hurt.[44] On informing him he would not, he then sent an Indian after him and in a few days he came with rather bad feelings from his last fall treatment. He brought some of the Chiefs with him who stated they had given Ryan Green River and as no treaty had ben made with them for their lands thought his right to be good but if it was not he did not want it—to settle this I advised him to compromise by binding in Bonds and leaving it to Washington or the superindendant of such business at Washington which he readily consented to and accordingly has done binding himself to keep peace and use his influence amongst the Indians to that effect—which has done and continues to do. He talk much to the Indians in favour of the Mormons. He seem[s] to take an interest in it. He will do anything I tell him and boast of it, for I am his friend as he says he wants peace and will do anything for us to effect it. He is one of the chieves of the Shoshonees and they consider him one of them and so do they think of all the Mountaineers who have squaws for wives—Jack Robertson tell[s] himto mind me and he will get along well. The Mountaineers all felt well. They say there has never been as good fee[l]ings here as now exists—there are manny of them who are the greatest of scamps but are as good to us as they can be—I do not know of a man on the River but what would come at a word to assist me in arresting any person. They many times come and offer their services and send word if I have anything to do with a large train just call on them—We have effected these feelings by telling them there

[44]John "Uncle Jack" Robertson (1806–1884), a veteran of the Pierres Hole 1832 fur trade rendezvous and battle, was a beloved character at Fort Bridger for four decades. Hafen, *Mountain Men*, 7:247–54. In a postscript to this letter, Hickman reported the Indians wanted "a trading post established on their lands near the buffaloo where they can trade and have something to eat at the same time. They want it on Snake River." Robertson agreed it was "a good place to raise grain and if we will make a settlement he will go with us so he can educate his children." Hickman said, "Robertson would be "the rite kind of a man to keep a post."

is good felling [*sic*] towards them and none will be tro[u]bled that some mormons talk an[d] act foolishly but not to mind it—this we had to do to get the good feeling of the Indians for they were so linked together we had not power to separate them. They are now working for us with the indians and will continue no doubt if some fool don't rip up what has been done.

Porter Rockwell is verry anxious to do it.[45] He says he dont care for w[h] at has been done if [he] could find the Indi[a]ns he would do as he was a mind to. We have ta[l]ked to him but to no effect—we have talked to Bro. Geo. Bean. He sees how thing[s] are here. He sees as we do and is satisfied and as we have taken much pains in explaining to him. I wish you would converse with him as he can give you satisfaction on anything I have not. Bros. Appleby Brown & myself have acted together and been agreed in all that has been done. We looke at things alike.

The Indians want to know what will be given them for their lands and w[h]at is going to be done for them—this is all they wish to know at this time. They feel well [and] are coming in to see you as soon as corn and mellons get ripe and have a feast and also some of the Mountaineers who have squaws with them. Ryan wished me to write to you that he would be a good man and use every exe[r]tion to make the Indians good and do just what you said.

As ever
Wm A. Hickman

Shortly after Porter Rockwell's visit, the Green River mission collapsed. The Mormons had learned the country was "a hard lonesome place." John Pulsipher claimed they were "all released to come home unless some wished to stay and save the crops."[46] Even James Brown complained the mission was "one of the most hazardous, soul-trying, disagreeable experiences of my life." Brown and Rockwell returned to Salt Lake Valley in July 1854, leaving the fort in the hands of Mormon mountaineers Barney Ward, Joshua Terry, and a few missionaries.[47]

Elisha Ryan became Hickman's "special friend" and interpreter: both enjoyed whiskey, deception, violence, and making money. Ryan proved "of great service," for he "could talk the Indian language as well as they could," Hickman recalled. "He came home with me and staid that winter. I had him

---

[45]In July 1854 Rockwell gave Brown a license from Brigham Young "to trade with the Indians" and delivered several "thousand dollars' worth of Indian goods," perhaps in response to Washakie's May request to "Bring out traid." The Shoshones "had disposed of their robes, pelts and furs for the season," so Brown stored the goods. Brown, *Life of a Pioneer*, 346–47.

[46]Pulsipher, Short Sketch, 43.

[47]Brown, *Life of a Pioneer*, 345–46. Isaac Baum, Amenzo Baker, Moses Sanders, and two others were living at Fort Supply when the missionaries returned. Pulsipher, Shoshone Mission Journal, 24 May 1855, 6.

with me on three trips to the Indians." Late that fall, they "had one starving trip through our foolishness" when they set out "to hunt up" Washakie," but "traveled eight days and found no Indians." This is the letter Young sent with them.[48]

BRIGHAM YOUNG TO WASH-E-KIK, 6 NOVEMBER 1854, BYC 17:15.

G.S.L. City, November 6th, 1854.

To Wash-e-kik.

I send this my letter to you by your good friends Mr Ryan & Mr Hickman. I was sorry to learn that your people are so disposed to break up & scatter about. I love the Shoshones, and therefore wish to tell you and your people some of my ideas which I think will be for your good. I think it is a poor plan for the Shoshones to scatter so much, & roam about in such small parties. This plan exposes you more to the attacks of your enemies. I also think it unwise for you to depend entirely upon hunting, & fishing for your living, for game is often scarce, and often hard to be caught, and in such cases you suffer from hunger, and sometimes starve. Now I would like to see your people collect into larger bands, & begin to cultivate the earth that you may not suffer, or starve when you are unfortunate in hunting. You have many good places that you can settle upon to raise grain & vegetables. Mr Ryan tells me that a place on Green River called Brown's Hole is [a] good spot for raising wheat, corn, potatoes, pumpkins, & many other things which are good to eat. If you wish to begin to farm, so that you may have plenty to eat in the long winters, without being obliged to hunt in the cold, I will send good men of my people to help you ~~Mr Ryan, Mr Hickman & Mr Brown~~ make farms, & help show you how to raise grain. I hope you will see that this is for your good, and conclude to begin to till the earth next spring, and I will help you to seed, tools, & such aid as you may wish to give you a good start.

During the coming winter I think it will be a good plan for you to go to some good hunting grounds, not in too small parties, and lay up plenty of meat, and dress skins, & robes, and next spring I will send men with blankets, powder, lead, beads, & such trade as you may wish, which you can purchase with your robes, skins, & such other articles as you may have to exchange. I hope you will understand that I am your friend, and brother, & that I desire to do you all the good I can. I also wish you to understand that Mr Ryan, Mr Hickman, & Mr Brown, and such of my friends & brothers as I may send to you, are your friends & brothers, and wish to do you good, & I presume your hearts will be good towards them, & that you will use them well, & open your ears to their good counsel.

Now Wash-e-kik & the Shoshones I want you to remember these my

---

[48]Hickman, *Brigham's Destroying Angel*, 105–106.

words to you, & open your ears well to understand them, & do not forget that I am your friend & Brother. [49]

SULLEN SULKINESS: SUBJUGATING THE NORTHWESTERN SHOSHONES, 1854

After Fort Supply closed in July, Mormon focus on Shoshones shifted west. At Manti, Nelson Higgins reported, "yesterday a Utah Indian came to me and stated that the (Snakes) or Shoshonee Indians had lately fell uppon a band of Utahs east of this place and killed five of the Utahs, drove off about fifty head of horses, stole a number of blankets and other articles of Indian trade that Walker had left with the band." Among the Utes killed "was one big Captain who was as big as Walker"—Quletes wanted Superintendent Young "to talk to the Shoshonees, and to assertain if they still intend to continue falling on them and kill them off and drive away their property." The Shoshones promised to be friendly, "yet they kill all that they possibly can and steal all the property that is in their power to get."[50]

Major David Moore of Ogden was always anxious "to Carry out whatever orders that may be presented by my Superior Officers." As 1854 began, he directed "forting up." Of eight Weber County forts, only three were underway: "the Rest have done nothing towards building their walls unless talking about them, but as soon as the earth is unchained from Jack Frost, I intend to Stir this people up, *as with a sharp stick*, and if the Lord will, keep doing so, untill every fort is well fortified and safe from Indian depredations," he reported. The Northwestern Shoshones were quiet but seemed "to have a kind of Sullen Sulkiness hanging about them, that I have not seen in any season before." Since fall 1853 the Weber bands had complained "about the whites using up all their lands and wood & some of them seem more sulky about it than they have been heretofore."[51] James Ferguson expected the grumbling Indians to listen to reason:

> I regret to learn of the spirit of the Indians in your vicinity. It requires in all places and with all classes of the aborigines a straight forward, mild, and at the same time, independent policy to be pursued. If they grumble about their lands shew them that those lands were created that they might

[49]See also James, "Brigham Young—Chief Washakie," 249–50.
[50]Higgins to Young, 2 September 1854, BYC 23:13.
[51]Moore to Ferguson, 13 February 1854, UTMR.

be cultivated and give them an opportunity by fair wages for the work they do to partake of the products. Shew them the use to which we put the timber and teach them to do likewise. With them as with white men idleness begets discontent; and Industry begets Peace and Contentment. Keep them at work if possible and pay them as you would your own species, and their grumbling will cease by degrees. Do not allow the energies of the people to relax, nor the work to be stayed till your settlements are properly fortified. You are not safe till then.[52]

The Lamanites proved unreasonable. In November 1854 Moore was "Called upon again this morning to remove the Indians from near Binghams fort, in Consequence of their burning up the fences" enclosing the farms of prominent Mormons, "as they have done frequently before for the two past years."

I have also been informed that the Utahs & some of the Shoshonees have killed several head of young Cattle about that section, and when the people remonstrate with them on the subject, they only Give them impertinant answers, such as, the Walker Utes have killed men & Cattle & that your Excellency has made them many presents, & they (the Soldier & Band) intend to do the same, that they may have presents also, they also say that the fence poles is their wood and they have a right to burn them & will do so, this is the prevaling spirit that is in them.

Moore wanted "express Council," since "removing an encampment of Indians often excites them very much," making the task a "rather hazarding job." His position "in respect to the Indians" was precarious, but Moore promised to carry out the prophet's orders to the best of his ability.[53] This apparently inspired Young's letter to Katattoo, "Chief of the Band of Shoshones Indians, about the Weber River north, and all the Shoshones Indians in that vicinity."

I Brigham Young write a few lines to you to let you know my council is to you, for this winter and next Spring. It will be rather difficult to get a living where you are this winter because you have not raised any grain; nor is there any game of importance near you. I therefore advise you to go to the Buffalo country this winter where you can hunt and get plenty of meat and skins, and in the Spring early select your location where you will feel satisfied to settle down and raise grain and we will assist you to open a farm where you can raise grain. I would also advise you to trade for cattle, cows &c, and raise stock, so that you might have meat and bread without having to go off

[52]Ferguson to Moore, 21 February 1854, Vault MSS 731, BYU Library.
[53]Moore to Young, 23 November 1854, BYC 23:15.

hunting for it. I hope by another winter that you will not be obliged to go away to hunt but will have enough to live on that you have raised, but this winter, I think you had better go and hunt.

Their "friend & brother" wished them good luck and hoped "that God will prosper and bless you."[54]

Young soon heard "that Little Soldier and his band are quit[e] troublesome in pilfering, burning fence poles, &c." The best thing to do "with that band is to distribute them out among the inhabitants of the district to labor and earn a living"—a task easier said than done. Americans justified taking harsh measures against Indians by arguing it was for their own good. So was reducing the Shoshones to indentured servitude.

> If the Indians will stay where you place them with the brethren, it will very much improve their condition, and there will be no fear of them going hungry or naked. Just take them and distribute them in families to the brethren; and tell them they must work, and tell the brethren they must exercise patience and forbearance, but require them to work, pay them reasonable wages in food and clothing day by day, and in such articles as they need, for themselves and families. In this way they will be disposed of very much to their own advantage and benefit and to the relief of the community, who will also find it much cheaper to support them in this manner, and they will do something towards their own support! as it is, the people have them to sustain. As to making them presents, it cannot be done. If they want things they must work and pay for them like other people.

That is, white people. Young denied giving the Utes presents for bad acts, claiming Wakara had "not at any time done anything." If a few of his men had, "they have been mostly used up for it, and the rest probably will be if they do not quit." Young called on "the people to aid and sustain" Moore, and if they managed the Indians properly, it would "very materially assist in bringing them to an understanding of our design in doing them good." From the safety of his new mansion, Young made the major's task harder: "You must have them disarmed, take from them their Guns, bows and arrows, and not permit them to have them." He would "send down Wm. Hickman with Mr. Ryan, and probably D. B. Huntington to talk to and preach to them, and explain to them our wishes." This would "probably cause them to comply with our wishes with little or no difficulty. But be this as it may you must have it done."[55]

---

[54]Young to Ka-tat-too, 24 November 1854, BYC 2:1, Letterbook 2:751.
[55]Young to Moore, 27 November 1854, BYC 2:1, Letterbook 2:756–57.

James S. Brown returned to Weber County from Fort Supply and on 28 August 1854 interpreted for Governor Young on his visit "to Chief Catalos' camp of Shoshones, four miles north of Ogden." Katattoo had "grievances to settle, and particularly desired to ask favors and get a better understanding with the white men through their big chief." Young gave the band "a liberal present of assorted Indian goods, talked friendship," Brown recalled, and "advised them to be good people, and to live at peace with all men, for we had the same great Father."

> Governor Young told them it would be good for them to settle down like the white man, and learn of him how to cultivate the land as he did, so that when the game was all gone they could live and have something to eat and to feed their families on. The Indians said this was "heap good talk," and their hearts felt good; so we parted with them in the best of feelings, notwithstanding that some of their bad Indians had stolen my only horse from where I had picketed him on the bottoms. I did not learn the facts in the case in time to get redress, and all the consolation I could obtain was that the thief did not know it was my animal—"heap no good Indian steal your horse."

On 20 November Brown, Bill Hickman, Elisha Ryan, and Dimick Huntington delivered "an order to Major Moore and the citizens of Weber County to disarm Chief Little Soldier and his band of Indians," distribute them among the Mormons "best able to feed and clothe them for the winter, and set them to work." The Shoshone families "had become very troublesome to the citizens of that county, by killing cattle, burning fences, and intimidating isolated families." Moore sent Brown to Little Soldier's camp, "and with considerable talking we got the Indians to accompany us to Ogden City," Brown recalled. "Still, they felt very warlike and stubborn, being unwilling to give up their arms." He allowed the Indians "to go with their arms across the Ogden River and camp among the willows."

Brown tried again with a posse in December but found the Shoshones "so hostile that we had to make a show of arms before they would submit to our proposition of distributing them among the whites." He devised a scheme to deceive and disarm the warriors, but "there was not a man who obeyed the order." Brown personally "went through the crowd of Indians and took every weapon with my own hands," and locked them in the tithing office. Brown and Moore next disarmed a "small party of Indians camped in the center of what was called Bingham Fort." Brown grabbed "a big Ute's gun" and wrestled it away. "He was full of wrath and a desire for vengeance. I found him to be one of the strongest men I had ever grappled with anywhere." Brown "vainly tried to talk the red men into reconciliation." Returning to Ogden, he "found the whites and Indians on the streets," with the Shoshones "as discontented as ever." Brown and Moore "tried to pacify them, but they were very stubborn and sullen." Brown recalled that Katattoo's brother explained why:

> "Here are my wife, my children, my horses and everything that I have. Take it all and keep it, only give me back my gun and let me go free. I will cast all the rest away. There is my child," pointing to a little three-year-old, "take it." The little innocent held up its hands and cried for the father to take it, but he frowned and looked at it as with a feeling of disgust, saying, "Go away. You are not mine, for I have thrown you away, and will not have you any more. . . . we are only squaws now. We cannot hunt or defend our families. We are not anybody now."

Brown knew his demand was humiliating, but the ends justified the means. The sullen Indians "went home with the whites and pitched their tents in the back yards." It was "hard to have them feel so bad, but they had no means of support for the winter, the citizens could not afford to have their stock killed off and their fences burned, and it was the better policy to feed the Indians and have them under control." The Shoshones "could husk corn, chop wood, help do chores, and be more comfortable than if left to roam; but for all that, they were deprived of that broad liberty to which they and their fathers before them had been accustomed, therefore they felt it most keenly." Brown began teaching Shoshone to dozens of Mormons, bought and fenced an Ogden lot, closed his Indian trading business, "and settled with D. H. Wells for the goods."[56]

"Feeling that you would be happy to hear how we are progressing with Soldier and his band," Major Moore told Brigham Young he had "not as yet been enabled to Get them fully divided out by families" but rejoiced accomplishing "some of the purposes of heaven Concerning this Lamanite Band." They had been "very discontented untill Pah-bush Returned from the City with the Tobacco & Letter." Little Soldier and his men "formed a Circle in front of the door" of Moore's house "& had a good smoke." Jim Brown explained Young's letter: "Soldier then Got up & shook hands with

---

[56]Brown, *Life of a Pioneer*, 346–50.

all present saying that he was fully satisfied and wanted to live in peace with all. Joy was on every Countinance present Both of the Brethren & Natives and we felt thankful to our Heavenly Father that he had thus far Blessed the undertaking." Moore advised the brethren "to not push them too hard at first with Labour, as they are unacostumed to work and as a matter of Course it will Come hard to them at first." Some Shoshones resisted: "Old Pipeagins and his band took a great fright and ran off to Box Elder in the night Saying that they did not know what the Americans intended to do with the Indians."[57]

As these events unfolded, Wilford Woodruff visited. He "saw the Indians who were lately distributed among the people for the purpose of bettering their condition by feeding them and clothing them and learning them to work." Most were at the forts, "very mad, and uneasy, fearing that some evil was designed against them; and while we were holding a meeting many left their wickeups standing and went down to Weber River."[58] The apostle claimed the Shoshones became "reconciled," but as long as northern Utah remained contested ground, tension and conflict endured.

A month later, David Moore felt it was his duty to report "our progress with the Soldier" and the Shoshone leader's reaction to a note from Brigham Young, who had disarmed and essentially enslaved his people.

> Bro. James Brown 3d undertook to Read it to Soldier undertook to Read it to Soldier but he was entirely deaf to it. Saying that the whites had endeavoured to talk to him for 3 years back & he was tired of their talks. The Indian that brought the tobacco & letter [Pah-bush] told something that has displeased them very much; they have been very sulky since but keep silent as to the Cause. Every now & then throw some hints about the Mormons taking away all their Lands &c. They are very angry about their Guns and tease me much for them. I told that when the Big Captain tells me to Give them back their Guns then I will do so, & not before. Some of the families have left the places where I had them distributed, and went into the brush again. It seems a hopeless Job to do any thing in General with them, but I don't feel to stop talking & doing what I Can for them yet by a Considerable.[59]

Moore added that he had "been to see the Shoshones" with James Brown and "Gave them Quite a preach & left them feeling first rate."

---

[57]Moore to Young, 5 December 1854, BYC 23:15.

[58]"Brief Account," *Deseret News*, 28 December 1854, 3/1.

[59]Moore to Young, 25 January 1855, BYC 24:08

THE WRITING OF THE WOLFS, 1855

By 1855 Brigham Young had too many irons in too many fires and too few resources to tend them all. Determined to "sanctify Israel" and build an army to handle the violent onset of the millennium, he dedicated manpower to Indian missions at Fort Limhi, Las Vegas, and Elk Mountain. As famine stalked Utah's settlements, the Steptoe Expedition, with its hundreds of recruits and camp followers, wintered in the territory.[60] Young's term as governor had expired, and on 18 February 1855 he gave two discourses: Thomas Bullock read the first, expressing Mormon "views concerning the government of the United States," which "sustained" the laws and Constitution but "used a sharp two edged sword against wickedness & wicked men." Young "followed with a lengthy sharp Cutting Oral Speech which was more pointed than his written," noted Wilford Woodruff.[61] President Pierce offered the office to Steptoe, who declined the honor and endorsed reappointing Young. Pierce did not, so Young remained governor by default.

On Blacks Fork, the year 1855 began violently. After his stay with Hickman in the settlements, Elisha Ryan returned to Fort Bridger where Hosea Stout noted "Joe a Spaniard" fatally shot "the man who made so much trouble & excitement at Green River Ferry."[62]

At conference, Brigham Young "Blessed & Set apart" at least seventeen men "to go on a mission to the Shoshone Nation & the other Tribes" at Fort Supply. He called James S. Brown "to Preside over the mission," and now women joined the venture. Brown reached Smiths Fork on 17 May 1855 and set out twelve days later with six men to deliver Brigham Young's letters to Washakie. One read:[63]

> Now we have come here into these vallies of the mountains, just at the right time to do good if you will harken to our instructions. The Lord directed us to come here and when you got well acquainted with us and our people, you will understand why. Now, you pray to the Lord and ask him to open your eyes so that you can see and understand about us, and see if he don't manifest to you that what I tell you is true. We can learn you how to get

---

[60]Steptoe started with "three hundred men, sixty wagons, and seven hundred horses and mules," John Bernhisel wrote Young on 12 May 1854, BYC 60:15. "The Overland Troops," *Sacramento Union*, 13 July 1855, 2/1, reported Steptoe's Salt Lake force "numbered some five hundred men."

[61]Van Wagoner, *Complete Discourses*, 18 February 1855, 2:913.

[62]Brooks, *The Diary of Hosea Stout*, 19 January 1855, 2:549.

[63]Pulsipher, Shoshone Mission Journal, LDS Archives. These probably included the November 1854 letter Hickman failed to deliver.

a good living. If you will do as we tell you—and that is to plant and sow grain, and take care of it when it ripens, and raise stock and not ramble about so much, but make farms and cultivate them. We will not disturb you when you make farms and settle down but now no matter where we settle you feel that it is an infringement upon your rights but it is not so, the land is the Lord's and so are the cattle and so is the game; and it is for us to take that course which is the best to obtain what he has provided for our support upon the earth. Now we raise grain and stock to last us year after year, and work to do so, but you depend upon hunting wild game for your support, that was all right when you had plenty of game, and it was to your own country, and you did not have to go so far away off into the Sious and Pawnees Country after it, and before the Lord sent us to do you good, but now you see it is different, and you should make locations on good land and raise grain and stock and live in houses and quit rambling about so much? The Creek and Cherokees have done so long ago and now many of them are very rich, have good comfortable houses and plenty of property. If you do so the Lord will be pleased with and bless you which I desire with all my heart. My heart is good towards you and your people and I wish to do you good and so do my brethren. We want you to be our brethren also. Bad men will give you whiskeys and when you drink it, it makes you mad, you must not do so, it is always bad for Indians to drink whiskey it kills them off. You ask the Lord to tell you if this is not so. I am well pleased with you for you have always been friendly and good so far as I know and I hope that you will continue to be so.[64]

John Pulsipher summarized Brown's second mission to Washakie as soon as his men "returned from their visit to the Shoshoni Tribe" on 14 June. Brown said they "had a firstrate visit with Washekets & the Shoshoni tribe."

JOHN PULSIPHER, SHOSHONE MISSION JOURNAL, 1855–1857,
LDS ARCHIVES.

After we left here on the 29th of May we traveled in the supposed direction of Waheketes camp. When we got about a 100 miles from here we left the wagon & 4 of the boys, Bros. [Elijah] Ward, [Joshua] Terry & myself started on horse back in search of the camp. We arrived there on the morning of the 8th of June just as the company was packing up to start. When they saw us, the men that were on their horses, charged at us armed with bows and arrows & guns. We were not frightened, we waited til they came up. They led us, or excorted us up to Washeketes tent. The crowd opened ranks as we came up & we passed right through the midst of them. They seamed much pleased clapped their hands & shouted tiaboo, tiaboo, which is, white man, white man.

---

[64]Young to Wash-e-kik, 1 May 1855, in James, "Brigham Young–Chief Washakie," 251–52.

The chief was glad to see us, we showed him the letters we had for him. He said they were just starting over to another creek & invited us to go with him. We went—they camped. [At] 2: oo oclock the chief called a council of 18 men—We gave them a piece of tobacco to smoke they laid it away & smoked their own, we wondered why they did so. We then presented the letter & a Book of Mormon to them. They wished us to read them. We read & interpreted the letters as well as we could, tho not perfect. We gave them a little idea of the Book, who wrote it & what the contents are.

The chief asked the council what they had to say. They spoke, some thot they did not want the book or letters! One of the Principal men motioned that these men be sent back & the letters &c with them. The chief then began to talk to them, he understood what we said, & they did not understand all, so he explained what we said. He was filled with the spirit & preached to them good.

He said the reason why they did not smoke that tobacco was, because The mountaineers had told them that the mormons was coming with poizen Tobacco to kill the Indians. When they saw the plug, it was the same size that had been described, so they thot it was poizen. Bro. Barney then took it, & took a chew of it & said it was not Poizen, then they thot the mountaineers had lied. The chief said he believed thise to be good men & they tell the truth. The letters are good & the Book of Mormon is a good book, it was written by our forfathers.

The council seamed to be all agreed & of the same mind of the chief. They wanted to trade for powder & lead &c. Bro. Brown promised to take them some trade, & meet them in about 20 days on Green River. The chief said they had been gathering together as Bro. Brigham wished them to. He was also wiling for his men to go to farming. Said he was wiling for a few mormons to live on his land. He wished to know if we would help them & learn them to build houses & raise grain & be friends to them?

Bro Brown said we would if they would do as we say. He said they would, & chose Bros. Brown, Ward & Tery to Select a place for them to make their farm.

President Brown sent a similar report to President Young. He described calmly facing a traditional "full Charg" Shoshone greeting, a terrifying display of skill and power. A band of Mountaineers and Nez Perces "riding with that mad speed only an Indian or a trapper can ride, yelling, whooping, dashing forward with frantic and threatening gestures" had used a similar display to "meet and greet" Narcissa Whitman and Eliza Spalding at South Pass on 4 July 1836.[65]

---

[65]Victor, *The River of the West*, 201–202.

JAMES S. BROWN TO BRIGHAM YOUNG, FORT SUPPLY,
16 JUNE 1855, BYC 23:20.

Fort Supply, Green River Co. June 16th 1855

Brother Young Dear Sir

As we have just returned from the Shoshoney Camps I feel it my duty, and [*illegible*] to send a report of our mission to you that you may know of our prosperity among the Lamanites. We taken our departur from this plase on the 29 of May and returned her on the 14 of June.

After having visited Washakeeks Camp of 113 lodges and a bout 2,000 Soles. We came to their camp Just as they ware packing up in the morning to moov Camp.

And Just before we got in their camp Some of the Chief men and a number of warers [warriors] met us on the full Charg with their poneys and armed with their Bows arrows and fire arms. Their was but 3 of us who a proached their camp namely E. B. Ward, Joshuway Terry, and my Self.

And as we were a quainted with their customs we did not feel a larmed but proceeded on their camps being *thickly* crowded a round by the warers [warriors] who slaped their hands and shouted as if filled with rage, Crying out (Tibu, Tibu) which was Whites, Whites. They then hileted [escorted?] us to where Washakeek and famley was packing up to move.

Washakeke then met us with a smiling countinence. Shook hands with us and then very politely invited us to lite [dismount]. We did so and the principle part of the men Gethered a round us. Then Washakeke Said all these men have come a round to here what you have Got to say; we then presented your letter to him and told him what our Busness was. He then said that they was a going a cross to another Brook and their we would hav a talk. He invited us to go along with them and they pitched camp a bout 2 clock P.M. And then called in their Council of 18 men and past the pipe a round at which time we a gane presented your letter to the council all So lade the Book of Morman down in the circle, they then wished to hav us read and interpit one of your former letters to them. We did so and they Said that was good and now they wanted to her [hear] the other one and see if they a greed or not. We then red and interpted it to them and left it for them to de cide whether they would receive it or not, and after they had talked a bout it for a while they told us that they had heard of our coming and that E. B. Ward had pison Tabaco for them and that the letters was pison, So they refused to Smoke the Tabaco untill Br ward taken a harty Chew of it. And one of the prisable [principle] men preposed that they sent the letter and all Back and have nothing to doo with any of it nor us but send all away to Gether. This motion was sustained by a number of the Council But the Same man that made the motion picked up the Book of mormon and looked at it and then pased it a round untill Washakeeke got a hold of it. Who opened it and said this is the Writing of the Wolfs that wrome over the plains. Now these Indiens have a tradision that when theire for Fathers depart this life that they are changed into a Wolf and Wrome ore the plains and when we told them that this Book was the writings of theire fore fathers they said yes it was the writings of the Wolfs. He (Washakeeke,) opend the Book a gane and Said that it was Good and from that he seemed to be filled with the Spirit of the Lord and he Spake with that power that all of the Council harkend to what he had to say and Submited to his disision and he Said they had nothing to comence to work like the whites but he wanted the letter and to Hear all we had to say for it was Good and right. He then refured the council to difrent Tribes that had become partly civilized and said he wanted to do as they done and So far he was willing to Abide our council and we to Befriend them when they had done right, and he wanted us as the Whites was a Judg of good land to hunt a place for them and next Spring they would come and Setle on it.

We told them that we would do so and let them know after we had Seen you: that seemed to suit them and they Said they wanted a nuf of whites or mormons to come on their lands to show them how to work and a sist them, and they was then Gethering in from all parts of their land and was not a going to stay to Gether as your letter said for them to do and as they was then out of aminition and in such a large camp of them that it would not be wisdom for them to come into the Setlements of the whites to traid for they could not sustain them Selfs. In so doing their fore they wished us to return home and Bring out traid for them wher they could Traid and hunt Game. So we promest to meet to meet them about 125 miles from this plase up on Green River with what Traid we have hear. We was to meet them in twenty days from that date, the 10, we shall all so leave some 4 or 5 of the Brethren with them to travel with them.

Washakeek said that they quit Slaying any more game than they could consoom, for it was getting very Scarce.[66] Now this is a Small Scetch of our mission and less I wery [weary] your pations [patience] I will conclud by Saying that All is well with us at present and our crops look promising whilst our hearts is filled with Gratitude to our father in heaven for his Blessings and manifestations of his Spirit and will towards us and the Spirit that has

[66]This was not so. "The immense herds of antelope I remember having seen along the route of the new road, in 1854 and 1857, seem to have disappeared," no less an authority than F. W. Lander observed in 1860. The Shoshone now had to travel twelve hundred miles roundtrip to "visit the border ground between their own country and the Crows and Blackfeet for the purpose of hunting elk, antelope, and stray herds of buffalo." They seemed "to have no discretion in the killing of game. The antelope 'surrounds,' in which the whole tribe often engages, are made at that season of the year when the antelope is heavy with young, or has the fawn by her side." In 1858 Lander saw Washakie lead a surround on Green River "during which the whole herd of antelope was slaughtered indiscriminately." Lander, "Report of F. W. Lander," in Sen. Exec. Doc. 42 (36–1), Serial 1033, 1860, 121–22.

been made manifest among the hous of Isrell. We feel from all a pearances at present that The Harvest is and will be Great, but the labors is fiew in this part of the vineyard.

May God Add his Blessings to you and all his Saints for Christ Sake
Amen. James Brown 3rd.

The missionaries met the next day and choose seven men "to take the trade to the Indians, & as many of them Stay with the tribe as the spirit shall dictate." Then they assembled on Smiths Fork, "the pure stream of water E. of the Fort to renew our covenants by baptism." After baptizing four-teen Saints, including Barney Ward's wife "Marry a Shoshoni woman," the congregation met again at 5:00 P.M. to bless them. John Pulsipher described an apparent epilepsy seizure:

> While we were confirming, an evil spirit came up[on] Prest. Brown, he sat down & was administered to, lay down & commenced cramping & gnashing his teeth, & continued so for about 20 minutes altho we administered to him a number of times & anointed him with oil. He was in awful pain all the time. It seamed almost impossible to drive the devil away, but thro the faith & prayer of all & the power of the Priesthood he was started.[67]

On the Fourth of July, Brown, Bullock, and Sanderson returned from "trading with the Indians. They were tired & hungry & were right glad of a good feast." The celebration had just "got well commenced to giving orations & speeches, [when] John Alger, Moroni Cole & James M. Brown came in, having stayed with the Indians 2 days." They "found it was not wisdom to stay any longer at present. The Indians were almost starving, & they would feel bad to see others eat when they had nothing to eat. So the boys gave them their flour & returned to wait til the Indians go to the Buffalo country." Twelve reinforcements arrived on 1 August, and the mission spent the rest of the summer exploring the country "to find a place for the Indians to make their farm," marrying three Shoshone women and baptizing a few more, and holding a "General Election for Green River Co" that polled twenty-five votes. By mid-month, some "30 or 40" Shoshones "were eating with us more or less every day. Provisions were getting low." On the 20th, "The Indians started to see Brigham & learn if he was their friend," while others "went to work for Bro. Robinson to earn something to help themselves. We keep busy taking care of our crops & cutting hay &c," Pulsipher wrote.[68]

[67]Pulsipher, Shoshone Mission Journal, 10–12.
[68]Ibid., 12–19.

Tabooachaget, or
Sun at Noon Day, 1873.
This unattributed photograph may
portray Ute leader Tabby-to-kwanah.
Courtesy American Antiquarian Society.

A political farce played out in September 1855 when some sixty Shoshones and thirty Utes met in Salt Lake. Senioroach—Arapene—"the Utah Chief in Walker's place," came "to make a treaty of peace with Ti-be-bu-tow-ats, the Chief of the Snakes," so White Man's Son, not Washakie, attended the Salt Lake festivities. Katattoo of the Weber band and Pocatello represented the "northern Snakes." Tsharpooeent (White Eye) and Antaro of the Yampas, Tintic, Sowietts's son Toquana, Tabby, and Peteetneet spoke for the Utahs. Dimick Huntington managed to get the Utes, who were painted for war, to stack their guns, but "many of them commenced concealing their bows and arrows under their blankets. When Pocatello saw this, 'he lifted up the pipe of peace towards Heaven, as high as he could raise his arm and shouted in a loud voice, 'THIS IS THE WEAPON I COME TO FIGHT WITH.'" The peacemakers talked, smoked, and "spent the remainder of the day in eating and refreshing."[69] When the negotiations ended five days later, everyone shook hands, Arapene's men raised "their hands toward Heaven as a token or covenant of peace," Brigham Young spoke, Garland Hurt distributed

[69]*Deseret News,* 12 September 1855, 5/3–4; Brown, *Life of a Pioneer,* 319.

provisions and presents, and all appeared satisfied. The Utes said they had "not had so good a treaty for twenty years."[70]

Meanwhile, trouble was brewing at Fort Supply. Agent George W. Armstrong left Provo on 3 October 1855 to visit Washakie's band. On the way, he heard "that Fort Supply was Surrounded by a Hostile band of Indians" threatening to burn the stockade and murder the Mormons. Armstrong, known to the Shoshones as "their great Father's Papoose," was not a bold soul and feared his nine-man guard was not enough to protect him at "the place of excitement."[71]

Isaac Bullock explained the trouble. On 10 October the Shoshones "demanded a present of potatoes and wheat from Brother Brown, telling him that he had promised it to them." When Brown said "he had made no such promise," the Shoshones "told him that he lied and were very bold and impudent." Zera Pulsipher actually had promised them "we would give them some wheat and potatoes that grew on their land" to stop the Shoshones from digging potatoes "before they were as big as hazle nuts." Tababooindowetsy, also known as White Man's Son, "was in a bad humor," for two of his children had died at Salt Lake and he "partly laid it to Brigham's talk killing them." Bullock said Pulsipher, not Brown, made the promise, which "partially reconciled them, at least to all appearances." Bullock and Tababooindowetsy went "to dig some potatoes for the chief," and "his whole band followed and commenced grappling all around me," destroying the patch. Tababooindowetsy claimed "he had no eyes and could not see" what happened. Bullock could see and had "worked very hard to water and rise them and that it did not make my heart feel good to have them do that way" when he was about to give them some. The Shoshones left, but their "feelings were not first rate." James S. Brown let three Indians into the field after they agreed to "keep the path and not run over the grain. They passed through and went galloping over the wheat, saying it was good to run over the 'Mormon's' grain." Bullock and Brown confronted them:

> One bold, impudent fellow said, Yes, he had run over it and would do it again and it was good to run over the Whites' grain. Pres. Brown told him if it was good for him to run over it and if he did it any more that they would go for him to whip him. He spoke up and said, "Whip me, whip me." And

---

[70]*Deseret News*, 19 September 1855, 5/3. For Huntington's complete reports, see Morgan, *Shoshonean Peoples*, 212–16.

[71]Armstrong to Young, 31 December 1855, in Morgan, *Shoshonean Peoples*, 217–20.

the other little chief said for [us] to whip him. They pressed and insisted that Brown should whip him, daring him to strike him. Coming close to Brother Brown to get him to strike the first blow, Pres. Brown told him to go away and leave the fort. He got so mad at Pres. Brown that he drew his bow and arrow and was about to shoot him, when Pres. Brown cried out to the brethren to get to their arms. They had not any more than got to them till another order to come quick with our arms. This happening close to my room door, I quickly stepped in and got my revolver and handed it out to Pres. Brown. As soon as they saw him with a pistol, they broke out of the fort. Brown followed close after them, telling them not to go through the field, when they instantly asked where they might go. He showed them to go around and they were perfectly cornered, and turned and went around. By this time the excitement had run like wild fire. The Indians came running with their bows and arrows. None seemed to be mad but these three, but still to see all the "Mormon" boys coming out with their arms in a bustle which they never had seen before, waked them up. A strong guard was placed around the fort and kept up all night.

The next day, "Our orders were to have our guns ready, for we might expect an attack." That afternoon a large dust cloud inspired fear: "The Indians are coming." The Mormons "mustered to arms in a hurry." Learning the band included whites "gave our hearts another flutter," Bullock wrote, for the Saints presumed they were mountaineers. Soon "it was authentically declared that it was the Indian agent" and his escort.[72] The "origin of the difficulties," White Man's Son told Armstrong, was "that 'Jim Brown,' as the Indians call the president, had a few days previous whipped one of his men." He admitted "some of his men did not behave well but had thrown down the fence and rode through the fields of grain and Commited sundry other depredations to retaliate for the whipping of the Indians." Brown "justified himself," saying "that the Indians behaved very rudely in his house and would not leave when he told them." Had "more mild measures been used in the first instance," Armstrong felt, "no difficulty would have taken place." The Shoshones "stated that they had no hostile feeling against any person at the Fort"—except James Brown.[73]

Armstrong first visited the Shoshone camp. On the way, a "splendidly attired" messenger gave "a sign that something very unusual was at hand by galloping his horse round making a circle three times, then bringing him

[72]Bullock to Smith, 20 October 1855, in Morgan, *Shoshonean Peoples*, 406–408.
[73]Armstrong to Brigham Young, 27 October 1855, BYC 55:20, 18, 21.

suddenly to a halt." At the camp, White Man's Son extended "his hand in a friendly manner," welcoming the agent to visit this "small portion of Wash-a-keek's band numbering one hundred warriors with their squaws and children" who had been at Fort Supply since summer. Armstrong headed for the stockade with thirty warriors "armed with bows and arrows as a guard." At the fort, Armstrong and his disarmed escort held "a council of about three hours duration."

The band demanded "a large quantity of provisions," he wrote, which "would have left the fort destitute," for grasshoppers had "entirely destroyed" the wheat crop. The Mormons had promised the Shoshones "when the crops were harvested that they were to have much the largest portion." The citizens "admitted that they had promised a certain amount," to which "the Indians took exceptions and threatened that if their demands were not Complied with to possess themselves at all hazzard with as much as they desired." The Shoshones confessed behaving "in a rude manner on several occasions by throwing down fences, riding their horses through the grain, making threats &c against the citizens," but "as the rightful owners of the Soil," they felt justified. Armstrong rebuked "the impropriety of their course" and said if "the great chief at Washington (the President of the U.S.)" heard about their conduct, he "would be much displeased and would look upon them as bad Indians."

White Man's Son expressed "their determination to renew their friendship with the people of the fort and promised not to disturb the property of the citizens for the future." Armstrong "returned their bows and arrows when they all left for their camp well Satisfied with the proceedings of the Council." He "sent for the entire band and gave them presents at the same time assuring them that if they should renew their hostilities that the President would not send them any more presents and that I would be under the necessity of resorting to measures to enforce peace." The band departed to hunt bison, while Washakie "left on a war party against the Crow Indians," which "proved very profitable to him as he has taken about seventy five horses and a large amount of skins and furs from the Crows. Many of the Sho-sho-nee Indians expressed a great desire to be instructed in farming having learned by the example of the white man that it is much better to raise their bread than to depend upon the chase for their Subsistence." Armstrong hoped to see Washakie "in the Spring as soon as the snow on the mountains will admit of traveling."[74] Upon his return, Washakie tried to collect his share of the presents distributed at Fort Supply but complained Armstrong paid no attention to him. The next summer, Young sent Bill Hickman, which Washakie liked "much better than if Armstrong had come."[75]

In October President Brown "spoke plain about whining to go home," but three weeks later he departed himself, leaving "John Pulsipher in chg of fort to preside til winter sets in." Most of the missionaries were "very anxious to go home as a great many have nothing but potatoes & water to live on." A handful of brave souls "Stayed at Ft. Supply thro' the winter," surviving brutal weather, with snow banked up around the stockade "15 ft. high in some places." It was "So bad that Bro. Terry & co. were prevented from going to Washekekes camp, so there was no news from them during the whole winter." Perhaps to celebrate Christmas, "John Phelps took a Lamanitish Woman to wife." James Brown "was released from the mission" in April 1856, and Isaac Bullock "was appointed & set apart to preside over the Shoshone mission & Green River County." Most of the settlers, including Bullock and Pulsipher, wintered in Salt Lake and returned after the country thawed with additional forces "to strengthen Ft. Supply & make a strong Settlement in Green River County." The "Duties of the mission changed. We are now sent to open farms & build mills 'good houses, &c. & make a permanent location," Pulsipher wrote.[76]

His Brother His Friend His Big Friend, and His True Friend, 1856

As 1856 began, Brigham Young put more irons into his many fires. The Shoshone Mission's new purpose reflected his plan to launch "a daily express and passenger communication between the western States and California, or, more extendedly, between Europe and China," soon known as the B.Y.X., which Young may have hoped to use "as an instrument to control the economic life of much of the West."[77] He began establishing "ranch forts" to serve as supply stations for Utah's new mail contract, his express, and his plan "to make hand-carts, and let the emigration foot it," which would be

[74]Morgan, *Shoshonean Peoples*, 217–20.
[75]Washakee to Brigham Young, 17 August 1856, BYC 25:9.
[76]Pulsipher, Shoshone Mission Journal, 27.
[77]"Mass Meeting," *Deseret News*, 30 January 1856, 4/4; Furniss, *The Mormon Conflict*, 52.

"just as quick, if not quicker, and much cheaper" than teams and wagons. The prophet called forty-six men to Fort Supply in February, where the new settlers began erecting grist and saw mills. As part of the express project, T. D. Brown surveyed a station between Fort Bridger and Fort Supply.[78] In December the legislature granted rights to the Green River ferries for three years to Isaac Bullock and Lewis Robison.[79]

Robison "found the Road dry & dusty the most of the way" when he returned to Fort Bridger in April. The snow "was gone in all the low lands & the streams are as destitute of watter as they wer[e] last fall," but snow-melt from higher elevations might provide enough water for irrigation. Fort Supply had only a small surplus of grain left. All was "Peace with the Indians," but the apostates who had "got Enough of mormonism and ar[e] Hell bound for the States" told tales of "the distresses of the inhabitants of the valleys." They claimed "Thousands of People ar[e] leaveing the vallyes & the rest are starving to Death & the grass Hoppers & crickets will destroy all the ballence," Robison reported. "Such Lyars should never live to reach the States."[80]

As the fort's leaders came and went, on 23 June frost "killed many of our tender plants," John Pulsipher wrote: farming at 7,201 feet was problematic. Except for a dance, the Fourth of July "passed without much noise," but on the 24th the fort "had a fine celebration"of the eighth anniversary of Brigham Young's arrival in Salt Lake Valley. A bugle call began the commemoration and "a salute was fired by the rifle co." A procession formed at 8:00 A.M. carrying banners proclaiming, "We are always ready," the riflemen had "come to teach the Lamanites the Gospel," and twenty-four ladies flew a banner that said, "We instruct our sisters of the forest." E. B. Ward's company of Indians flag read, "We shall become a white & delightsome people," "& an Indian painted, with bow & arrow," brought up the rear. "The Procession Marched around the fort & halted at the big house" to listen to speeches. "Bazil a Shoshone chief, made a very friendly speech. A speech also from Shoshone John, a good spirit was manifested they were glad we were here, liked to see our crops growing." The party moved to a table "loaded with substantial meal, new potatoes, peas, bread & butter, cheese cakes, pies, pud-dings, custard, sugar & coffee &c & plenty of meat also." Speeches, "15 or 20"

---

[78]Bagley, *South Pass, 171, 192*; Jenson, "Fort Bridger and Fort Supply," 36–39.
[79]Young to Bullock, 22 December 1855, BYC 17:19.
[80]Robison to Wells, 17 April 1856, BYC 25:5, 4.

beer toasts by the "brethren & some of the sisters," dancing, "cakes, cheese pies & beer again. All went off first rate commenced & closed by prayer."[81]

The business of the American West was now business. Diarist J. Robert Brown met Shoshones in August 1856 who understood this perfectly.

> I soon picked out Wassakee by his appearance. We found out through Brazil which was Wassakee for certain; an Indian will not tell his own name. I was somewhat disappointed in the appearance of this chief; I thought he was an old Indian, very large, and possessing great dignity. On the contrary, Wassakee is a medium sized man, aged about 35 or 40 years, but of a perfect form, straight, muscular and firm, and possesses the most beautiful set of teeth I ever saw. He was out on a hunt, and was dressed in a kind of coat and pants made of an old white blanket. Yates made the whisky flow freely now, and Wassakee drank much, but he would pour some into a tin cup and then fill it up with water, and then portion out a little to each Indian except Brazil, whom he allowed to take the raw material. I could not see that it affected Wassakee any; but Brazil's eyes began to brighten. After the Indians had drank he would wave his hand, and the Indians would mount and [ride] away. About 35 visited us during the morning. Wassakee could speak but a few words of American, but promised us "antelope, heap," after Yates told him about where we would camp. I told Yates I was afraid he would get these Indians drunk.

Washakie impressed Brown "as great a man as Tecumseh, Blackhawk or Phillip—he is, no doubt, a much better man." The Shoshone lord had a message:

> Wassakee wanted us to tell Brigham Young and the Mormons that he was *mad* at them. When a chief says that he means no child's play, for it is their declaration of war. (I have since learned that the Mormons had to make him many presents to keep him from fighting.) Yates says Wassakee is rich, and can dress as fine as any chieftain in the mountains.

Five days later, J. R. Brown met Bill Hickman "in charge of the presents for Wassahu, two wagon loads sent by Brigham to pacify the chief." Hickman was "a most foul and bloody murderer, but one would never suspect it from his appearance. Old man Hatch, who lives here, says Bill H. killed his son, and then came and sympathized with him and his aged wife about it." The young overlander had heard Hickman was "the leader of the 'Danites,' or, as they are called in the Mormon language, 'Destroying Angels.' I have heard some most atrocious stories concerning him and his gang of robbers,

---

[81]Pulsipher, *Shoshone Mission Journal*, 56.

thieves and murderers."[82] When James S. Brown's memoir appeared in 1900, Hickman had evolved from Mormon hero to "human hyena," but Brown felt Bill's "cunning and the cool head" averted much bloodshed. As Green River County sheriff, Brown recalled, Hickman "was always ready to support the law"—or at least Mormon law.[83] He also knew how to win the trust of the Shoshones.

BRIGHAM YOUNG TO WASHAKIE, 11 AUGUST 1856, BYC 17:26.

G.S.L. City August 1856

Wash-e-kik Chief of the Shoshonees

I send out by Bro Wm A Hickman a few Presents which I trust will be satisfactory to you. I have heard a good report from you and your tribe, and am glad to hear of your friendly feelings towards the whites, and that you are willing to have them settle on your land and raise grain. I am your brother and want to do you good. I want to have all the Indians live at peace with each other and be at peace with the whites. I have thought a great deal about you and have seen that you have a great deal of difficulty to support yourself and tribe [when] you have to go and hunt Buffalo to get a living. This brings you into collission with other Indians who are perhaps hostile and exposes you to danger. Moreover the game is continually getting scarce, which makes it more and more difficult for you to get a living. Owing to all these difficulties I have considered that it would be a good plan for you to have some of your Men to cultivate some land and raise grain such as wheat corn & potatoes and raise stock so that when the Game fails or it becomes dangerous to go after Buffalo you can have some food laid up from some other source upon which you can rely—Now our People will show your men to cultivate the land and assist them a little to get a start if you will have your men work as the whites do. This you will find will be the best policy for you to pursue, and you will also want to build some houses to live in and settle down and have schools wherein your young men and women and children can learn to read and write so that they can communicate their ideas to one another as I do now to you.

Wash-e-kik think of these things and ask the Great Spirit to tell you if it is true, and then act as the great Spirit shall dictate. I should like very much to see you but I cannot come out just now and I suppose that you cannot come to see me but if your men were cultivating the earth so that you did not have to go out on those long hunts every year we might see each other oftener. I remember you well and know that you are a good man wishing to do right and wishing to have your men to do so to[o]—I bless you and all of your tribe and ask God My Heavenly Father to bless you also.

[82]J. R. Brown, *Journal of a Trip across the Plains*, 6, 7, 12 August 1856, 71–72, 76.
[83]J. S. Brown, *Life of a Pioneer*, 336.

Washakie's response reflected his anger, frustration, and diplomatic skill as he recounted his experiences since the Fort Laramie Treaty of 1851 and the government's unfair treatment of the Shoshone. He said all he had "to say to Brigham now."

WASHAKIE TO BRIGHAM YOUNG, 17 AUGUST 1856, BYC 25:9, 21–28.
On the evening of the 17 of Aug./56 after the Council and a distribution of presents to the Shoshonees Washakee who had been previously invited came to dictate a letter to Gov. B. Young which he requested should go by the return of Sub. Agent Hickman—Washakee came with some 20 of his principal men who were comfortably seated by Mr. Lewis Robison in one of his rooms at Fort Bridger. Wm. A. Hickman Lewis Robison and Isaac Bullock were call[ed] together with interpreter Joshua Terry to to [sic] hear what said Washakee had to say [sic] [with] several other white men being present.

Washakee was notified that they were ready to hear him upon which he said who am I that I should talk (reply a friend). He then sat some minutes silent and says that I am not studying to lie but give you my true sentiments.

He commenced as follows.

1st. When you first came to my land you saw me and my people. We were not powerful—we were friends then and have been so ever since.

2nd. Say that since they have received their presents their hearts are all good. That he feels good and his children all feel good and that the whites must not be affraid when they see him or any of his men for they will not hurt them—

3rd. Says that here is the road the whites may Pass and repass as much as they are a mind to, and the whites may pass also on the North road to California or any whe[re] else they wish; that Indians may also pass and none shall be hurt, that their horses and cattle shall not be stolen, that they see plenty of horses and Cattle which they could steal but have not stolen any and neither will they hereafter—

4th. Says that when he is at Laramie or on Platt he does not charge on his enemies but wait to see if they char[g]e on him. He has to fight sometimes to save his life and the lives of his people and he dont know but he does wrong but does not know how else to do. Say that it makes his heart feel bad to have to fight—

5th. Says that his Country is good for all men [and] that they can lay down and sleep in peace and not be afraid nor have their horses stolen—

6th. Says that the soldiers sent for him to come to Platte last spring, he went [but their country was not good). They were all at war and he asked them what they wanted with him. (They told him nothing only wanted to see him.] Says he set there like a fool and had to watch his horses till his eyes were sore and after all their watching the Crows killed one of their young men. He then left—

7th. Says in /51 at the big treaty there were 9 tribes at Laramie and they all agreed to be friends and at peace with one another and with the whites. Says they all got presents but his people they got nothing and that they had all broken it except his tribe. Says he and his my [sic] men heard it good althoug[h] we got nothing. We have not lied or acted like wolves—

8th. Says now he is tired of going down in that Country and holding treaties for they are all the time breaking them. Says he is now going to stay at home in his own Country and attend to his own business.

9th. Says he is now going to talk about the Utes—says that they are just like wolves. That they will meet together and smoke and talk and agree to be friends and make the greatis [sic] of promises but just as soon as ~~they can catch~~ 2 or 3 of his people are discovered by them the Utes will kill them. This is the way they have always done. But when a good body of his men are together they are verry good but when they part they (the Utes] are like wolves

10th. Says that the Utes never did talk to him that the[y] always lied and that he is not going to hunt them up to make friends or to make war but if any of them come to his lodge they will not be hurt and he will hear them and they may talk as much as they are a mind to but he will not believe it for they always lie and never tell him truth not even one truth and he has no more confidence in them than wolves—

11th. Says that he hears that they serves his mates his good friends the mormons the same way. That when they catch 2 or 3 of them out or in the Canknons [sic] after wood they kill them just as they do his men—he then called on Joshua Terry and Elijah B. Ward who he said had been in the Country long to say if the Utes had not always done so, to which they answered yes.

12th. Says he the Utes are all the time stealing the mormons Cattle and horses and they are killing cattle. Now say he we do not do that way. We have plenty of chances to steal. We see plenty horses and plenty Cattle passing and in our Country all the time but we doe not touch anything belonging to the whites—says that when they find horses or Cattle that belongs to whites they bring them in and hunt the owner and sometimes they pay them something and sometimes they do not pay anything—Says that he keeps his people out of settlements and does not let them run round and steal. Says that they do not want to steal—

13th. Says that last fall Armstrong who they told him was their father Came here and sent for him to come that he had some presents for him but he was far off and did not hear it soon [enough] but when he did he came and on learning that Armstrong had gone back to the Valley he went round North of Salt Lake Valley, and sent to Armstrong but he paid no attention to him. He went away and came this time and sent for him and he has not come yet but his good friend and father Brigham Young has sent Bill Hickman with many presents to him which he likes much better than if Armstrong had come. Say[s] that Brigham Young is his father his Brother his friend his big friend, and his true friend, that has sent him these presents, that Brigham will not be like the Utes. That he always intends to hear him—

14th. Says that he will stay here till Hickman leaves then he will travel round in his country till the leaves fall. Then he will [go] for the Buffalos Somewhere far off but don't know where—

15 Says send your men among us anywhere in our country. Do not be afraid, that one man would be as safe as many or if he was at home in his own house. Says that is all I have to say to Brigham now.

Washakee Chief
Of the Shoshones Nation

To Brigham Young
Gov. of Utah Territory

We the undersigned Certify the above to be true as Spoken by Washakee and interpreted by Joshua Terry and that the interpretation is correct having heard and understood the same.

Isaac Bullock
E. B. Ward

O Heavens What a Time: The Big Whisky Day

Before going on his fall bison hunt, Washakie "intended to have a Spree."

Lewis Robison to Daniel H. Wells, 25 August 1856, BYC 25:5, 26–29.

Fort Bridger Augst 25th 56.

D.H. Wells Esqr
Dear Brother

Having a leasure moment (for the first in tenn days) I thought that I would tell you a little about matters hear since the sub Agent left us.

On the day after Brother Hickman left Washakick an[d] a large amount of his people came to the Fort as I supposed to trade, but since I have learned that they intended to have a Spree. After trade had commensed a little Washakick had a fuss with Razease & commensed fi[gh]ting in the Store. I interfeerd & Plead for the old man & finally succeeded in gitting them out of the Store & stoped the fight. Washakick hit me several times in the face, which is moore than I am accostomed to take from enny man. But I was not hurt, to make anny marks on my face.

I then closed the Store & thought the Difficulty over. But Washakick made me open the doore & when in he said he would have Whiskey. All objections & refusels was in vain. He would have it. He commensed drinking & giving to a few of his men. For several hours he only gave it to his faverites

& then gave it to all. About one Oclock in the day I thought best to send for Brother Bullock & some of his men, which come as soon as they could git their Horses & git hear which was near knight.

I had come to the conclusion to let them have all they wanted & keep peace if possible & When the Breathren kindly came to my relief they wer[e] of the Same opinion.

They kept on drinking till dark, when Washakick told them all to leave the Fort (except four men to stay & talk with him) which was done as quick as possible by all that could Walk & them that could not wer[e] soon dropped out.

As near as I can judge they drinked about 20 Gallons of Liqr. I will not try to Portray before you the sceans of the day. Nor my feelings & that of my friends dureing the day, (which lasted at Least a week). But O Heavens what a time. Washakick & council left about 10 Oclock. After assureing us that no harm should be done by anny of them & that they should drink no more. Thus passed one of the longest days of anxiety & fear that I ever Experienced. We Kept up a guard during the knight but all was peace.

I must say that I never saw as menny drunk men behave as well as they did. All was Peace not a bit of quarreling among them.

Brother Bullock & Breathren from Fort Supply have bin hear for 3 days & Rendered us assistance that will never be forgotten by me & my Family.

On yesterday morning their appeared to be considerable feelings in the camp. Some wanted to gow to fight the Utahs & Washakick opposeng the war. The chief said if they would not hear him he would leave whereuppen he gave orders to his Squaws to take down the Lodge. His Mother in Law was Preasant & told the Squaws not to gow, which caused some quarreling & Washakick stuck a butcher Knife in to the Old Ladys Side betwen the hip bone & the Ribs. This raised considerable Esxcitement in camp & some of the men wanted to kill him immediately. But others said wait & if she Diyes we will help you kill him. Washakick & Family left the encampment alone.

About 40 men started to war with the Utahs on the same day. But I believe they have mostly come back.

The Vilage of Indians is know broken up & nearly all gone, in different directions.

I have bin to see the wounded squaw & think it doubtful about hur recovering.

All has passed off & the Indians gone from us with the best of feelings for which we feel grateful to our Heavenly Fathe[r] for his preserving Care over us & the wisdem which he has given to us to bear all things that is nessessary for the sake of Peace.

August 26th The Squaw is still alive. The mail has just arrivd. Only Stops for dinner.

The crops at Fort Supply ar[e] Late but look very well. Oat Harvest has commenced. Wheat will not be ready for Har[v]est for a week or 10 Days.... All is Peace & Prosperity in this part of the World. Since the Big Whisky Day. Please Wright by return mail & let me know how things are going....

Wells's reply congratulated Robison on his "very narrow escape for if the least most trifling occurrence had taken place to rouse the anger of any of the Indians the consequences might have been direful indeed." The incident made "a pretty strong argument against keeping liquor at all at that place, we have always had some misgiving as to its propriety and are now more than ever satisfied that it is impolitic." Robison had bought "2 barrels Whiskey of a good Article at 3.75 per gallan" in late July, and Wells admitted that since Robison had "it on hand you could do no different": he had to give the Shoshones what they wanted. Wells knew its problems but did not order Robison to abandon the whiskey trade.[84]

CONFUSION, VEXATION, TERROR AND DISMAY

Winter at Fort Supply brought 1856 to a catastrophic close. It "Snowd 30 hours & cleard off cold as greenland" on 5 November. Six days later, the fort got "up a feast in honor of Bro Bullock," but the "careless & indiferent were not invited." Seventy people assembled, and "Altho we were in our poverty because of the failure of crops &c, we truly had a Sumptuous feast," Pulsipher recorded.

> While we were Seated at the table—the news come that the last cos, of hand carts were perishing in the Snows on Sweet water, & that the teams Sent from the valley had turned back before meeting them—Prest. Bullock called for Volunteers to go & Save that perishing people—Evry man present was ready to Start with all his team & Seams anxious to do all in their Power to help them.

Fort Supply's Saints bore the brunt of this humanitarian disaster. "About 400 persons are at Bridger without teams to go to the Valley & they are nearly out of Provision & we have not the assistance for them," Pulsipher wrote on 4 December. The mission leaders took charge of those going to Salt Lake "that have froze their feet so they will have to be cut off."[85] After getting the handcart survivors past Fort Bridger, Lewis Robison faced dealing with

---

[84]Robison to Wells, 26 July 1856, BYC 25:5, 17; Wells to Robison, 30 August 1856, BYC Letterbook 3:43.
[85]Pulsipher, *Shoshone Mission Journal*, 53–56.

more than 435 people still east of Green River: President Young had "not bin rightly informed with respect to their situation & the amount of supplyes on hand in this country. I think your informants must have bin taking a little Opium." Fifteen to twenty cattle with "the back trains" died every day, and the people had "had no Bread nor Salt" for days. They appeared trapped. Supplies at Forts Supply and Bridger were gone or dangerously low. "I cannot conseive what 4 or 5 hundred People can git to winter on in this country," Robison reported.[86]

A break in the weather allowed most of these trains to reach Salt Lake by mid-December, but the Saints at Fort Supply spent the winter enduring the ordeals of the Reformation, which required them to confess their sins. Hunger apparently turned the fort into a den of thieves. Ralph "Rowlin" Bowman confessed he had stolen a sack of flour, two cheeses, potatoes, and "Wood from a number of the neighbors," and he had milked a neighbor's cows at night. "If any of u find me Stealing again," he said, "just *kill me.*"[87]

When rescuer Thomas Steed met the Willie Company east of Fort Bridger, it was a "sight I shall never forget: they looked like Indians from afar," but we have no idea what Shoshones made of the disaster.[88] It is equally difficult to determine how Washakie viewed his dealings with Brigham Young, the Mormons, and the U.S. government. All parties in this triangle said what they believed their listeners wanted to hear. At South Pass in June 1860, overlander Clara Downes met a mail agent, "quite an intelligent man," who told her "many of his adventures with the indians as he had been living with them eleven years." The Shoshone had "two fathers the president & Brigam Young. One lies where the sun rises the other where it sets."[89] Washakie had to manage both leaders but never chose between fathers: he extracted tribute and supplies from both. Despite his many statements to federal agents and Mormons, what he believed is anyone's guess. Washakie's political and economic relations with the Mormons "focused on maximum gain for minimum commitment," observed historian Henry Stamm. He used their settlements as trading posts and enticed Brigham Young and other officials "with vague promises about farming or settling down in order to keep the 'presents' flowing. Covertly, he opposed any attempt by the Mormons to

[86]Robison to Young, 27 November 1856, BYC 25:5.

[87]Pulsipher, *Shoshone Mission Journal*, 65.

[88]Steed, *The Life of Thomas Steed*, 22.

[89]Downes, Journal Across the Plains, 23 June 1860, Bancroft Library. My thanks to Professor Melody Miyamoto for sharing her transcription.

control or limit the 'mountaineer' establishments—which for years had been outlets for the Shoshone fur and robe trade."[90] Without a doubt, Washakie used his power to protect his peoples' land and ensure their survival.

For believers living in the Mormon West, the events of 1856—the Reformation, the handcart disaster, the demand for statehood or "independant sovereignty," and the flight of hundreds of apostates from Zion—signaled the approach of the Last Days. Brigham Young thought so: "As confusion, vexation, terror and dismay pervade the nation, I discern the hard dealing of the Lord in answer to the prayers of His servants." America was "going to destruction at rail road speed." The faithful should "be prepared for the great events shortly to come to pass."[91] It must have felt like riding an avalanche that would sweep the Mormons and the United States into an apocalyptic confrontation.

---

[90]Stamm, *People of the Wind River*, 33–34.
[91]Young to Smith, Bernhisel, & Taylor, 30 August 1856, BYC Letterbook 3:19–20.

Chapter 10

WAKE UP THE
SONS OF LAMAN
The Utah War, 1857–1859

In Utah folklore, a "chief" told a local congregation, "Mormons weino. Mormons tick-a-boo. Make-em water-ditch. Plant-em grain. Feed-em Indians. Mormons tick-a-boo," meaning the Mormons and Indians were good friends. But "White man — of a ———.'"[1] Whether LDS missionaries drilled this perspective into Native peoples, as federal agents charged, or the Indians simply responded to how Latter-day Saints treated them, as Brigham Young insisted, the issue inflamed federal-Mormon relations.

At Las Vegas in July 1855, missionary Thomas D. Brown reported federal contractor James Leach "gave the Indians a few Blankets and other presents which caused them to say 'The Americans sometimes very good, give us clothes' &c." It was hard to explain to the Paiutes "why U.S. nincompoops had frequently more in their power to do them good than we had, but by our united & unfeigned attention and kindness to them, we gained upon their affections." Brown observed "cruelties, shootings & killings among them by the American emigrants, far outweighted the paltry presents now bestowed upon them." "United & unfeigned attention and kindness" won over the Indians, who "exclaimed 'The American no good, they won't allow us to come into their camps as the Mormons do, they are not our friends, but you are; We are Mormons & no longer Pahutes.'"[2]

The Southern Indian Mission had purposes beyond transforming Paiute identity: it helped Brigham Young dominate Indian trade and achieve economic self-sufficiency for his isolated kingdom. When "Govr. Young

---

[1]Brooks, "Indian Relations on the Mormon Frontier," 19.
[2]Brown, *Journal of the Southern Indian Mission*, 133.

& suite" visited Fort Harmony in May 1854, he told the settlers, "You are sent, not to farm, build nice houses & fence fine fields, not to help white man, but to save the red ones."[3] Young used the Indian superintendency to support his economic plans. Iron Mission president Isaac Haight "gave a writeing holding himself responsible" for the goods "brought down last fall for the Indians." When "those brethren labouring on the Iron works became almost destitute of clothing," Haight gave most of the apparel to his workers. The remainder was "disposed of to the Indians."[4] Thomas Brown dutifully credited $124.75 "for Indian clothing" to the Iron Company books and $161.64 "for Harmony Ind. Clothg" to Rufus C. Allen. He then transferred $286.39 to Brigham Young.[5]

Despite its scarcity of arable land, Young wanted Utah to produce its own food and clothing. Hamblin and company were "building a stone fort on the Santa Clara, and intend entering at once into raising cotton in the warm rich bottoms bordering on that stream, and probably, at an early day, sugar cane, olives and other fruits of warm climes."[6]

Mormon-Indian relations took center stage in 1857 as a cause of the Utah War. Provocative acts—the territorial legislature's January nullification ultimatum, which the new secretary of the Interior considered "a declaration of war"; the flight of every non-LDS federal officer save Garland Hurt from Utah; the ongoing Mormon Reformation; and Superintendent Brigham Young's spring expedition deep into Oregon Territory—had enduring consequences.[7]

THE SOUTHERN INDIAN MISSION, 1854–1856

Brigham Young "wanted to plant a colony wherever the water, timber and arable land would support one," Juanita Brooks observed.[8] Southern Utah settlement began with the Iron Mission in January 1851. When Young visited in May, he found some settlers "disposed to scatter out from the Forts," risking their lives and peace in the territory.

---

[3]Ibid., 29–30.
[4]Rufus C. Allen to Brigham Young, 13 August 1855, BYC 28:18.
[5]Brown to Young, 28 May 1855, BYC 23:20, 67–70.
[6]"Improvements in the South," *Deseret News*, 5 March 1856, 10/3.
[7]MacKinnon's "And the War Came" and *At Sword's Point*, 1:53–150, and Bigler's "A Lion in the Path" examine the conflict's causes.
[8]Brown, *Journal of the Southern Indian Mission*, ix.

We are located in the midst of savage tribes who for generations untold have been taught to rob plunder and kill and the gratification of every lustful appetite for Blood and revenge success in which among themselves paves the way to distinction and influence. They are moreover ignorant and degraded living in the lowest degree of filthiness practicing extreme barbarity to all such as unfortunately fall into their hands, under circumstances peculiar we have been shown into their midst. They are of Isreal [sic] so are our position among them furnishes abundant opportunities of doing good. We can here become saviours in very deed saviours of our brethren.[9]

In October 1853 Brigham Young appointed Rufus C. Allen president and called twenty-one men as missionaries to southern Utah's "poor, ignorant Lamanites who surround us, and are in our midst, at our own doors." They "must live with them, teach them, and counsel them in all things, and be on hand to do them all the good that lies in your power." After reaching Cedar City on 1 May, the next day they placed their farm and fort at New Harmony.[10]

None of America's Native peoples traveled a harder road than the resilient *Nuwuvi*, the Southern Paiutes. Mormons called them Paiutes, Pahutes, or Piedes, perhaps derived from the Pietes, a band living near Mountain Meadows. Their close relations gave Mormon missionaries a higher regard for the tribe than was common: "The Piutes is in my Judgment the most intelligent race of Lamanites that I have ever bin acquainted with," William Riley wrote from Las Vegas. [11]

Understanding them requires appreciating how overgrazing produced the harsh landscape of today's *Nuwuvi* homeland. The earliest accounts praise southern Utah's grassy range and lush meadows: Thomas Brown called Page Ranch near today's Pinto "the 'garden of the World,'" a circular valley on a fine stream "covered with a beautiful crop of green hay." Amid the "lofty turrets; temple spires; elevated ramparts; forts inaccessible; bastions & outworks impregnable" at the headwaters of the Virgin River, David Lewis described "Nature's grandeur in this Southern land" with valleys "covered with good grass—& the land fertile but water scarce."[12]

Brigham Young "spoke nearly as follows" on 19 May 1854 at Fort Harmony, outlining "the duties of this mission." God sent the Mormons "to save the

[9]Young and Kimball to the Iron County Saints, June 1851, BYC 16:22.
[10]Brown, *Journal of the Southern Indian Mission*, 2–3.
[11]Riley to Young, 14 December 1856, BYC 25:4.
[12]Brown, *Journal of the Southern Indian Mission*, 16, 93.

remnants of Israel in these mountains; the people of the western Isles are of Manasseh or most [of] them." They were "not to help white men, but to save the red ones. Learn their language" and "let them live with you. Feed them, clothe them and teach them as you can" and "when they go off in parties you go with them." He found his interpreters deficient and told the missionaries to learn Native tongues perfectly. "Don't let the natives go off in bands, you go with them, and thus you will tame them and learn their language, and when those Indians crowd in upon you, who are driven from the east and from the west, if you have tamed these and have their language, see your influence and power."

Zadoc Judd recalled the Southern Indian Mission's history in 1891.

> The settlement of Santa Clara was began in 1854 by the missionaries to the Lamanites. Their names were Rufus Allen President, Jacob Hamblin, Ira Hatch, Samuel Knight, Thales Haskel, Prime Coleman, Gus [Augustus] Hardy & some others. The Lamanites on the creek then must have numbered several hundred. They carried on farming quite extensive for lamanites. In their way they used all the water yet by the influence of the brethren they were prepared to be a little more economical & let the missionaries have water so that in 1854 they planted a little mellon patch. The Indians done no stealing of the mellons. They also procured several hundred grape cuttings which were brought from California. They were valued at 5 cts each. From this [came] the start of grapevines in that country. As to the cotton seed I cannot say who furnished it. I think there was bot about 2 or 3 doz[en] seeds. T D Brown got 3 seeds of the Sea Island or Black seed variety from a Sister Anderson in Parawon. The cotton seed was planted in 1855 & watched with much anxiety. In the Autumn of 1855 some of the missionaries moved their families there. It was thought to be unsafe for families with out a protection from the indians. A good stone quirey [quarry being] close at hand the church authorities called to our aide Elias Morris, Samuel Bradshaw, Samuel Atwood missionaries masons & 2 other stone masons from Cedar City with the assistance of Richard Robinson. The first families were Jacob Hamblin, Oscar Hamblin, Dudley Leavitt.[13]

James A. Little's 1881 *Jacob Hamblin: A Narrative* includes intriguing stories he probably heard from Hamblin about the mission's attempt to establish "as good a form of government among the Santa Clara Indians, as their circumstances would permit." The Paiutes "worked for a living and promised to be honest. If any one stole, he either paid a price for what he had taken, or

---

[13]Judd, Settlement of Santa Clara, Huntington Library. Commas inserted between names. The remaining two-thirds of Judd's account says nothing about Indians.

was stripped, tied to a tree and whipped, according to the magnitude of his offense. The Indians did the whipping," while Hamblin "generally dictated the number and severity of the lashes." By 1857, "after the Indians had been trying for some time to follow our counsels, they said to [Hamblin], "We cannot be good; we must be Piutes. We want you to be kind to us. It may be that some of our children will be good, but we want to follow our old customs." They again "began to paint themselves and to abuse their women, as they had done before we went among them."[14]

Pahvant leader Kanosh mastered the art of power in a theocracy. Harmony leader Samuel Atwood described how Kanosh brutalized Enos, an Indian "freebooter" who had been indicted for the Gunnison murders.

"HARMONY,—KANOSH'S VISIT TO THE PIEDES—HIS SPEECH—ENOS PUNISHED FOR STEALING," 16 JULY 1856, 4/1–2.

EDITOR DESERET NEWS:—

June 1, 1856

Dear Sir—Kanosh, chief of the Pah-van-tes on Corn creek, and a part of his band arrived here about noon on the of 26th of May. He came in his covered wagon, with a span of horses and driver; the rest of the band were horseback. They spent the afternoon in the Fort, where they had camped.

In the evening Kanosh requested the privilege of holding a meeting in the meeting house which was granted by Prest. [John D.] Lee. Several assembled at early candle-light, also all the Piedes near the fort. Kanosh then spoke quite at length to the Indians, and his remarks were interpreted to us by Lemuel, an Indian living with Prest. Lee. He spoke about the situation of the Indians when the whites first came among them contrasting, it with their present condition. Also about the great change for the better with himself and his tribe, and with the Utahs generally.

He told them that when the whites first came among they were all very poor, and that they had no clothes, nor wheat, corn, potatos [sic], squashes, melons &c., but had to live on grass, seeds, lizards, locust, mice &c., and much of the time go very hungry. But now they had got many things like the whites, and they could have many more if they would work like them.

He said that if they would not stop stealing cattle, horses, sheep, flour, wheat corn, squashes, and melons, he wanted them to go away off into the mountains and never come back. He further told them that if they did not stop stealing they would all be sick and die off.

His whole speech was very creditable, both in sentiment and delivery, and the Indians paid good attention during the whole of it.

---

[14]Little, *Jacob Hamblin*, 46–47.

During the following day he spent a part of his time with the Indians in their field showing them how to farm, talking with them about the benefits to be derived from raising their own grain and living like the whites.

On the next day Enos, a young Indian living sometimes with the Pah-van-tes and at other times with the Piedes, arrived from Corn creek. In the evening Kanosh began of his accord to talk to him about his stealing.

After talking for about an hour and a half, and telling him of many of the mean tricks that he had been guilty of since he had been in the Southern country among the Piedes, he gave him the privilege of making his plea. After Enos was through, Kanosh ordered one of his men to bind him, which was quickly done and he was placed apart, while Kanosh held a council with his men. In this council it was decided that Enos should receive twenty lashes with a lariette on his bare back. Enos was then brought into the ring, stript and required to lay down with his face to the ground. A buckskin lariette was first brought, but Kanosh, thinking that not hard enough, brought a rawhide one, which was applied to the back of Enos with such force that it caused him to writhe and groan with pain.

As soon as Enos was sufficiently composed, Kanosh commenced talking to him again. He told him that he had been stealing for a long time and that he had learned the Piedes to steal, for they had never done so before he came among them. That he had been like a wolf and a dog for he would steal and eat what he could and then go and bury the rest, and he ought to be killed.

He told him that he had talked to him before, and that the whites had talked to him and put a chain on him, but that he would not listen to any of them; neither himself nor the whites liked him, and would not, unless he would stop killing other people's cattle, sheep, &c. But if he would stop now he would be free and travel about as heretofore but if not he would have him put into the big stone house with a chain on him, or he would have his head cut off.

When Kanosh first arrived, he sent for Tot-se-go-bits and Mo-ro-van-tes, chiefs on the Santa Clara, wishing to hold a council with them, but as they did not come he started this morning for Fillmore, having done much good among the Lamanites in this country, and behaved himself like a gentleman. Much credit is due him for what he has done since he has been with us, more especially because he did it of his own free will.

Yours respectfully,
S. F. Atwood.

Ragnarök West: Paiutes, Lead Mines, and Las Vegas

Like Norse mythology, Mormon theology climaxed with its own Ragnarök. Preparations for this frontier apocalypse—the proliferation of Indian missions, the intensity of the Mormon Reformation, and the drumbeat of millennial militarism—led to the theocratic kingdom's confrontation with the United States in 1857. Everything after the Utah War stands in the shadow of its prophetic failure. The Mormon mission founded at Las Vegas in today's Nevada combined all these elements.

William Bringhurst and twenty-seven missionaries reached Las Vegas Creek, then in New Mexico Territory, in June 1855. They "laid off a fort 150 feet square on rise of ground near the creek" and "sent word to the Lamanites in our neighborhood to come in and have a talk." About thirty Southern Paiutes "came together & seemed very glad to find that we desired to settle here," Bringhurst reported. "They gave us full permission to settle where we pleased [and] to use the water, grass, timber &c." He found "many more Lamanites in this Country than has been represented by travelers." They were "perfectly honest & simple hearted and manifest a great inclination to take up with our manner and customs." They already raised "a little grain, but they are generally very poor having little or no clothing. Their highest ambition being a shirt or pair of moccason soles." The "Elders on a Mission to benighted Israel" evaluated local resources—the nearby mountains had "inexhaustible quantities" of the finest pine timber—and farming prospects. Bringhurst had no thermometer, but it was hot. The Paiutes harvested "green corn roasting ears" by 25 June.[15]

The Southern Indian Missions enjoyed singular success because the Mormons protected the Paiutes from slave raids. Both peoples lived in magical worlds where angels and spirits animated the earth and its holy places. Spiritually, early Latter-day Saints had more in common with the pantheistic Paiutes than they would with their twenty-first-century descendants. Bringhurst sent four men and a Native guide "to explore the Big Mountain," today's 11,916-foot Charleston Peak, thirty-five miles northwest of Vegas Creek. His report summarized local Paiute lore of this sacred summit from a Mormon perspective.

WILLIAM BRINGHURST TO YOUNG, 6 AUGUST 1855, BYC 23:20, 9–14.
This Mountain is famed throughout the Piedes and Utah Nations as being the dwelling place of the Lord and his younger brother the Devil, before they had their quarrel. The brethren finding their exploration led them to within half a days travel of the Lords Temple concluded to visit it. The superstitious guide tried to dissuade them from it but finally showed them the way. The description of the temple is as follows. In a deep kanyon near a

---

[15]Bringhurst to Young, 10 July 1855 and below.

grove of tall pines is a large natural cave about 100 feet in length and 30 feet wide. The entrance was 6 feet wide by 10 high. Also there was an opening of about two thirds in length of one side. The greatest height was about 15 feet. The guide explained to Bro Geo Bean the different apartments as they were when the house was occupied by the Great Spirit but it is so long since he was here that there remains no vestige of the different partitions told of by the guide. The Indians all invest this place with a great deal of sanctity. We were shown the Lords kindlingwood piled up in one place & they [say] it was never removed since he placed it. They also showed us the tracks of the Lords deer that were so gentle they would come to the door of his house. In the course of the travels the guide pointed out the rock where the (Shenoub) Devil pushed (Tervots) the Lord off a ledge [and] supposed that he was killed but after three days the Good Spirit returned and then commenced the war between them which has continued to this day. We also saw the rock on which Shenoub slew his wife. Also at another place the Lord's and Devil's wives were seen standing together in the shape of two large rocks. It appears to almost offend the Indians to see that we are incredulous on the points of belief. This Exploration set our minds at rest upon this matter for the Indians had told us so often of these things that we had got an idea that there were some ancient ruins in this neighborhood which had given rise to the tradition among the Indians.

I will now proceed to give you a short history of our manner of dealing with the Lamanites in this part of the vineyard. We have endeavored to set an example of sobriety and industry and honesty before them at all times and they appear to manifest an anxiety to understand and practice upon all that they see and hear. Our acquaintance with them extends in every direction, Strange ones coming in to see us every few days. They are very poor having no clothing & not understanding the use of firearms and we have been careful to withhold such knowledge from them judging it to be your will and knowing that it is for our preservation in the midst of these deserts & mountains. They have great faith in all that we tell them. For instance: the Great Chief of the Country (Onetump) came a few days and said he was sick & wanted some Medicine. Our interpreter Bro bean told him we had none but when the Mormons were sick they asked the good spirit to heal us. He said he wanted to be healed we accordingly administered by laying on of hands and the Lord heard our prayers & he experienced immediate releif [sic]. Since then he thought he was dying they sent for the Indians to come in for fifty miles round he sent for us again some of the brethren went and administered to and prayed for him and the disease left him and he is now apparently well and has the best of feelings towards us & strives to use his influence in our behalf. The Lamanites about here are all ready to obey the ordinance of baptism if it was thought proper. We have considered it not worth while to perform that ordinance with them until they were better able to understand the duty and obligations imposed by such performance. If you think differently I would be happy to receive a hint of the same when convenient.

I will give you account of a tradition extant with these Indians of this Country as it has been told by our interpreter Bro bean.

The Indians say that a long time ago before Piedes or any other Indians lived on this land, there were two brothers lived in the cave on the mountain near here. the Older brother Tervots, was good and friendly, but the younger Shenoub was evil. Tervots had a wife & Shenoub wanted her & so one time Tervots was out hunting & Shenoub came up behind secretly & pushed him off a precipice & supposed he was killed. Shenoub went back and by imitating his brothers voice he got into the upper chamber along with Tervots wife but after three days the older brother came back and then the war commenced which has continued up to the present time. However the older brother had to flee for his life & the Piedes know not where he went, but the other is round about them all the time watching for opportunity to punish them when they displease him.

They offer sacrifice and make Medicine to Shenoub not through love but fear of him, and when they found that the Mormons were acquainted with Tervots the Good Spirit they felt to rejoice and were willing to believe every word.

The missionaries discovered lead during their first winter at Las Vegas. The next spring Brigham Young began pouring men and resources into mining lead, which was "very scarce, high-priced, and much needed in our various operations."[16] The ore proved to be a fatal attraction, for it introduced bitter power struggles and distracted from the Indian Mission's purpose, which the Paiutes noticed. Nathaniel V. Jones admitted the lead was a "very strange compound," which when smelted was "very hard & brite" and had "a very Sharp ring to it," for "it contained a much larger ammount of *Silver*."[17] In February 1857 the enterprise collapsed:

the Indians have manifested a hostile Spirit towards us, they are determined to Steal & Kill all of our animels: about the 17th or 18th of last month a friendly Indian fetched me word that they had collected togeather at some springs East of us about three hours travel from the Mines one hundred Strong, & had been counciling for Sevral days & that they was agoing to come uppon us take our animels & drive us out of the country.[18]

---

[16]Young to Jonathan Wright, 13 June 1856, BYC 17:25.

[17]Jones to Young, 13 December 1856, BYC 25:5.

[18]Jones to Young, 17 February 1857, BYC 25:19. William Dame and Amasa Lyman reactivated this operation in February 1858. The mine produced enough lead to make 121,000 bullets. For an astute analysis, see MacKinnon, *At Sword's Point*, 1:258, 2:208.

DIMICK HUNTINGTON: THE LORD HAD COME OUT
OF HIS HIDING PLACE

Dimick Baker Huntington was the official interpreter of the Indian Office's Utah superintendency for years; in 1855, the job paid five dollars per day in gold.[19] He worked for Indian agents Holeman, Bedell, Rose, Hurt, Forney, and more. As his diary shows, Huntington was Young's main operative with both Utes and Shoshones. "The condition of the Indians from 1856 to 1858 was just as bad as could be for human beings to live," he recalled. "The settlers were very poor, and unable to help them much."[20]

Huntington's journal covering August 1857 to May 1859 is among the most mysterious documents in LDS church archives. It describes the critical meeting between Brigham Young and Utah Indian leaders on 1 September 1857, providing an insider's view of Mormon policy and its relation to the Utah War. It is not a daily diary, but a journal apparently composed in two later sessions, both in Huntington's handwriting. The first section is written in pencil in a large, rough style, while the ink entries after April 1858 are more carefully composed in a tighter hand. The content—especially the many misdated entries—indicates Huntington composed the pencil section between November 1857 and April 1858. He apparently compiled the rest from memory shortly before he delivered the journal to the Church Historian's Office on 24 May 1859, as the rescue of the surviving Mountain Meadows orphans ignited yet another political crisis.

The homemade, hand-sewn journal is bound in leather, perhaps buckskin. The document has forty-two unpaginated leaves. It measures 3.75 inches (9.4 cm) by 5.75 inches (14.5 centimeters). The cover has a paper label:

Dimick B. Huntington
Journal 1857–8–9

This is repeated on the inside cover with the note, "Deposited May 24, 1859." "D.B.H." is etched on the back cover. Huntington's text begins dramatically.

DIMICK B. HUNTINGTON, JOURNAL, 1857, MS 1419–2, LDS ARCHIVES.

August 10/57

Went to East Webber to visit Little Soldier & Band. Found him much Excited in consequience of an emagrant going from Calafornia to the States, who told

---

[19]U.S. Secretary of State, *Register of Officers and Agents*, 1855, 90.
[20]Davies, "Accounts of Brigham Young," 11.

the Indians that Brigham[21] was a going to cut all the mens throats & take their women to wife. I told Soldier to be Baptised & then he could tel when the Gentiles told him a lie. He said Tom had been Baptised & he lied all the time. He said that Brigham wanted to kill him when he took their guns away from them in 53 [December 1854] but Durst not. I told him that B fore saw that the time was near when the Game would be scarce & a famine was comeing & he wanted them to learn to farm it as the Mormans Did. Gave them Good homes but they set down on their buts & Howled like so many woolvs until he saw it was of no use and told me to go & give up your guns again.

I asked him if he knew that the U S troops were a coming. He said yes but he was a fraid of them & he would like to go a way off in to the Mountains & wait to see how the Mormans Come out. I told him that that was right for the troops would kill them as quick as they would us. I told him to Gather all the Berrys that they could & then Glean all the wheat they could & prepare for 7 years seage [siege] for B said so. & he sayed it was good & he would do it.

11 [August 1857] Went to Boxelder or the city of Brigham to visit the Shoshonies in Company with my son C A Huntington. Found Kortatto PibiGand Kotant-neah[22] & their different bands 400 in number men women & children. Found them much excited [and] afraid of being Poisend. Made them a feast. Killed 6 Beeves & 3 wagon loads of Bread Potatoes corn & other vegetables. Gave them the Presidents instructons to Gather all the Berries & wheat & cash [cache] it. I had under stood that some of the tribe had stolen some of the Calafornians horses & mules. The Chief looked much down and after a little he said he had heard a little that they had and asked me if I was mad. I told him no he than asked if Brigham was mad. I told him no [and he] could then tell me all about it to even show me whare the Horses was cashed in the mountains & left them feeling quite well.

12 [August 1857] Came to Ogden City stayed all Knight with C West Bishop.[23] Met Judson Stoddard & Geo Grant a going to scirtt [scout?] & wanted an Indian guide.[24] We went back to Ogden Hole to Katattos camp to get a g[u]ide. He said he had no man that he would trust & sent a man up to Boxelder to get us a gide. Stoped at Odgen Hole & mad a feast for a 100 more Indians thare. The Breathren done first rate by the Indians. Came home & found Breathren a leaving going out east to meat our Emigration.[25]

---

[21]The journal begins in ink, but from the "m" in Brigham it continues in pencil until 9 April 1858.

[22]Huntington named "Little Soldier and band," "Pi-be-gand, and band, Box Elder," and "Ke-tant-mah, and band, East Weber," in a 9 August 1857 voucher in Davies, "Accounts of Brigham Young," 81.

[23]In August 1857 Nauvoo Legion colonel Chauncey Walker West (1827–1870) was Weber County's presiding bishop.

[24]Stoddard and Grant were apparently assessing possible army routes into Utah.

[25]The "hole" is now Ogden Valley. Brigham Young charged U.S. soldiers "would abuse men, women and children. We have sent out our Men to bring in the emigration." Van Wagoner, *Complete Discourses*, 16 August 1857, 2:1,322.

16 [August 1857] Antero Qyeahoo & wife & 8 more Yam=pah Uts came to see Brigham & to have a talk. Exprest great fears about the troops & said he would go to the mountains & wait & see how we gut along through the fight. I told him that was good for [we] did not want any help with these. We could get along with them but he might look out [for] when the troops had killed us they would then kill all of them, but the Indians might runn off but God would feel after them & they had gut to fight them when the Lord wanted them to fight & they would not then be a fraid of them. I told them how the Gentiles had treated the Indians in times past & [Antero] said he would think of it.

18 [August 1857] 5 Goshah Uts came from Toeilla stayed all Knight [and] had a talk with them. They exprest great sorrow on account of the Lack of Amunition. Said they was afraid of the troops & would go home & wait and see how the troops came out. I told them that if the troops killed us they would then kill them. I told them all that they & the mormans was one but the Lord had thrown the Gentiles a way.

Sept 30 [August 1857]

An expres came in from Webber vally stating that thare was a great many Indians a gathering at that place & their intentions ware not known. The Presitent told me to go & see to it. I started the same day & went to Farmington stayed all Knight with Thomas Smith.[26] Next morning Brother Shepherd took his Horses & Carriage & carryed me to the place whare the Indians ware encamped Accompanyed by Bishop Stoker & Hes whare We found one hundred & twenty lodges & about one thousand men Women & Children. We met Bishop C West from ogden with 4 Waggon Loads of Corn & mellons for the Indians.[27] We gave them 4 beef Cattle & stayed all Night & never saw so good a spirit before. I told them that the Lord had come out of his Hiding place & they had to commence their work. I gave them all the Beef Cattle & horses that was on the Road to Cal Afornia the North Rout that they must put them into the mountains & not kill any thing as Long as they can help it but when they do Kill take the old ones & not kill the Cows or young ones. They sayed it was some thing new. They wanted to Council & think of it.[28] Ben Simons a Delaware Indian was thare. I told him all a Bout the Book of Morman & he said his Father had told him about the same thing that they would have to rise up to fight but he did not think it was so near. He said tell Brother Brigham that we are his friends & if he says the soldiers must not come it is anough. The[y] wont come in. He

---

[26]This was Col. Thomas S. Smith (1818–1890), who was in Utah recruiting new settlers for Fort Limhi.

[27]Marcus Lafayette Shepherd (1824–1904) and John W. Hess (1924–1903) were Mormon Battalion veterans. Hess was bishop of Farmington and an Indian missionary. John Stoker (1817–1881) was bishop of Bountiful's North Creek Ward.

[28]For an analysis of the violence raging on the Humboldt River during 1857 related to Huntington's gift, see Barrett, "Stony Point," 3–23, especially 5–6.

said tell B that he can Depend upon us & I come down to see & if he talk as you do it is enough.[29]

Tuesday 1st Sept 57.

Konosh the Pahvant Chief, Ammon & wife (C[hief] Walkers Brother) & 11 Pahvants came in to see B & D[30] & find out about the soldiers. Tutseygubbit a Piede Chief over 6 Piedes Band,[31] Youngwuds another Piede Chief & I gave them all the cattle that had gone to Cal [by] the southe rout it made them open their eyes. They sayed that you have told us not to steal. So I have but now they have come to fight us & you for when they kill us they will kill you. They sayd the[y] was afraid to fight the Americans & so would raise grain and we might fight.[32]

Sept 1/57. Anterro came to see the Pres & he told him to be at peace with all men except the Americans. & when an Indian stole from an other not to be mad with any one else but the one that stole & when a Ute stole from the Snakes give up that man that stole to the Snakes & let them do with him as they had a mind But be at peace with all other tribes.

Sept 8 Powder wich a Gosha Ute came to see us & was told the same.

10 [September 1857]. Tutsegubbets & Yungweids 2 Piede Chievs came from the Santa Clarra. Brigham ordained Tutsegubeds an elder[33] & said that the 2Nephites that was to tarry should administer to him & to let him to go & preach the Gospel & Baptise among the House of Israel.[34]

---

[29]Ben Simons, a Cherokee, French-Cherokee, or Delaware in Little Soldier's band, sported a large black beard. See Morgan, *Shoshonean Peoples*, 239. Simons reported this conversation to Indian Agent Garland Hurt: "some time in the early part of September, Dirnie [*sic*] B. Huntington, (interpreter for Brigham Young,) and Bishop West, of Ogden, came to the Snake village, and told the Indians that Brigham wanted them to run off the emigrants' cattle, and if they would do so, they might have them for their own." Simons said he advised the Snake chiefs "to have nothing to do with the cattle," and implied that the Mormons hired Little Soldier to seize some four hundred animals from a Missouri emigrant. See Garland Hurt to Jacob Forney, 4 December [1857], Senate Exec. Doc. 42, Serial 1033, 1860, 96–97.

[30]Probably Brigham Young and Daniel Wells or Dimick Huntington.

[31]John D. Lee identified "Tatsegobbotts" as "the Head Chief of the Piedes in this range."

[32]In contrast to Huntington's account, Young claimed, "A Spirit seems to be taking possession of the Indians to assist Isreal. I hardly restrain them from exterminating the 'Americans,'" Cooley, *Diary of Brigham Young*, 71. Juanita Brooks, *John D. Lee*, 203, thought the meeting's "purpose was to make sure that the Indians would be active allies in the coming conflict. They would be back in the south to overtake the Fancher train at Parowan." Whether any of the Indians at this meeting joined the mayhem at Mountain Meadows is hotly debated, but Ammon was at Corn Creek on 5 September and at Beaver days later. See *Los Angeles Star*, 17 October 1857, 2/4. Mormon sources universally deny any Pahvants participated in the massacre, but Kanosh's location on 11 September remains a mystery.

[33]"We ordained Tutsegabbotts an Elder this Evening," George A. Smith informed William Dame on 13 September. Dame, Papers, LDS Archives. Wilford Woodruff, *Journal*, 5:98, dated the ordination to 16 September 1857.

[34]In *The Book of Mormon*, 3 Nephi 28:7, Christ called twelve apostles in America and assigned three of them to live until his Second Coming. They are usually called the Three Nephites, but the manuscript clearly reads "2 Nephites."

Sept 16 57

Some Bannocks from Oregon City came in to see Brigham one Chief by the name of Piut & Chief by the name of Korokokee. They sayed that the Banack Prophet had sayed a great many things of late about Gods cutting off the Gentiles & that the tribes must be at peace with one another & that the Lariet of time was to be Broke.[35] That the sun was a going to fall & the moon to be turnd in to Blood [and] that the Lord had cut off all the Gentiles & throwed them all away.

20 [September 1857] Arapene came to see Brigham. Brigham told him now was the time to helps himself to what he wanted but he sayes he was a squaw. He sayes the Americans had not hurt him & he did not want to hurt them but if they would only hurt one of his men then he would wake up. He told me that the Piedes had killed the whole of an Emigrant Company & took all of their stock & it was right. That was before the news had reached the City. He sayed he would go off & stand still & see how the Battle went. I told him he might go as far as he could get but the Lord would fetch him out & he must doo the work that God & the prophets had said they must & Josephs Blood had got to be Avenged & they had got to help to do it.

Jacob Hamblin: The Scene of Blood and Carnage

"I will here say that Brother Hamlin is doing a good work with the Indians," Isaac Haight wrote after visiting the Santa Clara in July 1857. "They love him and he has more influence than any other Man South." Haight attributed this to his "even straight forward course with them," but an incident Hamblin described to Brigham Young indicates the Paiutes feared and respected him for his fearlessness.[36]

I would say by way of incouragement the Mission is in a prosperous condition at present on the Santa Clara. Two Chiefs rebelled against the Saints at the Fort and went to the Mountains. They threatened to kill me or some of my Family and drive off our cattle. I asked the head Chief to go withe me and see them. He refused. Every thing bid fair for trouble. Bro. Thales Haskell volunteered to go. He and myself traveled until near night when we found about 100 Indians old and young. They was mutch surprised to see us. We told them to get us some thing to eat. I then went to the chief that had taken the most active part in the fus [and] asked him if you wanted my blood. Toled him I was a Shamed of him. I had p[l]owed land for him and we ben friends so long he was a fool for actin so. He trembled like a leef and

---

[35]For the Bannock prophet, see Smoak, *Ghost Dances and Identity*, 75–77.
[36]I. C. Haight to Brigham Young, 24 July 1857, BYC 25:17.

reeled like a druncan man. The Lord gave us power over them. We realized your promises [that] you gave us at Harmony [in May 1854]. This has given us more influence than we ever had before.[37]

Brigham Young had appointed Hamblin to lead the Southern Indian Mission in August 1857. He immediately "started for Great Salt Lake City in company with Thales Haskell and Tutsegabit (the Yannawant Chief)," who "had felt anxious for a long time to visit Brigham Young." After an inflammatory tour that visited Mountain Meadows, George A. Smith met Hamblin, along with Kanosh. "Other Indian Chiefs also joined our company," Hamblin wrote, and "encamped on Corn Creek" near the southbound Fancher Party. Hamblin was present when the Indian leaders "went up to see Brigham Young the Great Mormon Chief."

Hamblin and Smith met the Fancher party on 25 August 1857. Two pages describing the encounter have disappeared from Hamblin's narrative, but text from his daybook suggests what the missing section might have said:

we encamp on corn Creek while on our way nere a company of emigrants from Arcan Saw on thare way to Calaforia. Thare was a Strang atmosphere Serounded them. George A Spoke of it Said he beliedd [sic] Some evle would befall them before they got through. [In Salt Lake] the Chiefs was treted with mutch resect was taken to the work Shops gardens orchards and other plases to Show them the advantages of industry and incourag them to [do] the Same or induce them them to labor for a living. While I was in the citty I was Several times invited in in [sic] to the council of the first presidency and questioned conceining the mision and cashing [caching].[38]

Lost evidence, such as Haight's 7 September letter asking Young what to do while the Mountain Meadows attack was underway, is common in any attempt to obstruct justice. Hamblin's narrative resumed with his return south about 29 September. He claimed he tried to protect the wagons following in the Fancher party's wake and "let the company pass uninterrupted." He heard "the indians in the south were determined to have a spoil upon the first opportunity, and that several of the brethren of the mission had gone with the company but they thought it would be impossible to get them through with their stock. I told them to go and do the best they could."[39]

---

[37]Hamblin to Brigham Young, March 1857, BYC 25:17, 20.

[38]The manuscript in the Jacob Hamblin Papers, MS 1951, folder 1, file 3, LDS Archives, 78–79, and the typescript ends here, replaced with random lists.

[39]Hamblin, Autobiography, MS 14654, LDS Archives.

The best they could was to steal every loose animal, for "the policy of robbing the passing emigrants was clearly a part of the general war tactics," Juanita Brooks observed long ago.[40] In an unpublished manuscript of his 1859 report, James Carleton came to a similar conclusion:

> It will without a doubt be found *that these men were sent forward to run off the stock themselves*: that the train which followed the one destroyed, was taken through the mountains from Cedar City above Mountain Meadows to Harmony by Mormon guides:—and there down the valley of the Virgin River [via Ash Creek] and up the Santa Clara through a pass called *Jacob's Twist* on to the road again which leads to California; thus avoiding the mountain meadows where the massacre had taken place, and where the unburied remains of the victims would have been seen by this company. That in a cañon south of the Muddy, in the night these Mormon interpreters and guides, ostensibly conducting the train through the Indians, themselves *stampeded* the loose stock, consisting of over three hundred head of cattle and nine mules, and left the emigrants to pursue their way over the desert with only the cattle then attached to the wagons.[41]

Hamblin found his family at Mountain Meadows "in a bad situation," with his wife Rachel nursing a "wounded child constantly having small children of her own, it made her situation extremely disagreeable." He went

> to the place of slaughter! Where those unfortunate people were slain, Oh! horrible, indeed, was the sight—language fails to picture the scene of blood and carnage. The slain, numbering over one hundred, men, women and children, had been intered by the inhabitants of Cedar City. At three places the wolves had disintered the babies and stripped the bones of their flesh, [and] had left them strewn in every direction. At one place I noticed nineteen wolves pulling out the bodies and eating the flesh.

"The Gloom, that seemed to diffuse itself through the air and cast a shade over the hills and vales, was dismal in the extreme," he recalled. The letter Hamblin sent during "one of the gloomiest times [he] ever passed through" reflected none of this.[42] In mid-October he seemed excited at the prospect of carrying out his instructions, which appear to be to finish Fort Clara and secure Mormon relations with southern tribes.

---

[40]Brooks, *Mountain Meadows Massacre*, 122.

[41]This note is initialed "J.H.C." and dated "Aug. 1/59." Collected Material, MS 2674, Folder 1, LDS Archives, 14–15, contains a handwritten version with Carleton's additional comments.

[42]Hamblin, Autobiography, MS 14654, LDS Archives.

JACOB HAMBLIN TO BRIGHAM YOUNG, 14 OCTOBER 1857,
BYC 25:17, 22–23.

Ft Clara the 14th [October] 1857

to Pres. Brigham Young
Dear Brother

It may be of benefit to let you know the course I have taken [*sic*] since my return. If ever thare was a time when we can doe good among the Natives it is now. The mudy and vagos Indians are not onely anxious but vexet [vext?] to think that thare is no Mishionarys sent to them. The Iats [Mohaves] and orabes [Hopis] on the Colerado have sent several invitacions for us to come a mong them. Bro [Ira] Hatch has seen a few of them. I caled on all that conciderd them selves on that Mission ~~to come~~ to come to this Fort and help finish it exception [excepting] those that Speek Indian language and to Visit the diferant bands Piute as thare is some [*illegible*] bands of Piutes all expecting visits from us this fall and Winter which will consume the time of one half of the Misionarys. Bro. Hach and a few[?] others will start for the Vagos and Muddy in a few days. Orparaguats [?] an Indian Chief is ready to Pilot us through to the Moquich nacion so soon as the Brotheren arive that are agoin from the Citty. He is acquainted with the rought and the Moquiche. Thare is some of the orabes [with] a band of Piutes living on the Colerado that speek the Moquich language that will interpret for us. I doe not know of a band of Indians but what we will be able to talk with through diferant interpreters. Bro Richard Roberson will superintend building the Fort. Thare will be 7 or 8 men left with him.

The Indians here are very hostile to all Strangers all most ungoverenable. I dar not go to far with them or to much aginst the spirit of them for fear of loosing influance and govermant ove[r] them. The last company of emigrants went without any loss of life but they took all of thare loos cattle but 100 head of ~~losse~~ lame ones. They divided them out to the diferants bands. They brought 400 cows to us to keep to rase calves. If any movements we have taken does not meet your aprobacion please let us know. A word from you is incouragein to the Boys especially these times.

Jacob Hamblin

Two years later U.S. troops from Fort Tejon and Camp Floyd met at Mountain Meadows to exchange the Army of Utah's pay and investigate the worst wagon-train massacre in the California Trail's history. On 20 May 1859 Hamblin sent his adopted son Albert, whose Shoshone name meant hungry (perhaps bohoriyêxa or behodyai), to Maj. James Carleton's camp. He blamed the atrocity on the Southern Paiutes:

John and I could see where the Indians were hid in the oak bushes and sage right by the side of the road a mile or more on their route; and I said to John, I would like to know what the emigrants left their wagons for, as they going into "a worse fix than ever they saw." The women were on ahead with the children. The men were behind. Altogether 'twas a big crowd. Soon as they got to the place where the Indians were hid in the bushes each side of the road the Indians pitched right out onto them and commenced shooting them with guns and bows and arrows, and cut some of the men's throats with knives. The men run in every direction, the Indians after them, and yelling whooping. Soon as the women and children saw the Indians spring out of the bushes they all cried out so loud John and I heard them.[43]

Albert's story, Carleton observed, was "artfully made up; evidently part truth and part falsehood" and identified its elements that could not be true. "Some account had to be made up, and the one most likely to be believed was that the whole matter had been started by the Indians and carried out by them," he observed. "A Pah-Ute chief, of the Santa Clara band named 'Jackson,' who was one of the attacking party, and had a brother slain by the emigrants from their corral by the spring," confirmed Carleton's suspicions. Jackson said, "orders came down in a letter from Brigham Young to the same effect," allegedly "brought down to the Virgin River band by a man named Huntingdon." He reported "there were 60 Mormons led by Bishop John D. Lee, of Harmony, and a prominent man in the church named Haight, who lives at Cedar City. That they were all painted and disguised as Indians. That this painting and disguising was done at a spring in a canyon about a mile northeast of the spring where the emigrants were encamped, and that Lee and Haight led and directed the combined force of Mormons and Indians in the first attack, throughout the siege, and at the last massacre."[44]

In August 1859 Jacob Forney reported white men "concocted" the massacre, which was "consummated by whites and Indians." He listed Hamblin and his wife "at Santa Clara" as his source. Perhaps Hamblin recognized it was counterproductive to deceive the Indian superintendent who employed him.[45]

When in 1859 Jacob Hamblin described the Mountain Meadows massacre to federal authorities, he attributed what he knew to Albert, his adopted

---

[43]John was a Las Vegas Paiute who lived with Samuel Knight.

[44]Carleton, *Special Report of the Mountain Meadow Massacre*, House Doc. 605, Serial 4377, 6–10. Many of these charges are suspect: Huntington did not deliver orders, and Jackson apparently confused stake president Haight, who was not present, with Maj. John Higbee, who was.

[45]Compton, *A Frontier Life*, 155.

Western Shoshone son, whom Mormon historians charge "either witnessed or participated in" the murder of two teenage twin girls.[46] As Hamblin left Santa Clara in March 1863, Albert predicted he would be "dead and buried when you get back." When Hamblin returned, his beloved Native son was, in fact, dead at about age twenty-two; his vision of "preaching the gospel to a multitude of his people" would have to "be realized in the world of spirits." Hamblin recalled, Albert was "a faithful Latter-day Saint; believed he had a great work to do among his people; had many dreams and visions, and had received his blessings in the house of the Lord."[47] Faithful chroniclers attributed his death to pneumonia, but Hamblin's teenage bride told another story in her old age. "Albert had been the main eyewitness to the terrible massacre for Jacob and other authorities, he had a hard time adjusting to life again. I have always felt that some of those involved in the terrible tragedy were the ones who made sure that Albert didn't live to testify at the court trial. He was found dead in a cactus patch."[48]

On the Side of Those Wicked Men

Ben Simons met Brigham Young during one of the most intense moments in the Utah War. After Lot Smith's raiders burned army supply wagons and engaged in a bloodless shootout with Capt. Randolph Marcy's "jack-ass Cavalry" in October 1857, two Mormons stumbled into Marcy's camp carrying Nauvoo Legion orders. U.S. officers concluded they authorized "violent & treasonable acts," proving Utah was "in a state of rebellion."[49] Young soon learned of the captured orders, so the letter sent in early November seems drafted as much for federal eyes as for Washakie's.

BRIGHAM YOUNG TO WASHAKIE, 2 NOVEMBER 1857, BYC 18:9.

G.S.L. City, Nov. 2nd, 1857.

Wash-e-keek,
Head Chief of the Shoshonees:—
     Our friend Ben. Simons is about to make you a visit, and I am pleased with the opportunity for sending you a few lines to let you know how I feel and how the Mormons feel.

[46]Walker, Turley, and Leonard, *Massacre at Mountain Meadows*, 267.
[47]Compton, *A Frontier Life*, 224–25, 234; Little, *Jacob Hamblin*, 93.
[48]Stuart-Hirschfield, "Life and Death of Albert Hamblin," 70.
[49]Bigler and Bagley, *The Mormon Rebellion*, 219–20.

Wash-e-keek, I love you and your people, for you have a good heart and your people are a good people and love peace. I and the Mormons love peace, and we wish to live in peace with our red brethren and do them all the good we can, and we want the Indians to be at peace with one another. Some of the whites in the United States are very angry at the Mormons because we wish to worship the Great Spirit in the way in which we believe he wants us to and have more than one wife, and they have sent some soldiers to this country to try to make us get drunk, to ~~lay with~~ abuse women, and to swear and ~~believe and~~ dispute and quarrel as many of them do. ~~These soldiers~~ Now we do not want to fight them, if they will only go away and not try to abuse and kill us when we are trying to do right. But if they try to kill us we ~~intend~~ shall defend ourselves, but we do not want you to fight on the side of those wicked men.

Wash-e-keek, you know that the Mormons do not want to fight, and you know that we never have fought, only when some bad Indians have stolen our animals and property and abused and killed our people, and then we have only fought for peace. We want to live with you in peace, and we wish you to live in peace. We also love to live in peace with ~~all men if they did not try~~ all ~~good~~ white men, but if bad white men try to kill us ~~for being~~ because we are trying to do good, you know that we ~~must~~ ought to defend ourselves and our wives and children. You know that when the Americans come to you they want to lie with your ~~wives~~ squaws, but the Mormons do not. And when white men come to you and want to lie with your squaws, you know that they are not Mormons. And if they lie and swear, you may know they are not Mormons.

Brother Beckstead and brother Davis [?] are going to you with our friend Simons, and I wish you to treat them well.

I do not want you to fight the Americans nor to fight us or them, for we can take care of ourselves. I am your Brother. B.Y.

Young failed to win over the Shoshones or at even keep them neutral. "There are a great number of Shoshones or Snake Indians here," U.S. Army captain Jesse Gove wrote at Green River. One "of the most warlike tribes this side of the mountains" was "down on the Mormons" and Washakie asked to meet commanding general. "He wants to take 1200 warriors into the field," Gove reported. "They are a splendid set of men."[50]

War would seemingly compel Utah Territory's tribes to pick a side, but Native leaders told the military and the Mormons what they thought each wanted to hear. Pvt. Theodore Boos recalled meeting "whole tribe of the Snake Indians perhaps three thousand in all" when the U.S. Tenth Infantry

---

[50]Gove, *The Utah Expedition*, 27 September 1857, 66.

reached Green River on 27 September. "I never have seen any cleaner better looking and finer shaped Indians than these and I have seen a great many different tribes." There Washakie told Bvt. Lt. Col. Edward Canby "that he had seen heap of Mormons trying to steal or destroy our trains, but they prevented them and a part of his tribe was watching the advance trains at the present." Canby knew the way to Wasakie's heart, for he gave him "a new Springfield rifle loaded it and fired at a hill about a mile distant. We could see the dust fly up where the ball struck and the chief was enthusiastic over his present."[51]

Indians in Utah County expressed different sentiments. Mormon Charles Hancock told of Ute support in October.

> Uingokkin an Indian wished me to write to you, stating that he knows you, and that he is friendly to us, and wishes to do all he can to make the other indians so. He never stole any cattle and does not intend to, but desires to live with us. He states that Peteetneet has gone, but that he will come back if he is wanted, and fight against the Americans but that Arapene is their captain, and they want him to lead out, and then they are ready to follow. He also says that Dr *Hurt lied* to them before he left for he told them that the Mormons wanted to kill the Indians, and they have proved to the contrary.[52]

Indians felt accommodating Brigham Young was essential. During the Utah War, the most powerful Ute showed the way. "All is wright with me," Arapene wrote from Payson in 1857. "I have put a ball & chain on one Indian for stealing Horses—If you have any Tobacco, powder, lead, caps & a little whiskey to send me I would like it if not all right with me." He gave Young beaver and buckskins, saying, "If you want any thing more done with the Indian in chains, I want you to write—I think his throat ought to be cut."[53] Arapene soon wrote one of the proudest statements a Ute leader ever dictated. "I feel well when I think about you as I know that you feel well towards me," he told Brigham Young.

ARAPENE TO YOUNG, 3 JANUARY 1858, BYC 26:3, 62–64.

. . . I prey to the Great Spirit to bless you & all the good Mormons. I do not understand what the Americans can want to come here & fight the Mormons for. I do not know whare the Mormons have don[e w]rong that

---

[51]Boos, "*My Life in the Army*," 16–17.
[52]Hancock to Young, 13 October 1857, BYC 25:17, 46. A postscript noted Uingokkin needed "some clothing and Tobacco &c &c."
[53]Arropene to Young, 25 November 1857, BYC 25:10, 78.

the Americans can be justified in such a cource. I want you to write to them & tell them for me to throw away their guns & be friendly & trade with the Mormons & with the Utahs & ask them whare I have Killed any of them or whare the Mormons have. I do not know any thing that has ever done bad but I know that the Mormons treated them well & traded them wheat & Cattle & horses & money for their goods & they have fed them when they ware hungry & it is not good for them to come & fight but to some & trade & be brothers & do right but if they will not hear what you & I say to them & throw away the papers & want to fight tell them that I am not afraide of them & know how to fight. Tell them that I am not afraid of them. I know how to fight & under stand all about the mountains. Tell the Americans that I have got aplenty of Powder & lead Guns & Caps & know how to use them & that they must not come on my Land to shead blood. Tell them that I am a big Chief & am not afraid to fight. I have be[e]n shot seven times with bullets & not a boan broken & twice with arrows & I am alive still & able to fight & if they will not hear good counsil they will find me & my men a verry formidabil fo[e]. Tell Col. Johnston that he is a white man & that he had a good education & aught to set a good example & not come & fight a good people as the Mormons are but go away & let them raise their wheat & corn & live in peace. I am not a white man as you are. I cannot read or wright but I know better than to do such things as you are trying to do. Tell Johnson that the roads to Calafornia has been open so that the Americans could travail across my land & not be disturbed & that they could travail in peace & go & get money that they loved so much & why do they come here & fight my brothers. You could go and get money & trade & who hindered your people[?] I did not neither did my people nor the mormons but some of your people Killed some of Kanoshes me[n] & they killed some of your me[n] in turn on that road in [*illegible*] swap & why do you keep making a fus about it? I do understand when Judg Kinney was here & Col Stepto[e] & they took 2 Parvants & tried them by the Kord [court] and [p]ut them in prison. Why did they not to do the same to the Americans that kild the Indians. Brother Brigham Ammon & Spoods my brothers have been & seen the Navaho Chief 3 moons ago & he had got a letter that you gave me which I gave to him & he carries it in his boosom & loves a great deal & say his peac is good all the time & he want[s] to see me very much & wantd me to come & trade with him & if the Americans go away & leave us in peace. I want you to let me have some Ammunition to trade with them & I will go and see him in the spring. The Elk Mountain Utes are fighting with the Navijoes all the time & I do not like that. I remain your brother

Arropene[54]

---

[54]For background, see MacKinnon, *At Sword's Point*, 2:55–60, 231.

After Apostle Ezra T. Benson visited and "heard him preach," Arapene apparently dictated this letter.

ARAPENE TO YOUNG, 28 FEBRUARY 1858, BYC 26:3, 65–66.

Manti U.T. Feb, 28th 1858

President Brigham Young Dear Brother

I write to let you know that I am well although I have been very Sick with the Distemper. My Peace is good. I wish to be at peace with all mankind. Still I do not want to give up my home and the home of my father & friends without a strugle. No I will fight first. I do no want the American to come upon my Land, unless for Peace. Some of the Utahs hang around the american Camp. They promise them great Preasants and are trying to hire to Indians to take the Mormon Cattle & Horses in the Spring. I talk good to the Utahs and tell them to stay away from them. Bro Benson sent for me to day So I have been with him. Was at meeting in Manti. He Blesed me and I felt good under his instructions and council after which I went with him to ft Ephraim. I want a Mormon wife that understands the Books and can make Bread, Butter, and wash and make things comfortable in my house. I am very Poor and in Destitute circumstances as regards my wives and children. If you could send me a little tobacco or anything else I should be very thankfull [and] a Little Whiskey if you please.

I want you to write to Bro [Indian Agent George] Armstrong and tell him I want some more team[s] and Ploughs on the farm here as the time to put wheat in is close at hand, and I want to have my Boys at work to Learn them to raise wheat. I have been dreaming a good deal Lately and Dream that peace will soon be made, but if the americans come here and want to drive the mormons from the Land I will geather all the indians from the sorounding mountains and fight them untill they will be glad for peace. Why cant they go home and let us alone.

We Dont want to fight. They are the ones that dont have good Peace and that want to fight. When have I even went the [to] their land to fight never but they have drove you and your people from your homes [in the Midwest] to my Land and I want you to stay and raise cattle horses sheep wheat and Build houses and every thing else. I claim this country still it is not mine nor any body's else but the Lords, and he dont want Blood to be spilt on it. He Loves this country. I want to talk a good deal to you. I am full, and my heart is good. Where is the american i have killed no or stole any thing from them no. I wont sell this Land to them. The Lord says *no, no.*

May God bless you and Heber and Daniel and all this people togeather with me and mine.

Write to me

Arapine

The Army of Utah faced hard times after Albert Sidney Johnston reached Fort Bridger on 18 November 1857. He quickly determined he had enough supplies to last until more could arrive, but the army had lost virtually all its animals. Within ten days, Capt. Randolph Marcy was bound for New Mexico with sixty-four volunteers to get livestock and supplies from Fort Union. On 9 December Johnston sent Benjamin Ficklin north to the Beaverhead to try to buy cattle from the mountaineers and ponies from the Indians.

No Utah War controversy is murkier than white attempts to enlist Indian support. As William MacKinnon observed, "both sides denied using Indians as auxiliaries and argued that they urged all tribes to remain neutral." Yet Dimick Huntington's journals document Mormon officials encouraging attacks on wagon trains, and Brigham Young's Utah War strategy collapsed when the raid on Fort Limhi ended his dream of a Lamanite alliance. The U.S. Army also contemplated enlisting Indian auxiliaries. By 14 January 1858, Colonel Johnston had for "some weeks" tried to use "the Uintah Indians as allies against the Mormons" if they "attempted to interfere with our movements in the Spring, or threatened the safety of the caravan under Marcy," journalized Fitz-John Porter, Johnston's chief of staff. The army had credible reports "that the Mormons designed an attack upon Capt. Marcy, and were going to organize a party of some two hundred men to capture or stampede and scatter his animals. This determined Col. J. to rely upon the Indians, and as an auxiliary to the force expected with Capt. M. and had Dr. Hurt, the Indian Agent of the tribe approached on the subject." Porter thought the army was powerless to protect Marcy's expedition, but Randolph Marcy proved ready to deal with whatever forces the Mormons threw at him.[55] On 3 March 1858 Johnston authorized Washakie's Shoshones to "protect and run the ferries upon Green River and Hams Fork." Johnston "abruptly cancelled both the invitation and his plan to use Indian auxiliaries" on 26 April 1858, probably because of the controversy about the Fort Limhi attack.[56]

During the Move South in June 1858, Apostle George A. Smith sent a distillation of fact and fantasy to a Mormon journalist working at the *New York Herald*.

[55]"Extracts from the Diary of Maj. Fitz-John Porter," Porter Papers, Library of Congress, 10. Porter later claimed the charges against Hurt and Ficklin "for inciting the Indians against the Mormons" were false. For Marcy, see MacKinnon, *At Sword's Point*, 2:45–54, 558.

[56]MacKinnon, "'Lonely Bones,'" 159–62.

SMITH TO STENHOUSE, 7 JUNE 1858, CHURCH HISTORIAN'S
OFFICE LETTERPRESS COPYBOOK, 518–22.

Provo, June 7, 1858

Brother T.B.H. Stenhouse. . . .

June 1st, 110 lodges of Indians (being the bands of Peteetneet and old white eye, composed of the Timpanoga and Yempa Utes) arrived and camped on the Provo river, they were *towidge* (very) hungry, and immediately spread through the town begging everywhere. They said that Washington's youngest brother at the soldiers camp had given them some shirts and blankets, but as they were dressed in soldiers clothes, dragoon and infantry caps, and had some Sibley tents along, it excited a little curiosity to learn how they procured them.

Namp-puds (cripple foot) Indian Doctor at Springville, who has a fair reputation for truth, says that San pitch hired out his squaw to the U.S. soldiers for prostitution, until she became so tired that she ran away, and came over to the Weber, he followed and found her, and wanted her to go back to the soldiers, she refused, and said she would rather die, he shot her dead.

Many of the squaws received considerable amounts of money from the soldiers, the Indians took the money from their squaws and bought liquor from the suttlers and got drunk. The squaws procured dragoon and infantry caps, soldiers coats and pants, and a number of Sibley tents in exchanges for venal favors.

Pete Berry, an Indian Interpreter known as shower shockets brother, says that Garland Hurt, Indian Agent, made $500 one night by gambling, and that on one occasion, he gave the Indians liquor enough to get them drunk, when the soldiers turned in and ravished their squaws: the term soldier with the Indians means the entire army and attaches [camp followers].

From the manner in which the Indians are dressed, we judge a very extensive business has been transacted at Camp Scott in stolen horses &c., and from the visible appearance of venereal taint already manifested, it is readily perceived that "the immaculate and sinless soldiery of U.S." have extensively planted the seeds of misery and premature death among these untutored savages.

On account of this nefarious traffic and open abuse, Little Soldier, chief of the Cumumbaks or Snake diggers, was compelled to return from Camp Scott, he informed the ~~soldiers~~ Interpreters that if the soldiers saw an Indian leave his tent to hunt, they would go and lay hold of the squaw and ravish her, and in several instances drove the Indians from the tents by the point of the bayonet, and prostituted the squaws, while others stood guard at the lodge door awaiting their turns.

This conduct astonished Little Soldier & the Indians, who have for the last 10 years camped in the neighborhood of Mormons, whose undeviating policy has been to preserve sacred the chastity of the Indians.

On Friday last the Indians attacked an unarmed party of 4 men and 1 woman and killed Messrs. Teckleson and Carruth, and Mr. James Yonkerson and wife, near the head of Salt creek kanyon, on the road to San Pete valley, a young man escaped, Yonkersons body was roasted.[57]

May 26, a party of Indians stole a band of horses in Beaver Co., 220 miles South of this place; a few citizens from Beaver followed, but were unable to overtake them; this news reached Manti, upon which Warren Snow took 32 men, and rode a hundred miles east (being satisfied they would take them immediately to Camp Scott) and struck the trail an hour a head of the thieving band, whom they surrounded, and captured the animals, the Indians fired 14 guns at Snow & his company, but only succeeded in shooting a horse, the brethren did not return fire. Col. Johnston will fail to receive this expected recruit.

This mode of warfare upon the Mormons, which has been so extensively adopted north and south, and so destructive of life and property, we had hoped was only a usurpation of authority on the part of the officers now in our Territory, but we were undeceived by the official publication by Congress of the instructions of the administration to brevet Brig. Gen. [William S.] Harney dated June 29, 1857. "The necessities of such an occasion would furnish the law for your guidance."

It is rumoured that Gov. [Alfred] Cumming has arrived at G.S.L. City, accompanied by Gov. [Lazarus] Powell and Maj. [Ben] McCullough [McCulloch], and that the President of the U.S. offers pardon for all treason which has been committed, in the Territory by the Mormons, provided, they admit the 6000 troops now en route, into the settlements: we shall know more about this in a day or two.

Offers of pardon sent by an army of 6000 men, are rather questionable, especially when they are pardons for offences which have never been committed.

Arrowpine, the Utah Chief, who leads in Agricultural life and is disposed to be peaceable, has received a message by an Indian from Camp Scott, that if he does not repair thither, he will have his throat cut, and that small pox would be introduced among his family. He called upon the settlers to know if they could help him to cure the small pox if the soldiers should carry out their threat.

If Mr. Buchanan could atone for the innocent blood which his Indian allies have shed, or even wipe away the tears of widows and orphans, made so by his zeal and enthusiasm to destroy a "false religion"; and, his savage barbarity in employing the Indians to murder, butcher, roast and eat his countrymen, his fellow citizens, because peradventure the necessities of *such*

---

[57]"Jens Jorgensen and wife, Jens Terklesen and Christian E. Kjerluf were massacred by Indians in Salt Creek Canyon, June 4th, 1858 while traveling unarmed on their way to Sanpete Valley." The Utes killed two men and burned them with their wagon. Gottfredsen, *History of Indian Depredations*, 107–108.

an occasion require it, he might talk of pardoning the innocent, but his offers of pardon to the guiltless, while his own hands are dripping with the blood of the innocent, comes with an ill grace, and his talk of treason while he is using the army of the U.S. to crush out the liberties of its citizens, which he was sworn to preserve, coupled with his false assertions in his proclamation as excuses for it; are unparralleled [*sic*] in the history of executive infamy.

After Mormon leaders accepted Buchanan's presidential pardon and ended the Utah War, the region's Native peoples joined the ranks of Mormon villains—federal officials, the army, and the "blacklegs gamblers and idlers loafing" at Salt Lake. George A. Smith expressed official LDS resentment at the Lamanites' failure to become one people in a day: "The Indians seem astonished at the peace, as they [had] come into the valleys for the purpose of plundering, robbing and destroying the families while the Mormons were away fighting the 'Mericats.'" Superintendent Forney gave the Utes a steer "and some flour, as a feast at the expense of the U.S.," but they "numbered about 1000 souls." Forney then sent them "to get something to eat (from the settlers)." Local citizens had to give "them 12 beeves, and several thousand pounds of flour, as they were very hungry, and they have stolen 20 or 30 more." The June murders on Salt Creek happened, Smith claimed, because the Utes felt "the advance of the army was the signal to commence the extermination of the Mormons."[58]

DIMICK HUNTINGTON: IT IS POISON

As 1857 ended, Huntington's journal described Ben Simon's visions, which reveal how Mormon and Native magical worlds interacted.

> Nov 1 [1857]. Benjamine Simonds came me down to get a pass to in company with 2 mormons to see Washakeek.[59] Brigham gave him the pass & talked good to him. Ben sayed that the Banark prophet was his father & saw that thare was or he had seen a great Light or that thare was a deal of powder a going to Burn in the west. He sayed that thare was 3 Gentiles went from Calafornia to see the prophet and they Laught at him a made Derision of him. When he asked them what they came for [as] he was not their father but [was] to the Indians when they commenced to cry & felt verry bad. Then they handed him a letter. He took it and looked at it when a large portion of

---

[58]Smith to Stenhouse, 8 July 1858, Smith Papers, 5:16.

[59]Brigham Young's 15 September declaration of martial law banned travel in Utah "without a permit from the proper officer."

the Letter droped off like ashes & he said what thare remain was good & that which dropt off was good for nothing. Ben says he has got the Book of Mormon & is a going to take it to the prophet in the spring, & if it Drops to peaces then it is good for nothing but if it Dont then he will be a mormon.

Here Huntington jumped to April 1858 with no mention the winter's transformative events—raising the "Standing Army of Israel," the February Bannock raid on Fort Limhi, the Mormon switch from planning an aggressive spring campaign to searching for a new refuge in the Great Basin, and when that failed, seeking a political solution. If Huntington composed his journal in two sessions, the break might have happened here, on page 24 of the scanned manuscript. Huntington's handwriting shifted from loose pencil text to a tighter, more legible ink script. The journal resumed in the middle of the "Move South," which emptied northern Utah to implement a projected "scorched earth" policy.[60] The narrative preserved in the Church Historian's Office Journal illuminates details and dates, along with Brigham Young's dreams and nightmares as James Buchanan's ultimatum compelled him to accept a pardon and capitulate to the federal government. Huntington's purpose changed from seeking Native allies to exploiting their resentment of the federal army and Indian agents.

DIMICK HUNTINGTON, JOURNAL, APRIL TO DECEMBER 1858, 24–34.
April 9 [1858] Family moved to Springville & I stayed at the City.
17 I went & visited my family.
28 Returned. Indians all out to Fort Bridger (Camp Scot).
    May 8 visited my family & visited Pintets, Petetenete sone & his uncle. Campt on Tantnoquint (Spring Creek).[61] Pintets sayed his Father had gone out to the soldiers & acted Bad. Got drunk & throwed him & the Mormans a way & said he had found out the Americans was good & the Mormons no good. Indians stole mutch of our stock in March, Aprile, & May. It was the Cumumbars [Western Shoshones] & Gosha Uts [Goshutes]. The principle actors was Tabbywepup, Ibim-muzup, Pooah-nan-kubbah [of the] Gosha Uts, & Lego-ets, Naracoots, & others of the Cumumbars.
    May last or June 1 about 300 of the uts came in to Utah Co. down Provo Canion from Camp Scot. The principal men ware White Eye,

---

[60]For the best account of the Standing Army and Move South, see Mackinnon, At Sword's Point, 2:66, 69–72, 309–45.

[61]Pintets (or Pintuts) was Peteetneet 's son. "Old Peteetneet called on Prest. Young" on 2 June 1858 at Provo. "The President introduced him to his Son Joseph A. Peteetneet asked the Prest. how many children he had. He made signs that he had 47, which made the old man laugh. He made signs that he had but 2." Church Historian's Office Journal, 2:73.

Tshap-pant-no-quint, Tabby, Anterro, Tintick & commenced their stealing Horses & killing cattle.[62] Brother Brigham told me to give them some flour for they all came into his office one by one and shook hands with him & the first Presidency. They sayed the solders was bad. They gave them nothing to eat & all they did was to use their squaws & had made them all sore.[63] When they had done talking I gave them 1200 lbs of flour & they mooved on to Springville whare B[rother] Brigham gave them 6 Beevs. In a few days they moved on to Spanish Fork & all the while they were verry saucy & ugly. Wah-toe-bick shot at Brother P. J. [Philander Jackson] Perry at Springville & shot at the Breathren at Spanish Fork & Pond Town. [They] stole the Breathrens Horses cattle & sheep all the time.

Some time in June thare was many sick a mong them. The Bishops A[aron] Johnson, [William] Miller, [Alexander Findlay] MacDonald, Doct France myself & others carryed them over a load of Bread.[64] On ariving at camp we found their Horses in the Breathrens wheat. Tshappantnop-quint [was] verry sick & the whole village mad. We gave them the Bread when they would come to me & Jam a piece of bread in to my mouth & say eat it for it is poison & you want to kill us. I told them it was good—give me more for I was hungry when Tabby the only one that would talk with me asked me what it ment they was all sick & Brigham & I had talked to the Great Spirit to make them all sick & die. I told him it was not so for when B & all the good mormons prayed they prayed for them. He sayed o shit you Lie. When a curious feeling came over me & I told him to stop. Now sayd I look thare & see your horses in our wheat. Are we mad no. How many stolen horses have you now in your Band of horses[?] Now if you will give up all stolen property & keep your horses out of the Mor[mon]s wheat your sickness shall leave you & all get well. The horses was taken out of the wheat in quick time.

We then went to the Lodge of the sick chief Tshappant-noquint whar we found him verry sick. Doctr. France sayed it was the Last stage of the quick Consumption [tuberculosis]. Evry time he cought he raised a Bloody froth to a great amount. Tabby wanted us to give him some medicin. I told him Tabby no for if he died they would say we killed him. Sayed he it is true. Don't do it & after a talking for some time Tabby sayed give it to him. We gave him one powder & left 2 more & the Doctor & I Layed our hands upon his head. I was mouth in Indian & we came a way & left them feeling quite Different. Soon after when the sick chief recoverd of his sickness they

---

[62]Commas inserted. The *Deseret News*, 12 September 1855, identified "T-shar-poo-e-ent (White Eye)" and An-ta-ro as "Chiefs of the Yampa Utes." Huntington tried to blame the U.S. Army for the 1858 raids, but they had deeper roots.

[63]A reference to venereal disease.

[64]All these men served as bishops, except for University of Glasgow graduate William France (1814–1860), who practiced surgery after reaching Utah in 1853.

all moved up Spanish Fork Kanion & took mutch of the Breathrens stock with them.

In August some of this Band went out to Camp Scot [Floyd] & stole some of the Goverment stock. The Draggoons followed them but found them not. About this time Antero, Tintic & about 12 Indians went out to Camp Scot when the Troops took them prisoners disarmd them & the soldiers marcht them a bout by the point of the bayonet. Marched them to the Colonels quarters when he talked to them. Made them agree to go and get the stolen stock. As soon as the[y] gut out of the fort they past for the vally & about this time 2 Indians attacted a Danish woman & Daughter. Ravished them & abused them in a Dreadful manner.[65] The Last of Sept Gov A Cummin sent to Col. Johnson to send a detachment of Draggoons & make the arrest. The troop surrounded the In[dian] Camp in the Knight. Took the principal men all but Pinttets. He refused to be taken & runn for Spanish Fork settlement & one Draggoon [went] after him calling on him to stop fired his revolver in the air. When P was a[l]most to the town the Draggoon shot him Dead. The 2 prisoners were given up & the others released when they all put to the Mountains.[66]

In Sept Arapene & quite a number of other Indians went to the Navyhoes (Pahwich) to trade. Petetenete says he will have pay for his sone & has gone to see Arapene & as Arapene says so it will be. The 7 of Oct Samuel Brown & Josiah Call was on their way from this City to Filmore City whare they lived & on the way 2 miles south of Chicken Creek Bridge they was shot scelpt throats cut & stript of most of their cloathing when they found be [by] the marksthat they was mormons. They left them feeling verry bad. Stuck up a stick & put a handkerchief upon it that they might be found. The Indians thought them soldiers by their cloathing.[67]

Oct 14 a messenger arrived at Ben Simons Camp from the uts to get his forces to go & help the uts. But Ben sayed no wait until they the soldiers killed some of them then he was ready. The messenger says they are a gathering up all the strength they can.[68]

---

[65]On 10 September 1858 Namowah (Looking Glass) and Pangunts (Mose) raped Anna Maria Markham and her nine-year-old daughter. Governor Cumming ordered Garland Hurt to "assemble the chiefs of the various bands, and demand peremptorily" the immediate delivery of the offenders. On 2 October the army executed these orders with the results Huntington described. Floyd, "Report of the Secretary of War," Serial 975, 152–60.

[66]At Manti in November 1858, Arapene "spoke of the death of *Pin Tuts* as a warrior much respected and beloved." Pintuts was "the fast friend and protector of the white man." For this, "death had been awarded him." Arapene pointed to "the Military squads encamped near his hunting grounds, and to the picket guards, upon the surrounding mountains, and asked for what was this?" *Valley Tan*, 10 December 1858, 1/2.

[67]Believing they came from Camp Floyd, Utes killed Brown and Call, but not before Call mortally wounded their leader, Tomac. Temple garments identified the men as Mormons, so the Utes marked the bodies with a white flag. Moorman and Sessions, *Camp Floyd*, 199–200.

[68]After the Markham rapes, the army struggled to prepare for winter and an Indian war. General Johnston concentrated the Utes on reservations and fed them.

Dec 8/58 Tnacks or Tibabu-undoah or Tibun=doah (the white mans sone) came to visit me from the salmon River Country.[69] Went to see Brother Brigham. Sayed his heart was good towards the mormans but he had heard the mountaineres say a great many hard things about us but they promised a great deal & did but Little. Doctor Forny gave him nothing which made him mad. Had a Draggoon revolver stolen from off his saddle before Radford & Cabbot's store. I told him that Brigham had been superintendant but the Americans thot he was to[o] good friends & gave the Indians to[o] many things so they put him out of office & sent Forny [so] that Washington had thrown B away & Forny had throwd me away. I told him wait [and] banby [by and by] the Americans would go away & then they would see B again for he was a friend to all good Indians.

Dec 19 a Band of Ibim Indians came in from the west [with] nothing of importance.[70] They say Brigham was asleep Dimick was asleep but Doctor Forney DF. D.F. D.F. was all they could hear.

Dec 25 Arapene [and] Wahuooner [came] from Manti or rather from Camp Floyd. He stayed thare 3 knights [and] sayed the soldiers talked good but he did not know who they was. They gave him whiskey & wanted him to go in the spring two ways. One way was to New Mexico & the other to Cal.[71]

About the 1st of Oct Pintets was killed at the Spanish Fork by the Soldiers or Draggoons & just before Arapene went away. He sayed the mormons was the cause of his Death. I asked him who told him so. He sayed nothing [and] tried to turn it off but Wahuooner sayed Doct Hurt told him so.[72] I told him that he knew we were his friends so he sayed D.H. [Doctor Hurt] sayed the mormans kept all the time a punching up D Forny & the Governor to send the soldiers so they had to do it to please the mormons. I told him it was a lie for Doct Forny sent his Boy down to my house in the knight for Clark Allen Huntington to go & carry the letter over to Col Johnsons camp in the knight & had to get thare by Daylight & the mormons Did not know what was in the letter & the first we knew we heard that Pintets was Dead.

Jacob Forney's duties as Utah Territory's second superintendent of Indian Affairs proved overwhelming. He had to protect tribes, wagon roads, and mail routes in today's Nevada, Wyoming, and Colorado; restore Utah's Indian farms; negotiate the contested political ground between Governor Cumming and

---

[69]Probably Tiwandoah, the Lemhi Shoshone leader known as "Old Snag."

[70]The "Ibm Pah" came from Deep Creek, now site of the Confederated Tribes of the Goshute Reservation at Ibapah, Utah. Nicholson, "The Lamanites." *Millennial Star*, 150.

[71]Capt. James Simpson probably discussed having Arapene guide road surveys for the Topographical Engineers.

[72]After Garland Hurt's commission expired in August 1858, he practiced law and defended Mose and Looking Glass in federal court. *Valley Tan*, 26 November 1858, 2/3.

A GROUP OF UTAH INDIANS
In January 1859 Samuel C. Mills took this daguerreotype, identified as "A Group of Utah Indians, including Arrapene (Sinnearoach), the head chief of the tribe, and Luke the interpreter, taken on the outskirts of Camp Floyd looking northwest toward the Oquirrah Mountains." Historian Ephriam D. Dickson III found the image in the *National Archives, #77-F-149–11.*

General Johnston; and recover the seventeen surviving children of Mountain Meadows. Huntington's journal shows Forney got no help from the Mormons.

In November 1858 rumor said that Utah's tribes "had assembled in large numbers near the Sevier Lake, for the purpose of attacking the whites, and to commit other depredations as might best suit their savage propensities." Forney set out to visit the territory's three reservations. At the Spanish Fork Indian Farm, "not a solitary Indian was to be found and all signs of their former habitations had disappeared." At Manti Forney explained "the penalty of disobedience" to Arapene "and extracted from this War-like Chieftain implicit compliance and obedience." The Utes had "suffered much" in their wanderings: extreme weather and hunger "caused much sickness among the Indians." Peteetneet, Tintic, and their families "lay in the mountains sick."

Arapene "made no demands for the accidental killing of sub chief Pin-tete, (his half brother,) last September by a soldier at Spanish Fork." At Corn Creek Kanosh and his warriors "all promised continued peace." A friend praised Forney for stopping an Indian conflict "in the bud." Forney called a conference hoping to establish a permanent peace, but it never happened.[73]

Despite their conflicts, Agent Forney benefited from how well General Johnston managed events that threatened to pitch the territory into another Indian war. As his men finished their winter quarters in January 1859, Johnston invited four Ute leaders to visit Camp Floyd, where Johnston promised to protect their reservations and hunting grounds if they avoided wagon roads and settlements. Johnston showed them the post's long line of artillery, wined and lavishly dined them, staged a sham battle, and let the Utes help themselves to all they could carry from the quartermaster's ample warehouse. Everything "was made satisfactory" to Arapene, "and after strolling around the Camp and seeing the curiosities he was suddenly impressed with the idea that his little band of Utes couldn't whip the 'sojers.'"[74] Arapene dropped his demand for a blood price for "sub chief Pin-tete, (his half brother)" and "said many things had been told him calculated to prejudice him and his people against the soldiers," but "in the future he would listen to no talk against the soldiers."

In 1859 many LDS leaders fled into the mountains to avoid federal investigations into the Fancher and Aiken party murders. George A. Smith charged that U.S. marshals hired Tabby's band "to go into the mountains and hunt them up." Smith claimed the 120 Utes who appeared at Nephi on 16 April were "engaged (Jackal like) to hunt up innocent men," to "satisfy the blood-thirsty revenge of Soldiers" and stir up a new confrontation.[75] Meanwhile, Dimick Huntington's attention shifted northward. His journal described several Mormon-Indian confrontations documented in the other source.

HUNTINGTON, JOURNAL, 1859, LDS ARCHIVES, 34–42.

Feb 19th [1859] She-ah-gand a snake chief from the North & 33 men came to see me. [Had] mutch to say about Doc Forny.

20th Little Soldier Sheat-gand & 4 others went to see Brigham. Called him their Father. Sheat-gand never saw him before [so Young] told them to raise grain. I told them about the vision that Charles Shumway Indian Boy

---

[73]*Valley Tan*, 10 December 1858, 1/3.

[74]*Valley Tan*, 25 January 1859, 3/1, 2/4. For Johnston's "Indian Diplomacy," see Moorman and Sessions, *Camp Floyd*, 195–203.

[75]Church Historian's Office Journal, 18 April 1859, BYC 2:22, 285–86.

had had & about the famin [and] about the thousands that would come here for bread both whites & Indians. For them to ask Forny to build them places to put up grain against the day of famin. Told them about Earth quakes in Different places [and] signs of war, the commet, the Eclips of the sun & moon[, and] the design of the Goverment towards us & them.[76]

March 1ˢᵗ Wah-nah & his brother came & stayed at my house 2 days & on their way a American over took them & told them that in 160 days the solders would come & kill all the mormons off. Wahnah told him he was a fool that the soldiers would all be killed off.

March 29 Little Soldier came down to see what was a going. [He] could hear a great many things but could not tel what was the truth. He went to see Brigham. LS said mutch about the Torpusers [Trousers] (the soldiers). He said that he had had a great talk with the snakes with the chievs & they was ready to help us. He said he had sent word to the Gosha Uts to Let the M[ormon]s cattle & horses alone but consider & think about the Tarpuacers stock. He said that thare had 8 of the US cattle started for the Humbold & he asked me if they would follow their stock if it was to go away. I told him no not if they had no horses to ride. He said that is a fact. He said if the Torpuacers commenced on our people [to] rite him a letter & he would see what the snakes would say to it. He said they had no amunition & he wanted to know if Brigham or DH Wells would let them have some. I told them yes if they wanted them to help us. Little S[oldier] said that Wahr-a-gi-kah the great Banark Prophet had said to all the Snakes & Banarks to be ready when he should call for them.[77]

April the Diggers campt in City Creek Kanion & Burnd off the Presidents noor pile to the amount of 100$. About the 1st of May they mooved over Jordan & encampd about 1 miles from the Bridge. Wah-to-e-bich a tinpanny ute one of the meanest & most dangerous of all Indians I know of gut drunk & kicked up a row with Yuads Wanships sone. Piched onto Yuadses mother & pounded & beat her in a most horable manner until she spit Blood when yuads was sent for who came & throwed a blanket over him & tried to pull him off but all to no purpose when he Drew an Allens revolver & commenced to shoot & shot all the loads at him & then Wahtoebich run & yuads gut his rifle & went in pursuit of him in the dark & met him a comeing back badly wounded when W recognized Yu & asked Yu what he wanted to kill him for when he was told he had lived enough & must die so yuads shot him twice & killed him Dead & in the morning Ws friends shot five (5) head of Horses & the Mormans buryed him near camp.

---

[76]Latter-day Saints regarded Donati's Comet of October 1858 as one of many millennial portents.

[77]Pashego is usually identified as the Bannock prophet. Huntington apparently confused Pashego's name with the Bannock "Sun-Flower Seed Eaters" band name, Wahr-a-gi-kah.

Girn Eurwintys [Uinta's] sone & wife came to see me from Spanish fork. Says the Indians are all a gathering up to the Indian farm for they are all most starved & White eye sow-ey-et Anterro & all hands was a comeing in soon & Girn says that Doctor Hurt was a Great deal better than the mormons for he had made a poppoos for Miles Googers old wife now Sampichs wife. She carryed the child in to D Hurt & said here is your poppoose. No said he it is not mine it is a solders. She put her face up close to his & said are you a soldier & repeated it 3 or 4 times over a getting closer & closer every time.[78]

Wah-to-e-bich the man that yuads killed was the same one that stole somany horses from the Emigrants other Indians & from our folks. He was a most notorious Chief & a mean man. 2 days after he was killed J Forny Superintendant called on me to go over with him to talk to the Indians. Said he would call on me in a short time & went & gut Prezeus a one eyed french man to go with him the next day & met the band on the Jordan Bridge for I had told the Indians to go North for I was a fraid that Wahtoibichs friend would be mad (but the truth was I did not want their horses a eating up the grass from the City Cows) & fall upon them & kill them all off. 21 [May 1859?] a company of US soldiers went North it is said to recover some stolen horses that the Banarks had stolen from Col Steptoe.[79] But the truth is the Banarks have drove all the mountaineers in here & wont let them live in their country so the mountaineers have gone & told this story to Gen Johnson to get his troops to go & Chastise the Indians for Driving them out of the country.

& may God turn away our enemies from us & all that are not of us to Gather Israel. Wake up the sons of Laman make them a defence to Zion & Let Zion be redeemd the Jews be gatherd to Jerusalem & it be rebuilt. The 10 tribes come from the North. Amen.

Dimick B. Huntington

After six lines of obliterated text, Huntington's journal ends with a final mystery: why did the Church Historian's Office preserve it? Many of Huntington's acts appear to be criminal. Perhaps Mormon eyes saw the situation differently. In May 1859 military officers, Indian officials, and a federal judge returned from Mountain Meadows with seventeen orphans, some able to identify their parents and siblings' murderers. Perhaps Huntington's journal was created to present Mormon conduct in the best possible light.

---

[78]Peteeteneet's daughter Pamona (*Pamamaci*, Water-woman), had children with fur trader Miles Goodyear in 1846 and 1848; she was with him when he died in California in 1849. Noting Hurt's religious faith and the story's source, her tale may be "highly unlikely." Bigler, "Garland Hurt," 168n67. But the story is possible, believable, and funny.

[79]On 17 May 1859 Johnston ordered Capt. R. H. Anderson north to investigate recent "depredations committed by a party of Bannack Indians." Floyd, "Report of the Secretary of War," Serial 1024, 176–77.

CHARGE AND COUNTERCHARGE:
THE END OF THE UTAH WAR

The Utah War had enormous consequences in Utah Territory. The establishment of Utah's first army post challenged previously unchallenged power. Brigham Young's failed predictions of victory drove the Mormon leader into a long depression and cast doubt on his prophetic powers. The failure of his millennial dreams transformed the political landscape Native leaders had to negotiate, but they quickly adapted and once again played both sides against the middle in their struggle to survive.

"The Mormon and Indian Fight at Salmon River" demonstrated the growing dissonance between western reality and Brigham Young's dreams of a Lamanite alliance. When the news of it arrived in March 1858, Young abandoned his plan for an aggressive spring campaign literally overnight.[80] John W. Powell, "a mountaineer who resides with the Bonnack Indians, and whom the Mormons allege led on the party who attacked the Salmon River settlement" gave an account of the affair, probably to surveyor David A. Burr.

"THE MORMON AND INDIAN FIGHT AT SALMON RIVER,"
15 APRIL 1858, 12 JUNE 1858, 1/1–2.

[John W. Powell] says that a large band of the Bonnacks were camped with him some four miles below the Salmon River Fort, where they had been for several weeks, when a war party of the Nez-Percés agreed to make friends and disclosed the villainy of their Mormon allies. The following night the Nez-Percés stole all the Snakes' horses and returned to their country. The Snakes thereupon immediately organized a war party to follow these thieves. Before starting, six Bonnacks of this war party determined to revenge themselves upon the Mormons, and came to POWELL and asked him whether the Americans were not at war with the Mormons, and told him that they wished to fight for the Americans. POWELL told them that "Big Captain JOHNSTON" said that he wanted the Indians to keep perfectly quiet,—that he was able to whip all the Mormons alone, and that he did not wish the Indians to take any part in it; that the Americans and Mormons wished to fight it out themselves. These Bonnacks then told him that they intended to attack the Mormons and drive off their stock. POWELL told them that if they did so it would be on their own responsibility, and WASHINGTON would be displeased at it. At the same time, he said, they were fools to go

---

[80]In 1967 David Bigler proposed what became the standard interpretation in "The Crisis at Fort Limhi," 121–36.

off only six in number, to attack so large a number of Mormons; they would all be killed. They, however, said they were not afraid; that Mormon bullets could not hit them; and that the Mormons were cowards, squaws, and afraid to fight; and so they started off.

On approaching the fort, when within a mile of it, they overtook three wagons loaded with wood and hay, drawn by oxen. They immediately rode up to these, killed two of the Mormon teamsters, and severely wounded the other one; and, unyoking the cattle, threw the yokes onto the wagons, and set them on fire. They then charged up onto the herd, which was guarded by a large party of Mormons, and sounded the war-whoop. The Mormons believing that it was the whole band of Snakes coming on them, dropped their guns and fled to the fort. But one shot was fired by them, and that was from a pistol. Several of them were wounded in their flight by the Indians, but none were killed. The Indians drove off the herd, numbering some 400 head of cattle and about 60 head of horses. As they passed the fort with the cattle, the Mormons hailed them, and begged them to sell them enough of the cattle for flour, to enable them to move away with. The whole depredation was committed by six Bonnack Indians. Two Mormons only were killed and a great many were wounded.

Jacob Forney assembled Shoshone, Bannock, and Ute leaders "in Council at Camp Scott" on 13 May 1858.[81] Forney apparently gave James W. Simonton of the *New York Times* this account of Washakie's speech:

[WASH-A-KEE] declined accepting any presents for himself, saying that he had money sufficient to purchase all that he needed. The quiet dignity with which he refused, satisfied the Superintendent that to press the gifts upon him would be an insult. When an effort was made to reconcile his tribe to the "Utes," with whom he has been many years at war, he replied in a brief, sententious speech, full of poetic fire and beauty, displaying rare power as an orator, almost reconciling one to faith in the truthfulness to nature of that remarkable production which an American statesman has placed in the mouth of Logan. He frankly declared that he had no confidence in the Utes,—that he feared any treaty with them would lead only to temporary peace, for they had made repeated treaties, and always violated them. The contemptuous scorn with which these suggestions were made could spring only from the heart of one to whom bad faith is a loathing. At the request of the Great Father at Washington, however, he was willing to make peace again. He evidently had a high appreciation of the Great Father—the chief of so powerful a people—and he especially charged Dr. Forney to write to the President, and tell him that WASH-A-KEE had always been a friend to the white man, and that he made peace with his red brethren now only

---

[81]Commissioner of Indian Affairs, *Annual Report*, 1858, Serial 974, 209–13.

because he wished it. He was perfectly willing, he said, to comply with his request; henceforth let their horses drink from the same stream, and feed together upon the same grass,—that they should sit together in the same wick-a-ups, (lodges,) smoke the same pipe, and hunt the elk, the mountain sheep, the deer and the beaver together in the mountains. He proudly declared that he had no apologies to make and no favors to ask of the Utes,—that he had in no single instance ever broken his word to them,—that they had invariably commenced hostilities with his people by stealing their horses or attacking some of his hunters while alone in pursuit of their game. It was to him matter of indifference whether they decided upon having peace of war. If they wished peace and would preserve it, so let it be. The Chief's whole bearing, as he stood out in front of the assembled tribes, was characterized by consciousness of truth, honesty, and unflinching courage.[82]

DICK JAMES

Richard W. James might be the most intriguing of the forgotten renegades who tangled with Mormon theocracy. He came to Utah in 1853 as a convert and gave many of the public prayers as a missionary at Elk Mountain two years later. When the Utes expelled the Mormons, he wandered for weeks in the Wasatch with Clark Huntington and William Sterrett before staggering into Provo, having eaten a dog and most of a horse. Along the way, he learned enough Ute to serve as an official interpreter. James eventually jumped the fence separating Utah's sheep from its apostate goats. He was with Garland Hurt on 25 October 1856 when he and James White, who were "not Americans, but Mormons," survived after Fillmore's Saints "began to stone the house, some of the rocks passing through the windows and smashing the lights," judging "that they were no better than Americans." James helped Hurt escape from Spanish Fork in September 1857. James Ferguson numbered "Dick James" among Hurt's "numerous staff of like vagabonds," who stood "aloof under the shades of the locust trees watching" as the army entered Great Salt Lake City in 1858. [83]

Historian John A. Peterson thoroughly researched Richard James's colorful life. He considers him "a bad and dangerous man" who "was known to have been involved in Black Hawk's operations." After Congress authorized

---

[82]Simonton, "Interesting from Utah," 12 June 1858, New-York Times, 8 July 1858, 1/4–5.

[83]Ferguson to Young, 26 June 1858, BYC 26:9; U.S. House, The Utah Expedition, Serial 956, 181; O'Neil, "A History of the Ute Indians," 52.

the Uinta Reservation in May 1864, James worked for Utah Indian super-intendent Franklin H. Head. Peterson reports James was "known to have carried on a brisk trade in stolen cattle, sometimes using the Overland Trail market based at Fort Bridger as an outlet. Head later admitted that he knew that James, an apostate Mormon and former Indian missionary, "had been guilty of theft some 6 or 8 years before I employed him."[84]

Governor Brigham Young declared martial law in September 1857 and decreed "no person shall be allowed to pass or repass into or through or from this Territory without a permit." At Provo next May, Young wrote, "I am willing that Richard James should go with the Indians [to] fort Bridger." After James arrived at Bridger on 23 May 1858 with Pintuts and Shorneguner, he gave James Simonton "one or two chapters of Mormon horrors" about the Aiken party.

"Important from Utah," 28 May 1858, 24 June 1858, 1/4.

Last November, six young men from California arrived at Salt Lake with the intention of coming out to Camp Scott. They were arrested at Box Elder, robbed of their horses, imprisoned for some time and in December were released, and four of them started for California again, under a Mormon guard, consisting of Porter Rockwell, John Murdock and two others, ostensibly to protect them from the Indians. Mr. James went with them as they were coming out of the city. Rockwell told him he would take them as far as Salt Creek, whence the "boys" in that direction would take care of them. James noticed that the Californians all wore red morocco leggings of peculiar shape and make, three pair of which were subsequently seen upon the limbs of Mormons. A few days afterwards, Pintuls [sic] and Aropeen, another Ute Chief, met a Mormon wagon going from Salt Creek towards the mountains. Supposing from the blood they saw dripping from the body of the wagon that it contained beef, Aropeen stopped it, threw up a quilt which lay there, and discovered the dead bodies of two men, whom he recognized at once as two of those he had seen going to the other direction with Porter Rockwell a few days before. Aropeen asked why they killed Americans, and demanded some of the "plunder," of which he got a part, consisting of clothing. He then proceeded to Salt Creek, and accused Bishop Bigler of murdering Americans. Bishop did not deny the fact, but justified his conduct. The Indians subsequently learned that the four Californians went as far as Sevier River, where they were attacked by Mormons in ambush. Two were killed on the spot, and two escaped for the time and went back to Salt Creek where they were also murdered. These last were those whose

---

[84]For Peterson's work on James, see *Utah's Black Hawk War*, 203–205, 237–38, 264, 301–302, 308, 310, 326.

bodies the Indians saw. There is scarce a doubt that two of the party were the brothers AIKEN, of California.[85]

In February last Mr. JAMES had an interview with KENOSH, the Chief of the Paravant band of Indians, who have for some time past been willing instruments of BRIGHAM YOUNG's murderous purposes in the South. KENOSH was on his way to Salt Lake. JAMES offered his hand, and was refused, the Chief saying he would not shake hands with an American, as they call all Gentiles. He was dressed at the time in civilized clothing, which JAMES identified as lately belonging to a teamster. He asked KENOSH where he got his clothes. KENOSH replied that he had killed an American, and that he had taken the clothes from his body, and, to prove his assertion, showed a hole in the side of the coat, and another in the pants, made by the bullets of his rifle, when he shot his victim. KENOSH proceeded to say that he had killed a good many Americans, and had plenty of wagons and cattle, and $1,500 in money, which he had taken from Americans, of whom he intended to kill all he could find. He said BRIGHAM was his father now, that BRIGHAM talked good to him, and was the only man that he would listen to.

PINTUTS having requested JAMES to ask BRIGHAM for some ammunition, JAMES preferred the request to Brigham's interpreter, DIMICK HUNTINGDON [sic], who said, "Why don't PENTULS do as KENOSH does, and then he won't be begging all the time. He is an old fool and won't listen to what BRIGHAM says. If he does as BRIGHAM tells him, and has all he wants—wagons, horses, cattle and $1,500 in cash. You tell him from me, that if he will turn out with all his band, as KENOSH has done, in two months he will be a rich man." James related the answer to PINTULS, who said he would prefer to beg rather than follow such advice.

Such tales made Richard James a pariah among the Mormons; faithful Latter-day Saint historians still damn him as a thief and liar. James spent the winter of 1866–67 camped on the Colorado among bands "of Uinta, Grand River, Yampa, Tabaguache, and Shiberetch Utes, and presumably with Black Hawk himself." That spring he led Antero's Utes to Denver, perhaps to sell stolen Mormon livestock. These "Salt Lake Utes" stayed all summer, telling Colorado's new governor that "their relations were at war with the Mormons, whom they, the Indians, seemed to regard as a different people from other White men, and not desiring to fight have moved over to this region." They remained sympathetic to James, the mysterious "vagabond whitemen" who sold them whiskey.[86]

---

[85] To check these details, see Bigler, "The Aiken Party Executions," 427–76.
[86] Peterson, *Utah's Black Hawk War*, 205.

Richard James deserves another look, for he won the trust and affection of the Indians whose cause he adopted as his own. He wrote a stirring defense of himself to the Nauvoo Legion's Gen. Aaron Johnson:

> And now a word for myself. I have heard by Report that the Mormon People think that I and others out Here are Inciting the indians to mischief and they will not Believe anything I or others may say. All that I can say and I speak for myself that it is an *Infamous Lie.* I have done all I could to make peace and to preserve it. This is what I am here for, and if I have influence With the Indians, I use it for a good purpose. I have done all I can and would do more to help the people if I could. If I can be of any servis to them in any way I will do it with pleasure. Give my Respects to Wm Huntington, and Receive the same Yourself.[87]

---

[87]R. W. James to Aaron Johnston [*sic*], 21 June 1866, BYC 31:6.

Chapter 11

DRIVE THE WHITE MEN
FROM THE COUNTRY

The Utah War settled everything and nothing. Native peoples managed Americans and Mormons brilliantly but still found their resources disappearing and their families trapped between white power struggles that threatened their survival. Amid national turmoil, American Indian policy followed a twisted path. President Abraham Lincoln's agents signed treaties with compliant "chiefs" that promised annuities and reservations but served as quitclaim deeds for Indian lands and rights. Tribes that resisted Lincoln's open hand experienced the military's iron fist, which obliterated entire bands in the new territories of Idaho, Colorado, and Montana. Many Native leaders in Mormon Country did not survive the Civil War; their fates illuminate the hard choices facing Great Basin peoples. New leaders dealt with the West's new balance of power and its intensified assault on Indians

Much of the Native response was visionary. At Fort Limhi, "We often heard of a great prophet among the Western Indians who prophesied of great events which shall take place among the Indians," recalled Lewis Shirtleff.[1] The "peculiarities of this latitude and locality" and the Great Basin's "mysterious powers" inspired its own oracles.

"AN INDIAN TRADITION—A PROPHET," *VALLEY TAN*,
12 NOVEMBER 1858, 2/1.

The report is among the Indian tribes, west of the Rocky Mountains, that a miraculous and mysterious being has been developed among the tribe known as the Bannacks, and a confident belief in his existence in tangible human form, has gained possession of the minds of nearly all the surrounding

---

[1]Shurtliff, Life and Travels, 42.

tribes.—The name of this copper colored or red skinned prophet, as given to us, by an old mountaineer and interpreter, is Waragikah, and he is regarded with great awe by those who believe in his wonderful powers.

The story runs, that immediately after birth he overstepped the tedious period of childhood and youth, with their long train of feebleness and dependence, and like Minerva, who sprang from the brain of Jove, he stepped at once into perfect manhood. It is related that his mother scarcely had time to encase him in the board upon her back, ere his limbs had grown so large that they snapped the buck skin thongs with which they were fettered, and he stood before his maternal ancestor fully grown. He is represented as being very large and perfectly developed, but has not a resemblance to the people of his tribe, and is said to be a California Indian. His proselytes claim for him the power to heal the sick, by blowing his breath upon them, while every variety of wild animals, are perfectly under his control as well as the elements of fire and water; he rebukes the winds and they obey him, and at his command the Mountains sink to a prefect level with the plain.

It is also related of him that he never deviates from a straight line and has been seen ascending perpendicular cliffs, hundreds of feet high, which his horse ascends with perfect ease. He makes powder and bullets out of dirt, and is impervious to the arrows of his enemies; and that upon one occasion when in battle he fell, and after it was over his comrades sought his supposed dead body, but in vain, and repairing to the village found him in his wigwam quietly smoking his pipe. Waragikah, with the sagacity which surrounds modern prophets, keeps himself perfectly secluded, thus adding an additional prestige and a more mysterious curiosity to his supposed miraculous powers. Who will dare say after this that the region on the sun set side of the Pacific slope of the Rocky Mountain is not a "ger-reat and gel-lorious kedentry?"

Leaving only a sergeant's guard at Fort Bridger, the U.S. Army withdrew from Utah in July 1861, giving Mormons and Indians a fourteen-month holiday from federal power. Withdrawing most of the army from the American West caused violence to rage as raiders disrupted transcontinental communications.

Violence heated up on the overland trails in 1862. Bishop Alvin Nichols of Brigham City reported attacks that left four Californians dead. "A few days ago Sagwich & Sanpitch's bands came in" and after a few days "began to show their money," all in twenty-dollar gold pieces.[2] "They were very anxious to buy fast horses" but were "very well supplied with the ammunition." Weber Jack warned Nichols to "to stay at home and not go out on the road" as the

[2]This Sanpitch was not the San Pete Valley Ute leader.

Shoshones prepared to fight the Cheyennes. Jack "had in his saddle Bags on one side as much as fifteen pounds of bullets and a good amount of powder & caps on the other side." An express from Washakie asked them to "make all possible speed to join him as the Cheyanes had killed some of his men and they also say that a camp of emigrants poisoned three of their Indians and they swear they will have their revenge and there is no doubt in my mind but what they intend to plunder and kill the emigration," Nichols wrote. The bands "had a war dance all night" and headed east on 30 July. "Sanpitch says he does not want to kill our men [and] that he never has washed his hands in a Mormon's blood and does not want to, but at the same time he recommended our men to stay at home." Miners were fair game: packers bound for Salmon River found "a Waggon all broken to pieces and three dead men laying near it with a great many Pony tracks all around." They left the bodies unburied and "made all possible speed" to Brigham City. Nichols had "no doubt what the Emigration will seee [sic] much trouble as I never before saw these Indians so bent on mischief and so anxious to fight." Washakie was very mad, and the way "the Indians have been carrying on some time back proves to me that they intend to make all they can off the emigration and make the balance by stealing and begging from us."[3]

A day later, Little Soldier, who had "always been a good friend to the white people," reported:

That the Shoshone, or Snake Indians, and the Bannack Indians, inhabiting the northern part of this Territory and the southern portion of eastern Washington Territory, have united their forces for the purpose of making war upon, and committing depredations on the property of, the white people, settlers in this Territory, and the emigrants to the Pacific coast by the northern route; that, for this purpose, the Shoshone Indians have set aside Wash-i-kee, the great chief of that nation, because he is a man of peace and a friend to the whites, and have chosen in his place as their leader Pash-e-go, because he is a man of blood; that they are trying very hard to get the Cum-um-bahs, the Gos Utes, and Shoegars, or Bannack Diggers, to join them; that they have already killed a number of emigrants, and committed many depredations on the property of the settlers and emigrants, stealing horses, cattle, &c.; that lately they have stolen and run off one hundred and fifty horses and mules at and about Fort Bridger, a large number in the northern part of the Territory, and three head north of and within ten miles, and seven head within fifty miles, of Great Salt Lake City; that they are now removing

---

[3]Nichols to Young, 1 August 1862, BYC 85:3, 2–5.

their families to the Salmon river country to get them out of danger, and that when the leaves turned red in the fall is the time they have agreed upon to assemble, and, when the leaves turn yellow and begin to fall, the time they are to fall upon and exterminate all the settlers in the Territory; that all these war movements are instigated and led on by War-i-gika, the great Bannack prophet, in whom the Bannacks and Shoshones have unbounded confidence and faith, who lives in the vicinity of Walla-Walla, in Oregon or Washington Territory.[4]

Dimick Huntington's "Banack Prophet" said "the Lariet of time was to be Broke." He gave the prophet's name as Wahr-a-gi-kah, confusing it with the Bannock "Sun-Flower Seed Eaters" band. F. W. Lander specifically identified Pash-e-co—Sweet Root—as "medicine-man, and head of all the Bannacks or Pannakees; thought a wonderful prophet by the Snakes."[5]

The simultaneous outbreak of violence and the appearance of prophets reflected the desperation confronting Numic peoples across the West. The hope and power visionaries like Pashego offered Native survivors foreshadowed the Pan-Indian phenomenon called the Ghost Dance.[6]

Fire among the Natives: Death Finds Arapene and Peteetneet

Aropene was "sick but is recovering and the natives here are friendly disposed toward the whites," John Eagar reported in April 1859. The agent at the Manti Indian farm was "rather limited in feeding the natives and in such cases they draw largely upon our settlements and Tithing office in the way of beging." The Utes insisted they had "a prior Claim" on Coal Canyon and would not let the Mormons mine it "unless we give them 2 Beef Creatures. I suppose they are hungry for meat." All was peace at present, Eagar wrote, but "excitable Reports have been in Circulation and effect the nervous though they are without foundation."[7]

---

[4]James Doty, 5 August 1862, in Morgan, *Shoshonean Peoples*, 278–79. Little Soldier died near Ogden on 22 April 1884. At his funeral, George W. Hill, his friend for thirty-five years, praised him as "an honest, upright man" who was "truthful and unswerving in his integrity," at least after he swore off Christian firewater and Hill baptized him in 1874. Born in Red Butte Canyon "near Salt Lake City about the year 1821," Little Soldier "received all the ordinances of the church." "An Exemplary Indian," *Deseret News*, 7 May 1884, 6/4–5.

[5]Lander, in Sen. Exec. Doc. 42, 1860, Serial 1033, 138.

[6]For the best analysis, see Smoak, *Ghost Dances and Identity*.

[7]Eagar to Young, 23 April 1859, BYC 26:21, 2.

As 1860 began, Warren Snow warned Brigham Young that the Sanpete Utes were starving and demanded provisions from local settlements daily.

> They will soon consume the Vegitables and a large quanity of wheat if their calls are supplied to sustain them. I have dealt out sparingly unto them & put them off as much as possible. Some of them are dying daily. Arropine is friendly and wishes to hear from you by letter as he is very sickly at present, & I do not think he will live long & if he dies we may see fire among the Natives, for while he lives he holds them in Check from Committing many depredations, and warns us if any of the disaffected have any evil designs or finds there are some threats made by some of the natives to kill some of our best men if some of them dies & would have tried to accomplish their designs had it not been for Arropine. We are on our guard against any attack that may be made.[8]

Arapene spent his last days hoping to steal the mules powering the army's evacuation of Utah while navigating the straits dividing his people and their neighbors. Death claimed him in December 1860.

> *Death of the Great Chief.*—On the fourth inst. Arrapeen, the chief of all the Utahs, departed this life. He had been on a visit to the Navajoes, and during his whole journey had been afflicted with consumption. Being apprehensive of his approaching dissolution, he gave instructions that no white man should be killed at his death. Pursuant to this instruction his brother, San Pitch, who now takes command of the tribe, had four horses killed, and, it is said, five head of cattle to accompany Arrapeen to his anticipated hunting grounds. He died fifty miles south of Manti. In the days of the great chief Walker, Arrapeen was said to be the greatest brave of all the Utes.[9]

It did not pay to be a "well known Utah Chief." Peteetneet died in Cedar Valley, "on or about" 23 December 1861. The Utes killed no horses as they often did "when an indian of distinction" died, the *Deseret News* claimed, but "a novel and brutal ceremony, by his express order, was instituted instead"—the murder of his wife, "who was dispatched by beating out her brains with an axe, a squaw being the executioner. The Chief was buried after the manner of Indian sepulture in the mountains adjacent and his murdered wife in the valley beneath."[10]

---

[8]Snow to Young, 26 February 1860, BYC 27:20, 8.
[9]*The Mountaineer*, 15 December 1860, 2/3–4.
[10]"Death of Chief Peteetneet," *Deseret News*, 1 January 1862, 1/4.

The White Plume: Pocatera's Two Fathers

The ten Northwestern Shoshone bands had dynamic leaders drawn from a population of about 1,500, notably Tooto'omitch, "War Chief of the Snakes"; Wirasuap, "Bear Spirit," known to whites as Bear Hunter; and Pocatello or Pocatara.[11] While leading the Pacific Wagon Road survey in 1859, Frederick Lander "made fruitless endeavors to find Pocatara's band" near City of Rocks to determine "whether his warriors were engaged in the Miltimore and Shepherd massacres or not," which he doubted. Pocatello was "a very wild and reckless chief," but he spoke "some words of English," had "great influence in the country," and had cooperated with the surveyors. Lander contacted "ten warriors, an outlying party of the band of Pocatara, or the 'White Plume'" and sent "a few small presents to Pocatara, inviting him to come to me, and have a talk. He came with fifty-five mounted warriors, and treated me and my small party with the utmost respect and consideration."

> He said to me his tribe had received what he termed in the Indian language, so far as I reach the interpretation, 'assaults of ignominy' from the white emigrants on their way to California; that one of his principal men had his squaw and his children killed by the emigrants quite recently; that the hearts of his people were very bad against the whites; that there were some things that he could not manage, and among them were the bad thoughts of his young men towards the whites, on account of the deeds of the whites towards his tribe. Many of the relatives of his young men had been killed, and nothing but the death of white men could atone for this; nevertheless, I had come to him like a man, and he would meet me like a man; that his father, 'Big-um,' (referring to Brigham Young, of the Mormon population,) had sent to him many presents; but he knew, for all that, that there was a greater man than Big-um, the Great Father of the Whites, before whom Big-um was as a little finger to the whole hand, and much frightened. Big-um, with all his warriors, had run away towards the South when the blue caps, or soldiers, the bands of the White Father, came in sight; therefore, he knew and respected the power of the White Father, and that whenever he should feel certain that the White Father would treat him as well as Big-um did, then he would be the kindest friend to the Americans that they had ever known. I told him that, if after the conclusion of the present year I heard good accounts of him and his people, I would endeavor to bring to him full proof of the estimation of the Great Father of the Whites when I came to see him the succeeding season.[12]

---

[11]Madsen, *The Shoshoni Frontier and the Bear River Massacre*, 6–7.
[12]Lander, 16 August 1859, in U.S. Senate, *Massacre at Mountain Meadows*, Serial 1033, 133–34.

BAND OF "INDIAN HUNTERS"
The child in the middle of this band of "Indian hunters" is said to be Reuben Van
Ornum. His alleged uncle, Zachias, sits to his left, with Maj. Edward McGarry to
his right. *Courtesy Special Collections & Archives, Merrill-Cazier Library, Utah State University.*

TO STOP ALL TRAVEL UPON THE OVERLAND:
MASSACRE AT BEAR RIVER

Threats to overland communications brought the California Volunteers to
Utah in October 1862 under Col. P. Edward Connor. Indians had "manifested
decided evidences of hostility toward the whites," reported Superintendent
James Doty, and showed "a determination to stop all travel upon the overland routes." It was now "unsafe even for the Mormon settlers to go into
the canyons for wood; and the Bannack prophet said the Indians would
combine and drive the white men from the country."[13]

Marching across Nevada Territory, the volunteers smashed hostile bands,
reaching Great Salt Lake City in October 1862, where they built Camp
Douglas. In November Maj. Edward McGarry led one hundred cavalrymen

---

[13]Doty to Dole, 24 October 1863, Commissioner of Indian Affairs, *Annual Report, 1863*, 539–40.

north to rescue a child said to be a survivor of a brutal attack on the Snake River; the Shoshones said he was the child of Washakie's sister and a Frenchman. In December McGarry returned to retrieve stolen livestock and give the Shoshones "a little taste of the fighting qualities of the volunteers." He did no fighting but seized and shot four hostages: if he "meant to teach the Shoshonis a lesson, his action had the opposite effect" and began a new cycle of violence. Warriors vowed "to kill every white man they met north of Bear River" and often did.[14]

Before dawn on a bitterly cold 29 January 1863, the California Volunteers attacked Boa Ogoi, the winter camp of the Northwestern Shoshone on the Bear near today's Preston, Idaho. There was no love lost between the army and the Mormons, but Brigham Young's bodyguard, Porter Rockwell, led the soldiers north to the Shoshone camp. Before leaving Salt Lake, Connor announced he would take no prisoners.

Frostbite disabled almost a third of the soldiers before they reached Brigham City, and the approach of the army was no secret to the Indians. Three Indians from Bear Hunter's band visited his father's farm the evening before the attack, William Hull recalled. When he saw the approaching *Toquashes*, or soldiers, Hull said, "Maybe you will all be killed."

"Maybe Touquasho be killed too," said one warrior.[15]

As the troops prepared to charge, "the Indians seemed to look upon the coming struggle with particularly good humor. While one of the chiefs rode up and down in front of the ravine brandishing his spear in the face of the volunteers, warriors in front sang out: 'Fours right, fours left; come on you California sons of b—hs!'"[16] The troops launched a costly frontal assault before flanking the Shoshones and cutting off their retreat. By 8:00 A.M. "the Indians were out of ammunition and the soldiers shot down the survivors with their revolvers." When resistance collapsed, the battle became a massacre.

PETER MAUGHAN TO BRIGHAM YOUNG, 4 FEBRUARY 1863,
BYC 29:10, 72–73.

I send you a note per J. H. Martineau. Bro Israel J Clark has just returned from visiting the Battlefield and give[s] the most sickening accounts of the inhuman acts of the Soldiers, as related to him by the squaws that still remain

---

[14]"Another Expedition after Indians," *Deseret News*, 10 December 1862, 4/2; Miller, *Massacre at Bear River*, 54–58.

[15]Bagley, "Bear River Massacre Haunts Utah History," *Salt Lake Tribune*, 26 January 2003, B1.

[16]*Deseret News*, 11 February 1863, 5/1.

on the ground. After they had routed the Indians, they killed the wounded by Knocking them in the head with an Axe and then commenced to ravish the Squaws which was done to the very height of brutality, they affirm that some were used in the Act of dying from their wounds.

The above reports are substantiated by others that were present ~~on the~~ at the time. We are unable to say what will be the future course of the Indians as the men have left for the Bannack Country with the intention of a big council and the Squaws are affraid to come into our Settlements lest the Soldiers should come back again. We sent 60 men on friday to bring our Herd home, which all arrived safe in Cache this evening without any interception from the Indians in that region. As near as we can find out there were about 120 Indians killed and about 90 squaws & children, several have counted them to about that number. I feel my skirts clear of their blood, they rejected the way of life and salvation which have been pointed out to them from time to time (especially for the last two years) and thus have perished relying in their own strength and wisdom.

We have pretty good reason to believe that if they had gained the victory over the Soldiers their intentions was to take our Herd and drive it right to the Salmon River Country for their own special benefit, this testimony we got from a friendly Indian. Bear hunter and Lehi are among the dead.

Everything about the Bear River Massacre is controversial, including that the massacre began as a battle. Claims the volunteers raped women and murdered children are hotly debated. Maughan's letter offers the best evidence for both charges, but another contemporary partisan source reported:

> Col. Connor gave strict orders against killing women and children, of whom, contrary to precedent, there were quite a large number in camp. A few were slightly wounded, and I believe one killed by a member of the cavalry, who was immediately notified that if the offense was repeated he would have his BRAINS BLOWN OUT. At the conclusion of the engagement, 114 women and children were allowed to go.[17]

Kass Fleisher's *The Bear River Massacre and the Making of History* argued rape played a major role in the atrocity, but one of her few Shoshone sources, Mae Timbimboo Parry, said rape "was never mentioned by the Indians. And I don't believe it's true." The intense cold froze whiskey rations in the soldier's canteens, so Dr. John Gary Maxwell argued under such extreme circumstances "rape would have been almost impossible," unless it was object rape.[18]

---

[17]*Stockton Daily Independent*, 17 February 1863, in Hart, *The Bear River Massacre*, 116.

[18]Maxwell's *The Civil War Years in Utah*, 185–94, is a balanced analysis.

Army surgeon John Vance Lauderdale arrived in Utah in 1864 but sent his sister Frances what was probably a popular perspective among the volunteers:

> Our boys have participated in but two [Indian fights], the one at Spanish Fork and the one a year ago last winter at *Bear river.* [The] latter which was by far the hardest fought battle *was instigated* without a *doubt by the Mormons.* The latter being unfriendly to our army thought they would betray us into the hands of the indians. They thought by so doing they would make a little speculation out of it themselves. They made the indians believe they could capture us most easily & agreed to reward them finely if successful. These Mormons acted as spies and did what they could to keep the indians informed of the movements of the soldiers. The sequel of the story proved the destruction of the indians. The only regret is, that the three hundred bodies of dead indians which lay along the shore and floated down the stream during the following summer were all of them Indians.[19]

Soon after the fight, Ute interpreter Peter Berry asked Connor "what he intended to do with the Indians." Conner said "all good Ind[ians] he would let alone but the bad ones he would kill, & he would have a plenty of soldiers this fall to do it." Antero, Tabby, and all the Utes were ready to resist, Pete told Brigham Young, "if you wanted them. Just send them word." They rejected Superintendent Doty's presents, "for they had heard that Doty had got the smallpox in them to give the Indians. Peet said if they did do it they would come in to the city to kill conner & Doty in the street."[20] The crucial difference between Connor's and Brigham Young's plans to kill all the bad Indians was that Connor had skilled soldiers prepared to do it. Utes at Pleasant Grove attacked five soldiers on 11 April 1863. They took shelter in an adobe as hundreds of settlers watched, "apparently pleased at the prospect" of their deaths. Reinforcements chased the Utes into Spanish Fork Canyon and believed they killed "about 30 warriors."[21]

On 10 June 1863 Utes attacked an overland stage and murdered Wood Reynolds and Thomas O'Shonnison about two miles west of the Jordan River ford. They soon appeared at Nephi, where Phebe Westwood saw them display "the scalps of the poor men they killed" and "a great many other things belonging to the stage. You had better believe it made me feel mad. I got dreadfully excited." The bishop "treated the Indians with tobacco and ordered the people to feed them, and it made me so mad that I pitched

---

[19]Lauderdale to Dear Frank, 15 June 1864, Lauderdale Papers, Beinecke Library.
[20]D. B. Huntington to Young, 25 September 1863, BYC 29:9.
[21]Maxwell, *The Civil War Years in Utah,* 199–200.

into them and told them what I thought of them, and then I felt better," she wrote.[22]

After speaking with the raiders at Manti, G. W. Bradley reported to Salt Lake.

> *Tabby said*—"I was leader of the war party that attackd the Mail lately and want you to know that I am sorry and ashamed to learn that a Mormon was killed in that affair, but now I am willing to listen to *your* councel and do as *you* say, that is if the Soldiers will listen too, and quit seeking Indians to kill them; we will take *your* advice and not molest the Mail Line nor Emigrants any more; but if the Soldiers will not *listen* we will not, but will try which are the best Warriors, they or us. Sanpitch, Konosh, Little Soldier and other Chiefs are not present, but I can vouch for them to back up what I say and agree to; I will send runners to them and if any should disagree, I will let you know. I wish to have another letter from *you* immediately, and till I receive it I do not want to say much more, only I want it known that my people are hungry and that we would like some Tobacco."[23]

Superintendent Doty described the Bear River Massacre as "the severest and most bloody of any which has ever occurred with the Indians west of the Mississippi." It "struck terror into the hearts of the savages hundreds of miles away from the battle-field." Doty considered Connor's extreme violence marked a turning point in the Great Basin's Indian wars, for it "effectually checked" the tribes "and severely and justly punished them for the wanton acts of cruelty." After Bear River, Doty reported several Utah bands were "willing and desirous to become settled, as herdsmen or husbandmen, on the Uinta reservation." The government should arrange the relocation of tribes near "the present routes of travel though this Territory." This would insure peace "with a people strongly inclined to agricultural pursuits, but who have, from unknown causes, at several times this season, attacked the stages and killed the drivers." As long as they lived near white settlements, however, conflict was certain. Doty wanted to abandon the Spanish Fork Indian farm as "a waste of public money." With Connor he had made "treaties of peace and friendship" under "difficult and hazardous" conditions, but it appeared "as though peace was again permanently established with all of the tribes." Emigrants, the overland stage, and telegraph lines and were now safe, and the tribes regarded "the Americans as the masters of this country."

---

[22]Connor to Drum, 28 June 1863, *War of the Rebellion*, Series 1, Vol. 50, Part II, Serial 3584, 500.
[23]Bradley to Young, 23 June 1863, BYC 29:7.

But only "regular, liberal, but just appropriations" and "a strong military force upon the main routes of travel through this city, and especially on the routes north" would keep the peace.[24]

Except when killing Indians, Utah Territory waged its civil war with words. The Camp Douglas newspaper charged ill-deposed persons had "manufactured out of the whole cloth" and "industriously bruited" tales of Native outbreaks as part of "strenuous efforts used by white liars to precipitate the Indians into hostilities" with "utterly false" reports. The "shameless mendacity" of the Mormons sought to set loose "the savage Indian" on the emigrants flooding into the territory and inaugurate a reign of terror.[25] No matter who wielded white power, Utah's Indians needed little encouragement to resist it, but they preferred to exploit its fractures.

FOR THE COMFORT OF THE INDIANS: THE SPANISH FORK TREATY, 1865

President Lincoln designated the Uinta Basin—"a vast contiguity of waste"—as the Ute reservation in 1861. Three years later Congress opened the Spanish Fork Indian farm to settlers and appropriated $30,000 to create a "permanent" home for the Utahs in the Uinta Basin.[26] As Robert E. Lee surrendered on 9 April 1865, John Lowry Jr., known to the Utes as the "man who drinks whisky," pulled Jake Arapene off his horse and ignited the last great Mormon-Indian war. Named after Black Hawk—Antonga, Antongur, or Noonch to his people—the bloodshed began when Ute raiders seized cattle at their now-defunct San Pete farm, killed Peter Ludvigsen, and decamped to Salina Canyon, where before sunset they met, murdered, and mutilated James Anderson and Elijah "Barney" Ward, the famous Mormon mountain man. Antonga quickly rallied some eighty men, seized 125 cattle, and routed the Nauvoo Legionaires sent to recover them.[27] Tabby might not have known where the hostiles were, but he and Antonga played both sides for years.

Within days of Barney Ward's murder, Sanpitch told Nephi's bishop he had "an agreement with him that if anything should happen to Ward,"

---

[24]Doty to Dole, 24 October 1863, *Report of the Commissioner*, 1863, 539–40.

[25]"Indian Hostilities," *Union Vedette*, 8 June 1864, 2/2.

[26]Bigler, *Forgotten Kingdom*, 237.

[27]Peterson, *Utah's Black Hawk War*, 16–22.

he could marry his daughters. Sanpitch wanted Brigham Young's approval and assured him he did "not wish the *Soldiers* sent here to settle the present difficulty because he does not like to see them come with their big guns &c."[28] Orson Hyde claimed Sanpitch was lying and had engineered Ward's murder to get his daughters: "Sanpitch generaled the whole wicked plan."[29]

Early in 1865 Congress appropriated $25,000 to defray expenses to make a treaty with Utah Indians. Knowing how power worked in Utah Territory, Superintendent Orsamus H. Irish invited Brigham Young to negotiate a treaty to extinguish Indian titles in Utah Territory.[30]

Hundreds of Utes assembled at the Spanish Fork Indian farm in late May and were fed "flour at Govt expense, but no beef, which they want very much." Tabby, "lately arrived from Uinta," dictated a message to Brigham Young, recalling "the good friendship and counsel, received from you in bygone years." He hoped to see Young about "the prospective treaty with the government officials," for he feared "some advantage will be taken of the Indians." Tabby wanted Young to "assume ownership of all the land formerly occupied by the Utahs, upon the ground of the agreement made between yourself, and Chiefs Walker, Sowiett & others at Provo, 14 years ago." Young "obtained the right of location and ownership in connexion with the Utahs, to all the land, water, grass, timber, &c throughout these vallies." He proposed Irish "first treat with you, before coming to the Indians and whatever you agree to in relation to giving up possession of the *land* Tabbey says he and *all* the Indians will agree to the same." As "a good father of the Indians," Young had "never promised anything to them that you did not perform," which was more than Tabby could "say about some of the rest of their fathers." He knew "nothing of those Hostile Indians but is equally afraid of them" and promised "to keep a good look out for danger."[31] The hostiles were the Utes who chose fighting. Tabby chose talking.

---

[28]Charles Bryan to Young, 18 April 1865, BYC 30:9, 23–24.

[29]Hyde to Bryan, 26 April 1865, BYC 30:9, 28.

[30]Bigler, *Forgotten Kingdom*, 237.

[31]Bean to Young, 26 May 1865, BYC 30:8, 58. No such 1851 agreement is known, but on 23 December 1855, as Garland Hurt started the Indian farm on Twelve Mile Creek, Arapene "deeded the land of his fathers to Brigham Young as a trustee for the church." "Cultural extinction was to be the price of survival," observed historians Albert Antrei and Allen Roberts. *History of Sanpete County*, 72–73.

PROCEEDINGS AT THE SPANISH FORK INDIAN FARM, JUNE 1865, NARA.

Proceedings of a Council held by O.H. Irish, Superintendent of Indian Affairs with the Utah Indians for the purpose of negotiating a treaty with them for the extinguishment of their title to the lands within Utah Territory in pursuance of the Act of Congress of February 23ʳᵈ 1865, entitled "An act to extinguish the Indian title to lands in the Territory of Utah suitable for agricultural and mineral purposes."[32]

At a Council of the Utah Indians, held at Spanish Fork Indian Reservation, commencing on the Seventh of June 1865 at which the said Indians were represented by the following chiefs viz:

Sow-e-ett	(Nearly Starved)	Chief	Yampah Utes
Kon-osh	(Man of white hair)	"	Pah-vants
Tabby	(The Sun)	"	Yampah Utes
To-quo-ne	(Black Mountain Lion)	"do [ditto]	do
Sow-ok-soo-bet	(Arrow Feather)	"	Sanpitch Utes
An-Kar-tew-ets	(Red Boy)	"	Timpanogs Utes
Kibets	(Mountain)	"	Spanish Fork Utes
Amoosh		"	Cum-um-bahs
An-Kar-aw-Keg	(Red Rifle)	Subchief	Pah-vants
Nanp-peades	(Fool Mother)	"	Timpanogs
Pan-sook	(Otter)	Subchief	Utes
Pean-up	(Big Foot)	"	Pah-vants
Eah-gand	(Shot to pieces)	"	do
Nar-i-ent	(Powerful)	"	do
Que-o-gand	(Bear)	"	Utes
San-pitch	(Bull rush)		Chief Utahs

With Huntington interpreting, Irish's preamble complained "bad Indians come into San-Pete Valley and drove off cattle and killed some of the settlers." The Utes said "they wanted to be friends with the whites and protect them instead of committing depredations upon them. Irish made a great show of giving blankets to To-quo-ne and Joe (Sow-ok-soo-bet), for "in this time of trouble" they had "tried to keep peace between the Indians and the whites." He promised, "I shall give them more presents. This is just a commencement." He would "never forget those two men in their efforts to defend the whites."

---

[32]Before becoming Utah's Indian superintendent on 2 February 1864, O. H. Irish served as agent to the Omahas.

Two messengers from the Uintah Valley got more blankets, "to let them know I remember them again." He told "Tabby and his Indians" when they hunted "for stolen property and bring it in, and show they are good Indians," they would be rewarded.

"The great Father at Washington has directed me to call his Indian children together and talk to them of matters that concern their future welfare." As leaders, they stood before them "today to lead them into a road of prosperity or one in which they will be poor and weak and suffering." The Great Spirit, who controlled "you and me and the great Father at Washington," wanted the ground that "we stand upon" where "you and your father have lived, to be used for the purpose of producing grain, corn and such things as go to make his children comfortable, happy and prosperous." He put "into the hearts of white men to come here and open farms and build houses" and made them "prosperous and happy. The same Great Spirit that led them here, has put it into their hearts" to "propose to make a treaty" that "your friends and brothers the white children of the great Father may live happy, peaceful and unmolested upon it" while "other land shall be occupied by you and your children alone." If they signed the treaty, "you shall have farms and houses and goods" and decide for their peoples' welfare "whether they and you shall pursue the road to prosperity and peace or want and trouble and sorrow." They could "make your people happy and prosperous," or "poor, miserable and unhappy. We wish to know whether you will gain a living the same as white men do and prosper in the same way, or whether you will dwindle away in idleness and ignorance." The Interpreter had read the treaty to them yesterday and Irish now read it again and was "done for the present."

> Kon-osh, (Bean Interpreter): We have agreed that four chiefs shall do this talking. Here is the father of all the Utes, Sow-e-ett. He used to be the great chief and father of us all, but now he is very old poor and blind, he has no flesh on his bones, he is going down. We want Sow-e-ett to talk and all to listen, both Utes and whites. I am only a boy and do not know how to talk very well. I might talk two ways and think two ways. I do not understand things as the old men do, things that are good and right. We expect, now there is a chief come from Washington, who talks one way, understands things one way and understands them right, that he will always talk one way. In past times, the Washington chiefs that came here from the United States would think and talk two ways and deceive us: they always talked and thought different from Pres. Young. They have been liars, two tongues and

two hearts. I do not want to make any hard talk. I want the Washington chief who talked and thought straight and all his brothers and friends to hear and understand. In former times, this land, where I laid my father, was very poor, but now it is not poor, it has got to be a good land since Pres. Young and the Mormons came here. All their children have plenty to eat and they have plenty of property. I have but few brothers and friends, and do not see what use it would be to trade the land where there are so few of us. Whatever we would trade for would be all gone soon: whether blankets, or hats, or shirts, or money. The money would soon go in the stores and the other things would soon be done. If the Americans buy the land, where would the Mormons who live here go to? Will the Lord take them up to his country? I think this is the Mormons land the Bishops land, with the Utahs: Let them all live here together. I do not want to cut the land in two. Let it all remain as it is. Suppose the Americans do buy the land here, and put the Utes off over to Uintah, will the Utahs take the American squaws with them to raise American children. I have worked at Corn Creek a long time and I have got nothing. President Young gave me five cows, and when the grasshoppers came and eat up my grain I had to sell them to get something to eat. They did not bring me any blankets or anything but I did not quarrel about it. I suppose the Washington chief is not afraid to let us remain here, go to Sanpete or Uintah or where we like: that is what we want: I am glad we have come together here, I like to see the Washington chief and Brigham and all the Indians together. With regard to these troubles in Sanpete, I wish it understood that I am not in favor of it any more than you are; My fathers were very poor. My father wasswapt poor: he had nothing to trade: and my Indians now have got but little they can trade. It is all right to let us stay where we are. Let me stay at Corn Creek and visit back and forth: let the Spanish Fork Indians visit us and we visit them. If they do not want to work here let them come with me. Suppose Brigham, our eldest brother, was to die, where would the Indians all run to. When they know he is at Salt Lake City, it is all right. Brigham is the great Captain of all, for he does not get mad when he hears of his brothers and friends being killed, as the California Captains do. The best thing is for the Superintendent to give us our blankets and shirts, and not talk about trading the land, but let us live and be friendly together. Give all of us blankets and shirts squaws and all, and do not make us feel poor, but clothe us up.

The Indians asked: What time the treaty came from Washington.

Supt. Irish replied, A few weeks ago.

San-pitch (Bean Interpreter): I am not going to talk about the treaty: I do not question the paper, but I do not want to trade the land nor the title to the land. It used to be the Lord's land but now it is the Mormons land and ours. The Maker of the Land is probably dead, and buried now. It is not the Utes' land now. I am friendly to both parties, both the Americans and Mormons, and I do not care anything about the talk of the boys. The Americans do not want to trade the land for money: they are hunting money. I am a friend to everybody and do not care for small talk. Others have traded their land and quarreled about it in the Mexican country. But this is good, heavy land, lots of water and rocks and I want it to stay here and us to stay here with it. We do not want to be removed from the land. The Utes are not numerous compared with the people here. The whites make farms, get wood and live on the land and we never traded the land. They have two children to the Utahs one; they are double in numbers to us: let them live here and us live here too. If the talk is for us to trade the land in order to get the presents, I do not want any blankets or any clothing. If that is to be the way they are to be got, I would rather do without, than to give up my title to the land I occupy. We want to live here as formerly.

Ex-Governor Young (Huntington Interpreter): San-pitch, Sow-e-ett, Tabby and all of you, I want you to understand what I say to you. I am looking [out] for your welfare. Do you see that the Mormons here are increasing? We have been and calculate to be friends all the time. If you do not sell your land to the Government, they will take it, whether you are willing to sell it or not. That is the way they have done in California and Oregon. They are willing to give you something for it and we want you to have it. If you go to Uintah, they will build you houses, make you a farm, give you cows, oxen, clothing, blankets and many other things you will want. And, then, the treaty that Colonel Irish has here, gives you the privilege of coming back here on a visit: you can fish, hunt, pick berries, dig roots and we can visit together. Kon-osh, San-pitch, Tabby and the rest of you, can come and see me when you please. The land does not belong to you nor to me, nor to the Government: it belongs to the Lord. But our Father at Washington is disposed to make you liberal presents to let the Mormons live here. We have not been able to pay you enough, although we have helped you a good deal. We have always fed you, and we have given you presents just as much as we could: but now, the great father is willing to give you more: and it won't make one particle of difference whether you say they may have the land or not, because we shall increase, and we shall occupy this valley and the next, and the next, and so on till we occupy the whole of them: and we are willing you should live with us. If you will go over there and have your houses built, and get your property and money, we are perfectly willing you should visit with us. Do you understand that, Konosh?

Kon-osh (and others): We do.

We feel to do you good: and I know that this treaty is just as liberal and does everything for you and for your people that can be done. If it were not so, I would not ask you to sign it. But as for the land, it is the Lord's, and we shall occupy it, and spread abroad until we occupy the whole of it: and we want you and your children to live, so that you can live with us and our children. Now, if you can understand this, you can see at once that we do not want anything wrong of you Indians. It is enough.

Tabby (Bean Interpreter): The hearts of the Indians are full: they want to think: wait until tomorrow: Let us go back to our lodges and talk and smoke over what has been said today. The Indians are not ready now to give up the land: they never thought of such a thing.

Sow-e-ett (Bean Interpreter): Here you see the Mormons and the Utahs all mixed together, I am the father of you all. I have always been the friend of the Americans (Mr. Young, "He has,") I have never thrown away my friendship for the Americans: I always liked to be a great friend to them. (Supt. Irish—That is what everybody says of you.) Long ago I was the Americans friend. After a while Brigham and the Mormons came here: I saw him and he was my son, my friend. I have always been the same, and I was the American's friend long before that. When I met President Young we talked and understood each other, me and my children the Utahs, and Brigham and his children. When some of my children stole horses and acted bad, did I break my friendship? No: never, I have heard from Col. Irish time and time. I heard he wanted to see me, but I was too sick. When my sons die and the Americans die there was never any quarrel between them, I never felt like breaking friendship. I do not want to see it. I am old: my heart is very weak now, but it is good.

The meeting seperated and the Indians returned to their lodges very much excited, unwilling to talk any more about giving up their land.

During the afternoon and evening the different chiefs and Indians visited Supt Irish and talked about the treaty informally and Supt Irish visited them in their camp with the Interpreters.

THURSDAY JUNE 8TH, 10. A.M.

The Council reassembled, all present except San-pitch.

Supt Irish (Huntington Interpreter) I wish to ask the Utah chiefs this morning, if they have eyes that they can see? If they have ears that can hear? If they have hearts that can understand? If they have I will not have occasion to repeat what was said yesterday. Are you prepared to give me your answer, that I may tell the great father your decision. Shall I tell the great father, that when he stretches out his hands to you full of gifts and benefits, you reject them: that when he sends to you men in whom you have confidence to give you counsel and advice, you refuse to receive it; that having eyes, you refuse to see, ears, you refuse to hear and hearts, that you will not understand. The great father does not wish us to stand waiting. He has other interests and other business for me to attend to: and he desires that I shall be employed at something else. We have come here today to settle this question. Do as you please: Decide for yourselves. Give me your answer. Are you ready to take the advice that was given to you yesterday? Do you need to have anything more said? Are you not men that can think for yourselves: shall we waste time in taking? Now is the time to act. Say now what you will do.

Sow-e-ett, It is good, We will sign.

Supt Irish, "Sow-e-ett, you are an old man, but if you live a year, you will live long enough to be glad of having signed this treaty.

The chiefs then attached their marks to the treaty.

Supt. Irish (Huntington Interpreter) The treaty is made, and I trust it will be a bond of peace and prosperity between you and the people and the Government, as long as these hills, around us, endure. When the great father told me to come and see his children in Utah, I asked him what he wanted me to do. He told me to do such things as would promote the interests of the Indians and the people in these mountains. If you live up to this treaty, if you keep it, you commence today a career of prosperity for yourselves and your children and the time will not be far distant when, if you will work and make use of the advantages it affords, you will be living in houses of your own, when you will have little farms of your own, when you will be gathering into your barns the produce of your farms, and by the side of your own fires you will be surrounded with your children in comfort. The man who looks at you today, and will look at you a few years hence, would not think you the same people. All this will most assuredly be, if you do right, if the provisions of that treaty are kept sacred and inviolate by you.

Ex-Gov. Young (Huntington Interpreter): I have the same regard for you that I have for all who will be friends to God and righteousness. We can read and write, and we wish you to learn to do so too, and to increase in intelligence. I have looked for your welfare just as I would look for my own or my own children. I want you to remember what has been said to you here: and I shall do hereafter all that I can for your good. Supt Irish, who had been sent here by Government, has done everything that he possibly could for your welfare. We wish he could stay here always, but by-and-by he will go and somebody else will come and we do not know who it will be, but, remember, I shall always look for your welfare ready to give you good counsel and advice. You can always receive all you have received by kindness, be fed and nourished by the people here just as you have been. You know how you were when we came here, and that you are a great deal better off now than you were then. We have never sought to hurt you, to take anything that belonged to you nor to destroy anything of yours: but we have sought to save your lives: and we want you still to live and be good men, good women, good children, and grow up to enjoy your selves. But if you go and do as you are requested to do, your condition will still be better.

I want to say a word to you about this command of soldiers that is coming here. They are within 10 or 15 miles of us here, and they want to go to work in the Kanyon. They are waiting now just to please you. Are you willing they shall march through here? Will you be afraid if they do? Colonel [W. D.] Johns will come tomorrow this side of Payson: next day to the Kanyon. Supt Irish wants you to stay here and enjoy yourselves a few days. Now, I will promise you, if you will keep away from the soldiers, that they will not come nigh you, nor say a word to you. Will you keep away from them?

Indians—Yes.

Mr. Young—Stay here till you get your presents and make your display. I want you to remain here and enjoy yourselves, eat and drink, so that when you go away you will feel good, right, and in peace, as we have been all the time.

Indians—All right.

Mr. Young—Then we will be brothers. may the Lord bless you.

Kon-osh (Bean Interpreter): The talk has been all good. I have been thinking good. All our hearts are good, and alike. I like this good, friendly, council. I always liked a council where it is good and friendly and where all agree together: and my friends like it. It pleases me very much to see Supt Irish and Brigham agreeing on this treaty and traveling together and talking to the Indians. In former times it has been when an Agent came here President Young would stay at one side: and I was sorry that they could not agree. There are only a few children growing up. What they will be by and by I do not know: but they are only a few now. The whites are increasing all the time. I am very glad to see the soldiers traveling about the country friendly and not shooting the Indians, but all good peace. Formerly myIndians did not know what was the use of powder and lead and caps, but now they do. We hope our father will give us some in his presents. When I understand that I can travel back and forth in the country, can trade my lands and continue to visit the country. I like that. For many years I have plowed and worked at Corn Creek and did not get blankets nor anything: Brigham knows that. Agents have come from Washington but would stop and never come nor bring me blankets. They would send and make promises but never fulfil them. It is all right, in this treaty: the Americans can come and hunt their money and live here. We do not want to quarrel. It is all good peace and good friendship, and we all understand alike. Now we are ready for the presents: fetch them out and deal them out. We don't want the father to hide up anything. Fetch all out.

Supt Irish: You can go and see if anything is left, after they are distributed.

Kon-osh: That is all right.

Supt. Irish: The great father will see the name of "Tabby" and want to know what he says.

Tabby: What shall I talk about? I would say only the same as you talk, and as President Young talks. I do not want to talk any other.

Mr. Young: It is all right!

Tabby (Bean Interpreter): It is all right. It is good to see you two fathers and all of you think alike. I love all of you. The Mormons, the Americans and all of you, I always liked to see the Mormon boys working on the land and feeling good. I know that all of these want to go over to Uintah. Part will go now, but all will not go yet awhile. Old "White-eye" who is over beyond, when he understands, will come in and be with you. Fetch out your presents—all of them. We are not quarrelsome. What should I quarrel about? I love all of you, and I do not want to see blood shed on the land. I want you to send a good father to Uintah; one that won't quarrel with us. I would like one like you, Supt Irish, or President Young. There are some boys not like me and "Kon-osh"—boys that will steal and run away with stock, but they are not here. Here are boys that are poor, Don't be stingy with them. I think you won't lie like other chiefs who have been here. They would bring blankets and other things here to give to the Indians and would never give them. My Indians know nothing about money. They don't know how to use it when they get it. They do not hunt for money but for buckskin. Some of the boys, may want money, if you paymoney, but they can speak for themselves. I had two thoughts about his treaty. One, I thought you wanted to buy the land and drive us out of the country. But now that you buy the land and let us go about our business it is all right. My great brother ("Walker," dead) said long ago to the people to settle all over the country. It is all right the soldiers [are] making a road through the country. Let them go: they can make their road. Again I want you to send a good chief to Uintah. I will go there. I love that country, though there are some here that do not like it, yet I have not much to talk about. I am not quarrelsome and have not much to say. Those Indians who are fighting out here have not come to my camp. I have instructed my Indians to take them prisoners if they do. I love the people of all that country where they are doing damage.

Sow-ok-soo-bet (Bean Interpreter): You are all right, you, the father and that fighting chief (Colonel Johns) and President Young. You have all agreed. You now can see your children here are poor, but we are all the same flesh and blood. The land used to be good here and we were all plentiful but it has been bad lately. There has been blood spilt on it: but through this treaty I hope it will be good again. I hope the children of those who have them will grow up and live and be good: but for me, I have no children, when you see me you see all my flesh, My children have all died and gone into the ground: the earth takes them all. If I have no more children I should be glad to see my friends children.

It is all right that the papers from Washington have come, and that you and President Young feel alike and the Indians. I hope that war chief (Col Johns) understands the papers as you do and that you will all continue to understand them alike, so that whenever I and others traveling about will shake hands with them, they will not forget the treaty. Sometimes the American boys will forget and be quarrelsome, and my boys will forget and be quarrelsome and throw away good hearts and good peace, but it is not good. Wherever the war-chief goes, in making roads, if he meets Indians I do not want him to kill them, but to meet them as friends and all the other tribes of Indians let them all be friendly as we are. I hope there will not another paper come from Washington that will contradict this and bring bad talk: I would like all the time for these good feelings to continue.

Fetch on the things and let us have them.

Ex-Gov. Young (Huntington Interpreter): I want you and all good Indians to remember this that I have always taught you—never to punish the innocent for the crimes of the guilty. Let the innocent live and never meddle with women or children among yourselves nor anywhere else; and when any of your tribes or any other tribes commit depredations by stealing or killing or doing such like wrongs, we want you to catch them and bring them and deliver them up to the authorities of the whites and you shall receive presents. Do you think that is right?

Kon-osh—I have understood for a long time that it is right.

Supt Irish—(Huntington Interpreter): This paper will be submitted to all the other Indians, south you have spoken of. When you see those Indians who are not here, speak to them about it—Go and get your women and children and bring them here to receive your presents, they shall all have something; the oldest man or woman as well as the smallest child.

In the afternoon, the presents were distributed among the Indians, all receiving a share according to their rank, age or necessities.

Friday Morning

The chiefs assembled to have a talk with Supt Irish upon various matters pertaining to the treaty, their removal &c.

Supt Irish (Huntington Interpreter): I have brought you here, this morning, to talk with you about going to Uintah: when you will go, and what you ought to do when you get there, and what you should do, while you stay round here among the peoples. There are no houses out in Uintah and no road out there yet. The Agent and his employees, who go out there have first to fix up places where they can live themselves. They have got to build bridges and fix it so that they can take provisions in there: and that will take considerable time. I do not think that Kon-osh and those Indians who are living around here ought to go this summer. I think they had better stay where they are for a little. That is Tabbys country there and I think he wants to go and those with him. They can go anytime, and we will fix things for them just as fast as we can, and let them know when they are ready. Tabby and his Indians might go over there this summer and look at it and see where they would like to have their farms and houses. We want to make little farms for them all. We do not want to make a great big farm and have the Government work it, but to make little farms and have you work them and that the produce and everything on them will then be yours, and you will have it. We wish to arrange it so that every man will have his little patch of ground and take his family, his woman and boys and work it and live upon it. We may make a field, but when we get it ready, and will mark it off, into patches and let each one who will work have one. I would like to know what you think about it?

Kon-osh: I like it well.

Irish launched a long, patronizing sermon, admonishing the Utes who knew "what is best and right" to teach their children "to do this work, and in a few years they will see their children living like us white people. Their children will be able to plow, to raise grain, and to write letters for them." He said, "you need not go immediately into the Uintah Valley, and it is understood that you are to have the privilege of coming around and visiting the people here and hunting and fishing as heretofore, until arrangements are made for you to remove." He lectured on "how you should do in passing through the settlements." The Mormons "came here poor: they have worked hard for what they have got. Whatever you may think of all this land that is not in use, you know that the land enclosed belongs to the people whose houses are upon it. The fences are theirs, the potatoes, corn and vegetables are theirs: and no Indian should touch any one of these things that belong to the whites, without their permission." Indians had "a perfect right to go to the white man and ask for something to eat, and the white man has a right to say whether he will give it to you or not." If they asked "in the right way you will always get it." They were sometimes refused "because some bad Indian man or woman has been there before them and meddled with things that did not belong to them, and the people therefore dislike to see them." He told them to knock on doors: "Then the white people will shake hands with them and be glad to see them. It looks very strange to white people to see these Indians coming up to the window and putting their faces to them, peeking through. I am telling you these things because I want to have the white people love you and take care of you." Could they "expect the people to be your friends when you are the friends of those who are killing them and destroying their property?" They should not have "anything to do with those Indians. When you leave here, hunt, fish, go to your houses, but be careful and keep away" from bad Indians. "I may hear of your getting into very serious trouble if you do not remember what I say."

"You may not like to see all this country that your fathers have lived in and occupied for many years taken up by another people," Irish concluded. It was "like the storm, like the wind, like the cold which you cannot help." The Ute leaders acted "like wise men," but the "bad Indians out in the mountains have not been wise like you." Those "who refuse to make a treaty with their father, will be cold, hungry, shivering, you will see them wasting away."

"Kon-osh": "I have understood considerable of this before. I have been to California and have seen the benefits that come from doing as Supt Irish says.

Tabby: Now we are not afraid of the soldiers, shall we go and shake hands with them and see them?

Supt Irish: When you go to see the soldiers I will go with you.

The Indians here requested Supt Irish to give them some powder.

Supt Irish (Huntington Interpreter): Well, you will get some powder. Sanpitch went away mad. The man who refused to come here and shake hands with us, who refused to look us in the face and act like an enemy. I cannot but think he had something to do with those who have been killing our people. I am waiting here for him to come here and tell me what he meant. I am ready to shake hands with him: ready to let him sign the treaty when he comes. But if he wants to act like an enemy, let him: that is what I mean when I say, I will not give you all powder. Those men who have acted like friends, who have made the treaty with their great father need not be afraid; they will get all the powder we can give them; but those who act like enemies and the friends of those who shoot down our people will not get powder. If San-pitch has done nothing to be ashamed of, let him come like a man; I am here waiting and ready to receive him. I am willing to talk with him like a friend: but if he will act like an enemy of the white people, he must take the consequences. Let him come up and do what I have said: if he is not ashamed: let him come like a man. Those men who have signed the treaty are my friends, the friends of the people, and the friends of the great father, and he will take care of them. That is what I meant when I said, Keep away from the Kanyons that you may not get among the enemies of the great father and his people.

The chiefs expressed themselves satisfied with the explanation of Supt Irish as to the powder.

Supt Irish: I had seen but two of you previous to my coming down here; I had heard of you, however, and I heard you all wanted to see me. I heard San-pitch wanted to see me, and was coming up here to meet me. Has San-pitch acted as though he wanted to see me? Has not he acted as though he had done something. Why he was ashamed to look me in the face? When I went out there to shake hands with him in his lodge to see him among his people, as I did the other chiefs, did he act as though he was a man? Did not he act as though he was ashamed of something?

To-quo-ne: I thought he acted ashamed.

Supt. Irish: Since the snows began to melt in this valley and in these mountains, 13 of our people have been murdered, their property destroyed and their stock driven away. I did not intend to talk to you about it, because I thought you had nothing to do with it, that you were all innocent of it. But I am afraid, from what I have seen since I have been here, that there are men among you who knew too much about it. When a chief, a man that ought to be looked up to as the leader of his people, is ashamed to look me in the face, I am afraid he has something to do with it. How long can you expect the whites to be quiet and friendly and trust Indians, when the Indians are thus murdering their people and their friends? Have they done anything why they should be killed? Now, if San-pitch does not know anything of it, if he is not the friend of those who have done it, why does he hang his head and cover his face? This people, the friends and neighbors of those who have been murdered, are your friends. How long, however, will you be trusted, if they are to be thus murdered and destroyed? If you wish to assure them of your fidelity, of your truthfulness, you should not hide among you: nor let any man remain with you who is the friend of those who have been engaged in these murders. When a man among you acts like an enemy, and is ashamed to meet the whites like a friend, I much fear lest he has done something that might be charged to you if he remains with you. You should cast him away from you drive him out, lest you be held responsible for his crimes, or he should be delivered up to the whites for punishment. That would be better.

Tabby (Bean Interpreter): That is right. I want to talk now. I know there are men who have not done right. Go and take them up, and take up the Indians the same way. I won't keep anything back. I will tell you the whole of it. There were 44 Indians engaged in that fight. I wont say who (white man) acted bad with the Mormons at Manti.

Supt Irish: Tell me who it was,

To-quo-ne: He is a man who drinks whisky. John Lowry is his name, I will tell you all about it. I spoke Brighams heart, Irish's heart and my father, Sow-e-ett's heart at Manti. I said, Stop, Stop, Stop, John Lowry, you don't know, anything; Sow-e-ett's boy understands good. I have Brighams heart, Irish's heart and Sow-e-ett's heart in me: but John Lowry would not interpret what I said to them. I told them not to fight, but Stop, Stop, Stop. The chief there did not know much—I was mad. An-kor-tew-ets came there on a horse. He was there mourning for his father [Arapene] who was dead. That made him mad. John Lowry said he would take his pistol and shoot him: that made the Indian mad. Then the two men were fighting mad. That is all I say.

Tabby (Bean Interpreter): San-pitch's father-in-law was in it. None of them have come in to the treaty, nor have been in my lodge. They were the

Elk Mountain Indians, and a few Manti Indians. To-quo-ne has heard that some of four friendly lodges, that had no hand in the fight, have been killed since; I suppose by white men. This we have only heard.

Supt Irish—The innocent often suffer for the guilty. That is the reason why I want you to keep away from these bad Indians, and keep the bad Indians away from here.

Tabby: They are away from here.

Supt Irish: What is the reason, then you cover up your faces?

Tabby—It was only San-pitch that felt bad, all the rest felt right.

(Douglass, a messenger who had been dispatched to the Indian encampment, to ascertain if San-pitch had any intention of coming to the Farm, returned.)

Douglas, San-pitch says, when he pukes up all that is in him, he will come down in the evening.

Supt Irish. I have been there to see him: he covered up his face. I am going to Payson, and won't be here this evening. I have done running after him: I have done waiting for him. He need not come unless he wants to do right. If he is a bad man, I do not want to see him. I do not want to see any but good men. If a man has done bad and wants to do right, I am willing to see him. Tell him that I am not sending for him, it is his friends, the Indians, who are sending for him.

(The Indians sent another messenger and as Commissioner Irish was starting for Payson, San-pitch arrived.)

Supt Irish: How do you do?

San-pitch: I am ashamed.

Supt Irish: I went to see you the other day and to shake hands with you, and found you did not want to see me: you did not do right. I heard yesterday that you were sick, and I sent up to enquire after you: to see if there was anything I could do for you. I pitied you if you were sick. But you sent me word you were mad and not sick. That is the reason I have not felt as if you were my friend, nor the friend of the great father.

San-pitch: I was like as if I had whiskey, but I had not had any whiskey.

Supt Irish: A bad spirit and whiskey are much alike.

San-pitch: Where did I sit the last time I was Here? I am ashamed. What was I talking about when I was here?

Supt Irish (Huntington Interpreter): I came here to be your friend; and it does not make any difference with me whether you make a treaty or not. I do not want any of this land. By-and by, I will go back to the great Father. The great father sent me here to do you and your friends good. I came here for that purpose. The great father has understood for a number of years that these Indians here wanted to make a treaty. Heretofore, the matter has been all talk which has been forgotten before it got to the great father. But now the great father has heard that they wanted to do it, and he has sent me to make a treaty and put it in writing that it might be sent to him, that he might see it at all times. This man is sitting here (the Reporter) to take down what is said, that the great father may know what is said: and when he hears about a chief, San-pitch, or Tabby, or Kon-osh, he looks at what is here written and finds out what kind of a man he is. If he finds that they talk good words, that their acts are all good, he remembers them for it after he makes a treaty. That is why I thought San-pitch ought to be careful what he did and said. I wanted the great father, to remember him and think of San-pitch and all the Utah chiefs as good men.

San-pitch: When the talk was I was called upon to speak. I spoke what was in my heart; and if I said anything that was not right, I am ashamed of it.

Supt Irish: That is no matter. We all talk. But I did not think you did right when you hid your face from me, and did not rise up to shake hands with me. If you are coming as a friend I can forget it. Tell me how it is?

San-pitch: I will throw away everything that is bad, and let us have a good paper. Let the good paper stay.

Supt. Irish: Do you want to come and be one with the other chiefs?

San-pitch: I will not put my name to the paper now. If it is a good paper, that is enough. This is my land. I shall stay here on this land till I get ready to go away, and then I shall go to the "Snakes" or somewhere else. Old Sow-e-ett cried because I would not come here.

Supt Irish: With regard to the treaty, I want you to do as you please. But as you say you are a friend, I will give you presents.

(Presents for San-pitch were brought out.)

San-pitch: Put them back. By-and-by, I will come down again and see you.

Supt Irish: I shall only be down here once more, and that will be tomorrow. You can do as you please. If you don't want the presents from the great father, I will give them to somebody else.

The talk terminated at this point.

San-pitch came the next morning and received his presents and nothing more was said about his signing the treaty.

He followed Supt Irish to Great Salt Lake City and then came forward himself and signed the treaty in the presence of the same witnesses as were present at Spanish Fork Indian Farm.

We hereby certify that we were present at a council held by the Utah chiefs at the Spanish Fork Indian Farm on the 7th. 8th. 9th & 10th of June 1865, and that we acted as Interpreters at said council and that the foregoing is a true and correct copy of the record of the proceedings, conversations and speeches as they took place and were interpreted by us.

D.B. Huntington
U.S. Indian Interpreter
Geo W. Bean
U. S. Indian Interpreter

THE WAR ON BLACK HAWK

The Spanish Fork conference hoped to stop another war against Indians, but Congress never ratified the treaty. Starvation, brutal winters, and epidemics compelled them to resist the relentless seizure of their beloved lands. Black Hawk's "small band of outlaws" did not "at first exceed fifty men," but recruits "from among the more reckless"—and desperate—Indians supported Antonga's resistance in a border war that proved nasty, brutish, and long.[33]

Ute leadership could prove fatal. As the conflict intensified, Brigham Young and Daniel Wells tried taking hostages to compel peace, but violence bred violence. In March 1866 Warren Snow seized Sanpitch and eight Utes. "Sanpitch, himself, ought to be summarily dealt with, in my opinion," Apostle Orson Hyde had recommended.[34] Sanpitch had reluctantly signed the Spanish Fork treaty, but Brigham Young ordered his arrest with eight Utes nonetheless. Snow jailed them and forced Sanpitch to name three raiders, whom Snow executed. On 13 April Black Hawk attacked Manti, and the jailed Utes escaped in the chaos. Snow personally shot Arapene's son Ankawakets, and other settlers murdered at least two more Utes. They also wounded Sanpitch, and on 14 April local militiamen killed him on Sanpitch Mountain. The Mormons buried the last of the escaped Utes on 19 April.[35] "You may kill Black Hawk and all his band," Sanpitch had warned, "but if you kill me, you will never have peace."[36]

Brigham Young told Snow, "I do not know that any better course could have been taken in relation to Sanpitch."[37] But the murders had consequences.

TABBY TO YOUNG, 12 MAY 1866, BYC 31:6, 52–54.

Indian Agency Uinta May 12/66

President B. Young

Tabby the Indian Chief requests me to say that he cannot come in and talk with you as you request as his Boys are so much excited that it is almost impossible to restrain them, and that it would afford him much pleasure to comply with your request if it was safe to leave them. He has been told that the Mormons in the Settlements would kill him if he came in and if

---

[33]Commissioner of Indian Affairs, *Annual Report*, 1866, Serial 1284, 124.

[34]Hyde to Charles Bryan, 26 April 1865, BYC 30:9, 27.

[35]Peterson, *Utah's Black Hawk War*, 237–41.

[36]Carter, *Heart Throbs of the West*, 6:483.

[37]Turner, *Brigham Young*, 345; Gottfredson, *History of Indian Depredations*, 187–88.

his boys were quiet he dare not trust himself among them. You will please inform Col. [Franklin] Head that a visit to the Reservation would be very acceptable by all the Indians as they want to see him very much and get acquainted with him and that he will be perfectly safe for him.

Sowette & Tucowents also join in the invitation to Col. Head.

All the Indians on the Reservation are friendly and say that the reasons they dare not visit the Settlements is because the Mormons say that they will cut their throats and that you have said the same. Sowette is trying to restrain his boys and talks good, but his boys say that they will not be friends until they kill Col [Warren] Snow. This is harsh language but they say they mean every word of it. They say that they look upon the killing of their Brother Sand Pitch in no other light than murder as they know he was innocent and if you do not bring him to justice they will. Tabby now says that he intends to remain upon the Reservation and keep his boys as quiet as he can. You will please pardon me for writing this curious letter to an almost an entire Stranger but at the urgent request of Tabby, and the other Chiefs I have done so. Tabby wishes you would send Sand Pitches Children to Salt Creek and get his Cattle and send them to the Agency. There are twenty head in all. One was bought at Salt Creek and is now there. The major at Salt Creek knows them all. For Tabby and Other Chiefs

[L. B.] *Kinney*

Tocowints & Jo say that they will do all they can to keep their boys peaceable.

The largest massacre of Indians in Utah history took place about 24 April 1866 at Circleville. The settlers disarmed as many as thirty Paiutes of the Koosharem band, imprisoned them in the log church, and killed them. William Allred described the slaughter to George A. Smith, now a Nauvoo Legion cavalry general despite being unable to mount a horse.

I take this opportunity to write you a few lines to let you know how we are getting along in Circleville. After I left you in San Pete, I returned home. I called the brethren together and laid before them the subject of moving close together which was agreed to and we commenced to move our houses about the 22rd of April. We received an express from Major S. S. Smith stating that two of our friendly Indians had shot one of his men by the name of West and that one of the Indians had been killed. We immediately sent to the Camp and requested them to come in to town which some of them did. I informed them of what I had learned by the express. I further told them that it was our wish to live in peace with us. I wished them to loan us their guns and go to work for us and we would pay them in such things as they stood in need of, as they had told me they had not a charge of ammunition. We would take their guns and defend ourselves and stock, but they refused to do either. After reasoning some time with them, I took their arms which they parted with reluctantly. Major J. R. Allred placed a guard over them and then returned to the camp to look for two more Indians who were reported to be there. When they reached camp, the two Indians cocked their guns and started off. They were told in their own language that they would not be hurt, but they started to run and one of them was shot down. He fired in return and slightly wounded one of our men. The whole band was taken then and disarmed and put under guard and sent to Colonel Dame. The Indians confessed to be carrying ammunition to the hostile Indians. They say that Black Hawk is at the Red Lake or Fish Lake from 40 to 60 miles from Circleville with a large amount of stock and that the Pi Utes, Pahvants and the Navajoes have agreed to unite against us as a people [and] that our little valley will be fill of them on the 24th. At night fall our prisoners rushed on the guard with clubs striking them with the same. The guard killed 16 of them which was all of the band except four children which we have yet. We think of sending them north to some of the settlements. We are all in a fort around the meeting house and we feel to maintain our ground. About 40 head of horses and cattle have been taken by the Pi Utes from Marysvale and the families are in this place. Some of the people think we will have to leave here. A word from President Young or yourself of encouragement to the people will greatly assist me in holding our ground. We have no word from the Col. [William Dame]. I called on Major S. S. Smith to assist us, but he could not let them go.[38]

The crime reprised the mass murder at Mountain Meadows in 1857: Smith first incited the settlers, the slaughter of helpless innocents followed—for it was necessary to kill anyone who could tell the tale—and a dispatch arrived too late to stop the atrocity. Since the victims were Indians and the circumstances horrific, most historians have forgotten Circleville. The Paiute men, bound with sticks and ropes, were shot down as they allegedly attempted to escape. Their captors murdered at least eleven women and children as they were brought one by one from a cellar. A. C. Anderson "saw the whites slit the throat of the first victim brought up." Historian D. Michael Quinn noted, "Slitting the throats of only the women and children seemed to be a special application of LDS teachings," as if the Paiute men "did not deserve this rite of blood atonement." Perhaps both massacres were ritualistic murders calculated to save the victims' souls.[39]

---

[38]Allred to Smith, 5 May 1866, Journal History.

[39]Rogers and Turley, "Remembering the Circleville Massacre," 263–68; Quinn, *The Mormon Hierarchy: Extensions of Power*, 252; Winkler, "The Circleville Massacre," 17.

TABIYUNA
Alexander Gardner photographed
"Tabiyuna or one who wins the
race," when a Ute delegation visited
Washington, D.C., in 1872. Also
known as Tabiona, he was one of
Black Hawk's leading raiders and
is often confused with Tabby-
To-Kwanah. *Library of Congress.*

Before his death in 1972, Koosharem Paiute Jimmy Timmican gave an account
of the massacre he got from Wakara's son, Ammon. It is now engraved on a
2016 monument at Circleville. Phillip Gottfredsen's dogged research located
living descendants of Paiute survivor David Munson, who died in Saratoga,
Wyoming, in 1925.[40] They apparently told anthropologist Martha Knack:

> My Father was a full blood piute Indian his parents were killed by the whites
> in the spring of 1866 in Circle Valley. . . . he has told my mother how [they]
> killed his parents. They were taken out of a cellar and killed. He was a little
> boy so they save him and sold him or trated [traded] him for a horse to [P]
> eter Monsen of Spring City and when he was a young man he went with
> some folks to Castel Valley and lost all track of his people. But he was old
> enough to know and remember that he was a piute.[41]

Orson Hyde claimed "a strong force of the enemy" threatened the town
with extermination, complaining, "We have hardly a friend among Jews,
Gentiles or Lamanites." Being "thrown upon our own resources" against
"the miserable clans and hordes that fight against Mt Zion," Hyde felt
"Sanpitch and his Braves and the Piutes of Circleville have received that kind

---

[40]"'Indian Dave' Munson Dies Very Suddenly," *Saratoga Sun,* 19 February 1925. Thanks to Phil Gott-
tredsen for this source.

[41]Knack, *Boundaries Between,* 85–86.

of Gospel which they merit."[42] He wanted the army to resolve the conflict with the Utes, but Brigham Young refused: "it would be far better to have the Indians to war with and to deal with," he told Hyde, "than to have to war and deal" with American soldiers.[43]

TABBY: THEY COULD ONLY SUBMIT

In 1866 the San Luis Valley Tabequache Utes received a revised treaty different from the one they had signed. When Colorado governor Alexander Cumming told them they had agreed to the treaty *and* its amendments, "they said it was such an agreement as the buffalo makes with his hunters when pierced with arrows: all he can do is to lie down and cease every attempt at escape or resistance. They said the Great Father at Washington had sent them soldiers with guns and all the means of a terrible war, and they could only submit."[44] The Uintas now faced the buffalo's fate.

As Sowiette aged, leadership of the Utes fell to Tabby-To-Kwanah, who also survived to great age: in 1892 he claimed to be 113 years old. Of the nine treaties negotiated with the Colorado Utes, six became law. In contrast, the United States made only the never-ratified Spanish Fork agreement with the Utahs. Tabby negotiated a path through the ruthless war against Black Hawk and became the grand master of the three-dimensional chess game between Utah's Indians, federal officers, and Mormon leaders. In August 1866 he told Brigham Young he was "anxious to make Peace and abide by it," but "your People" had killed the father of his men Unger Tasapp and Tab Wooner "and they say that they have had no Redress."[45] They had not killed anyone "nor Stolen any Stock but have always talkd Peace." Ute leaders Anthrow, Sowiette, Tokowoner, and Douglass talked "good Peace all the time." Tabby blamed Warren Snow.

> Thare is Som of your People that talk as though they did not want Peace but wanted to Kill Indians whare Ever they See them. I want you to tell them not to Kill my Indians for they are Peaceable. I Blame Bishop Snow

---

[42]Hyde to Smith, 26 April 1866, BYC 40:5.

[43]Turner, *Brigham Young*, 343.

[44]Alexander Cumming, 10 October 1866, in Commissioner of Indian Affairs, *Annual Report*, 1866, Serial 1284, 155.

[45]Alexander Gardner photographed "Tabiyuna or one who wins the race," when a Ute delegation visited Washington D.C. in 1872. A great raider also known as Tabiona, he was often confused with Tabby-To-Kwanah. Peterson, *Utah's Black Hawk War*, 284, 355.

for all our trouble and if you will chastise him I will do the same with Black Hawk. I think as much of my Flock & Blood as you do of yours and if you dont chastise snow Black Hawk will go unharmed by me.[46]

About sixty Utes appeared in Heber Valley in 1866 with "Some of the Principle Indian Chieffs, Nameley Taby Atero Douglas Sou-yets Son Shough yan & Dick" to seek peace. Tabby let Brigham Young know:

He Talks good & feels good & wishes to be at Peace at good peace no more to be broken. He Says he has talked to his Indians all the time and told them it was not good to fight. He Says Some of them had no Ears that they could not hear but they begin to hear and to under Stand now. He Says he has felt bad at what has hapened nameley the Death of Sanpich and he expects Some of oure people has fealt bad for Similar Cause but he feals all right now and he wants us to do the Same and be good friends and let the past be forgoten. He Says he has Sent men to Black Hawk that he is in the Elk mountain country and that if he Black Hawk has got any Ears and wil listen to what he Says that he wil quit his fighting. He tells the Indians that they must not come about him with Stolen Horses. If they wil Steal they wil have to hunt another Land. He wants peace good peace. That ther has ben Enough done. He wants to be on terms with this [Mormon] people as he formaley was so that he can go and come &c.[47]

A tough winter left Tabby and Sowiette "very destitute, having lost their ponies" and unable to hunt, agent W. W. Cluff reported in July 1867. The Utes had "made a *little peace*" with the Mormons the previous summer, but "now wanted to make *big peace*."[48] Black Hawk met Superintendent Franklin Head on the Uinta Reservation in August 1867, along with Sowiette, Tabby, Kanosh, and Antero.[49] When the fight began, Black Hawk made a covenant "that he would not have his hair cut, and he had talked strong of Tabby and Kan-osh who had theirs cut like white men." When he made peace, Black Hawk asked "the Superintendent to shorten his locks for him."[50]

Mormon military power evaporated in September 1870 when territorial governor Wilson Shaffer banned the Nauvoo Legion's "unlawful military system."[51] Armed Utes had ridden roughshod over Utah's militia, but they feared U.S. troops. The war had killed perhaps seventy Mormons and several hundred Utes, Paiutes, Pahvants, and Navajos. Historical statistics are guesswork, but between 1865 and 1875, the Ute population fell from 23,000 to 10,000, reflecting

[46]Tabby to Young, 25 August 1866, BYC 31:15, 13.

[47]Murdock to Young, 12 September 1866, BYC 31:9. Black Hawk almost caught Snow on a trading expedition in March 1867. Snow never commanded troops again. Peterson, *Utah's Black Hawk War*, 327–29.

[48]Cluff to Young, 2 July 1867, BYC 31:20.

[49]Lyman S. Wood to Young, 14 August 1867, BYC 45:34, 67.

[50]"Black Hawk," *Deseret News*, 28 August 1867, 5/2.

[51]Bigler, *Forgotten Kingdom*, 286–87.

"an undeniable and tragic demographic trend." The war was calamitous: the slaughter of Native and white women and children led to lingering bitterness and the abandonment of more than twenty-five Mormon settlements. "Instead of fulfilling the sacred obligation to bring the Lamanites to Christ," wrote John Peterson, Brigham Young "found himself threatening to utterly destroy them." The Nauvoo Legion submitted $1,121,037 in war expenses for 1865 to 1867, which Congress ignored.[52]

Go to the Reservation and Starve to Death

Native resistance restarted when a spiritual revival swept the reservation in 1872 and starving Utes returned to their traditional homes. At Nephi on 5 July, they ignored Agent G. W. Dodge's order to return to the Uinta Basin, for "the Spanish Fork Treaty was never ratified, therefore," Tabby argued, the land the Utes held "before the coming of the white man, was theirs, and that the white man was only occupying the same by their permission." On the 4th of July "the Great Spirit" told them "they might remain away from their agencies two months longer when the 'Voice from the West' would appear to them, and give instructions about their future course." Dodge, now "pretty badly scared," gave them ten days to comply and "1,500 pounds of flour and two beeves at the same time."[53]

Dodge called on Sowoksoobet, the Timpanogos leader known as Indian Joe, at his camp "of about 25 lodges and required him to go forthwith to the Uintah Reservation." The Utes refused, for there was "nothing there for them to live on; that they were farming here" in Utah Valley: Dodge insisted and threatened to use force. Joe raised "his own bread, and he had his crop in" near Provo and wanted to stay until fall. "He said his men were industrious, they farmed, they did not steal and that they did no harm to the whites." Why should Dodge "be so hard as require them to give up everything and go there?" Joe asked. His orders were imperative, Dodge said. If the Utes did not go willingly soldiers "would drive them there with their bayonets." Alarmed, Sowoksoobet "ordered his squaws and children to the mountains," for "blood would be spilled." The Utes "did not want to fight" but "they would rather be killed by the soldiers here by their dead friends who were buried here, than to go to the reservation and starve to death, that they had suffered and had been abused enough at the Reservation

---

[52]Peterson, *Utah's Black Hawk War*, 241, 359, 361n48; Neff, *History of Utah*, 407–409.

[53]"Indian Matters in Sanpete," *Deseret News*, 25 September 1872, 10/2.

in the last six years and they didn't want to go there and have it repeated."

Tabby appeared the next day near Fountain Green "with 130 warriors and they had a very stormy time, talked no less than five hours." Dodge made promises "about what he was going to do for them on the reservation, and insisted they should immediately return to Uintah." The Utes argued "it was impossible to sustain themselves there at this time," telling Dodge:

they were on a visit to see their friends, to associate together, & would not return for 2 months; that they expected a visit from their Great Spirit from the West. That they had received late word from that person that he was about 100 miles distant. They told the agent they were not afraid of the American soldiers but they were afraid of displeasing that Spirit. They asked him what he would do if they did not go back to the reservation. He told them they must go, there was no alternative. They then said, "Send on your soldiers to kill us; our skins are black they are no account: our country is all taken from us. We will die here by our dead friends and relatives and perhaps we shall have a chance to come up by & by." That was one of their great many arguments. After pleading with them for four or five hours the agent gave the matter up.[54]

By and By All Will Die

Sowiette, "the father of all the Utes," was already ancient in 1855. "A long time ago he talked with Brigham & his heart felt good. He loved Brigham & all the mormons. Then he could talk much. He then felt young now he feels old. His Ears are not good, he has poor eyes is old & weary & can talk but little." He had not thrown Brigham away:

He loves him but feels old & cant talk much. He loves Bishop [Aaron] Johnson & has not thrown him away. Brigham & the Bishop talk one way that he likes. He loves the mormons & their Children. He feels like taking them & dandling them on his knee—would like to live here till he Dies. He cant talk much but has got two sons that can. He would like some powder & lead for his sons to kill game—do not want it himself.[55]

As settlers and soldiers systematically drove the *Nuche* from their land, able leaders defended the Utes. Superintendent Head reported Sowiette, "a worthy and reliable chief," was 132 years old in 1868, while Edward Tullidge claimed "the king of the Utah nation" died "at the remarkable age of 110 years,

---

[54]Judge Bean, Interview with Indians, 19 July 1872, BYC 49:37.
[55]Aaron Johnson to Young, 28 August 1855, 24:6. For Sowiette's legend, see Farmer, *On Zion's Mount*, 32–35.

according to his own count."[56] When John Wesley Powell visited Tsau'-wi-et on the Uinta Reservation in July 1869, the old chief was "but the wreck of a man, and no longer has influence. Looking at him, you can scarcely realize that he is a man." Sowiette's wife Bishop wielded great influence in council and "though wrinkled and ugly" remained vigorous and garrulous.[57] After Powell's note, Sowiette disappeared from the historic record.

Powell and George W. Ingalls, the Baptist agent to the Southern Paiutes, investigated the condition of Great Basin tribes as special commissioners in 1873. When agents and army officers threatened to force the Utes back to the Uinta reservation, they refused and challenged the officers to fight. They "had determined to fight rather than stay on the reservation and starve, for they feared hunger more than they did the soldiers." Under existing conditions, Powell concluded it was "unreasonable to expect these Indians to remain on the reservation." They "were preparing to commence a war of extermination against the whites," Utah settlers complained in May. Such charges were groundless, Powell wrote, for "the Indians themselves were much more terrified than the whites" and "had fled to the mountains for refuge." They could "no longer live by hunting, fishing, and gathering the native products of the soil." They believed white settlement was inevitable, and knew "the folly of contending against it; and they earnestly ask that they may have lands of their own and be assisted to become farmers and stock-raisers." They especially wanted to raise cattle. Powell knew the Uintah Basin well but overstated its "abundance of good soil," water, timber, and ability to raise "smaller grains and vegetables." Its cattle range was "practically unlimited—in fact, there is room enough for all the Indians of Utah. Perhaps there is no finer valley than the Uintah in the territory of the United States west of the hundredth meridian," Powell claimed.

The commissioners identified two Ute tribes, the "Pah-vants and Seuva-a-rits," as independent of the reservation. Thanks to Kanosh, the Pahvants fared better than other Utah Indians. Between the Green and Colorado rivers, the Sheberetch still ranged free: Powell had met thirty-one lodges on the Sevier River "who live by hunting and fishing, and collect seeds and fruits. They are well mounted, are a wild, daring people, and very skillful in border warfare." Under Black Hawk, they had "been the terror of the settlers" for

---

[56]Commissioner of Indian Affairs, *Annual Report*, 1868, 150; Tullidge, "History of Spanish Fork," 141.
[57]Powell, *Exploration of the Colorado*, 42.

POWELL-INGALLS COMMISSION WITH SOUTHERN PAIUTES
The Powell-Ingalls Commission met with Southern Paiutes near St. George, Utah, in September 1873. Powell is the cropped figure standing on left. *J. K. Hillers photograph, Smithsonian Museum.*

ten years, subsisting "chiefly on the spoils of war." The Sheberetch had driven "eight or ten thousand white people" from their Sevier and San Pete valley homes. They refused to go to the Uinta Basin, but in early summer 1873, "a terrible scourge"—perhaps smallpox—"swept off great numbers of this tribe, until but 144 remain." The "terrified and humble" survivors sued for peace. The commissioners counted 528 Paiutes, 556 Utes, 134 Pahvants 134, and 256 Goshutes, for a total of 1,474 Indians in Utah. They recommended moving them to the Uintah Basin, and the Northeastern Shoshones to the Wind River and Fort Hall reserves.[58]

A. K. Thurber visited the central Utah camps of Angutseib and Sowoksoobet in 1876. "Chief Jo from Thistle vally" had "lost 25 horses last winter." Angutseib and his band of "about 125 indians (nearly one half of whome are Piedes)" had raised about 200 bushels of wheat in Grass Valley that summer. The Indians had done "remarkably well for four years past," and had quit "stealing or killing a head of stock either of cattle or horses during that time." Angutseib described the visionary elements of Lamanite Mormonism: He believed in the church, had spiritual beings visit, and had "many dreams and vissions under a powerful influence of the spirit of the Lord."

> An-gut-seib made me take down in writing the following while at his camp and also made me promise to send it to you. He said he had been doctrin a sick child and had layd down in his lodge and was alone, that he had been asleep when a person entered. He was small at first then expanded to a fair sized man with fine flowing beard and hair, verry white, [and] told An-gut-seib to make a fire as he wished to talk with him. Asked him if he was a Mormon and if the indians here and at Uinta had been baptized and if they were all good. Was answered that the indians here were all mormons & some at Uinta, that some indians and some mormons were not good. He then told him that a long time ago he was the red mans father and that he had come to visit. Why are you so poor [when] the big canons and the earth is full of gold and silver, sell it and trade. There is no acasion to be stingy [for] by and by all will die and then they would not need it. Told him that [neither] Washington nor the mormons paid that attention to the indians that they should but for them to be patient and cultivate a spirit of peace, not thirst for blood, not steal nor quarrel and that if they got so poor that they had to dress in rabit skins after a while they would be remembered. Told him the time might come when this country would be left desolate and much more which I do not deem necessary to trouble you with.

---

[58]Powell and Ingalls, "Report of Special Commissioners," 1873, Serial 1626, 42, 44, 56.

"Since the indians have ceased depredating upon the mormons they have greatly improved," Thurber continued. "Now there is verry little sickness among them."[59] He ignored the childhood epidemics that devastated Mormon and Native families throughout Utah. Sowoksoobet "had a little girl die last night" near Richfield, Thurber reported in 1877. She "was his last child and was between 2 & 3 years of age. She died with Diptheria which has been quite prevalent in this vally." Kanosh and Angutseib "comforted him verry much They all feel quite humble and in this case wholely abandon their old traditions and seek consolation from the Lord." Joe asked Thurber to tell Brigham Young "of his bereavment and that his heart was not dead," although "he did not understand why his last child should again be taken from him."[60]

By and by all will die, but some linger longer than others. Tabby-To-Kwanah presided over the hardest years of his proud nation and survived into the twentieth century.

> *SALT LAKE HERALD*, 29 OCTOBER 1902, 1/1.
>
> Price, Oct. 28:—Old Tabbey, Chief of the Uinta Utes as far back as the mind of the oldest inhabitant runs, died out near White Rocks Agency one day last week, aged 104 years. He was in early days the special friend Prophet Brigham Young and did much in his time to preserve peace between his people and the whites. He had been blind for a number of years. His squaw died some twenty-five years ago, and until his death the old fellow had never taken another. His personal effects were buried with him in his grave, and after the body had been put beneath the ground, forty horses belonging to the old fellow were fed and driven to the scene and shot over his grave. His successor as chief of the Uintah tribes has not been named, and will likely not be, says Indian Agent [Howell P.] Myton, until the annuity money now being distributed is all disbursed. His son Tecumseh is not in good favor as the old fellow's successor, he being considerable of a drunkard and gambler.

LEMUEL'S GARDEN

The irrepressible George Washington Hill's "good-natured bravado," wrote David Bigler, "was like catnip to Indians."[61] No missionary to the Lamanites matched Inkapompy, the "Man with Red Hair." While camped on

---

[59]Thurber to Young, 15 December 1876, BYC 37:3.

[60]Thurber to Young, 11 February 1877, BYC 37:16.

[61]Bigler, *Confessions*, 186.

the Portneuf River in 1855 on the way to establish Fort Limhi, Hill spotted approaching Indians and "told the Boys that were with me that there came some of my children and that I was going to Baptise them." They laughed at his prediction. Despite knowing but "few words of the Language" (and "not enough to do any good"), Hill baptized "the first Indians we saw." Hundreds would follow.[62]

Utah had spent a hundred times more "than any other Territory" on Indians. "What have we got for it? A song and had to sing it ourselves," Brigham Young complained in 1869. Yet the aging prophet remained committed to redeeming "the Lamanites, who are degraded and cast down to the lowest depths of filth," for they were "of the House of Israel."[63] During the 1870s he sent hundreds of men on Indian missions: they ignited "a religious awakening" among Utah's tribes and recruited Indians from the Shoshone, Kiowa, Lakota, and Cheyenne nations. Their success had consequences. At Deep Creek in 1874, Elder Lafayette Ball listed eight hundred Goshutes and Western Shoshones, many "from quite long distances," who came to be "buried in water" at Ibapah. In June 1875 a bishop baptized eighty-five Pahvants, and Kanosh spoke "with much earnestness, exhorting his followers to industry and good works." In March 1875 the *Salt Lake Herald* reported the baptism of the "entire tribe of Sheebit Indians, numbering 147, with the exception of a few who were lame and unable" to walk to St. George, perhaps "the result of some supernatural influence through their prophets and 'medicine men' similar to demonstrations in other parts of the territory," meaning the 1872 Ghost Dance gatherings in Sanpete. But the "work of developing Christian character and civilized habits in the mountain Indians," historian B. H. Roberts complained, was "a slow and toilsome process, and so far with but few examples of satisfactory success."[64]

George Washington Hill, "patriarch to the Lamanites," succeeded. He baptized 102 Shoshones at Bear River City on 6 May 1873, and the next day "another band of about twenty and still they come and the work is extending like fire in the dry grass." According to family lore, in May 1875 Brigham Young told "Brother Hill, there has been a load resting on my shoulders for

---

[62]Christensen, *Sagwitch*, 85; Hill, Incidents in the Life, 42.

[63]Van Wagoner, *Complete Discourses*, 5:2677, 2743.

[64]Roberts, *Comprehensive History*, 5:164–65; "Baptism of Indians" 20 March 1875, and "St George Items," 28 March 1875, both *Salt Lake Herald*, 3/5. These articles show that Charles Savage took his famous Shivwits photos on 19 March.

some time. I have tried to shake it off. Now I am going to give it to you. It is going to be your load from now on." Hill resigned his railroad job and established Indian farms at Franklin, Idaho, and at Bear River City near Corrine, the "Gentile Capital of Utah." By June 1875 the Lamanites were "coming in by hundreds," wrote Dimick Huntington. "There has been 2,000 baptisms already. I have more or less to baptize every week." With "nine tribes on their way to be baptized," Huntington "hired builders to erect a baptismal font in his front yard."[65]

U.S. troops ordered the Shoshones and Bannocks to leave Hill's farm in August 1875. Hill told Brigham Young they were "anxious to fight the soldiers and want me to go with them." The warriors volunteered to be *The Book of Mormon's* "young lion among the flock of sheep" and fulfill the promise "that the Indians would succeed in battle because of their allegiance to God." After quoting 3 Nephi to Hill, they said, "Now you lead us, and we will do that," saying they would "heap kill um dam Gentile." Hill told his charges if they fought now they would be "killed off and I do not want it done." He contemplated reclaiming the farm by force but reported there were "but a few indians here now, namely old Tsyquitches band of maybe seventy Lodges and they are poorly armed with very Little Ammunition and not prepared for any kind of a fight." He was torn between reality and the scriptural challenge to "gather the Indians in from their long dispersion and make of them one nation again." He suggested they "scatter one in a place all over the country": God "would gather them back from there again" if they went to Fort Hall.[66]

The revival intensified in 1877. At "Lemuels Garden" in April, Hill received an invitation to meet "as far from the white man as they can get easily get to preach to and baptise them" with three hundred lodges of "Pabby Utes" and "Boise Indians, the Northern Shoshonees, the Bannocks, walla wallas, Cyuse, Nezperces [and] Flat heads and I do not know what other tribes."[67] In May on "a Little trip to the north of nine days," Hill baptized 249 Indians and had to turn away another hundred, "as we were wright under the Agents nose." His converts wanted to join Hill at Lemuels Garden, but grasshoppers had destroyed the crops. Local donations and

---

[65]Christensen, *Sagwitch*, 88, 91, 96, 108.
[66]Ibid., 130–31.
[67]Hill to George Reynolds, 12 April 1877, BYC 37:9, 17.

Brigham Young's gift of twenty-three "very old" cows were not enough to feed Hill's flock.[68]

Critics often charged that Mormons colluded with Indians. Hill certainly did.

HILL TO YOUNG, 15 AUGUST 1877, BYC 37:9, 33–35.

Ogden, August 15th/77

President Young

Dear Br. our Indians in the north are very anxious to have a council with Cheeves [Chiefs] from the south to meet at my camp. They think they can see something approaching that is uncomfortable and they want a treaty of alliance made as soon as they can get it. Strictly they want to unite and become one nation for self protection and for a one other purpose. They wished the Navahoe chiefs called and the Utah Cheeves Kanosh Joe and tabby una Hanroads [Tabiuna?] and those from uintah and other places where ever they can be reached. They are sending west for the same purpose. They want the Nahvahoe chiefs to bring along their blankets and other things to exchange with them for what they have got to bind their contact as this is an ancient custom on all the important treaties to make private presents and to exchange commodities to bind their bargain. The chiefs that send this request are pagwite, Wehegond, tyhe, tetoba, tintowets, towenseah, topeshepo, pok-e-tell-O, Tom, Echupiny, sagwitch, and several smaller chiefs.[69] They want to gather in and bundle around us. They say they do not sleep well at all where they are. Tintowetz [Tosowitz?] the head Bannock chief told all the Indians sometime ago that they could not stay at the Agencies mutch Longer that it was only a question of time [before] they had got to come to me. The clouds Look a little ominous. The Indians in the Distance say that Inkapompy has brought his children through that narrows safely. They want to do the same but have not the money to secure themselves and the Gras hoppers have eaten us up so badly we have not the provisions to feed them with untill it will grow again and they do not know what to do.

Excuse my bad writing. My hand is so nervous this morning I can barely write. Please answer if you can. Have these chiefs called and about what time they can be here that I may send a runner after the chiefs from the north so that they need not stay any Longer than can be helped. Also if you can get any word for me from the court as I am aware they are trying hard to get up an

---

[68] Hill, Quarterly Report, 1 July 1877, BYC 37:9, 30. Between April and June, ten missionaries put in 478 days' worth of labor at Lemuels Garden.

[69] Historians and treaty interpreters used similar names for Hill's Northwestern Shoshone and Bannock "chiefs": Pagwite, Weratzewonagen, Tyhee, Tatober, Taboonsheya, Toopsepowot, Pocatello or Pokotel Tom, Echupwy, and Sagwitch. In 1890 Maj. E. R. Kellogg identified Bannock Jim (alias Pagwite) as the "Indian Christ" and "a Mormon, and it is not unreasonable to suppose that his attempts to stir up strife have been instigated by the Mormons." The charge is unlikely, but Pagwite was "a thorn in the government's side until his death in 1891." Smoak, "The Mormons and the Ghost Dance of 1890," 273.

indictment against me if they have not already done so so. Direct hamptons station unrr [Utah Northern Railroad]. If you have any instructions shall be pleased to receive them. Truly your brother in the Gospel

G. W. Hill

George W. Hill had reason to be nervous: on 14 August the *Salt Lake Tribune*'s front page denounced "The Scalpers Around Corinne" and ridiculed the "Muddled Excuses of the Danite Hill."[70] Investigations seemed to target Brigham Young, but the prophet died on 29 August 1877. A grand jury continued investigating Mormons and Indians in general and Hill in particular. The U.S. attorney general ordered Utah's U.S. attorney, Sumner Howard, to investigate. Utah Indians were "under the protection, and are the objects of the care and attention of the Mormon Church," Howard reported on 11 September 1877. Many had been through the faith's "peculiar ceremonies" in the Endowment House, so it was "not strange that every Indian looks upon the Mormons as their friend; and the 'Americans' as their enemies, and are led to believe that a conflict is pending between them." Mormons had established "a sort of protectorate over the Indians," and Howard wanted to prosecute George W. Hill. Hill escaped indictment, but his career as an Indian missionary died with Brigham Young.[71]

Mormon millennial hopes for American Indians persisted after Young's death. His successor, John Taylor, worked to redeem Lamanites until his own death in 1887. In November 1882 he sent Apostles Moses Thatcher and Lorenzo Snow "on a mission to the Shoshone Lamanites" in Idaho and possibly to "some tribes in Oregon and Washington." Snow went to Idaho, while Thatcher met Absaroka and Blackfoot bands in August, noting "very nice looking Squaws" among the Crows, who were "lighter skinned than the Shoshonies." He visited Yellowstone, Red Lodge, the Big Horn Basin, killing bison and a grizzly bear on his way to see missionary Amos Wright's secret congregation on the Washakie Reservation. In October 1884 he returned with presents for the Shoshones. Bishop Wright reported meeting with seventy-five Mormon Shoshones at Wind River and passed on some gossip:

Washakee got drunk last fall & Struck Officer over head with pistol. And told him to bring on soldiers. Sixteen Crow Chiefs visited Washakee and

---

[70]"Mormon Indians," *Salt Lake Tribune*, 14 August 1875, 1/4.
[71]Christensen, *Sagwitch*, 153–59.

INDIAN WAR VETERANS AT UTAH LAKE, 1903.
George Edward Anderson, Indian War veterans at Utah Lake, 1903. Some of the
men dressed as Indians may actually be Indians. *Editor's collection.*

Counseled with him [illegible] and did not want to be removed to the Big
horn—Subsequently Washakee had Counsel and it was decided to send to
Prest T for advise. Quewit (man without a wife) was to be the Messenger.[72]

What Taylor advised is unknown, but Wilford Woodruff spent 1885
hiding in Arizona Territory from federal marshals under the alias Lewis
Allen while trying to convert Navajos, Hopis, Apaches, and Zunis.[73] At
Tuba City in 1882, Christian Christianson "Baptized 27 Lamanites of late
and Messengers had appeared to one of them a lame Man and told him
there soon would be a great war all over the Land Except in Zion." The
Indians "must all be Baptized and work with the Mormons," for "there
would soon be a great famine. There would be a good Crops with the

[72]Thatcher, Diary, August 1883, October 1884, LDS Archives.
[73]Woodruff, *Journal*, 16 January 1886, 7:558.

Mormons for three years then times would be worse & worse throughout the Land."[74] After Woodruff publicly abandoned polygamy in September 1890, Mormon beliefs about the prophetic destiny of American Indians became artifacts of an evolving faith. "God will deal out to this Nation the measure they deal out to us," hardliners such as Moses Thatcher still insisted. "The battle axe of the Lord, the Lamanites, will have a hand in humbling this nation."[75]

A Gesture of Compassion: Washakie Settlement

History never stops. The LDS church bought 1,700 hundred acres in a barren Malad River valley in 1880 and moved Sagwitch and other Shoshone survivors to a settlement named Washakie, where forty of them patented homestead claims. With its sawmill, brick kiln, schoolhouse, chapel, canal, and cemetery, the village developed its own hardscrabble economy. It operated much like an Indian plantation, but it gave the band a place to call home. Its benevolent patriarchy declined when better opportunities opened during the 1940s. It ended when the LDS church defaulted on the implicit promise that Washakie "would be there for the Shoshone in perpetuity." On 24 November 1960 the LDS church sold its land at Washakie, which become a private cattle ranch. "In a gesture of compassion for the Washakie residents, the Northwestern Shoshone Band was given 184 acres of land purchased by the LDS church in the vicinity of Washakie." It is now the community cemetery, the only land Indians own.

Mae Timbimboo Parry, Sagwich's great-granddaughter and a Washakie School graduate, taped a meeting in June 1974 of former residents whose Washakie property was destroyed in 1960. Most of the Indians' humble dwellings, which "appeared to be abandoned but were not," were burned to the ground to ready the land for sale. "I looked around and when I saw our car sitting there all burned black. I started to cry," recalled Alice Pubigee. "Although my home may have looked like a shack to some people, it was my home." Whenever her family passed Washakie, "we cry and feel bad. This was our hometown."

---

[74]Woodruff, *Journal*, 6 December 1882, 8:136.

[75]Heber J. Grant, Journal, 30 September 1890, LDS Archives, Smith Research Associates, *New Mormon Studies CD-ROM*.

"All my personal papers had gone up in flames," said Leona Peyope Hasuse:

> Such things as records of my people, birth certificates, all my church records and other important papers. My blankets, clothing, mattresses, beds, stove, dishes, cupboard, refrigerator, table and chairs, and even our food was gone. As I stood looking at my burned stove and metal beds and my refrigerator sitting in the ashes, I cried. I mean, I cried out loud. I felt real bad.

Most of Washakie's dispossessed families moved north to Bannock Creek, one of five districts on the Fort Hall Reservation, where the Shoshone-Bannock peoples maintain a dynamic presence. When the Washakie survivors met in 1974, many were still devout Latter-day Saints. "We are living at Bannock Creek, Idaho, and are going to church there. We still believe in the church but it hurts when we remember what they did to us. We are not angry at the church. We still pray and pay our tithing," said Alice Pubigee. She was called to serve in the Bannock Creek Relief Society. "Although I cannot read or write, I am trying very hard to do as I am told. Leona Peyope is our president." The Pubigees bought a home for their children and grandchildren, but if the LDS church bought land "somewhere near Washakie for another community, I am sure we will come back. We hope this comes true." Alice and her husband Elias had visited the Washakie Cemetery the day before they testified. "We did not want to go back to Idaho. It was so quiet and peaceful here. We like it here at Washakie," Alice said. "We need a home here with a lot. I cannot forget how hard I cried. I cried very loud."[76]

Today the State of Utah has plans to pump water twenty miles from the Bear River, build dikes in the Washakie Valley, and create a shallow reservoir prone to eutrophication that smells like rotting eggs, and then pipe the water one hundred miles south to irrigate Salt Lake Valley lawns.[77] This will serve the developers who own the state legislature and be a windfall for the current landowners, the Kingston Clan, a wealthy polygamous cult known as The Order.

---

[76]Perry, in Cuch, *Utah's American Indians*, 58–67.

[77]Brett Prettyman, "Looking north to quench the Wasatch Front's thirst," *Salt Lake Tribune*, 12 March 2015.

AFTERWORD

Generations of American Indians have struggled to defend their families and keep their cultures vibrant. This volume describes but one episode in a war that began about 985 C.E., when the sagas say Norsemen landed in Newfoundland and began murdering the people they called *skrælingi*, barbarians. Two decades later, Thorvald Eiriksson's men killed or captured many *skrælingi* before a Native arrow pierced his gut. "We've found a land of fine resources," he said before becoming the first known European to die somewhere in North America, "though we'll hardly enjoy much of them." His prophecy proved true: the single verified Norse site at L'Anse aux Meadows did not last a decade. After 1492 this ten-century conflict became a war to control the Western Hemisphere. Native peoples initially won, for in the centuries before Columbus, Europeans failed to establish a single enduring outpost, even in Greenland.[1] As Old World diseases wreaked havoc in the new, Christians conquered continents and destroyed empires as millions of Native peoples fought and died to defend their lives, homes, and families from invasions often invisible (like unknown diseases) but always brutal.

The Great Basin witnessed one episode in this human catastrophe. "Because there was a religious theme to the settlement of this part of the West, the Utes came out looking as an embarrassing impediment," said Floyd O'Neil, who pioneered telling the Indian history of Utah honestly. Mormons did not spare Native peoples from the abuse that tribes suffered elsewhere. "It is very much the mentality of the South that all slaves were treated nicely. Much the same rhetoric is used here, that the Indians were

---

[1]Diamond, *Collapse*, 216–19.

[2]Monte Whaley, "Utes Resent Top Billing of Pioneers in Utah History," *Salt Lake Tribune*, 11 February 1997, A1, A8.

treated very well," he observed. "That is utter nonsense."[2]

This book's documents describe what happens when technically advanced societies encounter cultures with less sophisticated technology. "When two civilizations collide," historian John Gray observed, "action at their interface generates a frontier, whose turbulence is proportional to the dissimilarities in the two civilizations and the forces driving them to collision."[3] This is an interesting thesis but not an excuse.

Anyone doing creative work—and even editing a documentary history is creative work—is aware of his or her creation's flaws. This is true of . Historians—even documentary historians—should draw conclusions, but I will leave it to the readers to answer the first of the questions that began this volume: "Can such mediated documents reveal anything worth knowing about American Indians?" Others require only short, obvious responses: "How did the Mormon invasion affect the Great Basin's long tradition of violence?" Increasing competition for land and resources increased violence. "Did Latter-day Saint theology affect how Mormons treated Indians?" Marginally. "What differences existed between White-Native conflicts Mormon Country and elsewhere?" The details differed but had the same results.

"Was Brigham Young a friend of the Indians?" Sometimes. U.S. land claims are based on international law, especially the rights of discovery and purchase. The United States conquered Spanish and Mexican territories in Florida and the Southwest with force of arms but later paid for them. This ignored, as international law did until the late twentieth century, the indigenous rights first recognized when Juan Ginés de Sepúlveda lost his debate with Bartolomé de las Casas over whether Native peoples had any right to the lands they inhabited. Technically, the United States acquired its national domain based on treaties with Indian nations and subsequent purchases, but this is a legal fiction. Young claimed the Lord owned the land, and as God's agent he distributed "stewardships" of land as he saw fit. He told Ute leaders in 1865 the Mormons would "occupy it, and spread abroad until we occupy the whole of it," but he wanted "you and your children to live, so that you can live with us and our children."

Despite its complicated racial doctrines, Mormonism has connected with generations of American Indians. In 2013 *The New York Times* noted the success the LDS church enjoyed in the Navajo Nation as "an antidote to

[3]Gray, *Centennial Campaign*, 1.

heartaches and hardships" of "a land troubled by dysfunction and despair," including rampant unemployment, domestic violence, and alcoholism. Membership in the faith's Tuba City Stake had grown 25 percent in five years. Nora Kaibetoney explained the feeling of "reconnecting to our traditions," despite Mormonism often compelling Navajo converts to abandon rituals integral to their identity, such as healing ceremonies and the cleansing rites of sweat lodges. "In Navajo culture, the most important things we have are life and our family," said longtime Latter-day Saint Linda Smith, daughter of a Navajo code talker and hand trembler. Smith said converting "wasn't about turning away and embracing an entirely different tradition; it was about reconnecting." What set Mormons apart from other Christian evangelists, the article observed, was the role their holy scriptures ascribed to American Indians as descendants of the Lamanites whose conversion could help build God's kingdom. "There's this paradoxical sense in which the Lamanites are both a rebellious and wicked people, but they're also key central actors in the Mormon scriptural drama." American Indians hold the key "to the consummation of history," observed religious studies scholar Peter J. Thuesen. "No other form of Christianity gives the native people such a unique place in their story."[4]

This was also true historically. In his imperial chronicle of Mormonism's colonization of southern Utah, James Bleak suggested at least one Southern Paiute absorbed enough LDS doctrine to understand the basics of "atonement by the shedding of blood," as Brigham Young called the controversial Mormon doctrine better known as blood atonement. John Nebeker, who described the death of thirty-six Indians from measles in 1847, had charge of Mormon towns on Utah's western border in 1866. Mormons at Panaca, Nevada, had seized an Indian named Okus, who was wearing the clothes of a murdered miner. Okus led his captors the scene of the crime. On the way, the posse "met fifteen armed miners coming in from Pahranegat to take vengeance on the Mormons for suffering their friend, Rogers, to be killed by Danites." The miners seized Okus, put "one end of a chain around his neck," tied the other to a saddle, and dragged him ten miles to Meadow Valley. Okus implicated two other Indians, who the miners quickly hunted down and killed. "On the return of the company to Panaca, Okus saw, by the

[4]Fernanda Santos, "Some Find Path to Navajo Roots through Mormon Church," *New York Times*, 30 October 2013, A12.

preparations," that he was to be hanged, Bleak wrote. He told "an interpreter, that he knew he had bad blood in him and that it ought to be poured out, but he asked to be shot instead of hanged." Ignoring his request to be blood atoned, the miners hanged Okus, who "died without a struggle."[5]

The record provides plenty of evidence to condemn Mormon treatment of American Indians, but honest history demands a fair assessment of Brigham Young's actions as an Indian superintendent, militia commander, and prophet of a religion whose doctrines placed the children of Israel at the center of its theology. Historians who shift accountability for the brutality shown to Native peoples from leaders to followers have a point. There was nothing exceptional about the fear and hatred frontier Mormons shared with settlers across the West. Like all conquerors, Mormons despised the peoples whose lands they seized, often with good cause. "Baurank known here as Blanco" stole Levi Hancock's team at Manti in 1852, entered his home, and "undertook to pull up Emelies clothes." Hancock found his fourth wife fighting Blanco "with a Rock; he saw me, and ran and threw a stone at her head but just mist." Hancock had complained angrily but appreciated "the gentle Letter" he received from Young, "for the spirit it breaths is such as I admire." Hancock thanked God he was "under the care of so watchful and so wise and so good a man as your self." Young had the "pleasing Countanance, that bound my hart to the lovely Prophet Joseph Smith."

> No man can breath that same fatherly spirit and write it as you have to me and that too about a race of beings so much detested and hated as the poor Indians are; for while the genral cry of all people has bin to kill them; I see your hand is streched out in mercy for them. You say we aught to seek to reclaim them; not by makeing ourselves infearior but superior to them.[6]

Brigham Young stands astride the history of the American West like a colossus, including its Native history. No one since William Penn had "managed the Indians better than Governor Young," John Bernhisel argued: he "always treated them justly and kindly" and taught them "the arts of civilized life."[7] Did Young say, "with wonted shrewdness," as Gen. James F. Rusling wrote in 1866, "I can kill more Indians with a sack of flour than a keg of powder, and twice as many with a bale of blankets as an equal number

[5]Bleak, Annals of the Southern Utah Mission, 310–313, transcription courtesy of Melvin and Halli Johnson.

[6]Hancock to Young, 17 November 1852, BYC 21:16.

[7]Bernhisel to Young, 10 March 1857, BYC 61:1.

of guns"? Probably.[8] Did Native leaders believe Young was a good father to the Indians who never promised them anything he did not deliver? The sources are rife with contradictions, but Indians respected power, and they considered "Big-um" a great shaman. Young could pour out his feelings for the people he saw as fellow Israelites and advise Wakara in November 1849, "Be at peace one with another—dont fight, but love one another and you will soon be taught to become a great, united, and good people"—and soon order their extermination during the Fort Utah fight.[9]

I am too much of an iconoclast to make an unbiased assessment of such a beloved historical icon as "Brother Brigham." Historians will argue over who ordered the Mountain Meadows massacre to the end of time, but what is beyond doubt is that Mormons blamed Indians for an atrocity that Young knew his followers committed. The last word is best left to a Southern Paiute leader: "Now, nobody'd listen to an Indian anyway," said Eleanor Tom. "The whites, they won that story."[10]

Historians are argumentative and will debate whether facts actually exist, so the question of whether Mormons poisoned defiant Indians invites controversy. The tactic was ruthless but not exceptional: the historic record is circumstantial but suggests Anglo-Americans have poisoned Indians since at least 1623, when Dr. John Potts killed hundreds of Powhatans at Jamestown with doctored liquor. Strong evidence indicates British officers deliberately spread smallpox among American Indians.[11] In the 1830s American merchants began selling strychnine, which was soon widely available at western trading posts. George W. Hill's 1877 dictionary identified the Shoshone word for it: *esupnatsue*.[12] Overland travelers including Byron N. McKinstry, Elizabeth Knowlton, John Henry Brown, and Fanny Kelly described poisoning Indians, usually using strychnine, which had quick and horrific effects.[13] Frontier newspapers often printed poison stories: The *Deseret News* warned its readers on 2 April 1852 about fox furs tainted with strychnine, which produced "hydrophobia, canine madness."

[8]"Affairs in Utah and the Territories," House Misc. Doc. 153 (40:2), Serial 1350, 1867, 23. "Do not fight them, but treat them kindly," Young said, ". . . and it will get rid of them much quicker than by fighting them." *Journal of Discourses*, 9 April 1871, 14:87.

[9]Young to Cap. Walker, 22 November 1849, BYC 16:18.

[10]Hebner, *Southern Paiute*, 79.

[11]Gill, "Colonial Germ Warfare," unnumbered digital copy.

[12]Hill, *Vocabulary of the Shoshone Language*, 16.

[13]Editor's research notes and files.

Did Mormons poison Goshute, Shoshone, and Ute peoples? Nauvoo Legion captain William McBride's 1852 demand for strychnine indicates they did, but such claims are challenged. Other facts defy denial. Near Brigham City in August 1857, Dimick Huntington found four hundred "much excited" Shoshones "afraid of being Poisend." Utes at Spanish Fork jammed bread into his mouth in June 1858 and said, "eat it for it is poison & you want to kill us," for they believed Mormons used poison on them. Walker Ammon told LaVan Martineau he found an Indian camp near Manti with "no one around. The horses were out in the meadow grazing and were not fenced in. When he arrived at the camp no one was there, just blankets and belongings. There were not even any dogs to be found." Indians at Nephi said, "the white men had given the Indians poisoned meat and flour and it had killed them all."[14]

The Anglo-American invasion led both religious and government authorities to trample Indian land rights, confining them to smaller and smaller reservations. U.S. agents assigned no lands at all to Northwestern Shoshones and Southern Paiutes. By 1887, with the passage of the Dawes Severalty Act, the drive to break up reservations accelerated. The Utes were particularly anxious about their lands. Their fears were well founded, for following the arrival of permanent settlers in 1847 came displacement and expulsion, the exile and indoctrination of Native children, the imposition of dependency and allotments, and the continual erosion of reservation lands and resources. A Ute born in 1828 would have been age 20 when the United States acquired the Great Basin and 77 when it opened the Uinta Reservation to white settlement in 1905. She would have seen the federal government "cancel Indian rights to lands and place them on smaller and yet smaller reservations." Ute fears "were well founded, for by 1905 the process had gone full cycle," Floyd O'Neil observed in 1971. "From stone age to early 20th Century technology was a leap so great that most Indian people had difficulty comprehending what had happened to them." As the historian fondly remembered as Fearless Floyd said of Mormon exceptionalism in 2017, "The local conditions were different, but the results were the same."[15]

The fantasy of forging Native peoples into the sword of Jehovah to slay their latter-day enemies was the only exceptional feature of Mormon Indian theology. Brigham Young attempted to militarize American Indians in 1857.

---

[14]"Poisoning of Indians at Manti," Martineau, *The Southern Paiutes*, 59.

[15]O'Neil, "A History of the Ute Indians," 184–85; editor's notes, 5 June 2017.

He regarded cancelling the U.S. mail contract and "sending forth an army against us as strong indications that the Lord is hastening his work, and that the 'Redemption of Zion draweth nigh.'" On 4 August he directed William Felshaw in "Nebrasky" to tell Cheyenne and Lakota leaders:

> If they permit our enemies to kill us they will then kill them also. Let them understand this, but move in wisdom and be discreet in all you do, not to bring them nor yourselves into difficulty but open up communication with them as fast as you can conciliate them and make them your friends, for the prospect is *that all Israel* will be needed to *carry on the work of the last days.*[16]

Racism inspired a singular feature of latter-day-saint millennialism: the belief that their shared blood of Israel would unite the red sons of Ephraim and the white tribe of Manasseh to usher in the end times. The notion that British Israelism, a mythical nineteenth-century ideology, made the frontier Saints show exceptional benevolence to their Native neighbors is preposterous. Weaponizing the Lamanites became the fever dream driving Mormon apocalyptic beliefs. "Ephraim is the battle ax of the Lord," David Lewis told his fellow Southern Indian missionaries in 1854. "May we not have been sent to learn to *use* this ax with skill?"[17] Brigham Young's Indian policy sought to transform Lamanites into white and delightsome children of Israel. Otherwise Mormons adopted Protestant ideology, which killed the Indian to save the man. Ironically, the plan to deploy the Lamanites as the Lord's host blunted the murderous edge of genocide practiced across the American West, but it encouraged the racism that still thrives in Mormon Country.

The myth of Christian persecution has deep American roots, but few pilgrims fled England seeking religious freedom: they came to enforce their own absolutism in lands they seized in bloody wars with New England Natives. As the after-clap of Puritanism, Mormonism disguised the border wars it provoked with tales of persecuted innocence and a benevolent patriarchal dictatorship, still celebrated as holy writ in its legends. The violent history of Utah's forgotten kingdom long ago began its transformation into a mythical lost paradise. Floyd O'Neil "never met a Utahn whose ancestors were not friends of the Indian." Almost every pioneer Mormon family, including mine, venerates its tales of how Grandma Smith gave Native neighbors "huge slices of freshly baked bread spread liberally with butter and molasses"[18]

---

[16]Young to Felshaw, 4 August 1857, CHO Letterpress Copy Book 3:759–60.

[17]Brown, *Journal of the Southern Indian Mission,* 14 May 1854, 25.

[18]Bagley, "Revising the Revisionists," *Salt Lake Tribune,* 25 April 2004, B2.

This has been the hardest history I have ever struggled to present fairly and honestly. Too often historical records confirm harsh truths, such as the corrosive and corrupting influence of power on mortal men. It has forced me to reconsider the pioneer prophet and the "King of the Eutah nation" not as culture heroes but as ravenousness gangland warlords.

Even the darkest stories of the human experience include incidents that speak to our better natures. When writing about so many atrocities, it has been inspiring to hear the eloquence, intelligence, and compassion with which Native leaders spoke of their love for "the country of their fathers, the land where their fathers and mothers have died." The ground was hard "and we cannot eat it, and we cannot take it away," said Towombugah, "but we love the land where our fathers and mothers have died, and we cannot bear the thought of selling it. We want to live here and be brethren together." He "always heard what Br. Brigham has told him: his ears have not been stopped, but he says there is a great many mormons that have stopped up their ears, and many of my people have stopped up their ears, and they have got ears like stone." The man the Mormons called High Forehead had "one ear, one mouth, one heart, but some of the mormons and some of my people have got two ears, two mouths, two hearts." He wanted "all those who have got no ears to get some, for they should not have any mouths till they have ears."

Some Americans dreamed the great theme of the twenty-first century would be a revolution of reclamation to restore our only planet. War, hatred, and fear seem triumphant and humanity appears ever-more hellbent on making our planet unable to support human life. At Spanish Fork in 1865, Native leaders condemned Americans who wanted "to trade the land for money: they are hunting money." Sanpitch did "not want to trade the land nor the title to the land." He concluded the "Maker of the Land is probably dead, and buried now." If the Utes must "trade the land in order to get the presents, I do not want any blankets or any clothing." He preferred to "do without, than to give up my title to the land I occupy. We want to live here as formerly." Whatever his people could trade for their lands "would be all gone soon: whether blankets, or hats, or shirts, or money," said Kanosh. "The money would soon go in the stores and the other things would soon be done." The Indians, said Tabby, were "not ready now to give up the land: they never thought of such a thing." But Brigham Young said, "If you do not sell your land to the Government, they will take it, whether you are willing to sell it or not."

Whatever scars energy exploitation and mining have inflicted on Indian lands, the land will endure and ultimately heal. Ironically, the poverty and hardship of reservation life has prepared Native peoples to be the ultimate survivors. Condors have returned to soar in Utah's skies, and American Indians still speak truths about their past. As long the Great Basin's first human inhabitants can commune with the land, tribal elders say, their people will have a faith and a future. If Americans understood history, they would not still be fighting, dying, and killing in Afghanistan. Let us learn a great lesson from the crimes of our collective past: There is only one race, the human race.

Selected Bibliography

Books

Alexie, Sherman. *The Toughest Indian in the World*. New York: Grove Press, 2000.

[Alley, John R., et al.]. *Nuwuvi: A Southern Paiute History*. S.L.C.: Inter-Tribal Council of Nevada, 1976.

Alter, J. Cecil. *Jim Bridger*. Norman: University of Oklahoma Press, 1962.

Anonymous. *Minutes of the Apostles of The Church of Jesus Christ of Latter-day Saints, 1835–1893*. 5 vols. S.L.C.: Privately published, 2010.

Antrei, Albert, and Allen D. Roberts. *History of Sanpete County*. S.L.C.: Utah State Historical Society, 1999.

Bagley, Will. *Frontiersman: Abner Blackburn's Narrative*. S.L.C.: University of Utah Press, 1992.

———. *The Pioneer Camp of the Saints: The 1846 and 1847 Mormon Trail Journals of Thomas Bullock*. Spokane, Wash.: The Arthur H. Clark Co., 1997.

———. *Scoundrel's Tale: The Samuel Brannan Papers*. Spokane, Wash.: The Arthur H. Clark Co., 1999.

———. *South Pass: Gateway to a Continent*. Norman: University of Oklahoma Press, 2014.

Bancroft, H. H. *History of Utah, 1540–1886*. San Francisco: The History Company, 1889.

Barney, Ronald O. *One Side by Himself: The Life and Times of Lewis Barney, 1808–1894*. Logan: Utah State University Press, 2001.

Bean, George W. *Autobiography of George Washington Bean*. Flora Bean Horne, ed. S.L.C.: Utah Printing Company, 1945.

Beecher, Maureen Ursenbach, ed. *The Personal Writings of Eliza Roxcy Snow*. S.L.C.: University of Utah Press, 1995.

Bennett, Richard E. *Mormons at the Missouri*. Norman: University of Oklahoma Press, 2004.

Bigler, David L. *Forgotten Kingdom: The Mormon Theocracy in the American West, 18470-1896*. Spokane, Wash.: The Arthur H. Clark Co., 1998.

———. *A Winter with the Mormons: The 1852 Letters of Jotham Goodell*. S.L.C.: Tanner Trust Fund, 2001.

———. *Fort Limhi: The Mormon Adventure in Oregon Territory, 1855–1858*. Spokane, Wash.: The Arthur H. Clark Co., 2004.

————. *Confessions of a Revisionist Historian: David L. Bigler on the Mormons and the West*. Ed. by Will Bagley, with an appreciation by Polly Aird. S.L.C: Tanner Trust Fund and the Marriott Library, 2015.

Bigler, David L., and Will Bagley. *Army of Israel: Mormon Battalion Narratives*. Spokane, Wash.: The Arthur H. Clark Co., 2000.

————*The Mormon Rebellion: America's First Civil War, 1857–1858*. Norman: University of Oklahoma Press, 2011.

Blackhawk, Ned. *Violence over the Land: Indians and Empires in the Early American West*. Cambridge, Mass.: Harvard University Press, 2006.

Blanchard, Mark. *Going to My Grave: The Life and Mysterious Disappearance of the Mormon Scout Levi Gregory Metcalf*. Springville, Utah: Hobble Creek Press, 2011.

Boos, Theodore. *"My Life in the Army": Campaigning in the West with the Utah Expedition's Private Theodore Boos, 1857–1862*. Ed. by William P. MacKinnon. South Jordan, Utah: Bear Hollow Books, 2017.

Boughter, Judith A. *Betraying the Omaha Nation, 1790–1916*. Norman: University of Oklahoma Press, 1998.

Bradley, Martha Sonntag, and Mary Brown Firmage Woodward. *Four Zinas: A Story of Mothers and Daughters on the Mormon Frontier*. S.L.C.: Signature Books, 2000.

Brooks, Juanita. *John Doyle Lee: Zealot, Pioneer Builder, Scapegoat*. Glendale: Arthur H. Clark Co., 1961.

————. *On the Mormon Frontier: The Diary of Hosea Stout*, 2 vols. S.L.C.: University of Utah Press, 1964.

————. *The Mountain Meadows Massacre* Revised edition, Norman: University of Oklahoma Press, 1972.

————. *Not by Bread Alone: The Journal of Martha Spence Heywood, 1850–1856*. S.L.C.: Utah State Historical Society, 1978.

Brown, J. Robert. *Journal of a Trip across the Plains of the U.S. from Missouri to California in the Year 1856, Giving a Correct View of the Country, Anecdotes, Indian Stories, Mountaineers' Tales, Etc*. Columbus, Ohio: For the Author, 1860.

Brown, James S. *Life of a Pioneer, Being the Autobiography of James S. Brown*. S.L.C.: Geo. Q. Cannon & Sons, Printers, 1900.

Brown, Thomas D. *Journal of the Southern Indian Mission: The Diary of Thomas D. Brown*. Ed. by Juanita Brooks. Logan: Utah State University Press, 1972.

Brown, William R. *An Authentic Wagon Train Journal of 1853 from Indiana to California*. Ed. by Barbara Wills. Riverside, Calif.: Horseshoe Printing, 1985.

Burton, Richard F. *The City of the Saints and across the Rocky Mountains to California*. New York, N.Y.: Harper & Brothers, Publishers, 1862.

Bushman, Richard L. *Joseph Smith, Rough Stone Rolling: A Cultural Biography of Mormonism's Founder*. New York: Alfred A. Knopf, 2005.

Caballeria, Juan. *History of San Bernardino Valley: From the Padres to the Pioneers, 1810–1851*. San Bernardino: Times-Index Press, 1902.

Campbell, Eugene. *The Essential Brigham Young*. S.L.C.: Signature Books, 1992.

Carter, D. Robert. *Founding Fort Utah: Provo's Native Inhabitants, Early Explorers, and First Year of Settlement.* Provo, Utah: Provo City Corporation, 2003.

————. *From Fort To Village: Provo, Utah, 1850–1854.* Provo, Utah: Provo City Corporation, 2008.

Carter, Kate B., ed. *Heart Throbs of the West,* 12 vols. S.L.C.: Daughters of Utah Pioneers, 1939–1951.

Carvalho, Solomon Nuñes. *Incidents of Travel and Adventure in the Far West with Colonel Fremont's Last Expedition.* New York: Derby & Jackson, 1856.

Chandless, William. *A Visit to Salt Lake; Being a Journey Across the Plains, and a residence in the Mormon settlements at Utah.* London: Smith, Elder, and Co., 1857.

Chisholm, Clive Scott. *Following the Wrong God Home: Footloose in an American Dream.* Norman: University of Oklahoma Press, 2003.

Christensen, Scott R. *Sagwitch: Shoshone Chieftain, Mormon Elder, 1822–1887.* Logan: Utah State University Press, 1999.

Clark, Thomas D., ed. *Gold Rush Diary: Being the Journal of Elisha Douglass Perkins on the Overland Trail in the Spring and Summer of 1849.* Lexington: University of Kentucky Press, 1967.

Clayton, William. *William Clayton's Journal: A Daily Record of the Journey of the Original Company of "Mormon" Pioneers from Nauvoo, Illinois, to the Valley of the Great Salt Lake.* S.L.C.: The Deseret News for the Clayton Family Association, 1921.

Cleland, Robert Glass, and Juanita Brooks, eds. *A Mormon Chronicle: The Diaries of John D. Lee 1848–1876,* 2 vols. San Marino, Calif.: Huntington Library, 1955, 2003.

Compton, Everett L., ed. *A Frontier Life: Jacob Hamblin, Explorer and Indian Missionary.* S.L.C.: University of Utah Press, 2013.

Conetah, Fred A. *A History of the Northern Ute People.* Uintah-Ouray Ute Tribe, 1982.

Cooley, Everett L., ed. *Diary of Brigham Young, 1857.* S.L.C.: Tanner Trust Fund, 1980.

Crawley, Peter L. *The Essential Parley P. Pratt.* S.L.C.: Signature Books, 1990.

Cross, Whitney R. *The Burned-over District: The Social and Intellectual History of Enthusiastic Religion in Western New York, 1800–1850.* Ithaca, N.Y.: Cornell University Press, 1950.

Crum, Steven J. *The Road on Which We Came: A History of the Western Shoshone/Po'i Pentun Tammen Kimmappeh.* S.L.C.: University of Utah Press, 1994.

Cuch, Forrest, ed. *A History of Utah's American Indians.* S.L.C.: Utah State Division of Indian Affairs/Utah State Division of History, 2000.

Diamond, Jared. *Collapse: How Societies Choose to Fail or Succeed.* New York: Viking, 2005.

Drown, William. "A Trumpeter's Notes." In Theodore F. Rodenbough, *From Everglade to Canyon with the Second Dragoons.* New York: D. Van Nostrand Co., 1875, 207–30.

Drury, Clifford M. *Marcus and Narcissa Whitman and the Opening of Old Oregon,* 2 vols. Seattle: Northwest Interpretive Association, 1994.

Egan, Howard R. *Pioneering the West, 1846 to 1878: Major Howard Egan's Diary. Also, Thrilling Experiences of Pre-Frontier Life among Indians; Their Traits, Civil and Savage, and Part of Autobiography, Inter-Related to His Father's, by Howard R. Egan. Edited, Compiled, and Connected in Nearly Chronological Order by Wm. M. Egan.* Richmond, Utah: Howard R. Egan Estate and S.L.C.: Utah: Press of Skelton Publishing Co., 1917.

Fabian, Ann. *The Skull Collectors: Race, Science, and America's Unburied Dead.* Chicago: University of Chicago Press, 2010.

Farmer, Jared. *On Zion's Mount: Mormons, Indians and the American Landscape.* Cambridge, Mass.: Harvard University Press, 2008.

Farnham, Thomas Jefferson. *Travels in the Californias, and Scenes in the Pacific Ocean.* New York: Saxton & Miles, 1844.

Faulring, Scott H., ed. *An American Prophet's Record: The Diaries and Journals of Joseph Smith.* S.L.C.: Signature Books, 1989.

Firmage, Richard A. *A History of Grand County.* S.L.C.: Utah Centennial County History Series, Utah State Historical Society, 1996.

Fleisher, Kass. *The Bear River Massacre and the Making of History.* Albany: State University Press of New York, 2004.

Frémont, John Charles. *Memoirs of My Life.* Chicago and New York: Belford, Clarke & Company, 1887.

————. *The Expeditions of John Charles Frémont,* 4 vols., plus map portfolio. Ed. by Mary Lee Spence and Donald Jackson. Chicago: University of Illinois Press, 1970–1984.

Gibbs, Josiah. *Lights and Shadows of Mormonism.* S.L.C.: Salt Lake Tribune Publishing Co., 1909.

Gottfredson, Peter. *History of Indian Depredations in Utah.* S.L.C.: Skelton Publishing, 1919. Reprinted as *Indian Depredations in Utah.* Foreword by Phillip B. Gottfredsen. Tucson: Fenestra Books, 2002. Digital copy accessed 3 July 2013, http://www.archive.org/details/historyofindiandoogottrich.

Gove, Jesse A. *The Utah Expedition, 1857–1858: Letters of Capt. Jesse A. Gove, 10th Inf., U.S.A., of Concord, N.H., to Mrs. Gove, and Special Correspondence of the New York Herald.* Ed. by Otis G. Hammond. Concord, N.H.: New Hampshire Historical Society, 1928.

Gowans, Fred R., and Eugene E. Campbell. *Fort Bridger: Island in the Wilderness.* Provo: Brigham Young University Press, 1975.

————. *Fort Supply: Brigham Young's Green River Experiment.* Provo: Brigham Young University Press, 1975.

Gray, John Stephens. *Centennial Campaign: The Sioux War of 1876.* Fort Collins, Colo.: The Old Army Press, 1976.

Green, Nelson Winch, ed. *Fifteen Years among the Mormons: Being the Narrative of Mrs. Mary Ettie V. Smith* [Marietta Coray]. N.Y.: H. Dayton, 1858.

Grow, Matthew J., Ronald K. Esplin, Mark Ashurst-McGee, and Jeffrey D. Mahas, eds. *Administrative Records, Council of Fifty, Minutes, March 1844–January 1846.* S.L.C.: Church Historian's Press, 2016.

Grunder, Rick. *Mormon Parallels: A Bibliographic Source.* LaFayette, N.Y.: Rick Grunder—Books, 2008.

Gudde, Erwin G., and Elisabeth K. Gudde, eds. and trans. *Exploring with Frémont: The Private Diaries of Charles Preuss, Cartographer for John C. Fremont on his First, Second, and Fourth Expeditions to the Far West.* Norman: University of Oklahoma Press, 1958.

Gunnison, John W. *The Mormons, or, Latter-day Saints, in the Valley of the Great Salt Lake.* Philadelphia: Lippincott, Grambo & Co., 1852.

Hafen, LeRoy R., ed. *The Mountain Men and the Fur Trade of the Far West*. 10 vols. Glendale, Calif.: Arthur H. Clark Co., 1965–72.

Hämäläinen, Pekka. *The Comanche Empire*. New Haven: Yale University Press, 2008.

Harrington, H. D. *Western Edible Wild Plants*. Albuquerque: University of New Mexico Press, 1972.

Hart, Newell. *The Bear River Massacre: Being a Complete Source Book and Story Book of the Genocidal Action Against the Shoshones in 1863*. Preston, Idaho: Cache Valley Newsletter Pub. Co., 1983.

Harwell, William S., ed. *Manuscript History of Brigham Young, 1847–1850*. S.L.C.: Collier's Publishing Co., 1997.

Hebner, Logan. *Southern Paiute: A Portrait*. With photographs by Michael L. Plyler. Logan: Utah State University Press, 2010.

Heap, Gwinn Harris. *Central Route to the Pacific*. Ed. by LeRoy R. and Ann W. Hafen. Glendale, Calif.: Arthur H. Clark Co., 1957.

Hickman, William Adams. *Brigham's Destroying Angel: Being the Life, Confession, and Startling Disclosures of the Notorious Bill Hickman, The Danite Chief of Utah. Written by Himself, with Explanatory Notes by J. H. Beadle, Esq., of Salt Lake City*. New York: Geo. A. Crofutt, 1872.

Hill, George Washington. *Vocabulary of the Shoshone Language*. S.L.C.: Deseret News Steam Printing Establishment, 1877.

Holt, Ronald L. *Beneath These Red Cliffs: An Ethnohistory of the Utah Paiutes*. Logan: Utah State University Press, 1996.

Huntington, Dimick B. *Vocabulary of the Utah and Sho-Sho-Ne or Snake Dialects, with Indian Legends and Traditions. Including a Brief Account of* THE LIFE AND DEATH OF WAH-KER, THE INDIAN LAND PIRATE, BY D. B. HUNTINGTON, *Indian Interpreter*. 3rd ed., revised and enlarged. S.L.C.: Printed at the Salt Lake Herald Office, 1872.

Johnson, Don Carlos. *A Brief History of Springville, Utah, From its First Settlement September 18, 1850, to the 18th Day of September, 1900*. Springville, Utah: William F. Gibson, 1900.

Johnson, Melvin C. *Polygamy on the Pedernales: Lyman Wight and the Mormon Polygamous Villages of the Antebellum Texas Hill Country*. Logan: Utah State University Press, 2006.

Jones, Daniel W. *Forty Years among the Indians: A True and Thrilling Narrative of the Author's Experiences among the Natives*. S.L.C.: Juvenile Instructor Office, 1890.

Jones, Sondra. *The Trial of Don Pedro León Luján: The Attack against Indian Slavery and Mexican Traders in Utah*. S.L.C.: University of Utah Press, 2000.

Kane, Elizabeth. *Twelve Mormon Homes Visited in Succession on a Journey through Utah to Arizona*. Philadelphia: By the author, 1874.

Kane, Thomas L. *The Mormons: A Discourse Delivered Before the Historical Society of Pennsylvania: March 26th 1850*. Philadelphia: King & Baird, Printers, Sansom Street, 1850.

Kent, James. *Commentaries on American Law*. 4 vols. New York: O. Halsted, 1826–1830.

Knack, Martha C. *Boundaries Between: The Southern Paiutes, 1775–1995*. Lincoln: University of Nebraska Press, 2001.

Laird, Carobeth Tucker. "Chemehuevi Religious Beliefs and Practices." *Journal of California Anthropology* 1:1 (Spring 1974), 19–25.

Larson, Carl V. *A Database of the Mormon Battalion: An Identification of the Original Members of the Mormon Battalion*. S.L.C.: U.S. Mormon Battalion, Inc., 1997.

LeSueur, Stephen C. *The 1838 Mormon War in Missouri.* Columbia: University of Missouri Press, 1987.

Little, James A. *Jacob Hamblin: A Narrative of His Personal Experiences as a Frontiersman, Missionary to the Indians and Explorer.* S.L.C.: The Juvenile Instructor, 1881.

Lowe, Percival G. *Five Years a Dragoon.* Kansas City, Mo.: F. Hudson Publishing Co., 1906.

MacKinnon, William P., ed. *At Sword's Point, Part 1: A Documentary History of the Utah War to 1858.* Norman, Okla.: Arthur H. Clark, 2008.

———, ed. *At Sword's Point, Part 2: A Documentary History of the Utah War, 1858–1859.* Norman, Okla.: Arthur H. Clark, 2016.

Madley, Benjamin. *An American Genocide: The United States and the California Indian Catastrophe.* New Haven, Conn.: Yale University Press, 2016.

Madsen, Brigham D., ed. *B. H. Roberts: Studies of the Book of Mormon.* Urbana: University of Illinois Press, 1985. With a biographical essay by Sterling M. McMurrin.

———. *Chief Pocatello, The "White Plume."* Salt Lake City: University of Utah Press, 1986.

———, ed. *Exploring the Great Salt Lake: The Stansbury Expedition of 1849–50.* S.L.C.: University of Utah Press, 1989.

———. *Gold Rush Sojourners in Great Salt Lake City, 1849 and 1850.* S.L.C.: University of Utah Press, 1983.

———. *The Bannock of Idaho.* Caldwell, Idaho: The Caxton Printers, Ltd., 1958.

———. *The Shoshoni Frontier and the Bear River Massacre.* S.L.C.: University of Utah Press, 1985.

McCall, Ansel J. *The Great California Trail in 1849: Wayside Notes of an Argonaut.* Bath, N.Y.: Steuben Courier Printing, 1882.

McNitt, Frank. *The Indian Traders.* Norman: University of Oklahoma Press, 1962.

Manly, William Lewis. *Death Valley in '49. Important Chapter of California Pioneer History. The Autobiography of a Pioneer.* San Jose, Calif.: Pacific Tree and Vine Co., 1894.

Marquardt, H. Michael. *The Coming Storm: The Murder of Jesse Thompson Hartley.* Norman, Okla.: Arthur H. Clark, 2011.

Marcy, Randolph B. *Thirty Years of Army Life on the Border.* New York: Harper & Bros., 1866.

Martineau, LaVan. *The Southern Paiutes:Legends, Lore, Language, and Lineage.* Las Vegas: KC Publications, 1992.

Maxwell, John Gary. *Robert Newton Baskin and the Making of Modern Utah.* Norman: Arthur H. Clark, 2013.

———. *The Civil War Years in Utah: The Kingdom of God and the Territory that Did Not Fight.* Norman: University of Oklahoma Press, 2016.

Miller, Rod. *Massacre at Bear River: First, Worst, Forgotten.* Caldwell, Idaho: Caxton Press, 2008.

Missouri General Assembly. *Document Containing the Correspondence, Orders, &c., in relation to the disturbances with the Mormons* Fayette, Mo.: The Office of the Boon's Lick Democrat, 1841.

Moorman, Donald R., and Gene A. Sessions. *Camp Floyd and the Mormons: The Utah War.* S.L.C.: University of Utah Press, 1992.

Morgan, Dale L. *The Humboldt: Highroad of the West.* New York: Farrar & Rinehardt, 1943.

———. *Shoshonean Peoples and the Overland Trail: Frontiers of the Utah Superintendency of Indian Affairs, 1849–1869.* Ed. by Richard L. Saunders, with an ethnohistorical essay by Gregory E. Smoak. Logan: Utah State University Press, 2007.

Neff, Andrew Love. *History of Utah, 1847 to 1869.* S.L.C.: Deseret News Press, 1940.

Owens, Kenneth N., ed. *John Sutter and a Wider West.* Lincoln: University of Nebraska Press, 1994.

Peabody, Oliver. *Life of John Sullivan.* Boston: Little, Brown, 1955.

Pease, Ora Merle Hawk, comp. *History of Caldwell and Livingston Counties, Missouri.* St. Louis: National Historical Company, 1886.

Peterson, John Alton. *Utah's Black Hawk War.* S.L.C.: University of Utah Press, 1998.

Piercy, Frederick Hawkins. *Route from Liverpool to Great Salt Lake.* Ed. by James Linforth. Liverpool: Franklin D. Richards, 1855.

Pratt, Parley P., Jr. *The Autobiography of Parley Parker Pratt.* S.L.C.: Deseret Book Co., 1938.

Pritzker, Barry M. *A Native American Encyclopedia: History, Culture, and Peoples.* New York: Oxford University Press, 2000.

Quinn, D. Michael. *The Mormon Hierarchy: Origins of Power.* S.L.C.: Signature Books, 1994.

————. *The Mormon Hierarchy: Extensions of Power.* S.L.C.: Signature Books, 1997.

Ramsey, Jarold, ed. *Coyote Was Going There: Indian Literature of the Oregon Country.* Seattle: University of Washington Press, 1977.

Remy, Jules. *A Journey to Great-Salt-Lake City, by Jules Remy, and Julius Brenchley, M.A.; with a sketch of the history, religion, and customs of the Mormons, and an introduction on the religious movement in the United States.* 2 vols. London: W. Jeffs, 1861.

Roberts, Brigham H. *A Comprehensive History of The Church of Jesus Christ of Latter-day Saints,* 6 vols. S.L.C.: Deseret News Press, 1930.

Russell, Osborne. *Journal of a Trapper, Or Nine Years Residence among the Rocky Mountains Between the years of 1834 and 1843, Being a General Description of the Country, Climate, Rivers, Lakes, Mountains, Etc., and a View of the Life led by a Hunter in those Regions.* Boise, Idaho: Syms-York Company, 1921.

Schiel, Jacob H. W. *Journey through the Rocky Mountains and the Humboldt Mountains to the Pacific Ocean: A Sketch by Dr. J. Schiel.* Schaffhausen, Germany: Brodtmann'schen Buchhandlung, 1859. 80–81. Ed and trans. by Norman: University of Oklahoma Press, 1959.

Schindler, Harold. *Orrin Porter Rockwell: Man of God, Son of Thunder.* S.L.C.: University of Utah Press, 1983.

Sganyodaiyo. *The Code of Handsome Lake, the Seneca Prophet.* Ed. by Arthur C. Parker. Albany, N.Y.: State Education Department, Bulletin 530, 1913.

Smart, William B., and Donna T. Smart, eds. *Over the Rim: The Parley P. Pratt Exploring Expedition to Southern Utah, 1849–1850.* Logan: Utah State Univ. Press, 1999.

Smith, Joseph Jr. *History of the Church,* 7 vols. Ed. by Brigham H. Roberts. S.L.C.: Deseret News, 1902.

Smoak, Gregory E. *Ghost Dances and Identity: Prophetic Religion and American Indian Ethnogenesis in the Nineteenth Century.* Berkeley: University of California Press, 2006.

Spencer, Diana Major, ed. *Saga of the Sanpete.* Manti, Utah: Sanpete Historical Writing Committee and Universal Impression, 1997.

Stamm, Henry E., IV. *People of the Wind River: The Eastern Shoshones, 1825–1900.* Norman: University of Oklahoma Press, 1999.

Stansbury, Howard. *Exploration and Survey of the Valley of the Great Salt Lake.* Philadelphia: Lippincott, Grambo & Co., 1852.

Steed, Thomas. *The Life of Thomas Steed from His Own Diary.* Farmington, Utah: Privately Printed, 1935.

Steele, Raymond. *Goshen Valley History.* By the author, 1960.

Stenger, Wallace. *The Sound of Mountain Water: The Changing American West.* New York: E. P. Dutton, 1980.

Steward, Julian H. *Basin-Plateau Aboriginal Sociopolitical Groups. Bureau of American Ethnology Bulletin 120.* Washington, D.C.: Government Printing Office, 1938.

Stone, William Leete. *Life and Times of Sa-go-ye-wat-ha, or Red-Jacket. By William L. Stone. With a memoir of the author, by his son.* Albany, N.Y.: J. Munsell, 1866.

Stott, Clifford L. *Search for Sanctuary: Brigham Young and the White Mountain Expedition.* S.L.C.: University of Utah Press, 1984.

Talbot, Theodore. *The Journals of Theodore Talbot.* Ed. by Charles H. Carey. Portland: Metropolitan Press, 1931.

Tullidge, Edward W. *Tullidge's Histories, (Volume II.) Containing the History of all the Northern, Eastern, and Western Utah; also of the Counties of Southern Idaho; and Supplemental Volume, Biographies of the Founders and Representative Men of Northern, Eastern and Western Utah, and Southern Idaho.* S.L.C.: The Press of the Juvenile Instructor, 1889.

Turner, John G. *Brigham Young: Pioneer Prophet.* Cambridge, Mass.: Harvard Univ. Press, 2012.

Twain, Mark. *Roughing It.* Hartford, Conn.: American Publishing Company, 1872.

Van Wagoner, Richard, ed. *The Complete Discourses of Brigham Young.* 5 vols. S.L.C.: Smith-Pettit Foundation, 2009.

Victor, Frances Fuller. *The River of the West: Life and Adventure in the Rocky Mountains and Oregon.* Hartford, Conn., and Toledo, Ohio: R. W. Bliss and Co. 1871.

Walker, Ronald W., Richard E. Turley, and Glen M. Leonard. *Massacre at Mountain Meadows: An American Tragedy.* New York: Oxford University Press, 2008.

Wilcox, Adelia Almira. *Memoirs of Adelia Almira Wilcox: One of the Plural Wives of Heber C. Kimball.* Ed. by Stanley H. B. Kimball. New York: By the editor, 1956. Also cited as Adelia Almira Wilcox Hatton Wood Kimball, Memoirs, 1849–1868. Typescript, MSS A 1824, Utah State Historical Society.

Woodruff, Wilford. *Wilford Woodruff's Journal,* 10 vols. Ed. by Scott G. Kenney. Midvale, Utah: Signature Books, 1983.

Woolsey, Nethella Griffin. *The Escalante Story: A History of the Town of Escalante, 1875–1964.* Springville, Utah: Art City Publishing Company, 1964.

Yarrow, H. C. *Introduction to the Study of the Mortuary Customs among the North American Indians.* Washington, D.C.: Government Printing Office, 1880.

Young, John R. *Memoirs of John R. Young, Utah Pioneer 1847, Written by Himself.* S.L.C.: Deseret News, 1920.

CHAPTERS, ARTICLES, AND REPORTS

Alley, John R., Jr. "Prelude to Dispossession: The Fur Trade's Significance for the Northern Utes and Southern Paiutes." *Utah Historical Quarterly* 50:2 (Spring 1982), 104–23.

Barrett, Chuck. "Stony Point: Nevada's Bloody Landmark on the Overland Trail," *Overland Journal*, 25:1 (Spring 2007), 3–23.

Bennett, Richard E. "Mormon Renegade: James Emmett at the Vermillion, 1846." *South Dakota History* 15:3 (Fall 1985), 217–33.

———. "Lamanism, Lymanism, and Cornfields." *Journal of Mormon History* 13 (1986), 44–59.

———. "'Cousin Laman' in the Wilderness: The Beginning of Brigham Young's Indian Policy." *Nebraska History* 67:1 (Spring 1986), 69–82.

Bigler, David L. "A Lion in the Path: Genesis of the Utah War, 1857–1858." *Utah Historical Quarterly* 76:1 (Winter 2008), 4–21.

———. "Garland Hurt, the American Friend of the Utahs." *Utah Historical Quarterly* 62:1 (Spring 1994), 149–70.

———. "Mormon Missionaries, the Utah War, and the 1858 Bannock Raid on Fort Limhi." *Montana Magazine* 53 (Autumn 2003).

———. "The Aiken Party Executions and the Utah War, 1857–1858." *Western Historical Quarterly* 38:4 (Winter 2007), 457–76.

———. "The Crisis at Fort Limhi, 1858." *Utah Historical Quarterly* 35:2 (Spring 1967), 121–36.

Boyle, C. E. "The Gold Rush Diary of Dr. Charles E. Boyle," 1849. Serialized in the *Columbus (Ohio) Dispatch*, 2 October–11 November 1849 and 2 October–11 November 1949.

Brooks, Juanita. "Indian Relations on the Mormon Frontier." *Utah Historical Quarterly* 12:1–2 (January–April 1944), 1–48.

Carter, D. Robert. "Fish and the Famine of 1855–56." *Journal of Mormon History* 27:2 (Fall 2001), 92–124.

Christy, Howard A. "Open Hand and Mailed Fist: Mormon-Indian Relations in Utah, 1847–52." *Utah Historical Quarterly* 46 (Summer 1978), 216–35.

———. "The Walker War: Defense and Conciliation as Strategy." *Utah Historical Quarterly* 47:4 (Fall 1979), 394–420.

———. "'What Virtue There is in Stone' and Other Pungent Talk on the Early Utah Frontier." *Utah Historical Quarterly* 59:3 (Summer 1991), 300–19.

Clemmer, Richard O. "Tosawihi Quarry." Report, Elko, Nevada BLM, February 1990.

Coates, Lawrence G. "Refugees Meet: The Mormons and Indians in Iowa." *BYU Studies* 21:4 (Fall 1981), 491–514.

Cooley, Everett L., ed. "The Robert S. Bliss Journal." *Utah Historical Quarterly* 27:4 (October 1959), 381–404.

Culmer, Frederic A. " 'General' John Wilson, Signer of the Deseret Petition, Including Letters from the Leonard Collection." *California Historical Quarterly* 26:4 (December 1947), 321–48.

Defa, Dennis R. "The Goshute Indians of Utah." In Cuch, *A History of Utah's American Indians*, 73–122.

Duncan, Clifford. "The Northern Utes of Utah." In Cuch, *A History of Utah's American Indians*, 167–224.

Duffy, John-Charles. "The Use of 'Lamanite' in Official LDS Discourse." *Journal of Mormon History* 34:1 (Winter 2008), 118–67.

Ehat, Andrew F. "'It Seems Like Heaven Began on Earth': Joseph Smith and the Constitution of the Kingdom of God." *Brigham Young University Studies* 20:3 (Spring 1980), 253–79.

Farmer, Jared. "Crossroads of the West." *Journal of Mormon History* 41:1 (January 2015), 156–73.

———. "Displaced from Zion: Mormons and Indians in the 19th Century." *Historically Speaking: The Bulletin of the Historical Society* (January 2009), 40–42.

Flint, Thomas. "Diary of Dr. Thomas Flint: California to Maine and Return [1853]." Ed. by Waldemar Westergaard. *Annual Publications of the Historical Society of Southern California.* Los Angeles: The Historical Society of Southern California, 1923, 52–127.

Gates, Susa Young. "The Courtship of Kanosh, a Pioneer Indian Love Story." *Improvement Era* 9:1 (November 1905), 21–38.

Gibbs, Josiah. "Gunnison Massacre . . . Indian Mareer's Version of the Tragedy, 1894." *Utah Historical Quarterly* 1:3 (July 1928), 67–75.

Gill, Harold B. "Colonial Germ Warfare." *Colonial Williamsburg* (Spring 2004). Digital copy accessed 25 September 2017 at http://www.history.org/foundation/journal/spring04/warfare.cfm.

Harris, Henry, Jr. "The Walker War." *Utah Historical Quarterly* 39:2 (Spring 1971), 178. An interview by Floyd O'Neil.

Harrison, Merry Lycett. "The Botanical Parts of the Patterson Bundle: An Herbalist's Discovery." *Utah Archaeology* 16 (2003), 53–61. Digital copy accessed 17 December 2018, http://digitallibrary.utah.gov/awweb/awarchive?type=file&item=34203.

Heaton, John W. "'No Place to Pitch Their Teepees': Shoshone Adaptation to Mormon Settlers in Cache Valley, 1855–70." *Utah Historical Quarterly* 63:2 (Spring 1995), 158–71.

Higbee, Marilyn, ed. "'A Weary Traveller': The 1848–1850 Diary of Zina D. H. Young," *Journal of Mormon History* 19 (Fall 1993), 86–125.

Hines, Celinda K. "Life and Death on the Oregon Trail." *Covered Wagon Women.* Ed. by Kenneth L. Holmes. Spokane, Wash.: The Arthur H. Clark Co., 1986, 6:77–136.

Hitt, Jack. "Mighty White of You: Racial Preferences Color America's Oldest Skulls and Bones." *Harper's Magazine* (July 2005): 39–55.

Huntington, O. B. "A Trip to Carson Valley." *Eventful Narratives: The Thirteenth Book of the Faith-Promoting Series.* S.L.C.: Juvenile Instructor Office, 1887.

———. "Elk Mountain Mission." *Juvenile Instructor* 30:7, 9, 10, 12 (1 April to 15 June 1895) 224–27, 279–83, 306–10, 363–66.

———. "First Battle with IndiansinUtah." *Parry's Monthly Magazine* 6:6 (March 1890), 219–29.

Hurt, Garland. "Indians of Utah." In James H. Simpson, *Report of Explorations across the Great Basin.* Washington, D.C.: Government Printing Office, 1876, 457–64.

James, Rhett S. "Brigham Young–Chief Washakie Indian Farm Negotiations, 1854–1857." *Annals of Wyoming* 39:2 (October 1967), 245–56.

Jennings, Warren A. "The First Mormon Mission to the Indians." *Kansas Historical Quarterly* 37 (Autumn 1971), 288–99.

Jenson, Andrew. "History of Fort Bridger and Fort Supply." *Utah Genealogical and Historical Magazine* 4:1 (January 1913), 32–39.

———. "The Elk Mountain Mission." *Utah Genealogical and Historical Magazine* 4:4 (October 1913), 188–89. Includes "The Journal of O. B. Huntington," 189–200.

Johnson, Thomas H. "Chief Washakie's Mormon Baptism at Wind River, Wyoming, 1880."*Annals of Wyoming* 80:2 (Spring 2008), 14–19.

Jones, Sondra. "'Redeeming' the Indian: The Enslavement of Indian Children in New Mexico and Utah." *Utah Historical Quarterly* 67:3 (Summer 1999), 220–41.

Jorgensen, Danny L. "Building the Kingdom of God: Alpheus Cutler and the Second Mormon Mission to the Indians, 1846–1853." *Kansas History* 15:3 (Autumn 1992), 192–209.

Kelly, Charles. "We Found the Grave of the Utah Chief." *Desert Magazine* 9:12 (October 1946), 17–19.

Kenner, S. A. "Resources and Attractions of Utah, As Inviting the Attention of Tourists and Those Seeking Permanent Homes." In *The Meears Prize Essay*, S.L.C.: George A. Meears, 1881.

King, Jeffery S. "'Do Not Execute Chief Pocatello': President Lincoln Acts to Save the Shoshoni Chief." *Utah Historical Quarterly* 53:3 (Summer 1985), 217–47.

Kimball, Spencer W. "Of Royal Blood." *Ensign* (July 1971), 7–10.

———. "The Day of the Lamanite." *Improvement Era* (December 1960), 922–23.

Lewis, Hyrum S. "Kanosh and Ute Identity in Territorial Utah." *Utah Historical Quarterly* 71:4 (Fall 2003), 332–47.

Ludlow, Daniel H. "Of the House of Israel." *The Ensign* (January 1991), 51–55.

Lyman, Edward Leo. "Chief Kanosh: Champion of Peace and Forbearance." *Journal of Mormon History* 35:1 (Winter 2009), 157–207.

MacKinnon, William P. "And the War Came: James Buchanan, the Utah Expedition, and the Decision to Intervene." *Utah Historical Quarterly* 76:1 (Winter 2008), 22–37.

———. "'Lonely Bones': Leadership and Utah War Violence." *Journal of Mormon History* 33:1 (Spring 2007), 121–78.

———. "Sex, Subalterns, and Steptoe: Army Behavior, Mormon Rage, and Utah War Anxieties." *Utah Historical Quarterly* 76:3 (Summer 2008), 227–46.

Madsen, Brigham D. "B. H. Roberts's Studies of the Book of Mormon." *Dialogue* 26:3 (Fall 1993), 77–86.

———. "Shoshoni-Bannock Marauders on the Oregon Trail, 1859–1863." *Utah Historical Quarterly* 35:1 (Winter 1967), 3–30.

Mauss, Armand. "In Search of Ephraim: Traditional Mormon Conceptions of Lineage and Race." *Journal of Mormon History* 25:1 (Spring 1999), 131–73.

Morgan, Dale L. "The State of Deseret." *Utah Historical Quarterly* 8:2, 3, 4 (April, July, October 1940).

———. "The Administration of Indian Affairs in Utah, 1851–1858." *Pacific Historical Review* 17 (November 1948), 383–409. In Morgan, *Shoshonean Peoples*, 57–83.

Miller, Jay. "Numic Religion: An Overview of Power in the Great Basin of Native North America." *Anthropos*(1983), 337–54.

Murphy, Thomas W. "Other Mormon Histories: Lamanite Subjectivity in Mexico." *The Journal of Mormon History* 26:2 (Fall 2000): 179–214.

Newell, Linda King. *History of Piute County*. S.L.C.: Utah State Historical Society, 1999.

Nicholson, John. "The Lamanites." *Millennial Star* (February–March 1875), 97–99, 131–32, 150–51.

O'Neil, Floyd. "The Reluctant Suzerainty: The Uintah and Ouray Reservation." *Utah Historical Society* 39:2 (Spring 1971), 129–44.

Palmer, Grant. "Did Joseph Smith Commit Treason in His Quest for Political Empire in 1844?" *John Whitmer Historical Association Journal* 32:2 (Fall/Winter 2012), 52–58.

Palmer, William R. "Indian Names in Utah Geography." *Utah Historical Quarterly* 1:1 (January 1928), 5–25.

Peterson, Charles S. "Jacob Hamblin, Apostle to the Lamanites, and the Indian Mission." *Journal of Mormon History* 2 (1975), 21–34.

Quinn, D. Michael. "The Council of Fifty and Its Members, 1844 to 1945." *Brigham Young University Studies* 20 (Winter 1980), 163–97.

Robinson, John. "Traders, Travelers and Horse-Thieves on the Old Spanish Trail." *Overland Journal* 15:2 (Summer 1997), 27–42.

Rogers, Jedediah, and Richard E. Turley Jr. "Remembering the Circleville Massacre." *Utah Historical Quarterly* 84:3 (Summer 2016), 263–68.

Sloan, William K. "Autobiography." *Annals of Wyoming* 4:1 (July 1926), 235–64.

Smith, Christopher C. "Playing Lamanite: Ecstatic Performance of American Indian Identity in Early Mormonism." *Journal of Mormon History* 41:3 (July 2015), 132–67.

Smoak, Gregory E. "The Mormons and the Ghost Dance of 1890." *South Dakota History* 16:3 (Fall 1986), 269–94.

Stewart, Omer C. "Temoke Band of Shoshone." *Nevada Historical Quarterly* 23:4 (Winter 1980), 246–61.

Taylor, Samuel W. "Who Done It? The Nagging Mystery of Brigham Young's Last Moments." *Restoration* 6 (January 1987), 3–7.

Tom, Gary, and Ronald Holt. "The Paiute Tribe of Utah." In Cuch, ed. *A History of Utah's American Indians*, 123–65.

Trennert, Robert A. "The Mormons and the Office of Indian Affairs: The Conflict over Winter Quarters, 1846–1848." *Nebraska History* 53 (1972): 381–400.

Tullidge, Edward. "History of Provo City." *Tullidge's Quarterly Magazine* 3 (July 1885), 233–66.

———. "History of Spanish Fork." *Tullidge's Quarterly Magazine* 3 (April 1884), 137–70.

———. "Utah and California: Original Proposition to Unite Them as One State." *The Western Galaxy* 1:1 (March 1888), 88–90.

Van Hoak, Stephen P. "Waccara's Utes: Native American Equestrian Adaptations in the Eastern Great Basin, 1776–1876." *Utah Historical Quarterly* 67:4 (Fall 1999), 309–30.

———. "And Who Shall Have the Children? The Indian Slave Trade in the Southern Great Basin, 1800–1865." *Nevada Historical Quarterly* (Spring 1998), 3–25.

Walker, Ronald W. "Seeking the 'Remnant': The Native American during the Joseph Smith Period." *Journal of Mormon History* 19:1 (Spring 1993), 1–33.

———. "The Tintic War of 1856: A Study of Several Conflicts." *Journal of Mormon History* 42:3 (July 2016), 35–67.

———. "Wakara Meets the Mormons, 1848–52: A Case Study in Native American Accommodation." *Utah Historical Quarterly* 70:3 (Summer 2002), 215–37.

Winkler, Albert. "The Circleville Massacre: A Brutal Incident in Utah's Black Hawk War." *Utah Historical Quarterly* 55:1 (Winter 1987), 4–21.

Wilson, Edmund. "Apologies to the Iroquois." *New Yorker*, 17 October 1959, 49–128.

GOVERNMENT DOCUMENTS

"Affairs in Utah and the Territories," House Misc. Doc. 153 (40:2), Serial 1350, 1867.

Beckwith, Edward G. *Explorations and Surveys for a Railroad Route from the Mississippi River to the Pacific Ocean.* House Exec. Doc. 129 (33:1). Serial 737. Washington, D.C.: A. O. P. Nicholson, 1854.

Burr, David H. *Annual Report of Surveyor General of Utah, September 30, 1856.* House Exec. Doc. 1 (34–3), Serial 893, 543.

Carleton, James Henry. "Special Report of the Mountain Meadow Massacre Massacre, by J. H. Carleton, Brevet Major, United States Army, Captain, First Dragoons," House Doc. 605 (57-1), Serial 4377.

Commissioner of Indian Affairs. *Annual Report,* 1849 (31:1). House Exec. Doc. 5, pt. 2, Serial 570. Washington, D.C., 1849.

————. *Annual Report,* 1850 (31-2). House Exec. Doc. 1, Serial 595.

————. *Annual Report,* 1851 (32–2). Sen. Exec. Doc. 1, pt. 3, Serial 636.

————. *Annual Report,* 1852 (32–2). Sen. Exec. Doc. 1, pt. 1, Serial 658.

————. *Annual Report,* 1853 (33–1). Sen. Exec. Doc. 1, pt. 1, Serial 690.

————. *Annual Report,* 1854 (33–2). Sen. Exec. Doc. 1, pt. 1. Serial 746.

————. *Annual Report,* 1855 (34–1). Sen. Exec. Doc. 1, pt. 1, Serial 810.

————. *Annual Report,* 1856 (34–3). Sen. Exec. Doc., Vol. 2,Doc. 5, Serial 875.

————. *Annual Report,* 1858 (35–2). Sen. Exec. Doc. 1, pt 1, Serial 974.

————. *Annual Report,* 1861 (37–2). Sen. Exec. Doc. 1, pt. 1, Serial 1117.

————. *Annual Report,* 1863 (38–1). House Doc. 1, pt. 3, Serial 1182.

————. *Annual Report,* 1866 (39–2). House Exec. Doc. 1, pt. 2, Serial 1284.

————. *Annual Report,* 1868 (40-3) H. Exdoc. 1, pt. 2, Serial 1366.

Davies, Benjamin. "Accounts of Brigham Young, Superintendent of Indian Affairs in Utah Territory." House Exec. Doc. 29 (37–2), Serial 1128. Washington, D.C.: Government Printing Office, 1862.

Floyd, John B. "Report of the Secretary of War." In *Message of the President of the United States,* 35th Congress, 2nd Sess., Senate Exec. Doc. 85, vol. 2, Serial 975. Washington, D.C.: William A. Harris, Printer, 1858.

————. "Report of the Secretary of War." In *Message of the President of the United States,* 36th Congress, 1st Sess., Senate Exec. Doc. 2, vol. 2, Serial 1024. Washington, D.C.: George W. Bowman, Printer, 1860.

Lander, Frederick William. "Report of F. W. Lander," in Sen. Exec. Doc. 42 (36–1), Serial 1033, 1860, 121–38.

Powell, John Wesley. *Exploration of the Colorado River of the West.* Washington, D.C.: Government Printing Office, 1875.

Powell, John Wesley, and G. W. Ingalls. "Report of J. W. Powell and G. W. Ingalls." Commissioner of Indian Affairs, *Annual Report,* 18 December 1873, Serial 1626, 41–66.

Rood, Ronald J. *The Archaeology of a Mass Grave from Nephi, Utah and One Event of the Walker War, Utah Territory: A Report on the Excavations.* S.L.C.: State of Utah, 2016.

Simpson, James H. *Report of Explorations Across the Great Basin*. Washington, D.C.: Government Printing Office, 1876.

U.S. House. *Message from the President of the United States: California and New Mexico*. House Exec. Doc. 17 (31–1), 1850, Serial 673.

———. *Register of Officers and Agents, Civil, Military, and Naval, in the Service of the United States on the Thirtieth of September, 1855*. Washington, D.C.: A. O. P. Nicholson, Public Printer, 1855.

———*The Utah Expedition. Message of the President* (35:1, Serial 956), Exec. Doc. 71, 1858.

———. *Utah Territory. Resolution of Hon. John Bidwell, Relative to Affairs in Utah Territory*. (39:2, 1866, Serial 1284–2). House Misc. Doc. No. 75. Washington, D.C.: Government Printing Office, 1867.

U.S. Senate. *Message of the President of the United States, Communicating, in compliance with a resolution of the Senate, information in relation to the massacre at Mountain Meadows, and other massacres in Utah Territory.*Armstrong, John Christopher. Southern Utah Exploration Diary, 1 December 1849 to 9 January 1850. Typescript, MS 1759, LDS Archives.

THESES AND DISSERTATIONS

Brown, Ralph O. "The Life and Missionary Labors of George Washington Hill." Master's Thesis, Brigham Young University, 1956.

Denison, Brandilyn. "Remove, Return, Remember: Making Ute Land Religion in the American West." Ph.D. Dissertation, University of North Carolina, 2011.

Garrett, Matthew R. "Mormons, Indians and Lamanites: The Indian Student Placement Program, 1947–2000." Ph.D. Dissertation, Arizona State University, 2010.

O'Neil, Floyd A. "A History of the Ute Indians of Utah Until 1890." Ph.D. Dissertation, University of Utah, 1973.

Skousen, Christina. "Toiling among the Seed of Israel: A Comparison of Puritan and Mormon Missions to the Indians." Master's Thesis, Brigham Young University, 2005.

Stuart-Hirschfield, Rachel. "Life and Death of Albert Hamblin." Bachelor of Arts Honors Thesis, Emory University, 2015.

Taylor, Lori Elaine. "Telling Stories about Mormons and Indians." Ph.D. Dissertation, State University of New York at Buffalo, 2000.

Wimmer, Ryan E. "The Walker War Reconsidered." Masters Thesis, Brigham Young University, 2010.

MANUSCRIPTS

Armstrong, John Christopher. Southern Utah Exploration Diary, 1 December 1849 to 9 January 1850. Typescript, MS 1759, LDS Archives.

Atkin, Thomas. Life Sketch. MSS A 6019/5, USHS. See also A Brief Record Of Indian difficulties In Tooele County, MS 9262, LDS Archives. Digital copy at https://dcms.lds.org/delivery/DeliveryManagerServlet?dps_pid=IE3741193.

Bagley, Will. Notes of Paiute Elders Meeting, Santa Clara, Utah, 5 February 2004.

————. Papers, 1836–2008. Accn1937, Special Collections, J. Willard Marriott Library, University of Utah.

Barney, Lewis. Autobiography, "History of Lewis Barney," Ada Barney Plumb Typescript, Family History Library.

Bean, George W. Diary and Autobiography, 1852–1878MSS A 68, Utah State Historical Society.

Best, Christy. "Report of the Survey of Selected Territorial Records Extant at the Utah State Archives." S.L.C.: Utah State Archives, 1987.

Bleak, James. Annals of the Southern Utah Mission. MS 318, LDS Archives.

Bullock, Isaac. Diary, 1854–1857. MS 1478, LDS Archives.

Call, Anson. Statement, November 1853, Papers Concerning Gunnison Massacre, BYC 47:37.

Campbell, Robert Lang. Diary, July 1849 to March 1850, MS 1222, LDS Archives.

Carter, William A. "Remarks . . . by one of Carter's children." Papers, BANC MSS 99/75, 5:5.

Church Historian's Office (LDS), 1844–1972, CR100. Journal 1844–2012, CR100 1; Letterpress Copybooks, CR100 38; Reports of Speeches, 1845–1885, CR100 317; General Church Minutes, 1839–1877, CR100 318; Correspondence Files, 1856–1926, CR100 394; Minutes and Reports (Local Units), 1840–1886, CR100 589. LDS Church History Library, The Church of Jesus Christ of Latter-day Saints, S.L.C., Utah.

Collected Material Concerning the Mountain Meadows Massacre 1859–1961, MS 2674, LDS Archives.

Cutler, Sheldon Bela. Elk Mountain Journal, 1855–1856. MS 14561, Typescript, LDS Archives.

Davis, George W., Leslie J. Perry, and Joseph W. Kirkley, eds. *The War of the Rebellion: A Compilation of the Official Records of the Union and the Confederate Armies.* Series 1, Vol. 50, Part 2, Serial 3584. Washington, D.C: Government Printing Office, 1897.

Egan, William Monroe. Observations & Experiences among the Utes [of the] 'Fifties. WA MSS 159, Beinecke Library.

Gallup, Luke W. Reminiscences and Diary, 1842–1891. MS 8402, LDS Archives.

Goold, Luther. Overland from California to Omaha, 1862–1863. Typescript and digital transcription in author's possession, courtesy of Stafford Hazelett and Janet Skidmore.

Grant, Heber J. Journal, MSS 62, Vault Manuscript Collection, BYU Library.

Hamblin, Jacob. Papers, MS 1951, LDS Archives.

————. Journal, 1854–1858. MS 14654, LDS Archives.

Hancock, Charles Brent. Reminiscences and Diary, MS 1569, LDS Archives; and Autobiography, 1882, Frances Cart Yost typescript, MS 5285, LDS Archives.

Hill, George Washington. Incidents in the Life. MS 8172, LDS Archives.

Holeman, Jacob. Papers, MS 2178, LDS Archives.

Huntington, Dimick Baker. Journal, 1857 Aug–1859 May. MS 1419–2, LDS Archives.

Huntington, Oliver Boardman. Diary and Reminiscences. Eighteen volumes, 1843 to 1900. MSS 162, BYU Library.

Harker, Joseph. Reminiscences and Journal. MS 1560, LDS Archives.

Jackman, Levi. Diary, 1847 to 1849. Vault MSS 79, BYU Library.

Judd, Zadoc Knapp. Account of settlement of Santa Clara, Utah. 27 March 1891, Mormon File, Huntington Library. (The biblical spelling is Zadok, but this Judd's spelling.)

Kimball, William H. Nauvoo Legion Papers, 1853 July–August. Southern Military Department, William H. Kimball Detachment. MS 17208, LDS Archives.

LDS Church History Department. Historical Department Office Journal, 1844–2012. CR 100 1, LDS Archives. Digital copies at https://eadview.lds.org/findingaid/000083518/.

Lauderdale, John Vance. Papers, MSS S-1317, Beinecke Library.

Livingston, La Rhett L. Letters to James G. Livingston, 17 May, 18 June, 6 July, 12 July, and 24 August 1854. WA MSS S-1852, Beinecke Library.

Love, Andrew. Diary, 18 September 1852 to September 1875. MS 1675, LDS Archives.

McEwan, John. Elk Mountain Mission, 1855 Diary. MSS 1051, BYU Library, 27–120.

McKenzie, George. Ballad of the Walker War. Utah Humanities Research Foundation records, 1944–1954, Marriott Library.

Morris, Robert M. Journal of an Overland Trip to California and Other Army Assignments. MSS 1738, Beinecke Library.

Olney, Oliver H. Papers, 1842–1843. MSS 364, Beinecke Library. Includes Dale L. Morgan Foreword and Calendar of the Documents typescript, written for book dealer Edward Eberstadt.

Nebeker, John. Green River Company Journal, 1853–1854. MS 2038, LDS Archives.

Pace, William Byram. Autobiography and Journals, 1847–1857. MS 1658, LDS Archives.

———. Journal, 30 June 1855, MS 10424, LDS Archives.

Pettit, Ethan. Diary, May 1855 to June 1856. MS 419:2, LDS Archives.

Pulsipher, John. A Short Sketch of the History of John Pulsipher, Utah State Historical Society.

———. Shoshone Mission Journal, 1855–1857. MS 418, LDS Archives.

Salt Lake Stake Papers, Minutes, 1847–1849. LR 604 107, LDS Archives.

Salt Lake Stake Minutes, LR 604 109, LDS Archives. See also "Proceedings of Stake Presidency and High Council in Executive, Legislative and Judicial Capacity, Great Salt Lake Stake 1847–48, Minutes of the High Council, Albert Carrington—Clerk," in Kate B. Carter, comp., Our Pioneer Heritage, vol. 17 (S.L.C.: Daughters of Utah Pioneers, 1974), 89–112.

Sanderson, Henry Weeks. Diary. Typescript, BX 8670.1.Sa56, BYU Library.

Shurtliff, Lewis Warren. Life and Travels, ca. 1871. MS 7161, LDS Archives.

Smith, Albert. Reminiscences and Journals, 1876–1892. MS 1835, LDS Archives.

Smith, Joseph, Jr. The Joseph Smith Papers. http://josephsmithpapers.org/. LDS Archives.

Smith, George A. Smith Papers, MS 1322, LDS Archives.

Snow, Erastus. Journal 1847. MS 1329, LDS Archives.

Spencer, Daniel. Diaries, February 1847 to March 1849. MS 1566, LDS Archives.

Sterrett, William Wilson. Autobiography, ca. 1897. MSS SC 879, BYU Library.

Taylor, W. B. "Pioneer Reminiscences [sic]: W. B. Taylor Writes of his Experience Crossing the Plains in '49." Weekly Reveille (Cloverdale, California), 7, 14, 21, 28 March, 11, 18, 25 April 1896. Dale L. Morgan typescript, MSS 69/146 c, Bancroft Library.

Thatcher, Moses. Diary, 1883–1884. MS 3009, LDS Archives.

Thomas, Robert T. Autobiography. In William Thomas, Historical sketch and genealogy of the Thomas families. Typescript, MS 1598, LDS Archives. Digital copy at https://dcms.lds.org/delivery/DeliveryManagerServlet?dps_pid=IE3157909.

Wall, William Madison. Report of Captain Wm Wall, Commander of a Detachment of the Nauvoo Legion Cavalry on the Expedition to the extreme Southern Settlement of the Territory of Utah to the Adjutant General Office at Great Salt Lake City, 24 April to 11 May 1853, UTMC, 177.

Whitaker, George. Autobiography, 1820–1907. Special Collections, Marriott Library.

Whitney, Horace. 1847 Journal. MS 15256, LDS Archives.

Young, Brigham. Brigham Young Collection, CR 1234. Church History Department and Library, The Church of Jesus Christ of Latter-day Saints, S.L.C., Utah.

INDEX

It seems few English speakers spelled Native names the same way twice. This fact poses a number of challenges to indexing this book. This index uses the most common spelling of the subject's name (a judgment call) and includes some, if not all, of the variant spellings in parenthesis. References to portraits and other illustrations are *italicized*. Generally, if the subject's name occurs on fewer than three sequential pages, the index shows those pages; references over a larger number of pages are expressed as a range (e.g., 525–32).